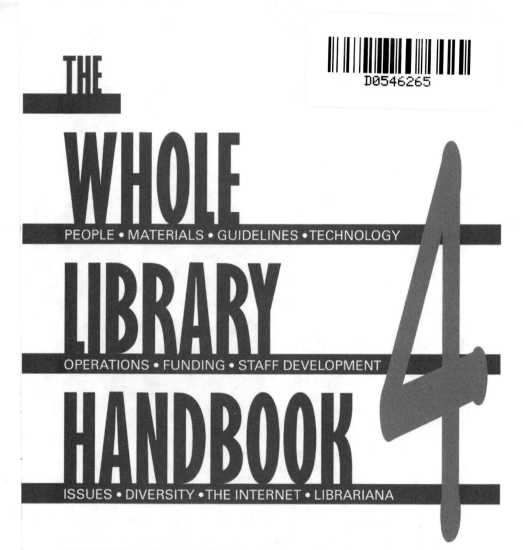

THE
WHOLE
PEOPLE • MATERIALS • GUIDELINES • TECHNOLOGY
LIBRARY
OPERATIONS • FUNDING • STAFF DEVELOPMENT
HANDBOOK
ISSUES • DIVERSITY • THE INTERNET • LIBRARIANA

4

CURRENT DATA, PROFESSIONAL ADVICE, AND CURIOSA ABOUT LIBRARIES AND LIBRARY SERVICES

EDITED BY **George M. Eberhart**

AMERICAN LIBRARY ASSOCIATION
Chicago   2006

While extensive effort has gone into ensuring the reliability of information appearing in this book, the publisher makes no warranty, express or implied, on the accuracy or reliability of the information, and does not assume and hereby disclaims any liability to any person for any loss or damage caused by errors or omissions in this publication.

Composition by Priority Publishing using Adobe PageMaker 7.0 on a Windows platform. Selected artwork from ClipArt.com.

The paper used in this publication meets the minimum requirements of American National Standard for Information Sciences—Permanence of Paper for Printed Library Materials, ANSI Z39.48-1992.

Library of Congress Cataloging-in-Publication Data

The whole library handbook 4 : current data, professional advice, and curiosa about libraries and library services / edited by George M. Eberhart.
  p.   cm.
Includes bibliographical references and index.
ISBN 0-8389-0915-9
  1. Library science—United States—Handbooks, manuals, etc.
2. Libraries—United States—Handbooks, manuals, etc.

Z665.2U6W49 2006
020.0973—dc22   2005033619

Printed in the United States of America.

10   09   08   07   06   5   4   3   2   1

CONTENTS

PREFACE

The Whole Library Handbook 4

George M. Eberhart

SIX YEARS HAVE PASSED since the *Whole Library Handbook 3* appeared, and in many ways it seems as if we are living in a different bibliographic era. In 2000, blogs were relatively unknown, 24/7 digital reference services were largely untested, and the USA Patriot Act and the Children's Internet Protection Act were not around to bedevil intellectual freedom advocates. Y2K forced everyone to upgrade their operating systems, and Google became the world's largest search engine in June with the creation of a billion-page Web index.

Many excellent books and articles on library history, theory, and practice have been written in the past six years, and I have tried offer a selection of the most informative, practical, and entertaining. About 97% of *WLH4* is completely new or substantially revised, with 16 more pages than the last edition.

However, there are still perfectly valid articles in the earlier handbooks, so I'd recommend keeping them on the shelves a few years more. *WLH3* has a complete list of library-related movies prior to 1999, how to identify a first edition, tips on preparing a bibliography, and a history of the card catalog. *WLH2* (1995) offers suggestions on how to photograph your library, a salute to Ranganathan, and an overview of 20th-century bookbindings. Even the first handbook (1991) contains still-insightful essays on Soviet librarianship, methods for moving books, and how barcodes work.

This edition maintains the same 10-chapter structure as the others:

Chapter 1 looks at basic library statistics and types of libraries, and provides a new definition of libraries for the Information Age.

Chapter 2 examines library jobs and people, from managers to volunteers, and offers 10 reasons to be a librarian, while crediting the essential work of support staff, Friends, and trustees.

Chapter 3 covers library conferences, education, and professional writing, and contains a comprehensive list of scholarships, grants, and awards offered by professional associations.

Chapter 4 reviews the types of materials found in a library, from books to multimedia. Ever wonder what the first printed book in the Basque language was? You'll find out here.

Chapter 5 takes up the varied operations library workers engage in, such as reference and cataloging, with basic information on metadata, Cutter numbers, and preservation storage.

Chapter 6 surveys a number of underserved users, including Hispanic youth, Asian-language speakers, gay and lesbian teens, and homeless persons.

Chapter 7 offers promotion and fundraising suggestions for all types of libraries.

Chapter 8 summarizes the state of technology in libraries, from paper clips and staplers to internet filters and RFID tags.

Chapter 9 outlines the major issues facing libraries in the 21st century, including copyright, intellectual freedom, privacy, literacy, patron behavior, and ethics.

Chapter 10 provides some comic relief with bizarre book titles, famous librarians' favorite books, libraries and librarians on film, library postcards, haunted libraries, and other stimulating trivia.

In short, there's something in here for everyone who loves libraries and wants to discover their mysterious ways. As in the earlier editions, please keep in mind that many of the selections are only extracts of longer books or articles. The originals in their full glory are always worth seeking out.

If I have, through lack of space or unconscious editorial preference, neglected to include a topic or reprint a particularly magnificent checklist, let me know and I will consider it for a future edition. Send ideas to me c/o *American Libraries*, 50 E. Huron St., Chicago, IL 60611, or email geberhart@ala.org.

Finally, I would like to thank the many authors in this edition, especially Denise Davis, Lori Ayre, Norman Stevens, Larry Nix, and Jeff Baskin, who made original contributions. Also, my deepest appreciation goes to my wife and occasional collaborator, Jennifer Henderson, who has offered tremendous moral support; and all of the library students, librarians, support staff, and library advocates who have found something useful in these handbooks over the years.

LIBRARIES
CHAPTER ONE

"When you are growing up, there are two institutional places that affect you most powerfully—the church, which belongs to God, and the public library, which belongs to you. The public library is a great equalizer."

—Rolling Stones guitarist Keith Richards

BASIC INFORMATION

What is a library?

by George M. Eberhart

A LIBRARY IS a collection of resources in a variety of formats that is (1) organized by information professionals or other experts who (2) provide convenient physical, digital, bibliographic, or intellectual access and (3) offer targeted services and programs (4) with the mission of educating, informing, or entertaining a variety of audiences (5) and the goal of stimulating individual learning and advancing society as a whole.

SOURCES: Heartsill Young, ed., *The ALA Glossary of Library and Information Science* (Chicago: American Library Association, 1983), p. 130; Robert S. Martin, "Libraries and Learners in the Twenty-First Century," Cora Paul Bomar Lecture, University of North Carolina at Greensboro, April 5, 2003, www.imls.gov/scripts/text.cgi?/whatsnew/current/sp040503.htm; Deanna B. Marcum, "Research Questions for the Digital Era Library," *Library Trends* 51 (Spring 2003): 636–651.

What we know about libraries

by Denise M. Davis

FOR MORE THAN 100 YEARS the library community has been reporting figures on its services, collection, staff, and facilities. These data have been collected by a myriad of associations and agencies, but the most consistent data are available from the U.S. National Center for Education Statistics (NCES), a branch of the U.S. Department of Education. These reports include: *Academic Libraries: 2002* (2003); *Public Libraries in the United States: Fiscal Year 2003* (2005); *State Library Agencies: Fiscal 2003* (2004); and *The Status of Public and Private School Library Media Centers in the United States: 1999–2000* (2004). Additional sources are cited where appropriate.

How many libraries are there?

Keeping track of the various types of libraries throughout the United States and its territories is no small task. In addition to the sources noted above for academic, public, state, and school libraries, the single best source of information about special, armed forces, and government libraries comes from the *American Library Directory,* compiled annually by the R. R. Bowker Company.

Libraries in the United States		
College and university libraries		3,527
Public libraries		9,211*
Centrals*	9,062	
Branches	7,479	
Buildings	16,541	
Bookmobiles	866	
School library media centers		93,861
Public schools	76,807	
Private schools	17,054	
State libraries		50
Special libraries		8,208
Armed forces libraries		314
Government libraries		1,225
Total		**116,396**

* The number of central buildings is different from the number of public libraries because some public library systems have no central building and some have more than one.

These libraries also may participate in cooperative arrangements, either formally or informally, to provide services to their communities. Libraries may share collections, technology, and staff expertise or may cooperatively acquire collections by leveraging the economies of scale possible with group purchases. The International Coalition of Library Consortia reported as its members in 2005 more than 170 consortia around the world and nearly 100 in the United States alone. In addition, a 1987 NCES study reported approximately 760 library networks and cooperatives existed in the U.S. at that time (*Survey of Library Networks and Cooperative Library Organizations, 1985–1986*).

Most college, university, and public libraries and many school libraries belong to at least one network, cooperative, or consortium, and many participate in more than one. Detailed information on this participation will be reported in the *Academic Libraries: 2002* report, which was not yet released at the time of this publication. Readers are encouraged to review the report online at nces.ed.gov/surveys/libraries/Academic.asp.

State libraries also play an important role in providing or supporting library services in the 50 states. The agency may have a library or may contract with a public or academic library to act as a resource or reference/information center. Forty-four state library agencies reported in 2003 that they supported some form of reference referral services to public libraries, 37 to academic and special libraries, 33 to school libraries, and 25 to systems. Many states have begun virtual digital reference services, and state libraries are providing support either through direct coordination or funding. All 50 states and the District of Columbia administer federal Library Services and Technology Act (LSTA) funding, and 50 states support Universal Service (e-rate discount) program reviews.

How much are they used?

The 3,527 **college and university libraries** submitting gate count figures to NCES for 1999–2000 reported that more than 16.5 million people visited these libraries in a typical week. In 2002, this figure is expected to decline, while remote use of academic libraries is expected to continue climbing. During 1999–2000, more than 193,962,856 items circulated from academic libraries, and it is estimated that a decline in print circulation will be reported in the 2002 study. This decline reinforces the increased use of digital content that does not need to be borrowed from academic libraries.

The 2002 NCES report on **public libraries** shows more than 1.2 billion visits in that year, an increase of 3.9% over the 2001 figures. In 2002, the average circulation for public libraries was 6.8 items per capita. The total number of items circulated nationally from public libraries in 2002 was nearly 1.9 billion, an increase of 5.6% over what was reported in 2001.

The 1999–2000 NCES survey estimated that for the 76,807 **public school library media centers** in the United States:

- more than 33.3 million students visited the libraries per week;
- each student averaged .74 visits to the library per week.

Almost all public schools have library media centers (92%), but many of the 27,223 **private schools** have small enrollments and are less likely to have a library. The 1999–2000 NCES survey estimated that:

- of the 25,120 private schools with less than 500 students, 60% had libraries;
- of the 2,102 private schools with 500 or more students, 92% had libraries;
- more than 5.3 million students visited private school libraries per week;
- each student averaged 1.01 visits to the library per week.

In 2004, NCES released a survey of 10th and 12th graders' use of school media centers, *School Library Media Centers: Selected Results from the Education Longitudinal Study of 2002* (nces.ed.gov/pubsearch/pubsinfo.asp?pubid= 2005302). This ELS study reported that 31% of school library media centers had 100–249 student visits in a typical week, 25% had 250–499 student visits per week, 19% had 500–999 student visits per week, and 11% had over 1,000 student visits during a typical week.

During the 1999–2000 school year, all **public school libraries** in the United States:

- circulated a total of more than 56.7 million items in a school year;
- circulated an average of 605 items per school in a school year.

In the 2002 ELS study, the mean circulation per week was 280. Despite this decline, 88% of school library media centers reported access to reference and bibliographic databases, and 82% reported access to general article and news databases.

It is clear that school libraries are providing very broad access to electronic resources that students do not have to borrow from the library.

Who uses public libraries?

In March 2002, KRC Research and Consulting conducted a survey for the American Library Association. The purpose of this survey was to measure the public's usage and perception of public libraries. One thousand people over the age of 18 were interviewed by phone. The study has a margin of error of plus or minus 3%. It found that:

- the library is most often used for educational purposes (46%), followed by entertainment (46%);
- 62% of respondents have a library card;
- 66% of all respondents reported using the public library at least once in the last year in person, by phone, or by computer.

Of those respondents who reported using the public library in person in the last year:

- 67% said they had taken out books;
- 47% had consulted a librarian;
- 47% used reference materials;
- 31% read newspapers or magazines;
- 26% connected to the internet;
- 25% took out CDs or videos;
- 14% heard a speaker, saw a movie, or attended a special program;
- 31% of the respondents had children; and
- 69% of these respondents said that they brought their children to the library.

The most current national study of library usage was published by the National Center for Education Statistics as part of its 1996 National Household Education Survey (nces.ed.gov/pubsearch/pubsinfo.asp?pubid=97446). The survey used a sample of 55,708 households. An adult member of each household was asked whether any household member had used the public library.

Sixty-five percent reported that individuals in the household had used the library in the last year, and 44% reported using it in the month prior to the interview; 61% of households with children under the age of 18 reported using the public library in the previous month; and only 35% of households without children under the age of 18 reported using the public library in the previous month.

In the month prior to the survey, 36% of all households reported borrowing from or dropping off a book to the public library, 18% reported visiting the library for some other purpose like a lecture or story hour, 14% reported calling to renew a book or to get information, and 4% reported using a home computer to link to the public library.

This survey can be downloaded at the NCES website at nces.ed.gov/pubsearch/pubsinfo.asp?pubid=97446.

Public Libraries in the United States: Fiscal Year 2003 (nces.ed.gov/pubsearch/pubsinfo.asp?pubid=2005362) contains the most recent usage statistics *as reported by libraries*. The 9,212 U.S. libraries and four U.S. territorial libraries reported:

	Users	Rate
Total visits	1,284,352,169	4.5 per capita
Total circulation	1,965,115,778	6.9 per capita
Circulation of children's materials	700,007,111	35.6% of total circ.

Unpublished statistics concerning library use by persons of different racial or ethnic groups based on data from the survey described above were included in "Using Public Libraries: What Makes a Difference?" in the November 1997 issue of *American Libraries*. The following table is taken from that article.

	White	Black	Hispanic	Asian/ Pacific	Indian/ Alaskan	Other
Used in last month	44%	45%	41%	53%	46%	51%
Used in last year	65%	63%	58%	72%	65%	66%

Librarians have long believed that when the economy goes down, public library use goes up. In February 2002, ALA contracted with the University of Illinois Library Research Center to study library use over the last five years, at the 25 U.S. public libraries serving populations of 1 million or more. Using data from 18 of those large libraries, the study found that circulation has increased significantly since March 2001, when the National Bureau of Economic Research pegged the beginning of the latest recession. Using statistical analysis, the LRC found that circulation in March 2001 was 8.3% higher than would be expected from the trend line that started in January 1997. It stayed well above that trend line, an average of 9% above, for the rest of the year.

Finally, the KRC study mentioned earlier found that:

- 91% of the total respondents believed libraries will exist in the future, despite all of the information available on the internet;
- 91% believe libraries are changing and dynamic places with a variety of activities for the whole family;
- 90% believe libraries are places of opportunity for education, self-help, and offer free access to all.

What do library collections look like?

For many years libraries have acquired and made available a range of resources, primarily books and serials (newspapers, magazines, journals). Although the content is largely unchanged, the method of delivery and formats are evolving. In August 2004, the Association of Research Libraries reported that electronic resource expenditures have grown by almost 400% from 1994–95 to 2001–02 to almost $1.4 million. Further, electronic journals represent 26% of total serials expenditures. Although this is not representative of all libraries, it does demonstrate a clear trend by libraries to include electronic resources as part of their general collections. For public libraries, audiovisual materials have evolved from cassette tapes to CD, DVD, MP3, and other digital transportable formats. In the 2003 NCES study, public libraries reported spending approximately $86.6 million for electronic materials, or 1% of total operating expenditures. This is an increase of $12.6 million from FY2002 expenditures.

So, are library collections more electronic than print? Some are, but most are not. The 3,527 **college and university libraries** reporting to NCES in the fall of 2000 held a total of 913,546,999 volumes of books, bound serials, and government documents. Collections ranged in size from 414 libraries with less than 5,000 volumes to 197 with 1 million or more. The academic libraries held nearly 7.5 million serial subscriptions and 87.5 million audiovisual materials.

Of the 9,212 **public libraries** in the United States included in the 2003 NCES report, slightly more than half had collections of less than 25,000, but 2,003 had collections of 500,000 or more. These libraries held a total of 230.4 million print, audio, video, and serial subscriptions.

Libraries in Canada	
College and university libraries	357
Public libraries	2,104
Special libraries	1,075
Government libraries	318
Total	**3,854**

SOURCE: *American Library Directory 2004–2005* (New York: R. R. Bowker, 2004).

Book collections in **public school library media centers** range from an average of 5,850 for schools serving fewer than 100 students to an average of 17,116 for schools serving 1,000 students or more. The average public school library in 1998–1999:

- held 10,232 volumes;
- checked out 605 items per school;
- spent $5,683 on books (65% of all library expenditures).

The average **private school library**:

- held 7,192 volumes;
- checked out 224 items per school;
- spent $2,660 on books (60.6% of all library expenditures).

Access

Libraries of all types have borrowed materials for their clients from other libraries through a cooperative arrangement known as interlibrary loan. Guidelines and forms devised by ALA facilitated this service, which is now largely automated. Rather than complete paper forms to request materials not owned by a library, clients request materials online. Libraries continue to provide interlibrary loan services to their clients even with the increased access to information in aggregated databases, electronic journals and books, and general information available on the internet. During the 2000 academic year, **academic libraries** in the United States:

- delivered more than 1.2 million documents to clients from commercial services;

- loaned nearly 9.5 million items to other libraries;
- received nearly 7.7 million items from other libraries.

During the 2002 academic year:

- more than 9.2 million items were loaned to other libraries;
- nearly 7.5 million items were received from other libraries.

In 2003, the 9,212 **public libraries** in the United States:

- provided more than 26.2 million items to other libraries;
- received more than 26.1 million items from other libraries.

In the figures above, the number of items provided is not equal to the number received for each type of library. This is due to several factors, such as lending across library types (including types for which no statistics are available).

Answers to questions

Librarians find answers to questions or help library users do so—either in person or virtually. During 2003, **public libraries** in the United States answered more than 305 million reference questions. The 3,527 **academic libraries** reporting in the fall of 2000 answered more than 75 million reference questions, approximately 1.5 million per week.

We are only beginning to capture reference transaction data from virtual digital reference services. Preliminary research indicates higher precision in responses to reference questions. See Neal Kaske, "The Ubiquitous Library Is Here," *portal: Libraries and the Academy* 4 (April 2004): 291–297. As we move forward with this technology, reference transaction data will reflect both in-person and virtual service to clients.

The electronic library

Since the late 1980s, libraries have been providing access to electronic resources—CD-ROM databases, then web-based delivery of commercial databases, and now internet-wide access to resources. Understanding the costs of these services has been challenging. Aside from database license or subscription costs, infrastructure, training, and maintenance costs have been more difficult to capture. What we do know about library purchasing and use of electronic resources includes:

- In 2005, 48% of public libraries in the United States connected to the internet at speeds of 769 kbps or higher, with those connecting at 1.5 mbps or higher increasing to 20.3% since the 2002 study. In 2002, 49% of public libraries reported access at speeds of T-1 or higher—77% in urban, 59% in suburban, and 33% in rural areas (see John Carlo Bertot, Charles R. McClure, and Paul T. Jaeger, *Public Libraries and the Internet 2004: Survey Results and Findings*, www.ala.org/ala/washoff/oitp/GatesFinalJun05.pdf; and John Carlo Bertot and Charles R. McClure, *Public Libraries and the Internet 2002: Internet Connectivity and Networked Services*, www.ii.fsu.edu/Projects/2002pli/2002.plinternet.study.pdf).
- In FY2003, public libraries reported to NCES having over 155,000 public-use internet computers and nearly 280 million users of electronic resources.

- In FY2002, academic libraries reported to NCES expenditures of more than $285 million on electronic serials, and nearly $42 million on other electronic materials.
- The Association of Research Libraries reported in August 2004 that electronic journals now account for 26% of overall serials expenditures of its members (see Mary M. Case, "A Snapshot in Time: ARL Libraries and Electronic Journal Resources," *ARL Bimonthly Report,* no. 235, August 2004, www.arl.org/newsltr/235/snapshot.html).
- In 2002, 94% of high school library media centers had PCs available for students to use, and 75% reported having one or more electronic database subscriptions, ebooks, or ejournals accessible from the library (see *School Library Media Centers: Selected Results from the Education Longitudinal Study of 2002*).

A number of projects have been underway in the early 2000s to describe and measure electronic resources and services. The National Information Standards Organization has a standard on library statistics that includes a number of regularly used electronic metrics. The standard is a web-based database of terms, methods of measurement, and best practices located at www.niso.org/emetrics/current/toc.html. In addition, ARL has studied its members' use of electronic resources and provides substantive guidance on its website at www.arl.org/stats/newmeas/emetrics/. Finally, Project COUNTER is an international initiative of publishers to better understand content usage and to provide normalized, consistent usage data to its customers. More information is available at www.projectcounter.org.

SOURCE: Special report for *The Whole Library Handbook 4* by Denise M. Davis, Director, ALA Office for Research and Statistics.

Library workers: Facts and figures

compiled by the AFL-CIO Department for Professional Employees

IN 2004, there were 151,857 librarians, 115,080 library technicians, and 102,310 library assistants. In 2012, there will be 184,000 librarians, 139,000 library technicians, and 146,000 library assistants, according to Bureau of Labor Statistics projections.

Between 2002 and 2012, the number of librarians is expected to increase by 10.1%, while library technicians increase by 16.8% and library assistants by 21.5%. Total employment in the U.S. is expected to increase by 14.8% over this period.

These projections for library workers are consistent with those for 2000–2010, when the number of librarians was expected to increase by 7%, while the number of technicians increased by 19.5% and the number of library assistants by 19.7%.

This trend points to "deprofessionalization": Work once performed only by librarians is now performed by support staff. In a recent American Library Association Support Staff Interests Round Table survey of 212 library support staff, 73% stated that they are now performing tasks previously performed by master's of library science (MLS) librarians at their library, or have the same or similar duties as MLS librarians at other institutions. The decrease in the number of projected librarians underscores this trend.

Employment

Most *librarians* work in school and academic libraries, but nearly one-third work in public libraries. The remainder work in special libraries or as information professionals for companies and other organizations.

More than two out of 10 librarians work part-time. Public and college librarians often work weekends and evenings, as well as some holidays. School librarians usually have the same workday and vacation schedules as classroom teachers. Special librarians usually work normal business hours, but in fast-paced industries such as advertising or legal services, they often work longer hours when needed. This applies also to *library technicians*.

More than half of all *library assistants* are employed by local government in public libraries; most of the remaining employees work in school libraries. Nearly half of all library assistants work part-time.

Women's work

Library workers have been, and will continue to be, mostly female. Most students of library science are women. Women comprise 80.2% of ALA-accredited master's of library science enrollment. Gender distribution is more equal for the master's of information science degree, where men account for 51.8% of all students.

In 2004, women accounted for 83.2% of all librarians, 83.2% of all library assistants, and the vast majority of library technicians.

An Association of Research Libraries survey found 64.3% of research librarians are female; 35.7% male. While female research librarians now outnumber male librarians among directors (53%), men still predominate as the head of computer systems departments (65.6%).

In academic libraries, 68% of all librarians are women. In public libraries, 79% are women, and in school libraries, 92% are women.

While men accounted for only 15.6% of librarians in 2003, they accounted for 47% of library directors in academic settings and 35% in public libraries.

Diversity

In 2004, 14.7% of all librarians were minorities: 5.6% were black or African American, 4.6% were Hispanic or Latino, and 4.5% were Asian.

Minorities accounted for 20.9% of all library assistants in 2004: 6.8% were black or African American, 5.0% were Asian, and 9.1% were Hispanic or Latino. While the Bureau of Labor Statistics does not have these percentages for library technicians, it is safe to assume that they are mostly white.

In public libraries, 6.3% of the staff is black or African American, 3.0% is Hispanic or Latino, 3.9% Asian/Pacific Islander, 0.25% American Indian/Alaskan Native, and 86.6% white, according to an American Library Association survey.

In ARL libraries, 12.9% of the professional staff is composed of minorities. Asian/Pacific Islanders account for 5.8% of the professional staff, blacks or African Americans for 4.3%, Latinos or Hispanics for 2.5%, and American Indian/Alaskan natives for 0.3%. The number of minorities in managerial or administrative positions in the largest U.S. academic libraries is far lower: 8% are directors, 7% are associate or assistant directors, and 10% are branch librarians. The percentage of minorities varies significantly between geographical regions. Minorities make up 20.3% of professional employees in ARL libraries in the South Atlantic Region, while comprising 3.1% of professionals in the East South Central ARL libraries.

An aging workforce

Fifty-eight percent of librarians in the United States are projected to reach the retirement age of 65 between 2005 and 2019. Forty percent of library directors plan to retire in less than nine years.

Women's pay

Pay inequity remains a persistent and pervasive problem in our society. In 2003, women earned 76% as much as men. For women of color, the gap was wider: African-American women earned 66% and Latina women 55% of men's earnings. While Asian women do better, they still made only 80% of men's earnings.

In 2004, the median annual income of a woman with a bachelor's degree who was age 25 and older and who worked full-time was 24% (or $13,104) less than that of a similarly qualified man, according to Census Bureau data. A woman with an advanced degree—master's, professional, or doctoral degree—earned 28% (or $20,176) less than a similarly qualified man.

Workers in predominantly female occupations earn less than others with similar qualifications, experience, and responsibility who work in fields that are predominantly male. This is certainly the case for library workers.

In 2001, new MLS graduates from ALA-accredited programs earned an average annual salary of $36,818; their median salary was $35,000. The average starting salary for a systems analyst or database administrator with a master's degree in computer science was $61,000. These are professions that are more than 82% male.

The median hourly wage for *librarians* in 2003 was $21.50 (an annual wage of $44,720 for those working full-time); the median hourly wage for similarly qualified computer systems analysts was $31.28 (an annual wage of $65,062), that of electrical engineers was $34.05 ($70,824 a year), that of computer and information systems research scientists was $39.81 ($82,804 a year), and actuaries earned $36.19 ($75,275 a year). These (mostly male) professionals have education and responsibilities comparable to those of librarians.

The median hourly wage of *library technicians* was $11.95 (an annual wage of $24,865 for those working full-time); the median hourly wage for civil engineering technicians was $18.38, while that of respiratory technicians was $17.29. Paralegals earned $18.48 an hour.

In a 1999 ALA survey of library support staff, 56% of respondents had a bachelor's or higher degree. The mean hourly wage was $11.28.

Library assistants had a median hourly salary of $9.61 (amounting to $19,988 annually for full-time work) in 2003, while loan interviewers and clerks earned $13.70 ($28,496).

The wage gap

In addition to library workers being poorly paid because they are predominantly female, those library workers who are women may well be paid less than those who are men.

In a 2003 survey of academic librarians, even when years of experience in a particular job category are accounted for, men still outpace women in salary by almost 6%: $56,199 for women and $59,417 for men. The average years of experience for women: 17.0; for men: 16.8. This pattern is repeated for minority librarians. The average salary of minority men is higher than that for minority women in seven of the 10 cohorts.

The average salary for male directors in ARL libraries was higher than that of their female counterparts. The overall salary for women research librarians was 94.4% that of men in 2003, compared to 94.1% in 2002.

In 2004, male librarians had median weekly earnings of $854 while the median weekly earnings for women were $823.

Benefits

Nearly 12% of public libraries do not offer a pension and 17.4% do not offer retirement savings. Among academic libraries, 23.3% do not offer a pension and 20% do not offer retirement savings.

Almost 40% of public libraries do not offer vision insurance and 16% do not offer dental insurance. Among academic libraries, 42.9% do not offer vision insurance and 17.9% do not offer dental insurance.

Almost 34% of public libraries do not offer disability insurance and almost 17% do not offer prescription coverage; in academic libraries, 19.7% do not offer disability insurance and 23.1% do not offer prescription coverage.

Unionization

In 2004, 26% of librarians were union members; 30% were represented by unions. Seventeen percent of library technicians were union members—more than twice as many as in 2003—and 17% were represented by unions.

Union librarians earned an average of 39% more than nonunion librarians in 2004. Union library assistants earned an average of 38% more than nonunion in 2004.

Through the New York Public Library Guild, Local 1930, American Federation of State, County and Municipal Employees (AFSCME) library workers won an 8% pay increase in April 2001, in addition to the two 4% raises negotiated for citywide employees, after a three-year campaign and negotiating with city officials.

The Orange County, Florida, Library System organized and affiliated with the Service Employees International Union (SEIU).

Management spent $100,000 to defeat the union. Workers got the first pay raise in nine years as a result of bargaining, as well as an extra floating holiday and a grievance procedure that mandates binding arbitration.

According to ALA, 65.7% of libraries surveyed reported that no one in their library was covered by a collective-bargaining agreement, and that all professional staff were covered in only 16.4% of libraries surveyed. All support staff were covered in 20.3% of the libraries surveyed.

For more information, contact Pamela Wilson, pwilson@dpeaflcio.org.

SOURCE: Pamela Wilson, "Library Workers: Facts and Figures," www.dpeaflcio.org/policy/factsheets/fs_2005_library_workers.htm.

ACADEMIC LIBRARIES

The largest university research libraries, 2004

THE FOLLOWING FIGURES are based on an index developed by the Association of Research Libraries (ARL) to measure the relative size of its university library members. The five categories used in the rankings were determined by factor analysis of 22 variables and represent the elements in which ARL university libraries most resemble one another. The index does not attempt to measure a library's services, quality of collections, or success in meeting the needs of users.

The five data elements are: numbers of volumes held, number of volumes added (gross), number of current serials received, number of professional and support staff, and total operating expenditures.

This rank order table is only for 113 university library members of ARL, which has approximately 10 nonuniversity library members. Nonuniversity libraries are not gauged by the same index formula as the universities, and are sufficiently different that it would be misleading to incorporate them into the table.

ARL does not claim that this ranking incorporates all the factors necessary to give a complete picture of research library quality. However, it is a measuring device that has proven reliable over the years for specific internal and comparative purposes.

Volumes in library does not include microforms, manuscripts, audiovisual and computer resources, maps, or certain other items central to research library collections and services. It includes government documents in some (but not all) cases. It is thus not a complete indicator of library resources.

Total staff includes professionals, nonprofessionals, and student assistants; however, only the first two groups are used to calculate the rank score.

Total expenditures include money spent on materials purchases, salaries, and general operations, but does not include capital expenditures for buildings, expenditures for plant maintenance, and some kinds of computing and administrative services; these are often part of the main university budget and not directly allocated to the library. However, such additional expenditures are crucial to an effective library and reflect the total commitment of an institution to providing and preserving research information. Figures for Canadian libraries are expressed in U.S. dollars.

	Rank	Volumes in library	Volumes added	Current serials	Total staff	Total expenditures
Harvard University	1	15,391,906	302,173	100,009	1,137	$100,892,145
Yale University	2	11,389,504	280,572	66,867	604	65,212,582
University of Toronto	3	10,032,197	230,073	62,023	539	47,556,426
University of California at Berkeley	4	9,812,997	200,310	79,394	426	53,263,903
University of California at Los Angeles	5	7,988,925	168,335	78,161	432	47,691,633
University of Illinois at Urbana-Champaign	6	10,191,895	178,221	89,444	400	33,557,443
Columbia University	7	8,650,258	162,166	65,650	479	46,200,379
University of Michigan	8	7,958,145	171,154	67,554	475	46,737,671
Cornell University	9	7,365,268	171,803	72,788	433	42,560,694
University of Texas at Austin	10	8,482,207	174,190	48,096	436	36,316,124
University of Wisconsin at Madison	11	7,807,097	126,373	55,164	402	39,251,812
Indiana University	12	6,770,498	145,288	70,370	362	32,340,522
University of Washington	13	6,546,072	186,227	48,269	351	34,780,704
Pennsylvania State University	14	4,975,339	98,771	58,549	527	40,610,081
Princeton University	15	6,373,184	154,045	44,634	354	35,256,274
University of North Carolina	16	5,601,436	120,688	52,454	339	29,619,061
New York University	17	4,642,734	126,576	49,044	344	34,462,180
University of Chicago	18	7,124,379	156,259	41,790	243	27,878,919
University of Minnesota	19	6,374,293	130,964	35,801	298	31,640,604
University of Pennsylvania	20	5,473,472	112,214	42,031	291	32,130,433
Ohio State University	21	5,809,505	145,968	35,561	280	28,509,784
University of British Columbia	22	5,207,841	111,213	48,430	312	25,964,851
University of Pittsburgh	23	4,640,279	147,594	44,924	291	25,664,536
University of Virginia	24	4,987,437	82,997	52,192	309	29,354,994
Duke University	25	5,471,919	115,778	33,934	299	30,156,928
University of Iowa	26	4,474,826	138,899	50,675	235	24,118,906
North Carolina State University	27	3,389,517	160,830	54,799	233	25,042,984
University of Alberta	28	6,011,574	89,221	40,328	295	24,105,116
Rutgers University	29	4,107,538	80,462	41,942	345	29,564,707
University of Arizona	30	5,201,065	104,508	36,060	259	27,064,875
University of Georgia	31	4,028,611	82,420	67,268	268	21,544,004
Northwestern University	32	4,545,038	100,317	39,944	254	25,630,720
Texas A&M University	33	3,310,840	92,518	49,197	261	25,842,504
Emory University	34	2,935,654	88,469	53,602	256	27,797,992
Johns Hopkins University	35	3,606,254	62,142	50,097	292	28,165,251
Arizona State University	36	4,058,675	81,631	34,482	288	24,614,964
Washington University in St. Louis	37	3,647,459	60,850	47,266	238	29,416,653
University of Florida	38	4,075,290	85,371	25,330	320	25,112,380
Michigan State University	39	4,747,959	71,996	37,880	204	22,557,590
University of Utah	40	3,185,910	68,199	40,753	266	22,230,041

	Rank	Volumes in library	Volumes added	Current serials	Total staff	Total expenditures
University of California at San Diego	41	3,071,461	75,716	30,461	282	25,945,519
University of Kansas	42	4,039,645	72,518	41,830	215	19,076,650
Université de Montréal	43	3,047,014	61,822	29,188	382	21,949,251
Brigham Young University	44	3,538,205	101,287	27,161	175	22,382,454
University of Tennessee	45	2,920,485	58,394	42,230	232	20,933,676
University of California at Davis	46	3,424,040	65,012	36,647	218	19,557,745
University of Cincinnati	47	3,050,113	87,357	39,787	168	19,502,676
University of Miami	48	2,515,732	68,540	43,939	205	19,986,430
McGill University	49	3,515,795	100,375	17,900	230	21,475,347
University of Maryland	50	3,082,973	69,910	33,438	208	20,033,947
Florida State University	51	2,874,988	92,637	38,271	196	13,697,817
University at Buffalo	52	3,360,036	61,241	34,126	185	18,720,435
Vanderbilt University	53	2,964,214	67,296	28,754	210	20,048,886
University of Oklahoma	54	4,736,213	66,488	31,325	147	17,232,008
University of Connecticut	55	3,211,431	51,464	37,621	159	23,488,601
University of Kentucky	56	3,092,616	58,371	29,633	216	19,270,355
Texas Tech University	57	2,399,479	51,904	44,327	212	18,527,587
University of Notre Dame	58	3,122,187	76,471	22,377	218	18,764,762
Georgetown University	59	2,407,125	66,659	28,173	211	22,184,204
University of California at Santa Barbara	60	2,818,424	55,107	38,223	187	18,208,284
Université de Laval	61	2,658,127	91,134	27,952	215	14,454,499
Louisiana State University	62	3,315,748	55,884	58,918	142	12,790,170
Boston University	63	2,396,362	56,230	34,214	198	19,977,770
University of Colorado	64	3,484,982	86,270	20,677	160	18,390,430
University of California at Irvine	65	2,398,455	74,436	25,464	203	18,542,297
University of South Carolina	66	3,436,445	63,439	24,152	182	17,271,058
Dartmouth College	67	2,434,788	50,810	37,893	175	18,807,974
University of Hawaii	68	3,356,031	74,036	29,679	150	14,786,274
University of New Mexico	69	2,627,815	67,615	14,901	251	19,396,595
Oklahoma State University	70	2,572,044	77,050	41,608	134	12,883,426
University of Southern Calif.	71	3,354,954	57,616	16,999	174	21,788,025
Massachusetts Institute of Technology	72	2,741,944	50,289	22,312	191	19,953,776
Wayne State University	73	3,348,242	35,799	20,940	194	21,297,891
Southern Illinois University	74	2,840,324	47,704	40,588	145	14,220,244
University of Western Ontario	75	3,056,875	37,758	38,517	169	14,382,653
Purdue University	76	2,459,943	54,003	20,829	219	17,745,361
University of Illinois at Chicago	77	2,236,632	44,089	31,236	215	15,603,117
Boston College	78	2,076,844	58,755	32,936	155	16,588,659
Iowa State University	79	2,416,670	52,692	33,914	147	16,076,113
Brown University	80	3,305,324	48,600	18,149	179	17,504,112
University of Rochester	81	3,370,854	43,358	22,770	158	16,324,549
Ohio University	82	2,550,511	85,974	25,557	139	12,445,639
University of Missouri at Columbia	83	3,205,927	60,290	19,746	165	14,231,832
Syracuse University	84	3,136,964	42,117	20,980	208	14,444,432

	Rank	Volumes in library	Volumes added	Current serials	Total staff	Total expenditures
University of Nebraska–Lincoln	85	2,807,194	47,806	31,571	153	13,446,172
University of Houston	86	2,256,863	63,906	22,052	162	15,650,925
Temple University	87	2,971,988	48,287	23,567	152	14,619,227
University of Louisville	88	1,950,624	60,513	24,872	141	17,319,156
Auburn University	89	2,767,765	47,258	39,318	109	12,518,579
University of Alabama	90	2,465,217	47,603	31,199	135	13,248,722
George Washington University	91	2,129,332	54,518	12,005	213	20,547,370
University of Massachusetts	92	3,158,359	32,688	37,716	126	11,654,629
Queen's University	93	2,410,869	49,097	21,092	155	13,312,409
University of California at Riverside	94	2,305,526	53,954	23,783	140	12,069,545
State University of New York at Albany	95	2,064,576	40,752	34,486	131	12,236,201
York University	96	2,476,701	56,411	10,965	171	17,445,868
Washington State University	97	2,193,803	36,548	30,936	142	12,775,271
Colorado State University	98	1,967,035	83,905	16,505	109	16,098,539
Tulane University	99	2,403,728	51,814	16,588	160	13,262,398
University of Oregon	100	2,636,234	38,956	18,180	151	14,294,319
University of Manitoba	101	2,025,342	40,484	15,809	196	14,806,890
Virginia Polytechnic Institute and State University	102	2,210,645	40,648	30,072	126	11,687,071
Kent State University	103	2,667,683	56,368	14,602	128	12,821,827
Rice University	104	2,394,131	52,497	16,013	123	14,266,058
University of Delaware	105	2,623,554	40,445	12,476	164	14,828,278
University of Saskatchewan	106	1,950,582	64,404	15,509	153	11,286,852
Georgia Institute of Technology	107	2,370,825	45,909	26,068	109	10,622,028
Case Western Reserve University	108	2,452,731	32,503	20,678	113	13,988,420
State University of New York at Stony Brook	109	2,192,704	26,551	29,091	115	12,383,254
McMaster University	110	1,968,168	34,542	20,401	142	11,383,561
University of Waterloo	111	1,992,700	25,744	16,689	136	11,395,352
Howard University	112	2,194,804	33,410	10,122	119	10,191,433
University of Guelph	113	1,555,385	28,797	12,505	117	9,179,417

SOURCE: Martha Kyrillidou and Mark Young, *ARL Statistics 2003–2004* (Washington, D.C.: Association of Research Libraries, 2004).

Denison
University Library,
Granville, Ohio, 1878

ACRL data from non-ARL libraries, 2004

THE FOLLOWING STATISTICS are selected from a sample of 1,119 of all types of North American academic libraries surveyed by the Association of College and Research Libraries. Those shown here are the 35 largest institutions that do not appear in the Association of Research Libraries statistics. Institutions are arranged by number of volumes in the library and not by a ranking similar to the ARL list, although the same measures are shown.

	Volumes in library	Volumes added	Current serials	Total staff	Total expenditures
Concordia University	2,996,256	24,455	12,339	165	$11,261,460
Southern Methodist University	2,807,991	60,026	11,635	158	11,993,718
University of Calgary	2,481,808	55,055	23,164	228	21,686,352
Claremont Colleges	2,390,598	91,249	16,308	99	8,271,363
Baylor University	2,165,992	35,601	20,027	223	12,027,240
College of William and Mary	2,118,870	40,156	11,507	116	8,710,757
Mississippi State University	2,074,652	25,015	16,551	152	9,753,602
Northern Illinois University	2,068,449	41,452	18,456	179	10,329,860
University of Wisconsin at Milwaukee	2,045,502	49,571	27,126	131	8,223,810
Western Michigan University	2,040,692	40,149	9,715	130	11,344,511
University of South Florida	1,983,472	64,917	21,592	220	14,628,877
Cleveland State University	1,943,895	100,838	4,269	74	4,580,907
St. Louis University	1,878,213	37,730	13,999	108	9,017,129
University of Victoria	1,856,987	22,934	14,473	153	11,936,770
State University of New York at Binghamton	1,845,181	36,149	6,233	132	9,637,059
Loyola University of Chicago	1,792,825	31,999	9,230	150	5,041,857
University of Toledo	1,769,403	27,456	11,092	77	5,203,524
Wake Forest University	1,766,301	34,399	15,889	131	10,590,170
University of New Hampshire	1,762,922	32,274	35,681	123	9,278,866
University of Arkansas	1,714,085	67,866	22,485	163	10,790,959
Université d'Ottawa	1,688,620	39,715	16,494	155	16,722,787
University of Windsor	1,687,823	17,919	23,562	99	7,141,253
University of North Dakota	1,658,824	73,039	20,270	106	5,828,552
Virginia Commonwealth University	1,647,775	54,008	12,973	126	8,862,921
Marquette University	1,570,290	46,258	18,678	122	10,040,742
Indiana University–Purdue University Indianapolis	1,568,290	53,158	9,974	178	13,984,627
Georgia State University	1,542,304	31,983	10,213	175	10,476,026
Oregon State University	1,529,693	25,435	14,062	121	9,463,898
West Virginia University	1,498,864	28,660	31,419	175	9,795,027
California State University at Long Beach	1,470,843	13,853	3,045	90	7,057,187
City University of New York– City College	1,444,400	28,611	29,990	56	4,040,512
Univ. of California at Santa Cruz	1,438,892	36,386	21,924	176	10,640,074
Florida Atlantic University	1,424,810	51,361	29,523	119	6,821,125
Western Washington University	1,377,949	20,137	4,516	78	4,836,059
Smith College	1,355,349	23,832	10,103	82	6,196,573

SOURCE: ALA Association of College and Research Libraries, *2004 Academic Library Trends and Statistics* (Chicago: ACRL, 2005).

Standards for libraries in higher education

IN 2004, the Association of College and Research Libraries approved standards that were significantly different from those it had adopted previously. The new standards were intended to apply to all types of libraries, they were intended to allow libraries to establish individual goals, they focused on the library's contribution to institutional effectiveness and student learning outcomes, and they suggested points of comparison against comparable institutions. Here is an extract from the new document.—*GME.*

Each library is encouraged to choose its own peer group for the purpose of comparisons. Peer groups may already be identified for benchmarking purposes by the institution. If not, a peer group could be identified using criteria such as the institution's mission, reputation, selectivity for admission, size of budget, size of endowment, expenditure for library support, and/or size of collection. Once a peer group has been determined, "points of comparison" can be made to compare the strength of the library with its peers. Suggested points of comparison for input and output measures are provided. This list is not to be considered exhaustive; other points of comparison can be determined by the institution. If comparisons are going to be conducted on an annual or other regular basis, the same categories should be used each time to assure a consistent and usable result.

Points of comparison: Input measures

- Ratio of volumes to combined total student (undergraduate and graduate, if applicable) and faculty FTE.
- Ratio of volumes added per year to combined total student and faculty FTE.
- Ratio of material/information resource expenditures to combined total student and faculty FTE.
- Percent of total library budget expended in the following three categories:
  1. materials/information resources, subdivided by print, microform, and electronic.
  2. staff resources, subdivided by librarians, full- and part-time staff, and student assistant expenditures. Federal contributions, if any, and outsourcing costs should be included here. When determining staff expenditures, care should be taken to consider comparable staff (i.e., including or excluding media, systems or development staff) and fringe benefits (within or outside the library budget).
  3. all other operating expenses (e.g., network infrastructure, equipment).
- Ratio of FTE library staff to combined student and faculty FTE.
- Ratio of usable library space (in square feet) to combined student and faculty FTE.
- Ratio of number of students attending library instructional sessions to total number of students in specified target groups.
- Ratio of library seating to combined student and faculty FTE.

- Ratio of computer workstations to combined student and faculty FTE (consider that institutional requirements for student ownership of desktop or laptop computers could affect the need for workstations within the library).

Suggested points of comparison: Output measures

- Ratio of circulation (excluding reserve) to combined student and faculty FTE.
- Ratio of interlibrary loan requests to combined student and faculty FTE (could be divided between photocopies and books).
- Ratio of interlibrary loan lending to borrowing.
- Interlibrary loan/document delivery borrowing turnaround time, fill rate, and unit cost.
- Interlibrary loan/document delivery lending turnaround time, fill rate, and unit cost.
- Ratio of reference questions (sample week) to combined student and faculty FTE.

Services

The library should establish, promote, maintain, and evaluate a range of quality services that support the institution's mission and goals. The library should provide competent and prompt assistance for its users. Hours of access to the library should be reasonable and convenient for its users. Reference and other special assistance should be available at times when the institution's primary users most need them.

Questions. How well does the library establish, promote, maintain, and evaluate a range of quality services that support the academic program of the institution and optimal library use?

Are reference, circulation, and government document services designed to enable users to take full advantage of the resources available to them?

How do student and faculty expectations affect library services?

How well do interlibrary loan and document delivery services support the needs of qualified users?

Does the library maintain hours of access consistent with reasonable demand?

What library services are provided for programs at off-campus sites? How are the needs of users and their satisfaction determined at those sites?

How are students and faculty informed of library services?

Does the library maintain and utilize quantitative and qualitative measurements of its ability to serve its users?

When academic programs are offered at off-campus sites, what are the standards or guidelines used to assure success? Are the *ACRL Guidelines for Distance Learning Library Services* (www.ala.org/acrl/guides/distlrng.html) used to consider existing and potential services?

SOURCE: "Standards for Libraries in Higher Education," *College & Research Libraries News* 65 (October 2004): 534–543.

PUBLIC LIBRARIES

Public library records

Most bookmobiles:	St. Louis Co. (Mo.) Library	10
Most branches:	Toronto (Ont.) PL	99
Highest director's salary:	Brooklyn (N.Y.) PL	$203,600
Highest entry-level salary:	Santa Clara (Calif.) PL	$60,936
Most reference transactions:	Los Angeles (Calif.) PL	9,856,120
Most interlibrary loans to others:	Madison (Wis.) PL	472,966
Most interlibrary loans from others:	Madison (Wis.) PL	648,884
Highest expenditures per capita:	Hampton Library, Bridgehampton, N.Y.	$286.11
Most generous Friends group:	Toledo–Lucas Co. (Ohio) PL	$800,000
Largest income from a foundation:	Free Library of Philadelphia	$17,486,909
Highest registrations as a percentage of population served:	Commerce (Calif.) PL	225.6%
Highest circulation per registered borrower:	Peninsula (Ohio) PL	51.2%
Highest program attendance:	PL of Charlotte & Mecklenburg Co., N.C.	568,557

SOURCE: Statistical Report 2005: Public Library Data Service (Chicago: ALA Public Library Association, 2005).

The 20 largest public libraries

THE NUMBER OF VOLUMES a library owns is not a measure of the quality of library service. But as the late Herman Fussler noted in 1949, "Yet the reverence for size continues. The library that has the most books is likely to be regarded as ipso facto, the best." Volume counts do have a certain fascination. The following are among the largest public libraries in North America, according to 2005 data in the annual *Public Library Data Service Statistical Report*, which surveyed 938 libraries. (The New York Public Library's Research Libraries, which has topped the list in the past, did not participate in this year's survey; nor did Dallas Public Library, which recorded 5,916,549 volumes in the 2004 survey.)—*GME.*

Boston (Mass.) Public Library	15,332,025
County of Los Angeles (Calif.) Public Library	9,619,692
Public Library of Cincinnati and Hamilton County, Ohio	9,178,249
Toronto (Ont.) Public Library	7,572,786
Detroit (Mich.) Public Library	7,371,078

Queens Borough (N.Y.) Public Library	6,651,821
Free Library of Philadelphia (Pa.)	6,307,978
Los Angeles (Calif.) Public Library	6,234,988
New York (N.Y.) Public Library, the Branch Libraries	5,796,978
Brooklyn (N.Y.) Public Library	4,927,341
Chicago (Ill.) Public Library	4,896,854
Miami-Dade (Fla.) Public Library	4,809,818
Houston (Tex.) Public Library	4,202,200
Cleveland (Ohio) Public Library	4,130,495
Cuyahoga County (Ohio) Public Library	3,676,286
Buffalo & Erie County (N.Y.) Public Library	3,644,761
King County (Wash.) Library System	3,466,000
Hawaii State Public Library System	3,372,589
St. Louis (Mo.) Public Library	3,340,550
Mid-Continent Public Library, Independence, Mo.	3,329,842

SOURCE: *Statistical Report 2005: Public Library Data Service* (Chicago: ALA Public Library Association, 2005).

How the states rank, 2003

DATA ON PUBLIC LIBRARY expenditures and operations are given for FY 2003. The rankings were compiled by the National Data Resource Center of the National Center for Education Statistics (NCES) using data submitted through the Federal-State Cooperative System (FSCS) for public library data. States are ranked by expenses per capita (total operating expenditures divided by the official state population estimate). Other measures are for local government income, circulation transactions, reference transactions, personnel costs, and expenditures for materials in electronic format.

State	Number of PLs	2003 operating expenditures	Expenses per capita	Rank	Rank local income	Rank circ. trans.	Rank ref. trans.	Rank total staff $	Rank electr. mats. $
Ohio	244	$ 612,345,118	$53.94	1	17	2	5	3	4
D.C.*	1	27,057,375	48.03	2	40	51	38	41	42
N.Y.	751	864,334,461	45.66	3	2	3	2	2	2
Conn.	194	147,811,480	42.71	4	20	23	24	20	17
N.J.	308	343,520,282	40.83	5	5	13	11	6	10
Ind.	238	247,453,696	40.70	6	9	7	13	12	9
Wash.	55	243,871,583	39.99	7	8	8	15	10	7
Ill.	629	483,347,529	38.92	8	3	5	6	4	3
Alaska	85	24,898,084	38.37	9	43	50	51	45	40
R.I.	48	39,181,855	37.38	10	39	42	42	35	37
Colo.	104	167,858,642	37.16	11	12	19	16	17	12
Oreg.	122	127,899,532	36.49	12	23	17	28	22	22
Wyo.	23	17,983,600	36.06	13	44	49	46	46	47
Md.	17	190,174,365	35.42	14	18	14	14	14	8
Mass.	370	225,173,501	35.03	15	10	16	17	11	23
Wis.	377	177,543,276	32.34	16	14	12	19	15	20
Minn.	129	159,026,294	31.59	17	16	15	21	16	21

* NCES includes data for the District of Columbia to be comprehensive, but the Public Library of the District of Columbia might more legitimately be compared to libraries in other large cities.

State	Number of PLs	2003 operating expenditures	Expenses per capita	Rank	Rank local income	Rank circ. trans.	Rank ref. trans.	Rank total staff $	Rank electr. mats. $
Mich.	379	308,471,923	31.04	18	7	11	12	8	13
N.H.	230	39,334,128	30.45	19	36	36	43	34	35
Kans.	325	82,819,183	30.41	20	27	27	29	27	19
Utah	53	64,851,117	27.97	21	32	24	26	31	33
Mo.	166	155,991,025	27.87	22	15	20	25	21	16
Va.	78	201,654,530	27.67	23	11	10	8	13	14
Nev.	19	63,019,387	27.44	24	33	33	34	33	26
Iowa	539	76,872,988	26.11	25	29	25	32	28	31
Calif.	166	917,330,786	25.77	26	1	1	1	1	1
Vt.	187	14,989,318	24.62	27	49	48	47	50	50
La.	65	110,147,704	24.50	28	24	30	18	24	28
Maine	273	30,719,060	23.84	29	42	39	44	40	45
Pa.	453	290,897,534	23.69	30	13	9	10	9	6
Fla.	53	403,685,124	23.65	31	4	4	3	5	5
Ariz.	86	124,376,460	22.73	32	21	21	20	23	15
Nebr.	275	38,797,422	22.67	33	35	34	39	37	30
Dela.	19	17,436,972	22.25	34	48	46	49	48	51
S.Dak.	125	15,958,521	21.14	35	46	45	45	47	41
Hawaii	1	25,337,130	20.35	36	51	43	41	42	48
S.C.	41	83,345,473	20.29	37	28	29	22	26	25
Ky.	116	81,671,776	19.95	38	25	28	30	30	27
Idaho	102	27,205,392	19.91	39	41	37	40	43	44
Ga.	58	160,113,986	19.66	40	22	22	9	18	29
Okla.	112	63,647,450	18.45	41	31	32	31	32	38
N.C.	64	149,848,216	18.00	42	19	18	7	19	24
Mont.	79	15,821,088	17.57	43	47	44	48	49	49
N.Mex.	90	31,172,458	16.63	44	38	40	37	39	32
Ala.	207	73,599,169	16.55	45	30	31	27	29	36
Tex.	552	332,030,374	15.24	46	6	6	4	7	11
Tenn.	184	86,735,945	14.88	47	26	26	23	25	18
N.Dak.	82	9,390,517	14.62	48	50	47	50	51	46
W.Va.	97	26,288,578	14.54	49	45	41	36	44	43
Ark.	43	37,073,325	13.87	50	34	35	33	38	39
Miss.	48	37,592,786	13.09	51	37	38	35	36	34

SOURCE: Public Libraries Survey: FY 2003 (Washington, D.C.: National Center for Education Statistics, June 2005), nces.ed.gov/pubsearch/pubsinfo.asp?pubid=2005362.

Great American public libraries, 2004

by Thomas J. Hennen Jr.

THE SEVENTH EDITION of Hennen's American Public Library Ratings (HAPLR) is based on data filed by libraries in 2004 concerning 2003 activities. The first edition in 1999 was based on data filed in 1997. The Federal-State Cooperative System compiles the annual reports as reported by state library agencies for nearly 9,000 libraries into a single dataset.

The HAPLR scores are based on six input and nine output measures. Each factor is weighted and then scored. Only libraries serving comparably sized populations are compared with one another. The author adds the scores for each library within a population category to develop a weighted score in each population category. A 95th-percentile score for all 15 measures would put the library at the top of its population category with a score of 950. A fifth-percentile score for all measures would place the library at the bottom with a score of 50. Most scores are between 250 and 750. Further details on the rating methods are available at www.haplr-index.com. Scores for the top five libraries in each population category are provided here.

Serving a population over 500,000
1. Columbus (Ohio) Metropolitan Library   867
2. Multnomah County (Oreg.) Public Library   858
3. Denver (Colo.) Public Library   838
4. Cuyahoga County (Ohio) Public Library   824
5. Baltimore County (Md.) Public Library   822

Serving a population of 250,000–499,999
1. Howard County (Md.) Library   917
2. Santa Clara County (Calif.) Library   896
3. Johnson County (Kans.) Library   828
4. St. Charles City-County (Mo.) Library District   814
5. Madison (Wis.) Public Library   807

Serving a population of 100,000–249,999
1. Naperville (Ill.) Public Libraries   940
2. Medina County (Ohio) District Library   886
3. Douglas County (Colo.) Libraries   870
4. St. Joseph County (Ind.) Public Library   867
5. Monroe County (Ind.) Public Library   866

Serving a population of 50,000–99,999
1. Washington-Centerville (Ohio) Public Library   947
2. Lakewood (Ohio) Public Library   929
3. Euclid (Ohio) Public Library   914
4. Newton (Mass.) Free Library   907
5. Westerville (Ohio) Public Library   896

Serving a population of 25,000–49,999
1. Westlake Porter (Ohio) Public Library   913
2. Upper Arlington (Ohio) Public Library   888
3. Suffern (N.Y.) Free Library   881
4. Middleton (Wis.) Public Library   877
5. St. Charles (Ill.) Public Library District   877

Serving a population of 10,000–24,999
1. North Canton (Ohio) Public Library   942
2. Twinsburg (Ohio) Public Library   937
3. Bexley (Ohio) Public Library   923
4. Brown Deer (Wis.) Public Library   910
5. Hays (Kans.) Public Library   910

Serving a population of 5,000–9,999
1. Wright Memorial Public Library, Oakwood, Ohio   939
2. Bridgeport (W. Va.) Public Library   926
3. New Cumberland (Pa.) Public Library   897
4. Morris (Minn.) Public Library   896
5. Dover (Mass.) Town Library   881

Serving a population of 2,500–4,999
1. Bell Memorial Public Library, Mentone, Ind.   914
2. Mount Pleasant (Utah) Public Library   913

3. James Kennedy Public Library, Dyersville, Iowa	908
4. Yoakum County (Tex.) Cecil Bickley Library	906
5. Tracy Memorial Library, New London, N.H.	903

Serving a population of 1,000–2,499

1. Flomaton (Ala.) Public Library	929
2. Sodus (N.Y.) Free Library	897
3. Seneca (Kans.) Free Library	889
4. Conrad (Iowa) Public Library	886
5. Angola (N.Y.) Public Library	883

Serving a population of under 1,000

1. Clayville (N.Y.) Library Association	896
2. Hardtner (Kans.) Public Library	894
3. New Woodstock (N.Y.) Free Library	893
4. Poland (N.Y.) Public Library	886
5. Brunswick (Nebr.) Public Library	869

SOURCE: Thomas J. Hennen Jr., "Great American Public Libraries: The 2005 HAPLR Rankings," *American Libraries* 36 (October 2005): 42–48.

Staying public:
The real crisis in librarianship
by John Buschman

LIBRARIANS AND THE INSTITUTIONS for which we speak have long prided ourselves on our integral relationship to democracy. We quote Madison and Jefferson approvingly and credit their ideas as the inspiration for what libraries do within and for a democratic society. This is not false pride or an illusion.

Librarianship, in many important ways, makes possible the ideal of the democratic public sphere through the rational organization of the cultural products of humanity—in effect keeping the ideal alive by embodying it in the multiplicity of voices and perspectives librarians consciously select. Historically, it is an imperfectly realized vision of librarianship—and always will be—but it has deep connections to the functioning of a legitimate democracy.

This view of librarianship is grounded in the ideas of German social theorist Jürgen Habermas, who has written extensively on the historical development of democracy and the public sphere. Habermas's ideal of unfettered communication is a natural fit for librarianship: By building diverse voices, perspectives, and arguments into our collections and services, we keep alive the means of realizing true democracy—by transcending our nation's historical shortcomings of exclusion and discrimination, and our profession's similar shortcomings, through the struggle to include censored works and underserved groups.

Jürgen Habermas

Our social role, our essence, our founding and reason for being are intimately tied to the needs of supporting and replicating democracy: The motivations behind the founding of public cultural institutions in 19th-century America closely followed the emergence of a democratic public sphere, and librarianship enacts what Habermas spelled out as its actual functioning.

All is not well with the democratic public sphere of today, however. Habermas has studied the corruption of communicative processes—think Jerry Springer here—and the consequent effects on democracy. The erosion has hit librarianship as well, in the form of an unacknowledged (and serious) narrowing of information outlets as evidenced by the handful of multinational conglomerates that control most information resources—both print and online.

However, there is a different vantage point on which I wish to focus: Without much debate, policymakers in the nation and in our own field have recast the purpose of libraries in economic instead of democratic terms. Like education, our field has been called upon to play a so-called crucial role in bringing about the information society and the new economy, but without the public funding for that expanded economic mission.

The model of the market, business management, and entrepreneurial practices has all been ascendant for some time now—especially in support of the new economy and information capitalism. Librarians have had to address that new role and the funding problems that stem from it. In the process we have transformed library users into "customers" and then adopted the corollary business practices of marketing and public relations. We have also embraced the market model of vying with other libraries and flashy bookstores for those customers, as well as taking an entrepreneurial approach to funding shortages and library practices.

Spherical argument

Without a larger view of what is happening to most public functions and all public cultural institutions, debating the specifics of these shifts (for example, the Barnes and Noble model as competition for libraries) is futile—rather like rearranging the deck chairs on the *Titanic*.

Over the last 25 years or so, the missions and operations of public cultural institutions have been redefined. In "The New Public Philosophy" (*Democracy*, Oct. 1981, pp. 29–37), political scientist Sheldon Wolin wrote, "Economics now dominates public discourse . . . in virtually every sphere of public activity, from health care, social welfare, and education to weapons systems, environmental protection, and scientific research." Management theorist Henry Mintzberg put his finger on a core issue in "Managing Government, Governing Management" (*Harvard Business Review*, May-June 1996, pp. 75–83): We're intoxicated with the "triumph" of capitalism over communism and as a result, we have unthinkingly imported business models on a massive scale into public enterprises.

What actually won out in this redefinition was not the pure market/business model. Rather, Mintzberg insists, it was *balance:* We had strong private *and* public sectors, as well as strength in hybrid institutions (for example, a private research university taking the lead in national matters such as public health with public research funding and support). Operating public cultural institutions such as libraries on business-based models assumes, among other things, that performance can be measured objectively. But as Mintzberg points out, some activities are publicly funded for the simple reason that they are extraordinarily difficult to measure: What objective criteria determine what makes a good teacher or children's librarian?

We are a society out of balance—tilted too much toward business and market solutions and too far from the ideals of a true public and a democratic society. Perhaps more disturbing is our unawareness of the historical fact that we as a society used to regard our public institutions differently and managed them with the goal in mind of furthering the public good. The new economic model of public philosophy has become both the reason and the method to reform and shape public policy for a generation now, directly shaping priorities that determine the spending for and mission of public cultural institutions.

The money pit

This is all well and good, you say—and you might even agree—but what does it really have to do with librarianship in general, or your library in particular? Libraries share a common fate with archives, schools, universities, orchestras, and museums—whether they recognize it or not and whether they are nominally private or not—and these broad trends do not stop at the school board or university or museum doorstep. They form the basis of public policy and funding for libraries too. Imitating business-management schemes to run a library is inappropriate and it recasts the nature of tax-exempt institutions as quasieconomic entities.

Boards and provosts all over the country are encouraging libraries away from public (or tuition-based, which is similar) funding sources and toward entrepreneurial strategies. One prominent proponent of this approach in the field, Charles Robinson, assumes that larger public libraries will—and should—serve primarily the middle class and raise 15% of their operating revenues themselves through grants and fund-raising. Specific funding for technological resources is seen as central to the new economy and therefore easier to come by (think Gates Foundation), while public funding for more traditional needs such as buildings, furniture, and retrospective cataloging has become much more difficult to acquire.

An ideology is being pursued here: Buildings and collections (and sometimes, hours and popular services) are held static or defunded to move libraries toward networked resources. It is essentially a way to position the library within dominant economic trends so that we seem relevant, or worth funding. Our acceding to this model is, in many ways, an active dismantling of the democratic public-sphere discourse that libraries enact and represent.

Victoria Public Library, Victoria, B.C.

The current vogue of the customer-service creed in librarianship is just another way of moving us toward a business model and is a good example of what I mean by "dismanding." It presumes a number of things—among them, that libraries do not currently serve their publics well or that they lack the motivation (profit incentive, in business terms) to improve their performance. The whole notion of "customer" presumes, as John Budd notes ("A Critique of Customer and Commodity," *College & Research Libraries*, July 1997, pp. 310–321), prior knowledge of what a client needs and a quick turnaround in delivering it (the vaunted "McDonald's of information" or "hardware store" model). We know full well that instant information is *not* the same as research or actually learning something, yet that is the model we are urged to pursue. Responding purely to popular demand forces us to abandon any notion of outreach to underserved populations or providing alternative resources on our shelves and in our services—a basic, democratic tenet of fairness.

We're looking for a return on investment from those we serve, and that is a radically reconceptualized notion of libraries. In the process, the democratic public and social function of libraries subtly but surely changes: from a space for research, reflection, and reading to the social capital of a community (or a splashy recruiting locus for a university). When we don't structure our services and collections around public purposes, but around the needs of the economy and the economic well-being of our library, we are not only abandoning the democratic public sphere—we are actively dismantling the essential core of our institutions.

We are a public institution and profession, founded for democratic purposes, and we simply cannot be true to our raison d'etre and our democratic role while unthinkingly and enthusiastically embracing an economic one. I am not suggesting that adopting appropriate business practices to acquire supplies or discounts on books corrupts us, or that seeking to better serve our constituencies automatically shifts us to a customer focus, with all that implies. Nonetheless, here's a measure of how far out of balance the current environment is: A private consulting firm suggested that the word "public" be dropped in describing schools because it "has come to have negative connotations" with such entities as public libraries, public radio, and public assistance (Michael W. Apple and James A. Beane, eds., *Democratic Schools*, Association for Supervision and Curriculum Development, 1995, p. 101). We should stand apart from—and even in opposition to—the shift to a democracy of consumers where the only voters are those who can afford the privilege.

As a society, do we really need another model of media- and market-driven consumer space, or do we need an alternative in the public sphere? Mintzberg put it well: "When the enterprises are really free, the people are not." Our boards and our sponsoring institutions need to be reminded that the impact of a library—like good teaching—is extraordinarily difficult to quantify (monetarily or in terms of quality). The effects may be profound but latent for many years. Informed deliberation and communication remain the essence of both education and democracy, and we play a pivotal—if undervalued—role in both. Our ideas about our profession and our institutions should be more expansive, more democratic, truer to our principles, and not merely limited to what is good for the economy.

Libraries were founded—and funded—as essential to the democratic public sphere. Can we move away from those purposes and maintain our funding? Thanks to multinational corporations, the public airwaves can pull off such a trick, but I doubt we can.

SOURCE: John Buschman, "Staying Public: The Real Crisis in Librarianship," *American Libraries* 35 (August 2004): 40–42.

SCHOOL LIBRARIES

Roles and responsibilities of the school library media specialist

AS TEACHER, THE LIBRARY MEDIA SPECIALIST collaborates with students and other members of the learning community to analyze learning and information needs, to locate and use resources that will meet those needs, and to understand and communicate the information the resources provide. An effective instructor of students, the library media specialist is knowledgeable about current research on teaching and learning and skilled in applying its findings to a variety of situations—particularly those that call upon students to access, evaluate, and use information from multiple sources in order to learn, to think, and to create and apply new knowledge. A curricular leader and a full participant on the instructional team, the library media specialist constantly updates personal skills and knowledge in order to work effectively with teachers, administrators, and other staff—both to expand their general understanding of information issues and to provide them with specific opportunities to develop sophisticated skills in information literacy, including the uses of information technology.

As **instructional partner**, the library media specialist joins with teachers and others to identify links across student information needs, curricular content, learning outcomes, and a wide variety of print, nonprint, and electronic information resources. Working with the entire school community, the library media specialist takes a leading role in developing policies, practices, and curricula that guide students to develop the full range of information and communication abilities. Committed to the process of collaboration, the library media specialist works closely with individual teachers in the critical areas of designing authentic learning tasks and assessments and integrating the information and communication abilities required to meet subject matter standards.

As **information specialist**, the library media specialist provides leadership and expertise in acquiring and evaluating information resources in all formats; in bringing an awareness of information issues into collaborative relationships with teachers, administrators, students, and others; and in modeling for students and others strategies for locating, accessing, and evaluating information within and beyond the library media center. Working in an environment that has been profoundly affected by technology, the library media specialist both masters sophisticated electronic resources and maintains a constant focus on the nature, quality, and ethical use of information available in these and in more traditional tools.

As **program administrator**, the library media specialist works collaboratively with members of the learning community to define the policies of the library media program and to guide and direct all activities related to it. Confident of the importance of the effective use of information and information technology to students' personal and economic success in their future lives, the library media specialist is an advocate for the library media program and provides the knowledge, vision, and leadership to steer it creatively and energetically in the 21st century. Proficient in the management of staff, budgets, equipment, and facilities, the library media specialist plans, executes, and evaluates the program to ensure its quality both at a general level and on a day-to-day basis.

Editor's note: For much more information on school libraries, refer to Blanche Woolls and David V. Loertscher, eds., *The Whole School Library Handbook* (Chicago: American Library Association, 2004).

SOURCE: ALA American Association of School Librarians and Association for Educational Communications and Technology, *Information Power: Building Partnerships for Learning* (Chicago: American Library Association, 1998), pp. 3–5.

School librarians and student performance

by Keith Curry Lance, Marcia J. Rodney, and Christine Hamilton-Pennell

IF YOUR SCHOOL HAS a well-developed library media center, student achievement on standardized tests will increase from 15% to 18%, according to this 2000 survey, known as the Second Colorado Study.—*GME.*

Colorado Student Assessment Program (CSAP) reading scores increase with increases in the following characteristics of library media (LM) programs: LM program development, information technology, teacher/library media specialist (LMS) collaboration, and individual visits to the library media center (LMC). In addition, as participation increases in leadership roles, so does

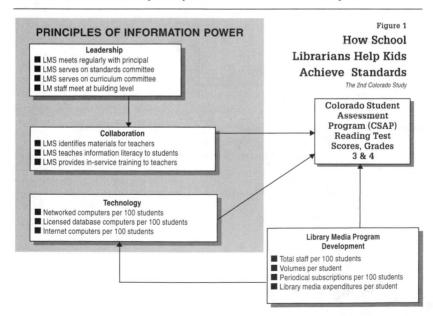

PRINCIPLES OF INFORMATION POWER

Leadership
- LMS meets regularly with principal
- LMS serves on standards committee
- LMS serves on curriculum committee
- LM staff meet at building level

Collaboration
- LMS identifies materials for teachers
- LMS teaches information literacy to students
- LMS provides in-service training to teachers

Technology
- Networked computers per 100 students
- Licensed database computers per 100 students
- Internet computers per 100 students

Figure 1

How School Librarians Help Kids Achieve Standards
The 2nd Colorado Study

Colorado Student Assessment Program (CSAP) Reading Test Scores, Grades 3 & 4

Library Media Program Development
- Total staff per 100 students
- Volumes per student
- Periodical subscriptions per 100 students
- Library media expenditures per student

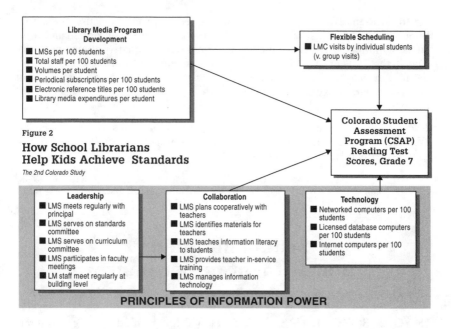

Figure 2

How School Librarians Help Kids Achieve Standards

The 2nd Colorado Study

collaboration between teachers and LMSs. The relationship between these factors and test scores is not explained away by other school or community conditions.

Library media program development

CSAP reading test scores increase with increases in:

- LMS hours per 100 students (7th grade),
- total staff hours per 100 students,
- print volumes per student,
- periodical subscriptions per 100 students,
- electronic reference titles per 100 students (7th grade), and
- library media expenditures per student.

Information technology

Where networked computers link library media centers with classrooms, labs, and other instructional sites, students earn higher CSAP reading test scores. These higher scores are particularly linked to the numbers of computers enabling teachers and students to utilize:

- LMC resources, either within the LMC or networked to the LMC,
- licensed databases, and
- internet/World Wide Web.

Collaboration

A central finding of this study is the importance of a collaborative approach to information literacy. Test scores rise in both elementary and middle schools as library media specialists and teachers work together. In addition, scores also increase with the amount of time library media specialists spend as in-service trainers of other teachers, acquainting them with the rapidly changing world of information.

Test scores increase as library media specialists spend more time:

- planning cooperatively with teachers (7th grade),
- identifying materials for teachers,
- teaching information literacy skills to students,
- providing in-service training to teachers, and
- managing a computer network through which the library media program reaches beyond its own walls to classrooms, labs, and offices (7th grade).

Flexible scheduling

Students have greater freedom in middle school, and are often able to choose whether or not they visit their school's LMC and use the resources there or take them home. Choosing to visit the LMC as an individual, separate from a class visit, is also a strong indicator of higher test scores. Middle schools with high test scores tend to have LMCs that report a high number of individual visits to the LMC on a per student basis.

Indirect effects

While not having a direct effect on test scores, leadership involvement on the part of the library media specialist (LMS) has a strong impact on whether or not the LMS is working closely with teachers and students. At both elementary and middle school levels, the more the LMS is involved in school and library media professional activities, the higher the level of collaboration. Collaboration, in turn, does have a direct impact on test scores.

Higher levels of collaboration result from:

- meeting regularly with school administration,
- serving on standards and curriculum committees,
- working with faculty at school-wide staff meetings, and
- meeting with library media staff at the building level.

At the elementary level, library media program development (levels of staffing, collections and expenditures) and technology are strong predictors of each other as well as of test scores. The seventh grade level sees a strong relationship between library media program development and flexible scheduling. These predictors of academic achievement cannot be explained away by school differences, including:

- school district expenditures per pupil,
- teacher/pupil ratio,
- the average years of experience of classroom teachers, and
- their average salaries; or

community differences, including:

- adult educational attainment,
- children in poverty, and
- racial/ethnic demographics.

How much will a school's test scores improve with specific improvements in its library media program? The answer depends on the library media (LM) program's current status, what it improves, and how much it is improved. When LM predictors are maximized (e.g., staffing, expenditures, and information resources and technology), CSAP reading scores tend to run 18% higher in fourth grade and 10–15% higher in seventh.

SOURCE: Keith Curry Lance, Marcia J. Rodney, and Christine Hamilton-Pennell, "Executive Summary," *How School Librarians Help Kids Achieve Standards: The Second Colorado Study* (Denver: Library Research Service, Colorado State Library, April 2000). For information on how to obtain the complete report, visit www.lrs.org.

SPECIAL LIBRARIES

Personal competencies for special librarians: Applied scenarios

by the Special Libraries Association

PERSONAL COMPETENCIES represent a set of attitudes, skills, and values that enable practitioners to work effectively and contribute positively to their organizations, clients, and profession. These competencies range from being strong communicators, to demonstrating the value-add of their contributions, to remaining flexible and positive in an ever-changing environment. The ideal special librarian:

Seeks out challenges and capitalizes on new opportunities.
- Actively pursues new roles in the organization that require an information leader.
- Demonstrates that their professional knowledge and skills solve a variety of information problems in a wide range of settings.
- Foresees changes impacting clients or patrons and aggressively explores services and programs, options and offerings.
- Helps others develop their new ideas.
- Views and uses technology as an enabler of new information ideas, products, and services.

Sees the big picture.
- Understands the environment in which her/his parent organization is operating and how the library or information services contribute towards those operations.
- Views the library and its information services as part of the bigger process of making informed decisions; gives the highest priority to demands and projects critical to the organization's competitive advantage.
- Monitors major trends and world events that may impact the parent organization and/or the library profession; considers the impacts of these trends and proactively realigns library and information services to take advantage of them.

Communicates effectively.

- Presents ideas clearly, succinctly, and enthusiastically, either verbally or in writing, always in the language of the audience, and with an understanding of their perceptions and perspectives.
- Demonstrates a professional, approachable presentation style with all audiences.
- Actively listens, considers, and then responds.
- Requests feedback on communications skills and uses it for self-improvement.

Presents ideas clearly; negotiates confidently and persuasively.

- Conveys effective, clear, and assertive messages and coaches others to do the same.
- Believes in his/her ability to provide the best possible information service and relays that message to staff, management, and clients alike.
- Demonstrates well-honed negotiation skills and the ability to secure the terms most beneficial for all concerned.

The *USA Today* library, McLean, Va.

Creates partnerships and alliances.

- Seeks alliances with other functions in the organization, such as information technology or human resources, to optimize complementary knowledge and skills.
- Forms partnerships with other libraries or information services inside or outside the organization to optimize resource sharing.
- Seeks alliances with content and technology suppliers and other information providers to improve products, services, and operations.
- Seeks alliances with researchers in faculties of library and information studies to conduct relevant and practical studies.

Builds an environment of mutual respect and trust; respects and values diversity.

- Treats others with respect and values diversity.
- Knows own strengths and the complementary strengths of others.
- Delivers on time and on target and expects others to do the same.
- Creates a problem-solving environment in which everyone's contribution is valued and acknowledged, and helps others optimize their contributions.
- Advocates for a work environment that encourages and supports ongoing knowledge development and that values the contribution of people.

Employs a team approach; recognizes the balance of collaborating, leading, and following.

- Works as part of the team regardless of his/her position or level.
- Develops and uses leadership and collaboration skills.
- Keeps abreast of trends in leadership skills and styles, using this knowledge to help self and others develop the most effective and appropriate approaches in different contexts. Willing to share leadership or to follow

when this is in the best interests of all involved.
- Mentors other team members and asks for mentoring from others when it is needed.

Takes calculated risks; shows courage and tenacity when faced with opposition.
- Shows courage when faced with opposition.
- Works closely with those in power who may say "no" to clearly understand what's required to arrive at "yes."
- Asks "what's the worst that can happen?" and, if they can live with the answer, goes for it.

Plans, prioritizes, and focuses on what is critical.
- Recognizes that in order to use resources (including human resources, content, and financial resources) most effectively, ongoing, careful planning is required.
- Refuses to let the "cry of the urgent" drown out the "drone of the critical" if the urgent is not aligned with where the library or service organization is strategically headed.
- Incorporates strategic imperatives into the individual goals and objectives of self and others to ensure long-term plans drive daily decisions and operations.
- Regularly reviews plans to ensure the organization is still on track or is responsive to unforeseen developments.

Demonstrates personal career planning.
- Is committed to a career that involves ongoing learning and personal growth. Takes personal responsibility for finding these opportunities for learning and enrichment as well as for long-term career planning. Maintains a strong sense of self-worth based on the achievement of a balanced set of evolving personal and professional goals.
- Seeks out performance feedback from management, clients, and/or mentors and uses it for continuous improvement.
- Envisions his/her individual "preferred" future and maps a path to arrive there successfully.

Thinks creatively and innovatively; seeks new or "reinventing" opportunities.
- Pursues positions or projects outside the information service department or library to gain a better understanding of how other functions apply information in their work; uses this understanding to create inventive services and programs that are indispensable to patrons and clients.
- Regularly scans for new ideas both within and beyond the library field to anticipate the future, "guesstimate" the implications, and carve out new opportunities.
- Looks at existing operations, processes, and services and asks "why?" Examines changes to these operations, processes, and services and asks "why not?"

Recognizes the value of professional networking.
- Actively contributes to and participates in SLA and other professional associations, sharing insight, knowledge, and skills; benchmarks against other information service providers; and forms partnerships and alliances.

- Recognizes the need for a forum where information professionals can communicate with each other and speak with one voice on important information policy issues, such as copyright and the global information infrastructure.
- Contributes towards the building and maintenance of a strong profession, thereby enhancing its value in the eyes of colleagues, clients, and the broader community.

Balances work, family, and community obligations.
- Supports self and others in the continual search for a balanced lifestyle.
- Optimizes opportunities for all those involved to lead healthy and satisfying professional and personal lives.

Remains flexible and positive in a time of continuing change.
- Willingly assumes different responsibilities at different points in time that respond to changing needs.
- Maintains a positive attitude and helps others to do the same.
- Seeks solutions and initiates problem-solving processes.

Celebrates achievements for self and others.
- Nominates employees and colleagues for awards in the organization, association, or community.
- Creates and contributes towards an environment where achievements, large and small, are acknowledged, celebrated, and rewarded.
- Knows that "little things count" and encourages mutual support and sharing in the organization and within the profession.
- Celebrates own success and that of others; takes pride in a job well done.

SOURCE: Special Libraries Association, "Applied Scenarios," *Competencies for Information Professionals of the 21st Century,* January 2004, www.sla.org/content/learn/comp2003/index.cfm. Reprinted with permission.

Library of Congress 2004 fact sheet

IN FISCAL YEAR 2004, the Library of Congress—

Welcomed more than one million on-site visitors.

Provided reference services to 682,264 individuals (in person, by telephone, and through written and electronic correspondence).

Held a total of 130,198,420 items in the collections, including:

19,729,698   cataloged books in the Library of Congress classification system.

9,821,216   books in large type and raised characters, incunabula (books printed before 1501), monographs and serials, music, bound newspapers, pamphlets, technical reports, and other printed material.

100,647,514 items in the nonclassified (special) collections, including:
  2,710,882 audio materials, such as discs, tapes, talking books, and other recorded formats,
 58,479,431 total manuscripts,
  4,807,827 maps,
 14,047,798 microforms,
  5,190,359 music, and
 13,914,990 visual materials, including 957,794 moving images, 12,338,513 photographs, 89,241 posters, and 529,442 prints and drawings.

Registered 661,469 claims to copyright.

Completed 899,284 research assignments for the Congress through the Congressional Research Service.

Recorded more than 3.3 billion transactions on all of the Library's public computer systems, including more than 218 million hits on America's Library, the Library's interactive website for children and families. A monthly average of 12 million transactions were recorded on the public legislative information system known as Thomas and 50 million transactions each month on the American Memory website. At year's end, the Library's American Memory online historical collections contained 9.2 million digital files.

Employed a permanent staff of 4,120 employees.

Operated with a total fiscal 2004 appropriation of $559,299,548, including authority to spend $36.3 million in receipts.

SOURCE: Library of Congress.

The German national libraries

by Jürgen Seefeldt and Ludger Syré

IN CONTRAST TO MANY OTHER COUNTRIES, no national library was formed for a long time in Germany because of territorial fragmentation and internal political contradictions. The Deutsche Bücherei, founded by the Association of the German Book Trade with support from the city of Leipzig and the Kingdom of Saxony in 1912, could not fulfill its tasks of being both a national library and center for national bibliography for the Western zones after the division of Germany in 1945. Thus, on the initiative of publishers and librarians, the German Library (die Deutsche Bibliothek, or DDB) was created in 1946 in Frankfurt am Main. These institutions merged after German reunification in 1990. The newly created German Library carries the same name. Though its tasks are distributed in three different places—the Deutsche Bücherei in Leipzig, the Deutsche Bibliothek in Frankfurt, and the Deutsches Musikarchiv in Berlin (established in 1970)—these three institutions combine to fulfill many of the responsibilities of a national library.

Die Deutsche Bibliothek

With approximately 18 million bibliographic units, of which 9 million are in Leipzig, 8 million in Frankfurt, and 1 million sets of sheet music and recordings in Berlin, die Deutsche Bibliothek is by far the largest library in Germany. Its task since 1913 is the collection, archiving, and bibliographical indexing of

- all items published, printed or electronically, in Germany, totally independent of their medium, including publications on the internet, and German-language publications published in another country,
- German-language items translated into another language and published abroad,
- publications in other languages about Germany published abroad, and
- all printed items published or written by German emigrants between 1933 and 1945.

In order to fulfill these tasks, the DDB has the status of legal depository for the Federal Republic of Germany. The law requires each publisher to deliver two copies of each new publication—in paper form, microform, sound recordings, audiovisual media, or electronic publications. The clearly defined legal charge to collect these items makes the DDB into a German-language universal library that collects and catalogs literature in all areas of knowledge. The library does not lend items, but offers its collections to the public for use onsite.

The DDB also serves as the German national bibliographic center and fulfills this part of its task by compiling and publishing the *German National Bibliography*, which is divided into several series. Bibliographic data can be purchased in different media, from the printed catalog card via CD-ROM to the online Bibliodata database. In 2003, a "New Publications Service" (*Neuerscheinungsdienst*) was launched jointly with the German Booksellers Association (*Buchhändler-Vereinigung*), which publishes the German version of *Books in Print*.

Deutsche Bücherei, Leipzig, 1962

The DDB devotes special attention to documenting expatriate German-language authors in exile during the National Socialist regime from 1933 to 1945. The Collection of Exile Literature (*Sammlung Exil-Literatur*) in Leipzig and the German Exile Archive (*Deutsches Exilarchiv*) in Frankfurt contain published books, brochures, and journals of Germans abroad, as well as the personal records of individual emigrants and the archives of exile organizations.

The Deutsche Bücherei in Leipzig houses an international research library of documentation on the Holocaust. The Anne Frank Shoah Library pursues the goal of making available all literature published worldwide on the persecution and destruction of European Jews by the Nazis. Publications on other peoples and groups who were persecuted because of ethnic, political, religious or other reasons also fall into this collection emphasis.

The German Book and Writing Museum in the Leipzig library is a documentation center for the history and culture of the book. Founded in 1884—which makes it the oldest book museum in the world—the museum showcases its extensive and valuable collections, including the largest assemblage of watermarked papers in the world, to a wide audience in both special and permanent exhibitions.

The Center for Book Conservation in Leipzig was part of the Deutsche Bücherei until 1998 and has since become an independent corporation concerned with the conservation and restoration of books as physical objects. Tens of thousands of books made of wood-pulp paper have been threatened by acidification since the middle of the 19th century. The center uses deacidification processes and microfilming to preserve the contents of endangered books.

In its function as national library, the DDB participates in such national and international projects as codifying of standards and guidelines, creating authority file databases, developing methods of mass deacidification, defining a metadata standard for digital resources, and acting as a national ISSN center (serials) for Germany.

In addition to the DDB, Germany has two other major collections that serve as national libraries: The State Library of Berlin–Prussian Cultural Heritage Foundation, founded in 1661, and the Bavarian State Library in Munich, founded in 1558. Both have evolved from the court libraries of princes. With their comprehensive German and international older collections, their numerous special collections, and their participation in the Special Subject Collection Program of the German Research Council, they can be designated as national libraries. For the applied sciences, they are augmented by the three Central Subject Libraries, in Hannover (technology), Köln (medicine), and Kiel (economics).

The State Library of Berlin, 1959

The State Library of Berlin

The State Library of Berlin–Prussian Cultural Heritage Foundation (*Staatsbibliothek zu Berlin–Preußischer Kulturbesitz*) continues the tradition of the Prussian State Library, which was one of the largest and most important European libraries before the Second World War. Its successful development came to an abrupt end after the war with the division of Germany. The separate development of the German State Library (*Deutsche Staatsbibliothek*), which in East Berlin had shared the tasks of a national library with the State Library of the Prussian Cultural Heritage and the Deutsche Bücherei in Leipzig, was finally ended with the reunification of Germany.

In both its current buildings—on the Unter den Linden and at Potsdamer Platz—the State Library is making an attempt to reestablish its former rank as a major research library in a reunified Berlin and to take on central functions for German librarianship. It possesses an impressive collection of nearly 10 million books and journals from all areas of knowledge, countries, periods, and languages. Areas of emphasis include Eastern European literature, East Asian materials, official publications and parliamentary papers, the publications of international organizations, journals and newspapers, and children's literature.

The State Library also produces the international Union Catalog of Incunabula, maintains a central catalog of handwritten manuscripts, participates in the cataloging and classification of German imprints of the 16th and 17th centuries, maintains the German Periodicals Database (*Zeitschriftendatenbank*), and runs the national ISBN (books) and ISMN (music) agencies.

The Bavarian State Library

With some 7.6 million volumes of national and international literature, the Bavarian State Library (*Bayerische Staatsbibliothek*) in Munich is the second-largest scholarly library in the Federal Republic of Germany. At the same time, it is the central state library for Bavaria and the state service center for public libraries in all areas concerning Bavarian librarianship; since 1663, it has collected the legal depository copies of all works published in the region. With its more than 40,600 journals and newspaper subscriptions, it is the largest periodicals library in Europe after the British Library.

Founded in 1558 as the court library of the House of Wittelsbach, this library has used its present name since 1919. Special areas of focus include studies of antiquity and archaeology, history, music, East and Southeast Europe, East Asia, pre-1700 manuscripts and imprints, and foreign literature of the post–World War II era.

Similar to the State Library of Berlin, the Bavarian State Library in Munich participates in numerous cooperative projects, and maintains partnerships with international associations and foreign libraries. It also supports both the Institute for Book and Manuscript Restoration (*Institut für Buch- und Handschriftenrestaurierung*) as well as the Munich Digitization Center (*Münchener Digitalisierungszentrum*).

SOURCE: Jürgen Seefeldt and Ludger Syré, *Portals to the Past and to the Future: Libraries in Germany* (Hildesheim, Ger.: Georg Olms Verlag, 2003), pp. 36–41. Reprinted with permission.

Presidential libraries

THROUGH THE PRESIDENTIAL LIBRARIES, which are located at sites selected by the presidents and built with private funds, the National Archives and Records Administration preserves and makes available the records and personal papers of a particular president's administration. In addition to providing reference services on presidential documents, each library prepares documentary and descriptive publications and operates a museum to exhibit documents, historic objects, and other memorabilia of interest to the public.

Herbert Hoover Presidential Library and Museum, 211 Parkside Drive, P.O. Box 488, West Branch, IA 52358-0488; (319) 643-5301; hoover.library@nara.gov; hoover.archives.gov.

Roosevelt Library   Truman Library

Franklin D. Roosevelt Presidential Library and Museum, 4079 Albany Post
Road, Hyde Park, NY 12538-1999; (845) 486-7770; roosevelt.library
@nara.gov; www.fdrlibrary.marist.edu.

Harry S. Truman Presidential Library and Museum, 500 West U.S. Hwy.
24, Independence, MO 64050-1798; (816) 268-8200; truman.library
@nara.gov; www.trumanlibrary.org.

Dwight D. Eisenhower Presidential Library and Museum, 200 S.E. 4th
Street, Abilene, KS 67410-2900; (785) 263-6700; eisenhower.library
@nara.gov; eisenhower.archives.gov.

John F. Kennedy Library and Museum, Columbia Point, Boston, MA 02125-
3398; (617) 514-1600; kennedy.library@nara.gov; www.jfklibrary.org.

Lyndon B. Johnson Library and Museum, 2313 Red River Street, Austin,
TX 78705-5702; (512) 721-0200; johnson.library@nara.gov; www.lbjlib.
utexas.edu.

Richard Nixon Library and Birthplace, 18001 Yorba Linda Boulevard, Yorba
Linda, CA 92886; (714) 993-5075; archives@nixonlibrary.org; www.
nixonfoundation.org. NARA is scheduled to take over this private library in
2006.

Richard Nixon Presidential Materials Staff, National Archives, 8601 Adelphi
Road, College Park, MD 20740-6001; (301) 837-3290; nixon@nara.gov;
nixon.archives.gov/index.php.

Gerald R. Ford Library, 1000 Beal Avenue, Ann Arbor, MI 48109; (734) 205-
0555; ford.library@nara.gov; www.fordlibrarymuseum.gov.

Gerald R. Ford Museum, 303 Pearl Street, N.W., Grand Rapids, MI 49504-
5353; (616) 254-0400; ford.museum@nara.gov; www.fordlibrarymuseum.
gov.

Jimmy Carter Library and Museum, 441 Freedom Parkway, Atlanta, GA 30307;
(404) 865-7100; carter.library@nara.gov; www.jimmycarterlibrary.
gov.

Ronald Reagan Presidential Library and Museum, 40 Presidential Drive,

Carter dedicating the JFK Library, 1979   Clinton Library

Simi Valley, CA 93065-0600; (805) 577-4000; reagan.library@nara.gov; www.reagan.utexas.edu.

George H. W. Bush Presidential Library and Museum, 1000 George Bush Drive West, College Station, TX 77845; (979) 691-4000; bush.library @nara.gov; bushlibrary.tamu.edu.

William J. Clinton Presidential Library and Museum, 1200 President Clinton Avenue, Little Rock, AR 72201; (501) 374-4242; clinton.library@nara.gov; www.clintonlibrary.gov.

Presidential libraries not administered by NARA are:

National First Ladies' Library, Saxton McKinley House, 205 Market Avenue South, Canton, OH 44702; (330) 452-0876; regulam@firstladieslibrary.org; www.firstladies.org.

New Hampshire Political Library, 20 Park Street, Concord, NH 03301; (603) 225-4617; info@politicallibrary.org; www.politicallibrary.org.

Abraham Lincoln Presidential Library and Museum, 112 N. Sixth Street, Springfield, IL 62701; (217) 558-8844; www.alplm.org/home.html.

Jefferson Davis Home and Presidential Library, Beauvoir, 2244 Beach Boulevard, Biloxi, MS 39531; (800) 570-3818; www.beauvoir.org/prezlib.html. Damaged significantly by Hurricane Katrina in 2005.

Rutherford B. Hayes Presidential Center, Spiegel Grove, 1337 Hayes Avenue, Fremont, OH 43420; (419) 332-2081; hayeslib@rbhayes.org; www.rbhayes.org/library.htm.

James A. Garfield National Historical Site Memorial Library, 8095 Mentor Avenue, Mentor, OH 44060; (440) 255-8722; www.nps.gov/jaga.

McKinley Memorial Library, 40 N. Main Street, Niles, OH 44446; (330) 652-1704; www.mckinley.lib.oh.us/library/.

Theodore Roosevelt Collection, Houghton Library, Harvard University, Cambridge, MA 02138; wfdailey@fas.harvard.edu; hcl.harvard.edu/houghton/ departments/roosevelt.html.

William Howard Taft National Historic Site, 2038 Auburn Avenue, Cincinnati, OH 45219; (513) 684-3262; www.nps.gov/wiho/.

Woodrow Wilson Presidential Library, 18-24 N. Coalter Street, Staunton, VA 24402-0024; (540) 885-0897; woodrow@woodrowwilson.org; www. woodrowwilson.org.

Calvin Coolidge Presidential Library and Museum, Forbes Library, 20 West Street, Northampton, MA 01060; (413) 587-1014; coolidge@forbeslibrary. org; www.forbeslibrary.org/coolidge/coolidge.shtml.

Presidential, yes; libraries, not really

by Lynn Scott Cochrane

PRESIDENTIAL LIBRARIES OFTEN MAKE newspaper headlines, especially when sites for new libraries are under consideration or when new libraries are dedicated. The libraries are often the targets of media exposés. For decades, columnists for such publications as the *Washington Post*, the *Nation*, and the *Chronicle of Higher Education* have raised two issues: mingling public and private dollars to support presidential libraries, and the timeliness and impartiality of the release of presidential papers to researchers.

The official Presidential Library System, a division of the National Archives and Records Administration (NARA), includes 12 presidential libraries that are actually museums and archival repositories, rather than libraries in the usual sense. They are built with private money and the archival functions are then maintained in perpetuity with federal money.

During the U.S.'s first 150 years, preservation and management of public records was generally neglected, including that of the papers of the presidents. When presidents left the White House, they took their official documents with them. Many documents and artifacts found homes in state libraries, university libraries, state historical societies, and, most prominently, the Library of Congress. Beginning in 1834 and continuing for a century, the Library of Congress undertook major and minor purchases of presidential papers: $45,000 for Washington's and $65,000 for Madison's were among the largest expenditures. Fire destroyed the collections of several former presidents, including those of William H. Harrison, John Tyler, and Zachary Taylor.

Privately built, publicly maintained

Since presidential libraries are not actually libraries, there has been some debate over the misnomer. According to author and historian Donald R. McCoy, a group of scholars met on December 17, 1938, to discuss the Franklin D. Roosevelt Library in Hyde Park, New York. For months, everyone had referred to the proposed facility as a repository or an institution, neither of which seemed appropriate. Almost incidentally, the lone librarian, Randolph G. Adams, director of the William L. Clements Library at the University of Michigan, was the first to try out the term "library," citing the example of "Mr. Hoover's Library" at Stanford University.

After some wrangling, the committee decided to recommend the name Franklin D. Roosevelt Library to the president. FDR countered with the Hyde Park Library but realized that would cause confusion with the town library near his estate. He also jokingly suggested the Crum Elbow Library, referring to the bend in the Hudson River near the Roosevelt home. Nevertheless, the decision was finally made to follow the committee's suggestion.

In 1914, the first presidential library, paid for largely by the state of Ohio, opened in Fremont as the Rutherford B. Hayes Memorial Library. The library is maintained jointly by the Rutherford B. Hayes–Lucy Webb Hayes Foundation and the state of Ohio. Similarly, the Hoover Library of War, Revolution, and Peace was established in 1919 on the campus of Stanford University to house documents related to Herbert Hoover's public service beginning in 1914. Hoover's presidential papers were housed at Stanford for more than 30 years, from the end of his term in 1933 until the Herbert Hoover Presidential Library opened at his West Branch, Iowa, birthplace in 1964.

By 1937, President Roosevelt had adapted the Hayes and Hoover models to develop his concept of a privately built, publicly maintained presidential library. In 1939, federal legislation chartering the Franklin D. Roosevelt Library was enacted and the completed library became a federal facility July 4, 1940. FDR was the only president to see completion of his library during his term of office. Several of his fireside chats were broadcast from there.

Truman, aware that he was establishing the precedent for future presidents, followed Roosevelt's lead and created a Missouri corporation to establish his presidential library on the FDR model. Before the Truman Presidential Library was completed, Congress enacted the Presidential Libraries Act of 1955, and President Eisenhower signed it into law. All subsequent federal presidential libraries trace their statutory authority to this legislation. Until passage of the Presidential Records Act in 1978, this 1955 legislation gave former presidents the authority to designate which papers were to be considered presidential, and they retained complete ownership and control over them after leaving office.

In 1978, Congress passed the Presidential Records Act, which defined what presidential records are and how they are to be preserved and made available to the public. The law also established public ownership of all presidential records and materials created on or after January 20, 1981. President Ronald Reagan's papers were the first to be subject to the provisions of the 1978 law. Ironically, they were also the first to be withheld, under a 2002 executive order by President George W. Bush.

During the late 1970s, public and congressional discontent mounted over the benefits bestowed upon former presidents and their families. In addition to office support and Secret Service protection, one of the main concerns was the cost of maintaining and staffing the presidential libraries. As each new library joined the system, it tended to eclipse its predecessors in size and grandeur.

After several years of congressional investigations, the Presidential Libraries Act of 1986 was enacted. The new law placed fiscal limitations on future presidential libraries, architectural and design conditions, reporting requirements, and the establishment of operating endowments for "any President who takes the oath of office as President for the first time on or after January 20, 1985." The George H. W. Bush Presidential Library and Museum in College Station, Texas, was the first to be subject to all provisions of the 1986 reforms.

It turns out that NARA's Presidential Library System is a quintessentially American system. The libraries are set up as federally supported public institutions but they cannot really succeed without continual private funding. The archival functions of the libraries are supported by the federal budget and operated according to federal policies and procedures. The museum and educational functions are supported with private money and are subject to the influences that accompany such funding. Thus there is always tension between researchers, who complain that the libraries are geographically dispersed and archival materials inaccessible, and the general public, who enjoy visiting them.

The federal government is content to have the private sector fund the construction and endowment of the facilities in return for private interest groups having a measure of influence over what takes place there. The system is preserving presidential archives for posterity, and the American people through their representatives have decided the trade-offs are worth the costs.

SOURCE: Lynn Scott Cochrane, "Presidential Libraries: Presidential, Yes; Libraries, Not Really," *American Libraries* 33 (May 2002): 58–62.

STATE LIBRARIES

What state library agencies do

A STATE LIBRARY AGENCY is the official agency of a state that is charged by state law with the extension and development of public library services throughout the state and has adequate authority under state law to administer state plans in accordance with the provisions of the Library Services and Technology Act (LSTA) (P.L. 104–208).

Beyond these two roles, state library agencies vary greatly. They are located in various departments of state government and report to different authorities. They are involved in various ways in the development and operation of electronic information networks. They provide different types of services to different types of libraries. They provide important reference and information services to state governments and administer the state libraries and special operations such as state archives, libraries for the blind and physically handicapped, and the State Center for the Book.

The state library agency may also function as the state's public library at large, providing library services to the general public. This report provides

North Dakota State Library

information on the range of roles played by state library agencies and the various combinations of fiscal, human, and informational resources invested in such work. Some state library agencies perform allied operations, services not ordinarily considered a state library agency function. These special operations may include maintaining state archives, managing state records, conducting legislative research for the state, or operating a museum or art gallery.

The state library agencies of the District of Columbia, Hawaii, and Maryland are different from the other state libraries in a variety of ways. They are administrative offices without a separate state library collection. In the District of Columbia, which is treated as a state for reporting purposes, the Martin Luther King Memorial Library, the central library of the District of Columbia Public Library, functions as a resource center for the municipal government. In Hawaii, the state library is located in the Hawaii State Public Library System. State law designates Enoch Pratt Free Library's central library as the Maryland State Library Resource Center. The state library agencies of the District of Columbia, Hawaii, and Maryland administer LSTA funds and report LSTA revenue and expenditures. The District of Columbia and Maryland state library agencies administer and staff the Library for the Blind and Physically Handicapped (LBPH). The Library of Congress owns the LBPH collections.

Governance

Nearly all state library agencies (49) are located in the executive branch of government. Two state library agencies are located in the legislative branch. Sixteen state library agencies are independent agencies within the executive branch. Of the state library agencies located in the executive branch, almost two-thirds (33) are part of a larger agency. Of the 33 state library agencies that are part of a larger state agency, 14 are part of the state department of education. Four state library agencies were located in a department of cultural resources, and five states were part of a department of state.

Collections and services

State library agency collections averaged 531,000 uncataloged government documents in 2003. State library agencies averaged 457,000 book and serial volumes. The median number of books and serial volumes held by state library agencies was 179,000. State library agencies also held audio or visual materials or serial subscriptions. The average number of such materials held by state library agencies varied by format: 3,700 audio materials, 3,000 video materials, and 1,300 serial subscriptions.

During the 2003 fiscal year, state library agencies averaged 37,000 library visits. State library agencies averaged 61,000 circulation transactions. The median number of circulation transactions was 9,400. State library agency staff responded to an average of 26,000 reference transactions in fiscal year 2003. The median number of reference transactions was 14,000.

Service outlets and staff

State library agency service outlets have regular hours of service in which staff are present to serve users. The state library agency, as part of its regular operation, pays the staff and all service costs. The main or central outlet is a single unit library where the principal collections are located and handled. Other outlets have separate quarters, a permanent basic collection of books and/or other materials, permanent paid staff, and a regular schedule of hours open to users. Bookmobiles are trucks or vans specially equipped to carry books and other library materials. They serve as traveling branch libraries.

State library agencies reported a total of 134 service outlets—47 main or central outlets, 71 other outlets (excluding bookmobiles), and 16 bookmobiles. The user groups receiving library services through these outlets, and the number of outlets serving them, included the general public (95 outlets); state government employees (77 outlets); blind and physically handicapped individuals (56 outlets); residents of state correctional institutions (31 outlets); and residents of other state institutions (27 outlets).

The total number of budgeted full-time-equivalent (FTE) positions in state library agencies was 3,600. Librarians with American Library Association-accredited master of library science degrees represented 1,100 positions; other professionals accounted for 718 FTE positions; and other paid staff represented 1,700 FTE positions.

SOURCE: *State Library Agencies, Fiscal Year 2003* (Washington, D.C.: National Center for Education Statistics, December 2004).

SMALL & RURAL LIBRARIES

Small libraries, big ideas

by Christine Watkins

RURAL LIBRARIES AND THEIR URBAN AND SUBURBAN counter-
parts are in different places, not on different planets. Clearly, they face different challenges. But *small* is not the same as *less.*

Being small cuts both ways—there are disadvantages, but there are also
some built-in advantages. "In small towns, in very rural areas," says Ruth Solie,
"people still know what's going on in the world. Their children have to graduate from high school and inhabit the same world as other children who grow
up in cities. People tend to wear multiple hats, and connections can be made
quickly. Institutions are often interwoven, and if someone has a good idea, it
doesn't take months of preparation to get it on the table."

Solie directs the Northern Lights Library Network (NLLN) in northwest-
ern Minnesota. NLLN is one of seven multitype library cooperatives in the
state and serves 9% of Minnesota's population in an area encompassing nearly
one-third of the state. Among NLLN's 300 participating libraries, many serve
communities of fewer than 2,500 people.

NLLN's 40 public libraries are grouped into four regional systems, with
the remaining members drawn from school, academic, and special libraries.
Whether NLLN is atypical or representative, this article offers glimpses of
ways that rural libraries overcome their geographic isolation with a mix of technology, imagination, and perseverance.

While local connections for rural librarians are highly personal, electronic
communications have greatly increased the ease with which library practitioners can reach well beyond the local community. In rural Minnesota, this has
meant a statewide network that offers internet access for patrons and librarians alike. While public-access computing is often stressed, professional access is at least as significant: When you are the sole staff member, it can make
a world of difference to have colleagues as close as the other end of an email
message.

Density vs. intensity

A January 2003 University of Washington study on the impact of public-
access computing found that while rural libraries generally welcomed and
embraced the technology, reactions ranged from libraries seeing the initial
installation as an end in itself to those that view getting wired as just the
first step. The study, conducted for the Bill and Melinda Gates Foundation
and focusing on the Gates Library Program, identified a group dubbed "can-
do" librarians. Not surprisingly, the study found that the "can-do" spirit char-
acterizes not only the library's use of technology, but its overall vision and
delivery of library service.

Not only can NLLN librarians talk to each other, offer online resources to their patrons, and explore what other and bigger libraries are up to, they can make their own communities more accessible to the outside world. Lina Belar directs the History Museum of East Otter Tail County in Perham, Minnesota. The museum is a special-library member of NLLN, and Belar is one of those people who wears multiple hats.

When she saw that the Minnesota Historical Society had digitized its photo collections and put them on the Web, Belar decided, "If they could do it with 64,000 photos, I figured we could do it with the 2,000 or so in our collection." She added, "We're now doing something similar with local newspapers. Sometimes being small makes it easier, because the scale of the project is conceivable."

Belar describes Perham as an entrepreneurial town that personifies the "can-do" spirit. Despite its population of roughly 2,500, it boasts strong local manufacturing and civic enterprises. "Perham was never the county seat, or even near the county seat. It had to make it on its own. Rather than wait around for something to happen, we just do it."

The Pelican Rapids Public Library, another NLLN member library, offers another can-do case in point. Roughly a quarter of the town's 2,300 current residents speak a first language other than English, a far cry from the largely homogenous community of Scandinavian descent that populated the town only a decade or so ago. No one's quite sure why it became a destination of choice for such a varied influx, but postings on an online immigrant grapevine might read, "Go there—the library is cool."

The library's internet access gives patrons from Somalia, Serbia, Croatia, Russia, Vietnam, Laos, and elsewhere the means to stay in touch with their families and keep up with news from their home countries. "Just because we are located in rural Minnesota doesn't mean that our patrons aren't sophisticated," says librarian Pamela Westby. "Many immigrants are computer savvy." Besides providing a dozen computer workstations, the renovated and expanded library houses a coffee bar and meeting rooms, a fireplace to gather around, and quiet places to study. ESL classes are offered through a welfare-to-work program, and the collections include bilingual books, movies, and language cassettes and CD-ROMs. The library also displays a tapestry of needlecraft and fiber art made by 21 local contributors representing all the countries from which people have recently immigrated to Pelican Rapids. "Tapestry of Friendship" was the brainchild of the local Friends group, which won for it the 2003 Barbara Kingsolver Award from Friends of Libraries USA.

Pocket change

Director Solie doesn't talk about how tough things are, but about what it takes to get things done. The phrase she uses again and again to describe the nucleus of change she's observed in towns like Perham, Pelican Rapids, and Detroit

Tapestry of Friendship, Pelican Rapids PL

Lakes is "pockets of people" that find each other and make things happen. The phrase conjures a topographical map not with mountains and rivers, but elevations made of bulging pockets stitched over a town with heads poking up and hands waving.

The kind of people that make the pockets bulge are ones with a passion for something—and not necessarily for books or libraries or information or the internet. "It can be a passion for licorice," Solie says, referring to the main manufacturing business in a nearby town. "There's a lot cooking in these towns, and it's traceable to the people who want their town to be terrific—they convey that what they're doing is so important that other people can't resist."

Solie's own passion for writers and literature prompted a series of programs she organized while director of the Detroit Lakes Public Library that brought in well-known authors—small towns, big names. After moving to NLLN, Solie realized there were two obstacles for other small-town libraries wanting to do the same thing. First, their staff members didn't think it was possible. And second, they had no idea how to begin. So Solie started posting tips and information on the NLLN website, and now there are big names popping up in small towns all up and down U.S. Highway 10.

The NLLN website (nlln.org) has separate blogs for general postings and children's issues that put state and national conferences, publications, issues, and expertise into local hands. "This kind of knowledge empowers

---

Survey of Rural Libraries, 2003

The ALA Task Force on Rural School, Tribal, and Public Libraries designed and administered a survey in 2003 to explore the resource needs, perceived challenges, and developmental needs of rural librarians. This survey was distributed to the rural school librarians, rural tribal librarians, and rural public librarians.

Survey respondents were most likely to be representatives of rural school or public libraries from the Great Lakes/Plains or West/Southwest regions of the United States. Most respondents serve communities with a population smaller than 10,000.

Poverty was the issue that was of greatest concern for survey respondents, particularly those representing rural tribal libraries. Although depopulation was an issue identified by rural school and public libraries, this was not a concern for rural tribal libraries. Unemployment/underemployment was a concern that was identified as well in the qualitative responses.

Survey respondents identified a lack of money as their greatest challenge and computer training as their most pressing training need. Inadequate space was a challenge identified in the qualitative responses. "Basic library skills" was identified as a pressing training need for both rural tribal and school libraries. Computer hardware, technical support, and technical training were all identified as significant technological needs.

Survey respondents identified "current nonfiction" as a significant collection development need. However, rural tribal libraries identified "local history, reminiscences, folklore, and traditions" as their most pressing collection development need. Rural school libraries identified "school curriculum materials" as a significant collection development need.

The majority of respondents reported collaborating with civic organizations, nonprofits, and governmental agencies. A strong minority also reported collaborating with colleges and universities. Schools and other libraries were identified as sources of collaboration in the qualitative data. Nearly half reported being members of the American Library Association, while a significant minority belongs to the Public Library Association.

SOURCE: Evan Leach, "Rural Library Survey Summary Report," June 28, 2004, www.ala.org/ala/olos/outreachresource/ruratf_surveysumpt1.pdf.

people in unexpected ways," Solie says. "Suddenly they can speak with confidence about the importance of library services for very young children because they know that a big-deal economist is saying the same thing."

Peg Werner directs the Viking Library System, one of the four systems that make up NLLN, and the one to which both Perham and Pelican Rapids belong. Werner has been instrumental in statewide telecommunications issues, and is an important link for member libraries in accessing LSTA grants and funds, as well as providing such low-tech services as ensuring that materials get delivered—even if it sometimes means hitching a ride to a person's home.

Other venues

It's no different in rural northeast Pennsylvania, where Moll Rodgers is the system administrator for the Wayne Library Authority, which serves roughly 750 square miles with seven libraries. Until four years ago, WLA's seven members were independent libraries struggling for survival. "When we started meeting to discuss a dedicated library tax, it took a couple of years of meetings to overcome distrust and negotiate distribution if the referendum were to pass," Rodgers explains. "It did pass in 2000, and even though an antitax backlash later revoked the tax, we managed to keep the system together."

The benefits have been noticeable and significant—longer operating hours, libraries meeting state standards, librarians having access to continuing education, materials delivered to patrons regardless of library locations, and joint grant applications and shared staffing to extend resources. "Despite continued threats to our funding from both local and state cuts," Rodgers says, "there is a commitment to save the system, no matter what!"

The experiences of Susan Rawlins, director of the Colusa County (Calif.) Library, demonstrate a similar combination: Libraries benefit from both collective and individual action, with a healthy dose of creativity thrown in. Rawlins credits former California State Librarian Kevin Starr for his awareness of and responsiveness to rural libraries through grants and projects, as well as the Gates Foundation for their technology grants. "Without Gates funds and state library grants, we'd still be in the 1960s," Rawlins notes.

Another of Rawlins's strengths is the ability to mix high- and low-tech problem-solving. "Our literacy program just traded a new refrigerator and HP color printer for a retired transit bus—we're converting it into a mobile literacy lab. We can't afford to buy a custom vehicle, but we'll repaint the bus, have local children design the external graphics, and voilà! We will have the ImagiBus."

It all goes to show that the formula for rural library success isn't dependent on a particular geographic, political, or even economic environment, although all those things contribute. Resources and technology are necessary, but not sufficient unless there are powerful human elements in the mix. This is not the same as saying that all it takes is a charismatic leader— or even an MLS librarian. Rather, the alchemy requires both the ability to imagine and deliver excellence in library services and a local population that supports and demands quality.

SOURCE: Christine Watkins, "Small Libraries, Big Ideas," *American Libraries* 35 (March 2004): 28–30.

MOBILE LIBRARIES

Bookmobile service in Ohio

by John Philip

THIS IS A REVIEW OF OHIO'S most significant contributions to extending library service to the citizenry. To best capture the underlying spirit of bookmobile service, this effort would be appropriately done in a fictional format. At least one novel has been done in this setting, *The Girl on the Bookmobile*, by Natalie King (Avalon, 1964); however, it does not focus on Ohio.

Ohio was not the home of the first bookmobile in the United States. That honor goes to Hagerstown, Maryland, which started bookmobile service in

Washington County (Md.) Free Library

1905 (left). Ohio libraries were not far behind in using bookmobiles. The list in Table 1, which shows public libraries operational in 1939, is from the *County Library Primer*, written by Mildred Sandoe and published by the H. W. Wilson Company in 1942. It was not possible to determine which Ohio library was the first to initiate bookmobile service in any document. To approximate this "number one" with the available resources, letters were written to those libraries on the 1939 list requesting verification of the date bookmobile service commenced in that library. Table 1 also shows the result of this effort, with the library's name and the year service started.

It is apparent from the list that a major growth of bookmobile service happened in 1938. This expansion was due to a program set up by then Governor Martin L. Davey in 1937 designed "to encourage the spread of library services to rural communities." The State Library of Ohio managed the program with discretion left to the libraries to determine individual county needs.

An interesting memorandum dealing with early bookmobiles was written by Electra C. Doren, Director of the Dayton Public Library, dated November 16, 1923.

Six Weeks of the Dayton Public Bookwagon
October 1–November 14, 1923

To have a bookwagon at all we had to take the most inexpensive thing we could get. This was a Ford one-ton truck with closed sides. The janitor fitted up bookshelves four to each side; on one side the shelves

Table 1

Library	Bookmobile service
Dayton–Montgomery County	1923
Cleveland Public Library	1926
Cincinnati[1]	1927
Mansfield–Richland County[2]	1931
Springfield–Clark County	1933
Maumee–Lucas County	1937
Canton–Stark County	1937
Lorain[3]	1939
Circleville–Pickaway County	1938
Lane–Hamilton County	1938
Lima–Allen County	1938
Martins Ferry–Belmont County	1938
Middletown Public Library[4]	1938
Newark–Licking County	1938
Nelsonville–Athens County	1938
Portsmouth–Scioto County	1938
Warren–Trumbull County	1938
Troy–Miami County	1938

1. Cincinnati discontinued traditional bookmobile service in 1992, to focus on a variety of outreach services to people with special needs.
2. Mansfield discontinued bookmobile service in favor of expanded branches and a branch-mobile until 1989.
3. The Lorain Public Library discontinued its bookmobile in 1971 until 1990, when a new bookmobile was put into service.
4. The Butler County bookmobile service was rendered by both Middletown Public and Lane Hamilton Libraries. Middletown dropped the service in 1998 in favor of special services. The Lane Hamilton Libraries continue the service.

were six inches wide and on the other eight inches wide. These are belted to the floor of the truck in such a way that they may be removed if necessary. The books are held into place on the shelves by strong double canvas tapes 1-1/2 inches wide, stretched across the front and buttoned on carriage curtain buttons screwed into the bookcase uprights.

We are able to carry 600 volumes and 100 current magazines, two folding metal seats, a very substantial small folding table, a charging tray, a book truck and three people. We have had two chauffeurs trained, both of them high school graduates who have been pages and desk clerks for three or four years in our libraries. Hence they were able to help with the work of charging and discharging books and holding the discipline, while the young woman assistant who is a good reference worker as well as a good publicity agent, "sells the books," interviews prospective patrons and incidentally develops reference questions to be answered from the main library or either of the two Carnegie branch libraries.

In the beginning we sent only the chauffeur and the young woman assistant. We are now finding it necessary because of the increasing business and the short period stops to send a third person, usually a well-trained page. Of course the bookwagon is a novelty in Dayton, having been in operation practically only since October first. In the month we have established regular calling stations in each of the three bookwagon districts all of which will provide us shelter in bad weather, without charge. Everywhere there is interest and a welcome from business stands but residence streets, even the plainer ones, are much more difficult to develop.

Thus far we have registered 901 patrons who have not been using the Main Library or any of the branch libraries and have circulated 4,032 books and magazines. At first, lest we run out of books on our trip and also to encourage registration of more members of the family especially of adults, we allowed only one book and one magazine to each card but we are now extending the privilege to two books and a magazine for each card.

The first month's work (October) showed a total registration of 695 borrowers, being more than the gain of book borrowers at a Carnegie Branch Library for the entire year of 1922 and nearly three times as many the Main Library registered in the same month (Oct.).

The memorandum goes on to make optimistic projections for the future. Among these are plans for a larger vehicle with outside shelving and a panel that can shelter patrons in inclement weather while advertising the library's programs when not opened. Bookmobile managers will appreciate Ms. Doren's budget. The cost of the wagon was $687, and salaries for one year were $2,600. For the first month, vehicle expenses were $12.10 for gas and repairs. Her final statement speaks for itself: "Library personnel, especially in the initial stages, is an even greater factor in this type of work than at almost any other point of the library system."

Some statistics

- By 1939, the libraries in Table 1 had circulated 1,495,771 items to 59,909 people.
- By 1973, there were 60 libraries in 69 counties that circulated 6,187,339 items.
- Sixty libraries provided their own bookmobile service; 21 counties contracted for the service provided by the State Library of Ohio. In 1976, the recently created regional system, Ohio Valley Area Libraries, absorbed service to four counties in contracts with the system contributing toward the costs. The Library Services and Construction Act (LSCA) funds helped this process as part of the system financing by the State Library of Ohio.
- In 1993, 63 libraries provided bookmobile service, circulating 4,001,340 items. The State Library served 17 counties, and Ohio Valley Area Libraries provided service to four. The total circulation figure above includes the State Library and the Ohio Valley Area Libraries system circulation.
- In 2001, there were 54 libraries in 49 counties providing bookmobile service, circulating 3,089,150 items. Seven libraries still contracted for bookmobile service from the State Library of Ohio, and one, Champaigne, contracted with Springfield Clark County Library.
- In 2002, the State Library ceased offering bookmobile service to Adams, Brown, and Clinton counties.

One encouraging event (at least to a bookmobile/outreach enthusiast) has been the return to bookmobile service in major urban libraries. In recent years, Dallas, Chicago, and Detroit have returned to bookmobile service. Cleveland, Ohio, can be added to this list; it restarted its program in 2001 after ceasing the service in 1986.

Lest there be any misunderstanding about the previous data, it is appropriate to note that not all current bookmobile service looks like "traditional" bookmobile service. This is stated without intending to diminish the current services bookmobiles offer, but administrators and trustees have recognized the various targets for this form of service delivery. A bookmobile typically visits day care centers, senior service centers, the homebound, and various other focuses where the personal and informational service is well received. The numbers listed here reflect much community activity of the traditional type.

In 1958, the Board of the Ohio State Library, with strong leadership from State Librarian Walter Brahm, initiated a broad plan to close some of the gap in service with six regional centers, which eventually included bookmobile service to 22 counties. By 2002, all of these had been gradually phased out or turned over to local libraries. By this time, library budgets had improved, and, in some cases, branch and central libraries had expanded.

Leadership in construction and design

Since 1946, Ohio has had the advantage of being the center of bookmobile manufacturers. Located in Wooster, the Gerstenslager Company led the country in constructing and selling bookmobiles until it ceased doing so in 1986. Other companies tried to fill the gap, but none were able to establish themselves as "the maker of bookmobiles" as Gerstenslager had.

Missoula (Mont.) PL bookmobile, 1950s

In 1988, the Ohio Bus Company captured an impressive portion of the business. Also in 1988, the Farber Specialty Vehicles Company stepped in and has its significant share of the business. There have also been competitive companies based out of state. The most successful of these are Moroney Bookmobiles in Worcester, Massachusetts, which has been building bookmobiles since 1940, and Matthews Specialty Vehicles in Greensboro, North Carolina, which entered the bookmobile market in 1992.

The Rehabilitation Act (1973) raised the question to libraries of access to the bookmobile for persons with mobility handicaps. The proposed answer to this was the wheelchair lift designed into the bookmobile during construction. The bookmobile manufacturers responded, and the lift became a standard option by all manufacturers. The State Library of Ohio purchased a bookmobile with this wheelchair lift, even before an "informal guidance" paper was issued by the United States Justice Department in 1993, under the strong encouragement of Eunace Lovejoy, a state library consultant. Even though the 1993 Justice Department letter did not require the lift if the library offered other access successfully, most libraries seriously consider this enhancement when purchasing a bookmobile.

In 1995, the Farber Company introduced a low floor design with a ramp to accommodate persons using wheelchairs, or with other mobility limitations. The first libraries to purchase these bookmobiles were the Troy–Miami County Library, Auglaize County District Public Library, and the Public Library of Steubenville and Jefferson County.

National conferences and media appearances

In 1985, the State Library of Ohio convened the first National Bookmobile Conference. There has been a national conference, with the exception of one year, ever since. In 1994, Clarion University of Pennsylvania held its first Great American Bookmobile Conference. Under the leadership of Bernard Vavrek, director of the Center for the Study of Rural Librarianship, the office has continued sponsorship of this annual conference, renamed in 2001 as the Great American Bookmobile and Outreach Conference. Complementary to this, the Ohio Library Council established an Outreach Award in 1994, emphasizing the importance of outreach service to the community.

SOURCE: John Philip, "An Overview of the History of Bookmobile Service in Ohio: A Mirror of the National Scene," *Bookmobile and Outreach Services* 7, no. 1 (2004): 29–36. Reprinted with permission.

Donkey-drawn libraries in Zimbabwe

by Thelma H. Tate

THE DONKEY-DRAWN BOOK SERVICES were a direct response to the community's demand for library outreach and extension services in rural Zimbabwe. The first cart was launched in Nkayi District in 1995. It was designed by the Rural Libraries and Resources Development Programme and constructed by Mr. Hlabangana, a local smith, who generally specializes in making ordinary carts. To date, the RLRDP operates four ordinary donkey-drawn mobile libraries in Nkayi.

The donkey-drawn mobile libraries, including an electro-communication cart, were developed to provide library extension and outreach services to communities that are remote from the static library communities. They are affordable because they exclude the consumption of fuel and inevitable wear and tear incurred on running motorized bookmobiles, given the rough terrain in the district.

Each cart serves an average population of 3,000–4,000. Their goal is to stimulate and affirm reading interests among their communities. The electro-communications cart, besides serving as a mobile library, works as a media center, offering radio, television, video, telephone, fax, email, and internet.

Electrical power for operating the equipment is supplied by renewable solar energy, provided by a solar unit installed on the roof that charges a battery.

SOURCE: Thelma H. Tate, *The Donkey Drawn Mobile Library Services in Zimbabwe, August 6–13, 2001* (The Hague, Neth.: International Federation of Library Associations and Institutions, 2002), pp. 10–13.

FACILITIES

Library design trends

by Sam Demas and Jeffrey A. Scherer

LIBRARIANS AND ARCHITECTS use many strategies to enhance the functionality of the library and the sense of place and enjoyment it provides. Academic libraries are reclaiming their roles as agents in community building by borrowing ideas from their colleagues in public libraries, who never lost sight of the library's importance as a gathering place. Public libraries are increasing their roles in information literacy and strengthening their virtual library presence.

Given the variety of activities that take place in a library, one key challenge is achieving a balance among an opposing range of functions and needs. Some examples include: solitude versus interaction; quiet versus noise; conservation versus food and drink; order versus mess; existing physical barriers versus no barriers; durability versus comfort; openness versus security; and limited hours versus 24/7 expectations. In addressing these apparent tensions, it is much too easy to either opt for the status quo or succumb to the latest fad and introduce the changes for the wrong reasons. The successful library meets all its needs through a careful, iterative process of consultation, compromise, and design.

Some specific examples of solutions to these design quandaries include:
* the gossip corner at the Detroit Lakes (Minn.) Public Library;
* the computer-free zone of the Carmel Clay Public Library in Carmel, Indiana;
* the athenaeum of the Carleton College Library in Northfield, Minnesota.

In the Detroit Lakes example (shown below), the community desired a space for local citizens to meet informally—much like the agora of ancient Greece. At Carmel Clay, citizens expressed a strong desire to get away from the computer and read, resulting in a computer-free zone. These design examples illustrate how old ideas have been updated in response to community needs, interests, and tastes.

The following is a list of design trends that help to make libraries more useful, distinctive, and attractive places.

Reading and study spaces. Studying is both a private and a communal act. Increasingly, the trick is to design a range of choices for reading and study that meet the continually changing needs of the populations served. In academic libraries, many students go to the library because peer pressure and the overall ambiance put them in the mood to study. The mix of study seating is shifting from the individual study carrel to more table-and-chair ensembles (traditional reading rooms are places to see and be seen while doing serious work) and more soft seating (comfortable armchairs and couches). Comfortable seating needs to reflect such newer technologies as laptop computers, which, like books, can sit on one's lap as well as on a table or desk. And libraries are always expected to provide that increasingly rare commodity—the quiet area within a public space.

Collaborative workspaces. Study rooms and informal spaces, wholly or partially secluded from the view of others, are popular for group study, tutoring, and conversations. Although some libraries are experimenting with designs for collaborative computing spaces—allowing small groups to view, manipulate, and create information collaboratively—others are simply making spaces that can be easily and economically altered as the needs of the student body or community change.

Spaces for groups. The demand for community spaces for collective study, conversation, or meeting rooms continues to grow. These often accommodate small gatherings (5–10 people) for book clubs, tutoring or literacy programs, investment clubs, homework services, and other activities. They also include larger meeting spaces for community groups.

Learning and teaching spaces. Information literacy is taught in smart classrooms, fully wired and flexibly designed. These rooms also serve as overflow public access computing labs when not being used for instruction. As computing becomes more ubiquitous, large centralized computer labs are giving way to a more widely distributed configuration of computing resources. Wireless technology allows network access anywhere in the building.

Technology-free zones. Although much of the current debate centers on accommodating technology and its effect on library use, many libraries are honoring patron and student requests by setting aside spaces (such as dedicated quiet rooms or zones) where computing is prohibited. The intimate act of reading requires both solitude and quiet.

Archives, special collections, and exhibit spaces. These invaluable parts of a collection increasingly take the form of prominently featured displays,

---

Most Popular Floor Colors in New Academic Libraries, 1995–2002

Blue	22.7%
Green	17.2%
Gray	16.6%
Multicolored	14.1%
Beige	14.1%
Brown	7.4%
Red	5.5%
Purple	1.8%
White	0.6%
Gold, yellow, orange	0.0%

SOURCE: Harold B. Shill and Shawn Tonner, "Creating a Better Place: Physical Improvements in Academic Libraries, 1995–2002," *College & Research Libraries* 64 (November 2003): 431–466.

which celebrate local history, the continuum of the book, knowledge, and the community of ideas. Whether it is genealogy, local history, local authors, the history of local crafts, foods, industries, or natural history, every library has some special collecting niche that contributes to the "national collection." These spaces also allow for "quick response" to topical issues that may surface—such as how terrorist attacks have brought attention to Islamic cultures and religion.

"What's new" spaces. People appreciate the library's qualitative screening and gravitate to spaces that build on some design principles of retailing and marketing. Because of this, libraries are emulating the marketing techniques used by bookstores, through the use of prominently featured "recommended by staff" services, video and CD rental collections, and popular reading collections that cater to the interests of a particular reading community.

Cultural events spaces. Libraries bring together communities of interest to peruse, discuss, debate, and celebrate the world of learning and the creative arts. They increasingly provide elegant spaces designed for lectures, author readings, films, concerts, book arts, and dramatic events. In effect, libraries are re-embracing the role of the ancient institution, the athenaeum. The Carleton College Athenaeum (right) was created by converting a little-used room into an elegant reading room and venue for cultural events. Several times each week, in conjunction with the college's academic departments, the library cosponsors lectures, book and poetry readings, and panel discussions that serve to highlight the library as a cultural center of the college.

Age-specific spaces. Designing spaces for specific ages presents challenges and opportunities. For example, teens are in an interesting place—caught between their fading childhood and emerging adult years. Each teen is also different in his or her stage of development. It is this "between-ness" that makes the design of space for the teenager so crucial and fascinating. For older adults, considerations include temperature control, glare-free lighting, seating that is perceived as secure (older adults prefer their "backs to a wall"), and lounge seating grouped for conversation. Other considerations include:

1. accommodating the display of materials based on genre categories rather than a traditional classification system;
2. increasing the number of books and materials that are displayed face-out—despite the often limited amount of space available;
3. focusing on personal preferences of users over the "system" of the library;
4. providing increased availability to privacy—despite the anxieties about illicit activity;
5. allowing users to have control and ownership of the space;
6. creating a balance between independence and guidance; and
7. isolating the space while simultaneously providing connection to the rest of the library.

Shared spaces. The age of the highly individualized, use-specific space is giving way, for reasons of efficiency and economics, to multiuse spaces. Today, we are seeing public libraries partnering with city halls, schools, university libraries, and senior centers. In many ways this trend evokes the fer-

**Nonlibrary Facilities Included
in New Academic Libraries, 1995–2002**

Conference room	82.7%
General computer lab	69.9%
Seminar room	53.2%
Multimedia production center	45.1%
Snack bar or café	32.4%
General use classroom	31.8%
Educational tech center	26.0%
Art gallery	24.9%
Auditorium	20.2%
Writing lab	16.8%
Research institute	5.8%
Bookstore	4.0%

SOURCE: Harold B. Shill and Shawn Tonner, "Creating a Better Place: Physical Improvements in Academic Libraries, 1995–2002," *College & Research Libraries* 64 (November 2003): 431–466.

ment of the amazing Carnegie library building boom, when libraries were designed to serve as full-service cultural and community centers—offering meeting halls, museums, recreation facilities, and teaching spaces. Today, academic libraries are experimenting with merging and/or co-locating with academic support services like IT operations, career centers, writing centers, learning and teaching centers, tutoring programs, media services, and language centers.

Another old idea that is coming around again is the design of buildings that co-locate academic and public libraries. The private Nova Southeastern University in Fort Lauderdale, Florida, has opened its new library as a combined university and public library. San Jose, California, and St. Paul, Minnesota, are designing joint public/academic library facilities with public universities in their communities. While they present design and operational issues, these shared spaces reflect the demographics of the student body, support real community needs, and promise savings through cost-sharing.

Art spaces. Libraries celebrate art as a metaphor for continuity, innovation, and creativity. As institutions concerned historically with text, we are expanding our scope to include visual information that contains power, beauty, and the ability to provoke beyond the word. Through collaboration with local artists and art guilds, "percent for art" programs, and a growing range of museum/library collaborations, libraries now offer opportunities for the public to engage with and enjoy artwork in busy public places. Spaces are being designed for permanent art commissions as well as galleries for short-term exhibitions. Collaboration with local arts groups helps libraries present art that speaks to the issues and aesthetics of the community. Design challenges include conservation (light and environmental conditions), security, and hanging surfaces.

Nature, natural light, and landscapes. Natural light, views of nature from the inside, and plants and aquaria give vitality to a library. For example, the Boulder (Colo.) Public Library has an ensemble of aquaria that depicts the ecology of the Boulder River watershed. Both the siting of library buildings and the exterior landscaping are sometimes designed to evoke the notion of the cultural institution in a garden or parklike setting, or the notion of a "cultural park" or "civic center," with museums and other civic and cultural institutions located nearby.

Decorative arts and interior design trends. Before the 1940s, libraries were designed as a totality. The container (architecture) was given equal attention to the contents (the books and readers). The contents were seen as worthy of special display and space for the reader was treated with special rooms that communicated the idea of the pursuit of truth and knowledge. The container reflected civic grandeur and virtues. Who is not in awe of the Rose Reading Room at the 42nd Street New York Public Library or the great hall and reading room of the Library of Congress? While this may be seen as nostalgic reminiscence, people really respond to and respect a sensitively presented sense of historical reference and civic grandeur, This "totality" in design is reemerging, updated to reflect contemporary tastes and styles. Library users consistently respond to features that give libraries a sense of warmth, style, and locality.

This expresses itself in a wide range of interior and decorative touches, including fireplaces, decorative stairwells, beautiful lighting fixtures and lamps, and the use of local materials for floors and countertops.

Just as every community has its "living room"–quality spaces for special public occasions, there is a need for "library" or "drawing room"–quality space open for members of the community to use for cultural events, for learning, and to meet their informational needs. While these "library-quality" spaces look and feel very different from place to place, the successful ones have in common a tangible sense of the history and ethos of the place and the diversity and strivings of the people that they serve. The *quantity* of space in a library is not as important as the *quality*. Librarians, architects, and the users of libraries are learning that by reflecting and understanding the unique history, traditions, features, and needs of its patrons, a library can design programs and buildings that embody and enhance the *esprit de place* that is each library's unique contribution to its community.

SOURCE: Sam Demas and Jeffrey A. Scherer, "Esprit de Place," *American Libraries* 33 (April 2002): 65–68.

27 rules for good and evil in library architecture

by Fred Schlipf and John Moorman

1. Few libraries have ever built enough storage space on purpose.
2. The right number of entrances to a library is anything up to one.
3. Echoes are not our friends.
4. Even if it's stupid, as long as it's legal, you can have whatever you want.
5. Never buy a chair until you've spent at least 15 minutes sitting in it.
6. Never sign a completely open-ended contract with a professional.
7. When citizens enter a library, they want to see librarians and books.
8. The layout of a good building is intuitively obvious.
9. You can't match your carpet.
10. Reject traditional architectural forms at your peril.
11. Always show your plans to your custodians.
12. A service desk is a service desk, not a monument.

13. No matter what you call it, EIFS is still an eighth of an inch of stucco over plastic foam.
14. Carpet squares tend to look like squares of carpet.
15. Any sign worth making is worth making well, and lots of signs aren't worth making at all.
16. Never hire a consultant who works for your architect.
17. Today's trendy color scheme is tomorrow's avocado and orange.
18. Skylights cause impossible glare, but they make up for it by leaking.
19. Creating excitement with light in a library is like creating excitement with steps in a nursing home.
20. Never create a cozy corner you don't want occupied by a bag lady.
21. Even if your books are about pears and your staff are pear-shaped, you still don't want a pear-shaped library.
22. You can turn HID lighting off, but you can't turn it back on again.
23. Watch your sightlines. The romantic dreams of Grace Livingston Hill fans do not include unexpected glimpses of the men's room in action.
24. No matter what turns a designer on, a library is not an airline terminal, a torpedo factory, or a Chuck-E-Cheese.
25. Task lighting and down lighting aren't completely evil, but they come close enough for all practical purposes.
26. Buy strong. There is no theoretical upper limit to the number of teen-agers who can occupy a chair.
27. Ars longa, technologia brevis.

SOURCE: Fred Schlipf and John Moorman, "(Un)desiderata: 27 Snappy Rules for Good and Evil in Library Architecture," presented at the 2000 Public Library Association conference, urbanafreelibrary.org/fredunde.htm.

THE PAST

Bookmen of Babylon

by D. N. Marshall

ANOTHER MATTER which needs to be mentioned concerns the librarians of the time. There was always a special functionary in charge of each of the very many libraries found in the region. George Herbert Bushnell, in *The World's Earliest Libraries* (Grafton, 1931), gives the name of Nebo-zuqub-Yukin as one of the chief librarians of the Nineveh library when it was situated at Nimrud, prior to its transfer from that place to Nineveh. It seems he held office from the sixth year of the reign of Sargon II (716 B.C.) to the 22nd of Sennacherib (684 B.C.), that is for about 32 years, a pretty useful inning. James Westfall Thompson, in his *Ancient Libraries* (University of California, 1940), tells us that librarians were known by the title of Nissu-duppi-satri, an Akkadian term meaning "man of the written tablets." He adds that the first of them who bore this title was a Babylonian named Amil-anu, who lived 1,000 years before the date of the libraries in Nimrud and Nineveh.

At Nimrud, one library seems to have been collected under the direction and care of Nebu-zuqub-gina, son of Mamdak Mubagar the librarian, and grandson of Gabbu-llani-Kamis the great librarian. Nebu-zuqub-gina also acted as librarian for a number of years. It appears that most of these were professional scribes who also served as interpreters and were, in more ways than one, very helpful scholarly guides. Indeed, Bushnell mentions that the office of librarian was of very great importance and was probably a well-paid post. Having regard to these extra duties of interpretation and inscribing of books and the fact that an elaborate system of cataloging and classification existed, the post, obviously, was no sinecure.

Samuel Kramer, in his *From the Tablets of Sumer* (Falcon's Wing, 1956), gives interesting details about the book lists prepared at the time. On a tablet 2½ inches in length and 1½ inch in width, 62 titles were inscribed in a very minute script. A. H. Sayce, in his *Babylonians and Assyrians* (Scribner's, 1899), describes somewhat in detail the process of cataloging, which had to provide for the fact that a work consisted of a number of tablets. Series of tablets had to be correlated while retaining each one's identity. This was done by coupling with the title the first line of each tablet and the parts of the work. This aided readers in finding the work and also any particular part of it. The tablets were arranged on shelves. Sayce cites the fact that at Lagash, 32,000 of them were discovered still in the order in which they were placed in 2700 B.C.

Now let us turn to another library. We have just seen the most magnificent in these regions. We now turn to the oldest. Sargon I (2300 B.C.) is regarded by scholars as the father of libraries in Asia, as libraries of dates earlier than this have not yet come to our knowledge. It was he who founded the great library at Akkad, and we have in Paris, even today, a beautiful seal of one of the librarians of this library. His name was Ibnisarru. A portion of the catalog of this library is available even today. From the instructions to readers given therein, we find that a system very similar to the one followed at present was prevalent at the time in this library. Each reader had to write on a piece of papyrus, provided for the purpose, his name and particulars of the work he wanted to consult; the librarian then took out the tablet and handed it over to him. Each tablet was classified and the perfection of the system had grown out of long experience. These facts prove that the library profession is a very ancient one.

SOURCE: D. N. Marshall, *History of Libraries: Ancient and Mediaeval* (New Delhi, India: Oxford & IBH, 1983), pp. 27–29.

Libraries of the early church

by M. Cecchelli Trinci

BETWEEN THE LATE 2nd century and the first half of the 3rd, among the greatest power-houses of Christian theology were, first, Alexandria, then Palestinian Caesarea and Jerusalem. At Alexandria, where a *scriptorium* and a library were attached to the school, Clement and Origen taught. To Origen we also owe the foundation of the school of Caesarea.

The library of Jerusalem was founded by its bishop Alexander, who also contributed to the school of Caesarea. Here the library was celebrated for its abundance of volumes, on which Eusebius drew in compiling his *Ecclesiastical History*. In the East, especially Egypt but also Palestine, in the coenobia founded there from the second half of the 4th century, were also important libraries. In the West, e.g., in Gaul, collections of books—the indispensable equipment of scholastic structures—were organized in coenobitic institutions, especially through the influence of St. Martin of Tours (317–397).

Notable among the private libraries was that of St. Augustine (354–430), which the North African town of Hippo preserved until the Vandal irruption in 431.

The history of the origins of the Roman ecclesiastical library is not rich in information. Up to Innocent I (pope, 402–417), indeed, data on the formation of archives is very unilluminating, though it goes back to the pontificate of Antherus (235–236). This lack of information is partly due to the destruction of the archives themselves, especially during the period of Diocletian's persecution (303–311); however, the library of the Apostolic See must have been well-stocked with materials for some time, and not just this library, if Pope Hilarus (461–468) was busy creating one *ex novo* in the cloister of San Lorenzo al Verano.

In Rome, from the late 5th through the 6th century, were being perfected the organization of the archive of the Apostolic See and the criterion of choice and selection of the books of which libraries should consist. Popes like Gelasius I (492–496), under whose name goes the decree *De libris recipiendis et non recipiendis (Decretum Gelasianum)*, and Agapetus I (535–536), creator of the library near the slope of Scaurus on the Coelian hill, certainly gave a considerable boost to the establishment of theological and humanistic culture in the city. Finally the uniting of the papal libraries at the Lateran by Gregory the Great (590–604) increased the importance, among all the Roman libraries, of the pontifical library of the Apostolic See. Moreover, Rome in the 7th century became a center of cultural attraction of undoubted importance; the young frequented its schools and the book trade flourished, with a lively contribution from Greek culture.

Pope Gregory I

From the 6th to the 7th century in the West, thanks above all to the monks of the Benedictine order, schools, *scriptoria*, and libraries began to become increasingly numerous. In Italy there was Cassiodorus's foundation at Vivarium in Calabria, closely linked to St. Benedict. At Bobbio, St. Columbanus, thanks partly to the precious contribution of the Langobard kings—the barbarians, starting with Odoacer and then with Theodoric, had never neglected the organization of education in their territories—founded an abbey that soon became famous for its school of writing and its precious library.

New libraries were also founded in Gaul; Spain owed its strongest cultural boost to the work of St. Isidore (560–636), whose library was in the archiepiscopal palace of Seville and whose bibliographical knowledge was so vast as to suppose immense materials *in loco* for consultation.

1

Finally, the libraries of St. Columba's numerous monasteries in Scotland and the very important library of Iona, that of Lindisfarne in northeast England, those of Canterbury and Jarrow, also in Britain, but also the collections of books preserved in Germany in centers like Fulda and Mainz, or at St. Gall in Switzerland, do not exhaust a subject that really requires much fuller treatment.

SOURCE: Angelo Di Berardino, ed., *Encyclopedia of the Early Church* (Cambridge, Eng.: James Clarke, 1992), vol. 1, p. 486. Reprinted with permission.

Types of libraries in America, pre-1876

by Haynes McMullen

THIS LIST OF LIBRARIES includes definitions of terms used before 1876 and terms used by recent writers on American library history.

Apprentices' library. A library for the use of apprentices, usually planned and supervised by older businessmen or employees and usually containing a general collection of books. Often open to others besides apprentices.

Asylum library. The term *asylum* was widely used for any institution where handicapped or disadvantaged children or adults lived and were cared for. Many were maintained by charitable societies; others were operated by federal, state, or local governments.

Athenaeum library. Athenaeums were societies, partly social and partly cultural. Their libraries were like social libraries because both kinds were general and because the operation of a library was often one of the main objects of the athenaeum. If the athenaeum library differed, it was because it might put more emphasis on current journals and newspapers.

Bray libraries. The libraries sent from England to Church of England parishes, mostly in Maryland beginning around 1700 through the efforts of Anglican clergyman Thomas Bray (1656–1730).

Church library. A library maintained by a particular church in a town or city.

Circulating library. Originally, any library from which books could be taken home. The term was used to designate two main types: a *commercial circulating library*, operated for profit, and a *social library*, operated for the benefit of its users. In recent years, historians have usually limited the term to mean the former.

College student society library. A library belonging to a society of students in an institution of higher education. These societies, often called literary societies, held meetings for social or educational purposes and typically owned general collections of books. A few such societies, mainly in theological seminaries, had libraries containing books on religion. Collections on other special subjects were rare.

Commercial circulating library. A library owned by an individual or firm and containing books that were circulated to individuals for a fee. The fee was usually in the form of a subscription, payable monthly, quarterly, or annually. The collections were almost always general and popular in nature.

Education library. A few state governments operated libraries that were on the subject of education or were intended for education professionals, beginning in the 1850s. The libraries operated by a few city boards of education at about the same time may have had an educational emphasis, but several of them were general in content.

Fraternal organization library. A library belonging to a lodge of the Masons, the Independent Order of Odd Fellows, or other fraternal group.

Hotel reading room. Hotels sometimes maintained reading rooms containing a few books, current journals, and newspapers.

Lyceum library. A lyceum was an organization made up of people who met together to debate and listen to lectures and who usually established a general library.

Mercantile library. A library formed for the use of clerks in business firms. Ordinarily formed by the clerks themselves and ordinarily general in content.

Mill library. A library maintained in a factory by its owner, for the use of employees. Sometimes a small fee was charged. Such a library was more often found in New England than elsewhere.

Proprietary library. A term that was never in general use in the 19th century. It was used interchangeably with the term *subscription library* by Edward

---

The First U.S. Library Conference
by Wayne A. Wiegand

In June 1853, five men began planning the first library conference on the North American continent: Smithsonian Institution Library Director Charles Coffin Jewett, New York publisher Charles Benjamin Norton, New York Mercantile Library Director Seth Hastings Grant, Brown University Library Director Reuben Aldridge Guild, and recent Yale University graduate (and later Johns Hopkins University president) Daniel Coit Gilman. On September 15, 82 delegates met in New York City and unanimously elected Jewett conference president.

"We meet to provide for the diffusion of a knowledge of good books, and for enlarging the means of public access to them," Jewett told the crowd that morning. "I unite most cordially in

the hope which I have heard expressed this morning, that this convention may be the precursor of a permanent and highly-useful association." Ambitious plans.

Those participating in the conference (mostly white males from Northeast and Middle Atlantic states, many of whom represented the book trade) established professional friendships, resolved to exchange catalogs and annual reports, shared information about the latest technologies that promised to improve their practice, committed themselves to compile a librarians' manual, and planned for a permanent librarians' association. They also discussed catalogs, indexes, government documents, and popular libraries, and then returned to their respective homes charged with enthusiasm.

Norton, Gilman, and Grant

That enthusiasm, however, soon dissipated. Within a year Congress passed the Kansas-Nebraska Act, a congressional bill establishing the territories of Kansas and Nebraska, which represented one more step toward a civil conflict that eventually tore the nation apart and preoccupied the attention of its citizens for an entire generation.

Yet the conference of 1853 was not a total failure. Although it did not generate "the formation of a permanent librarians' association" that a conference resolution promised, it did serve as a precedent. Librarians had met once and they would meet again. In fact, given the track record the American Library Association established since it organized in 1876, one might say again, and again, and again, and again.

SOURCE: Wayne Wiegand, "This Month, 149 Years Ago," *American Libraries* 33 (June/July 2002): 122.

Edwards in his book *Memoirs of Libraries* (London: Trübner, 1859). Apparently, the two terms were both used to describe social libraries until Charles K. Bolton published a pamphlet, *Proprietary and Subscription Libraries* (Chicago: American Library Association, 1912), and began to employ the term *proprietary library* if the users of the collection owned stock in it; he employed the term *subscription library* for one in which the users paid annual fees. Writers since his day have accepted his idea, apparently ignorant of the fact that, for many social libraries, the proprietors were called subscribers and paid an annual fee. They sometimes permitted others to use the collection for a fee.

Public library. Before 1876, this term was ordinarily used to mean any library other than one owned by an individual for his or her own use. In its more recent sense, it means a library, usually general in content, which was almost always owned by a local government and was open to most or all of the citizens without charge.

Saloon reading room. Saloons sometimes maintained reading rooms as added attractions for their customers.

Social library. A library owned by an association formed to establish and operate a library intended for its members' use. Usually, the members subscribed for stock in order to purchase the initial collection, which was often general in subject matter. Then they were assessed a smaller sum or tax each year to keep up the collection. Some social libraries were for a particular part of the population (children, Germans, ladies) or for those with a particular subject interest (agriculture, history, religion).

Society library. A library belonging to an association formed because of its members' subject interest, that is, an association that was not formed primarily to operate a library. A few societies seem to have been general in interest; others had specialized subject interests (agriculture, antiquarian, engineering, history, literature, medicine, music, religion).

Subscription library. This term has been used by some modern writers to mean a *social library* in which the users did not own the collection but paid an annual fee, in contrast to a *proprietary library*, which was owned by the users. Actually, in a typical library, the proprietors paid annual fees.

Workingmen's library. A library for the use of laborers. Most of these collections were in Indiana and were established with the aid of funds left in the will of geologist and educational reformer William Maclure (1763–1840).

SOURCE: Haynes McMullen, *American Libraries before 1876* (Westport, Conn.: Greenwood, 2000), pp. 163–171. Reprinted with permission.

The five laws of library science

by S. R. Ranganathan

1. Books are for use.
2. Every person his or her book.
3. Every book, its reader.
4. Save the time of the reader.
5. A library is a growing organism.

SOURCE: S. R. Ranganathan, *The Five Laws of Library Science* (1st ed., Madras, India: Madras Library Association, 1931).

Books for doughboys:
World War I service of the ALA

by Theodore Wesley Koch

LIFE IN THE CAMPS AND CANTONMENTS lacks many of the pleasures or diversions to which the average new-coming soldier has been accustomed. To a great extent the cantonments are isolated, and sometimes far distant from the home states of the troops there assembled. To take away some of the dreariness of this isolation, varied provision has been made for the leisure hours of the boys in khaki. A novel and effective effort along this line has been the establishment of the American Library Association Camp Libraries.

Upon the entrance of the United States into the war in 1917, the president of the ALA [Walter Lewis Brown] appointed a War Service Committee which made its first report at the annual conference of the Library Association at Louisville in June. The committee was at that time further organized and its work formulated. Subcommittees on finance, publicity, and book collecting (among others) were appointed.

On learning of these plans, the Commission on Training Camp Activities by an unanimous vote invited the ALA to assume the responsibility for providing adequate library facilities in the camps and cantonments. It seemed natural to ask the Association to handle this problem for the government because as an organization it could call to its services the necessary trained help.

The Secretary of War having appointed 10 nationally known men and women as a Library War Council to aid in an appeal for funds, it was decided to raise by private subscription a million dollars with which to carry on the work. It was felt that this was the least amount for which the needed buildings could be erected, equipped, and administered, the soldiers supplied at the front, in the field, in cantonments and training camps, and on board the troop ships.

The financial campaign was successful in raising the money asked for—and half as much again. A campaign for books was conducted at the same time as the campaign for funds, resulting in the receipt of over 200,000 volumes for immediate service. These were collected at central points and delivered, either at the camps or at designated depots for transportation abroad. It was planned to use the funds largely for books of a serious nature, as it was anticipated that the lighter books would be largely supplied by gift. The campaign for books was to continue as long as the war lasted, as would also the need for funds if the war were to last as long as some people predict. The Carnegie Corporation made a grant of $10,000 for each of the proposed 32 camp libraries, and a similar sum was received from another source for a library building at the Great Lakes Naval Training Station, north of Chicago.

Administration and personnel

In October 1917, at the request of the War Service Committee of the American Library Association, Dr. Herbert Putnam, Librarian of Congress, took over the direction and control of the War Service work. Headquarters were established in the Library of Congress. Here there is competent oversight of the work at the camps, careful administration of the Fund, with a scrutinizing accounting of all expenditures. Prompt attention is paid to the needs and opportunities for service as reported by the librarians in charge at the camps.

The camp librarian

Some of the camp librarians are volunteers; others are paid a small salary—$1,200 per year, in addition to subsistence—an amount less than a second lieutenant receives. There is also a paid assistant provided with subsistence. Some provision is likewise made for janitor service and the expenses of the local volunteers, making a total cost of about $250 per month for each camp library. Multiplying this by 31 brings the amount up to about $8,000 per month, less than $100,000 per year for this branch of the service.

Although the work has been simplified as far as possible at headquarters, additional men are still needed for this Camp Library service, since the employment of women is not permitted by the rules of the War Department. Women are, however, permitted to do volunteer work in connection with library service. Where the camp is adjacent to a town, the supervision of the camp library has in some cases been entrusted to the woman who is chief librarian of the local public library. Women librarians desiring to proffer volunteer service of this permitted type are requested to communicate with the camp librarian. In Camp Sherman (Chillicothe, Ohio) the technical work of getting the books ready for the library was placed under the direction of the daughter of the Commanding Officer. She is a graduate of Pratt Institute Library School. Her volunteer assistants were recruited mainly from the wives of officers at the camp, many of whom welcomed the opportunity to help. This volunteer staff does its work at the Chillicothe Public Library and is capable of preparing about 300 books a day.

Books are sent to the camp librarian from libraries which have been collecting books from citizens. All books must be delivered at storehouses of the Quartermaster's Corps, and must be taken from platforms every day. No assistance can be given in the matter of delivery to the library building either by the Quartermaster or the express companies. It has been found expedient to supply each camp library with a low-priced automobile with delivery box attached.

The call for books

Do the men in the camps read? When do they find time for it?

Some people have been raising the one question, and others have been doubtful about the second point. Major General Glenn, the commanding officer at Camp Sherman, wrote to Mr. W. H. Brett, librarian of the Cleveland Public Library, asking him to take steps to correct the erroneous impression that had gone abroad that the men did not have time for reading on account of the demands of military training. He wished to have it known that there is no one thing that will be of greater value to the men in his cantonment in producing contentment with their surroundings than properly selected reading matter.

One officer wrote to headquarters that he needed books for his men so badly that he was quite willing to pay for them himself. Another officer said that if the ALA would supply his regiment with books, he would see to it that a room and a competent man to take care of the books would be provided, for all seem agreed that the men in the new American army are very eager to read. Even before the regular camp libraries were opened a hundred books placed in a YMCA building of an evening would usually be borrowed before the building closed for the night.

That men who have been drilling, marching, and digging trenches all day are liable to be too tired in the evening to wish to walk any great distance for books has been recognized in efforts to bring the books as near to the soldiers' barracks as possible. In some instances traveling libraries have been resorted to with very great success.

Types of service

Evidences of the appreciation of the efforts of the camp librarian are beginning to come in from many sides. When a machine gun company went into quarantine on account of measles, the major was pleased to have a hundred books and a lot of magazines sent over to him. The camp librarian was aware of the fact that the medical officer might not permit the return of this material, but he was willing to stand the loss.

ALA Library at Camp Lewis, Washington State

A soldier detailed to call for a box of books at a public library, said: "Gee, Lady, you mean to *give* us all those books! Say, you people know what to do for a soldier! Some people just talk an' talk about entertainin' soldiers, but say, you have just hit the nail right on the head—without sayin' a word, too!"

The librarian at Camp Upton (Yaphank, N.Y.) reports that officers have come to the library for help in the technical aspects of their particular branch of the service and have expressed appreciation of the value of good propaganda material in building up the morale of the men.

A man at Camp Devens (Ayer, Mass.) said that what he wanted was a place where he could sit down in peace and quiet, with a book or two and a chance to read and dream. "Your alcoves are godsends," said he to the librarian. "The barrack's social room in which 75 to 125 men are talking and playing cards, where a piano and phonograph are rivaling one another, and where at any moment a basketball may knock your head sideways, is certainly no decent place to read, let alone trying to do any studying."

The librarian at Camp Logan (Houston, Tex.) writes that there is immediate need for books of live present-day interest, bearing on all phases; books of travel and histories of France, England, and the United States; mathematics (arithmetic, geometry); French conversation; automobiles; army engineering; manuals of army organization; the poetry of Robert Service, Alfred Noyes, John Masefield, John Greenleaf Whittier, Henry Wadsworth Longfellow; collections of war poetry; and inspirational books on modern, social and religious questions. He adds that he would be glad to receive a consignment of books of this character, with titles duplicated from five to 15 times. He is of the opinion that there should also be eight or ten good war atlases.

From other sources comes the word that maps are studied and handled until they are in shreds. A group of a dozen men is frequently seen around one map. The men not only want maps of their home district, but of the place where they are and the places where they have reason to believe they are going, including the maps of the scene of conflict. Good atlases and wall maps have now been supplied to all the camp libraries. The post route maps

1

of the various states in which the different camps are located, and the topographic survey maps of the immediate vicinity are *very* helpful and popular with the men.

Another camp librarian writes that French manuals, military manuals not published by the government, aviation, physical training, sanitation, bookkeeping, simple textbooks of English, histories, and books about the stars are much needed, while from another camp comes the request for French magazines and French songs. A special interest is manifested in books of travel and description about France. The men want to know about the customs of the country they expect to visit, the kind of money used, and the mode of life.

A private in the Engineers' Corps at Camp Devens asked for books which would explain the psychology of camouflage. He was something of an artist and had been successful with color photography. He wanted to know, for example, why the eye fails to recognize a shadow when light patches have been painted where the shadow would naturally fall. Material was found for him and he succeeded in hiding guns so well with paint that he deceived his own captain.

SOURCE: Theodore Wesley Koch, *War Service of the American Library Association* (Washington, D.C.: ALA War Service, Library of Congress, 1918), pp. 4–10, 20–22, 31–32.

THE FUTURE

Top issues facing academic libraries
by W. Lee Hisle

IN 2002, the ACRL Focus on the Future Task Force collected data concerning the most important issues facing academic libraries. Some 300 librarians were involved in generating ideas for this list, which represents the most often expressed issues, not necessarily in priority order.

1. Recruitment, education, and retention of librarians. The need to find and retain quality leadership for libraries is a core issue for the future. Even as retirements increase, fewer librarians are entering the academic library field in particular. Ensuring education of new librarians and reeducating existing librarians with skills and knowledge to support new roles in a digital information age is a challenge for the profession. Indeed, the continued relevance of the MLS to academic librarianship may be in question. In addition, low salaries and the lack of diversity in the profession were relevant subtopics, often mentioned as problems that need collective action.

2. Role of the library in academic enterprise. Librarians are dedicated to maintaining the importance and relevance of the academic library as a place of intellectual stimulation and a center of activity on campus. Even so, some feel that libraries are becoming marginalized. Librarians believe that it is essential that we emphasize information literacy instruction and the importance of the teaching role of librarians. We must find ways to promote the values, expertise, and leadership of the profession throughout the campus to ensure appreciation for the roles librarians do and can play. Though access to information is increasingly decentralized, and computer labs now compete with libraries as campus gathering points, librarians must demonstrate to the campus community that the library remains central to academic effort.

3. Impact of information technology on library services. Librarians are aware that an appropriate institutional balance needs to be maintained between traditional library materials and services and those services represented by instructional and information technology departments. Should libraries house campus information commons? Should libraries report through an "information czar," rather than through the traditional academic hierarchy? It is also important, though difficult, to maintain technological currency in the face of decreasing resources, rising costs, and differing views about institutional funding priorities.

4. Creation, control, and preservation of digital resources. Methods to determine what should be digitized, to find resources to do the work, and to develop appropriate bibliographic control mechanisms for digital materials offer complex challenges. In addition, librarians want to ensure that digital materials are preserved appropriately and that permanent access to those materials can be provided.

5. Chaos in scholarly communication. Librarians advocate the need for fair scholarly communication models as copyright laws change or are reinterpreted and challenges to fair-use in a digital context continue to be made. Traditional library/publisher relationships may change substantially. The consolidation of the information industry under a few large vendors is a substantial threat as it represents possible homogenization of information and the potential for monopolistic business practices. The rise of the Web as the first choice for student and faculty researchers represents a departure from traditional scholarly research patterns.

6. Support of new users. Librarians articulate the need to provide appropriate services and resources to new users, whether distance education students or those involved in new teaching and learning methods. The organizational patterns of academic libraries are thought to be a barrier to providing these students with access to instruction and information appropriate to their educational style. Librarians would like to take advantage of student enthusiasm, creativity, and technical skills. At the same time, librarians observe the growing lack of literacy among students, along with flexible ethics that tolerate plagiarism and copyright violations.

7. Higher education funding. Considering the current state of the economy, librarians face the possibility of reductions in funding that could have a deleterious effect on library programs, salaries, and resources. Creative thought and action will be required to compensate for the already low pay of librarians, as well as the rising costs of materials and technology. The question asked is, "How can libraries provide access to the information students and faculty need when the cost of resources is rising so precipitously?" In addition, librarians must face the challenge of competition from other organizational units during these times of scarce resources.

SOURCE: W. Lee Hisle, "Top Issues Facing Academic Librarians: A Report on the Focus on the Future Task Force," *College & Research Libraries News* 63 (November 2002): 714–715, 730.

PEOPLE
CHAPTER TWO

"We are librarians, and therefore the elect of God. To read is human, to catalogue divine."

—Charity Blackstock, *Dewey Death* (1956)

RECRUITMENT

How many people work in libraries?

by Denise M. Davis

THE LIBRARY WORKFORCE includes librarians and other professionals, paraprofessionals, and clerical and technical personnel. Statistics are not available for each category of personnel in each type of library. This is a summary of the latest available statistics on the two major categories—librarians and other professionals, and other paid staff—in the four types of libraries for which reliable national figures are available from the National Center for Education Statistics (NCES) (nces.ed.gov/surveys/libraries/index.asp).

The figures for public, academic, school, and state librarians are from five NCES surveys: *Public Libraries in the United States, Academic Libraries, Schools and Staffing Survey, State Library Agencies,* and *Digest of Education Statistics.* The most current information about staffing for public and academic libraries is available from such web-based peer comparison tools as the Public Libraries Peer Comparison Tool (2002) (nces.ed.gov/surveys/libraries/compare/Index.asp? LibraryType=Public) and the Academic Libraries Peer Comparison Tool (2002) (nces.ed.gov/surveys/libraries/compare/Index.asp?LibraryType=Academic). The figures on school library staffing are from unpublished tabulations in the *Schools and Staffing Survey, 1999–2000* (2002) (nces.ed.gov/surveys/SASS/ question9900.asp) and *Digest of Education Statistics, 2003* with data collected in 1999–2000 (nces.ed.gov/programs/digest/d03/list_tables.asp).

Each source uses a different definition of "librarian." The report on public libraries distinguishes the 29,086 persons with master's degrees from programs of library and information studies accredited by the American Library Association (ALA's definition of librarian) from the 15,406 staff who have the title of librarian but not an ALA MLS. The report on academic libraries gives a figure for "librarians and other professionals." We have reason to believe that the majority of these persons do have an ALA MLS. The figure for school libraries includes only state-certified library media specialists.

	Librarians	Other paid staff	Total staff
Academic libraries	25,152	70,291	95,443
Public libraries	44,920	91,300	136,220
School libraries	66,471	99,557	166,028
State libraries	1,201	2,631	3,832
Total	**137,744**	**263,779**	**401,523**

Comparable figures for employment in special libraries (e.g., libraries serving businesses, scientific agencies, hospitals, law firms, and nonprofit organizations) are not available. The Special Libraries Association reported in 2003 it had more than 12,000 members in 80 countries (www.sla.org/content/SLA/ pressroom/factsheet.cfm). It further reported that 80% of its members do work in libraries, while "as many as 18% of the Canadian and U.S. SLA members surveyed do not work in a library or information resource center. This compares with 13% in 1999" (www.sla.org/content/resources/research/researchlinks/moveout.cfm).

ALA estimated that in 2001 approximately 15,307 librarians worked in special libraries, bringing the total number of librarians to over 136,000, based on information available from several related associations. Going back further, a 1982 study of the library workforce (*Library Human Resources: A Study of Supply and Demand*) prepared for NCES found that total paid staff in special libraries was 47,410 with 18,600 identified as "librarians" and 28,819 identified either as other professionals or technical, clerical, and support staff. It was not then, nor is it now possible, to estimate the number of the other paid staff in special libraries.

However, a study sponsored by the Institute of Museum and Library Services that is underway in 2005 will provide detailed information about many types of librarians. Visit the Future of Librarians in the Workforce website at libraryworkforce.org.

SOURCE: Special report for *The Whole Library Handbook 4* by Denise M. Davis, Director, ALA Office for Research and Statistics.

Retirement and recruitment

by Mary Jo Lynch, Stephen Tordella, and Thomas Godfrey

IN MARCH 2002, *American Libraries* sounded an alarm about the need to bolster recruitment efforts with an article titled, "Reaching 65: Lots of Librarians Will Be There Soon," based on data from the 1990 census—the most recent information available at that time. The article has been used heavily to support recruitment efforts, most notably in the argument for legislation that gave the Institute of Museum and Library Services $10 million in 2003 to spend on recruitment projects. Newly published data files from the 2000 census confirm the prospect of a surge of retirements in the near future.

The first two figures are a repeat from the earlier article, except that they are based on the new data. Here we take a deeper look at the issue of retirement and recruitment by presenting an analysis of "age cohorts," or age groups of librarians, that combines census data from 1990 and 2000. All of the data analyzed and presented are based on the authors' analysis of the 1990 and 2000 census Public Use Microdata Sample (PUMS) files. The analysis was supported by a Small Business Innovation Research grant from the National Institutes of Health (NIH) to develop software usable for analysis of any occupational group.

In reviewing these new data, it is important to remember that the census labor force information reflects *what employed people say they do.* For example, 197,089 people said they were librarians in the 1990 census, and this figure

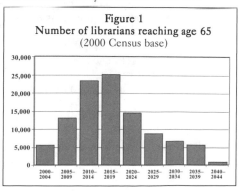

Figure 1
Number of librarians reaching age 65
(2000 Census base)

often was used in articles on the retirement problem. But in working with Decision Demographics on the pilot phase of their NIH project involving the demographics of various occupations, the American Library Association learned that only 87,409, or less than half, of those reported librarians had the master's degree or higher. Degrees by discipline are not reported in the decennial census, so we do not know how

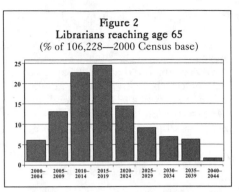

Figure 2
Librarians reaching age 65
(% of 106,228—2000 Census base)

many have an MLS itself. But possession of a master's degree or above in some field of inquiry seems a reasonable surrogate for the MLS. In 2000, the number of people who said they were librarians and also said they had a master's degree or above had increased to 106,228.

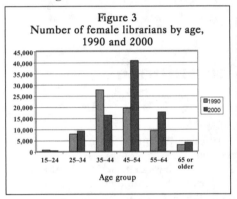

Figure 3
Number of female librarians by age, 1990 and 2000

The 1990-based analysis predicted a significant wave of retirement that would peak in 2010–2014. Updating the forecast with 2000 census data, as shown in Fig. 1–2, predicts a similar retirement surge in the near future. The main difference is that retirements now appear to peak slightly later—between 2015 and 2019. In total, the 10-year period beginning in 2010 will see 45% of today's librarians reach age 65. This surge of retirement represents the early wave of baby-boom librarians reaching the traditional retirement age.

In addition to the wave of retirements, several other related trends became evident in our analysis. Between 1990 and 2000, the number of working librarians with master's degrees grew by 18,819—an increase of nearly 22%. Much of this growth came from librarians following a career path that included

a late entry or reentry into the field—a sharp contrast from more traditional pathways to careers. The pattern was more pronounced with female librarians, as shown in Fig. 3–4.

Fig. 3 shows the number of female librarians by age in 1990 and 2000. During the 1990s, the number of female librarians grew by 30%, or 20,202—from 67,239 to 87,441. The largest net increase occurred among women in their late 30s and early 40s. Of particu-

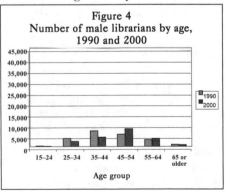

Figure 4
Number of male librarians by age, 1990 and 2000

lar note are the 27,469 female librarians age 35–44. A decade later when they had aged to 45–54, their ranks had swelled to 40,465, a 47% increase. A simi-

Retirements: What We Can Expect

The researchers in the accompanying article found that the greatest estimated retirement wave will occur between 2010 and 2020, creating a potential deficit of library and information science graduates between 2015 and 2019.

Current graduation rates reported by ALA-accredited library school programs indicate that LIS graduates will not keep pace with potential retirees in 2015–2019. Estimated retirements outpace graduations in the United States, even accounting for reduced growth in professional-level library staffing in public and academic librarians.

We know that LIS programs attract a large number of second-career individuals, and it is reasonable to assume that the average age of an LIS graduate is 30–35. Based on this assumption, and using the 2000 census projections of estimated retirements (at the age of 65) for library professionals, we can calculate the potential net loss to retirement in the critical years of 2015–2019 at 5,085 (by subtracting the estimated retirements for those years from the number of LIS graduates in 1985–1989). If this method of prediction is reliable, we will begin to see a surplus of graduates to retirees in 2019, but it may take until 2023 before we really recover from the deficit years. The average annual graduation rate for the period 1980–2002 is 4,608.

Muddying somewhat this vision of the future is the fact that this method does not take into consideration growth in the number of libraries, possible reductions in the number of positions for qualified professionals, or the siphoning off of LIS graduates into nonlibrary settings.—*Denise M. Davis, Director, ALA Office for Research and Statistics.*

lar pattern was found among the group of female librarians who started off at age 25–34 in 1990 with 7,785. By the time they reached age 35–44 in 2000 their numbers had grown to 16,179. This increase of nearly 8,400 more than doubled the size of that group.

Patterns of change among male librarians provide a sharp contrast. The total number and share of male librarians identified in the census dropped over the last decade. In 1990, 20,170, or 23% of librarians were men; by 2000, this had declined to 18,787, accounting for only 18% of all librarians. In Fig. 4, men display a small tendency toward midcareer entry from ages 35 to 54, but it pales in comparison to the women's pattern. Men generally start their library careers earlier and retire or shift careers earlier than women. Among men aged 45–54 in 1990 who aged to 55–64 by 2000, the number of librarians declined 33%—presumably because of retirements or field switching. The analogous decline in number of female librarians was only 9%.

The net influx of midcareer female librarians, and their later departure from the field, will do little to diminish the retirement surge looming in 2010. It has only served to delay it somewhat. The short-term supply of librarians appears to be bound up with the fate of baby-boom women, while the longer-term health of the field depends on those who follow them. Was the flooding of baby boomers into library science a unique phenomenon, or will succeeding generations of women make similar midcareer and midlife moves?

Part of the answer may lie in how library science competes with other opportunities available to women. Perhaps our field's competitive edge in the broader marketplace is in the ability of women to join the profession midcareer or as a second career; if so, it follows that there should be increased promotion of library science as a midlife career choice.

SOURCE: Mary Jo Lynch, Stephen Tordella, and Thomas Godfrey, *Retirement and Recruitment: A Deeper Look* (Chicago: ALA Office for Research and Statistics, 2004), www.ala.org/ala/ors/reports/recruitretire/recruitretire-adeeperlook.pdf.

White privilege in Library Land

by John D. Berry

HAVING JUST RETURNED from the April 2004 CARL (California Academic and Research Libraries) Conference, where I was a panelist on a diversity panel for reference service, I just had to stop and think to myself: What exactly is necessary to get across the ideals and values of diversity, not just in improved reference services, but profession-wide?

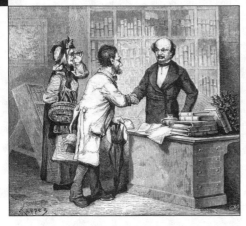

My copanelists were younger, probably more articulate, and female (all to the good), and they were most eloquent. We were all willing to do this session and believe in our profession's need for diversity, professionally and in regards to services to our communities.

At the end of our session, during the question and answer period, one academic librarian in the audience said (and I paraphrase), "So, if we just treat everybody nicely, that should do it," not particularly phrased as a question. I know this librarian did not mean this exactly, but they still apparently didn't get it. Superficially, the answer could be yes. But that doesn't really get it either.

Perhaps an adapted version of some of the questions from "White Privilege: Unpacking the Invisible Knapsack" by Peggy McIntosh (*Independent School*, Winter 1990, pp. 31–34) will help.

These are yes or no questions. If you can say yes to most of these questions, you possess "white privilege."

1. I can, if I wish, arrange to be in the professional company of people of my race most of the time.
2. If I should need to change jobs, I can be pretty sure of working in my library position in a library professionally staffed, primarily if not exclusively, with people of my race.
3. I can be pretty sure that my colleagues in such a location will be neutral or pleasant to me.
4. I can take a job with an affirmative-action employer without having co-workers on the job suspect that I got it because of race.
5. I can be pretty sure that the person in charge in a library will be a person of my race.
6. I can remain oblivious of the language and customs of persons of color who constitute the world's majority without feeling in my culture any penalty for such oblivion.
7. I can examine the majority of materials in my library, print, or media and see people of my race widely represented.
8. When conducting collection development, I can easily find materials featuring people of my race.
9. When I research national history or "civilization," I find that I am shown that people of my color made it what it is.

10. I can criticize my library or my profession and talk about how much I fear its policies and behavior without being seen as an outsider.
11. I can go home from most professional meetings or conferences feeling somewhat tied in—rather then isolated, out-of-place, outnumbered, unheard, held at a distance, or feared.
12. If my work day, week, or year is going badly, I need not ask myself of each negative episode or situation whether it has racial overtones.

If you can answer yes to most of these questions, you have social and institutional power, "white privilege," which you may not have earned, but nevertheless possess. Accepting this awareness is critical if you have a commitment to the goals and values of diversity and equity, not only within our profession, but also within our society and nation.

Attending diversity events are learning opportunities. Yes, they can challenge our perceptions and understandings. Yes, they can be uncomfortable. Change is never easy, but, if our avowed professional goals and ethics are to be sustained as our profession changes, these changes must be effected by each of us, personally.

SOURCE: John D. Berry, "White Privilege in Library Land," *Versed,* June 2004, pp. 1, 12.

Library degrees awarded by ethnic group, 2001–2002

Ethnic group	Gender	ALA-accredited master's		Post-master's		Doctorate	
American Indian/	Female	18	0.4%	1	1.8%	1	3.2%
Alaskan Native	Male	3	0.1%	–	–	–	–
	Total	21	0.5%	1	1.8%	1	3.2%
Asian/	Female	93	2.2%	1	1.8%	–	–
Pacific Islander	Male	25	0.6%	–	–	–	–
	Total	118	2.8%	1	1.8%	–	–
Black	Female	175	4.2%	2	3.7%	5	15.6%
	Male	33	0.8%	–	–	–	–
	Total	208	5.0%	2	3.7%	5	15.6%
Hispanic	Female	114	2.8%	18	33.3%	–	–
	Male	33	0.8%	3	5.5%	–	–
	Total	147	3.6%	21	38.8%	–	–
White	Female	2,897	70.4%	25	46.3%	17	53.1%
	Male	728	17.7%	4	7.4%	9	28.1%
	Total	3,625	88.1%	29	53.7%	26	81.2%
Total*	Female	3,297	80.0%	47	87.0%	23	71.9%
	Male	822	20.0%	7	13.0%	9	28.1%
	Total	4,119	100.0%	54	100.0%	32	100.0%

* This excludes international students and those for whom racial/ethnic category was not available.

Library degrees awarded by ethnic group, 1980–1981

American Indian/	Female	8	0.2%	–	–	–	–
Alaskan Native	Male	1	0.03%	1	0.8%	–	–
	Total	9	0.2%	1	0.8%	–	–

Library degrees awarded by ethnic group, 1980–1981 *(cont.)*

Ethnic group	Gender	ALA-accredited master's		Post-master's		Doctorate	
Asian/	Female	98	2.6%	6	5.1%	3	5.6%
Pacific Islander	Male	20	0.5%	1	0.8%	–	–
	Total	118	3.1%	7	5.9%	3	5.6%
Black	Female	129	3.4%	13	11.0%	5	9.3%
	Male	38	1.0%	1	0.8%	4	7.4%
	Total	167	4.4%	14	11.9%	9	16.7%
Hispanic	Female	48	1.3%	2	1.7%	–	–
	Male	15	0.4%	1	0.8%	–	–
	Total	63	1.7%	3	2.5%	–	–
White	Female	2,820	74.7%	74	62.7%	23	42.6%
	Male	599	15.9%	19	16.1%	19	35.2%
	Total	3,419	90.5%	93	78.8%	42	77.8%
Total	Female	3,103	82.2%	95	80.5%	31	57.4%
	Male	673	17.8%	23	19.5%	23	42.6%
	Total	3,776	100.0%	118	100.0%	54	100.0%

Library degrees awarded by ethnic group, 1973–1974

American Indian	Female	4	0.06%	–	–	–	–
	Male	2	0.03%	–	–	–	–
	Total	6	0.09%	–	–	–	–
Asian	Female	131	2.1%	–	–	1	2.1%
	Male	19	0.3%	–	–	2	4.3%
	Total	150	2.4%	–	–	3	6.4%
Black	Female	255	4.0%	9	12.0%	1	2.1%
	Male	52	0.8%	1	1.3%	1	2.1%
	Total	307	4.8%	10	13.3%	2	4.2%
Hispanic	Female	46	0.7%	1	1.3%	–	–
	Male	15	0.2%	–	–	1	2.1%
	Total	61	0.9%	1	1.3%	1	2.1%
White	Female	4,434	70.1%	43	57.3%	15	32.0%
	Male	1,245	19.7%	18	24.0%	24	51.0%
	Total	5,679	89.8%	61	81.3%	39	83.0%
Other	Female	77	1.2%	1	1.3%	–	–
	Male	45	0.7%	2	2.7%	2	4.3%
	Total	120	1.9%	3	4.0%	2	4.3%
Total	Female	4,947	78.2%	54	72.0%	17	36.2%
	Male	1,376	21.8%	21	28.0%	30	63.8%
	Total	6,323	100.0%	75	100.0%	47	100.0%

SOURCES: ALA Office for Human Resource Development and Recruitment, *Degrees and Certificates Awarded by U.S. Library and Information Studies Education Programs, 2001–2002* (Chicago: American Library Association, 2003); ALA Office for Library Personnel Resources, *Degrees and Certificates Awarded by U.S. Library Education Programs, 1973–1976,* and *1979–1981* (Chicago: American Library Association, 1977 and 1982).

Models for minority recruitment

by R. E. L. Spencer

THE URGENT NEED TO RECRUIT persons of diverse ethnic heritages to the library profession has grown. We know we need to recruit persons of varied cultural backgrounds, but the question arises—how? Indiana University's School of Library and Information Science in Bloomington has put the following strategies in place for recruiting people of color.

1. Start with a focus. The need to recruit can overwhelm. Selecting a focus can help. IU's SLIS made recruitment of African-American students a priority, and the experience has been a positive one.

2. Say something. Asking questions about race can be awkward, but conversation is a powerful means of inquiry. Inadequate statements are acceptable. Saying nothing is not. Talk to those around you.

Current students of African-American heritage were willing to talk about race. Their ideas helped. They stated the importance of having someone of their own heritage at orientation sessions. Being a new student is hard enough, but being a student of color in a room full of white people can be disconcerting. IU is a multicultural university that values people of all heritages, but persons of varied racial backgrounds may not be present at smaller meetings. Students also advised us to continue to include photographs of people with their racial heritage on the website and in brochures. Photographs help prospective students visualize themselves at our school.

Faculty members were also willing to provide copies of articles on minority recruitment strategies, help students pursue scholarship funds, speak to prospective students, and offer words of encouragement. Statements such as "Ask me if you need help" were important in recruitment plans.

Ten Recruitment Vows for Librarians

Take responsibility for the future of our profession. Promise yourself to:

1. Make a personal commitment to recruitment and diversity and encourage your colleagues to do the same.
2. Develop a positive vision and think creatively in ways that will excite potential students.
3. Reach out, encourage, coach, and counsel potential students.
4. Provide ongoing professional and emotional support and assistance to library school students.
5. Develop one-on-one relationships with nondegreed library staffers and others, encouraging them to consider librarianship as a career.
6. Provide as much flexibility as possible to accommodate subordinates pursuing the MLS.
7. Encourage and participate in the development and implementation of a first-rate mentoring program in your institution.
8. Get to know and work closely with a library school dean and staff.
9. Branch out from traditional settings to capture the attention of potential library school students.
10. Recruit actively, not passively.

SOURCE: Emma Bradford Perry, "Let Recruitment Begin with Me," *American Libraries* 35 (May 2004): 36–38.

3. Build a base of legitimacy. The next step was to meet or reconnect with campus units that support minority students. One campus director stated that if we wanted to recruit minority students, we needed to establish a strong legitimacy on campus. The importance of meeting campus advisers face-to-face was excellent advice. Several new students came to the school because their campus adviser recommended us. We held a Minority Student Open House in January 2001 with an advertisement for the event in the campus newspaper; fliers also helped potential students learn about our degrees.

4. Expand your invitation. "Come to our school: We want you here." Simple statements of welcome do work. Extending these welcomes via mailings to historically black colleges, African-American studies departments, and multicultural centers are ways to demonstrate commitment to minority recruitment. Ask your alumni for help and ideas. Alumni are key resources. One-on-one contact works.

5. Gather resources. Make lists and web links of minority scholarships. Know where students can go for help. Become an information broker on behalf of the services that aid minority students.

How do we recruit persons of all heritages to our profession? Start each year with a focus. Talk to the people around you about race. Ask questions. Ask what makes a person feel welcome. Get to know the resources of support on your campus and in your community. Network beyond your school with alumni, professional associations, and college career advisers. Don't worry. Our language is imperfect. Our ability to communicate is often awkward. But our willingness to say something will have meaning. Our willingness to say "Come to our school" is a good place to start.

SOURCE: R. E. L. Spencer, "Saying Something about Race: Models for Minority Recruitment," *American Libraries* 33 (August 2002): 54.

How to screen and appoint academic librarians

by the ACRL Committee on the Status of Academic Librarians

THIS GUIDELINE OFFERS suggestions on using a search committee effectively to fill an academic library position.

Personnel officer

The role of the personnel officer, if there is one, is to administer the search for the search committee. The personnel officer may serve as a regular or ex-officio member of all search committees.

Formation of search committees

The primary goal in the formation of a search committee, elected or appointed, should be to create a body representative of the constituencies affected by the position. Persons accepting appointment to the committee disqualify themselves as candidates for the position.

The administrator to whom the committee reports should give the following written information at the first meeting:

1. approximate date for submission of a list of nominees and proposed date of appointment;
2. number of finalists to be recommended;
3. affirmative action/equal opportunity requirements;
4. arrangements for payments, reimbursements, and clerical assistance;
5. standards for documenting committee actions and preserving those records;
6. importance of confidentiality and discretion;
7. concerns specific to the position; and
8. copy of the position description.

The position announcement

At the outset of the search, the supervisor of the position should write (or approve) a position description with equal opportunity and affirmative action considerations in mind. The description should serve as the standard against which the candidates are judged. It should list the responsibilities of the position in detail and describe the education, experience, and competencies that are required, preferred, and desired of candidates.

Posting the position

The library should advertise the position within the campus community and in appropriate regional and national publications, taking care to notify all potential groups of candidates protected by equal opportunity/affirmative action legislation. The advertisement should include a brief description of the responsibilities, qualifications, salary, and other benefits. It should also specify the date the position is available, application deadline, name of the person to whom to submit applications, and a list of items each candidate must submit. The library should advertise in print publications, on electronic discussion lists, and on the Web; it may consider using placement centers.

References

The search committee should solicit references only for qualified candidates under active consideration and from the list supplied by the candidate. The search committee may only contact additional referees with a candidate's permission. The search committee must hold all references in strict confidence and should advise each referee what information will be made available to the candidate in accordance with local practice. Each candidate should list only referees who can provide substantive information about his or her professional qualifications and should also list an administrator in the direct reporting line.

Selection, interview, and administrative procedures

Selection procedures. Each committee should screen and evaluate applicants according to library and institution-wide policies. All applications will undergo an initial screening for compliance with the qualifications and requirements stated in the position description. Unqualified candidates will not receive further consideration.

Fair, objective, and consistent procedures should be used to narrow the field of candidates to the desired number of finalists, whom the committee will invite for interviews. The search committee should be aware of institutional guidelines and all applicable laws when developing questions to ask the candidates selected for interviews.

Interview procedures. The committee and the appropriate administrative officer shall determine the interview agenda. All parties should adhere to this schedule in the interest of time and fairness.

Candidates invited for an interview should receive a copy of the interview schedule and information about the library and its parent organization in advance of the interview. Such information could include guides to the library, promotion and tenure guidelines, organizational charts, and bylaws.

The expenses of travel, meals, and lodging for the candidates should be borne by the inviting institution whether the interviews are held on or off campus. When this is not the practice, the candidate should be so apprised when an invitation is issued. If a presentation is required of the candidates, that requirement should be clearly communicated to each candidate when the interview is first scheduled.

Administrative procedures. The responsible administrator should instruct the committee chairperson in the prompt and accurate completion of all search-related reports. Sensitive files relating to the search should be treated in accordance with laws, regulations, and local practices.

Communications with candidates

Successful candidate. Only the proper administrator should contact the successful candidate after the interview. The initial notification of selection may be oral, but the official offer should be in writing and should include the specific terms of employment.

Unsuccessful candidates. A letter should be sent to all unsuccessful applicants thanking them for their interest and indicating that the search has concluded. Special acknowledgement should be accorded all interviewees.

Miscellaneous. All active candidates should be notified if the decision is made to close or extend the search.

SOURCE: A Guideline for the Screening and Appointment of Academic Librarians Using a Search Committee (Chicago: ALA Association of College and Research Libraries, 2003).

JOB SEARCH

Guide to library placement sources

CLASSIFIED ADS OF LIBRARY VACANCIES and positions wanted are carried in many of the national, regional, state and organizational library journals, newsletters, and periodicals. Members of associations can sometimes list "position wanted" ads free of charge in their membership publications. Listings of positions available are regularly found in *American Libraries, Chronicle* *of Higher Education, College & Research Libraries News, Library Journal, Library Hotline*, state and regional library association newsletters, state library journals, and foreign library periodicals.

Local newspapers, particularly the larger city Sunday editions, such as the *Washington Post*, the *New York Times*, *Los Angeles Times*, and *Chicago Tribune*, often carry job vacancy listings in libraries, both professional and paraprofessional. There are also online versions of the newspapers and journals.

In 2006, the American Library Association is launching a career website that consolidates advertisements listed in *American Libraries* and *College & Research Libraries News* and makes them searchable by job category, state, institution, library type, and salary. The ALA online career center, to be called JobLIST: Careers in Library and Information Science and Technology, www.joblist.ala.org, allows job seekers to create profiles that describe themselves and the positions they are looking for. Employers can post institutional profiles and search through résumés submitted by those seeking employment. The site also offers a communication tool that allows employers and job hunters to exchange messages anonymously without using email. JobLIST will also offer employment-related reading from the two magazines.

Many library-related discussion lists on the internet post library job vacancies interspersed with other news and discussion items. Two specialized library-related job search web links include:

- **LISjobs.com, Jobs for Librarians and Information Professionals,** compiled by Rachel Singer Gordon, at www.lisjobs.com; and
- **Library Job Postings on the Internet,** compiled by Sarah Johnson, at www.libraryjobpostings.org.

Specialized library associations and groups

Other organizations assist library job seekers with advertisements or placement services. Only website information is provided here; further details can be obtained from the organizations themselves.

Academic Position Network, www.apnjobs.com.

Advanced Information Management, www.aimusa.com/content/employment_services/hot_jobs.shtml.

Affirmative Action Register, www.aar-eeo.com/cgroups.html#library.

Alabama Public Library Service, www.apls.state.al.us/webpages/news/jobs.html.

American Association of Law Libraries, www.aallnet.org/hotline/hotline.asp.

American Libraries, www.ala.org/ala/education/empopps/careerleadsb/careerleadsonline.htm.

ALA Association of College and Research Libraries, www.ala.org/ala/acrl/acrlpubs/crlnews/crlcareeropps/careeropportunities.htm.

ALA Library Information Technology Association, www.lita.org/ala/lita/litaresources/litajobsite/litajobsite.htm.

ALA Office for Human Resource Development and Recruitment, www.ala.org/hrdr/placement.html.

American Society for Information Science and Technology, www.jobtarget.com/home/index.cfm?site_id=180.

Art Libraries Society/North America, www.arlisna.org/jobnet.html.
Asian/Pacific American Libraries Association, www.apalaweb.org/jobs/
apalajobs.htm.
Association for Educational Communications and Technology, www.
jobtarget.com/home/index.cfm?site_id=136.
Association for Library and Information Science Education, www.alise.org/
jobplacement/index.html.
Association of Research Libraries, db.arl.org/careers/index.html.
Black Caucus of the ALA, www.bcala.org/resources/jobs.htm.
British Columbia Library Association, www.bcla.bc.ca/Default.aspx.
C. Berger Group, www.cberger.com.
California Academic and Research Libraries, www.carl-acrl.org/Jobs/index.
html.
California Library Association, rsmart.ca/CLA_Members/jobmart.asp.
Canadian Library Association, www.cla.ca/careers/careeropp.htm.
Capital District Library Council, www.cdlc.org/Jobs/jobs.shtml.
Carney, Sandoe & Associates, www.carneysandoe.com.
Central New York Library Resources Council, clrc.org/jobs.shtml.
Chinese-American Librarians Association, www.cala-web.org.
Chronicle of Higher Education, chronicle.com/jobs/.
Clarion University of Pennsylvania, Department of Library Science, www.
clarion.edu/edu-humn/newlibsci/jobs/.
Cleveland Area Metropolitan Library System, www.camls.org/jobs/.
Colorado State Library, www.cde.state.co.us/cdelib/jobline.htm.
Connecticut Library Association, cla.uconn.edu/membership/clajobs.html.
Corestaff Services, www.corestaff.com/searchlines/.
Delaware Library Association, www.dla.lib.de.us/jobs.shtml.
Educause, www.educause.edu/jobpost/.
Florida Library Jobs, floridalibraryjobs.org.
Foothills Library Association, www.fla.org/jobline.html.
Georgia Public Library Service, www.georgialibraries.org/lib/jobs.html.
Gossage Sager Associates, www.gossagesager.com.
Greater Cincinnati Library Consortium, www.gclc.org/employment/index.
html.
Hawaii Library Association, www.hlaweb.org/html/jobs.html.
HigherEd Jobs.com, www.higheredjobs.com/default.cfm.
Idaho State Library, www.lili.org/forlibs/jobs.htm.
Illinois Library Association, www.ila.org/jobline/index.htm.
Indiana University, School of Library and Information Science, www.slis.
indiana.edu/careers/students.html.
InfoCurrent, www.infocurrent.com.
Information Media Jobs.com, www.informationmediajobs.com.
Iowa State Library, www.silo.lib.ia.us/for-ia-libraries/joblist.html.
Jinfo: Jobs in Information, www.jinfo.com.
John Keister and Associates, www.johnkeister.com.
K-12 Jobs.com, k12jobs.com.
Kansas Library Association, skyways.lib.ks.us/KLA/helpwanted/index.html.
Kentucky Department for Libraries and Archives, www.kdla.ky.gov/
libsupport/jobline.htm.
Labat-Anderson, www.labat.com/jobs/job-opening.htm.
Libjobs.com, www.libjobs.com.
Library Associates, www.libraryassociates.com/index.php4?page=jobs.

Library Co-Op, www.thelibraryco-op.com.
Library Journal, jobs.libraryjournal.com.
The Library Network, tln.lib.mi.us/jobs/.
Library of Congress, www.loc.gov/hr/employment/index.php?action= cMain.showJobs.
Long Island Library Resources Council, www.lilrc.org/jobs/joblistings.php.
Louisiana State Library, www.state.lib.la.us/Library/Employment/index.cfm.
Maine State Library, www.maine.gov/msl/libs/jobjar.htm.
Manitoba Library Association, www.mla.mb.ca/jobs.cfm.
Maryland Library Association, www.mdlib.org/job/index.htm.
Massachusetts Board of Library Commissioners, mblc.state.ma.us/jobs/ find_jobs/index.php.
Medical Library Association, www.mlanet.org/jobs/index.html.
Metropolitan New York Library Council, www.metro.org/magnet/.
Michigan Library Association, www.mla.lib.mi.us/development/jobline.html.
Minnesota Library Association, mnlibraryassociation.org/Jobs.htm.
Mississippi Library Commission, www.mlc.lib.ms.us/jobs/index.cfm.
Missouri Library Association, molib.org/Jobline.html.
Mountain Plains Library Association, www.usd.edu/mpla/jobline/.
Music Library Association, www.musiclibraryassoc.org.
Nebraska Library Commission, www.nlc.state.ne.us/libjob/adjobs.html.
Nevada Library Association, www.nevadalibraries.org/Jobs/jobs.html.
New England Jobline, www.simmons.edu/gslis/career/jobline/.
New Hampshire State Library, www.state.nh.us/nhsl/ljob/index.html.
New Jersey Library Association, www.njla.org/jobs.html.
New York State Library, www.nysl.nysed.gov/libdev/libjobs.htm.
North Carolina State Library, statelibrary.dcr.state.nc.us/jobs/ncjobs_current_ month.htm.
Ohio Library Council, www.olc.org/jobline.asp.
Oklahoma Department of Libraries, www.odl.state.ok.us/fyi/jobline/ jobline.htm.
Ontario Library Association, www.accessola.com/site/showPage.cgi?page= career/index.html.
Oregon Library Association, www.olaweb.org/jobline.shtml.
Pacific Northwest Library Association, www.pnla.org/jobs/index.htm.
Pennsylvania Library Association, www.palibraries.org/jobs/.
Pro Libra Associates, www.prolibra.com.
Reforma: National Association to Promote Library Service to the Spanish-Speaking, www.reforma.org/refoempl.htm.
Rhode Island Office of Library and Information Services, www.lori.ri.gov/ jobline/default.php.
Society of American Archivists, www.archivists.org/employment/index.asp.
South Carolina Library Association, www.scla.org/Documents/Jobs/.
South Carolina State Library, www.state.sc.us/scsl/jobs.html.
South Dakota Library Association, lib.sdstate.edu/lib18/SDLAPos.html.
Southeastern New York Library Resources Council, www.senylrc.org/ members/employment.htm.
Special Libraries Association, sla.jobcontrolcenter.com.
Tennessee Library Association, www.lib.utk.edu/~tla/tnjob.html.
Texas Library Association, www.txla.org/jobline/jobline.asp.
Texas State Library and Archives Commission, www.tsl.state.tx.us/ld/jobline/ index.html.

University of Western Ontario, Faculty of Information and Media Studies, www.fims.uwo.ca/employment/lis_can/index.htm.
USA Jobs, jobsearch.usajobs.opm.gov.
Utah Library Association, www.ula.org/jobline/jobline.htm.
Vermont Library Association, www.vermontlibraries.org/jobs.html.
Virginia Library Association, www.vla.org/jobline.asp.
West Virginia Library Commission, librarycommission.lib.wv.us/jobpostings. htm.
Western New York Library Resources Council, www.wnylrc.org/New/ jobswny.htm.
Wisconsin Employment, www.wisconsin.gov/state/app/employment.
Wontawk, www.wontawk.com.
Wyoming Library Association, www.wyla.org/jobboard.shtml.
Wyoming State Library, www-wsl.state.wy.us/libraries/libjobs.html.

How do I get there from here?

by Susanne Markgren and Tiffany Allen

HOW DO LIBRARIANS working in nonacademic institutions find their way into academic librarianship positions? How do technical service librarians move into public service roles or vice versa? Making the move from one type of position, or one type of library, to another can be a daunting prospect for many librarians today.

Whether you have a fear of being typecast or a fear of leaving your safety zone, the idea of transitioning to a new library can be as intimidating and overwhelming as starting over again in a new country. Recent graduates who would like to work in a specific setting, whether it is academic or special or public, often take the first job that comes along, even if it is not their desired position or their ideal environment. They want—and need—experience of any kind. After a few years, they find it difficult to break into a different setting and end up staying unhappily where they are.

The good news for librarians hoping to make the transition into a different library setting is that times, and roles, are changing. And the stereotypes, at least within the library world, are slowly dissolving. Librarian positions, on the whole, are becoming more and more diversified. Traditional roles are getting harder to find in today's rapidly changing environment as librarians (in survival mode) are forced to acquire a variety of skills and, in many cases, take on multiple roles within their libraries. The evolving nature of the current library landscape is helping to transform and, in some settings, abolish traditional roles and titles, while producing new titles, new career paths, and exciting opportunities for the future. All of this leads to more mobility and flexibility for librarians today.

As columnists for the "Career *Q&A* from the Library Career People" in the *Info Career Trends* newsletter, we have received several questions from frustrated librarians—recent graduates and 20-year veterans alike—wanting to know how to make the move from one library to another or how to transition into a different area of librarianship. In response to these questions and to address this common dilemma in librarianship today, we offer some advice for those transition seekers.

Assess your skills

What is it they say about good intentions? The pathway to library school is paved with good intentions? Seriously, a lot of us go into library school with one career plan in mind, and come out with a job in something else. We have all met the recent graduate who starts out wanting to be a reference librarian but discovers a passion for preservation, special collections or archives, or something else he or she stumbled across in the classroom or a field experience. The question is, once you have taken a job in one area and then decide to get back to your first love, how do you make that transition? How do I get there from here?

First you need to assess the skills you have. Think about it from a global perspective. For example, in your current position, you may work with individuals from the public or from a highly specialized field. Think of these people as your customers or patrons and consider the work you do for them in terms of public service. Do you work with them to answer their questions? Do you consult reference materials? Do you perform a mini-reference interview with your customers to gather more information regarding their requests? You need to examine your skill set outside of your current context to find transferable skills.

Transferable skills are skills that you pick up in one context and can carry to a new situation. Computer skills; customer service skills; budget, management, and supervisory experience—these are all examples of transferable skills. Think about the skills you have and how they may fit into the new career opportunity you are pursuing.

Do your homework

To assist you in your job search and to prepare you for interviewing, you may want to acquire more relevant experience and knowledge. This could include taking classes, finding a mentor, or simply doing some research.

The experience you crave may be right under your nose. Find out what you can do at your current job to gain experience in a different field or subject area. Is there someone who can mentor you or teach you new skills? Can you spend time learning and performing reference duties or technical services duties? Some libraries even offer exchange programs between departments, such as cataloging and reference or acquisitions and archives. Talk to your supervisor and find out if something like this is possible. Also, find out if your library or institution will pay for you to attend classes or workshops.

At the very least, do your homework and research the ins and outs of your desired position or field. Find competencies, best practices, guidelines, and standards dealing with library environments and librarian roles. Identify and read current literature to stay informed of trends and initiatives going on in your specific field. Showing a potential employer that you know what's going on in the field is a sure sign that you are interested in the position.

Job hunting

Keeping an open mind about librarian roles and titles may help to open more doors. Stop thinking of librarian roles in the traditional sense and consider looking for alternative roles and positions. For academic positions, how about considering a special academic library such as health sciences, law, or art?

If you are looking for a reference position, how about considering a position that includes reference duties, such as regular desk hours or instruction hours, as part of the position but not necessarily the majority of the position? You may find an electronic services position that includes regular reference desk hours.

Sometimes the more diverse a position is, the more interesting it will be. Also, diverse positions, which involve a variety duties and skills, may allow for more growth and more flexibility to move into different roles within the library. But be careful—don't apply for a job only for one part of it; you should be interested in all aspects of the job.

As you begin your job search, be as exhaustive and thorough as you can. Be sure to look closely at the descriptions, the qualifications, and the requirements for the position before applying. Titles can be deceptive, and may not accurately, or completely, describe the position. Don't rule out positions that sound too specialized because you think you are not qualified—you may be surprised to find out that you are qualified, or at least meet the requirements, for these specialized positions.

Take time to write a thorough and detailed cover letter that emphasizes your transferable skills and your experience as it relates to the position at hand. Include all related experience and skills even if they were obtained from classes, workshops, nonlibrary jobs, or school projects. Related experience of any kind will add weight to your résumé and show potential employers that you are motivated and willing to learn.

The interview

The interview is your opportunity to once again express your enthusiasm for the position and to reiterate how your skills closely match the needs of the position. Think of your experience in terms of the needs of the position and be sure to convey how the skills you possess will transfer from one context to another. Inevitably, someone will ask why you are making a switch, for example, from a special library to an academic library. Be sure to have an answer

prepared for this. And you'll need something more than, "It's what I went to library school for." Again, speak in terms of the position. Hiring organizations want to hear that you want *their* job, not just *any* job.

You can begin with something like: "I always thought I would work in a university library, but an excellent opportunity (the special library) came along and it was something I wanted to pursue to gain valuable skills and experience."

But then get more specific: "But I recently saw this opportunity and it reinforced my desire to get back to the university, working more directly with students and faculty. I like the challenges presented in the position and believe my experience in [x, y, and z] closely match the needs of this position." Bring your transferable skills into the conversation and match them to the position's required and preferred qualifications.

In any organization, people want to hire the best candidate, the candidate who most closely matches the needs of the position and the organization. It will be your job as the candidate to educate the individuals making the hiring decision that your skills, although gained in a different environment, will transfer to their organization and will make you the best qualified candidate.

Librarianship is an evolving profession, and those working in it know that change is not only inevitable, but it is around every corner and quickly coming up from behind. Because we are in this constant state of change, moving from role to role or institution to institution is not as difficult as it is perceived to be. Similar skills are needed in all libraries no matter what your constituency is, or your role is, or what subject matter you deal with. If you remember that skill sets are transferable and experience is relative, it is possible to "get there from here."

SOURCE: Susanne Markgren and Tiffany Allen, "How Do I Get There from Here? Changing Jobs, Changing Roles, Changing Institutions," *College & Research Libraries News* 65 (December 2004): 653–656.

Confessions of an interview junkie

by Saul J. Amdursky

I LOVE TO INTERVIEW. I enjoy identifying vacancies, developing cover letters, and speculating on whether my résumé meets the expressed job criteria. I'm ecstatic when I get an invitation to interview, participate in the interview, and make decisions on whether I want to stay in the hunt for a different job in a new location. My fascination with interviewing started at the beginning of my career.

I view the interview process as theater. Some may claim the process is a "Theater of the Absurd." I prepare in much the same way an actor prepares for an audition. I study my part, and script the questions and answers. I've been through enough interviews to know that at least 70% of the questions asked will be similar. Interviews will often contain the following questions in some form or another:

Q. Would you tell us a little something about yourself?

A. I try to answer by pulling highlights out of my résumé and adding one or two things about myself that are not apparent from the paperwork. I generally keep this answer short and light.

Q. Would you explain your management style?

A. I always approach management from a planning perspective. Once a plan has been adopted it's easier to discuss style. I talk about the types of plans I've employed, how they have worked, and how staff was engaged.

Q. What are your strengths?

A. I explain how I have run tax levies, managed building programs, dealt with legislators, and become heavily involved in automation. I am quick to point out that often my role is knowing how, and to whom, responsibility and authority should be delegated.

Q. What is your greatest weakness? Tell us where you need to grow.

A. Look the board square in the eye and talk about a strength that some might view as a weakness. "My wife tells me I work too hard and should take more vacations," is one response. "I know I'm too impatient for change," is another favorite. "I set my personal standards too high," works as well.

Q. What are your experiences managing personnel, developing budgets, or dealing with real or hypothetical crises related to one of these areas?

A. Questions about personnel and budget should be answered factually with specific examples. Questions about crises incorporate answers that address planning.

Q. How would you react to: a challenged material complaint; a sexual harassment incident; filtering the internet?

A. The importance of developing, maintaining, and enforcing policies is the appropriate answer to all of the above. The real question is, will the board support the staff and the director when policies need to be enforced?

Q. Why are you interested in this job?

A. Boards want to know both what interests you in the current vacancy as well as why you are considering leaving your current position. For me, the answer is always the opportunity to address new challenges and opportunities. I am very comfortable in my current position and inform boards that any new job will have to pique my curiosity and sense of adventure.

Q. Will you accept this job if it is offered?

A. I have never given an absolute yes or no answer to this question at an interview. The process always makes me want to take my time and reflect before making a commitment.

Boards usually ask candidates if they have any questions. I always have a few. I want to know why the last director left. Just because a director was fired  does not indicate a bad board or a bad situation. Often it's an indication of an intelligent and proactive board. I want the board to trace revenue streams. Is there a voted tax levy? Is the library dependent on an appropriation from a third party? Are there some "hidden" revenues that accrue to the library because of vagaries in local or state laws? The more the board can tell me about revenue the better. I ask boards to define micromanagement and rate themselves on a 1–10 scale. I want to know what the board thinks of its staff, its facilities, and its place in the community.

I enjoy a very well-prepared interview that allows me to interact with staff, peers, and community. The best interviews I have participated in required a full day or more. When boards are seeking a new director, no matter how small the community, they should make a real effort to involve the prospective director's peers and staff in the decision-making process.

Over a decade ago, I was involved in a process where I was interviewed first by peers (some of them were managers from nonlibrary departments that the director needed to work with regularly) and then by the board. In addition, all candidates were required to develop a 10–15-minute speech they might deliver to a service organization. The process also included a tour of several library agencies conducted by staff. Arrangements were made to have someone talk to candidates about the community, the cost of living in the area, and employment opportunities for spouses. The board also invited and paid for spouses to attend the three-day interview process.

Boards tend to be volunteers with limited insight into professional library service delivery and library leadership. Peers are happy to volunteer their expertise, and staff is thrilled to be included in the process. This method is expensive in the short term, but often ultimately pays for itself.

I see myself as a free agent. Free agency should not be limited to athletes. So, 300-average power hitters with strong fielding percentages are a hot commodity in baseball. Competent library directors with strong track records are equally important in Libraryland.

One rule I employ is to inform my board president whenever I choose to accept an interview. In this day of open meetings, I do not want my current board to be surprised by a call from a reporter about my candidacy for another directorship. This is a simple courtesy that protects my board and me.

I regard contract negotiations to be vital to decision making. Public employers will always have contractual restraints. Salaries can only rise to a certain level. Health benefits and retirement programs are usually dictated. However, boards often have flexibility over the length of a contract, the number of vacation and personal days permitted, or how a vehicle allowance is handled. The issue here is not how much the board is willing to give a new director, but how they choose to conduct the negotiations.

I have never accepted an interview where I would not consider employment. For me this is a matter of integrity. When attending an interview, I was always open to the possibility of accepting new employment. If a job offer is not forthcoming I must not have wanted the position.

I often learn something I can use in my current position while interviewing. Libraries are unique to their communities, but many of the issues they address are common to the profession. In discussions with boards and staffs, I've come away with ideas for a wide variety of programs and services, some wonderful personnel development concepts, and a variety of insights on how different libraries deal with difficult patrons, internet use, and more.

I worry that someday prospective employers will regard me as too old to be worthy of consideration. From my perspective, as long as I am willing to work I will never be too old to look at another job. However, my experience makes me very qualified to address the really challenging jobs. For 30 years I have been proud to be a librarian. I believe that my forays into the job market have helped me prosper and grow. Be that as it may, my confessions are at an end; further penance awaits.

SOURCE: Saul J. Amdursky, "Confessions of an Interview Junkie," *American Libraries* 32 (October 2001): 66–68.

The top 10 reasons to be a librarian

by Martha J. Spear

AS A HIGH SCHOOL LIBRARY MEDIA SPECIALIST, I have the good fortune to work with, and sometimes mold, young people. If I'm lucky, I discover what they do after graduation. Recently, one of my favorite students informed me that after earning her humanities degree at a tiny private college, she was pursuing a master's degree in museum studies. Congratulating her, I jokingly said, "Watch it. That's awfully close to a master's in library science." She laughed and said: "Oh, I'd never do that." Somewhat defensively, I replied, "You could do worse."

Long after this brief conversation, I wondered, where did we, as librarians, go wrong? Why is there such an onus on this profession that a bright, young person would choose, well, any career but that of librarianship? I think it's sad. Librarianship has much to offer, and I think we can do better in promoting our profession. Toward that end, I present my top 10 reasons for being a librarian.

10. **Ever-changing and renewing.** The single thing I like most about being a librarian is that it is, to paraphrase Ernest Hemingway, a movable feast. I've been employed in academic, public, and school libraries in three different states working in technical services, public services, and classrooms, and with street people, teachers, and young adults. I've booked psychics, mountain climbers, rock musicians, and landlords for programs. I teach, catalog, book talk, advise, troubleshoot, demonstrate, connect s-video cables, and shelve . . . in a single day. What I learned in my master's program bears little resemblance to what I actually do in my library today. Yet the principles remain; and, through conferences, professional literature, and  networking, I hold my own. If the new books don't excite me, the new technologies do. Most importantly, I learn something new every day. Can you say that about working at McDonald's?

9. **Romance.** Okay, so I may be stretching things a bit here. I married a librarian. (For the record, we met in a singles group; but our paths would have crossed in local library circles eventually, I'm sure.) My case may be extreme, but there is help for the lovelorn in libraries—either in the wonderfully interesting colleagues we meet (see reasons #2 and #7) or in the books and resources libraries offer.

8. **Useful skills.** I did not enter library school with a soaring heart. I viewed the degree less as graduate school and more as a kind of trade school. Truthfully, my library education was both. I learned the value of organization (I finally put my massive LP collection in alpha order by artist). I discovered the importance of collection development, equal access to resources, and intellectual freedom. I learned valuable skills in locating and using information that serve me to this day, whether I'm helping a patron write a paper on the Manhattan Project or figuring out the best place to buy a teakettle online.

7. **Great conferences.** Librarians host good conferences. I love the hustle and bustle of ALA's Annual Conference. I consider my state conference to be so necessary to my mental well-being that I often pay my own way. My husband's ties to the International Federation of Library Associations and Institutions have taken us to Nairobi, Tokyo, Havana, and elsewhere. What better way to see the world and recharge the professional batteries? Conferences are blessed events, and you don't have them when you work at Wal-Mart.

6. **Time off.** Librarians may not get great pay, but we do generally receive liberal vacations. As a public librarian, I got six weeks off and as a school media specialist . . . well, you don't want to know. In any case, these vacations have made it possible to visit Paris in April, and Beijing in

September, and to spend five weeks in Scandinavia. And when I'm not away, I've been able to repaper my hallway, paint the family room, and put in a patio.

5. **A job with scope.** As a child, when people asked me what I wanted to be, I have to admit I never said librarian. Although I used and enjoyed libraries, it never occurred to me to actually work in one. I *did* say that I wanted a job with scope. I am not sure what I meant by that then, but I know what it means now. It means being a librarian. I do dozens of different things every day. It's not a desk job and it's anything but routine. When you work with people, changing technologies, and always-new resources, how could it be?

4. **It pays the rent.** As a librarian, I will never get rich. However, it has allowed me to live alone (without the dreaded roommate), subsist moderately well, and be employable in different markets and in changing times. I have made a living as a librarian for almost 25 years and I'm not on the street corner selling pencils yet.

3. **Good working conditions.** I've worked in factories where I stood on my feet for nine hours. I've worked in kitchens where I came home smelling of puréed peas. I was a production typist where my derrière routinely fell asleep, not to mention my brain. In a library, you're clean, dry, warm, and working with people who are generally happy to be there.

2. **Cool coworkers.** I love librarians (also see #9). We are intelligent, cultured, well-read people who bring a myriad of skills, backgrounds, and interests to the job. Most of my fellow librarians, myself included, have degrees and/or work experience in other areas. I backed into librarianship after realizing that a major in English and German wasn't going to make me very employable. I know librarians who are former attorneys, truck drivers, teachers, and factory workers. This experiential, intellectual potpourri makes for an interesting mix. And librarians are readers. The conversational gambit "Read any good books lately?" is met with a din around librarians.

1. **Grand purpose.** As librarians, we support the freedom to read. We champion the right to access information for all people, regardless of race, creed, religion, or economic disposition. Libraries are everyone's university. These may feel like clichés to the converted (us librarians), but they remain truisms.

In sum, I feel very much like Evelyn Carnahan in the film *The Mummy.* To refresh your memory, our leading lady is in the midst of describing—and defending—what she does for a living to a roguish male. They have been drinking.

> *Evelyn:* Look, I—I may not be an explorer, or an adventurer, or a treasure-seeker, or a gunfighter, Mr. O'Connell! But I am proud of what I am!
> *Rich O'Connell:* And what is that?
> *Evelyn:* I am . . . a librarian!

I couldn't have said it better.

SOURCE: Martha J. Spear, "The Top 10 Reasons to Be a Librarian," *American Libraries* 33 (October 2002): 54–55.

Librarian salaries, 1999–2004

by Denise M. Davis

EACH YEAR THE AMERICAN LIBRARY ASSOCIATION conducts a sample survey of public and academic libraries to determine the change in salaries. The study samples six types of positions in medium and large public libraries, two- and four-year colleges, and university libraries.

Between 1999 and 2004, the average salary for librarians increased each year from a low of 2.3% to a high of .4%. The net average increase was approximately 18%, or $7,979. This is lower than the increase for comparable occupations reported each year by the U.S. Bureau of Labor Statistics in the *Monthly Labor Review*. The first-quarter earnings estimates were used for comparison with the *ALA Survey of Librarian Salaries*. The net average increase for civilian workers for the period 1999–2004 was approximately 20%. Librarian salaries increased at a higher rate than the national average for civilian workers in 2000, 2002, and 2003. The estimated increase in 2005 was 1.6%. Librarian and civilian annual salary changes are reflected in Tables 1 and 2.

Table 1. Librarian salary changes, 2000–2005

	2000	2001	2002	2003	2004	2005
Net change in mean salaries	+4.3%	+3.75%	+4.7%	+3.6%	+2.3%	+1.6%
Mean salary (all positions)	$46,121	$47,852	$49,866	$51,362	$52,188	$53,016

SOURCE: *ALA Survey of Librarian Salaries*, 2000–2005.

Table 2. Wages and salaries, civilian—12 month percent change

	1999	2000	2001	2002	2003	2004
All workers	3.3%	4.0%	3.8%	3.5%	2.9%	2.5%
State and local government	2.9%	3.8%	3.5%	3.4%	3.1%	2.1%

SOURCE: U.S. Bureau of Labor Statistics, www.bls.gov/cgi-bin/dsrv?ec.

The *ALA Survey of Librarian Salaries 2004* included 15,027 salaries ranging from $13,878 to $241,280 with a mean of $52,188 and a median of $48,792. Table 3 summarizes responses and compares the change with those reported in 2003.

Table 3. Rank order of position title by mean salary, 2003–2004

Title	2004 salary	2003 salary	%03–04	%02–03
Director	$80,823	$79,385	+1.8	+4.9
Deputy/associate/assistant director	66,497	65,665	+1.3	+4.5
Department head/senior manager	56,690	55,838	+1.5	+2.9
Manager/supervisor of support staff	46,648	46,246	+0.9	+3.8
Nonsupervisory librarian	45,554	45,210	+0.8	+2.1
Beginning librarian	38,918	36,198	+7.5	+3.3

SOURCE: Diane LaBarbera, *ALA Survey of Librarian Salaries 2004* (Chicago: ALA, 2004). The methodology beginning in 2005 shifted sampling away from regional to state-level estimates. Percent salary change by position title does not correlate to previous years.

Table 4 summarizes beginning public librarian salaries reported in 2004.

Table 4. Annual salaries for beginning public librarians, 2004

Public libraries serving	High	Low	Mean
over 1,000,000	$53,678	$28,008	$37,099
500,000 to 999,999	56,908	27,215	36,008
250,000 to 499,999	50,628	18,660	34,670
100,000 to 249,999	60,936	22,278	34,728
50,000 to 99,999	57,101	16,000	33,977
25,000 to 49,999	50,326	20,000	33,893
10,000 to 24,999	50,000	15,779	32,272
5,000 to 9,999	41,000	8,000	25,850
under 5,000	31,200	10,000	21,352

SOURCE: Statistical Report 2005: Public Library Data Service (Chicago: ALA Public Library Association, 2005).

The College and University Personnel Association for Human Resources is the national authority on compensation surveys for higher education HR professionals. The Association publishes four annual salary surveys, plus benefits and benchmarking surveys. Table 5 gives median salaries for librarian positions listed in its surveys.

Table 5. Median salaries for academic library positions, 2004–2005

Dean, library and information services	$114,067
Director, library services	$ 73,225
Director, educational/media services center	$ 58,746
Director, learning resources center	$ 53,687
Chief public services librarian	$ 54,652
Chief technical services librarian	$ 52,718
Acquisitions librarian	$ 50,678
Reference librarian	$ 47,925
Catalog librarian	$ 46,514

SOURCE: College and University Personnel Association for Human Resources, www.cupahr.org/surveys/salarysurvey04-05.html.

The Association of Research Libraries and the Special Libraries Association conduct annual salary surveys of all professional staff in their member libraries. Tables 6 and 7 summarize median salaries in recent years.

Table 6. ARL median salaries, U.S. and Canada, 2000–2005

	2000–2001	2001–2002	2002–2003	2003–2004	2004–2005
Median salary	$49,068	$50,724	$51,636	$53,000	$55,250
Median salary, U.S.	$49,753	$51,806	$52,789	$53,859	$55,600
Median salary, Canada*	$43,394	$42,928	$42,657	$45,310	$52,707
Net increase	3.3%	3.4%	1.8%	2.6%	4.2%

* Canadian salaries are converted each year to reflect U.S. dollars.

SOURCE: ARL Annual Salary Survey, www.arl.org/stats/salary/.

Table 7. Median salaries of special librarians by region, 2003–2004

Census division	2003 salary	2004 salary	% change
New England	$60,750	$64,000	5.0%
Middle Atlantic	$61,625	$63,000	2.2%
South Atlantic	$55,250	$60,000	7.9%
East South Central	$53,288	$46,625	–14.0%
West South Central	$50,809	$55,000	7.6%
East North Central	$54,000	$55,000	1.8%
West North Central	$48,000	$50,000	4.0%
Mountain	$52,000	$52,250	0.5%
Pacific	$62,000	$64,082	3.2%
All United States	$57,000	$58,258	2.2%

SOURCE: SLA Annual Salary Survey, 2004 (Alexandria, Va.: Special Libraries Association, 2004).

A source for school library staff salaries is *Salaries and Wages Paid Professional and Support Personnel in Public Schools*, conducted annually by Educational Research Service and reported by Education Week online at www.edweek.org/ew/index.html. Results of the 2004–2005 study indicate salaries for librarians ranging from a low of $19,018 to a high of $109,918. Not surprisingly, when distributed by community type, the mean salary was highest in suburban areas, $61,109, and lowest in rural areas, $44,976. The study also provides salary ranges for library clerks.

SOURCE: Special report for *The Whole Library Handbook 4* by Denise M. Davis, Director, ALA Office for Research and Statistics.

Ten graces for new librarians

by GraceAnne De Candido

GOOD EVENING. It is an honor and a pleasure to be with you. The last time I addressed a graduating class, it was as valedictorian at my own high school—31 years ago. Sister Bernadette, who was my speech coach and who rid me of my Bronx accent, gave me one sentence of advice: Be charming, she said, and be brief.

I will endeavor to follow her advice now, as I did then. But in seeking wisdom as to what to tell you, I sought some from my own colleagues and yours. I put a call out on the net. I sent a query via email to my various library discussion lists, and asked my fellow librarians online. I asked them what they thought I should tell you, newly minted, freshly picked librarians, as you take your degrees and go forth.

I got more than 80 responses, from 21 states and three foreign countries. They were, universally, heartfelt and upbeat and wonderful, in the original sense of full of wonder. Even though I am clearly not David Letterman (although Letterman and I are exactly the same age), here is a list of 10, well, let us call them admonitions or blessings, graces, if you will, for new librarians.

The first should be pretty obvious—join a discussion list! Actually, it is much broader than that—link yourselves to your colleagues in the field. There are many library-related discussion lists, and through them, you can be in touch with people who do the same work as you across the country and the world.

2

Particularly for new librarians, and those who find themselves in smaller libraries, that connection will keep you sane. Join your professional associations—your state association surely, but also the American Library Association, the Special Libraries Association, the Art Libraries Society of North America—whatever your particular library specialty is, find your colleagues and talk to them. As Sue Searing of the University of Wisconsin [now at the University of Illinois, Urbana-Champaign] says, "library work culture is basically collaborative. . . . Seize the opportunities for support." There are many such opportunities, and as you exploit them, hold fast, in your dealings with your colleagues, to the gentle rules of courtesy. Say "please" and "thank you" and "well done!" and "that was great!"

Number two. You have your degree, but you make your education every day. One of the great joys of being a librarian is that it is the last refuge of the renaissance person—everything you have ever read or learned or picked up is likely to come in handy. Realize that your degree is only the beginning. The world of librarianship is unimaginably different now from what it was in 1972 when I got my MLS from the late, lamented Columbia University; in fact, it is unimaginably different from what it was in 1991 when I got my first email address; or in 1994 when I first heard the words, "World Wide Web." Keep learning stuff; as a librarian, you are in a unique position to do so.

Number three. "Make your own luck" was the way Taina Makinen of Toronto put it. Take advantage of what comes your way, and put yourself in the way of opportunity. A positive attitude and a realistic sense of your own selfhood are tools at least as precious as the skills you have learned in school. Your first job won't be your last, but it is your first chance. Learn your own organization thoroughly—most libraries aren't very good at staff development. And learn, as soon as you can, how to speak up: at meetings, with trustees, before community boards. Find the courage to raise your voice and be heard.

Number four. Find and keep and nurture your sense of humor. People in service professions, especially in public service, need a finely honed sense of the absurdities of life, because you will deal with them every day, and many of them will not have an aroma of sweetness about them.

Number five. With Richard Palladino of Iona College, I say, "Be the librarian you would have wanted to encounter as a patron: approachable, attentive, facilitative, generous." And with Lisa Richland of the Library in Greenport, New York, I say that "public doesn't mean clean or sane or similar to ourselves, and that the public responds to a sincere interest and an open smiling face." We are a service profession, and we need a tender openness toward those we serve: students, faculty, children, adult learners, executives.

Number six. If you are a mom or a dad, if you're in love, I don't even have to tell you this. But with Kathy Deiss of the Association of Research Libraries [now at the Chicago Metropolitan Library System], let me remind you, "Keep your life and work in balance." Make sure that you have interests, hobbies, distractions, and passions outside of the workplace. They will enrich your life, and make the unbearable possible.

Number seven. Change is what happens. Change is the only surety. We can create and embrace change, or we can fear and fight it, but change will come in either case. It is far less stressful to frame change as an adventure. A corollary to this was expressed by two folks in very different fields of librarianship: John Haskell Jr. of the College of William and Mary, and Judy Jerome from a school library system in New York State. Judy said, "Work within the system, but be subversive." John was more direct: "Rules are meant to be bent and even broken; they can also be changed or discarded."

Number eight. Develop a strong sense of your own self-worth, and the worth of the profession. Honor and respect the women and men you work with. Take the values you learned in library school and apply them in the real world. As Sarah Pritchard of Smith College [now at the University of California, Santa Barbara] says: Don't permit a false dichotomy to be made of a "social issue" versus a "library issue"—examine how the issue affects equity and access and intellectual participation for our users and for ourselves as professionals. In the words of the ancient Jewish philosopher Hillel, "If I am not for myself, who will be for me? And if I am only for myself, what am I? If not now, when?"

Number nine. Make your particular vision part of the cultural memory of librarianship—write for publication. From book reviews to a column in the local newspaper, from Letters to the Editor in *American Libraries* to feature articles in *Library Journal* or your own library's website, write about what you have learned, what you want to share, how you think about what you do. It is the deepest legacy you can leave for those who stand beside you, and who will follow you.

Tenth, and last. I believe that librarianship is the connecting of people to ideas. Now, very late in the 20th century, it doesn't matter, often, where the people are, as they call up and dial in and fax over. It doesn't matter where the ideas are, either, in a book or on a video or over the net. And it's not just good ideas, not just worthy ideas, but bad ideas and lousy ideas and dangerous ideas and silly ideas. We particularly need to save the dangerous and silly ideas, because if we don't, who will?

Go and celebrate now, with your families and your loved ones. We share a great profession. And we get to buy books with other people's money. Rejoice in having the good fortune to be a librarian. If you let it, it will bring you joy.

SOURCE: GraceAnne De Candido, "Ten Graces for New Librarians," commencement address, SUNY/Albany School of Information Science and Policy, May 19, 1996.

Tips for part-time librarians

THREE MEMBERS of the Association of Part-Time Librarians—Kathleen Quinlivan, Linda Herman, and Anne Huberman—have put together a list of features which they feel an ideal position for a part-time professional librarian should have.

Prorated pay. The pay for part-time librarians should be proportionate to the pay received by full-time librarians having the same qualifications and performing the same work.

Health insurance. If full health benefits are not possible, then employers should contribute proportionately toward the premiums, or at the very least allow part-timers to purchase health insurance at the group rates.

Sick leave and vacation time. These benefits should be prorated for part-time librarians.

Training and orientation. It is in the best interests of libraries to offer thorough training and orientation to newly hired librarians. Often, part-time librarians work night and weekend hours when no other professionals are on duty. They may not have the luxury of asking more experienced librarians for help during their working hours, and they need to be totally familiar with the

Nonmonetary Rewards for Employees
by Joan Giesecke and Beth McNeil

In times of tight budgets or budget cuts, rewarding employees with monetary awards may not be possible. When funding is an issue, consider nonmonetary rewards.

Noncash incentives

Time off with pay (1 to 40 hours)
Tickets to local performances (may include movie, theater, sports event, etc.)
Gift certificates
Computer accessories, software, or office equipment
Professional development funds
Parking permit for one year
Campus recreation membership
Other choices to be determined by the employee, supervisor, and library director
Flexible scheduling (flextime, flexitour, variable day, variable week, etc.)
Job design (job rotation and job enrichment or enlargement)
Celebrations of milestones on the job
Providing desirable committee appointments or related assignments
Extending an invitation to coauthor a publication or work jointly on a special initiative

Different rewards for different generations

Veterans / Traditionalists
    Handwritten thank-you note
    Plaque
    Photo with the library director (or important visitor)
    Alternate scheduling
    Job security
Baby Boomers
    Time (errand service, dry cleaning pickup, etc.)
    Promotion and new job title
    Cash bonus
    Expensive symbolic gift (Rolex watch, etc.)
    Rewards that contribute toward plan for same standard of living at retirement
    Retirement and financial counseling
Generation X
    Challenging work
    Higher salary and better benefits
    Flexibility and freedom (work schedule)
    Daily proof that work matters
    Involvement in decision-making process
    Managers who allow flexibility and creativity
    Evidence of rewards tied directly to performance
    Clear areas of responsibility
Generation Y / Millennials / Nexters
    Meaningful work
    Learning opportunities
    Time for personal or family activities
    A fun place to work
    Desire for autonomy
    Want to be treated as a colleague, not a kid

SOURCE: Joan Giesecke and Beth McNeil, *Fundamentals of Library Supervision* (Chicago: American Library Association, 2005), pp. 139–145.

library procedures for which they are responsible and with the collections they are using.

Communication. Changes in procedures, policies, resources, and programs often take part-time librarians by surprise because they are not around to hear about these changes when they are discussed by the full-time staff. Further, they may miss out on valuable hints about the current "difficult questions" patrons are asking if full-time librarians don't have and use an effective means of communication. Inclusion of part-timers in staff meetings, use of email, and use of a reference desk notebook can improve communication.

Professional development. Library administrations should encourage part-time librarians to attend conferences and workshops and make it financially possible for them to do so.

Flexibility. Part-time librarians often work during night and weekend hours when important family and social events are likely to occur. Allowing part-timers to trade hours and rearrange their schedules for important events can make the difficulties of working unpopular hours much more manageable.

Retirement plan. Part-time librarians should have the same access to retirement plans as full-time librarians, and employer contributions should be made in proportion to the hours they work.

Professional recognition. Administrators and colleagues should recognize part-time librarians professionally by assigning them meaningful responsibilities that expand their skills and develop new ones, by listening to their ideas and opinions, by providing feedback on the quality of their work, by providing them with adequate facilities (e.g., office space; use of a computer, telephone, and email), and by avoiding assigning them nonprofessional duties.

Job security. A renewable contract for a specified period of time can give a part-time librarian the kind of job security that few now have.

SOURCE: Association of Part-Time Librarians, www2.canisius.edu/~huberman/goodjob.html. Reprinted with permission.

The legacy of Melvil Dewey

by Dee Garrison

MELVIL DEWEY (1851–1931) WAS A DRIVEN MAN, tense, complicated, concentrated, hounded by a fear of death and decay. He was a man for whom nothing was ever completed; each achievement was only a challenge to accomplish more. His dreams and projects were superhuman. To fulfill any one of them would have required the span of 10 lifetimes. Dewey was a librarian the like of which the country had never seen—a one-man profession. He was a man who bridged two Americas, his early years formed by the hard Victorian demand of duty to God and work, his final years devoted to the rationalization of a technocratic culture. From frontier farming America of the 1850s to the Depression of the 1930s, he spanned his time in a remarkable way, rashly moving from missionary  of culture to prophet of business. He was a man of massive influence, force, and enthusiasm, and of equally massive insecurity. The volume of his achievements never lessened the inner fears that impelled him to incessant activity.

He was a complex of incongruities. He achieved fame through the decimal system that bears his name, yet others did most of the work for him. He was highly intelligent and consecrated his life to education, but he lacked the flexibility of a first-rate mind and could not feel any real affinity to intellect. Although he was literally obsessed with the saving of time, his most striking characteristic was the manner in which he wasted it, in inordinate amounts, in his effort to save it. A lifelong apostle of thrift, once holding on to a post-card for 21 years before using it, he was incredibly reckless with his personal finances. While earning great wealth, he remained perpetually balanced on the very edge of financial ruin. Tall, powerfully built, handsome, personally magnetic, he was beloved by many and drew to him a group of unusually talented and otherwise self-sufficient women whose loyalty to him was supreme and who followed him, harem-like, for decades, from one of his homes to another. Yet he was fiercely hated by many others, to whom he had been cold, tactless, and cruel. No one who met him found it possible to hold a neutral opinion of Melvil Dewey, for he had "an indisputable . . . inner power—chemical or/and electrical—that was evidenced in a few seconds when in his presence." Georgia Benedict, a schoolgirl who saw him briefly in 1892, never forgot her impression:

> I was ushered into an office where a black-haired, black-bearded, black-eyed gentleman in a pepper-and-salt suit was working away with a kind of furious quiet at a big desk. I was struck by the speed and accuracy of his movements. It was like watching a fine machine, an electric machine—the air about him was vibrant with energy. . . . His decisiveness, the sparkling darkness of his face (dominated by his vivid eyes), his intense energy impressed me deeply. Indeed, I was a little awed . . . I had come into contact with an immense force.

More than any other single person Dewey shaped the development of the public library in the United States, forcing it forward into the path he believed it should take. Almost alone he set the pattern for library education. His paeans to professionalization not only affected the growth of librarianship but also influenced educational standardization in all the professions, especially in New York State. But we must remember that to Dewey the library was only one area of operation for his educational work. He decided when still a boy that he would be above all else a "seed-sower"—a man who expanded his own life many times by inspiring others to work toward new and great ends. Despite the grandiose nature of his goal, it is startling to discover how often he reached it. Wholly outside the library profession and entirely aside from the crusades he directly initiated, his influence propelled others to organizational activity in forms as varied as the establishment of Barnard College, the founding of the American Home Economics Association, and the bringing of the Winter Olympics to the United States in 1932—to mention only a very few of his sown seeds.

Dewey was intensely aware of his place in history and preserved the documentary vestiges of his life from the time he was 15 years old until his death 65 years later. Despite his belief that he would be remembered as a foremost educator, however, Dewey's name has survived almost entirely because of his identification with the decimal system of classification. He formulated this when he was 22 years old and an assistant at the Amherst College Library. Within the library profession, his reputation was permanently affected by the sexual scandal of 1905, which helped to force him out of active library work.

To some modern feminist librarians he has become almost an object of ridicule, remembered for his simplistic preaching of the library mission and his rakish reputation. ("Like what did you *really* have in mind, Mel baby, when you hotly defended the right of women to library education and then made the attractive young ladies put their bosom measurements on their application? . . . Your brother librarians have kept your more goatish gambols out of your authorized biography."—*Library Journal,* September 1, 1971.) His two biographers have indeed suppressed the remarkable Melvil Dewey. The offi-

cial biography by Grosvenor Dawe, *Melvil Dewey: Seer, Inspirer, Doer,* published the year after Dewey's death, is an unashamed romanticization of his life that was written under the general supervision of his second wife; the book's subtitle gives away its purpose. *Melvil Dewey,* a small book written by Fremont Rider in 1944, is more valuable because Rider, who married Dewey's niece, knew Dewey intimately, both personally and professionally. Rider's study is a sensitive and detached interpretation, but when he sent his manuscript to readers he was congratulated by them for his deliberate decision to delete any reference to Dewey's less glorious moments or to his "darker side."

Yet Melvil Dewey remains a figure of considerable historical interest despite the lack of attention paid to him by posterity. Aside from his effect upon the American library and his influence upon the larger professionalization movement that took place in the United States during his lifetime, his life can be studied for the insight it provides into at least one type of reforming "savior" mentality. Because he left such a wealth of evidential material and was a man of such unusual inner force, it is impossible to ignore Dewey's personal disorder and its connection to his social impact.

It is apparent that Dewey manifested in his personality a particular complex of thoughts, feelings, ideas, and behavior characteristic of a general mode of functioning that is most often dubbed "obsessive-compulsive." This personality structure is marked by a tendency toward order, perfectionism, and concentration on detail; an emphasis upon intellectualization; an overcompliance with and hyperconcern for rules; a reliance on verbal fluency; and an overriding commitment to work. The central idea is control—governance over oneself and over the forces outside oneself. The ordering of self and others is achieved in most instances through the assumption of grandiosity. This posture allays anxieties about being in danger either because one cannot meet the requirements of others or cannot be sure of their acceptance.

But how to tease from the biographical record these matters of compulsion? When evidence allows, the historian can trace the interaction and interdependence of three themes—the historical impact of the innovative "great man," the personality constants that reappear throughout his life, and the needs and characteristics of a particular period in history. In our post-Freudian age, it seems self-evident that the contribution of theory in any area of thought is inevitably stamped with the subjective concerns of the theorist.

Melvil Dewey's contribution to library development was related to his personal conflicts. But it will not do to merely dismiss him as a neurotic personality. Dewey was a prophet of the new professionalism, an evangel of efficiency and standardized methods, and a decisive contributor to the social upheaval that made mass culture a way of life. Let us simply recognize that here was an uncommon man whose attempts at resolving inner conflict stamped our library system, and hence our lives.

SOURCE: Dee Garrison, *Apostles of Culture: The Public Librarian and American Society, 1876–1920* (Madison, Wis.: University of Wisconsin, 1979, 2003), pp. 105–108. Reprinted with permission.

Melvil's heir: Eric Moon

by Kenneth F. Kister

FEW STUDENTS OF LIBRARY HISTORY would disagree that Melvil Dewey was the American profession's most prominent pioneer, the 19th-century prime mover who among many other accomplishments devised the

enduring Dewey decimal classification system, founded *Library Journal,* started the first library school in the United States, and played an indispensable part in establishing the American Library Association and the New York Library Association. Who among all the great and famous librarians since Dewey—Lester Asheim, Augusta Baker, Verner Clapp, Robert Downs, Michael Gorman, Frances Henne, Virginia Lacy Jones, E. J. Josey, Anne Carol Moore, Lawrence Clark Powell, Frances Clarke Sayers, Ralph Shaw, Jesse Shera, Louis Shores, Joseph Wheeler, Robert Wedgeworth, to name but a few—is Dewey's natural heir? Who is the 20th-century Melvil Dewey?

Eric Moon

A case can be made that Eric Edward Moon is that person.

Dewey (1851–1931) stood out as the commanding figure in American librarianship during the last 30 years of the 19th century (actually his career as a practitioner ended in 1905), a period of enormous youthful zeal and growing pains for the new profession. Moon (born in 1923) made his mark as American librarianship's most influential and durable leader during the 1960s and 1970s, a period of profound change at least equal in intensity to that experienced during Dewey's day. Dewey and Moon claimed center stage at very different times in the history of the profession and quite understandably confronted very different circumstances, issues, and challenges. On the other hand, the two men were quite similar in their philosophies and leadership styles.

Both men were passionately committed to their profession, viewing it not as work or a job but a high calling; both were generalists who believed librarians must take a leading role in shaping the intellectual and cultural destiny of their respective communities; both were activists/innovators/reformers whose deeds had a major impact on the future of the profession; both were journalists/editors/publishers whose words moved their colleagues; both were teachers whose opinions and arguments inspired the next generation; both were committed to associations as a means of advancing the profession; both possessed an astute business sense; both were brash and courted controversy;

both were hyperindustrious and keenly competitive—when ALA was formed in Philadelphia in 1876 Melvil rushed to sign the register, "Number one, Melvil Dewey"; both loved women; both were egocentric and boastful; both were leaders par excellence.

Of course there were differences between them too. Moon, for instance, believed in human equality and Dewey, a bigot, clearly did not; Moon adamantly opposed censorship in any guise and Dewey, who saw the librarian as an agent for moral betterment, did not; Moon never sexually harassed women and Dewey apparently did; Moon was not especially interested in classification whereas Dewey built his career around it. But these and any other differences Dewey and Moon might have had are historically insignificant: Both men were giants who enlarged the profession by their presence; both had that quintessential quality—some call it gravitas—that marks a born leader.

The record

Moon's remarkable library career, which began in 1939 on the eve of World War II, took him from a junior assistant (or clerk) position in his hometown of Southampton, England, to the heights of the profession in the United States in the raucous 1960s and 1970s. Among his major accomplishments: rejuvenation of a stale, foundering *Library Journal*, North America's foremost library periodical; creation of a fresh, honest, dynamic library journalism that changed the way librarians perceive themselves and their world; transformation of Scarecrow Press from a back-pocket operation into a formidable publishing enterprise; and election as president of the American Library Association, the world's largest and most influential library organization.

In addition, Moon's leadership was instrumental in exposing and eliminating institutional racism in American librarianship, and in democratizing ALA, hitherto the preserve of a narrow, conservative elite. He also contributed substantially to the debate on intellectual freedom and censorship in libraries, adopting the final sentence of *The Freedom to Read Statement* as his credo: "Freedom is a dangerous way of life, but it is ours."

Moon's impact on the profession as teacher and mentor was less readily apparent than his other achievements but no less significant. Except briefly in the 1950s when he lectured part-time at North-Western Polytechnic School of Librarianship in London, he did little formal teaching, resisting several opportunities to join library school faculties in the United States after gaining prominence as editor of *Library Journal*. Yet he was an inveterate teacher, his passion to educate infusing everything he did professionally. During Moon's editorship of *LJ*, for instance, the magazine took on the character of a lively national tutorial on the major issues confronting contemporary librarianship, with himself as master (or head tutor) and *LJ's* readers his students. In similar fashion, during the campaign to reform ALA in the late 1960s and early 1970s, he assumed the role of "guru," instructing young militants in tactics about how best to achieve their—and his—aims. Later he created the Eric Moon Flying Circus, a sort of traveling college of librarianship. His proteges—Arthur Curley, Pat Schuman, John Berry, Robbie Franklin, Judy Serebnick, John Wakeman, et al.—attest to his mentoring powers.

Moon did not win every battle nor slay every dragon. But neither did he shrink from taking on the truly tough problems. In the case of his most public defeat—an ambitious but ill-fated effort to promulgate an egalitarian national information policy during his ALA presidency—the failure was due as much to bad luck as to his own miscalculations. Moreover, like the strongest leaders, Moon refused to let defeat discourage or stop him. In the case of information policy, he continued to champion the cause long after his term as ALA president was over, battling against privatization and fees, which he considered forms of economic censorship, as recently as the 1991 White House Conference.

The last word goes to another great librarian, Lawrence Clark Powell, who died in 2001 at age 94 and will be missed. In a letter he wrote dated January 6, 1981, recommending Moon for the Lippincott Award, Powell said: "I now judge him [Moon] as one of the few creative librarians of our time, along with such as Ralph Shaw, Verner Clapp, and Keyes Metcalf. In a larger perspective I class Moon with Dewey and [John Cotton] Dana. He is truly one of our great ones, towering above the housekeepers, glorified and lesser, that librarians almost invariably are, God help us all!"

SOURCE: Kenneth F. Kister, *Eric Moon: The Life and Library Times* (Jefferson, N.C.: McFarland, 2002), pp. 405–406, 409–410. Reprinted with permission.

MANAGERS

Supervising: What they didn't teach you in library school

by Melinda Dermody and Susan Schleper

THE DECISION TO GET AN MLS usually is not motivated by the desire to manage or supervise people. Check out the courses provided at any ALA-accredited university program, and it's doubtful that you'll see classes that teach you how to deal with the real-life situations of being a supervisor in a library. And yet many of us out here in the real world of librarianship are asked to become supervisors overnight, often with little or no training. Here are some of the kernels of wisdom that we wish someone had told us before our responsibilities expanded from books to people.

I am the supervisor, right?

It's natural to expect that you will need some confidence building when coming into a new supervisory position. Confidence as a supervisor is gained through experience and learning how to deal with people in the work environment. This is unfortunate because initially, experience is the very thing you don't have. Don't let that stop you. Make a mental note that you were hired because you are the best-qualified person to fill the position, and remind yourself of this often. Be confident that you have the skills to get the job done and that eventually you will feel comfortable taking charge.

One way to jump-start the confidence-building process is to attend a supervising workshop that can help you gather important information about personalities and people's work styles. You may find that some of these workshops, especially those sponsored by national training companies, emphasize and cover the same basic information. Remember that learning to supervise is an ongoing process, and like any skill that is improved over time and with practice, you will need to continually hone your skills.

Confidence is required to address difficult supervisory challenges, so it is well worth the time, effort, and courage to develop it. Although it is sometimes easier to put a problem on the back burner, "situations" only grow worse if they are left unaddressed. By tackling a problem early and confidently, you can often stop it from escalating.

It also takes a sense of confidence to communicate to your colleagues the fact that you are in charge. Defining your territory with your colleagues can help you visualize the actions and course you need to follow in order to achieve the goals you have for your area of responsibility. It also demonstrates to them that you can work collegially while being a confident manager.

Who's got the monkey?

Especially for an unseasoned supervisor, learning how to delegate can feel like a monkey on your back, but it is an important part of supervising. For many of us, delegating is very difficult for various reasons. One reason may be that we feel we can do the job better. But the purpose of delegating is to allow you, as the supervisor, to be freed from certain tasks in order to orchestrate the direction of your area. Also, there is every possibility that the tasks you let go can be done more efficiently by those you supervise. Along with letting go of certain tasks, you should allow your staff to work in a style that is comfortable for them. When you give up a task, let it go for good.

Another reason that delegating can be difficult is that you may feel like you are imposing on your staff. But remember that, ultimately, the success of the

area you coordinate is your responsibility. Your training in the field and dedication to the profession have prepared you to see the big picture and will help you make decisions based on a comprehensive understanding of the library in which you work. Moreover, your employees may also share the larger sense of mission and indeed feel proud of their contributions.

As a new supervisor, be aware that your staff may inadvertently delegate tasks back to you. The literature on management calls this phenomenon "Who's got the monkey?" (See William Oncken Jr., *Managing Management Time*, Prentice-Hall, 1984.) If you find yourself reporting to your staff on any issue, you may find the task that you once delegated has returned to you. When staff members come to you with a legitimate problem, give them the initiative and leeway to find a solution until your direct action as a supervisor is needed. Doing this leaves the task with the appropriate person, allows you to use your time more constructively, and tells your staff that you rely on them to solve problems as well.

People . . . people who need people

By definition, supervising involves people, and it's a well-known fact that people can have conflicting personalities. Something to consider as you strive toward a good working relationship with your staff is that you don't necessarily have to be their friend. Of course, the ideal situation would be to get along socially and professionally with the people with whom you work on a daily basis. However, if that isn't feasible, settle for a good, professional working relationship. Define tasks and responsibilities based on the positions that are held by your staff, rather than on personalities. Being able to separate the personal from the professional is a very valuable skill to have as a supervisor and will gain you the respect of your staff.

When people are involved, another workplace reality is gossip—both positive and negative. It can be a good way to learn about the people with whom you work and to gain insights into the culture of the workplace. It's also possible to learn informal information without becoming involved or passing on anything that you learn. But don't repeat gossip! A good rule of thumb is to not say anything that you wouldn't want everyone to hear. Also, if you are uncomfortable with some information or topic that's being discussed, it is completely appropriate to point out your discomfort and ask that that topic be avoided.

Remember that you have an obligation to all of the individuals you supervise. Problem employees have a negative effect, so for the sake of the morale of all your employees, it is best to isolate the negativity of a problem employee as much as possible. Doing so minimizes their negative energy and helps to foster a better working environment for the others in your area. Of course, this can be a difficult task, but try to look at the big picture and think creatively to determine how best to limit the harmful impact of a difficult person on the rest of the employees for whom you are also responsible.

Is this thing on? Testing, one, two . . . testing . . .

Establishing good communication is one of the best things you can do as a supervisor. Formally, regular meetings can be scheduled with your employees, and informally, you can have an open-door policy, if that is consistent with your supervisory style. Either way, it is good to keep all necessary people, including your supervisor, in the loop to ensure that all staff members are getting the information they need to do their job and stay informed.

Regarding challenges, it is important to promptly communicate problems to the people involved. As further discussions develop, you may find it necessary to establish rules of interaction, so that overly emotional or upsetting situations do not arise. Another aspect of setting up these rules may be defining what is and is not open for discussion. Remember, however, that communication is a two-way street and what you are trying to communicate may be as important as what is being communicated to you, verbally and nonverbally, so listen and watch carefully.

It is imperative to acknowledge and communicate your recognition of the hard work and successes of your staff. Positive actions and events should be recognized and encouraged. This positive encouragement can be done in a variety of ways, including informally through personal contact and formally through evaluations.

A final word on communication is that it is very important to clearly establish and communicate the mission of your area with employees, patrons, supervisors, and colleagues. It is this clear mission that will guide the services, resources, and responsibilities that you manage.

Details, details, details

Maintaining accurate and consistent documentation is an important job of the supervisor. Make sure that employee evaluations and assessments are done on a timely basis and that they accurately reflect your employees' work and your assessment of their efforts. If an evaluation does not truly address an employee's work, then you are unfairly misleading the person, and leaving yourself without key documentation if further actions are necessary.

Goals, responsibilities, and expectations should be made very clear to the employee. If there is a problem, address it early either verbally or in writing, and keep it in your records, as well. Know and understand the human resource policies and procedures. Read the policies, union contracts, or any other documents that exist relating to your being a supervisor, from how to perform an evaluation to the steps taken for disciplinary actions. It is also helpful to have a good and knowledgeable contact in your human resources office.

Remember to keep a written record for yourself of every significant event, positive or negative, especially if you are in the midst of a challenging supervisory situation. Sometimes your memory fails or something may not seem important at the time. Take a moment to write down a quick summary of all situations, with the date, so that you can put them out of your mind and know that they are there if and when you need them.

Finally, you must recognize the confidential nature of your supervisory position. Discussion of your employees, incidents, evaluations, and the like should be avoided with individuals not involved in their supervision. You never want your supervisory situation to become a topic of gossip, so avoid any improper discussion to which that could lead. Of course, speaking with your supervisor or a mentor may be appropriate as long as it's understood that the conversation is confidential.

Hello, is there anybody out there?

Remember that even though you may feel like it, you are not the first supervisor in the process of gaining experience, so take advantage of the resources available to you. Talk to other supervisors, a mentor, colleagues, and friends who may have new and helpful perspectives. In fact, you might find a lot of help by simply talking with other supervisors in your library. They may be able to help you avoid pitfalls and give insights into the people you are supervising. A friend or family member can also be a good sounding board, even if they can't provide answers.

Most importantly, remember that being a supervisor is only one aspect of your life. Be able to walk away from the situation and put it out of your mind as much as possible when you are away from work. This may be harder than it sounds, but it is crucial in maintaining a balanced life. In fact, in walking away, you may be able to find a better perspective and maybe even some humor in the situation.

Ready, set, go!

You may find supervising is one of the more challenging aspects of your job, and library school may not have prepared you for it. But be assured that with experience comes knowledge and wisdom, and the moment you get started as a supervisor is the moment that you begin gaining experience.

These suggestions and bits of advice are meant to smooth the way and help guide you as you begin developing that inevitable experience of your own.

SOURCE: Melinda Dermody and Susan Schleper, "Supervising: What They Didn't Teach You in Library School," *College & Research Libraries News* 65 (June 2004): 306–308, 332.

2

The doghouse concept
by Will Manley

WHAT CAN LIBRARIANS DO to help the environment?

For one thing, we can stop buying books on management. Each year, entire forests are decimated for the purpose of producing a parade of new books that promise once and for all to unveil the hidden secrets of how to manage effectively.

The allure is quite tempting. Who among us doesn't want to learn the magic formula of how to square the management circle of keeping everybody happy— the public, board, and staff—while at the same time staying within budget and making sure all the work gets done? So, like every other sucker in business and government, we buy these books in hopes that this will be the year that the one, true guru of management wisdom will emerge like some wispy literary Aladdin from their poorly written pages.

The problem is, of course, that these books inevitably disappoint us. There is precious little magic in the field of management science, and there is more stability in the fashion industry. One year the experts tell us to rule through intimidation, the next year we're supposed to be touchy-feely. Today it's Theory X; tomorrow it's Theory Y. Still looking for your "inner coach"? If you haven't found him or her, don't worry, because next week it won't matter; you'll be looking for your "inner gladiator."

I suppose I'm like a lot of you. At one time in my life I took the whole management book du jour thing pretty seriously. But after spending a good part of my career consuming a whole alphabet soup of management acronyms— MBO (Management by Objective), PERT (Program Evaluation and Review Technique), and my favorite, MBWA (Management By Walking Around, aka AM, Ambulatory Management)—I realized the whole thing was the literary equivalent of vaporware. I never learned anything practical that I could actually use in my library.

For instance, nowhere in any of these books did I ever come across the concept of the organizational "doghouse." When you really think about it, you can't strategically plot your library career without coming to terms with the reality of the doghouse. As much as library directors and supervisors insist that they do not have a doghouse, the plain truth is that they do, and the louder they protest to the contrary, the larger their doghouses are. I'm even pretty sure that someone as saintly as the Pope has a doghouse reserved for cardinals and bishops that make his cup runneth over.

I once worked for a very dignified man who professed that he did not have anything as unseemly as a doghouse. Actually, he was partially correct. His organizational Siberia resembled more of a kennel than a doghouse. Out of a staff of 20, there could be as many as five or six people in the doghouse at any one time.

His saving grace was that he was forgiving. If you were willing to humiliate yourself enough by flattering him on a daily basis, you could get out of the doghouse in a week or two.

This was not the case with another director I worked for. Exile to the doghouse was a lifetime sentence. One reference librarian, over a few drinks at happy hour at a library conference, happened to say something mildly critical about the director's wife. The comment filtered back to the director (and his wife) and the librarian's career was pretty much over in that place. We took to calling him Rover and would leave doggie biscuits by his computer, which he now used mainly to update his résumé.

"Oh, yes, Helen, I've still got old Chuck in the doghouse."

How do you stay out of the doghouse? That's easy. Never be the bearer of bad news, and never do anything stupid. A corollary to that is that if you do something good, always give the credit to the director. It's also important to remember that no matter how many times your director or supervisor says, "I have an open-door policy, so please tell me exactly what is on your mind," do not believe him. What he really means is, "I have an open-door policy and I want you to make use of it to tell me how wonderful I am."

Another common expression that directors like to use is, "I believe strongly that all my employees should be empowered to make decisions." A fairly accurate translation of that phrase would be, "I believe strongly that all my employees should be empowered to do exactly what I tell them to do."

SOURCE: Will Manley, "The Doghouse," *American Libraries* 31 (December 2000): 96.

MEDIA SPECIALISTS

What does a school library media specialist do?

TODAY'S SCHOOL LIBRARY MEDIA SPECIALIST works with both students and teachers to facilitate access to information in a wide variety of formats, instruct students and teachers how to acquire, evaluate, and use information and the technology needed in this process, and introduces children and young adults to literature and other resources to broaden their horizons. As a collaborator, change agent, and leader, the school library media specialist develops, promotes, and implements a program that will help prepare students to be effective users of ideas and information, a lifelong skill. The many roles of a library media specialist are detailed in chapter one, "The Vision," of *Information Power: Building Partnerships for Learning* (Chicago: ALA, 1998).

These resources provide a more detailed description of the school library media specialist's job:

- "Roles and Responsibilities of the School Library Media Specialist," from *Information Power* (ALA, 1998), reprinted in this book on pp. 28–29.
- Kathleen de la Peña McCook and Margaret Myers, *Opportunities in Library and Information Science Careers* (Chicago: VGM Career Books, 2002).
- Betty-Carol Sellen, *What Else You Can Do with a Library Degree: Career Options for the 90s and Beyond* (New York: Neal-Schuman, 1997).
- Priscilla K. Shontz, *Jump Start Your Career in Library and Information Science* (Lanham, Md.: Scarecrow, 2002).
- "Librarians," U.S. Department of Labor, Bureau of Labor Statistics, *Occupational Outlook Handbook, 2004–2005*, online at www.bls.gov/oco/ocos068.htm.
- Also, read testimonials from three school library media specialists at www.ala.org/ala/aasl/aasleducation/recruitmentlib/learningabout/schoollibrary.htm.

Job outlook

You may also be interested in the status of school librarianship around the country as you explore school librarianship as a career. *School Library Journal* ran an article on school library staffing that may be of interest. Nancy Everhart in "School Staffing Survey 2000: Looking for a Few Good Librarians" (*SLJ*, September 2000) surveyed the states about school librarianship and found that there were more retirements including early retirements, and a prosperous economy and more lucrative job options had those interested in information careers looking elsewhere.

Nationwide, there was an average of one librarian for every 953 students, up from 887 two years previously. Reasons for the shortage cited by respondents to the survey included retirements, limited access to library education, stricter certification rules, heavy workloads, site-based management, increasing emphasis on standards and test scores, limited access to library education, and technology coordinators replacing LMS or doing double duty.

Two years later, in "Filling the Void" (*SLJ*, July 2002), Everhart found those surveyed reporting 68% of school library media specialists projected to leave the profession in 12 years or less. The reported shortage was no longer just in urban and rural areas. Since then, the economic downturn has impacted staffing, especially in states with no or limited staffing requirements for school library media specialists. For more information see:

- Marilyn L. Miller and Marilyn L. Shontz, "New Money, Old Books," *School Library Journal*, October 2001, pp. 50–60.
- Nancy Everhart, "The Prognosis, Doctor?" *School Library Journal*, August 1998, pp. 32–35.
- "Library Profession Faces Shortage of Librarians," key facts and figures from the American Library Association, October 2001, www.ala.org/ala/pio/piopresskits/recruitpresskit/libraryprofession.htm.

Are mentoring or job shadowing programs available?

Another way to learn about the job is to shadow a school library media specialist for a day. Contact your local schools or state professional organization to set
up a visit. Once you are in a job, connecting with a mentor will help the new
library media specialist navigate through the challenges of a new career.

The Colorado Power Libraries project (www.cclsweb.org) matches veteran
librarians with new librarians to help mentor them to learn collaboration skills
and techniques that will turn their school libraries into vital learning centers.
Click on the Power Libraries link for a description of the program.

Individual districts such as Atlanta Public Schools have mentoring programs
for their new employees (*Library Media Specialist Mentor's Guide*, www.atlanta.
k12.ga.us/parents_students/curriculum_areas/library_media/handouts/
mentor.pdf). Check with your district for local programs. In some states, districts are required to establish district-wide mentorship programs.

Reforma, the National Association to Promote Library and Information Services to Latinos and the Spanish Speaking, provides a mentoring program
(www.reforma.org/mentoringprogram.html) to assist those providing services
to Latinos.

Some professional organizations such as the Wisconsin Educational Media
Association and the Arizona Information Literacy discussion list are beginning mentoring programs or providing forums to seek mentors for new library
media specialists. Check with your state organization of school librarians for
local programs.

SOURCE: ALA American Association of School Librarians, "Learning about the Job," www.ala.org/
ala/aasl/aasleducation/recruitmentlib/learningabout/learningabout.htm.

National Board effects
on library education

by Gail Dickinson

THE NATIONAL BOARD for Professional Teaching Standards (NBPTS)
was formed in 1987 in response to the publication of *A Nation at Risk*. Two of
the problems that a subsequent Carnegie report identified as reasons why
teachers left the classroom were the lack of a career ladder for teachers and
poor pay and benefits. NBPTS addressed these and other issues
by creating rigorous standards for the teaching profession, devising a voluntary system of identifying accomplished teachers, and
encouraging policy changes to reward and sustain those skilled
teachers in the classroom.

To date, there are nearly 24,000 National Board Certified Teachers (NBCTs). Library media as a certification area first became
available in 2002. The first class of candidates produced approximately 435 library media–certified teachers, although there may
be others with library media licensure who are board certified in
areas such as early- or middle-childhood generalists.

If one were told that Jones Middle School was a good library
program, the immediate response might be, "What do they *have*?"
The assumption is that good school library media programs have

financial resources and supports—good facilities, sound and stable budget streams, current materials and technologies, and administrative backing (evidenced by best practices such as flexible access). The National Board standards take the opposite approach by examining school library media specialist (SLMS) performance irrespective of resources. The influence on school library media research and practice will be profound.

SLMSs who achieve accomplished teacher status through National Board Certification (NBC) are judged against the same rigorous standards as classroom teachers. They demonstrate outstanding competence at collaborating with classroom teachers to teach information skills, integrate technology, and encourage reading and love of literature. They exhibit knowledge of management practices, technology basics, children's and YA literature, collection development, ethical and legal tenets, and information literacy. There is good reason to be proud of those in our profession who have met and exceeded such high standards. Still, amidst the cheers, there are those of us who wonder what this means for school library media preparation programs and practices.

As awareness of the NBC process increases and more states follow North Carolina's pattern of having at least one certified teacher in each school, questions will arise on how to align school library media preparation programs with NBPTS standards. What and when should students be encouraged to apply? How should the NBPTS process be supported?

Accreditation of teacher education programs

The National Council for the Accreditation of Teacher Education (NCATE) offers an accreditation process for teacher education programs. Required in some states, but voluntary in most, NCATE's core propositions of what teachers should know and be able to do and their subject-specific standards also affect teacher preparation. In addition to covering the syllabi, schools of education must demonstrate that prospective teacher candidates, in NCATE's words, "know and can do" the basic building blocks of teaching. Phrases such as "performance-based," "conceptual frameworks," "knowledge, skills, and dispositions," and "assessment systems" are constantly revisited in faculty meetings in university and college preparation programs.

NCATE accredits teacher education units at both beginning and advanced levels. For initial licensure programs (first-time teachers), NCATE suggests alignment with the Interstate New Teacher Assessment and Support Consortium (INTASC) standards for beginning teachers. INTASC represents a group of state education agencies and national educational organizations dedicated to the reform of the preparation, licensing, and ongoing professional development of teachers. For advanced programs (licensed teachers seeking master's or post-baccalaureate degrees), NCATE advocates alignment with NBPTS standards. This poses an interesting dilemma.

School library media preparation programs are designed for beginning SLMSs, whether they are at the undergraduate or graduate level. In some states, SLMSs are required to hold a teaching license in another subject or grade level. In other words, they must have been a classroom teacher (or at least done practice-teaching) before they can begin their school library media career. In several states, no such previous licensure is required; first-time SLMSs are also new teachers. In contrast, NCATE states that preparation of SLMSs should always be considered advanced. If we are preparing first-time educators, then surely INTASC standards are more relevant. On the other hand, NBPTS library media standards are more applicable to the library media skills needed. Since NBPTS library media standards are for accomplished teachers, its place in school library media licensure is unclear. It is unreasonable to expect novice students to become accomplished media specialists within the short library school or graduate degree experience. An extensive dialogue among school library media educators is needed to agree upon the extent to which our preparation programs should be aligned with various standards, including NBPTS.

The role of preparation programs in supporting candidates

Teachers need at least three years of experience before applying for NBC, but prior state licensure in their certification area is not required. For example, students new to library media but experienced as teachers can apply for certification in library media or in any other certificate area. How should school library media educators respond when their students ask for assistance or advice concerning their application for NBC?

There are compelling reasons to seek licensure immediately. Experienced teachers may not want to wait for three years after graduation to apply for library media certification. One important consideration is that concepts and content underlying the field are fresh to current students. Three years later, a high school librarian will have to review areas that relate to elementary education, such as literature for young children. Similarly, certain aspects of learning theory, information literacy, and technology may need refreshing.

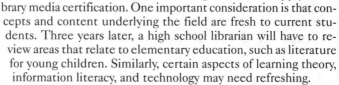

Secondly, as more school library media preparation programs become performance based, the assignments and activities used in preparation programs will grow to align closely with NBPTS requirements. If required to develop a literature-based instructional activity as part of a children's literature course, students working on their certification portfolio may want to enhance that same activity to submit for the literature appreciation portfolio entry.

Further, as a library school student, one has access to academic resources, learning opportunities, and mentors. While a professor may not be the best critical friend to read a portfolio entry, that person remains a source of information and advice.

Finally, students in library school are in a milieu in which writing, reading, and being assessed are everyday occurrences. After leaving graduate school, the emotional aspect of writing for another's review may feel like a difficult hurdle.

There are equally good reasons to discourage application for certification while in library school. First, NBPTS is designed to identify accomplished practice. While prospective SLMSs may show evidence that they will become accomplished library media specialists, they are not, yet. It is an oxymoron to designate inexperienced SLMSs as accomplished. Of future concern, if states begin to accept NBC in lieu of state licensure, SLMSs could become certified with only minimal training in the library profession.

Secondly, the focus of NBPTS is on teaching standards. While tying the program administration role firmly to student learning makes partial sense, some parts of an SLMS's job relate more closely to library science than teaching. Will alignment with NBPTS standards weigh the school library media field too heavily toward education, minimizing the important role that we play in the library and information sciences?

In addition, support for unsuccessful candidates is somewhat murky. While a certification candidate who does not achieve a passing overall score can bank passing scores and retake low-scoring sections, teacher education programs rarely take responsibility for NBPTS candidates who do not pass on the first try. NBPTS feedback is sketchy; a candidate may only learn that he or she did not provide "clear, consistent, and convincing evidence" of the required knowledge and skills. A "banker" may need guidance in designing a plan for improvement of an entry. School library media educators must ask themselves if they are prepared to accept responsibility for a graduate banker's NBPTS portfolio or assessment center exercises. Should continuing education be offered to retake candidates on children's and YA literature, collaboration, learning styles, or technology?

Compounding these issues is the fact that little information is available about the areas in which NBPTS candidates score poorly. Those who achieve certification are listed on the NBPTS website and publicly applauded. Retake candidates, already reeling from not achieving certification, must self-identify to receive assistance.

What if the knowledge needed is related more to education than library science? The school library media field asserts that teaching is an important role of the SLMS. How credible is it for educators in preparation programs to say, "Not our problem," if pedagogical expertise needs to be revisited by the candidate?

Further, we are long overdue for a discussion about the integration of education and library and information science precepts, principles, and practices in school library media education. Are students equally prepared as educators and library and information science professionals? Should they be? In discussion, we could clarify these issues. Unfortunately, these questions have not yet been articulated, much less discussed, in some programs.

Meeting multiple goals

In raising these questions, I am not suggesting that we ignore NBPTS requirements, nor completely redefine our preparation programs. Rather, many programs can incorporate the beginning skills without difficulty. For example, a typical assignment for a curriculum class asks a school library media candidate to develop a lesson plan that can be taught in a collaborative setting. To turn that into a performance-based assignment to satisfy NBPTS requirements, the candidate would be asked for evidence of developing and implementing a collaborative unit. By partnering with a classroom teacher and collaborating to develop and implement an information skills unit integrated into classroom content, the candidate would also satisfy NBPTS entry 1 on instructional collaboration. To further align some of the basic skills required for NBPTS entries, a preparation program could require a videotape of instruction and a reflective writing piece.

In teacher education programs, professors can lay the groundwork for writing, teaching, and action research in the early education courses, perhaps as early as the freshman year in college. Throughout the junior and senior years, these skills can be scaffolded. After teaching for a few years, the experienced but still fresh teacher could return for a master's degree, which could build upon both the academic base and the practical experience. Teacher as writer, teacher as researcher, teacher as leader—typical courses in an MEd program— align with NBPTS standards.

In an ALA-accredited program, only a few courses are designed specifically for the SLMS. Additional scaffolding is rare. If state regulations allow school library media licensure without previous teacher certification, those courses have to lay massive groundwork. The rare individual with an undergraduate degree in school library media may decide to return to school for an ALA-accredited MLIS or an advanced education degree. However, the former is considered to be an entry-level degree, while the latter may not even mention school library media.

Another significant difference concerns a shift in focus from working with teachers and content to focusing primarily on students. SLMS education programs ask the library school student to start the collaborative effort by identifying a teacher with whom they would work well, or by choosing a curricular area in which they are comfortable. In contrast, NBPTS applicants almost never write about the collaborating teacher or the subject area. Instead, they focus on the makeup of the class, student learning styles, demographics, special needs, and personality characteristics. In later entries they analyze the learning of one or two students. Turning from collaborating with teachers to teaching students alone requires a shift in thinking. Assessing the achievement of one student's learning of information skills is different from analyzing large-scale assessments of the impact of the library media center program.

Scholarly research opportunities

The school library media field has experienced two major shifts in preparation programs. The first was the Knapp School Libraries Project, which provided

National Library Power Program

An Initiative of the DeWitt Wallace - Reader's Digest Fund

models of school library media programs as well as insight into the preparation of SLMSs. Along with the impetus provided by the 1960 standards, the Knapp Project was responsible for defining the modern school library media program. Similarly, in the late 1980s and early 1990s, Library Power, a major school library initiative funded by the DeWitt Wallace–Reader's Digest Foundation, provided documentation and affirmation of collaborative work with teachers and administrators both in instruction and in program administration. Library Power and *Information Power* set the stage for the modern library media program.

NBC may represent a third major shift in the field. With both the Knapp Project and Library Power, emphasis was placed on building the structure of the library program. Adequate resources, budgets, facilities, technologies, and staff development for classroom teachers and administrators were seen as essential for the successful school library media program. If excellence in school library media programming fell short, it was because it was a good instructional program but lacked an adequate facility, or it had a superb facility but little technology, or wonderful technology and staff but no flexible access.

Now academic researchers can begin to answer questions about how the SLMS affects that equation. Through the portfolio entries, they have a window into how the SLMS encourages reading, collaborates with a classroom teacher, and integrates technology, regardless of grade levels, physical plant, budgets, community demographics, or other factors. Can SLMSs achieve excellence with a poor budget, few resources, and an unsupportive administration?

A proactive response

As a first step, educators in school library media preparation programs need to become informed about NBPTS library media standards and portfolio entries. Then, we must find natural congruencies between the NCATE and NBPTS standards. The third step involves assessing which skills required by the NBPTS process can be incorporated into the school library media preparation programs.

Let us begin a national conversation about the role of school library media preparation in NBC. Preparation programs should lead the way in carefully planned, research-based approaches to school library media certification candidacy. Our school library media students are demonstrating their expertise as accomplished teachers. Our role, as yet undefined, could determine their next steps as leaders in the profession.

SOURCE: Gail Dickinson, "National Board Effects on School Library Media Education," *Knowledge Quest* 32 (January/February 2004): 18–21.

Advocacy ABCs for trustees
by Ellen G. Miller

TELEVISION SCHEDULES. Footwear fashions. Diets for pets. These and other important aspects of our lives are subject to constant change, so it's reassuring that one thing stays the same: A library trustee's job. All we have to do is:
- Attend monthly meetings.
- Read the agenda beforehand.
- Evaluate the director in writing annually.

Right? Not any more. For decades, trustees got by on that light job description, but today the job has bulked up and includes advocating for dollars.

"Whoa," many trustees say. "Nobody told me I'd be twisting arms!" In fact, many of us became trustees precisely because the job looked easy. Why pay attention to this advocacy stuff now? The answer: S-H-O-R-T-F-A-L-L. Our communities need more information, but our libraries don't have enough money to provide it.

The three-legged stool

For too long, library staff have carried the advocacy burden alone. Year after year, directors and staff trekked to city council meetings and Legislative Day, telling the story of obsolete equipment, below-market pay scales, and out-of-date collections.

Too often, elected officials saw only vested interests, believing the staff just wanted to enlarge their little empire. The three-legged library-advocacy stool kept trying to stand on one leg, with predictable results.

What was missing? Friends and trustees, the stool's other two legs. As grassroots supporters, we trustees don't have a vested interest. Elected officials pay attention when grassroots folks team up with staff to tell how the community will benefit from longer hours or a new children's room. The director-trustees-Friends team has political clout because it has access to something officials love. That something is votes.

Regrettably, too many trustees still are reluctant to seek funds from their mayor, city council, county commission, or state legislature.

Fear of trying

Many barriers exist. Some of the main excuses trustees give for not doing advocacy include:

"I don't know how." Solutions abound. More advocacy workshops pop up all the time. If "advocacy" is a foreign word, start with your state conferences.

Then check out activities of ALA's Association of Library Trustees and Advocates (ALTA) at www.ala.org and ALA's Library Advocacy Now! campaign. Also see what Libraries for the Future (www.lff.org) is up to. Another tack: Advocacy training at your own board meetings. Under the leadership of chair Gail Dysleski, the East Brunswick, New Jersey, board spends part of its monthly meetings practicing answering tough questions. The library serves an estimated 43,000 people.

"I hate making cold contacts." So don't. While some folks are intimidated, others see advocacy as an everyday activity. "If you tell your neighbors or fellow PTA members what wonderful things are happening at the library, that's advocacy," says Dysleski. Talk with the local elected officials or candidates you know. Call Mayor Mike—your kids and his kids play T-ball together. Ask him for a brief meeting to discuss library needs and funding. Rehearse, then go do your best.

"I'm not sure what to say." Practice helps. Have your director prepare a fact sheet, with a budget. Then rehearse, especially anticipating cost questions. Does the mayor think 50 cents per person per year for libraries is fine? Point out that that doesn't even buy a cup of coffee at Billy Bob's cafe.

"I hate to bother elected officials in their off hours."  Stop right there! Across the United States, local elected officials will tell you that they want to hear from citizens. As Kansas state senator John Vratil (right) said, "If we don't hear from you, we think you don't care." Don't be thoughtless, though, haranguing county commissioner Kate at the grocery store while her ice cream melts. Instead, tell her you'll be calling for an appointment.

"It's an uphill fight." That's right, but you have to start by starting. Decide how to improve services to seniors, home-schoolers, or others. Then make a game plan, because the competition sure does—police, parks, water districts, and others want money, too. Put together a persuasive case for the city council. "If you sit out and don't do anything, nothing is what you'll get," commented Las Vegas–Clark County, Nevada, former trustee Moises Denis.

"Libraries are low priority." Beware this self-fulfilling prophecy! Too often, it's due to us library supporters confusing means with ends. Instead of talking about the winners, we drone on about multimedia collections and interlibrary loan. What's the goal? Showing elected officials how home-schoolers, seniors, families, and students of all ages (read: *voters and potential voters*) will benefit.

Advocacy must-do's

Unfortunately, some make advocacy sound like the quest for the Holy Grail, remote and unreachable. In fact, it's just a means toward an end, which is to carry out your library's up-to-date vision and strategic plan. What, you don't have one or both? Don't walk, *run* to put strategic planning on next month's agenda. Both planning and vision are part of POSCERV, the management model that covers planning, operations, staffing, communications, evaluation, resources, and vision.

Meanwhile, here are some points to keep in mind:

Long-term goals. Advocacy helps position your library with decision makers, specifically elected officials and voters. But realism must rule, as the Las Vegas–Clark County Public Library knows. The library's strategic plan showed the need for a facilities bond issue, and the June 2001 ballot looked like a good place for it until a prominent state legislator from Clark County started promoting his own town's library issue. Bowing to reality, the Las Vegas–Clark County library shelved its plans to get on the ballot . . . and benefited since voters nixed all library ballot issues. Denis foresees a four-partner Clark County library coalition in future elections. "We need to form on common grounds and get past our differences," he said.

Short-term goals. Start with your game plan (including deadlines and who's responsible for what). Then get your three-legged stool assembled and functional. Seek out advocacy partners as appropriate. Having your local home-school network, historical or genealogical society, or ministerial alliance speak out gets the city council's attention. Those groups' comments on how their constituents will benefit takes your library advocacy to a new level of political clout.

Tools of the trade. Decide which methods to use. They typically include:

- In-person contacts, whether at the elected official's office or out in the community.
- Letters, faxes, emails, telegrams, and mailgrams.
- Videos. In the late 1990s, the Lexington (Ky.) Public Library, which serves about 260,500 people, showed its short video, *Wings on Words*, to a newspaper's editorial board. "You need to have a good video and presentation by the board chair and library director," says chairman James Wyrick. "Present not only your needs but the positive things that the library is doing with its limited resources."
- Media coverage. Letters to the editor, guest columns, press releases, photos, and even paid information ads get your story across.
- Talk radio. Put an articulate advocate on the air to give facts and to answer questions.
- Community TV, public service announcements (PSAs).

- Presentations. Get on the agenda of business and civic groups such as the Chamber of Commerce and Rotary. A short video or PowerPoint presentation gets things started right.
- Special library events such as Teen Poetry Cafe, home-schooler web training, and Pajama Storytime featuring a local elected official.

Does every method need to be used? Of course not. Pick and choose what will work best with your targeted person or group. *Tip:* Some elected officials love email; others ignore it. Find out before you use this method extensively. How? Call them or their secretary!

Follow up. Don't argue, just do it! Follow-up includes:

- A handwritten letter to all elected officials you visit, thanking them for their time and reminding them of the specific action you seek.
- Special thanks to elected officials who voted for your cause, even if it didn't pass this time.
- Visibility in your library's own or state trustee association newsletter, naming those who voted "yes."
- Copies of emails, letters, faxes, etc., to your advocacy captain. Why bother? Because copies let your team see who's saying what to whom. The city council will pay extra attention to your presentation when you flip a stack of copies; they represent caring citizens who usually vote.

Staying power

Advocacy is like parenthood: It goes on . . . and *on* . . . and ON! I believe library advocacy must be led by the folks who live and breathe libraries 24 hours a day: the directors and staff. We supporters need input into plans, of course; but when the game plan is ready, it's time for us to play our position.

"Public libraries are the highest form of democracy that we have," said Lexington trustee Wyrick. "We serve all the people. There is no greater charge or responsibility than to provide information services to the total population, regardless of background, income, or social status."

Grassroots advocates make the difference between a library that limps along and one that sprints. The buck does stop with us.

Trustee association health quiz

What's *your* state's score? Need more library clout with elected officials? Worried about poor trustee turnout on Legislative Day? Afraid that trustees can't learn new tricks like advocacy?

If so, it's time to ratchet board members up to a new level.

A key player is your state trustee group. It may be a section of the state library association (as in Kansas and Georgia) or a stand-alone entity (New York and California). Whatever the organizational form, its members must be effective advocates for statewide library priorities.

Get out your stethoscope! Take this health quiz to find out if your statewide trustee group is robust, comatose, or somewhere in between.

True or false? Or don't know?

1. At least 25% of our state's trustees belong.
2. Offers 4–8 sessions at the annual library conference.
3. Offers 4–8 workshops per year around the state.

4. Works closely with the state library and other groups.
5. At least 10% of the members contacted state legislators last session.
6. Members get discounts for conferences and workshops.
7. Has an active, diverse board that gets things done.
8. Member communications include newsletter, email, website.
9. Conference and workshop attendance keeps growing.
10. Members from small libraries qualify for grants, stipends.

Scoring:
    True = add 10 points.
    False = subtract 5 points.
    Don't know = subtract 2 points (and contact your library director ASAP for
        the facts).

85–100	Other states need to find out what your trustee group is doing! Write an article for ALTA's *Voice.*
60–84	Pretty good, but avoid complacency. Find out what your group is offering this year.
30–59	Beware the slippery slope. Ask your director how you can help.
< 30	Call your state trustee group today! Offer to help it get back on track.

SOURCE: Ellen G. Miller, "Advocacy ABCs for Trustees," *American Libraries* 32 (September 2001): 56–59.

Meeting do's and don'ts

by Mary Y. Moore

MOST LIBRARIES HAVE MONTHLY BOARD MEETINGS. Unless your library is a private one, these meetings are mandated to be open to the public. That means they must be publicly announced—in the daily paper, on the local radio and TV stations, and certainly on the library's website—a specific number of days ahead of time. The amount of time required for notification is usually stipulated in your state's open public meeting legislation, a copy of which should be in your board notebook along with the other state and local laws pertaining to the library. If members of the community wish to attend any of the meetings, they need to be accommodated with chairs, copies of the agenda, and a time during the meeting when they may make comments or ask questions, should they choose to do so.

Your role

Library board meetings are important for many reasons, but mainly because the trustees set public policy and the public must be involved in that activity. Therefore, it is essential that the meetings be run efficiently and effectively. Follow these guidelines to make sure you are doing your part to make the meetings productive:

- Always be on time and do not leave early.
- Come to the meeting prepared.
- Stay on topic.
- Do not interrupt.
- Speak up when you have something to say, but don't hog the discussion.

- Note any tasks assigned to you as a result of a board decision.
- Speak with honesty and candor.

If you do your part to help a meeting along, you will be a good model for other trustees. Certainly the board chair will appreciate you.

The meeting agenda

Those who lead the board meetings, such as the chairperson and the director, are responsible for developing the agenda. It makes sense to set the agenda— with the exception of emergency items—at the preceding meeting. That way, everyone has a chance to provide input, and items are more likely to come up in a timely fashion. Five to 10 days prior to the meeting, board members should receive a copy of the finalized agenda along with any information needed for decision making. This is referred to as the *board packet*. Keep in mind that the information you receive will do you no good if you don't read it.

Setting an agenda with an eye to a meeting that runs smoothly can take some expertise. There was a time when agendas consisted of old business, new business, and reports. In the newer format, agenda items are arranged according to outcomes or expected reaction from the board members. The items are timed, and there is an indication of who will lead the discussion on each item. A typical library board agenda would look something like the following:

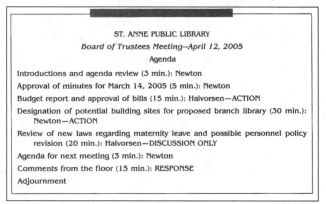

ST. ANNE PUBLIC LIBRARY
Board of Trustees Meeting—April 12, 2005
Agenda

Introductions and agenda review (3 min.): Newton

Approval of minutes for March 14, 2005 (5 min.): Newton

Budget report and approval of bills (15 min.): Halvorsen—ACTION

Designation of potential building sites for proposed branch library (30 min.): Newton—ACTION

Review of new laws regarding maternity leave and possible personnel policy revision (20 min.): Halvorsen—DISCUSSION ONLY

Agenda for next meeting (3 min.): Newton

Comments from the floor (15 min.): RESPONSE

Adjournment

With this type of agenda, you will know what is expected of you before the meeting. You can be well prepared and able to take part in the discussions and decision making.

Board leadership

The chairperson is usually designated to lead board meetings. The library director is expected to attend and take part in all board meetings. In some cases, the director takes the minutes of the meetings, but it is better to have an administrative assistant perform that task so that the director is free to enter discussions and provide reports. The chairperson needs to have good facilitation skills to run a successful meeting. Those skills include keeping people on track, dealing with those who interrupt or try to dominate the discussion, making sure everyone has a chance to speak, and ensuring that there is follow-through on any decisions that are made.

Executive sessions

The only meetings of a public library board not open to the public are executive sessions. Generally speaking, these need to be announced ahead of time following the normal meeting notification procedures, and the topic of discussion needs to be made public. However, the meeting itself is private. The reasons for an executive session usually have to do with personnel. Collective bargaining sessions with employee unions, grievance or mediation proceedings, or the director's performance evaluation may be held privately according to the majority of state laws on the subject. Executive sessions may also be held to consider publicly bid contracts or real estate transactions. Always check your state's Open Public Meetings Act before proceeding with any executive sessions.

Trivia

Even with the best meeting management and the most dedicated board members, things can still go wrong. The most typical error board members make is to dwell on the trivial rather than the big picture. For instance, the topic of a library fund-raiser may come up for discussion and possible action. The board might spend valuable time talking about the pros and cons of various foods to be served rather than paying attention to the desired result or the strategies for actually raising the money. When that happens, the chairperson should appoint a subcommittee to deal with the details of the project. Perhaps you feel more comfortable or more knowledgeable about the small stuff of life, but that is not the job of a library trustee.

Micromanagement

Emphasis on the trivial may waste time, but micromanagement can be even more damaging to the library and its staff. Micromanagement is defined as "controlling with excessive attention to minor details," and, sadly, it occurs in more libraries than we would like to think about. A library board of trustees exists for the purpose of governance, not management. Excessive attention to minor details may be appropriate for an accountant or a project director, but it is not appropriate in anyone who is responsible for many divergent programs or staff. The following examples of micromanagement have actually occurred in libraries across the country:

1. The library director provides board members with copies of the revised branch hours. The chairperson notices a change in the times of a particular branch and insists upon setting up a subcommittee to "explore" the matter.
2. A board member becomes concerned about the quality of the young adult books. She enters the main library in the evening, removes a professional tool from the director's office, and proceeds to check the library catalog for the top ten young adult books. Then, at the next board meeting, the trustee announces that the library only has seven of the top ten young adult books, and she wants to know why.
3. After reviewing the bills for a month, as is the custom in some libraries, a board member notices a purchase for pens. He notes the price per pack and takes the library director to task for not buying the pens at another store for a cheaper price.

Board members who insist on micromanaging either do not have a clear understanding of what they are supposed to be doing or they have lost trust in the management of the library. In either case, the behavior must be stopped because it is counterproductive and potentially destructive. If it involves mistrust of the library's management, that can be taken care of during the director's performance evaluation and might entail additional management training. If it is a behavioral issue, it is up to the chairperson to have a private talk with the person who has the problem.

Managing public comment

Another problem that might occur is the disruption of the meeting by people who are unhappy over something the board or the library has done or is about to do. Library trustees must deal with several contentious issues, including free speech, positioning of a library branch, and funding concerns. If a meeting cannot be conducted in an orderly fashion because of public outburst,

the board may order the meeting room to be cleared and continue in session. Final action can take place only on the matters listed on the agenda, and members of the media must be allowed to remain.

Management of public comment is an important board skill. There should always be a time on the agenda for public comment, preferably at the end. Courtesy and consideration need to prevail. There will always be those who disagree with something that a public entity is doing. It is an important aspect of democracy that these folks have a chance to speak their minds. And it is important for the library board members to hear these folks so that they can keep in touch with the library's constituents.

Methodology

In his book *Policy Making for Public Library Trustees* (Libraries Unlimited, 1993), James C. Baughman says, "A good trustee identifies problems, develops solutions, and makes decisions based on his or her knowledge of specific problems in relationship to the basic principles of trusteeship." That is absolutely true except for the fact that no trustee makes decisions independently of the rest of the board. The decisions are made together, in congress, and therein lies the rub.

The bylaws of your board should specify how decisions are to be made. Will you decide by majority rule or by consensus? Or perhaps you will try for consensus, and if that fails the majority opinion will hold. It is best to check out your bylaws before getting involved in any decision making. If the matter is not addressed in the bylaws, don't be afraid to ask. Your questions might lead the board to a better method for making decisions.

Many boards use a five-step process for problem solving and decision making.

1. Bring the necessary people together.
2. Define the problem.
3. Determine the most probable cause.
4. Develop possible solutions.

5. Determine the best option based on the library's strategic plan, customer desires, budget capabilities, and staff resources.

Sometimes the library director will bring up a problem for discussion and will present a number of options that he or she has already considered. In that case, your job is to decide which option is best for the library and its customers. To do so, you will have to understand the issue thoroughly and make sure the director has gone through a valid process in coming up with the options.

Follow-through

Decisions with no follow-through might as well not have been made. All too often, a group of people makes a decision and then everyone expects someone else to carry it out. Hasn't that happened to you? So a decision is not fully made until the participants decide who will do what, by what time or date. If one of the steps requires you to do something, make sure you record the task and the time by which you say you can get it done. Follow-up on decisions is one of the earmarks of a really efficient and effective board.

What happens if you do not like a decision that has been made? You need to ask yourself three important questions.

1. Am I unhappy with the decision or the process?
2. If it is the process, can I try to change it?
3. If it is the decision, can I live with it?

If you can answer yes to the second or third question, you should feel better. When you make decisions as a group, sometimes the decision made will not be to your liking. If your answer to the third question is no, you may have to consider resigning from the board. However, it won't have to come to that if you can get used to the change that may have occurred.

SOURCE: Mary Y. Moore, *The Successful Library Trustee Handbook* (Chicago: American Library Association, 2005), pp. 14–20.

FRIENDS

State Friends organizations

STATE FRIENDS GROUPS support the local Friends in their states with resources, programming, advice, and advocacy.

Arizona—Arizona Library Friends, 1333 E. Ellis Drive, Tucson, AZ 85719-1939.

Arkansas—Friends of Libraries Arkansas, 5000 Cliff Drive, Fort Smith, AR 72903.

California—Friends and Foundations of California Libraries, 11045 Wrightwood Place, Studio City, CA 91604; www.friendcalib.org.

Colorado—Colorado Library Association, Trustees and Friends Division, 12081

W. Alameda Pkwy., #427, Lakewood, CO 80228; (303) 463-6400; www.
cal-webs.org/trustees.html.

Connecticut—Friends of Connecticut Libraries, 786 S. Main Street, Middletown, CT 06457; (800) 437-2313; www.cslib.org/focl/.

Delaware—Friends of Delaware Libraries, P.O. Box 1319, Bethany Beach, DE
19930-1319.

District of Columbia—Federation of Friends of DCPL, 1423 Iris Street, N.W.,
Washington DC 20012.

Florida—Friends and Trustees Interest Group, c/o Florida Library Association, 1133 West Morse Blvd., Suite 201, Winter Park, FL 32789; (407) 647-
8839; www.flalib.org/friends/.

Hawaii—Friends of the Library of Hawaii, 690 Pohukaina Street, Honolulu,
HI 96813-3185; www.flhawaii.org.

Illinois—Friends of Illinois Libraries, 200 West Dundee Road, Wheeling, IL
60096-2799.

Indiana—Friends of Indiana Libraries, c/o Library Development Office, 140
N. Senate, Indianapolis, IN 46204; www.incolsa.net/~foil/.

Kansas—Friends of Kansas Libraries, 200 Arco Place, Building Box 132, Independence, KS 67301; (620) 331-8218; www.skyways.org/KSL/fokl/.

Maine—Friends of Maine Libraries, c/o Corrilla Hastings, 538 Malbons Mills
Road, Skowhegan, ME 04976; (207) 947-4051; www.friendsofmainelibraries.
org.

Maryland—Citizens for Maryland Libraries, P.O. Box 267, Funkstown, MD
21734-0267; www.citizensformarylandlibraries.org.

Massachusetts—Massachusetts Friends of Libraries, 29 Fairchild Drive,
Holden, MA 01602; www.masslib.org/mfol/.

Michigan—Friends of Michigan Libraries, 1200 S. Canton Center Road, Canton, MI 48188; (734) 397-0999, ext. 121; www.foml.org.

Minnesota—Minnesota Association of Library Friends, 1619 Dayton Ave.,
Suite 314, St. Paul, MN 55104-6206; www.malf.info.

Mississippi—Friends of Mississippi Libraries, 1221 Ellis Ave., Jackson, MS
39209; (601) 961-4111; www.mlc.lib.ms.us/advocacy/friends/index.htm.

Missouri—Missouri Trustees and Friends Council, c/o Missouri Library Association, 1306 Business 63 South, Suite B, Columbia, MO 65201.

New York—Empire Friends of New York State, c/o New York Library Association, 252 Hudson Ave., Albany NY 12210-1802; (800) 252-6952; www.nyla.
org/index.php?page_id=57.

North Carolina—Friends of North Carolina Public Libraries, 4640 Mail Service Center, Raleigh, NC 27699-4640.

Ohio—Ohio Friends of the Library, c/o Ohio Library Council, 2 Easton Oval,
Suite 525, Columbus, OH 43219-7008; (614) 416-2258; www.olc.org/
friends.asp.

Oklahoma—Friends of Libraries in Oklahoma, c/o Tulsa City-County Library,
400 Civic Center, Tulsa, OK 74103; www.okfriends.net.

Pennsylvania—Pennsylvania Citizens for Better Libraries, P.O. Box 752, Camp
Hill, PA 17001; (800) 870-3858; www.pcblpa.org.

Rhode Island—Coalition of Library Advocates, P.O. Box 3777, Cranston, RI
02910; www.bodees.com/COLA/COLA.htm.

South Carolina—Friends of South Carolina Libraries, P.O. Box 11121, Columbia, SC 29211; www.foscl.org.

Tennessee—Friends of Tennessee Libraries, 562 Riverfront Way, Knoxville,
TN 37915; www.friendstnlib.org.

Texas—Friends of Libraries and Archives of Texas, P.O. Box 12927, 1201 Brazos, Austin, TX 78711; (512) 463-5514; www.tsl.state.tx.us/friends/.

Virginia—Friends of Virginia Libraries, c/o Library of Virginia, 800 E. Broad Street, Richmond, VA 23219-1905; (804) 692-3763.

Washington—Washington Library Friends, Foundations, and Trustees Association, 4016 1st Ave., N.E., Seattle, WA 98105-6502; www.wla.org/igs/wlffta/.

Wisconsin—Friends of Wisconsin Libraries, 2367 S. 84th Street, West Allis, WI 53227-2501; cheesestate.com/friends/.

SOURCE: Friends of Libraries USA, "State Friends Organizations," www.folusa.org/html/statefol.html.

Friends' Literary Landmarks

THE LITERARY LANDMARKS ASSOCIATION was founded in 1986 by former Friends of Libraries USA president Frederick G. Ruffner to encourage the dedication of historic literary sites. The first dedication was at Slip F18 in Bahia Mar, Florida, the anchorage of the *Busted Flush*, the houseboat home of novelist John D. MacDonald's protagonist Travis McGee. In 1989, the Literary Landmark project became an official FOLUSA committee.

Dedications have included homes of famous writers, libraries and museum collections, and literary scenes. Local Friends groups or state Friends may apply to dedicate a Literary Landmark. When an appropriate landmark is identified, the sponsoring group can plan a dedication ceremony and apply to FOLUSA for official recognition. These are the landmarks that have been dedicated since 1987.

2005

Boston (Mass.) Public Garden. Here is where Robert McCloskey set his 1942 Caldecott Medal book, *Make Way for Ducklings*.

William Johnson House, Natchez, Miss. Home of William Johnson (1809–1851), a free African-American businessman whose diary, covering the period 1835–1851, contains an extensive description of everyday pre–Civil War life.

891 Post Street, San Francisco, Calif. Dashiell Hammett (1896–1961) lived in this building from 1926 until 1929 when he wrote his first three novels: *Red Harvest* (1929), *The Dain Curse* (1929), and *The Maltese Falcon* (1930). Sam Spade's apartment in *The Maltese Falcon* is modeled on Hammett's, which was on the northwest corner of the fourth floor.

Evergreen Cemetery, St. Augustine, Fla. Burial site of Randolph Caldecott (1846–1886). The Caldecott Medal, commissioned in 1938, was named in honor of English illustrator, artist, and sculptor Caldecott.

Bland Cemetery, Jordan's Point, Prince George County, Va. The burial site of revolutionary patriot and pamphleteer Richard Bland (1710–1776) who represented Virginia in the First and Second Continental Congresses and in all five of Virginia's Revolutionary Conventions.

William Carlos Williams Home, Rutherford, N.J. Lifelong home of William Carlos Williams (1883–1963), writer, physician, friend, and neighbor.

Tennessee Williams House, New Orleans, La. Thomas Lanier "Tennessee" Williams (1911–1983) owned this 19th-century townhouse from 1962 until his death in 1983.

Pearl S. Buck Birthplace, Hillsboro, W. Va. Pearl S. Buck (1892–1973) was the only American woman to win both the Pulitzer Prize (in 1932, for her book *The Good Earth*) and the Nobel Prize for Literature (1938).

McAlester, Okla. The birthplace on October 25, 1914, of John Berryman, poet and biographer, honored with the Pulitzer Prize, National Book Award, and Bollingen Prize.

Dorothy Parker Birthplace, West End, N.J. Site of the summer cottage of Dorothy Parker (1893–1967), short story writer, critic, poet, member of the Algonquin Round Table, and champion for social justice.

Union Stockyard Gate (right), Chicago, Ill. This site commemorates the centennial of the novel, *The Jungle* (1906), by Upton Sinclair. The book exposed the unsanitary conditions of the meatpacking industry.

2004

Tennessee Williams House, Key West, Fla. Residence of author, playwright, and poet Tennessee Williams from 1949 to 1983.

Casa Genotta, the Eugene O'Neill house, Sea Island, Ga. O'Neill (1888–1953) lived here with his wife from 1931 to 1936 during which time he completed two plays, *Ah Wilderness!* and *Days without End.*

Home of Angie Debo, Marshall, Okla. Debo (1890–1988) was a daughter of sodbusters, a courageous scholar, and first lady of Oklahoma history. This town served as the subject of *Prairie City* (1944), Debo's literary gift to her family and community.

Matilda Moseley Home, Eatonville, Fla. Site of the home of the childhood best friend of Zora Neale Hurston (1891–1960) who celebrated the town's rich culture as representative of rural, Southern people of African descent.

Tennessee Williams Visitors Center, Columbus, Miss. Williams was born in Columbus. This site was formerly the rectory of St. Paul's Episcopal Church.

The Langhorne House, Danville, Va. A tribute to the lives and accomplishments of Irene Langhorne Gibson (1873–1956, "The Gibson Girl") and Nancy Langhorne Astor (1879–1964, "Lady Astor"), and their families.

481 Laurel Avenue, St. Paul, Minn. The birthplace of novelist F. Scott Fitzgerald (1896–1940), internationally renowned for such works as *The Great Gatsby, Tender Is the Night,* and *This Side of Paradise.*

Theodore Roethke House, Saginaw, Mich. Birthplace, childhood home, and lifelong inspiration for Pulitzer Prize–winning poet Roethke (1908–1963).

Oklahoma State University Library, Stillwater, Okla. The home of the literary papers of Angie Debo (see above).

Rome/Floyd County Library, Rome, Ga. Ann Cornelisen, author of *Torregreca: Life, Death, Miracles,* and other works ardently and generously supported this library as a Friend and benefactor from 1969 to 2003.

2003

The Library Company of Philadelphia, Pa. America's first subscription library started by Benjamin Franklin.

Beluthahatchee, Fruit Cove, Fla. Woody Guthrie (1912–1967) wrote the final draft of his autobiographical *Seeds of Man* here, as well as the ballad "Beluthahatchee Bill."

Central Children's Room, Donnell Library Center, New York Public Library, New York City. Home since 1987 of the original Winnie the Pooh stuffed bear and four of his companions—Eeyore, Tigger, Piglet, and Kanga.

Nevada State Library and Archives, Carson City, Nev. The site Basque author Robert Laxalt considered his second home while he grew up.

Territorial Community of Claremore, Okla. Birthplace of playwright and poet Lynn Riggs (1899–1954) and the setting of his *Green Grow the Lilacs*, the play that became the Broadway musical *Oklahoma*.

St. George's Episcopal Church Rectory, Clarksdale, Miss. Here the writings of Tennessee Williams were influenced by the people, land, and spirit of Mississippi's Delta.

Bay St. Louis–Hancock County (Miss.) Library. Stephen E. Ambrose researched *Nothing Like It in the World: The Men Who Built the Transcontinental Railroad, 1863-1869* here as well as other titles.

2002

Home of Maxwell E. Perkins, 93 Park Street, New Canaan, Conn. Perkins (1884–1947) was a noted literary editor.

Lillian Hellman Home, New Orleans, La. Playwright Lillian Hellman (1906–1984) wrote *The Watch on the Rhine* and *Toys in the Attic*.

Sunnyside, Tarrytown, N.Y. Home of author Washington Irving (1783–1859).

Dr. Seuss National Memorial Sculpture Garden, Springfield, Mass. Children's author Theodor Geisel (1904–1991) was better known as Dr. Seuss.

Katherine Anne Porter home, Kyle, Tex. Short-story author Porter (1890–1980) won the Pulitzer Prize for fiction in 1966.

Margaret Mitchell Home and Museum, Atlanta, Ga. Mitchell (1900–1949) wrote *Gone with the Wind* in 1936.

Ralph Ellison Branch of the Metropolitan Library System, Oklahoma City, Okla. Author and educator Ellison (1914–1994) is best known for his *Invisible Man* (1952).

Walter Clinton Jackson Library, University of North Carolina at Greensboro.

St. Simons Island (Ga.) Library. Eugenia Price researched her first novel, *The Beloved Invader* (1965), and developed her St. Simon's trilogy here.

Little Red Lighthouse, New York City. The inspiration for the children's classic *The Little Red Lighthouse and the Great Gray Bridge* (1942), by Hildegarde H. Swift and Lynd Ward.

Marquette County (Mich.) Courthouse. To honor Michigan Judge John D. Voelker (1903–1991), author of *Anatomy of a Murder* (1958).

2001

Beauvoir, Biloxi, Miss. Home and Library of Confederate President Jefferson Davis (1808–1889).

Bank Street College of Education, New York City. Children's author Margaret Wise Brown (1910–1952) taught here.

Woody Guthrie birthplace, Okemah, Okla. The singer was born here in 1912.

McNichols Campus Library, University of Detroit Mercy. To honor poet Dudley Randall (1914–2000), founder of Broadside Press.

2000

Menger Hotel, San Antonio, Tex. Associated with Oscar Wilde, O. Henry, and Theodore Roosevelt.

Hall Branch, Chicago Public Library. Associated with Richard Wright, Langston Hughes, Anna Bontemps, Gwendolyn Brooks, and Zora Neale Hurston.

Oak Hill Cottage, Mansfield, Ohio. Was the basis for Shane's Castle in *The Green Bay Tree* by Louis Bromfield (1896–1956).

Chumley's, 86 Bedford St., New York City. This pub and speakeasy was a hangout for John Steinbeck, F. Scott Fitzgerald, Eugene O'Neill, John Dos Passos, William Faulkner, Anaïs Nin, Orson Welles, Edna St. Vincent Millay, James Thurber, and others.

1999

"Grip" the Raven, Rare Books Department, Free Library of Philadelphia, Pa. Pet raven owned by Charles Dickens that inspired Edgar Allan Poe's 1845 poem.

Waldemar Ager House, Eau Claire, Wis. Home of Norwegian-American author Ager (1869–1941).

James Dickey Library, University of South Carolina, Columbia, S.C. Poet Dickey (1923–1997) taught at the university for nearly 30 years.

Willa Cather Prairie, Highway 281, Red Cloud, Nebr. Mixed-grass prairie near author Cather's (1873–1947) hometown.

Wyndham Robertson Library, Hollins University, Roanoke, Va.

Hotel Monteleone, New Orleans, La. Associated with Truman Capote, Richard Ford, Eudora Welty, William Faulkner, and Tennessee Williams.

Pete's Tavern, 129 E. 18th Street, New York City. Haunt of O. Henry and Ludwig Bemelmans.

O. Henry House and Museum, Austin, Tex. Home of short-story author O. Henry (1862–1910) in the 1890s.

Ernest Hemingway Birthplace, Oak Park, Ill. Hemingway's (1899–1961) boyhood home.

1998

Sherwood Anderson's salon, Pontalba Apartments, New Orleans, La. Writer Anderson (1876–1941) rented part of these apartments.

Cossitt Branch, Memphis–Shelby County (Tenn.) Public Library. In honor of the library's influence on novelist Richard Wright (1908–1960).

Maine Women Writers Collection, University of New England, Portland, Me.

Library of Congress, Jefferson Building, Washington, D.C.

Heinold's First and Last Chance Saloon, Oakland, Calif. Author Jack London (1876–1916) wrote and drank at a corner table here.

Plaza Hotel, New York City. Kay Thompson lived here while she wrote stories about *Eloise*.

Sunnybank, Wayne, N.J. Home of writer Albert Payson Terhune (1872–1942).

Rachel Maddux, Erin, Tenn. Home of novelist Rachel Maddux (1912–1983).

1987–1997

Founders Library, Howard University, Washington, D.C. To honor poet and professor Sterling A. Brown (1901–1989).

John's Grill, San Francisco, Calif. Favorite eatery of Sam Spade, the gumshoe character in Dashiell Hammett's *Maltese Falcon* (1930).

Wallace Stevens, Key West, Fla. Poet Stevens (1879–1955) wrote "The Idea of Order at Key West" (1936).

Algonquin Hotel, New York City. The Round Table Wits.

John Hersey House, Key West, Fla. Home of author John Hersey (1914–1993).

Laura Riding Jackson Cottage, Vero Beach, Fla. Home of poet Jackson (1901–1991).

Rosenbach Museum and Library, Philadelphia, Pa. Marianne Moore (1887–1972) room.

Robert Frost Cottage, Key West, Fla. Winter home of poet Robert Frost (1874–1963).

Cliff Dwellers Club, Chicago literary scene.

San Carlos Institute, Key West, Fla. Cuban patriot José Marti delivered speeches here.

Little White House, Key West, Fla. President Harry S. Truman relaxed and worked here.

Center for Robert Penn Warren Studies, Western Kentucky University, Bowling Green, Ky.

Isaac Bashevis Singer apartment house, Miami, Fla. Home of Polish-American writer Singer (1901–1991).

Elizabeth Bishop House, Key West, Fla. Home of poet Elizabeth Bishop (1911–1979).

Thomas Hornsby Ferril house, Denver, Colo. Home of poet Ferril (1896–1988).

Rowan Oak, Oxford, Miss. Antebellum home of novelist William Faulkner from 1930 to 1972.

ROWAN OAK
Built c. 1848. From 1930 to 1962 home of novelist William Faulkner, who named it for the rowan tree, symbol of security and peace. Now maintained as a literary landmark by the University of Mississippi.

William Faulkner House, New Orleans, La. 624 Pirate's Alley was Faulkner's home in 1925.

Ernest Lyons House, Stuart, Fla. Home of journalist and outdoorsman Lyons (1905–1990).

City Lights Bookstore, San Francisco, Calif. Owned by Beat poet Lawrence Ferlinghetti.

Robert W. Woodruff Library, Clark Atlanta University, Ga.

Herbert Hoover National Historic Site, West Branch, Iowa.

Bridges of Chicago, Wacker Drive, Chicago, Ill. Associated with poet Carl Sandburg (1878–1967).

Walter Farley Wing, Venice Area (Fla.) Public Library. Named after the author of *The Black Stallion* (1941).

Stephen Crane House, Daytona Beach, Fla. Home of novelist Stephen Crane (1871–1900).

Slip F-18, Bahia Mar, Fort Lauderdale, Fla. Anchorage of Travis McGee's *Busted Flush* houseboat, in John D. MacDonald's series of mystery novels.

Marjorie Kinnan Rawlings Historic State Park, Cross Creek, Fla. 1930s home of the author of *The Yearling* (1938).

Edgar Allen Poe House, Philadelphia, Pa. Poe's home from 1838 to 1844.

Tennessee Williams House, New Orleans, La. 722 Toulouse is now part of the Historic New Orleans Collection.

SOURCE: Friends of Libraries USA, FOLUSA's Register of Literary Landmarks, www.folusa.org/html/literarylandmark.html.

SUPPORT STAFF

Are you the librarian?

by Jennifer S. Kutzik

SO JUST WHAT *DO* SUPPORT STAFF SAY when asked, "Are you the librarian"? "I do answer 'yes' to that question because the general public does not know the difference between a librarian and an information services assistant," related Padma Polepeddi of Arapahoe Library District in Englewood, Colorado. Linda Hearn, a 26-year library veteran without an MLS degree, holds the title of "assistant branch librarian" and always answers "yes." But Joan Neslund of Ellensburg (Wash.) Public Library countered: "If a patron asks, I say 'yes.' If I am asked by another professional, I say 'no.'"

Binary thinking, at the root of Western philosophy, leads most of us into either/or mode. A person is a librarian or isn't, is a professional or isn't. But the real world is more fluid and complex, with each person challenging or accepting boundaries all the time. "We are all performing jobs that only those with the MLS would have done just five years ago," states Mary T. Kalnin, a 33-year employee at the University of Washington in Seattle. "I also try to stop myself from saying 'I just work here.' It seems to belittle the job that nonlibrarians do," says Linda Patterson, circulation supervisor at Multnomah County (Oreg.) Library's Central Library.

How staff COPE

"I can remember it like it happened yesterday," recalls Dorothy Morgan, business manager of Liverpool (N.Y.) Public Library. As president of the American Library Association's fledgling Library Support Staff Interests Round Table (LSSIRT), she approached the ALA Executive Board in January 2001 to petition for a third Congress on Professional Education (COPE 3). "I felt so passionate about the issue.... I let them know I was speaking on behalf of LSSIRT; that I was only one voice out of thousands for support staff."

Oh, If!
by William Fitch Smyth (1910)

If I were made Librarian
    I'd bear me like a king.
I'd sit with folded arms and scowl;
    I'd never do a thing.
But if some visitor should dare
    To ask me for a book,
I'd thunder: "To the dungeon, knave!"
    And crush him with a look.

And should some reader seek for aid,
    I'd shout: "See here, my man!
I'd have you understand that I
    Am now LIBRARIAN!
Down on your knees, false villain, down!"
    I'd roar in rabid rage.
But oh, I'm *not* Librarian!
    I'm just a student page.

SOURCE: William Fitch Smyth, *Little Lyrics for Librarians* (Storrs, Conn.: University of Connecticut Library, 1974), p. 8.

In May 2003, over 150 delegates representing association leaders, administrators, educators, and support staff gathered at the third Congress on Professional Education to brainstorm future directions for the professional development of library workers. Their first task was to identify what support staff do well. Each small group generated extensive statement lists that included such attributes as "fill vital roles," "understand collections and materials," "understand users," "are the faces of the library," "use teamwork concepts," and "have a service attitude."

The stories of library workers are as diverse as the libraries represented within ALA. With terms of service ranging from three months to over 30 years, some feel the library calling early in life. "In 6th grade, I ran the Van Buren Elementary circulation desk during recess while the librarian took her afternoon break," reported James Farmer, head of access services at Colorado State University in Fort Collins.

"As a teenager, I volunteered in the library at the Cheyenne Veterans Affairs Medical Center," recalled Trish Palluck, resource-sharing specialist for the Wyoming State Library in Cheyenne. Many bring rich experiences to library service from previous posts as health care personnel, teachers, bus drivers, mail carriers, editors, bartenders, jewelers, herbalists, and full-time parents.

Many library support staff have earned advanced degrees up to the doctoral level. However, some MLS-holding delegates to COPE 3 were surprised to learn that not everyone working in a library aspires to obtain an advanced library degree. When the issue of upward mobility was discussed, support staff delegates made a strong case for a career lattice that offers parallel promotional opportunities. "I don't see any advantage in today's working environment in libraries to pursue a costly MLS degree," said one staffer who preferred to remain anonymous. "I like what I do as a principal library assistant," stated Ellen Brewer of Ocean County (N.J.) Library.

The perception that degreed librarians spend too many hours in meetings or compiling endless reports deterred Betsy Miller, senior library technician at Robins Air Force Base in Georgia, from pursuing her MLS. "I prefer to do 'library work' (a.k.a. 'play with the books')," she explained. Amy P. Underwood, who has served for 28 years at Ohio University–Zanesville/Zane State College, echoed that sentiment, saying, "I don't really want to do management, so I'm content not to pursue the MLS." "I had a choice," mused Steve Mitchell, a 19-year professional of the Estes Park (Colo.) Public Library. "Get an MLS degree and become a library administrator, or finish my novel and become rich and famous. I chose to finish my novel, *Steve McQueen Would Be Proud* [Xlibris Corporation, 2001]. I'm not rich or famous, yet."

In these times of shrinking budgets and retiring workers, many support staff administer the full gamut of library functions without possessing an MLS or MLIS degree. "I am the sole employee in this library," stated Eva Anderson, library administrator at Platte Canyon High School in Bailey, Colorado. "I order the books, catalog and recatalog the books, hold seminars for the faculty, work with the teachers on curriculum mapping, keep a nice display case, and do random bits of research." Even workers with advanced library degrees may find that a support staff position is the right fit for them, or is a necessity due to a lack of positions requiring an MLS or MLIS in their desired region.

Does loyalty pay?

Are long-term library employees rewarded for their loyalty, or do they choose to stay for the variety of work and adequate benefits despite a lack of perceived advancement opportunities? "I think it depends on the library system and if you can continue to grow and learn within that system," says Heather Rivera, a 26-year veteran of Newark (N.J.) Public Library. "I think if the work is engaging, challenging, and you are respected, then it always pays to stay," asserts Dee Wilson, who has worked 17 years at Duke University in Durham, North Carolina. Sue Knoche reported that East Tennessee State University in Johnson City awards a $100 longevity benefit for each year of employment to offset the lower salaries in that geographic area. Linda Patterson of Multnomah County Library testified, "We are paid more than most places that I am aware of. So, financially, it would not pay for me to move."

But the issue of the pay discrepancy between librarians and support staff continues to be a thorn in many a staffer's side. "You don't get paid for the work you do—it's very demoralizing," laments Irene Shown of New Mexico State University in Las Cruces. "Even after 20 years, I don't make what an entry-level librarian starts at." Given the latest salary statistics, library workers in general bemoan a "serve, suffer, and sacrifice" reality when it comes to compensation that is commensurate with that of their MLS-holding colleagues.

Does certification hold a key?

Numerous support staff rally behind library technical assistant (LTA) programs, or general certification of support staff skill sets, as tools to higher pay. Some workers believe job qualifications requiring the LTA degree or certification would facilitate moving to better-paying positions at other libraries.

In partnership with ALA's Office for Human Resource Development and Recruitment, LSSIRT's Certification Committee developed a survey instrument to help determine the level of interest in, and the perceived benefit of, a voluntary certification program. To provide more information on current practice, Jenifer Grady, director of the ALA–Allied Professional Association, recently began compiling the variety of certifications available to support staff nationwide. "There are conflicting currents," emailed Sarah Vaughn of the University of Northern Colorado in Greeley. "Do we want certification to take on more duties . . . or does that weaken our status by making us a cheap and ill-supported alternative to MLS-holding librarians?"

Growth by Association

ALA began targeting support staff recruitment in 2001 with an ongoing, reduced-rate offer of $59 for membership in ALA, LSSIRT, and either the Reference and User Services Association or the Association for Library Collections and Technical Services. "I joined when they offered a reduced price for support staff for a trial period," reported Jane Ternes of Walla Walla (Wash.) Public Library. In September 2004, the association introduced a new library support staff dues category and rate of $35. LSSIRT, in particular, experienced rapid growth from these initiatives.

Still, the ongoing recruitment challenges are numerous. To foster an "each one, reach one" effort, the ALA Member and Customer Service Center has prepared a peer-recruitment kit called "Sharing Connections," available at www.ala.org. Many support staff are not aware of the new rates and believe membership is still too costly. Others report they could never afford to attend national conferences, nor do they believe current conference programming addresses their continuing education needs. "Until recently, I didn't think ALA had much to offer for support staff, but it looks like they are starting to change," said Lisa Adams of Richland (Wash.) Public Library.

Certainly, ALA conference programming to address support staff needs has made noticeable strides. At the 2005 Annual Conference in Chicago, an inaugural ALA "Conference within a Conference" offered a reduced-rate experience to support staff. With more emphasis on the professional development of all staff, forward-looking library deans and directors are encouraging support staff to join their professional organization and, when feasible, attend conferences.

Through years of service and dedication to their libraries, support staff have chosen the career of information provision, a career of honor. However, it is a choice whose future holds many options and directions. The challenge will be for the profession—and ALA—to more clearly define that future.

Then, when a patron comes to a library service point and asks, "Are you the librarian?" without hesitation, the staff member will answer, "I *am* a library professional. How may I help you?"

SOURCE: Jennifer S. Kutzik, "Are You the Librarian?" *American Libraries* 36 (March 2005): 32–34.

Advice column: Only provoke

by Sylvia Skene

SUMMERTIME IS WHEN a library worker's thoughts turn to . . . fun. Why isn't working in this library more fun?—*Ride-Around-Sally*

Dear Sally,
See that coworker sneaking a piece of chocolate in a "no-food" zone? The one furtively sliding back from coffee a minute late? The supervisor reading through each Viagra spam email carefully before deleting it? Funsters all!

The NLAs (Naughty Library Assistants) rate dead people more fun than some librarians if the dead are former members of a rock band. Most library people *do* have a sense of humor: an inoffensive, politically correct, nice, nonsexual, no-practical-jokes sense of humor. Zzzzzz . . .

Fact is, the typical library worker is fun-challenged. Like any handicap it takes lots of effort, time, and often money to improve. And you need like-minded people around you who want to have the same sort of fun you do. As Peggy Lipe points out, "The only reason Ride-Around-Sally is even asking the question is because she does not work here at Cuesta College Library with me and Jennifer."

And as Jennifer Correa observes, "Library workers are urged, nay, expected to dress and be groomed conservatively. If library workers dressed like the cast of *Friends* (via a uniform allowance, of course) they too would have silly adventurous mishaps and stare at ugly naked men who live across the way, while at work."

Women get far too earnest about *organizing* fun. Get with it! "Earnest" and "fun" have not rented a room together since Oscar Wilde died.

With few men, library workers must be content with chocolate. Rita Gibson writes, "Hear hear for choco! The quickest path to sanity, taming the savage beast! And less messy than other forms of . . . well . . . guess I'd better not go there." (Darn.)

A warning: The worst peril to fun is your management institutionalizing it. The latest version is the Go Fish!—er, Fish!—philosophy, instituted by upper administration to make the lives of their staff even more miserable, by letting them know it's their fault if they're not having fun.

What a load of hooey.

Oops, did we just say that? We were just kidding. We suggest you take them at their solemn word and institute the following sacred Fishy!—er, Fish!—principles, with examples:

Make work like play

On a hot day, ask your patrons to show you if they have an "innie" or an "outie" belly button when they ask you a question. Mark it down as a quick reference question if they do.

Make their day

Begin by talking in a normal voice to a patron. Slowly lower your voice and lean forward until you're almost nose-to-nose and whispering. Then pause and say, "You know, you've got very nice eyes."

Choose your (happy) attitude

Even though you're spoon-fed these Cream of Wheat concepts on a regular basis rather than getting any tangible improvements in working conditions or funding.

Final advice from the NLAs

You want fun? Look outside your library. But do us a favor: When you retire or leave the library profession, send your notice in by Strip-O-Gram.

Yours provokingly,
The Naughty Library Assistants

SOURCE: Sylvia Skene, "Advice from the Naughty Library Assistants: Only Provoke," *Library Mosaics* 13 (September/October 2002): 28. Reprinted with permission.

VOLUNTEERS

A primer on volunteers

by Sally Gardner Reed

2

IT IS HARD TO IMAGINE running a small library without volunteers. In fact, in the very small library it is quite likely that volunteers outnumber paid staff. Volunteers can offer a library even more than their time, as valuable as that is. Your volunteers will have a vested interest in the health and vitality of the library. They will be among your most dependable supporters when you need to convince town government of your financial needs. Who better to send that message than those who love the library enough to donate their time and energy to provide service? When the chips are down, they will be there for you.

Because the volunteer workforce is (or should be) a critical asset to the small library, it is important that they are well managed to maximize their value and their potential to help you deliver excellent services. In managing volunteers, the view is often espoused that "Volunteers in the library should be recruited, evaluated, and in all other respects treated just as you would paid employees." Those of us who actually *do* manage volunteers know that nothing could be further from the feasible. Let's face a fact right now that makes it nearly impossible for directors of small public libraries to treat volunteers like paid employees: They're *not* paid! Although volunteers are people from the community who love the library and want to contribute to it, they are not accountable, and without that paycheck, it is very hard to make them accountable. Managing volunteers presents some unique challenges.

Criticizing and correcting job performance takes on a whole new light and requires special tact. For instance, demanding strict adherence to a schedule with vacation guidelines spelled out will probably discourage some volunteer services. Yet these are important components to the smooth running of the library. Because managing volunteers can get pretty sticky, there may be a temptation to do without them. Even if you can get along without their services financially, there are important extrabudgetary reasons to welcome the service of community citizens.

Volunteers bring the library so much more than their labor. For example, volunteers can offer wonderful new perspectives and may offer unique ideas for service delivery. It is quite possible that in a small library, volunteers give our staffs the greatest diversity in terms of background, age, and life experience. It would be a real waste not to capitalize on this. As creative as we may believe we are in designing and delivering service, we who have chosen this profession are likely to be constrained by our own experience and knowledge. Volunteers who come from all walks of life can broaden our perspectives. In addition, volunteers will come with a "patron's" perspective and may be able to help us improve our services because they know, as patrons, what is best about our services and what might be changed to make them better.

Another critically important role volunteers can and do play for the library is that of citizen advocate. Who better to support the library than someone who gives freely to deliver services? And who better to accurately send the message about the library's needs than an insider who really knows how important financial support is for the library? Your volunteers will send the message of the library's importance in informal ways—for instance, through casual word of mouth at other venues in which they participate—and often formally by speaking out at budget time.

Finally, bringing volunteers into the library will show those who fund you that you are sharing in the costs of running the library. When you make your case at budget time, the town leaders are likely to want to know how you are helping yourselves. You can talk about grants and gifts and . . . you can talk about volunteers! Be sure to keep track of all your volunteers' hours and calculate their time contribution in dollars.

While it is clear that volunteers are very important to libraries in many ways, it is critically important that they form only an *auxiliary* labor force. That is, volunteers should supplement paid staff; they should not replace them. If you attempt to round out an inadequate workforce with volunteers, you will lose the best bargaining chip you have to get the increased funding you need. No one is going to pay for something they can get for free. Even if you have a perfect volunteer in a position that ordinarily would be paid, you will pay for his services dearly when he leaves. It will be very hard to convince the town government that in addition to the usual increases, you need to add a new paid staff position as well.

When assessing the value of volunteers, do not make the mistake of assuming they are free. Volunteers take training, and in many cases significantly more supervision than staff. You can maximize their value to your library by ensuring that you provide a very thorough and professional orientation for new volunteers. Develop job descriptions for your volunteers so it is clear what you expect of them. Assign a member of the staff or a veteran volunteer to be a mentor for the first month of a new volunteer's service—this will not only improve their training, it will also make them feel more at home and help them become integrated into the library's culture more quickly. Finally, be sure a new volunteer understands the goals and mission of your library. A volunteer will often work only a couple of hours a week so the training and orientation they get in the beginning of their service will help tremendously in ensuring the highest quality performance in the years to come.

When considering volunteers, don't forget the children's services. Quite often, the children's room is the busiest place in the library; volunteers can make a tremendous contribution here. If you shake the right trees (try the Parent Teacher Association or the school newsletter), you may find someone who is great at storytelling or who has some background in children's services. Be sure, however, to spell out your requirements. If you want someone with some education in children's literature, say so. Present the volunteer opportunity in the exciting light it deserves. You might get lucky and find a retired person who misses working with children.

One caveat: No matter how desperate you may be for help in the children's room, remember that the people who work there will be contributing to the creation of a lifelong image of libraries for the children. Make sure that image is a good one by ensuring that everyone who works in the children's room (paid or not) clearly enjoys children.

SOURCE: Sally Gardner Reed, *Small Libraries: A Handbook for Successful Management,* 2nd ed. (Jefferson, N.C.: McFarland, 2002), pp. 41–43. Reprinted with permission.

THE PROFESSION
CHAPTER THREE

"We are often considered society's gatekeepers, but librarians are actually the gateways. We are the one profession dedicated to ensuring the right to know. We must never lose sight of this mission despite the seductive siren songs of our information age's mythology."

—Patricia Glass Schuman (1991)

EVENTS

Calendar to 2013

2006

May

2–7	Montana Library Assoc.	Missoula, Mont.
4–7	N. American Serials Interest Group	Denver, Colo.
5–9	Art Libraries Society/N. America	Banff, Alberta
8–10	Connecticut Library Assoc.	Wallingford, Conn.
16–17	Vermont Library Assoc.	Burlington, Vt.
17–19	Utah Library Assoc.	St. George, Utah
18–21	BookExpo America	Washington, D.C.
19–24	Medical Library Assoc.	Phoenix, Ariz.

June

11–14	Special Libraries Assoc.	Baltimore, Md.
11–15	Joint Conf. on Digital Libraries	Chapel Hill, N.C.
14–17	Canadian Library Assoc.	Ottawa, Ont.
21–24	American Theological Library Assoc.	Chicago, Ill.
22–28	American Library Assoc. (Annual)	New Orleans, La.

July

3–7	International Assoc. of School Librarianship	Lisbon, Portugal
15–20	American Assoc. of Law Libraries	St. Louis, Mo.
31–Aug. 6	Society of American Archivists	Washington, D.C.

August

4–6	Americas Conference on Info Systems	Acapulco, Mex.
9–12	Pacific Northwest Library Assoc.	Eugene, Oreg.
17–19	Shanghai International Library Forum	Shanghai, China
20–24	International Federation of Library Associations and Institutions	Seoul, Korea

September

19–22	Australian Library & Info Assoc.	Perth, W.A.
20–22	North Dakota Library Assoc.	Fargo, N.Dak.
20–22	South Dakota Library Assoc.	Rapid City, S.Dak.
27–29	Minnesota Library Assoc.	St. Cloud, Minn.

October

2–4	West Virginia Library Assoc.	Huntington, W.Va.
3–6	Illinois Library Assoc.	Chicago, Ill.

4–5	Idaho Library Assoc.	Moscow, Idaho
4–9	Frankfurt Book Fair	Frankfurt, Ger.
9–12	Educause	Dallas, Tex.
10–13	Michigan Library Assoc.	Detroit, Mich.
11–13	Iowa Library Assoc.	Council Bluffs, Ia.
11–15	Joint Conference of Librarians of Color	Dallas, Tex.
22–24	New England Library Assoc.	Burlington, Vt.
23–25	Internet Librarian Conference	Monterey, Calif.
26–29	Library & Info. Technology Assoc.	Nashville, Tenn.
31–Nov. 3	Wisconsin Library Assoc.	Wisconsin Dells

November

1–4	New York Library Assoc.	Saratoga Springs
3–9	American Society for Info Science & Tech	Austin, Tex.
8–11	Charleston Conference	Charleston, S.C.
10–13	California Library Assoc.	Sacramento, Calif.
13–19	Children's Book Week	
15–18	Pennsylvania Library Assoc.	Pittsburgh, Pa.
28–30	South Carolina Library Assoc.	Hilton Head, S.C.

2007

January

16–19	Assoc. for Library & Info Science Education	Seattle, Wash.
19–24	American Library Assoc. (Midwinter)	Seattle, Wash.

February

1–3	Ontario Library Assoc.	Toronto, Ont.

March

7–9	Tennessee Library Assoc.	Nashville, Tenn.
29–April 1	Assoc. of College & Research Libraries	Baltimore, Md.

April

9–13	Florida Library Assoc.	Orlando, Fla.
10–13	Catholic Library Assoc.	Baltimore, Md.
11–13	Kansas Library Assoc.	Topeka, Kans.
11–14	Texas Library Assoc.	San Antonio, Tex.
15–21	National Library Week	
24–25	New Jersey Library Assoc.	Long Branch, N.J.

May

2–3	Amigos Library Services	Dallas, Tex
15–17	Utah Library Assoc.	Provo, Utah
18–23	Medical Library Assoc.	Philadelphia, Pa.
23–26	Canadian Library Assoc.	St. John's, Newf.
31–June 3	BookExpo America	New York, N.Y.

June

3–6	Special Libraries Assoc.	Denver, Colo.

| 21–27 | American Library Assoc. (Annual) | Washington, D.C. |

July

| 14–18 | American Assoc. of Law Librarians | New Orleans, La. |

August

	International Federation of Library Associations and Institutions	Durban, S. Africa
2–6	Black Caucus of the ALA	Fort Worth, Tex.
27–Sept. 2	Society of American Archivists	Chicago, Ill.

September

| 26–28 | North Dakota Library Assoc. | Jamestown, N.Dak. |

October

3–5	West Virginia Library Assoc.	Morgantown, W.Va.
3–5	South Dakota Library Assoc.	Watertown, S.Dak.
3–6	Idaho Library Assoc.	Nampa, Ida.
6–10	Arkansas Library Assoc.	Little Rock, Ark.
10–14	Frankfurt Book Fair	Frankfurt, Ger.
14–16	New England Library Assoc.	Sturbridge, Mass.
16–19	Wisconsin Library Assoc.	Green Bay, Wis.
17–20	New York Library Assoc.	Buffalo, N.Y.
23–26	Educause	Seattle, Wash.

November

6–9	Michigan Library Assoc.	Lansing, Mich.
7–10	Charleston Conference	Charleston, S.C.
12–18	Children's Book Week	

2008

January

8–11	Assoc. for Library & Info Science Education	Philadelphia, Pa.
11–16	American Library Assoc. (Midwinter)	Philadelphia, Pa.
31–Feb. 2	Ontario Library Assoc.	Toronto, Ont.

March

| 25–28 | Catholic Library Assoc. | Indianapolis, Ind. |
| 25–29 | Public Library Assoc. | Minneapolis |

April

9–11	Kansas Library Assoc.	Wichita, Kan.
13–19	National Library Week	
15–18	Texas Library Assoc.	Dallas, Tex.
30–May 1	Amigos Library Services	Dallas, Tex.
30–May 3	Utah/Mountain Plains Library Assoc.	Salt Lake City

May

| 16–21 | Medical Library Assoc. | Chicago, Ill. |

| 21–24 | Canadian Library Assoc. | Vancouver, B.C. |
| 29–June 1 | BookExpo America | Los Angeles, Calif. |

June

| 26–July 2 | American Library Assoc. (Annual) | Anaheim, Calif. |

July

| 12–16 | American Assoc. of Law Libraries | Portland, Oreg. |
| 27–30 | Special Libraries Assoc. | Seattle, Wash. |

August

| 10–15 | International Federation of Library Associations and Institutions | Québec City, Qué. |
| 23–31 | Society of American Archivists | San Francisco, Calif. |

October

4–7	Arkansas Library Assoc.	Little Rock, Ark.
21–24	Michigan Library Assoc.	Kalamazoo, Mich.
28–31	Educause	Orlando, Fla.

November

5–8	New York Library Assoc.	Saratoga Springs
14–17	California Library Assoc.	San Jose, Calif.
17–23	Children's Book Week	

December

| 3–5 | West Virginia Library Assoc. | White Sulphur Sprs. |

2009

January

| 23–28 | American Library Assoc. (Midwinter) | Denver, Colo. |
| 29–31 | Ontario Library Assoc. | Toronto, Ont. |

April

1–3	Mountain Plains/Kansas Library Assoc.	Overland Park, Kan.
12–18	National Library Week	
14–17	Catholic Library Assoc.	Anaheim, Calif.
20–25	Texas Library Assoc.	Houston, Tex.

June

| 14–17 | Special Libraries Assoc. | Washington, D.C. |

July

| 9–15 | American Library Assoc. (Annual) | Chicago, Ill. |

August

| 1–9 | Society of American Archivists | Austin, Tex. |

October

| 27–30 | Educause | Denver, Colo. |

November

| 4–7 | Michigan Library Assoc. | Lansing, Mich. |
| 16–22 | Children's Book Week | |

2010

January

| 15–20 | American Library Assoc. (Midwinter) | Boston, Mass. |
| 28–30 | Ontario Library Assoc. | Toronto, Ont. |

April

4-10	National Library Week	
7–9	Kansas Library Assoc.	Wichita, Kan.
13–16	Texas Library Assoc.	San Antonio, Tex.

June

| 13–16 | Special Libraries Assoc. | New Orleans, La. |
| 24–30 | American Library Assoc. (Annual) | Orlando, Fla. |

October

| 12–15 | Educause | Anaheim, Calif. |

November

| 12–15 | California Library Assoc. | Sacramento, Calif. |

2011

January

| 28–Feb. 2 | American Library Assoc. (Midwinter) | Chicago, Ill. |

April

6–8	Kansas Library Assoc.	Topeka, Kan.
10–16	National Library Week	
12–15	Texas Library Assoc.	Austin, Tex.

June

| 12–15 | Special Libraries Assoc. | Philadelphia, Pa. |
| 23–29 | American Library Assoc. (Annual) | New Orleans, La. |

2012

January

| 20–25 | American Library Assoc. (Midwinter) | San Antonio, Tex. |

April

| 17–20 | Texas Library Assoc. | Dallas, Tex. |

June

23–29	American Library Assoc. (Annual)	Anaheim, Calif.

November

12–15	California Library Assoc.	San Jose, Calif.

2013

January

25–30	American Library Assoc. (Midwinter)	Seattle, Wash.

April

8–12	Texas Library Assoc.	San Antonio, Tex.

June

20–26	American Library Assoc. (Annual)	Washington, D.C.

SOURCE: For up-to-date meeting information, see the *American Libraries* datebook at www.ala.org/ala/alonline/datebook/datebook.htm.

Past ALA Annual Conferences

A LIST OF ALL ALA Annual Conference dates and locations, with attendance figures, contrasted with total ALA membership (from 1900).

Date	Place	Attendance	Membership
1876, Oct. 4–6	Philadelphia	103	[N/A
1877, Sept. 4–6	New York	66	for
1877, Oct. 2–5	London, England	21*	1876–
1878	[No meeting]		1899]
1879, June 30–July 2	Boston	162	
1880	[No meeting]		
1881, Feb. 9–12	Washington, D.C.	70	
1882, May 24–27	Cincinnati	47	
1883, Aug. 14–17	Buffalo, N.Y.	72	
1884	[No meeting]		
1885, Sept. 8–11	Lake George, N.Y.	87	
1886, July 7–10	Milwaukee, Wis.	133	
1887, Aug. 30–Sept. 2	Thousand Islands, N.Y.	186	
1888, Sept. 25–28	Catskill Mountains, N.Y.	32	
1889, May 8–11	St. Louis, Mo.	106	
1890, Sept. 9–13	Fabyans (White Mts.), N.H.	242	
1891, Oct. 12–16	San Francisco	83	
1892, May 16–21	Lakewood, N.Y., Baltimore, Washington	260	
1893, July 13–22	Chicago	311	
1894, Sept. 17–22	Lake Placid, N.Y.	205	
1895, Aug. 13–21	Denver & Colorado Springs	147	

* U.S. attendance

Date	Place	Attendance	Membership
1896, Sept. 1–8	Cleveland	363	
1897, June 21–25	Philadelphia	315	
1897, July 13–16	London, England	94*	
1898, July 5–9	Lakewood, N.Y.	494	
1899, May 9–13	Atlanta	215	
1900, June 6–12	Montreal, Québec	452	874
1901, July 3–10	Waukesha, Wis.	460	980
1902, June 14–20	Boston & Magnolia, Mass.	1,018	1,152
1903, June 22–27	Niagara Falls, N.Y.	684	1,200
1904, Oct. 17–22	St. Louis, Mo.	577	1,228
1905, July 4–8	Portland, Me.	359	1,253
1906, June 29–July 6	Narragansett Pier, R.I.	891	1,844
1907, May 23–29	Asheville, N.C.	478	1,808
1908, June 22–27	Lake Minnetonka, Minn.	658	1,907
1909, June 28–July 3	Bretton Woods, N.H.	620	1,835
1910, June 30–July 6	Mackinac Island, Mich.	533	2,005
1910, Aug. 28–31	Brussels, Belgium	46*	
1911, May 18–24	Pasadena, Calif.	582	2,046
1912, June 26–July 2	Ottawa, Ontario	704	2,365
1913, June 23–28	Kaaterskill, N.Y.	892	2,563
1914, May 25–29	Washington, D.C.	1,366	2,905
1915, June 3–9	Berkeley, Calif.	779	3,024
1916, June 26–July 1	Asbury Park, N.J.	1,386	3,188
1917, June 21–27	Louisville, Ky.	824	3,346
1918, July 1–6	Saratoga Springs, N.Y.	620	3,380
1919, June 23–27	Asbury Park, N.J.	1,168	4,178
1920, June 2–7	Colorado Springs	553	4,464
1921, June 20–25	Swampscott, Mass.	1,899	5,307
1922, June 26–July 1	Detroit	1,839	5,684
1923, April 23–28	Hot Springs, Ark.	693	5,669
1924, June 30–July 5	Saratoga Springs, N.Y.	1,188	6,055
1925, July 6–11	Seattle, Wash.	1,066	6,745
1926, Oct. 4–9	Atlantic City, N.J.	2,224	8,848
1927, June 20–27	Toronto, Ontario	1,964	10,056
1927, Sept. 26–Oct. 1	Edinburgh, Scotland	82*	
1928, May 28–June 2	West Baden, Ind.	1,204	10,526
1929, May 13–18	Washington, D.C.	2,743	11,833
1929, June 15–30	Rome and Venice, Italy	70*	
1930, June 23–28	Los Angeles	2,023	12,713
1931, June 22–27	New Haven, Conn.	3,241	14,815
1932, April 25–30	New Orleans	1,306	13,021
1933, Oct. 16–21	Chicago	2,986	11,880
1934, June 25–30	Montreal, Québec	1,904	11,731
1935, May 20–30	Madrid, Seville, & Barcelona, Spain	42*	
1935, June 24–29	Denver	1,503	12,241
1936, May 11–16	Richmond, Va.	2,834	13,057
1937, June 21–26	New York	5,312	14,204
1938, June 13–18	Kansas City, Mo.	1,900	14,626

* U.S. attendance

Date	Place	Attendance	Membership
1939, June 18–24	San Francisco	2,869	15,568
1940, May 26–June 1	Cincinnati	3,056	15,808
1941, June 19–25	Boston	4,266	16,015
1942, June 22–27	Milwaukee, Wis.	2,342	15,328
1943	[No meeting]		14,546
1944	[No meeting]		14,799
1945	[No meeting]		15,118
1946, June 16–22	Buffalo, N.Y.	2,327	15,800
1947, June 29–July 5	San Francisco	2,534	17,107
1948, June 13–19	Atlantic City, N.J.	3,752	18,283
1949:	Regional conferences	[N/A]	19,324
Aug. 22–25	(Far West) Vancouver, B.C.		
Sept. 2–5	(Trans-Miss.) Fort Collins, Colo.		
Oct. 3–6	(Middle Atlantic) Atlantic City, N.J.		
Oct. 12–15	(New England) Swampscott, Mass.		
Oct. 26–29	(Southeastern) Miami Beach, Fla.		
Nov. 9–12	(Midwest) Grand Rapids, Mich.		
Nov. 20–23	(Southwestern) Fort Worth, Tex.		
1950, July 16–22	Cleveland	3,436	19,689
1951, July 8–14	Chicago	3,612	19,701
1952, June 29–July 5	New York	5,212	18,925
1953, June 21–27	Los Angeles	3,258	19,551
1954, June 20–26	Minneapolis	3,230	20,177
1955, July 3–9	Philadelphia	4,412	20,293
1956, June 17–23	Miami Beach, Fla.	2,866	20,285
1957, June 23–30	Kansas City, Mo.	2,953	20,326
1958, July 13–19	San Francisco	4,400	21,716
1959, June 21–27	Washington, D.C.	5,346	23,230
1960, June 19–24	Montreal, Québec	4,648	24,690
1961, July 9–15	Cleveland	4,757	25,860
1962, June 17–23	Miami Beach, Fla.	3,527	24,879
1963, July 14–20	Chicago	5,753	25,502
1964, June 28–July 4	St. Louis	4,623	26,015
1965, July 3–10	Detroit	5,818	27,526
1966, July 10–16	New York	9,342	31,885
1967, June 25–July I	San Francisco	8,116	35,289
1968, June 23–29	Kansas City, Mo.	6,849	35,666
1969, June 22–28	Atlantic City, N.J.	10,399	36,865
1970, June 28–July 4	Detroit	8,965	30,394
1971, June 20–26	Dallas	8,087	29,740
1972, June 24–30	Chicago	9,700	29,610
1973, June 24–30	Las Vegas	8,539	30,172
1974, July 5–13	New York	14,382	34,010
1975, June 29–July 5	San Francisco	11,606	33,208
1976, July 18–24	Chicago (Centennial)	12,015	33,560
1977, June 17–23	Detroit	9,667	33,767
1978, June 25–30	Chicago	11,768	35,096
1979, June 24–30	Dallas	10,650	35,524
1980, June 29–July 4	New York	14,566	35,257
1981, June 26–July 2	San Francisco	12,555	37,954

3

Date	Place	Attendance	Membership
1982, July 10–15	Philadelphia	12,819	38,050
1983, June 25–30	Los Angeles	11,005	38,862
1984, June 23–28	Dallas	11,443	39,290
1985, July 6–11	Chicago	14,160	40,761
1986, June 26–July 3	New York	16,530	42,361
1987, June 27–July 2	San Francisco	17,844	45,145
1988, July 9–14	New Orleans	16,530	47,249
1989, June 24–29	Dallas	17,592	49,483
1990, June 23–28	Chicago	19,982	50,509
1991, June 29–July 4	Atlanta	17,764	52,893
1992, June 25–July 2	San Francisco	19,261	54,735
1993, June 24–July 1	New Orleans	17,165	55,836
1994, June 23–30	Miami Beach	12,627	55,356
1995, June 24–28	Chicago	19,146	56,444
1996, July 4–10	New York	18,027	56,688
1997, June 26–July 3	San Francisco	19,339	55,643
1998, June 25–July 1	Washington	24,844	55,573
1999, June 24–30	New Orleans	22,598	58,777
2000, July 6–12	Chicago	24,913	61,103
2001, June 14–20	San Francisco	26,820	63,424
2002, June 13–19	Atlanta	21,130	64,211
2003, June 19–25	Toronto	17,570	63,793
2004, June 24–30	Orlando	19,731	64,222
2005, June 23–29	Chicago	27,962	66,127

Helpful hints for ALA conferences

by Elisa F. Topper

WHILE THEY CAN BE INITIALLY OVERWHELMING, with some careful planning ALA conferences can be extremely rewarding. Follow the tips below and be assured you'll have an energizing experience—in fact, you'll likely ask yourself why you didn't go before!

Look through the preliminary conference program to map out a tentative schedule before you even arrive at your hotel. Be sure to allow for travel time

Rapt attendees in Montreal, 1900

between sessions and for meal breaks. Once at the conference, review the final program to verify your sessions, as times and locations may change.

An excellent way to get a quick overview of the conference is to attend the New Members Round Table orientation session.

Take advantage of the free shuttle buses between conference hotels and the convention center. Wear your badge at conference activities but not on the street. You do not want to advertise that you are a tourist.

Glance at name tags and try to strike up conversations on shuttle buses, while waiting in line, and during session breaks. You can meet some of the most interesting people in this manner, and you are likely to make valuable professional contacts.

Interested in getting involved in committee work, or want to find out more about a specific division or ALA office? Attend one of the committee's sessions or visit the ALA information booth.

Wear comfortable clothes—especially shoes. Bring a sweater or jacket, as often the air-conditioned meeting rooms can be quite chilly. And, of course, don't forget a tote bag to carry all of your conference "equipment," which should include energy bars and a water bottle to keep yourself nourished and hydrated.

Don't forget to attend the exhibits; you may even want to break the exhibits up into two or three half-day trips. Be selective in what giveaways you pick up, as freebies can get heavy. Also consider using ALA's post office in the exhibits area to mail back your materials. Caution here: The lines tend to be long, so expect to wait.

Library-school reunions held during conference are a great place to renew old acquaintances and meet new colleagues. Check your school's web page for location and advance notification of the event.

Interested in applying for a new job, or need career information, a critique of your résumé, or job-search advice? Take advantage of the ALA Placement Center.

Pick up daily issues of *Cognotes*, the conference newspaper, for additional conference information, last-minute session changes, and job listings.

Always keep a supply of business cards with you, and be sure to exchange them with colleagues you meet during the conference. Graduate students should consider having cards printed, making sure to get the school's permission to use its logo.

Take a few minutes on your return flight, train ride, or drive home to reflect on your conference experience. Jot a few notes to review before your next one. What did you especially like? Who did you meet? What would you do differently? What did you wish you had more time to do?

SOURCE: Elisa F. Topper, "Helpful Hints for ALA Conferences," *American Libraries* 34 (June/July 2003): 106.

End PowerPoint dependency now!

by Steven J. Bell

I'M CONVINCED THAT our profession's love affair with PowerPoint is stronger than ever. At the past three library conferences I attended, virtually every presentation by a librarian involved PowerPoint slides.

On the other hand, nearly every keynote presenter or invited speaker (almost always nonlibrarians) made little or no use of PowerPoint. Granted, keynotes differ considerably from research-based presentations, but these speakers connected with their audiences effortlessly.

The library profession seems oblivious to the global backlash against PowerPoint. Several articles over the past three years have led the movement against the dependence on slides as presentation standards. With titles such as "Ban It Now: Friends Don't Let Friends Use PowerPoint," "PowerPoint-Induced Sleep," and "Is PowerPoint the Devil?" the articles detail the same behaviors demonstrated at library conferences that lead to static, dull, audience-alienating presentations.

Edward Tufte's *The Cognitive Style of PowerPoint* (Graphics Press, 2003) generated further backlash against PowerPoint recently. Tufte's goal was to encourage presentations that are clearer, more useful, and more powerful, but he thoroughly illustrates how Power Point sabotages well-intentioned presentations. Tufte's Ask E.T. weblog (www.edwardtufte.com/bboard/ offers anecdotes about bad PowerPoint presentations.

The running theme of all these publications is that PowerPoint rarely enhances a presentation. Instead, it facilitates poorly designed communication graphics and can ultimately detract from a speaker's ability to connect with the audience.

Short of declaring an absolute ban on PowerPoint slides at our conferences, what can be done? As a PowerPoint user myself—and one who is likely guilty of those offenses condemned by anti-PowerPoint advocates—I still believe that PowerPoint slides can add value to a program. As in all things, moderation is the key.

But PowerPoint users must also pay attention to the importance of visual and graphic design in communication. Unfortunately, most librarians lack familiarity with these skill areas. In this article, I offer a few suggestions on how our profession can reduce its dependency on PowerPoint, or at least make sure our use of it enhances, rather than weakens, our presentations.

Go live or simulate it

Internet connections have improved vastly in the last few years. With dependable connectivity increasingly the norm, let's raise our expectations for live, dynamic presentations. Instead of giving the audience bullet points to explain why your library decided to implement a new web-based technology solution, provide a live demonstration that speaks for itself and excites your audience.

And please don't linger over several dozen PowerPoint slides only to rush through the most interesting portion of your presentation in the last five minutes. Start with a clear, visually informative demonstration that will allow attendees to make better sense of the rest of your remarks. Show the audience exactly what you are talking about.

Speakers who have qualms about going live during a presentation should think about providing a canned demonstration. A number of software products allow you to capture complete or partial web pages that can be used to simulate live connections or at least show the audience what's being discussed.

Even die-hard PowerPoint enthusiasts can use LiveWeb (skp.mvps.org/liveweb.htm), a free utility that painlessly captures current web pages and content into PPT slides. Live is better, because it allows for spontaneous innovation and responses to "what if" scenarios. Compared to the linear, start-to-finish predictability of PowerPoint, going live or simulating it can make a presentation truly dynamic.

Instead of serving up the usual series of bullet-point slides, try to integrate more "web evidence," or "webidence" for short. For example, suppose you want to make a point about the way students increasingly use the internet for their research. Instead of a PowerPoint slide that reduces the key findings from a national study of student Internet use to bullet points, locate articles found on websites that support your point. Possible sources in this case might include an actual Pew Research Center study that reported this data or a web page from a college newspaper with a story on the topic.

It can be far more powerful and effective to show the audience the evidence as you make a case in support of your presentation. This is where web-page capture software such as Net Snippets (www.netsnippets.com) is most helpful. If you come across a web page containing information that could be relevant to an upcoming or future presentation, capture it immediately. Delay even a week and you may find that the page no longer exists.

Should we dare to go retro-tech, low-tech, or no-tech? Walt Crawford, a sought-after keynote speaker, makes no secret of his preference for avoiding PowerPoint. In his book *First Have Something to Say* (ALA, 2003), he advises the reader to avoid leaning on PowerPoint as a crutch. If Crawford can succeed without PowerPoint, why shouldn't more of us be following suit?

In a recent thread on Tufte's Ask E.T. weblog, one respondent recalled that the best presenter he ever experienced simply used a continuous roll of transparency film on an overhead projector. This old technology allowed the presenter to jot down thoughts and talking points as they occurred and in reaction to audience questions and comments. What a refreshing experience that would be, assuming you could find such a device at a convention center.

Transparencies, 35mm slides, and other low-tech approaches are all potential visual aids, but you might consider talking without AV. It would certainly depend on your topic, but just think how dynamic this could be. If you need convincing, think of the best presenter or presentation you've ever experienced. Do you remember any content on the slides or what template was used? Or do you remember the dynamic speaking style of the presenter? Did PowerPoint or the speaker's visual technology make it memorable? Probably not.

If you must PPT

It would be unrealistic to expect the entire profession to stop cold turkey. So when you do use PowerPoint slides, consider some of the following suggestions:

Keep the number of slides to a minimum. As a guideline, create no more than 10 substantive slides (a cover slide does not count) per hour of presentation. If you assume four to five minutes of speaking per slide, 10 would consume nearly all of an hour-long presentation with only a short time for discussion.

It always spells trouble for the audience when the presentation begins in slide mode and the slides total 30–40 or more. In those situations, the speaker rarely has time to get through them all, so some important information is skipped. If a speaker chooses to exceed the 10-slide maximum, no slide should remain up for more than two or three minutes. Few things contribute to a static presentation like slides that persist for more than a few minutes. Remember: With fewer bullet points to cover, you'll have more opportunity to talk, and that's why the attendees are really there—to hear what you have to say.

Avoid PowerPoint templates that are used to death (for example, Blends, High Voltage, Notebook). It's actually quite simple to design your own template style or visit sites that offer new and different templates for download-ing. While you're at it, consider customizing your slides with the name or theme of the conference. Let attendees know you took the time to think about your slides.

Unless it's absolutely necessary, spare the audience details about your library. I attended a program where the speaker had only 20 minutes to present. Almost half of this was used to provide unnecessary details on multiple slides about her library's programs, the institution's student body, faculty, technol-ogy infrastructure, and more. It's true that speakers gain confidence by start-ing with familiar information that's easily recalled, and at times this informa-tion can add context to the talk. But keep it brief, and limit it to just one slide. Even better, start with the demonstration or show how your service operates, then work a few points about your library or institution into the opening se-quence. That could eliminate one or more slides right away.

Resist the urge to supply everyone with a printout of all your slides at the start of the program. The focal point of any presentation is the speaker. When handouts are available, the audience focuses on the text and jumps ahead to see what the speaker will be saying next. If you create slides or other forms of electronic visual support and want to make them available to attendees for later review, put them on a website. I do advocate supplying attendees with a presen-tation handout. It should contain on a single page the speaker's contact infor-mation, a list of related readings or web resources, and the URL where the presentation visuals can be viewed. This can be distributed at the start of the program without compromising what the speaker has to say. If a complete set of slide printouts is required, save the distribution for the end of the program.

There are dozens more tips for improving slide presentations (don't read from the slides, keep the text consistent, avoid meaningless clip art on every slide, limit the bullet points to three or four per slide, practice and time the presentation in advance), but this article is intended to encourage you to stop or reduce your use of PowerPoint. Using such tips merely makes the problems less noticeable. For further advice, visit staff.philau.edu/bells/ppt.html.

Few of us are natural presenters. We need to gain experience and build confidence. For some it comes at local conferences, while others hone presen-tation skills during library-instruction sessions. More national library confer-ences could benefit from offering instructional workshops for speakers, espe-cially those with limited presentation experience. ALA's Association of Col-lege and Research Libraries is a good model, as it offers just such a workshop at the ALA Midwinter Meeting prior to its own national conference (even if a significant portion of the program is devoted to creating effective PowerPoint presentations). If you've been selected to give a presentation at a library con-ference, consider a speaker's workshop if you're new to presenting.

If no such workshop is available, then take advantage of the myriad web resources devoted to helping individuals improve their presentation skills. But none of these sites will likely provide the encouragement you need to declare your freedom from PowerPoint. If you need such motivation, take time to read the literature that identifies and discusses the symptoms and causes of "PowerPoint-lessness." Then imagine your program without PowerPoint. Chances are you will be improving on your ability to achieve every speaker's ultimate objective—creating a memorable conference experience for your audience.

SOURCE: Steven J. Bell, "End PowerPoint Dependency Now!" *American Libraries* 35 (June/July 2004): 56–59.

GRANTS & AWARDS

Scholarships, grants, and awards

MANY OPPORTUNITIES EXIST in the field of library and information science for its practitioners to obtain assistance for their research and to gain recognition for their achievements. The following list provides information on grants, scholarships, and awards given by ALA and other national associations in the United States and Canada. Not all of them can be applied for, although most have some procedure by which others can be nominated.

The arrangement is topical under two major headings: **Grants and scholarships** (money awarded for things you are going to do); and **Awards** (honors and honoraria for things you have already done). Considered topically, this list can be also be viewed as a measure of what we value most in our profession.

Under Grants and scholarships, the subheads are:
   For education (pp. 153–156);
   For programs (pp. 156–158); and
   For publications, research, and travel (pp. 158–163).

Under Awards, the subheads are:
   To individuals or groups for achievement and service (pp. 163–170);
   To libraries for excellence (pp. 170–172);
   For publications and research (pp. 172–177);
   For service to children and young adults (pp. 177–178);
   For service to the underserved (pp. 179–180);
   For intellectual freedom (p. 180);
   For literacy and social responsibility (pp. 180–181);
   For documents and archives (p. 181); and
   For technology (p. 182).

Grants and scholarships

For education

AALL Educational Scholarships. Scholarships in support of library degrees for both law school graduates and non–law school graduates, minority stipends, and law degrees for library school graduates. American Association of Law Libraries, www.aallnet.org/services/scholarships.asp.

AILA Library School Scholarship. A $500 scholarship to an American Indian or Alaskan Native student who is enrolled in, or has been accepted in, an ALA-accredited master's degree program. American Indian Library Association, www.nativeculturelinks.com/aila.html.

AJL Rosalie Katchen Memorial Grant. A cash grant to support catalogers and library school students seeking to further their knowledge of Hebraica/Judaica cataloging or participate in and contribute Hebraica records to national cooperative cataloging programs. Association of Jewish Libraries, www.jewishlibraries.org.

AJL Scholarship. A $500 scholarship to a library school student who has taken Judaic/Hebrew courses. Association of Jewish Libraries, www.jewishlibraries.org.

ALA David H. Clift Scholarship. A $3,000 scholarship to an individual pursuing a master's degree in library science from an ALA-accredited program. ALA Scholarships, www.ala.org.

ALA Marshall Cavendish Scholarship. A $3,000 scholarship to an individual pursuing a master's degree in library science from an ALA-accredited program. ALA Scholarships, www.ala.org.

ALA Mary V. Gaver Scholarship. A $3,000 scholarship to an individual specializing in youth services who is pursuing a master's degree in library science. ALA Scholarships, www.ala.org.

ALA Miriam L. Hornback Scholarship. A $3,000 award given to an ALA or library support staff person to support studies toward a master's degree in library and information studies. ALA Scholarships, www.ala.org.

ALA Tom and Roberta Drewes Scholarship. Scholarship of $3,000 to a library support staff person currently working in a library, pursuing a master's degree in library science. ALA Scholarships, www.ala.org.

ALA Tony B. Leisner Scholarship. A $3,000 award to a library support staff person currently working in a library, pursuing a master's degree in library science. ALA Scholarships, www.ala.org.

ALA Women's National Book Association/Ann Heidbreder Eastman Grant. A $750 grant for a librarian to take a course or participate in an institute devoted to aspects of publishing as a profession or to provide reimbursement for such study completed within the past year. ALA Publishing, www.ala.org/ala/ourassociation/publishing/.

ALA/AASL School Librarians' Workshop Scholarship. A scholarship of $3,000 to a full-time student preparing to become a school library media specialist at the preschool, elementary, or secondary level. ALA American Association of School Librarians, www.ala.org/aasl/.

ALA/ALSC Bound to Stay Bound Books Scholarships. Four $6,500 awards to assist individuals who wish to work in the field of library service to children. ALA Association for Library Service to Children, www.ala.org/alsc/.

ALA/ALSC Frederic G. Melcher Scholarships. Two annual $6,000 scholarships established to encourage and assist people who wish to enter the field of library service to children. ALA Association for Library Service to Children, www.ala.org/alsc/.

ALA/ASCLA Century Scholarship. An annual award of $2,500 fund services or accommodation for a library school student with disabilities admitted to an ALA-accredited library school in order to fund services or accommodations that are either not provided by law or otherwise by the university. ALA Association of Specialized and Cooperative Library Agencies, www.ala.org/ascla/.

ALA/ERT Christopher J. Hoy Scholarship. A $5,000 award to an individual pursuing a master's degree in library science. ALA Scholarships, www.ala.org.

ALA/GODORT W. David Rozkuszka Scholarship. A $3,000 award for financial assistance to an individual currently working with government documents in a library and working on a master's degree in library science. ALA Government Documents Round Table, sunsite.berkeley.edu/GODORT/.

ALA/LITA Christian (Chris) Larew Memorial Scholarship. A $3,000 scholarship for qualified persons who plan to follow a career in library and information technology, and who demonstrate academic excellence, leadership, and vision. ALA Library and Information Technology Association, www.ala.org/lita/.

ALA/LITA LSSI Minority Scholarship in Library and Information Technology. A $2,500 scholarship for qualified persons who plan to follow a career in library automation and who are members of a principal minority group. ALA Library and Information Technology Association, www.ala.org/lita/.

ALA/LITA OCLC Minority Scholarship in Library and Information Technology. A $3,000 scholarship for qualified persons who plan to follow a career in library automation and who are members of a principal minority group. ALA Library and Information Technology Association, www.ala.org/lita/.

ALA/OFD Spectrum Scholarships. Provides 50 annual scholarships of $5,000 each to minority students representing African-American, Asian-Pacific Islander, Latino/Hispanic, and Native American populations to encourage admission to graduation from an ALA-accredited master's degree program in library and information studies. ALA Office for Diversity, www.ala.org/diversity/.

APALA Scholarship. Provides financial assistance to a student of Asian or Pacific background who is enrolled, or has been accepted in, an ALA-accredited master's or doctoral degree program. Asian/Pacific American Library Association, www.apalaweb.org.

ARL Initiative to Recruit a Diverse Workforce. A stipend of up to $10,000 to attract students from underrepresented groups to careers in academic and research libraries. Association of Research Libraries, www.arl.org.

ARLIS/NA Robertson Rare Book School Scholarship. An annual award of tuition waiver for one course at Rare Book School (RBS) at the University of Virginia. Art Libraries Society of North America, www.arlisna.org.

ASIS&T Thomson ISI Doctoral Dissertation Scholarship. An award of $1,500 to foster research in information science by assisting doctoral students in the field with their dissertation research. American Society for Information Science and Technology, www.asis.org.

BCALA E. J. Josey Scholarship Award. Two unrestricted grants of $2,000 awarded annually to African-American students enrolled in or accepted by ALA-accredited programs. Black Caucus of the American Library Association, www.bcala.org.

Beta Phi Mu Blanche E. Woolls Scholarship. Award of $1,500 to a student beginning library and information studies at an ALA-accredited school with the intention of pursuing a career in school library media service. Beta Phi Mu, www.beta-phi-mu.org.

Beta Phi Mu Doctoral Dissertation Scholarship. For doctoral students who have completed their course work, this $2,000 award offers funding to complete the degree. Beta Phi Mu, www.beta-phi-mu.org.

Beta Phi Mu Eugene Garfield Doctoral Dissertation Fellowship. Six awards of $500 to library and information science students working on doctoral dissertations. Beta Phi Mu, www.beta-phi-mu.org.

Beta Phi Mu Frank B. Sessa Scholarship. Award of $1,250 for continuing education of a Beta Phi Mu member. Beta Phi Mu, www.beta-phi-mu.org.

Beta Phi Mu Harold Lancour Scholarship. Award of $1,500 for graduate study in a foreign country related to the applicant's work or schooling. Beta Phi Mu, www.beta-phi-mu.org.

Beta Phi Mu Sarah Rebecca Reed Scholarship. Award of $2,000 for study at an ALA-accredited library school. Beta Phi Mu, www.beta-phi-mu.org.

CALA Huang Tso-ping and Wu Yao-yu Scholarship. A $200 award for students of Chinese heritage in an ALA-accredited program in library and information science. Chinese American Librarians Association, www.cala-web.org.

CALA Scholarship. A $1,000 award for students of Chinese heritage in an ALA-accredited program in library and information science. Chinese American Librarians Association, www.cala-web.org.

CALA Sheila Suen Lai Scholarship. An award of $500 for students of Chinese heritage in an ALA-accredited program in library and information science. Chinese American Librarians Association, www.cala-web.org.

CLA Dafoe Scholarship. An award of $5,000 (Can.) for a Canadian citizen or landed immigrant to attend an accredited Canadian library school. Canadian Library Association, www.cla.ca.

CLA H. W. Wilson Scholarship. An award of $2,000 (Can.) for a Canadian citizen or landed immigrant to pursue studies at an accredited Canadian library school. Canadian Library Association, www.cla.ca.

CLA World Book Graduate Scholarship in Library and Information Science. An award of $2,500 (Can.) for a Canadian citizen or landed immigrant to pursue doctoral studies at an accredited Canadian library school. Canadian Library Association, www.cla.ca.

CLA Rev. Andrew L. Bouwhuis Scholarship. A $1,500 scholarship for graduate study towards a master's degree in library science. Catholic Library Association, www.cathla.org.

CLA World Book Award. A $1,500 grant for up to three CLA members to attend continuing education in school or children's librarianship. Catholic Library Association, www.cathla.org.

CLIR A. R. Zipf Fellowship. A cash award to a student in the early stages of graduate school who shows exceptional promise for leadership and technical achievement in information management. Council on Library and Information Resources, www. clir.org.

CLIR Postdoctoral Fellowship in Scholarly Information Resources. Awarded to recent PhDs who believe there are opportunities to develop meaningful linkages among disciplinary scholarship, libraries, archives, and evolving digital tools. Council on Library and Information Resources, www.clir.org.

CNI Paul Evan Peters Fellowship. An award of $2,500 for two consecutive years to assist students pursuing graduate studies in information sciences or librarianship who demonstrate commitment to the use of networked information and advanced technology to enhance scholarship, intellectual productivity and public life; support of democratic values; humor and imagination. Awarded every two years. Coalition for Networked Information, www.cni.org.

MLA Continuing Education Awards. Grants of $100–$500 to develop MLA members' knowledge of the theoretical, administrative, or technical aspects of librarianship. Medical Library Association, www.mlanet.org.

MLA Scholarship. A scholarship of up to $5,000 for a student who is entering an ALA-accredited library school. Medical Library Association, www.mlanet.org.

MLA Scholarship for Minority Students. A scholarship of up to $5,000 for a minority student who is entering an ALA-accredited library school. Medical Library Association, www.mlanet.org.

MLA Thomson Scientific Doctoral Fellowship. A fellowship given every two years in the amount of $2,000 to encourage students to conduct doctoral work in an area of health sciences librarianship. Medical Library Association, www.mlanet.org.

NASIG Fritz Schwartz Serials Education Scholarship. A $2,500 scholarship to a library science graduate student who demonstrates excellence in scholarship and the potential for accomplishment in a serials career. North American Serials Interest Group, www.nasig.org.

Reforma Scholarships. Grants of $1,500 to Hispanic or Latino/a students attending an ALA-accredited library school. Reforma, www.reforma.org.

SLA Affirmative Action Scholarship. One $6,000 grant to a minority student for graduate study in librarianship leading to a master's degree at a recognized school of library or information science. Special Libraries Association, www.sla.org.

SLA ISI Scholarship. A $1,000 grant for beginning graduate study leading to a PhD from a recognized program in library science, information science, or related fields of study. Special Libraries Association, www.sla.org.

SLA Mary Adeline Connor Professional Development Scholarship. One or more scholarships, not to exceed $6,000 in total, granted for post-MLS certificate or degree programs in any subject area, technological skill, or managerial expertise relevant to special librarianship. Special Libraries Association, www.sla.org.

SLA Plenum Scholarship. A $1,000 grant for beginning graduate study leading to a Ph.D. from a recognized program in library science, information science, or related fields of study. Special Libraries Association, www.sla.org.

SLA Scholarships. Up to three $6,000 grants for graduate study in librarianship leading to a master's degree at a recognized school of library or information science. Special Libraries Association, www.sla.org.

ULC Joey Rodger Fund for Library Leadership. A grant of up to $5,000 will be awarded annually to provide financial assistance to a library leader for participation in a leadership development opportunity. Urban Libraries Council, www. urbanlibraries.org.

For programs

AIIP Roger Summit Award. Sponsors an industry leader to attend and speak at the annual AIIP Conference. Association of Independent Information Professionals, www.aiip.org.

ALA H. W. Wilson Library Staff Development Grant. $3,500 and a 24k gold-framed citation to a library organization for a program to further its staff development goals. ALA Awards, www.ala.org.

ALA World Book–ALA Goal Award. An award of $10,000 to ALA units for the advancement of public, academic, or school library service and librarianship through support of programs that implement the goals and priorities of ALA. ALA Awards, www.ala.org.

ALA/AASL ABC-CLIO Leadership Grant. Up to $1,750 for planning and implementing leadership programs at the state, regional, or local level to be given to school library associations that are affiliates of AASL. ALA American Association of School Librarians, www.ala.org/aasl/.

ALA/ALSC BWI Summer Reading Program Grant. A grant of $3,000 to an ALSC member to implement an outstanding public library summer reading program for children. ALA Association for Library Service to Children, www.ala.org/alsc/.

ALA/ALSC Maureen Hayes Author/Illustrator Visit Award. A $4,000 honorarium to pay for a visit from a nationally known author or illustrator who will speak to children who have not had the opportunity to hear an author or illustrator. ALA Association for Library Service to Children, www.ala.org/alsc/.

ALA/ALSC May Hill Arbuthnot Honor Lecture Award. An invitation to an individual of distinction to prepare and present a paper that will be a significant contribution to the field of children's literature and subsequently published in *Children and Libraries*. ALA Association for Library Service to Children, www.ala.org/alsc/.

ALA/LAMA Cultural Diversity Grant. Up to $1,000 to support the creation and dissemination of resources that will assist library administrators in developing a vision and commitment to diversity. ALA Library Administration and Management Association, www.ala.org/lama/.

ALA/ORS Loleta D. Fyan Public Library Research Grant. One or more grants up to $10,000 to a library, library school, association, unit or chapter of ALA, or an individual for the development and improvement of public libraries and the services they provide. ALA Office of Research and Statistics, www.ala.org/ors/.

ALA/PIO Scholastic Library Publishing National Library Week Grant. A $5,000 grant awarded to a library or library association for the best proposal for a public awareness campaign that supports the theme of National Library Week. ALA Public Information Office, www.ala.org/pio/.

ALA/PLA Baker & Taylor Entertainment Audio Music/Video Product Award. Designed to provide a public library the opportunity to build or expand a collection of either or both formats in whatever proportion the library chooses, the grant consists of $2,500 worth of audio music or video products. ALA Public Library Association, www.ala.org/pla/.

ALA/YALSA BWI Collection Development Grant. Up to two $1,000 grants for collection development materials to YALSA members who represent a public library and work directly with young adults. ALA Young Adult Library Services Association, www.ala.org/yalsa/.

ALA/YALSA Frances Henne Voice of Youth Advocates Research Grant. An annual grant of $500 to provide seed money to an individual, institution, or group for small-scale projects to encourage research on library service to young adults. ALA Young Adult Library Services Association, www.ala.org/yalsa/.

AMHL Small Grants Program. Enhances opportunities for members of AMHL to engage in research, scholarship, and creative endeavors. Association of Mental Health Librarians, www.fmhi.usf.edu/amhl/statement.html.

Amigos Fellowship Program. Grants of up to $7,500 to library and information professionals in Amigos member libraries to fund individuals' development projects. Amigos Library Services, www.amigos.org.

Beta Phi Mu Mary Jo Lynch Distinguished Lecture Award. An annual $2,000 award to an innovative and research-oriented faculty member, library/information center practitioner, or a member of the information industry to present either a lecture on original research completed or in process, or lecture/assess the state-of-the-art or future of LIS research. Beta Phi Mu, www.beta-phi-mu.org.

IAMSLIC Grants. Supports projects related to the recording, retrieval, and dissemination of information in aquatic and marine science through small grants ($200–$2,000) to IAMSLIC regional groups and members. International Association of Aquatic and Marine Science Libraries and Information Centers, www.iamslic.org.

IMLS Librarians for the 21st Century Grants. Grants to libraries or institutions of higher education in amounts from $50,000 to $1 million for library programs that support efforts to recruit and educate the next generation of librarians and the faculty who will prepare them for careers in library science. Institute of Museum and Library Services, www.imls.gov.

IMLS National Leadership Grants. Grants to libraries in amounts from $50,000 to $1 million for library programs that will help all individuals attain the knowledge, skills, attitudes, behaviors, and resources that enhance their engagement in community, work, family, and society. Programs must be in one of three categories: advancing learning communities, building digital resources, or research and demonstration. Institute of Museum and Library Services, www.imls.gov.

IMLS Native American Library Services Basic Grants. Annual grants to Indian tribes and Native Alaskan villages to support existing library operations and to maintain core library services. Institute of Museum and Library Services, www.imls.gov.

IMLS Native American Library Services Enhancement Grants. Annual grants to Indian tribes and Native Alaskan villages to enhance existing library services or begin new library services. Institute of Museum and Library Services, www.imls.gov.

IMLS Native Hawaiian Library Services Grants. Annual grants to nonprofit organizations primarily serving Native Hawaiians to expand and improve library services. Institute of Museum and Library Services, www.imls.gov.

IMLS Partnership for a Nation of Learners Community Collaboration Grants. Grants to libraries in amounts from $25,000 to $250,000 for programs that build and strengthen working relationships among libraries, museums, and public broadcasting licensees to enhance their roles within their communities. Institute of Museum and Library Services, www.imls.gov.

MLA Janet Doe Lectureship. Awarded for a unique perspective on the history or philosophy of medical librarianship. The selected lecture is presented at the MLA annual meeting and published in the *Journal of the Medical Library Association.* Medical Library Association, www.mlanet.org.

MLA John P. McGovern Award Lectureship. For a significant national or international figure to speak on a topic of importance to health science librarianship at the MLA annual meeting. Medical Library Association, www.mlanet.org.

MLA Joseph Leiter NLM Lectureship. For a lecture on biomedical communications. Medical Library Association, www.mlanet.org.

For publications, research, and travel

AALL Grants. To cover registration costs at association-sponsored educational activities. American Association of Law Libraries, www.aallnet.org/committee/grants/grants.asp.

AALL Minority Leadership Development Award. Given to an AALL member who is a member of a minority group for travel and registration expenses to the annual meeting and for an experienced AALL leader to serve as the recipient's mentor. American Association of Law Libraries, www.aallnet.org.

AECT Dean and Sybil McClusky Research Award. A cash award of $500 for the most outstanding doctoral research proposal in educational technology. Association for Educational Communications and Technology, www.aect.org.

AIIP Myra T. Grenier Award. This award offers a complimentary conference registration and up to a $500 stipend to enable new or aspiring independent information professionals to attend the AIIP Annual Conference. Association of Independent Information Professionals, www.aiip.org.

AIIP Sue Rugge Memorial Award. A complimentary conference registration and $300 cash stipend awarded to a full member of AIIP who has significantly helped another member through formal or informal mentoring. Association of Independent Information Professionals, www.aiip.org.

AJL Convention Travel Grant. To subsidize the cost of attending the AJL conference. Association of Jewish Libraries, www.jewishlibraries.org.

AJL Doris Orenstein Memorial Convention Travel Grant. Awards to international members who are planning to attend the AJL conference. Association of Jewish Libraries, www.jewishlibraries.org.

AJL Lucius Littauer Foundation Travel Grant. Awards to new members who are planning to attend their first AJL conference. Association of Jewish Libraries, www.jewishlibraries.org.

ALA Carnegie-Whitney Awards. Annual grants of up to $5,000 to individuals, official ALA units, and other groups affiliated with ALA for the preparation and publication of popular or scholarly reading lists, indexes, and other guides to library resources that will be useful to users of all types of libraries. ALA Publishing, www.ala.org/publishing/.

ALA EBSCO Conference Sponsorship. Ten awards of up to $1,000 allowing librarians to attend the ALA Annual Conference. An essay of no more than 250 words addressing, "How will attending this ALA Conference contribute to your professional development?" is required. ALA Awards, www.ala.org.

ALA/AASL Frances Henne Award. A grant of $1,250 to a school library media specialist, with less than five years in the profession, to attend an AASL national conference or ALA Annual Conference for the first time. ALA American Association of School Librarians, www.ala.org/aasl/.

ALA/AASL Highsmith Research Grant. Two grants totaling $5,000 to conduct innovative research aimed at measuring and evaluating the impact of school library media programs on learning and education. ALA American Association of School Librarians, www.ala.org/aasl/.

ALA/ACRL Coutts Nijhoff International West European Specialist Study Grant. An annual grant for an ALA member to study some aspect of Western European studies, librarianship, or the book trade. The grant covers air travel to and from Europe, transportation in Europe, and lodging and board for no more than 14 consecutive days. A maximum amount of 4,500 euros is awarded. ALA Association of College and Research Libraries, www.ala.org/acrl/.

ALA/ACRL Doctoral Dissertation Fellowship. An annual award of $1,500 presented to assist a doctoral student in academic librarianship for dissertation research. ALA Association of College and Research Libraries, www.ala.org/acrl/.

ALA/ACRL Haworth Press Distance Learning Librarian Conference Sponsorship Award. An award of $1,200 to a librarian working in the field of distance learning librarianship to defray the costs of attending an ALA conference. ALA Association of College and Research Libraries, www.ala.org/acrl/.

ALA/ACRL Samuel Lazerow Fellowship for Research in Acquisitions or Technical Services. An annual award of $1,000 to foster advances in collections or technical services by providing librarians a fellowship for travel or writing in those fields. ALA Association of College and Research Libraries, www.ala.org/acrl/.

ALA/ALCTS First Step Award/Wiley Professional Development Grant. A $1,500 award to allow librarians new to the serials field to attend an ALA Annual Conference for the first time. ALA Association for Library Collections and Technical Services, www.ala.org/alcts/.

ALA/ALSC Louise Seaman Bechtel Fellowship. Grant of $4,000 for ALSC members with eight or more years professional service to children to read and study at the Baldwin Library/George Smathers Libraries, University of Florida. ALA Association for Library Service to Children, www.ala.org/alsc/.

ALA/ALSC Penguin Young Readers Group Awards. Four $600 awards to children's librarians in school or public libraries with 10 or fewer years of experience to attend the ALA Annual Conference. ALA Association for Library Service to Children, www.ala.org/alsc/.

ALA/ALTA Gale Outstanding Trustee Conference Grant. Two awards of $750 each, to ALTA members currently serving on a local public library board, for first attendance at the ALA Annual Conference. ALA Association for Library Trustees and Advocates, www.ala.org/alta/.

ALA/FAFLRT Adelaide del Frate Conference Sponsorship. Award of $1,000 for attendance at the ALA Annual Conference, to encourage library school students to become familiar with federal librarianship and seek work in federal libraries. ALA Federal and Armed Forces Libraries Round Table, www.ala.org/faflrt/.

ALA/GODORT NewsBank/Readex Catharine J. Reynolds Research Grant. A grant of $2,000 to documents librarians for study in the field of documents librarianship. ALA Government Documents Round Table, sunsite.berkeley.edu/GODORT/.

ALA/IRO Bogle Pratt International Library Travel Fund. A $1,000 award to assist ALA members to attend their first international library conference. ALA International Relations Office, www.ala.org/iro/.

ALA/LAMA Diana V. Braddom FRFDS Scholarship. An annual grant of $1,000 to two individuals who have no previous formal financial development training and have a genuine need for fund-raising skills. The funds go toward attending the Fundraising and Financial Development programs at the ALA Annual Conference. ALA Library Administration and Management Association, www.ala.org/lama/.

ALA/LAMA YBP Student Writing and Development Award. A travel grant of up to $1,000 to attend the ALA Annual Conference to honor the best article on a topic in the area of library administration and management written by a student enrolled in a library and information studies graduate program. ALA Library Administration and Management Association, www.ala.org/lama/.

ALA/LRRT Ingenta Research Award. A grant of up to $6,000 to support research projects about acquisition, use, and preservation of digital information, and up to $1,000 for travel to a national or international conference to present the results of the research. ALA Library Research Round Table, www.ala.org/lrrt/.

ALA/LRRT Jesse H. Shera Award for the Support of Dissertation Research. A prize of $500 for exemplary library dissertation research designs that have been approved by the doctoral candidate's dissertation committee and that are about to be employed or are in the initial stage of use. ALA Library Research Round Table, www.ala.org/lrrt/.

ALA/NMRT Shirley Olofson Memorial Award. A $1,000 award to an NMRT member to help defray costs of attending the ALA Annual Conference. ALA New Members Round Table, www.ala.org/nmrt/.

ALA/NMRT 3M Professional Development Grant. A cash award to attend the ALA Conference for NMRT members to encourage professional development and participation in national ALA and NMRT activities. ALA New Members Round Table, www.ala.org/nmrt/.

ALA/OFD Diversity Research Grants. Three annual awards of $2,000 for original research in three selected topics on diversity issues within the library profession and a $500 travel grant to attend and present research results at the ALA Annual Conference. ALA Office for Diversity, www.ala.org/diversity/.

ALA/ORS Carroll Preston Baber Research Grant. Up to $3,000 for innovative research that could lead to an improvement in library services to any specified group(s) of people. ALA Office for Research and Statistics, www.ala.org/ors/.

ALA/PLA Demco New Leaders Travel Grant. Awards of up to $1,500 each, designed to enhance professional development and improve the expertise of public librarians new to the field by making possible their attendance at major professional development activities. ALA Public Library Association, www.ala.org/pla/.

ALA/RUSA Thomson Financial Student Travel Award. An annual travel award of $1,000 that will enable a student enrolled in an ALA-accredited master's degree program to attend an ALA conference, including a one-year membership in the Business Reference and Services Section. ALA Reference and User Services Association, www.ala.org/rusa/.

ALA/YALSA Baker & Taylor Conference Grants. Two annual grants of $1,000 each awarded to young adult librarians in public or school libraries to attend the ALA Annual Conference for the first time. ALA Young Adult Library Services Association, www.ala.org/yalsa/.

ALISE Doctoral Students to ALISE Awards. Up to two awards in the amount of $400 to defray travel expenses and conference registration. Association for Library and Information Science Education, www.alise.org.

ALISE OCLC Library and Information Science Research Grant Program. Awards of up to $15,000 to faculty of library and information science schools for independent research that helps librarians integrate new technologies into areas of traditional competence. Association for Library and Information Science Education, www.alise.org.

ALISE Research Grant Awards. One or more grants totaling $5,000 to support research broadly related to education for library and information science. Association for Library and Information Science Education, www.alise.org.

ARLIS/NA Andrew Cahan Photography Award. An award of $1,000 for information professionals in the field of photography to attend the ARLIS/NA conference. Art Libraries Society of North America, www.arlisna.org.

ARLIS/NA Conference Attendance Award. An award of $500 for committee members, chapter officers, and moderators to attend the ARLIS/NA conference. Art Libraries Society of North America, www.arlisna.org.

ARLIS/NA Getty Latin American Travel Award. An award of up to $2,675 for art librarians in Latin America to attend the ARLIS/NA conference. Art Libraries Society of North America, www.arlisna.org.

ARLIS/NA H. W. Wilson Foundation Research Grants. Awards of up to $2,000 in support research activities by ARLIS/NA individual members in the fields of librarianship, visual resources curatorship, and the arts. Art Libraries Society of North America, www.arlisna.org.

ARLIS/NA Howard and Beverly Joy Karno Award. An award of $1,000 for art librarians in Latin America to attend the ARLIS/NA conference. Art Libraries Society of North America, www.arlisna.org.

ARLIS/NA Puvill Libros European Travel Award. An award of $1,000 for art librarians in Europe to attend the ARLIS/NA conference. Art Libraries Society of North America, www.arlisna.org.

ARLIS/NA Research Libraries Group Asia/Oceania Award. An award of $2,000 to help finance attendance at the ARLIS/NA conference for someone in Asia or Oceania who has never attended. Art Libraries Society of North America, www.arlisna.org.

ARLIS/NA Student Travel Award. An award of $500 to help finance attendance at the ARLIS/NA conference for a library school student who has never attended. Art Libraries Society of North America, www.arlisna.org.

ASIS&T ProQuest Doctoral Dissertation Award. An award of $1,000 and up to $500 in travel support to recognize outstanding recent doctoral candidates, provide a forum for presenting their research, and assist them with some travel support. American Society for Information Science and Technology, www.asis.org.

ASIS&T Thomson ISI Citation Analysis Research Grant. An award of $3,000 to support research based on citation analysis. American Society for Information Science and Technology, www.asis.org.

ATLA Bibliography Grant. A grant of up to $1,500 to one or more bibliographers or indexers to aid in the development of a work that provides access to a significant body of literature within the fields of theological or religious studies. American Theological Library Association, www.atla.com.

BSA Fellowships. A stipend of up to $2,000 per month (for up to two months) in support of travel, living, and research expenses to support bibliographical inquiry as well as research in the history of the book trades and in publishing history. Bibliographical Society of America, www.bibsocamer.org.

CALA C. C. Seetoo Travel Scholarship. A $500 award for students of Chinese heritage in a graduate program in library and information science to provide mentoring and networking opportunities at the ALA Annual Conference. Chinese American Librarians Association, www.cala-web.org.

CALA Sally C. Tseng Professional Development Grant. Annual grants of up to $1,000 to CALA members in support of library research. Chinese American Librarians Association, www.cala-web.org.

CHLA Donald Hawryliuk Rural and Remote Opportunities Grant. A cash grant to support continuing education activities for members in rural or remote communities. Canadian Health Libraries Association, www.chla-absc.ca.

CLA Research and Development Grants. One or more grants totaling $1,000 (Can.) awarded annually to personal members of the Canadian Library Association, in support of theoretical and applied research in library and information science. Canadian Library Association, www.cla.ca.

CLIR Mellon Fellowships for Dissertation Research in Original Sources. Ten fellowships of $1,600 per month for 8–12 months to support dissertation research in the humanities in original sources. Council on Library and Information Resources, www.clir.org.

CLIR Rovelstad Scholarship in International Librarianship. Provides all expenses for a student of library and information science to attend the annual IFLA meeting. Council on Library and Information Resources, www.clir.org.

CSLA Pat Tabler Memorial Scholarship Award. Recognizes and pays conference expenses for a beginning librarian who has shown initiative and creativity in starting or renewing a congregational library. Church and Synagogue Library Association, worldaccessnet.com/~csla/.

Educause Jane N. Ryland Fellowship Program. Grants established to expand opportunities for information technology professionals to attend Educause events. Educause, www.educause.edu.

IASL Jean E. Lowrie Leadership Development Grant. $1,000 and conference fees for school librarians in developing nations to attend an IASL conference. International Association of School Librarianship, www.iasl-slo.org.

IASL Ken Haycock Leadership Development Grant. $1,000 and conference fees for school librarians in developing nations to attend an IASL conference. International Association of School Librarianship, www.iasl-slo.org.

IASL Takeshi Murofushi Research Award. A $500 grant to fund research in school librarianship. International Association of School Librarianship, www.iasl-slo.org.

MELA George Atiyeh Prize. An annual cash award to attend the annual meetings of MELA and the Middle East Studies Association of North America. Middle East Librarians Association, www.mela.us.

MLA Cunningham Memorial International Fellowship. A four-month fellowship for health sciences librarians from countries outside the United States and Canada to provide for observation and supervised work in one or more medical libraries in North America. The award is $6,000, with up to $2,000 additional for travel within these two countries. Medical Library Association, www.mlanet.org.

MLA David A. Kronick Traveling Fellowship. A $2,000 fellowship to cover the expenses involved in traveling to three or more medical libraries in the United States or Canada, for the purpose of studying a specific aspect of health information management. Medical Library Association, www.mlanet.org.

MLA Donald A. B. Lindberg Research Fellowship. An annual grant of $25,000 to fund research linking the information services provided by librarians to improved health care and advances in biomedical research. Medical Library Association, www.mlanet.org.

MLA EBSCO Annual Meeting Grant. Awards of up to $1,000 for travel and conference-related expenses to four health science librarians to attend the MLA meeting. Medical Library Association, www.mlanet.org.

MLA Research, Development, and Demonstration Projects Grants. These provide support for projects that will help to promote excellence in the field of health sciences librarianship and information sciences. Grants range from $100 to $1,000. Medical Library Association, www.mlanet.org.

MLA/HLS Professional Development Grants. Given twice a year, this award provides librarians working in hospital and similar clinical settings with the support needed for educational or research activities. Medical Library Association, www.mlanet.org.

MLA/MIS Career Development Grant. This award provides up to two individuals $1,500 to support a career development activity that will contribute to advancement in the field of medical informatics. Medical Library Association, www. mlanet.org.

MLA Dena Epstein Award. Awarded to support research in archives or libraries internationally on any aspect of American music. Music Library Association, www.musiclibraryassoc.org.

MLA Kevin Freeman Travel Grant. Conference registration fee and a cash award of up to $750 to support travel and hotel expenses to attend the MLA annual meeting. Music Library Association, www.musiclibraryassoc.org.

MLA Walter Gerboth Award. An award to MLA-member music librarians in the first five years of their professional careers, to assist research in progress. Music Library Association, www.musiclibraryassoc.org.

NASIG Horizon Award. Provides funding to attend NASIG annual conference for a practicing serials librarian. North American Serials Interest Group, www.nasig.org.

NASIG Marcia Tuttle International Grant. Provides funding for a NASIG member working in serials to foster international communication and education, through overseas activities such as research, collaborative projects, job exchanges, and presentation of papers at conferences. North American Serials Interest Group, www.nasig.org.

NASIG Student Grants. Encourage participation at NASIG conferences by funding students enrolled in an ALA-accredited school who are interested in pursuing some aspect of serials work upon completion of their professional degrees. North American Serials Interest Group, www.nasig.org.

NCIS Research Grants. Cash awards to independent scholars for research. National Coalition for Independent Scholars, www.ncis.org.

SAA Colonial Dames of America Scholarships. Three awards up to $1,200 for tuition, travel, and housing expenses at two annual Modern Archives Institutes for newcomers to the archival profession, who work in repositories with holdings in the period predating 1825. Society of American Archivists, www.archivists.org.

SAA Harold T. Pinkett Minority Student Award. Supports full registration and related expenses of hotel and travel to attend the SAA annual meeting. Awarded to a minority student who manifests an interest in becoming a professional archivist. Society of American Archivists, www.archivists.org.

SAA Oliver Wendell Holmes Award. Assists overseas archivists already in the United States or Canada for training, to travel to or attend the SAA annual meeting. Society of American Archivists, www.archivists.org.

SALALM Enlace Award. Assists Latin American or Caribbean librarians with travel to the SALALM conference. Seminar on the Acquisition of Latin American Library Materials, www.library.cornell.edu/colldev/salalmhome.html.

SALALM Presidential Travel Fellowships. Provides up to $1,000 for Latin American studies librarians for travel to the SALALM conference. Seminar on the Acquisition of Latin American Library Materials, www.library.cornell.edu/colldev/salalmhome.html.

SLA Diversity Leadership Development Program Award. A $1,000 stipend to assist in travel to the SLA Annual Conference awarded to active members of the Association from groups traditionally underrepresented in SLA who have the potential for leadership responsibilities. Special Libraries Association, www.sla.org.

SLA Steven I. Goldspiel Memorial Research Fund. Supports projects that promote research in library sciences, especially those focusing on SLA goals. Special Libraries Association, www.sla.org.

Awards

To individuals or groups for achievement and service

AALL Marian Gould Gallagher Distinguished Service Award. Recognizes sustained service to law librarianship, exemplary service to AALL, or contributions to the professional literature. American Association of Law Libraries, www.aallnet.org.

AALL Presidential Certificate of Merit. Awarded annually at the discretion of the AALL President in recognition of exceptional achievements and contributions to the profession and AALL. American Association of Law Libraries, www.aallnet.org.

AALL/ALL Frederick Charles Hicks Award. This award recognizes an individual or group who has made outstanding contributions to academic law librarianship through continued efforts to improve law librarianship. American Association of Law Libraries, Academic Law Libraries Special Interest Section, www.aallnet.org.

AALL/SCCLL Bethany J. Ochal Award. Given to a member who has made a significant contribution to law librarianship and who is nearing the end of his or her library career or who has recently retired. American Association of Law Libraries, State, Court, and County Law Libraries Special Interest Section, www.aallnet.org.

AALL/TS Renee D. Chapman Memorial Award. This award recognizes extended and sustained distinguished service to technical services law librarianship and to AALL. American Association of Law Libraries, Technical Services Special Interest Section, www.aallnet.org.

AASLH Award of Distinction. Given in recognition of long and distinguished service in the field of state, provincial, and local history to those who are recognized nationally as leaders in the profession. American Association for State and Local History, www.aaslh.org.

ACL Emily Russel Award. A certificate and plaque given to honor outstanding contributions to Christian librarianship. Association of Christian Librarians, www.acl.org.

ACMLA Honours Award. Recognizes distinguished service to the association. Association of Canadian Map Libraries and Archives, www.ssc.uwo.ca/assoc/acml/acmla.html.

AECT Distinguished Service Award. Granted to a person who has shown outstanding leadership in advancing the theory and/or practice of educational communications and technology for over 10 years. Association for Educational Communications and Technology, www.aect.org.

AECT Robert deKieffer International Fellowship Award. A cash award of $200 presented to an individual in recognition of professional leadership in the field of educational communications and technology in a foreign country. Association for Educational Communications and Technology, www.aect.org.

AECT Special Service Award. Presented to an individual who has shown notable service to AECT over the past 10 years. Association for Educational Communications and Technology, www.aect.org.

AIIP President's Award. Given in recognition of any person or institution that has demonstrated extraordinary support of the objectives of the association. Association of Independent Information Professionals, www.aiip.org.

AJL Fanny Goldstein Merit Award. Recognizes loyal and ongoing contributions to AJL and the profession of Jewish librarianship. Association of Jewish Libraries, www.jewishlibraries.org/ajlweb/home.htm.

AJL Life Membership Achievement Award. Recognizes outstanding leadership and professional contributions to AJL and the profession of Jewish librarianship. Association of Jewish Libraries, www.jewishlibraries.org/ajlweb/home.htm.

ALA Beta Phi Mu Award. A $500 award presented to a library school faculty member or an individual for distinguished service to education for librarianship. ALA Awards, www.ala.org.

ALA Elizabeth Futas Catalyst for Change Award. A citation and $1,000 award to honor a librarian who invests time and talent to make positive change in the profession of librarianship. ALA Awards, www.ala.org.

ALA Honorary Membership. Conferred on a living citizen of any country whose contribution to librarianship or a closely related field is so outstanding that it is of lasting importance to the advancement of the whole field of library service. ALA Awards, www.ala.org.

ALA Hugh C. Atkinson Memorial Award. An annual $2,000 award to recognize outstanding achievement (including risk-taking) by academic librarians that has contributed significantly to improvements in library automation, management, and/or development and research. Jointly administered by ALA's ACRL, LAMA, LITA, and ALCTS divisions. ALA Association of College and Research Libraries, www.ala.org/acrl/.

ALA Joseph W. Lippincott Award. A $1,000 award to a librarian for distinguished service to the profession, to include outstanding participation in professional library activities, notable published professional writing, or other significant activities on behalf of the profession. ALA Awards, www.ala.org.

ALA Ken Haycock Award for Promoting Librarianship. A citation and a $1,000 award to honor an individual for contributing significantly to the public recognition and appreciation of librarianship through professional performance, teaching, and/or writing. ALA Awards, www.ala.org.

ALA Melvil Dewey Medal. A citation presented to an individual or a group for recent creative professional achievement of a high order, particularly in those fields in which Melvil Dewey was interested, notably library management, library training, cataloging and classification, and the tools and techniques of librarianship. ALA Awards, www.ala.org.

ALA Paul Howard Award for Courage. $1,000 awarded every two years to a librarian, library board, library group, or an individual who has exhibited unusual courage for the benefit of library programs or services. ALA Awards, www.ala.org.

ALA/ACRL Academic or Research Librarian of the Year Award. A $3,000 award for outstanding contribution to academic and research librarianship and library development. ALA Association of College and Research Libraries, www.ala.org/acrl/.

ALA/ACRL Award for Career Achievement in Women's Studies Librarianship. A $1,000 award for significant career-long achievements and contributions in women's studies librarianship. ALA Association of College and Research Libraries, www.ala.org/acrl/.

ALA/ACRL Award for Significant Achievement in Women's Studies Librarianship. A $1,000 award for a significant one-time achievement or contribution in women's studies librarianship. ALA Association of College and Research Libraries, www.ala.org/acrl/.

ALA/ACRL Distinguished Education and Behavioral Sciences Librarian Award. This $1,000 award honors a distinguished academic librarian who has made an outstanding contribution as an education and/or behavioral sciences librarian. ALA Association of College and Research Libraries, www.ala.org/acrl/.

ALA/ACRL EBSCO Community College Learning Resources and Library Achievement Awards. Two awards of $500 to individuals, groups, or institutions to recognize significant achievement in the areas of programs and leadership. ALA Association of College and Research Libraries, www.ala.org/acrl/.

ALA/ACRL Innovation Award. This annual $3,000 award recognizes a project that demonstrates creative, innovative, or unique approaches to information literacy instruction or programming. ALA Association of College and Research Libraries, www.ala.org/acrl/.

ALA/ACRL Marta Lange/CQ Press Award. This $1,000 award recognizes an academic or law librarian for contributions to bibliography and information service in law or political science. ALA Association of College and Research Libraries, www.ala.org/acrl/.

ALA/ACRL Miriam Dudley Instruction Librarian Award. A cash award to an individual librarian who has made an especially significant contribution to the advancement of instruction in a college or research library environment. ALA Association of College and Research Libraries, www.ala.org/acrl/.

ALA/ALCTS Bowker/Ulrich's Serials Librarianship Award. An annual $1,500 award for distinguished contributions to serials librarianship, including leadership in serials-related activities through participation in professional associations or library education programs, contributions to serials literature, research in the area of serials, or development of tools to enhance serials access or management. ALA Association for Library Collections and Technical Services, www.ala.org/alcts/.

ALA/ALCTS Esther J. Piercy Award. An annual $1,500 award to recognize contributions by a librarian in technical services with not more than 10 years professional experience. ALA Association for Library Collections and Technical Services, www.ala.org/alcts/.

ALA/ALCTS Leadership in Library Acquisitions Award. This award of $1,500 is given to recognize the contributions by and outstanding leadership of an individual in the field of acquisitions librarianship. ALA Association for Library Collections and Technical Services, www.ala.org/alcts/.

ALA/ALCTS Margaret Mann Citation. An annual citation for outstanding professional achievement in cataloging or classification through publication, participation, or contributions over the past five years. OCLC will donate a $2,000 scholarship to the U.S. or Canadian library school of the winner's choice. ALA Association for Library Collections and Technical Services, www.ala.org/alcts/.

ALA/ALCTS Paul Banks and Carolyn Harris Preservation Award. A $1,500 award to recognize the contribution of a professional preservation specialist who has been active in the field of preservation or conservation for library or archival materials. ALA Association for Library Collections and Technical Services, www.ala.org/alcts/.

ALA/ALTA Major Benefactors Honor Award. Citation to individuals, families, or corporate bodies who have made major benefactions to public libraries. ALA Association for Library Trustees and Advocates, www.ala.org/alta/.

ALA/ALTA Trustee Citations. A citation presented to each of two outstanding public library trustees for distinguished service to library development on the local, state, regional, or national level. ALA Association for Library Trustees and Advocates, www.ala.org/alta/.

ALA/ASCLA Leadership Achievement Award. A citation for leadership in consulting, multitype library cooperation, and state library development. ALA Association of Specialized and Cooperative Library Agencies, www.ala.org/ascla/.

ALA/ASCLA Professional Achievement Award. A citation presented to one or more ASCLA members for professional achievement in the areas of consulting, networking, statewide services, and programs. ALA Association of Specialized and Cooperative Library Agencies, www.ala.org/ascla/.

ALA/ASCLA Service Award. A citation presented to recognize an ASCLA member for outstanding service and leadership to the division. ALA Association of Specialized and Cooperative Library Agencies, www.ala.org/ascla/.

ALA/FAFLRT Achievement Award. Recognizes achievement in the promotion of library and information service in the federal community. ALA Federal and Armed Forces Library Round Table, www.ala.org/faflrt/.

ALA/FAFLRT Distinguished Service Award. Recognizes a FAFLRT member for outstanding and sustained contributions. ALA Federal and Armed Forces Library Round Table, www.ala.org/faflrt/.

ALA/IRO John Ames Humphry/OCLC/Forest Press Award. This $1,000 award is made to a librarian or other person who has made significant contributions to international librarianship. ALA International Relations Office, www.ala.org/iro/.

ALA/LAMA Group Achievement Award. A citation to honor groups or committees that provide outstanding service in support of the division's goals. ALA Library Administration and Management Association, www.ala.org/lama/.

ALA/LAMA Leadership Award. A citation to honor an individual LAMA member for outstanding contributions to the goals of the division. ALA Library Administration and Management Association, www.ala.org/lama/.

ALA/LAMA President's Award. A citation to recognize extraordinary contributions to the goals of LAMA by outside organizations or by individuals who are not LAMA members. ALA Library Administration and Management Association, www.ala.org/lama/.

ALA/MAGERT Honors Award. Cash award and a citation to recognize outstanding contributions by a Map and Geography Round Table personal member to map librarianship, MAGERT, and/or a specific MAGERT project. ALA Map and Geography Round Table, magert.whoi.edu.

ALA/NMRT Student Chapter of the Year Award. Given to an ALA student chapter in recognition of its outstanding contributions. ALA New Members Round Table, www.ala.org/nmrt/.

ALA/OFD Achievement in Diversity Research. Complimentary ALA Annual Conference registration awarded to an ALA member who has made a significant contribution to diversity research in the profession. ALA Office for Diversity, www.ala.org/diversity/.

ALA/PLA Allie Beth Martin Award. An award of $3,000 to a librarian who, in a public library setting, has demonstrated extraordinary range and depth of knowledge about books or other library materials and has distinguished ability to share that knowledge. ALA Public Library Association, www.ala.org/pla/.

ALA/PLA Charlie Robinson Award. A $1,000 award to a library director who, over a period of at least seven years, has been a risk-taker, innovator, and/or change agent in a public library. ALA Public Library Association, www.ala.org/pla/.

ALA/RUSA Dun and Bradstreet Public Librarian Support Award. An award of $1,000 to support the attendance at ALA Annual Conference of a public librarian who has performed outstanding business reference service. ALA Reference and User Services Association, www.ala.org/rusa/.

ALA/RUSA Isadore Gilbert Mudge–R. R. Bowker Award. An annual award of $5,000 and a citation to an individual who has made a distinguished contribution to reference librarianship. ALA Reference and User Services Association, www.ala.org/rusa.

ALA/RUSA Margaret E. Monroe Library Adult Services Award. A citation to honor a librarian who has made significant contributions to library adult services. ALA Reference and User Services Association, www.ala.org/rusa/.

ALA/RUSA MARS Recognition Certificate. Given to an individual in recognition of service to the Machine-Assisted Reference Section. ALA Reference and User Services Association, www.ala.org/rusa/.

ALA/RUSA Thomson Gale Award for Excellence in Business Librarianship. A citation and $3,000 cash award to an individual who has made a significant contribution to business librarianship. ALA Reference and User Services Association, www.ala.org/rusa/.

ALA/RUSA Virginia Boucher–OCLC Distinguished ILL Librarian Award. An award of $2,000 to an individual for outstanding professional achievement and contributions to interlibrary loan and document delivery. ALA Reference and User Services Association, www.ala.org/rusa/.

ALISE Award for Professional Contributions to Library and Information Science Education. For contributions that promote and enhance the status of library/information science education. Association for Library and Information Science Education, www.alise.org.

ALISE Award for Teaching Excellence in the Field of Library and Information Science Education. For regular and sustained excellence in teaching library and information science. Association for Library and Information Science Education, www.alise.org.

ALISE Service Award. Given to an ALISE member for regular and sustained service through the holding of various offices and positions or accomplishing specific responsibilities for the organization. Association for Library and Information Science Education, www.alise.org.

ARSC Award for Distinguished Service to Historical Recordings. This award honors a person who has made outstanding contributions to the field of recorded sound, outside of published works or discographic research. Association for Recorded Sound Collections, www.arsc-audio.org.

ASI Hines Award. Honors those members who have provided exceptional service to ASI. American Society of Indexers, www.asindexing.org.

ASIS&T Award of Merit. A Revere bowl and certificate to recognize an individual for noteworthy contributions to the field of information science. American Society for Information Science and Technology, www.asis.org.

ASIS&T James M. Cretsos Leadership Award. To recognize a new ASIS&T member who has demonstrated outstanding leadership qualities in association activities. American Society for Information Science and Technology, www.asis.org.

ASIS&T Special Award. To recognize a public figure (a government or industry leader) for long-term contributions to the advancement of information science and technology which have resulted in increased public awareness of the field and its benefits to society. American Society for Information Science and Technology, www.asis.org.

ASIS&T Thomson ISI Outstanding Information Science Teacher Award. An award of $1,000 to recognize the unique teaching contribution of an individual as a teacher of information science. American Society for Information Science and Technology, www.asis.org.

ASIS&T Watson Davis Award. To recognize an ASIS&T member who has shown continuous dedicated service to the membership through active participation in and support of the association's programs. American Society for Information Science and Technology, www.asis.org.

BCALA Distinguished Service Award. Given to a BCALA member for outstanding service to the association. Black Caucus of the American Library Association, www.bcala.org.

BCALA Trailblazer's Award. Presented once every five years in recognition of an individual whose pioneering contributions have been outstanding and unique, and whose efforts have "blazed a trail" in the profession. Black Caucus of the American Library Association, www.bcala.org.

CALA Distinguished Service Award. To a CALA member for outstanding service to the profession. Chinese American Librarians Association, www.cala-web.org.

CALA President's Recognition Award. To a CALA member for service to the association. Chinese American Librarians Association, www.cala-web.org.

CBHL Charles Robert Long Award of Extraordinary Merit. Given to a CBHL member for distinguished service and achievement. Council on Botanical and Horticultural Libraries, www.cbhl.net.

CHLA Canadian Hospital Librarian of the Year. Recognizes the contribution of an individual hospital librarian to the advancement of health care and health librarianship in Canada. Canadian Health Libraries Association, www.chla-absc.ca.

CHLA Emerging Leader Award. Acknowledges the contribution of a librarian in the early years of a career in health librarianship in Canada. Canadian Health Libraries Association, www.chla-absc.ca.

CHLA Margaret Ridley Charlton Award for Outstanding Achievement. Honors an individual who has made a significant contribution to the field of health sciences librarianship in Canada. Canadian Health Libraries Association, www.chla-absc.ca.

CLA Outstanding Service to Librarianship Award. An award for distinguished service in the field of Canadian librarianship. Canadian Library Association, www.cla.ca.

CLA/CACUL Outstanding Academic Librarian Award. Presented to an individual member of CACUL who has made an outstanding national or international contribution to academic librarianship and library development. CLA Canadian Association of College and University Libraries, www.cla.ca.

CLA/CACUL Outstanding College Librarian Award. Presented annually to an individual member of CACUL who has made an outstanding national or international contribution to college librarianship and library development. CLA Canadian Association of College and University Libraries, www.cla.ca.

CLA/CAPL Brodart Outstanding Public Library Service Award. For outstanding service in the field of Canadian public librarianship. CLA Canadian Association of Public Libraries, www.cla.ca.

CLA/CASLIS Award for Special Librarianship in Canada. For an outstanding contribution to special librarianship in Canada through publication, research, teaching or any other noteworthy activity of benefit to the profession. CLA Canadian Association of Special Libraries and Information Services, www.cla.ca/caslis/.

CLA/CLTA Merit Award for Distinguished Service as a Library Trustee. Presented annually to a library trustee who has demonstrated outstanding leadership in the advancement of trusteeship and public library service in Canada. CLA Canadian Library Trustees' Association, www.cla.ca.

CLA/PCLSS Aggiornamento Award. For an outstanding contribution to the renewal of parish and community life. Catholic Library Association, Parish and Community Library Services Section, www.cathla.org.

CNI Paul Evan Peters Award. Biannual award that recognizes notable, lasting achievements in the creation and innovative use of information resources and services that advance scholarship and intellectual productivity through communication networks. Coalition for Networked Information, www.cni.org.

COLT Outstanding Support Staff of the Year Award. Presented annually for noteworthy service by a library support staff member. Council on Library/Media Technicians, colt.ucr.edu.

COLT Outstanding Supporter of Support Staff of the Year Award. Presented annually for outstanding service to library support staff. Council on Library/Media Technicians, colt.ucr.edu.

CSLA Award for Outstanding Congregational Librarian. Recognizes a church or synagogue librarian who exhibits distinguished service to his/her congregation and/or community through devotion to the ministry of congregational librarianship. Church and Synagogue Library Association, worldaccessnet.com/~csla/.

CSLA Award for Outstanding Contribution to Congregational Libraries. Given to a person or institution that has provided inspiration, guidance, leadership, or resources to enrich the field of church or synagogue libraries. Church and Synagogue Library Association, worldaccessnet.com/~csla/.

Educause Leadership Awards. Recognizes prominent leaders within the information technology field for broad leadership influence. Educause, www.educause.edu.

FLICC Federal Librarian of the Year. This award recognizes and commends active and innovative leadership and professionalism in the promotion and development of library or information services by a federal librarian or information professional. Federal Library and Information Center Committee, www.loc.gov/flicc/.

FLICC Federal Library Technician of the Year. This award recognizes and commends exceptional technical competency and flexibility under changing work conditions by a federal library technician. Federal Library and Information Center Committee, www.loc.gov/flicc/.

FOLUSA Baker & Taylor Awards. Three $2,000 awards to Friends groups that have completed outstanding projects in the previous year. Friends of Libraries U.S.A., www.folusa.com.

FOLUSA Barbara Kingsolver Award. $10,000 given annually to a Friends group of a small public library for outstanding community and volunteer involvement. Friends of Libraries U.S.A., www.folusa.com.

GIS Distinguished Service Award. Recognizes and honors significant contributions to the geoscience information profession. Geoscience Information Society, www.geoinfo.org.

MLA Distinguished Public Service Award. Presented to honor persons, most often legislators, whose exemplary actions have served to advance the heath, welfare, and intellectual freedom of the public. Medical Library Association, www.mlanet.org.

MLA Estelle Brodman Award for Academic Medical Librarian of the Year. A cash award that recognizes an academic medical librarian at mid-career level who demonstrates significant achievement, the potential for leadership, and continuing excellence. Medical Library Association, www.mlanet.org.

MLA Fellows and Honorary Members. Recognizes MLA members and nonmembers who have made outstanding contributions to the advancement of medical librarianship by conferring a special membership status. Medical Library Association, www.mlanet.org.

MLA Lois Ann Colaianni Award for Excellence and Achievement in Hospital Librarianship. Given to an MLA member who has made significant contributions to the profession through overall distinction or leadership in hospital library administration or service, production of a definitive publication related to hospital librarianship, teaching, research, advocacy, or the development or application of innovative technology to hospital librarianship. Medical Library Association, www.mlanet.org.

MLA Louise Darling Medal. Presented annually to recognize distinguished achievement in collection development in the health sciences. Medical Library Association, www.mlanet.org.

MLA Lucretia W. McClure Excellence in Education Award. Honors outstanding practicing librarians or library educators in the field of health sciences librarianship and informatics who demonstrate skills in teaching, curriculum development, mentoring, research, or leadership in education at local, regional, or national levels. Medical Library Association, www.mlanet.org.

MLA Marcia G. Noyes Award. Recognizes a career that has resulted in lasting, outstanding contributions to health sciences librarianship. Medical Library Association, www.mlanet.org.

MLA President's Award. Given to an MLA member for a notable or important contribution to medical librarianship in the past year. Medical Library Association, www.mlanet.org.

MLA Special Achievement Award. An award recognizing extraordinary service to the profession of music librarianship over a relatively short period of time. Music Library Association, www.musiclibraryassoc.org.

NSN Lifetime Achievement Award. Presented annually to individuals who have dedicated their lives to the art form of storytelling and who have demonstrated meritorious service to the National Storytelling Network, as well as to the community of storytellers at large. National Storytelling Network, storynet.org.

SLA Factiva Leadership Award–21st Century Competencies in Action. A $2,000 award presented annually to an individual SLA member who exemplifies leadership as a special librarian through examples of personal and professional competencies. Special Libraries Association, www.sla.org.

SLA Fellows. Bestowed to individual SLA members in recognition of leadership in the field of special librarianship and for outstanding contributions and expected future service. Special Libraries Association, www.sla.org.

SLA Hall of Fame Award. Granted to an SLA member at or near the end of an active professional career for an extended and sustained period of distinguished service. Special Libraries Association, www.sla.org.

SLA Honorary Member. Nonmember elected by SLA members at the Annual Conference. Special Libraries Association, www.sla.org.

SLA John Cotton Dana Award. Conferred upon individual members in recognition of exceptional service to special librarianship. Special Libraries Association, www.sla.org.

SLA Member Achievement Award. Presented to an individual SLA member for outstanding contributions by raising visibility, public awareness, and appreciation of the profession or the association. Special Libraries Association, www.sla.org.

SLA President's Award. Awarded to an individual SLA members for a notable or important contribution during the past association year. Special Libraries Association, www.sla.org.

SLA Professional Award. Given to an individual or group in recognition of a specific significant contribution to the field of librarianship or information science. Special Libraries Association, www.sla.org.

SLA Rose L. Vormelker Award. Given to an individual SLA member in recognition of exceptional services to the profession of special librarianship in the area of mentoring students and/or practicing professionals in the field. Special Libraries Association, www.sla.org.

TLA Distinguished Librarian Award. Given to individuals who have made extraordinary contributions to theater librarianship. Theatre Library Association, tla.library. unt.edu.

ULC Urban Player Award. A $1,000 honorarium that recognizes individuals in positions of library leadership who have provided substantive community leadership during the past two years. Urban Libraries Council, www.urbanlibraries.org.

To libraries for excellence

AALL West Excellence in Marketing Award. Honors outstanding achievement in public relations activities. American Association of Law Libraries, www.aallnet.org.

AASLH Albert B. Corey Award. Recognizes primarily volunteer-operated historical organizations that best display the qualities of vigor, scholarship, and imagination in their work. American Association for State and Local History, www.aaslh.org.

AASLH Award of Merit. Presented for performance deemed excellent compared nationally with similar activities. American Association for State and Local History, www.aaslh.org.

ALA Marshall Cavendish Excellence in Library Programming Award. An annual $2,000 cash award recognizing either a school or public library with programs that have community impact and respond to community needs. ALA Awards, www. ala.org.

ALA Thomson Gale Financial Development Award. A citation and $2,500 to a library organization that exhibited meritorious achievement in carrying out a library financial development project to secure new funding resources for a public or academic library. ALA Awards, www.ala.org.

ALA/ACRL EBSCO Community College Learning Resources Leadership and Library Achievement Awards. Two awards of $500 to individuals, groups, or institutions to recognize significant achievement in the areas of programs and leadership. ALA Association of College and Research Libraries, www.ala.org/acrl/.

ALA/ACRL Excellence in Academic Libraries Awards. Three awards of $3,000 granted annually to recognize outstanding community college, college, and university libraries. This award acknowledges the accomplishments of librarians and other library staff as they come together as members of a team to support the mission of their institution. ALA Association of College and Research Libraries, www.ala.org/acrl/.

ALA/LAMA AIA Library Building Awards Program. A biennial award presented by the American Institute of Architects and the ALA Library Administration and Management Association to encourage excellence in the architectural design and planning of libraries. Citations are presented to the winning architectural firms and to libraries. ALA Library Administration and Management Association, www.ala.org/lama/.

ALA/LAMA IIDA Interior Design Award. Presented by the International Interior Design Association and the ALA Library Administration and Management Association for excellence in interior design. ALA Library Administration and Management Association, www.ala.org/lama/.

ALA/LAMA John Cotton Dana Public Relations Awards. An annual citation honoring outstanding library public relations, whether a summer reading program, a year-long centennial celebration, fund-raising for a new college library, an awareness campaign, or an innovative partnership in the community. ALA Library Administration and Management Association, www.ala.org/lama/.

ALA/LAMA Swap and Shop "Best of Show" Award. To recognize the best individual pieces of public relations materials produced by libraries in the previous year. Many different categories and winners. ALA Library Administration and Management Association, www.ala.org/lama/.

ALA/PLA Excellence in Small and/or Rural Public Library Service Award. This $1,000 award honors a public library serving a population of 10,000 or less that demonstrates excellence of service to its community as exemplified by an overall service program or a special program of significant accomplishment. ALA Public Library Association, www.ala.org/pla/.

ALA/PLA Highsmith Library Innovation Award. This $2,000 award recognizes a public library's innovative and creative service program to the community. ALA Public Library Association, www.ala.org/pla/.

ALA/RUSA Thomson Gale Award for Excellence in Reference and Adult Library Services. A citation and $3,000 cash award to a library for development of an imaginative resource to meet patrons' reference needs. Resources may include a bibliography, guide to literature of a specific subject, directory, database, or other reference service. ALA Reference and User Services Association, www.ala.org/rusa/.

CLA/CACUL Innovation Achievement Award. An award of $1,500 (Can.) to recognize Canadian academic libraries which, through innovation in ongoing programs/services or in a special event/project, have contributed to academic librarianship and library development. CLA Canadian Association of College and University Libraries, www.cla.ca.

CLA/CACUL Micromedia Award of Merit. Presented annually in recognition of college libraries which, through innovation in ongoing programs or services or in a special event or project, have contributed to college librarianship and library development. CLA Canadian Association of College and University Libraries, www.cla.ca.

CLA/RSIG OCLC Canada Award for Resource Sharing Achievement. $1,000 (Can.) to recognize an individual, organization, or project team for outstanding professional achievement, leadership, and contributions to library resource sharing in Canada. CLA Resource Sharing Interest Group, www.cla.ca.

CLA/TSIG 3M Canada Award for Achievement in Technical Services. An award of $1,000 (Can.) to recognize achievement in technical services by any unit whose library has an institutional membership in CLA. CLA Technical Services Interest Group, www.cla.ca.

CSLA Award for Outstanding Congregational Library. Honors a church or synagogue library that has responded in creative and innovative ways to the library's mission of reaching and serving members of the congregation and/or wider community. Church and Synagogue Library Association, worldaccessnet.com/~csla/.

FLICC Federal Library/Information Center of the Year. Two awards recognizing and commending outstanding, innovative, and sustained achievements by a federal library or information center, one for agencies with 11 or more employees, and another for those with 10 or less. Federal Library and Information Center Committee, www.loc.gov/flicc/.

IMLS National Award for Library Service. Given annually to recognize a library's commitment to public service through exemplary and innovative programs and community partnerships. Institute of Museum and Library Services, www.imls.gov.

OHA Elizabeth B. Mason Project Award. Two biannual awards that recognize outstanding oral history projects. Oral History Association, omega.dickinson.edu/organizations/oha/.

ULC Highsmith Award of Excellence. A $1,000 honorarium that recognizes a ULC member library for the creation or adaptation of a service that meets an urban area's need, can be replicated easily, is not costly, and has proven results. Urban Libraries Council, www.urbanlibraries.org.

For publications and research

AAC&U Frederic W. Ness Book Award. A $2,000 award recognizing a book that contributes to the understanding and improvement of liberal education. Association of American Colleges and Universities, www.aacu.org.

AALL Joseph L. Andrews Bibliographical Award. For significant contribution to legal bibliographical literature. American Association of Law Libraries, www. aallnet.org.

AALL *Law Library Journal* Article of the Year. A cash award of $500 for outstanding achievement in research and writing published in *Law Library Journal*. American Association of Law Libraries, www.aallnet.org.

AALL Law Library Publications Award. Honors achievement in creating in-house library materials that are outstanding in quality and significance. American Association of Law Libraries, www.aallnet.org.

AALL Lexis/Nexis Call for Papers Awards. A cash award of $750 to promote scholarship and provide an outlet for creativity. American Association of Law Libraries, www.aallnet.org.

AALL *Spectrum* Article of the Year Award. A cash award of $500 to honor outstanding achievement in writing an article that contributes to topics relating to law librarianship, practical applications for library work, legal materials, legal information, or professional and staff training and development in *AALL Spectrum*. American Association of Law Libraries, www.aallnet.org.

AALL/ALL Outstanding Article Award. For contributions to the enhancement of academic law librarianship through publishing. American Association of Law Libraries, Academic Law Libraries Special Interest Section, www.aallnet.org.

AALL/SCCLL Connie E. Bolden Publications Award. An award given every third year for a scholarly publication that addresses the concerns of state, court, or county law librarians. American Association of Law Libraries, State, Court, and County Law Libraries Special Interest Section, www.aallnet.org.

ACA W. Kaye Lamb Prize. Awarded to honor the author of the best *Archivaria* article published during the past year. Association of Canadian Archivists, archivists.ca.

AECT James W. Brown Publication Award. A cash award of $500 to the author(s) of an outstanding publication in the field of educational technology. Association for Educational Communications and Technology, www.aect.org.

AIIP Thomson Gale Writer's Award. A $350 travel award to the AIIP Annual Conference is given to the writer of the best original article published in *Connections* each year. Association of Independent Information Professionals, www.aiip.org.

AJL Reference and Bibliography Awards. For outstanding bibliographies and reference books in Judaica. Association of Jewish Libraries, www.jewishlibraries.org/ajlweb/home.htm.

AJL Sydney Taylor Book Awards. Recognizes the best in Jewish children's literature each year. Association of Jewish Libraries, www.jewishlibraries.org/ajlweb/home.htm.

AJL Sydney Taylor Manuscript Award. A cash award of $1,000 for the best fiction manuscript appropriate for readers ages 8–11, written by an unpublished author. Association of Jewish Libraries, www.jewishlibraries.org/ajlweb/home.htm.

ALA Schneider Family Book Awards. Three annual awards of $5,000 each to honor an author or illustrator for a book that embodies an artistic expression of the disability experience for child and adolescent audiences. ALA Awards, www.ala.org.

ALA W. Y. Boyd Literary Novel Award for Excellence in Military Fiction. $5,000 to an author for the best fiction set in a period when the United States is at war. ALA Awards, www.ala.org.

ALA/ACRL Instruction Publication of the Year Award. This award recognizes an outstanding publication related to instruction in a library environment published in the preceding two years. ALA Association of College and Research Libraries, www.ala.org/acrl/.

ALA/ACRL Katharine Kyes Leab and Daniel J. Leab American Book Prices Current Exhibition Catalogue Awards. Three awards for outstanding catalogues published by American or Canadian institutions in conjunction with library exhibitions as well as electronic exhibition catalogues of outstanding merit issued within the digital/web environment. ALA Association of College and Research Libraries, www.ala.org/acrl/.

ALA/ACRL Oberly Award for Bibliography in the Agricultural or Natural Sciences. A biennial award of $350 for the best English-language bibliography in the field of agriculture or a related science. ALA Association of College and Research Libraries, www.ala.org/acrl/.

ALA/ALCTS Best of *LRTS* Award. Annual citation given to the author(s) of the best paper published in *Library Resources and Technical Services*. ALA Association for Library Collections and Technical Services, www.ala.org/alcts/.

ALA/ALCTS Blackwell's Scholarship Award. A $2,000 scholarship to a U.S. or Canadian library school to honor the author(s) of the year's outstanding monograph, article, or original paper in the field of acquisitions, collection development, and related areas of resource development. ALA Association for Library Collections and Technical Services, www.ala.org/alcts/.

ALA/ALSC Andrew Carnegie Medal. A medal presented annually to an American producer for outstanding video production for children issued in the United States in the previous calendar year. ALA Association for Library Service to Children, www.ala.org/alsc/.

ALA/ALSC John Newbery Medal. A medal presented annually to the author of the most distinguished contribution to American literature for children published in the United States in the preceding year. ALA Association for Library Service to Children, www.ala.org/alsc/.

ALA/ALSC Laura Ingalls Wilder Medal. A medal presented to an author or illustrator whose books, published in the United States, have over a period of years made a substantial and lasting contribution to children's literature. Presented every two years. ALA Association for Library Service to Children, www.ala.org/alsc/.

ALA/ALSC Mildred L. Batchelder Award. A citation presented to an American publisher for a children's book considered to be the most outstanding of those books originally published in a foreign language in a foreign country and subsequently translated into English and published in the United States. ALA Association for Library Service to Children, www.ala.org/alsc/.

ALA/ALSC Pura Belpré Award. Biennual award to a Latino/Latina author and illustrator whose works best portray, affirm, and celebrate the Latino cultural experience in an outstanding work of literature for children and youth. ALA Association for Library Service to Children, www.ala.org/alsc/.

ALA/ALSC Randolph Caldecott Medal. A medal presented annually to the illustrator of the most distinguished American picture book for children published in the United States in the previous year. ALA Association for Library Service to Children, www.ala.org/alsc/.

ALA/ALSC Robert F. Sibert Informational Book Medal. Awarded annually to the author of the most distinguished informational book published in English during the preceding year. ALA Association for Library Service to Children, www.ala.org/alsc/.

ALA/ALSC Theodor Seuss Geisel Award. Awarded to the author(s) and illustrator(s) of the most distinguished contribution to the body of American children's literature known as beginning reader books published in the United States during the preceding year. ALA Association for Library Service to Children, www.ala.org/alsc/.

ALA/EMIERT Coretta Scott King Awards. Awards given to an African-American author and to an African-American illustrator for an outstandingly inspirational and educational contribution. The awards consist of a plaque and $1,000 to the author and $1,000 to the illustrator. ALA Ethnic and Multicultural Information Exchange Round Table, www.ala.org/emiert/.

ALA/EMIERT David Cohen Multicultural Award. A $300 award to encourage and recognize articles of significant new research that increase understanding and promote multiculturalism in libraries in North America. ALA Ethnic and Multicultural Information Exchange Round Table, www.ala.org/emiert/.

ALA/EMIERT John Steptoe Award for New Talent. Citation for an outstanding book designed to bring visibility to a black writer or artist at the beginning of his/ her career as a published book creator. ALA Ethnic and Multicultural Information Exchange Round Table, www.ala.org/emiert/.

ALA/GLBTRT Stonewall Book Award–Barbara Gittings Literature Award. Cash awards to authors of fiction of exceptional merit relating to the gay/lesbian/bisexual/ transgendered experience published in the United States. ALA Gay, Lesbian, Bisexual, and Transgendered Round Table, www.ala.org/glbtrt/.

ALA/GLBTRT Stonewall Book Award–Israel Fishman Nonfiction Award. Cash awards to authors of nonfiction of exceptional merit relating to the gay/lesbian/ bisexual/transgendered experience published in the United States. ALA Gay, Lesbian, Bisexual, and Transgendered Round Table, www.ala.org/glbtrt/.

ALA/LHRT Donald G. Davis Article Award. An award presented every other year for the best article written in English in the field of United States and Canadian library history including the history of libraries, librarianship, and book culture. ALA Library History Round Table, www.ala.org/lhrt/.

ALA/LHRT Eliza Atkins Gleason Book Award. An award presented every three years to recognize the best book written in English in the field of library history, including the history of libraries, librarianship, and book culture. ALA Library History Round Table, www.ala.org/lhrt/.

ALA/LHRT Justin Winsor Essay Prize. An award of $500 to an author of an outstanding essay embodying original historical research on a significant subject of library history. The essay will be published in *Libraries and Culture*. ALA Library History Round Table, www.ala.org/lhrt/.

ALA/LHRT Phyllis Dain Library History Dissertation Award. A biennial award of $500 to outstanding dissertations treating the history of books, libraries, librarianship, or information science. ALA Library History Round Table, www.ala.org/lhrt/.

ALA/LITA Endeavor Student Writing Award. $1,000 given for the best unpublished manuscript on a topic in the area of libraries and information technology written by a student or students enrolled in an ALA-accredited library and information studies graduate program. ALA Library and Information Technology Association, www.ala.org/lita/.

ALA/LRRT Jesse H. Shera Award for Distinguished Published Research. A prize of $500 for an outstanding and original research article related to libraries published the previous year. ALA Library Research Round Table, www.ala.org/lrrt/.

ALA/PLA *Public Libraries* Feature Writing Awards. A first prize of $500 and a second prize of $300 to the authors of the best feature published in *Public Libraries* in the past year. ALA Public Library Association, www.ala.org/pla/.

ALA/RUSA ABC-CLIO Online History Award. A biennial citation and $3,000 cash award to recognize the production of a freely available online historical collection, an online tool tailored for the purpose of finding historical materials, or an online teaching aid stimulating creative historical scholarship. ALA Reference and User Services Association, www.ala.org/rusa/.

ALA/RUSA Dartmouth Medal. A medal presented to honor the creation of a reference work of outstanding quality and significance. ALA Reference and User Services Association, www.ala.org/rusa/.

ALA/RUSA Genealogical Publishing Company Award. A citation and $1,500 cash award to a librarian, library, or publisher to encourage professional achievement in historical reference and research librarianship. ALA Reference and User Services Association, www.ala.org/rusa/.

ALA/RUSA Louis Shores–Greenwood Publishing Group Award. A citation and $3,000 cash award to an individual reviewer, group, editor, review medium, or organization to recognize excellence in book reviewing and other media for libraries. ALA Reference and User Services Association, www.ala.org/rusa/.

ALA/RUSA Reference Service Press Award. $2,500 award presented to recognize the most outstanding article published in *RUSQ* during the preceding two-volume year. ALA Reference and User Services Association, www.ala.org/rusa/.

ALA/RUSA Sophie Brody Medal. An award for the U.S. author of the most distinguished contribution to Jewish literature for adults. ALA Reference and User Services Association, www.ala.org/rusa/.

ALA/YALSA Alex Awards. Citations to 10 authors of English-language adult books that appeal to young adults. ALA Young Adult Library Services Association, www.ala.org/yalsa/.

ALA/YALSA Margaret A. Edwards Award. A $2,000 award given to an author or coauthor whose book(s) over a period of time have been accepted by young adults as an authentic voice that continues to illuminate their experiences and emotions. ALA Young Adult Library Services Association, www.ala.org/yalsa/.

ALA/YALSA Michael L. Printz Award. Honors the highest literary achievement in books for young adults. ALA Young Adult Library Services Association, www.ala.org/yalsa/.

ALISE Bohdan S. Wynar Research Paper Competition. A $2,500 honorarium for a completed research paper concerning any aspect of librarianship or information science. Association for Library and Information Science Education, www.alise.org.

ALISE Eugene Garfield Doctoral Dissertation Award. A $500 award for a completed dissertation dealing with substantive issues related to library and information science. Association for Library and Information Science Education, www.alise.org.

ALISE Methodology Paper Competition. A $500 honorarium for papers that address a research methodology, related issues, and/or a particular technique. Association for Library and Information Science Education, www.alise.org.

APALA Awards for Literature. Given to the writers or illustrators of adult or children's books about Asian/Pacific Americans. Asian/Pacific American Library Association, www.apalaweb.org.

APHA Annual Awards. Honors an individual or institution for a distinguished contribution to the study, recording, preservation, or dissemination of printing history, in any specific area or in general terms. American Printing History Association, printinghistory.org/index.htm.

ARLIS/NA George Wittenborn Memorial Book Award. Annual award for outstanding art books published in North America. Art Libraries Society of North America, www.arlisna.org.

ARLIS/NA Gerd Muehsam Memorial Award. $500 cash and $300 in travel expenses to the ARLIS/NA conference to a graduate library student for a paper or project on a topic relevant to art librarianship. Art Libraries Society of North America, www.arlisna.org.

ARLIS/NA Melva J. Dwyer Award. Citation given to the creators of exceptional reference or research tools relating to Canadian art and architecture. Art Libraries Society of North America, www.arlisna.org.

ARLIS/NA Worldwide Books Award for Electronic Resources. To recognize outstanding electronic publications by ARLIS/NA individual members in librarianship, visual resources curatorship, or the arts. Art Libraries Society of North America, www.arlisna.org.

ARLIS/NA Worldwide Books Award for Publications. To recognize outstanding publications by ARLIS/NA members. Art Libraries Society of North America, www.arlisna.org.

ARSC Lifetime Achievement Award. Presented to an individual in recognition of a life's work in research and publication on recorded sound. Association for Recorded Sound Collections, www.arsc-audio.org.

ASI H. W. Wilson Company Indexing Award. A citation and $1,000 for the indexer, and a citation for the publisher to honor excellence in indexing of an English-language monograph or other nonserial publication published during the previous calendar year. American Society of Indexers, www.asindexing.org.

ASIS&T Award for Research in Information Science. To recognize an individual or individuals for an outstanding research contribution in the field of information science. American Society for Information Science and Technology, www.asis.org.

ASIS&T Best Information Science Book. To recognize the outstanding book in information science published during the preceding calendar year. American Society for Information Science and Technology, www.asis.org.

ASIS&T John Wiley & Sons Best *JASIST* Paper Award. A $1,500 cash award to recognize the best refereed paper published in the volume year of the *Journal of the American Society for Information Science and Technology* preceding the ASIS&T annual meeting. American Society for Information Science and Technology, www.asis.org.

ASIS&T Pratt-Severn Best Student Research Paper. Up to $500 for travel expenses and full registration for the ASIS annual meeting for research and writing in the field of information science. American Society for Information Science and Technology, www.asis.org.

BCALA Literary Awards. The two annual BCALA Literary Awards (fiction and non-fiction) of $500 each recognize outstanding works by African-American authors depicting the cultural, historical, or sociopolitical aspects of the Black Diaspora. Black Caucus of the American Library Association, www.bcala.org.

BSA Justin G. Schiller Prize for Bibliographical Work on Pre-20th-Century Children's Books. An award of $2,000 for scholarship in the bibliography of historical children's books. Bibliographical Society of America, www.bibsocamer.org.

BSA William L. Mitchell Prize for Research on Early British Serials. An award of $1,000 for bibliographical scholarship on 18th-century periodicals published in English or in any language but within the British Isles and its colonies and former colonies. Bibliographical Society of America, www.bibsocamer.org.

CBHL Annual Literature Award. Given to both the author and publisher of a work that makes a significant contribution to the literature of botany or horticulture. Council on Botanical and Horticultural Libraries, www.cbhl.net.

CLA Student Article Contest. An honorarium of $150 (Can.) and publication in *Feliciter* for articles by students in Canadian library schools. Canadian Library Association, www.cla.ca.

CLA/CACL Amelia Frances Howard-Gibbon Illustrator's Medal. For an illustrator of an outstanding children's book published in Canada the previous year. CLA Canadian Association of Children's Librarians, www.cla.ca.

CLA/CACL Book of the Year for Children Award. For an outstanding children's book published in Canada the previous year by a Canadian author. CLA Canadian Association of Children's Librarians, www.cla.ca.

CLA/YASIG Young Adult Canadian Book Award. Recognizes an author of an outstanding English-language Canadian book appealing to young adults. CLA Young Adult Services Interest Group, www.cla.ca.

CLA John Brubaker Memorial Award. For the best article in *Catholic Library World* in the previous year. Catholic Library Association, www.cathla.org.

CLA/ALSS Jerome Award. Presented annually for excellence in Catholic scholarship. Catholic Library Association, Academic Library Services Section, www.cathla.org.

CLA/CLSS Regina Medal. A silver medal awarded to an author or illustrator for a lifetime contribution to children's books. Catholic Library Association, Children's Library Services Section, www.cathla.org.

CSLA Helen Keating Ott Award for Outstanding Contribution to Children's Literature. A person or organization selected and honored for significant contribution in promoting high moral and ethical values through children's literature. Church and Synagogue Library Association, worldaccessnet.com/~csla/.

MLA Ida and George Eliot Prize. Award presented annually for a work published in the preceding calendar year that has been judged most effective in furthering medical librarianship. Medical Library Association, www.mlanet.org.

MLA Murray Gottlieb Prize. Awarded annually for the best unpublished essay on the history of medicine and allied sciences written by a health sciences librarian. Medical Library Association, www.mlanet.org.

MLA Rittenhouse Award. Given for the best unpublished paper (bibliographical, issue- or topic-based, or report of research results) or web-based project on health sciences librarianship or medical informatics written by a student in an ALA-accredited school of library science or a trainee in an internship. Medical Library Association, www.mlanet.org.

MLA Eva Judd O'Meara Award. An annual award for the best review published in *Notes*. Music Library Association, www.musiclibraryassoc.org.

MLA Richard S. Hill Award. An annual award for the best article on music librarianship or article of a music-bibliographic nature. Music Library Association, www.musiclibraryassoc.org.

MLA Vincent H. Duckles Award. Annual award for the best book-length bibliography or other research tool in music. Music Library Association, www.musiclibraryassoc.org.

NCIS Eisenstein Prize. A biannual prize for the best published article submitted by an NCIS member. National Coalition for Independent Scholars, www.ncis.org.

NSN Talking Leaves Literary Award. Presented to individuals who have made outstanding contributions to the literary body of storytelling as authors, editors, or collectors. National Storytelling Network, storynet.org.

OHA Article Award. Biannual award that recognizes a published article or essay that uses oral history to make a significant contribution to contemporary scholarship. Oral History Association, omega.dickinson.edu/organizations/oha/.

OHA Book Award. Recognizes a published book that uses oral history to make a significant contribution to contemporary scholarship. Oral History Association, omega.dickinson.edu/organizations/oha/.

OHA Outstanding Use of Oral History in a Nonprint Format. Recognizes a film, video, performance piece, radio program or series, exhibition, or drama that makes significant and outstanding use of oral history to interpret an historical event, person, place, or way of life. Oral History Association, omega.dickinson.edu/organizations/oha/.

SAA Fellows' Ernst Posner Award. Certificate and cash award that recognizes the author(s) of an outstanding article dealing with some facet of archival administration, history, theory, and/or methodology that was published during the preceding year in the *American Archivist.* Society of American Archivists, www.archivists.org.

SAA Preservation Publication Award. Recognizes the author(s) or editor(s) of an outstanding published work related to archives preservation published in North America during the preceding year. Society of American Archivists, www.archivists.org.

SAA Theodore Calvin Pease Award. Certificate and cash prize of $100 that recognizes superior writing achievements by students of archival administration. Society of American Archivists, www.archivists.org.

SAA Waldo Gifford Leland Award. Certificate and cash prize that encourages and rewards writing of superior excellence and usefulness in the field of archival history, theory, or practice. Monographs, finding aids, and documentary publications published in North America during the preceding year are eligible. Society of American Archivists, www.archivists.org.

SALALM José Toribio Medina Award. An honorarium of $250 for outstanding bibliographies, reference works, and sources which facilitate access to research or contribute to the understanding, use, or development of Latin American collections. Seminar on the Acquisition of Latin American Library Materials, www.library.cornell.edu/colldev/salalmhome.html.

SLA H. W. Wilson Company Award. A $500 cash award to the author(s) of an outstanding article published in *Information Outlook* during the publication year. Special Libraries Association, www.sla.org.

SLA Media Award. Recognizes a journalist who published an outstanding feature on the profession of special librarianship, preferably in a general circulation publication or radio or television production. Special Libraries Association, www.sla.org.

TLA Award. Given annually to the best English-language book about recorded performance, including motion pictures, television, and radio. Theatre Library Association, tla.library.unt.edu.

TLA George Freedley Award. Given for the best English-language work about live theater published in the United States. Theatre Library Association, tla.library.unt.edu.

For service to children and young adults

ALA Grolier Foundation Award. A $1,000 award to a librarian whose contribution to the stimulation and guidance of reading by children and young people exemplifies outstanding achievement in the profession. ALA Awards, www.ala.org.

ALA Sullivan Award for Public Library Administrators Supporting Services to Children. An annual award of a gift and citation to an individual who has shown exceptional understanding and support of public library service to children while having general management, supervisory, or administrative responsibility that has included public library service to children in its scope. ALA Awards, www.ala.org.

ALA/AASL Collaborative School Library Media Award. A $2,500 award to a school library media specialist who demonstrates exemplary collaborative efforts through joint planning of a program, unit, or event using media center resources. ALA American Association of School Librarians, www.ala.org/aasl/.

ALA/AASL Distinguished School Administrators Award. An award of $2,000 to a school administrator who has made worthy contributions to the operations of an exemplary school library media center and to advancing the role of the school library media center in the educational program. ALA American Association of School Librarians, www.ala.org/aasl/.

ALA/AASL Distinguished Service Award. A $3,000 award for and outstanding contribution to school librarianship and school library development. ALA American Association of School Librarians, www.ala.org/aasl/.

ALA/AASL National School Library Media Program of the Year Award. Three awards of $10,000 each to school districts (large and small) and a single school, for excellence and innovation in outstanding library media programs. ALA American Association of School Librarians, www.ala.org/aasl/.

ALA/AASL President's Crystal Apple Award. Given at the discretion of the AASL president to an individual or group who has had significant impact on school libraries and students. ALA American Association of School Librarians, www.ala.org/aasl.

ALA/ALSC Distinguished Service Award. A $1,000 award to honor an ALSC member who has made significant contributions to library service to children and/or ALSC. ALA Association for Library Service to Children, www.ala.org/alsc/.

ALA/ALSC Sagebrush Education Resources Literature Program Grant. One annual $1,000 award to an ALSC member for development and implementation of an outstanding library program for children, involving reading and the use of literature. ALA Association for Library Service to Children, www.ala.org/alsc/.

ALA/YALSA Great Book Giveaway. Each year the YALSA office receives approximately 1,200 newly published children's, young adult and adult books, videos, CDs and audiocassettes. YALSA and the cooperating publishers are offering one year's worth of review materials as a contribution to a library in need. ALA Young Adult Library Services Association, www.ala.org/yalsa/.

ALA/YALSA Sagebrush Young Adult Reading or Literature Program Award. $1,000 to a YALSA member for development and implementation of an outstanding library program for young adults, involving reading and the use of literature. ALA Young Adult Library Services Association, www.ala.org/yalsa/.

CLA/CASL Angela Thacker Memorial Award. Honors Canadian teacher-librarians who have made contributions to the profession through publications, productions, or professional development activities that deal with topics relevant to teacher-librarianship or information literacy. CLA Canadian Association of School Libraries, www.cla.ca/casl/.

CLA/CASL Margaret B. Scott Award of Merit. Honors an individual for development of school libraries at the national level in Canada. CLA Canadian Association of School Libraries, www.cla.ca/casl/.

CLA/CASL National Book Service Teacher-Librarian of the Year Award. Honors a school-based teacher-librarian who has made an outstanding contribution to school librarianship within Canada through planning and implementing school library programs, based on a collaborative model that integrates library and classroom programs. CLA Canadian Association of School Libraries, www.cla.ca/casl/.

CLA/HSYALSS St. Katharine Drexel Award. For an outstanding contribution to the growth of high school librarianship. Catholic Library Association, High School and Young Adult Library Service Section, www.cathla.org.

IASL ProQuest Information and Learning E-Library Commendation Award. A $500 award for outstanding and innovative projects, plans, publications, or programs that could serve as models for replication by individuals or associations. International Association of School Librarianship, www.iasl-slo.org.

IASL Softlink International Excellence Award. $1,000 to recognize significant contributions to school librarianship by school library specialists, educators, or researchers. International Association of School Librarianship, www.iasl-slo.org.

For service to the underserved

AALL/SCCLL O. James Werner Award for Distinctive Service to Persons with Disabilities. To honor a member who has made a significant contribution to serving directly or for arranging services to be provided to persons with disabilities. American Association of Law Libraries, State, Court, and County Special Interest Section, www.aallnet.org.

AILA Honoring Our Elders Award. An award to a current or former AILA member for distinguished service to Indian communities and extraordinary service to the association. American Indian Library Association, www.nativeculturelinks.com/aila.html.

ALA/ASCLA Exceptional Service Award. A citation presented to recognize exceptional service to patients, to the homebound, to medical, nursing, and other professional staff in hospitals, and to inmates, as well as to recognize professional leadership, effective interpretation of programs, pioneering activity, and significant research of experimental projects. ALA Association of Specialized and Cooperative Library Agencies, www.ala.org/ascla/.

ALA/ASCLA Francis Joseph Campbell Award. A citation and a medal presented to a person who has made an outstanding contribution to the advancement of library service for the blind and physically handicapped. ALA Association of Specialized and Cooperative Library Agencies, www.ala.org/ascla/.

ALA/ASCLA KLAS National Organization on Disability Award. A $1,000 award and certificate to a library for an innovative and well-organized project that has developed or expanded services for people with disabilities or to a library that has made its total services more accessible through changing physical and/or attitudinal barriers. ALA Association of Specialized and Cooperative Library Agencies, www.ala.org/ascla/.

ALA/EMIERT Gale Multicultural Award. $1,000 for significant accomplishments in library services that are national or international in scope and that include improving, spreading, and promoting multicultural librarianship. ALA Ethnic and Multicultural Information Exchange Round Table, www.ala.org/emiert/.

ALA/OLOS Diversity Fair Awards totaling $750 to outreach librarians for their institutions' diversity-in-action initiatives, including programs, activities, and services. ALA Office for Literacy and Outreach Services, www.ala.org/olos/.

ALA/OLOS Jean E. Coleman Library Outreach Lecture. An invitation to an individual of distinction to prepare and present a paper on a library access topic to ensure that all citizens, particularly Native Americans and adult learners, have access to quality library services. ALA Office for Literacy and Outreach Services, www.ala.org/olos/.

ALA/RUSA Dun and Bradstreet Award for Outstanding Service to Minority Business Communities. An annual award of $2,000 to a librarian or library that has created an innovative service for a minority business community, or has been recognized by that community as an outstanding service provider. ALA Reference and User Services Association, www.ala.org/rusa/.

ALA/RUSA John Sessions Memorial Award. A plaque given to a library or library system to honor significant work with the labor community and to recognize the history and contributions of the labor movement toward the development of this country. ALA Reference and User Services Association, www.ala.org/rusa/.

BCALA Demco Award for Excellence in Librarianship. An annual award of $500 presented to the librarian who has made significant contributions to promoting the status of African Americans in the library profession. Black Caucus of the American Library Association, www.bcala.org.

CLA W. Kaye Lamb Award for Service to Seniors. Biennial award recognizing a library that has developed an ongoing service, program, or procedure of benefit to seniors or a design and organization of buildings or facilities that improve access and encourage use by seniors. Canadian Library Association, www.cla.ca.

Reforma Arnulfo D. Trejo Librarian of the Year Award. Granted to an individual who has promoted and advocated services to the Spanish-speaking and Latino/a communities. Reforma, www.reforma.org.

Reforma Estela and Raúl Mora Award. A $1,000 stipend presented annually to the most exemplary program celebrating *Día de Los Niños/Día de Los Libros*. Reforma, www.reforma.org.

For intellectual freedom

AALL Public Access to Government Information Award. Honors the achievements of those who have championed public access. American Association of Law Libraries, www.aallnet.org.

ALA/AASL Intellectual Freedom Award. A $2,000 award to a school library media specialist who has upheld the principles of intellectual freedom. An award of $1,000 goes to a media center of the recipient's choice. ALA American Association of School Librarians, www.ala.org/aasl/.

ALA/IFRT Eli M. Oboler Memorial Award. $500 awarded biennially to an author of a published work in English, or in English translation, dealing with issues, events, questions, or controversies in the area of intellectual freedom. ALA Office for Intellectual Freedom, www.ala.org/ifrt/.

ALA/IFRT John Phillip Immroth Memorial Award for Intellectual Freedom. $500 and a citation honoring intellectual freedom fighters who have demonstrated remarkable personal courage. ALA Office for Intellectual Freedom, www.ala.org/ifrt/.

ALA/IFRT ProQuest/SIRS State and Regional Intellectual Freedom Achievement Award. $1,000 and a citation to state libraries or library associations, educational media associations or programs, legal defense funds, intellectual freedom committees, or coalitions for the most innovative and effective intellectual freedom project covering a state or region. ALA Office for Intellectual Freedom, www.ala.org/ifrt/.

ALA/OGR Eileen Cooke State and Local James Madison Award. To recognize state or local individuals, groups, or other entities that have championed access to government information and the public's right to know. Presented yearly on Freedom of Information Day. ALA Office of Government Relations, www.ala.org/washoff/.

ALA/OGR James Madison Award. To honor those who have championed, protected, and promoted public access to government information and the public's right to know. Presented yearly on Freedom of Information Day. ALA Office of Government Relations, www.ala.org/washoff/.

CLA Award for the Advancement of Intellectual Freedom in Canada. Recognizes outstanding contributions to intellectual freedom in Canada, by individual librarians or libraries. Canadian Library Association, www.cla.ca.

FTRF Roll of Honor Award. Recognizes those individuals who have contributed substantially to the Foundation through adherence to its principles and/or substantial monetary support. Freedom to Read Foundation, www.ala.org/ala/ourassociation/othergroups/ftrf/freedomreadfoundation.htm.

For literacy and social responsibility

ALA Equality Award. $500 to an individual or group for an outstanding contribution that promotes equality in the library profession in such areas as pay equity, affirmative action, legislative work, and nonsexist education. ALA Awards, www.ala.org.

ALA-APA Award for Outstanding Achievement in Promoting Salaries and Status for Library Workers. An annual award of $2,500 given to an individual, group of individuals, or an institution that has made an outstanding contribution to improving the salary and status of library workers in a local, regional, or national setting. ALA–Allied Professional Association, www.ala-apa.org.

ALA/ALTA Literacy Award. Citation to a library trustee or an individual who, in a volunteer capacity, has made a significant contribution to addressing the problem of illiteracy in the United States. ALA American Library Trustee Association, www.ala.org/alta/.

ALA/OITP L. Ray Patterson Copyright Award: In Support of Users' Rights. Honors those who have made significant and consistent contributions to the pursuit of balanced copyright principles while working in the area of academia, law, politics, public policy, libraries, or library education. ALA Office for Information Technology Policy, www.ala.org/washoff/.

ALA/PLA Advancement of Literacy Award. This award honors a publisher, bookseller, hardware or software dealer, foundation, or similar group (not an individual) for making a significant contribution to the advancement of adult literacy. ALA Public Library Association, www.ala.org/pla/.

ALA/SRRT Jackie Eubanks Memorial Award. An award of $500 and a certificate to honor outstanding achievement in promoting the acquisition and use of alternative information resources in libraries. ALA Social Responsibilities Round Table, www.libr.org/AIP/.

CLA/CLTA Stan Heath Achievement in Literacy Award. Presented annually to a Canadian public library board that has initiated an innovative program that is contributing significantly to the advancement of literacy in its community. CLA Canadian Library Trustees' Association, www.cla.ca.

IFLA Guust van Wesemael Literacy Prize. This award sponsors a public or school library in a developing country to perform activities in the field of literacy. International Federation of Library Associations and Institutions, www.ifla.org.

For documents and archives

ACA Honorary Membership. Recognizes individuals for distinguished service to the archival profession. Association of Canadian Archivists, archivists.ca.

ACA Membership Recognition Award. Given annually to an ACA member for professional achievements or significant contributions. Association of Canadian Archivists, archivists.ca.

ALA/ALCTS Paul Banks and Carolyn Harris Preservation Award. A $1,500 award to recognize the contribution of a professional preservation specialist who has been active in the field of preservation or conservation for library or archival materials. ALA Association for Library Collections and Technical Services, www.ala.org/alcts/.

ALA/GODORT Bernadine Abbott Hoduski Founders Award. Recognizes documents librarians who may not be known at the national level but who have made significant contributions to the field of state, international, local, or federal documents. ALA Government Documents Round Table, sunsite.berkeley.edu/GODORT/.

ALA/GODORT James Bennett Childs Award. An annual award presented to an individual who has made a lifetime and significant contribution to the field of government documents librarianship. ALA Government Documents Round Table, sunsite.berkeley.edu/GODORT/.

ALA/GODORT LexisNexis "Documents to the People" Award. $3,000 to an individual, library, organization, or noncommercial group that most effectively encourages the use of government documents in library services. ALA Government Documents Round Table, sunsite.berkeley.edu/GODORT/.

SAA C. F. W. Coker Award. Certificate and cash award for finding aids, finding aid systems, projects that involve innovative development in archival description, or descriptive tools that enable archivists to produce more effective finding aids. Society of American Archivists, www.archivists.org.

SAA Distinguished Service Award. Recognizes a North American archival institution, organization, education program, or nonprofit or governmental organization that has given outstanding service to its public and has made an exemplary contribution to the archival profession. Society of American Archivists, www.archivists.org.

SAA J. Franklin Jameson Archival Advocacy Award. Honors an individual, institution, or organization not directly involved in archival work that promotes greater public awareness, appreciation, or support of archival activities or programs. Society of American Archivists, www.archivists.org.

SAA Philip M. Hamer–Elizabeth Hamer Kegan Award. Certificate and cash award that recognizes an archivist, editor, group of individuals, or institution that has increased public awareness of a specific body of documents through compilation, transcription, exhibition, or public presentation. Society of American Archivists, www.archivists.org.

SAA Sister M. Claude Lane Memorial Award. Certificate and cash prize that recognizes individuals who have made a significant contribution to the field of religious archives. Society of American Archivists, www.archivists.org.

For technology

AACC David R. Pierce Faculty Technology Award. A $5,000 honorarium given to two outstanding community college faculty who promote the use of information technology. American Association of Community Colleges, www.aacc.nche.edu.

AALL New Product Award. Honors new commercial information products that enhance or improve access to legal information or procedures for technical processing of library materials. American Association of Law Libraries, www.aallnet.org.

AECT Annual Achievement Award. Honors the individual who during the past year has made the most significant contribution to the advancement of educational communications and technology. Association for Educational Communications and Technology, www.aect.org.

AECT Richard B. Lewis Memorial Award. Presented to a school district for outstanding utilization of technology. Association for Educational Communications and Technology, www.aect.org.

AIIP Technology Award. Recognizes innovative products that enhance the working environment of independent information professionals. Association of Independent Information Professionals, www.aiip.org.

ALA Information Today Library of the Future Award. An award of $1,500 to honor a library, library consortium, group of librarians, or support organization for innovative planning for, applications of, or development of patron training programs about information technology in a library setting. ALA Awards, www.ala.org.

ALA/AASL Information Technology Pathfinder Award. Awards of $1,000 to elementary and secondary library media specialists for demonstrating vision and leadership through the use of information technology to build lifelong learners. ALA American Association of School Librarians, www.ala.org/aasl/.

ALA/LITA Brett Butler Entrepreneurship Award. A prize of $5,000 to recognize a librarian or library that demonstrates exemplary entrepreneurship by providing an innovative product or service designed to meet the needs of the library world through the skillful and practical application of information technology. ALA Library and Information Technology Association, www.ala.org/lita/.

ALA/LITA Frederick G. Kilgour Award for Research in Library and Information Technology. $2,000 for research relevant to the development of information technologies, especially work which shows promise of having a positive and substantive impact on any aspect of information publication, storage, retrieval and dissemination. ALA Library and Information Technology Association, www.ala.org/lita/.

ALA/LITA Library Hi Tech Award. An award of $1,000 to recognize outstanding achievement in communication in continuing education within the field of library and information technology. ALA Library and Information Technology Association, www.ala.org/lita/.

ALISE Pratt-Severn Faculty Innovation Award. A $1,000 award to identify innovation by full-time faculty members in incorporating evolving information technologies in the curricula of accredited LIS programs. Association for Library and Information Science Education, www.alise.org.

CLA Information Today Award for Innovative Technology. $500 (Can.) given annually to honor a member or members of the Canadian Library Association for innovative use and application of technology in a Canadian library setting. Canadian Library Association, www.cla.ca.

CLIR Bill and Melinda Gates Foundation Access to Learning Award. An annual award of up to $1 million to a public library or similar organization outside the United States that has an innovative program offering the public free access to information technology. Council on Library and Information Resources, www.clir.org.

MLA Thomson Scientific Frank Bradway Rogers Information Advancement Award. Presented annually in recognition of outstanding contributions for the application of technology to the delivery of health science information, to the science of information, or to the facilitation of the delivery of health science information. Medical Library Association, www.mlanet.org.

SLA Innovations in Technology Award. Cash award of $1,000 granted to an individual SLA member for innovative use and application of technology in a special library setting. Special Libraries Association, www.sla.org.

LIBRARY EDUCATION

Accredited library programs

THE FOLLOWING GRADUATE LIBRARY and information studies programs are accredited (as of summer 2005) by the American Library Association under its *Standards for Accreditation.* All programs offer a master's-level degree; those marked with an asterisk (*) offer a doctorate or other post-master's program.

*Catholic University of America, School of Library and Information Science, 620 Michigan Ave., N.E., Washington, DC 20064; (202) 319-5085; slis.cua.edu. Martha Hale, dean.

Most Expensive Library Schools, 2003

In-state tuition and fees for a full ALA-accredited master's degree:

Drexel University	$33,000
Catholic University of America	31,265
Syracuse University	27,712
St. John's University	26,760
Simmons College	25,920
University of Michigan	25,151
Long Island University	23,688
Pratt Institute	23,616
Dominican University	20,700
Clark Atlanta University (closed in 2005)	19,018
University of Pittsburgh	15,564

Highest Student Enrollments, 2003

Number of full-time students in library science program:

	Male	Female	Total
University of Michigan	85	153	238
University of Toronto	85	135	220
San Jose State University	47	172	219
Indiana University	50	150	200
Kent State University	47	137	184
University of Texas	39	140	179
University of Illinois	47	112	159
Rutgers University	28	131	159
University of Maryland	42	110	152
University of North Carolina/Chapel Hill	36	113	149
Florida State University	42	104	146
University of Washington	42	103	145
University at Buffalo	36	106	142

SOURCE: Evelyn H. Daniel and Jerry D. Saye, eds., *Library and Information Science Education Statistical Report 2004* (Oak Ridge, Tenn.: Association for Library and Information Science Education, 2005), pp. 84–88, 225–227.

*Clarion University of Pennsylvania, Department of Library Science, 210 Carlson Library Building, 840 Wood St., Clarion, PA 16214-1232; (866) 272-5612; www.clarion.edu/libsci/. Bernard F. Vavrek, chair.

Dalhousie University, School of Information Management, Kenneth C. Rowe Management Building, Halifax, NS, Canada B3H 3J5; (902) 494-3656; sim.management.dal.ca. Fiona Black, director.

*Dominican University, Graduate School of Library and Information Science, 7900 W. Division St., River Forest, IL 60305; (708) 524-6845; www.gslis.dom.edu. Susan Roman, dean.

*Drexel University, College of Information Science and Technology, 3141 Chestnut Street, Philadelphia, PA 19104-2875; (215) 895-2474; www.cis.drexel.edu. David E. Fenske, dean.

*Emporia State University, School of Library and Information Management, 1200 Commercial, Campus Box 2045, Emporia, KS 66801; (316) 341-5203; slim.emporia.edu. Ann L. O'Neill, dean.

Florida State University, School of Information Studies, Shores Building, Tallahassee, FL 32306-2100; (850) 644-5772; www.lis.fsu.edu. Larry Dennis, dean.

*Indiana University, School of Library and Information Science, 1320 E. 10th Street, LI 011, Bloomington, IN 47405-3907; (812) 855-2018; www.slis.indiana.edu. Blaise Cronin, dean.

Kent State University, School of Library and Information Science, 314 University Library, P.O. Box 5190, Kent, OH 44242-0001; (330) 672-2782; www.slis.kent.edu. Richard E. Rubin, director.

*Long Island University, Palmer School of Library and Information Science, C. W. Post Campus, 720 Northern Boulevard, Brookville, NY 11548-1300; (516) 299-2866; cics.cwpost.liu.edu. John J. Regazzi, dean.

*Louisiana State University, School of Library and Information Science, 267 Coates Hall, Baton Rouge, LA 70803; (225) 578-3158; slis.lsu.edu. Beth Paskoff, dean.

*McGill University, Graduate School of Library and Information Studies, 3459 McTavish Street, Montreal, QC, Canada H3A 1Y1; (514) 398-4204; www.gslis.mcgill.ca. France Bouthillier, director.

North Carolina Central University, School of Library and Information Sciences, P.O. Box 19586, 1801 Fayetteville St., Durham, NC 27707; (919) 530-6485; www.nccuslis.org. Irene Owens, dean.

*Pratt Institute, School of Information and Library Science, 144 W. 14th Street, 6th Floor, New York, NY 10011; (212) 647-7682; www.pratt.edu/sils/. Tula Giannini, acting dean.

*Queens College, City University of New York, Graduate School of Library and Information Studies, 65-30 Kissena Boulevard, Flushing, NY 11367-1597; (718) 997-3790; www.qc.cuny.edu/GSLIS/. Virgil L. P. Blake, director.

*Rutgers, the State University of New Jersey, Department of Library and Information Science, 4 Huntington Street, New Brunswick, NJ 08901-1071; (732) 932-7500, ext. 8955; scils.rutgers.edu. Nicholas J. Belkin, director.

*St. John's University, Division of Library and Information Science, 8000 Utopia Parkway, Jamaica, NY 11439; (718) 990-6200; www.stjohns.edu/libraryscience/. Jeffery E. Olson, director.

San Jose State University, School of Library and Information Science, 1 Washington Square, San Jose, CA 95192-0029; (408) 924-2490; slisweb.sjsu.edu. Ken Haycock, director.

*Simmons College, Graduate School of Library and Information Science, 300

The Fenway, Boston, MA 02115-5898; (617) 521-2800; www.simmons.edu/gslis/. Michèle V. Cloonan, dean.

*__Southern Connecticut State University,__ School of Communication, Information and Library Science, Department of Information and Library Science, 501 Crescent Street, New Haven, CT 06515; (203) 392-5781; www.southernct.edu/departments/ils/. Edward C. Harris, dean.

*__Syracuse University,__ School of Information Studies, 245 Hinds Hall, Syracuse, NY 13244; (315) 443-2911; www.ist.syr.edu. Raymond F. von Dran, dean.

*__Texas Woman's University,__ School of Library and Information Studies, P.O. Box 425438, Denton, TX 76204-5438; (940) 898-2602; www.twu.edu/cope/slis/. Ling Hwey Jeng, dean.

*__Université de Montréal,__ Ecole de bibliothéconomie et des sciences de l'information, C.P. 6128, Succursale Centre-Ville, Montréal, QC, H3C 3J7; (514) 343-6400; www.ebsi.umontreal.ca. Marcel LaJeunesse, interim director.

3

Former Library Schools

Alabama Agricultural and Mechanical University
  Huntsville, Ala., closed 1981
Ball State University
  Muncie, Ind., closed 1985
Brigham Young University
  Provo, Utah, closed 1993
Carnegie Institute of Technology
  Pittsburgh, Pa., closed 1962
Carnegie Library of Atlanta
  Atlanta, Ga.
  Transferred to Emory University in 1930
Case Western Reserve University
  Cleveland, Ohio, closed 1986
Clark Atlanta University
  Atlanta, Ga., closed 2005
Columbia University
  New York, N.Y., closed 1992
Emory University
  Atlanta, Ga., closed 1988
Hampton Institute
  Hampton, Va., closed 1939
Los Angeles Public Library
  Los Angeles, Calif., closed 1932
Marywood College
  Scranton, Pa.
  Accreditation stopped 1956
New Jersey College for Women
  New Brunswick, N.J., closed 1952
New York Public Library
  New York, N.Y.
  Transferred to Columbia in 1926
North Carolina College for Women
  Greensboro, N.C., closed 1933

Northern Illinois University
  DeKalb, Ill., closed 1994
Our Lady of the Lake College
  Baton Rouge, La.
  Accreditation stopped 1957
Peabody College for Teachers
  Nashville, Tenn.
  Merged with Vanderbilt University in 1979
St. Catherine College
  St. Paul, Minn., closed 1959
St. Louis Library School
  St. Louis, Mo., closed 1932
State University of New York at Geneseo
  Geneseo, N.Y., closed 1983
University of California at Berkeley
  Berkeley, Calif., School of Information Management & Systems
  Not accredited since 1994
University of Chicago
  Chicago, Ill., closed 1990
University of Mississippi
  Oxford, Miss., closed 1984
University of Oregon
  Eugene, Oreg., closed 1978
University of Southern California
  Los Angeles, Calif., closed 1986
Vanderbilt University
  Nashville, Tenn., closed 1988
Western Michigan University
  Kalamazoo, Mich., closed 1983
William and Mary College
  Williamsburg, Va., closed 1948

SOURCE: ALA Office for Accreditation.

*University of Alabama, School of Library and Information Studies, Box 870252, Tuscaloosa, AL 35487-0252; (205) 348-4610; www.slis.ua.edu. Elizabeth Aversa, dean.

*University at Albany, State University of New York, School of Information Science and Policy, 135 Western Avenue, Draper 113, Albany, NY 12222; (518) 442-5110; www.albany.edu/sisp/. Peter A. Bloniarz, dean.

*University of Alberta, School of Library and Information Studies, 3-20 Rutherford South, Edmonton, AB, Canada T6G 2J4; (780) 492-4578; www.slis. ualberta.ca. Anna Altmann, director.

*University of Arizona, School of Information Resources and Library Science, 1515 East First Street, Tucson, AZ 85719; (520) 621-3565; www.sir. arizona.edu. Jana Bradley, director.

*University of British Columbia, School of Library, Archival and Information Studies, Suite 301, 6190 Agronomy Road, Vancouver, BC, Canada V6T 1Z3; (604) 822-2404; www.slais.ubc.ca. Edie Rasmussen, director.

*University at Buffalo, State University of New York, School of Informatics, Department of Library and Information Studies, 534 Baldy Hall, Buffalo, NY 14260-1020; (716) 645-2412; informatics.buffalo.edu/lis/. David Penniman, dean.

*University of California, Los Angeles, Department of Information Studies, Graduate School of Education & Information Studies Building, Box 951520, Los Angeles, CA 90095-1520; (310) 825-8799; is.gseis.ucla.edu. Anne Gilliland, chair.

*University of Denver, Library and Information Science Program, Wesley Hall, 2135 East Wesley, Suite 103, Denver, CO 80208; (303) 871-2747; www.du.edu/LIS/. Deborah S. Grealy, director.

*University of Hawaii, Library and Information Science Program, 2550 McCarthy Mall, Honolulu, HI 96822; (808) 956-7321; www.hawaii.edu/ slis/. Rebecca Knuth, chair.

*University of Illinois at Urbana-Champaign, Graduate School of Library and Information Science, 501 East Daniel Street, Champaign, IL 61820-6211; (217) 333-3280; www.lis.uiuc.edu. John Unsworth, dean.

University of Iowa, School of Library and Information Science, 3087 Main Library, Iowa City, IA 52242-1420; (319) 335-5707; www.uiowa.edu/~libsci/. David Eichmann, director.

*University of Kentucky, School of Library and Information Science, 502 King Library, Lexington, KY 40506-0039; (859) 257-8876; www.uky.edu/ CIS/SLIS/. Timothy W. Sineath, director.

*University of Maryland, College of Information Studies, 4105 Hornbake Building, College Park, MD 20742-4345; (301) 405-2033; www.clis.umd. edu. Jennifer Preece, dean.

*University of Michigan, School of Information, 304 West Hall Building, 550 East University Avenue, Ann Arbor, MI 48109-1092; (734) 764-9376; www. si.umich.edu. John L. King, dean.

*University of Missouri-Columbia, School of Information Science and Learning Technologies, 303 Townsend Hall, Columbia, MO 65211; (573) 882-4546; sislt.missouri.edu. John Wedman, director.

*University of North Carolina at Chapel Hill, School of Information and Library Science, CB #3360, 100 Manning Hall, Chapel Hill, NC 27599-3360; (919) 962-8366; www.ils.unc.edu. José Marie Griffiths, dean.

University of North Carolina at Greensboro, Department of Library and Information Studies, School of Education, 349 Curry Building, Greensboro,

NC 27402-6170; (336) 334-3477; lis.uncg.edu. Lee Shiflett, chair.

*University of North Texas, School of Library and Information Sciences, P.O. Box 311068, NT Station, Denton, TX 76203-1068; (940) 565-2731; www.unt.edu/slis/. Samantha K. Hastings, interim dean.

*University of Oklahoma, School of Library and Information Studies, 401 West Brooks, Room 120, Norman, OK 73019-6032; (405) 325-3921; www.ou.edu/cas/slis/. Kathy Latrobe, interim director.

*University of Pittsburgh, Department of Library and Information Studies, 135 N. Bellefield Ave., Pittsburgh, PA 15260; (412) 624-5142; www.sis.pitt.edu. Ronald Larsen, dean.

*University of Puerto Rico, Escuela Graduada de Ciencias y Tecnologías de la Información, P.O. Box 21906, San Juan, PR 00931-1906; (787) 763-6199; egcti.upr.edu. Nitza Hernández, director.

University of Rhode Island, Graduate School of Library and Information Studies, Rodman Hall, 94 W. Alumni Ave., Kingston, RI 02881; (401) 874-2947; www.uri.edu/artsci/lsc/. W. Michael Havener, director.

*University of South Carolina, School of Library and Information Science, Davis College, Columbia, SC 29208; (803) 777-3858; www.libsci.sc.edu. Daniel Barron, director.

*University of South Florida, School of Library and Information Science, 4202 East Fowler Avenue, CIS 1040, Tampa, FL 33620-7800; (813) 974-3520; www.cas.usf.edu/lis/. Vicki L. Gregory, director.

*University of Southern Mississippi, School of Library and Information Science, 118 College Drive, #5146, Hattiesburg, MS 39406-0001; (601) 266-4228; www.usm.edu/slis/. M. J. Norton, director.

*University of Tennessee, School of Information Sciences, 451 Communications Building, 1345 Circle Park Drive, Knoxville, TN 37996-0341; (865) 974-2148; www.sis.utk.edu. Edwin Cortez, director.

*University of Texas at Austin, School of Information, 1 University Station D7000, Austin, TX 78712-0390; (512) 471-3821; www.ischool.utexas.edu. Andrew Dillon, dean.

*University of Toronto, Faculty of Information Studies, 140 St. George Street, Room 211, Toronto, ON, Canada M5S 3G6; (416) 978-3202; www.fis.utoronto.ca. Brian Cantwell Smith, dean.

*University of Washington, The Information School, 370 Mary Gates Hall, Box 352840, Seattle, WA 98195-2840; (206) 685-9937; www.ischool.washington.edu. Michael B. Eisenberg, dean.

*University of Western Ontario, Graduate Programs in Library and Information Science, Faculty of Information and Media Studies, North Campus Building, Room 240, London, ON, Canada N6A 5B7; (519) 661-4017; www.fims.uwo.ca. Catherine Ross, dean.

*University of Wisconsin-Madison, School of Library and Information Studies, 4217 Helen C. White Hall, 600 North Park Street, Madison, WI 53706; (608) 263-2908; www.slis.wisc.edu. Louise S. Robbins, dean.

*University of Wisconsin-Milwaukee, School of Information Studies, P.O. Box 413, Milwaukee, WI 53201; (414) 229-4707; www.sois.uwm.edu. Johannes Britz, dean.

*Wayne State University, Library and Information Science Program, 106 Kresge Library, Detroit, MI 48202; (313) 577-1825; www.lisp.wayne.edu. Joseph J. Mika, director.

SOURCE: ALA Office for Accreditation, July 2005.

Critiquing the LIS curriculum

by Wayne A. Wiegand

AFTER READING LIBRARY AND INFORMATION SCIENCE research and watching LIS curriculum development for the past 30 years, I've concluded I differ fundamentally in two particular perspectives from most of my library-faculty colleagues.

First, I'm convinced that most of them think of libraries as part of a greater world of information. (Please bear in mind that I'm just trying to describe here, not criticize.) However, my study of American library history leads me to see information as only part of a larger library world, in which libraries have done three things especially well for the past century and a half: They have (1) made information accessible to millions of people on many subjects; (2) provided tens of thousands of places where patrons have been able to meet formally as clubs or groups, or informally as citizens and students utilizing a civic institution and a cultural agency; and (3) furnished billions of reading materials to millions of patrons.

Second, I'm convinced that most LIS faculty are inclined to think primarily of—as Douglas Zweizig famously put it—"the user in the life of the library." Evidence of this perspective abounds. Note, for example, the bureaucratic structure of ALA, or categories we use in the Association for Library and Information Science Education's Research Area Classification Guide to describe our teaching and research interests—phrases like "information resources management," "classification," "collection development," and "reference and information service." All reflect the discursive formations of the professional jurisdiction we claim; all manifest mostly a "user in the life of the library" perspective.

However, I am more inclined to think of "the library in the life of the user," adopting the conceptual frame Zweizig suggested 30 years ago. I do this for two reasons: to help me find and understand the influence their publics have had on libraries, and to help me focus on how the institution has historically functioned as a cultural agency in the everyday life experiences of ordinary people.

And the differences in our perspectives, I surmise, have led us in different directions over the past decades. While many library faculty have worked hard and successfully to carve out a research and curricular niche within the academy in a rapidly changing world of technology that places the study of libraries in a larger world of information, I have been following cutting-edge humanities research in two particular areas that inform "library in the life of the user" thinking: First, I've been focusing on reading—especially the social nature of this essential human behavior that libraries have been facilitating for generations. Second, I've been following humanities research on the role "place" plays as an agent in the construction of community.

The public sphere

Let me elaborate the latter first. These days one cannot begin to think about "place" without considering the ideas developed by social theorist Jürgen Habermas in *The Structural Transformation of the Public Sphere: An Inquiry into a Category of Bourgeois Society* (Blackwell, 1989). During the 18th century, Habermas argues, the growing middle class sought to influence government actions by assuming control of an emerging public sphere of deliberation that eventually found an influential niche between forces exercised by governments and marketplaces. Within this public sphere, members of the middle class developed their own brand of reason; and over time they created a network of institutions and a series of sites (e.g., newspapers and periodicals, political parties, academic societies, and, I would argue, libraries of all types) through which they refined this rationalized discourse into an expression of the public interest that governments and markets dared not ignore.

Once Habermas's theory established a foundation for understanding how a series of social and cultural preconditions shaped the public sphere, other scholars began to analyze the institutions and sites in which this rationalized discourse has been practiced by multiple communities and groups that have not been primarily concerned either with political ideology or with marketplace activities. And it is out of analyses of these institutions and sites that a refined concept of the role of "place" as cultural space has emerged.

Last year, two-thirds of this country's citizens visited at least one public library at least once per year. Grade and high school students frequented school library media centers 1.5 billion times, one-and-a-half times the visits of all people to state and national parks. Add in visits annually made to public and academic libraries, and that number jumps to 3.5 billion—more than twice the number of people annually attending movie theaters. Over 16 million patrons visit academic libraries weekly, and in the past decade, per-capita annual visits to public libraries have increased from 3.1 to 4.2.

A perpetually open place

In the fall of 2003, Library Director Ken Frazier announced that because of student demand, the 2002 pilot project for 24-hour library service in the University of Wisconsin at Madison graduate library was being extended to the undergraduate library. He added that the library would also open a new cafe. "The idea of a library as a place where people collaborate in intellectual work is an idea that was not really articulated by academic librarians in the past," said Frazier. "Presuming that it would be a good thing if people were able to gather around a table in a space where they could talk freely was not evident in the design of libraries."

Over the generations, millions of patrons have demonstrated their support for the library as a place by visiting it again and again, yet we don't know very much about why they do it. In LIS studies, we have some ideas and beliefs, but little solid evidence based on research to validate them. Explorations of the myriad ways people in libraries "exchange social capital"—a phrase that is so much a part of public-sphere thinking—are largely absent in our research and curricular agendas.

Or let's turn to "reading," which is reflected in circulation data. For academic libraries, circulation now totals nearly 200 million items per year. In 2004, 150 million Americans went to a public library to check out a book, and a substantial portion of them withdrew multiple titles. These statistics prove conclusively that the American library constitutes a major source and site for the act of reading.

Although they haven't always been sure why, librarians have always been advocates for reading. Scan any catalog from ALA Graphics and you'll find more than 50 posters with a variety of media darlings holding a book with the word "Read" displayed in huge letters at the top. Look at ALA's website and count the number of times the word "read" pops up in the association's program initiatives.

And there's plenty of evidence about reading to demonstrate what patrons expect from librarians. For example, in answer to a question ALA piggybacked onto an omnibus 2001 telephone survey of 1,000 adults about what skills librarians most needed, 76% (the highest percentage of any category) said "familiarity with a range of books and authors." The survey also asked what activities people do at public libraries; 92% (also the highest percentage in any category) responded, "borrow books." Admittedly, much of this reading is driven by popular fiction. Every year for the past century millions of library patrons have checked out billions of novels. In public libraries, fiction generally accounts for two-thirds of total circulation. As members of the LIS community, library faculty believe that providing patrons access to popular fiction is important. At the same time, however, the amount of attention paid to this service in our teaching and research demonstrates convincingly that it ranks much lower than providing access to "information" and "useful knowledge" (a term that has resonated in our professional discourse for generations).

But in the past 25 years, a growing body of scholarship has emerged outside our field that analyzes the subject of reading stories from a variety of perspectives, including literacy studies, reader-response theory, ethnographies of reading, the social history of print, and cultural studies. Reading scholars analyze who reads what stories, and why, by focusing on the complex ways readers from information cultures based on gender, race, age, class, and creed use what they read and how they apply that reading in their daily lives, revealing how reading functions as a cultural agency and practice in the everyday lives of ordinary people.

For example, Elizabeth Long's *Book Clubs: Women and the Uses of Reading in Everyday Life* (University of Chicago, 2003) explores reading's capacity to stimu-

late imagination and construct community through shared meaning. She argues that the modern construction of the solitary reader ignores the thoroughly social base for some kinds of reading. She says that this infrastructure includes shared interpretive frameworks, participation in a set of institutions, and social relations.

Long's research helps to explain why millions of people belong to hundreds of thousands of reading groups and books clubs, many now meeting via the internet. It also helps us explain the increasing number of book festivals in recent years across North America, and the popularity of "one book–one city" reading programs monitored by hundreds of public libraries in the past five years. Yet how many in LIS are doing research on "the library in the life of the reader"? How much attention are we paying in our core curriculum to this ubiquitous cultural practice, an essential human behavior that has been central to our professional enterprise for millennia?

Based on my alternative perspectives, I have concluded that by concentrating so much in our research and teaching on information (and especially on the type of information made accessible by computer technology), and by largely overlooking "reading" and "place" in our professional discourse, we deprive ourselves and our students of opportunities to develop a much deeper understanding of the library in the life of the user.

My conclusion is largely driven by two perspectives that appear to me relatively foreign to orthodox LIS thinking: If we intend to carry out research in the future that will address all of library practice, if we intend to provide a well-rounded education that prepares our students to take places in a world of librarianship, we have to start thinking outside our self-constructed box.

First, we have to make substantial adjustments in our research and teaching agendas (and especially in our core curriculum) to accommodate questions of place and reading that are (and have been) so important to our patrons. A cursory glance at the pages of *American Libraries* demonstrates that library practitioners and patrons intuitively know reading and place are important. Library educators and researchers have to begin explaining why. The best way to accomplish this, I would argue, connects to my second perspective: We have to look much more at the library in the life of our users (and conversely, nonusers) in order to deepen our understanding of the many roles it plays (or could play) in their everyday lives.

SOURCE: Wayne A. Wiegand, "Critiquing the Curriculum," *American Libraries* 36 (January 2005): 58–61.

RESEARCH & WRITING

Useful addresses

YOUR UNANSWERED QUESTIONS on library matters might be directed to one of the following organizations.

Alternative Press Center, P.O. Box 33109, Baltimore, MD 21218; (410) 243-2471; altpress@altpress.org; www.altpress.org.

American Association for Higher Education, 1 Dupont Circle, N.W., Suite 360, Washington, DC 20036-1143; (202) 293-6440; info@aahe.org; www.aahe.org.

American Association for State and Local History, 1717 Church St., Nashville, TN 37203-2991; (615) 320-3203; membership@aaslh.org; www.aaslh.org.

American Association of Colleges and Universities, 1818 R St., N.W., Washington, DC 20009; (202) 387-3760; www.aacu-edu.org.

American Association of Community Colleges, 1 Dupont Circle, N.W., Suite 410, Washington, DC 20036; (202) 728-0200; www.aacc.nche.edu.

American Association of Law Libraries, 53 W. Jackson Blvd., Suite 940, Chicago, IL 60604; (312) 939-4764; aallhq@aall.org; www.aallnet.org.

American Booksellers Association, 200 White Plains Rd., Tarrytown, NY

10591; (914) 591-2665, (800) 637-0037; info@bookweb.org; www. bookweb.org.

American Council of Learned Societies, 633 Third Ave., New York, NY 10017-6795; (212) 697-1505; www.acls.org.

American Council on Education, 1 Dupont Circle, N.W., Suite 800, Washington, DC 20036; (202) 939-9300; comments@ace.nche.edu; www.acenet.edu.

American Indian Library Association, c/o Lisa A. Mitten, *Choice* Magazine, 100 Riverview Center, Middletown, CT 06457; fax: (603) 649-6120; lamitten@yahoo.com; www.nativeculturelinks.com/aila.html.

American Institute of Architects, 1735 New York Ave., N.W., Washington, DC 20006-5292; (202) 626-7300, (800) 242-3837; infocentral@aia.org; www.aia.org.

American Libraries **Online,** 50 E. Huron St., Chicago, IL 60611-2795; (800) 545-2433, ext. 4216; americanlibraries@ala.org; www.ala.org/alonline/.

American Library Association, 50 E. Huron St., Chicago, IL 60611-2795; (800) 545-2433; library@ala.org; www.ala.org.

American Library Association, Washington Office, 1301 Pennsylvania Ave., N.W., Suite 403, Washington, DC 20004; (202) 628-8410, (800) 941-8478; alawash@alawash.org.

American National Standards Institute, 25 W. 43rd St., 4th Floor, New York, NY 10036; (212) 642-4900; info@ansi.org; web.ansi.org.

American Printing History Association, P.O. Box 4519, Grand Central Station, New York, NY 10163-4519; (212) 673-8770; sgcrook@printinghistory. org; printinghistory.org/index.htm.

American Society for Information Science and Technology, 1320 Fenwick Lane, Suite 510, Silver Spring, MD 20910; (301) 495-0900; asis@asis.org; www.asis.org.

American Society of Indexers, 10200 W. 44th Ave., Suite 304, Wheat Ridge, CO 80033; (303) 463-2887; info@asindexing.org; www.asindexing.org.

American Theological Library Association, 250 S. Wacker Dr., Suite 1600, Chicago, IL 60606-5889; (888) 665-2852; atla@atla.com; www.atla.com/ atlahome.html.

Americans for Libraries Council, 27 Union Square West, Suite 204, New York, NY 10003; (646) 336-6236, (800) 542-1918; alc@americansforlibraries. com; www.lff.org.

Amigos Library Services, 14400 Midway Rd., Dallas, TX 75244-3509; (972) 851-8000, (800) 843-8482; amigos@amigos.org; www.amigos.org.

Antiquarian Booksellers' Association of America, 20 W. 44th St., 4th Floor, New York, NY 10035-6604; (212) 944-8291; inquiries@abaa.org; abaa.org.

Art Libraries Society of North America, 232-329 March Road, Box 11, Ottawa, Ontario K2K 2E1, Canada; (613) 599-3074, (800) 817-0621; arlisna@igs.net; www.arlisna.org.

Asian/Pacific American Librarians Association, c/o Ling Hwey Jeng, 1807 N. Elm St., #444, Denton, TX 76201; (940) 898-2602; linghwey@yahoo. com; www.apalaweb.org.

Aslib, the Association for Information Management, Holywell Centre, 1 Phipp Street, London EC2A 4PS, United Kingdom; +44 (20) 7613-3031; aslib@aslib.co.uk; www.aslib.co.uk.

Asociación Mexicana de Bibliotecarios, Angel Urraza 817-A, Col. del Valle,

México, D.F. 03100; +52 (55) 55-75-33-96; correo@ambac.org.mx; www. ambac.org.mx.

Association des Bibliothécaires Français, 31, rue de Chabrol, 75010 Paris, France; +33 (1) 55 33 10 30; abf@abf.asso.fr; www.abf.asso.fr.

Association for Educational Communications and Technology, 1800 N. Stonelake Dr., Suite 2, Bloomington, IN 47404; (812) 335-7675; aect@aect. org; www.aect.org.

Association for Information and Image Management International, 1100 Wayne Ave., Suite 1100, Silver Spring, MD 20910-5603; (301) 587-8202, (800) 477-2446; aim@aiim.org; www.aiim.org.

Association for Library and Information Science Education, 1009 Commerce Park Dr., Suite 150, P.O. Box 4219, Oak Ridge, TN 37830; (865) 425-0155; contact@alise.org; www.alise.org.

Association for Recorded Sound Collections, c/o Peter Shambarger, P.O. Box 543, Annapolis, MD 21404-0543; shambarger@sprynet.com; www.arsc-audio.org.

Association of American Colleges and Universities, 1818 R Street, N.W., Washington, DC 20009; (202) 387-3760; info@aacu.org; www.aacu.org.

Association of American Publishers, 71 Fifth Ave., 2nd Floor, New York, NY 10003-3004; (212) 255-0200; www.publishers.org.

Association of Canadian Archivists, P.O. Box 2596, Station D, Ottawa, Ontario K1P 5W6, Canada; (613) 234-6977; aca@archivists.ca; archivists.ca/home/.

Association of Canadian Map Libraries and Archives, c/o Government Records Branch, Library and Archives Canada, 395 Wellington Street, Ottawa, Ontario K1A 0N3,Canada; (613) 996-7374; pmcintyre@archives.ca; www.ssc.uwo.ca/assoc/acml/acmla.html.

Association of Christian Librarians, P.O. Box 4, Cedarville, OH 45314; (937) 766-2255; info@acl.org; www.acl.org.

Association of Independent Information Professionals, 8550 United Plaza Blvd., Suite 1001, Baton Rouge, LA 70809; (225) 922-4611; info@aiip.org; www.aiip.org.

Association of Jewish Libraries, c/o NFJC, 330 Seventh Ave., 21st Floor, New York, NY 10001; (212) 725-5359; ajlibs@osu.edu; www.jewishlibraries. org/ajlwcb/home.htm.

Association of Mental Health Librarians, c/o Stuart Moss, Health Sciences Library, Nathan S. Kline Institute, 140 Old Orangeburg Rd., Orangeburg, NY 10962; (813) 974-4471; hanson@fmhi.usf.edu; www.fmhi.usf.edu/amhl/.

Association of Part-Time Librarians, c/o Anne Huberman, Andrew L. Bouwhuis Library, Canisius College, 2001 Main St., Buffalo, NY 14208-1098; huberman@canisius.edu; www2.canisius.edu/~huberman/aptl.html.

Association of Records Managers and Administrators International, 13725 W. 109th St., Suite 101, Lenexa, KS 66215; (913) 341-3808, (800) 422-2762; hq@arma.org; www.arma.org.

Association of Research Libraries, 21 Dupont Circle, N.W., Suite 800, Washington, DC 20036; (202) 296-2296; arlhq@arl.org; www.arl.org.

Associazione italiana biblioteche, c/o Biblioteca nazionale centrale, Viale Castro Pretorio 105, 00185 Roma, Italy; +39 (6) 446 3532; aib@aib.it; www.aib.it.

Australian Library and Information Association, P.O. Box 6335, Kingston ACT 2604, Australia; +61 (2) 6215 8222; enquiry@alia.org.au; www.alia. org.au.

Barahona Center for the Study of Books in Spanish for Children and Adolescents, California State University at San Marcos, Kellogg Library, 5th Floor, 333 S. Twin Oaks Valley Rd., San Marcos, CA 92096-0001; (760) 750-4070; ischon@csusm.edu; www.csusm.edu/csb/.

Barbara Bush Foundation for Family Literacy, 1201 15th St., N.W., Suite 420, Washington, DC 20005; (202) 955-6183; churd@cfncr.org; www.barbarabushfoundation.com.

Beta Phi Mu National Headquarters, School of Information Studies, Florida State University, Tallahassee, FL 32306-2100; (850) 644-3907; beta_phi_mu@lis.fsu.edu; www.beta-phi-mu.org.

Bibliographical Society (London), c/o Institute of English Studies, Room 304, Senate House, Malet Street, London WC1E 7HU, United Kingdom; secretary@bibsoc.org.uk; www.bibsoc.org.uk.

Bibliographical Society of America, P.O. Box 1537, Lenox Hill Station, New York, NY 10021; (212) 452-2710; bibsocamer@aol.com; www.bibsocamer.org.

Bibliographical Society of Australia and New Zealand, c/o Rachel Salmond, P.O. Box 1463, Wagga Wagga, NSW 2650, Australia; rsalmond@pobox.com; www.csu.edu.au/community/BSANZ/.

Black Caucus of the American Library Association, P.O. Box 1738, Hampton, VA 23669; membership@bcala.org; www.bcala.org.

Book Industry Study Group, 19 W. 21st St., Suite 905, New York, NY 10010; (646) 336-7141; info@bisg.org; www.bisg.org.

Booklist and *Book Links,* 50 E. Huron St., Chicago, IL 60611; bott@ala.org; www.ala.org/ala/booklist/booklist.htm.

British Association of Picture Libraries and Agencies, 18 Vine Hill, London EC1R 5DZ, United Kingdom; +44 (20) 7713-1780; enquiries@bapla.org.uk; www.bapla.org.uk.

Canadian Health Libraries Association, 39 River St., Toronto, Ontario M5A 3P1, Canada; (416) 646-1600; info@chla-absc.ca; www.chla-absc.ca.

Canadian Library Association, 328 Frank St., Ottawa, Ontario K2P 0X8, Canada; (613) 232-9625; info@cla.ca; www.cla.ca.

Catholic Library Association, 100 North Street, Suite 224, Pittsfield, MA 01201-5109; (413) 443-2252; cla@cathla.org; www.cathla.org.

Center for Applied Linguistics, 4646 40th Street, N.W., Washington, DC 20016-1859; (202) 362-0700; info@cal.org; www.cal.org.

Center for Book Arts, 28 W. 27th St., 3rd floor, New York, NY 10001; (212) 481-0295; info@centerforbookarts.org; www.centerforbookarts.org.

Center for Children's Books, GSLIS, University of Illinois at Urbana-Champaign, 501 E. Daniel St., Champaign, IL 61820; (217) 244-9331; ccb@alexia.lis.uiuc.edu; www.lis.uiuc.edu/~ccb/.

Center for the Book, Library of Congress, 101 Independence Ave., S.E., Washington, DC 20540-4920; (202) 707-5221; cfbook@loc.gov; www.loc.gov/loc/cfbook/.

Center for the History of Print Culture in Modern America, c/o James P. Danky, State Historical Society of Wisconsin, 816 State St., Madison, WI 53706-1482; (608) 264-6598; jpdanky@whs.wisc.edu; slisweb.lis.wisc.edu/~printcul/.

Center for the Study of Reading, Bureau of Educational Research, University of Illinois at Urbana-Champaign, 158 Children's Research Center, 51 Gerty Drive, Champaign, IL 61820; (217) 333-2552; csr.ed.uiuc.edu.

Chicago Book Clinic, 5443 N. Broadway, Suite 101, Chicago, IL 60640; (773) 561-4150; kgboyer@ix.netcom.com; www.chicagobookclinic.org.

Chief Officers of State Library Agencies, 201 East Main Street, Suite 1405, Lexington, KY 40507; (859) 514-9151; ttucker@amrinc.net; www.cosla.org.

Children's Literacy Initiative, 2314 Market St., 4th Floor, Philadelphia, PA 19103; (215) 561-4676; info@cliontheweb.org; www.cliontheweb.org/index-main.html.

China Society for Scientific and Technical Information, 15, Fuxing Ave., Beijing 100038, China; zhengyn@istic.ac.cn; www.istic.ac.cn.

Chinese American Librarians Association, c/o Sally Tseng, 49 Gillman St., Irvine, CA 92612; (949) 552-5615; sctseng888@yahoo.com; www.cala-web.org.

Choice, 100 Riverview Center, Middletown, CT 06457; (860) 347-6933; choicemag@ala-choice.org; www.ala.org/acrl/choice/.

Church and Synagogue Library Association, P.O. Box 19357, Portland, OR 97280-0357; (503) 244-6919, (800) 542-2752; csla@worldaccessnet.com; worldaccessnet.com/~csla/.

CILIP/Chartered Institute of Library and Information Professionals, 7 Ridgmount St., London, WC1E 7AE, United Kingdom; +44 (20) 7255 0500; info@cilip.org.uk; www.cilip.org.uk.

CILIP Cymru/Wales, Department of Information Studies, Llanbadarn Fawr, Aberystwyth, Ceredigion SY23 3AS, United Kingdom; +44 (1970) 622 174; scm@aber.ac.uk; www.dis.aber.ac.uk/cilip_w/.

Coalition for Networked Information, 21 Dupont Circle, N.W., Suite 800, Washington, DC 20036-1109; (202) 296-5098; clifford@cni.org; www.cni.org.

College and University Personnel Association for Human Resources, Tyson Place, 2607 Kingston Pike, Suite 250, Knoxville, TN 37919; (865) 637-7673; membership@cupahr.org; www.cupahr.org.

Consortium of Research Libraries in the British Isles, Room 1211, 12th Floor, Muirhead Tower, University of Birmingham, Edgbaston, Birmingham B15 2TT, United Kingdom; +44 (121) 415 8109; www.curl.ac.uk.

Copyright Clearance Center, 222 Rosewood Drive, Danvers, MA 01923; (978) 750-8400; info@copyright.com; www.copyright.com.

Council for Adult and Experiential Learning, 55 E. Monroe St., Suite 1930, Chicago, IL 60603; (312) 499-2600; www.cael.org.

Council for Higher Education Accreditation, 1 Dupont Circle, N.W., Suite 51, Washington, DC 20036; (202) 955-6126; www.chea.org.

Council on Botanical and Horticultural Libraries, c/o Charlotte Tancin, CBHL Secretary, Hunt Institute for Botanical Documentation, Carnegie-Mellon University, Pittsburgh, PA 15213-3890; (412) 268-7301; ctancin@cmu.edu; www.cbhl.net.

Council on East Asian Libraries, c/o Sarah S. Elman, East Asia Library, Sterling Memorial Library, Yale University, P.O. Box 208240, New Haven, CT 06520-8240; (203) 432-8210; sarah.elman@yale.edu; www.sois.uwm.edu/jeong/ceal/.

Council on Library and Information Resources, 1755 Massachusetts Ave., N.W., Washington, DC 20036-2217; (202) 939-4750; info@clir.org; www.clir.org.

Council on Library/Media Technicians, 28262 Chardon Rd., PMB 168, Wickcliffe, OH 44092-2793; (630) 257-6541; margaretrbarron@aol.com; colt.ucr.edu.

Early Book Society, Department of English, Pace University, 41 Park Row, New York, NY 10038; driver@pace.edu; www.nyu.edu/projects/EBS/.

Education Resources Information Center, c/o Computer Sciences Corporation, 4483-A Forbes Blvd., Lanham, MD 20706; (800) 538-3742; www.eric. ed.gov.

Educause, 4772 Walnut St., Suite 206, Boulder, CO 80301-2538; (303) 449-4430; www.educause.edu.

Electronic Frontier Foundation, 454 Shotwell St., San Francisco, CA 94110-1914; (415) 436-9333; information@eff.org; www.eff.org.

Electronic Privacy Information Center, 1718 Connecticut Ave., N.W., Suite 200, Washington, DC 20009; (202) 483-1140; info@epic.org; www.epic.org.

Equal Employment Opportunity Commission, 1801 L Street, N.W., Washington, DC 20507; (202) 663-4900, (800) 669-4000; www.eeoc.gov.

European Commission on Preservation and Access, Royal Netherlands Academy of Arts and Sciences, Kloveniersburgwal 29, P.O. Box 19121, NL-1000 GC Amsterdam, The Netherlands; +31 (20) 551 08 39; ecpa@bureau.knaw.nl; www.knaw.nl/ecpa/.

Federal Library and Information Center Committee, Library of Congress, 101 Independence Ave., S.E., Adams Building, Room 217, Washington, DC 20540-4935; (202) 707-4800; flicc@loc.gov; www.loc.gov/flicc/.

Freedom Forum, 1101 Wilson Blvd., Arlington, VA 22209; (703) 528-0800; news@freedomforum.org; www.freedomforum.org.

Freedom to Read Foundation, 50 E. Huron St., Chicago, IL 60611-2795; (800) 545-2433, ext. 4226; ftrf@ala.org; www.ftrf.org.

Friends of Libraries U.S.A., 1420 Walnut St., Suite 450, Philadelphia, PA 19102-4017; (215) 790-1674, (800) 936-5872; folusa@folusa.org; www.folusa.com.

Geoscience Information Society, c/o Jane Ingalls, Branner Earth Sciences Library, 397 Panama Mall/MC 2211, Stanford, CA 94305-2174; (650) 725-1103; jingalls@stanford.edu; www.geoinfo.org.

Great Books Foundation, 35 E. Wacker Dr., Suite 2300, Chicago, IL 60601-2298; (800) 222-5870; gbf@greatbooks.org; www.greatbooks.org.

Indexing and Abstracting Society of Canada, P.O. Box 664, Station P, Toronto, Ontario M5S 2Y4, Canada; jeadie1@cogeco.ca; www.indexingsociety.ca.

Institute for Bibliography and Editing, 1118 Main Library, Kent State University, Kent, OH 44242-0001; (330) 672-2092; editing@kent.edu; dept.kent.edu/ibewebsite/.

Institute for the Study of Adult Literacy, Pennsylvania State University, 102 Rackley Building, University Park, PA 16802-3202; (814) 863-3777; bdo1@psu.edu; www.ed.psu.edu/isal/.

Institute of Museum and Library Services, 1100 Pennsylvania Ave., N.W., Washington, DC 20506; (202) 606-8536; imlsinfo@imls.gov; www.imls.gov.

International Association of Aquatic and Marine Science Libraries and Information Centers, c/o Library, Harbor Branch Oceanographic Institution, Inc., 5600 US 1 North, Fort Pierce, FL 34946, (772) 465-2400, ext. 201; www.iamslic.org.

International Association of Law Libraries, c/o Ann Morrison, P.O. Box 5709, Washington, DC 20016-1309; (202) 662-6152; ann.morrison@dal.ca; www.iall.org.

International Association of School Librarianship, Secretariat, P.O. Box 83, Zillmere, Queensland 4034, Australia; +61 (7) 3633 0570; iasl@kb.iasl.com.au; www.iasl-slo.org.

International Federation of Library Associations and Institutions, P.O. Box

95312, 2509 CH The Hague, Netherlands; +31 (70) 314-0884; ifla@ifla. org; www.ifla.org.

International Literacy Institute, University of Pennsylvania, Graduate School of Education, 3910 Chestnut St., Philadelphia, PA 19104-3111; (215) 898-2100; editor@literacy.upenn.edu; literacy.org/ili.html.

International Organization for Standardization, 1, rue de Varembé, Case postale 56, CH-1211 Genève 20, Switzerland ; +41 (22) 749 01 11; central @iso.ch; www.iso.org.

International Reading Association, 800 Barksdale Road, P.O. Box 8139, Newark, DE 19714-8139; (302) 731-1600, (800) 336-7323; pubinfo@reading. org; www.reading.org.

ISBN Agency, R. R. Bowker, 630 Central Ave., New Providence, NJ 07974; (877) 310-7333; isbn-san@bowker.com; www.isbn.org/standards/home/ index.asp.

ISSN Agency, National Serials Data Program, Library of Congress, Washington, DC 20540-4160; (202) 707-6452; issn@loc.gov; www.loc.gov/issn/.

Library and Information Association of New Zealand Aotearoa, P.O. Box 12 212, Wellington, New Zealand; +64 (4) 473 5834; office@lianza.org.nz; www.lianza.org.nz.

Library and Information Association of South Africa, P.O. Box 1598, Pretoria 0001, South Africa; +27 (12) 481 2870; liasa@liasa.org.za; www. liasa.org.za.

Library Association of Ireland, 53 Upper Mount St., Dublin 2, Ireland; +353 (1) 061-202193; www.libraryassociation.ie.

Library Journal, 360 Park Ave. South, New York, NY 10010; (646) 746-6800; fialkoff@reedbusiness.com; www.libraryjournal.com.

Library of Congress, 101 Independence Ave., S.E., Washington, DC 20540; (202) 707-5000; lcweb@loc.gov; www.loc.gov.

Libri Foundation, P.O. Box 10246, Eugene, OR 97440; (541) 747-9655; libri@librifoundation.org; www.librifoundation.org.

Lumina Foundation for Education, 30 S. Meridian St., Suite 700, Indianapolis, IN 46204; (317) 951-5300; www.luminafoundation.org.

Medical Library Association, 65 E. Wacker Place, Suite 1900, Chicago, IL 60601-7246; (312) 419-9094; info@mlahq.org; www.mlanet.org.

Middle East Librarians Association, c/o William Kopycki, University of Pennsylvania Library, 3420 Walnut St., Philadelphia, PA 19104-6206; (215) 898-2196; secretary@mela.us; www.mela.us.

Modern Language Association of America, 26 Broadway, 3rd Floor, New York, NY 10004-1789; (646) 576-5000; membership@mla.org; www. mla.org.

Music Library Association, 8551 Research Way, Suite 180, Middleton, WI 53562; (608) 836-5825; mla@areditions.com; www.musiclibraryassoc.org.

National Archives and Records Administration, 8601 Adelphi Road, College Park, MD 20740-6001; (866) 272-6272; www.archives.gov.

National Association for the Education of Young Children, 1509 16th Street, N.W., Washington, DC 20036-1426; (202) 232-8777, (800) 424-2460; naeyc@naeyc.org; www.naeyc.org.

National Association of Government Archives and Records Administrators, 48 Howard St., Albany, NY 12207; (518) 463-8644; nagara@ caphill.com; www.nagara.org.

National Center for Education Statistics, 1990 K St., N.W., Washington,

DC 20006; (202) 502-7300; nces.ed.gov.

National Center for Family Literacy, 325 W. Main St., Suite 300, Louisville, KY 40202-4237; (502) 584-1133; ncfl@famlit.org; www.famlit.org.

National Center on Adult Literacy, University of Pennsylvania, Graduate School of Education, 3910 Chestnut St., Philadelphia, PA 19104-3111; (215) 898-2100; editor@literacy.upenn.edu; literacy.org/ncal.html.

National Church Library Association, 275 S. Third Street, Suite 101A, Stillwater, MN 55082; (651) 430-0770; info@churchlibraries.org; www. churchlibraries.org.

National Coalition Against Censorship, 275 7th Ave., 20th Floor, New York, NY 10001; (212) 807-6222; ncac@ncac.org; www.ncac.org.

National Coalition of Independent Scholars, P. O. Box 5743, Berkeley, CA 94705; ncis@mindspring.com; www.ncis.org.

National Commission on Libraries and Information Science, 1800 M St., N.W., Suite 350 North Tower, Washington, DC 20036-5841; (202) 606-9200; info@nclis.gov; www.nclis.gov/index.cfm.

National Committee on Pay Equity, 1925 K St., N.W., Suite 402, Washington, DC 20006-1119; (202) 223-8360, ext. 8; fairpay@pay-equity.org; www.pay-equity.org.

National Council for History Education, 26915 Westwood Rd., Suite B2, Westlake, OH 44145-4657; (440) 835-1776; nche@nche.net; www.nche.net.

National Council for the Accreditation of Teacher Education, 2010 Massachusetts Ave., N.W., Suite 500, Washington, DC 20036-1023; (202) 466-7496; ncate@ncate.org; www.ncate.org.

National Council of Teachers of English, 1111 Kenyon Rd., Urbana, IL 61801-1096; (217) 328-3870, (877) 369-6283; www.ncte.org.

National Council of Teachers of Mathematics, 1906 Association Dr., Reston, VA 22091-1502; (703) 620-9840; orders@nctm.org; www.nctm.org.

National Council on Public History, 327 Cavanaugh Hall-IUPUI, 425 University Boulevard, Indianapolis, IN 46202-5140; (317) 274-2716; ncph@iupui.edu; ncph.org.

National Endowment for the Arts, 1100 Pennsylvania Ave., N.W., Washington, DC 20506; (202) 682-5570; www.arts.gov.

National Endowment for the Humanities, 1100 Pennsylvania Ave., N.W., Washington, DC 20506; (202) 606-8400, (800) 634-1121; info@neh.gov; www.neh.gov.

National Federation of Abstracting and Indexing Services, 1518 Walnut St., Suite 1004, Philadelphia, PA 19102-3403; (215) 893-1561; nfais@nfais.org; www.nfais.org.

National Film Preservation Foundation, 870 Market St., Suite 1113, San Francisco, CA 94102; (415) 392-7291; info@filmpreservation.org; www.filmpreservation.org.

National Historical Publications and Records Commission, National Archives and Records Administration, 700 Pennsylvania Avenue, N.W., Room 111, Washington, DC 20408-0001; (202) 501-5610; www.archives.gov/nhprc/.

National Information Standards Organization, 4733 Bethesda Ave., Suite 300, Bethesda, MD 20814; (301) 654-2512; nisohq@niso.org; www.niso.org.

National Institute for Literacy, 1775 I St., N.W., Suite 730, Washington, DC 20006-2401; (202) 233-2025; www.nifl.gov.

National Science Teachers Association, 1840 Wilson Blvd., Arlington, VA 22201-3000; (703) 243-7100; www.nsta.org.

National Security Archive, Gelman Library, George Washington University,

2130 H St., N.W., Suite 701, Washington, DC 20037; (202) 994-7000; nsarchiv@gwu.edu; www2.gwu.edu/~nsarchiv/.

National Storytelling Network, 132 Boone St., Jonesborough, TN 37659; (423) 913-8201, (800) 525-4514; nsn@storynet.org; storynet.org.

National Technical Information Service, U.S. Department of Commerce, 5285 Port Royal Rd., Springfield, VA 22161; (703) 605-6000; info@ntis.gov; www.ntis.gov.

National Trust for Historic Preservation, 1785 Massachusetts Ave., N.W., Washington, DC 20036-2117; (202) 588-6000, (800) 944-6847; members@nthp.org; www.nationaltrust.org.

North American Cartographic Information Society, American Geographic Society Collection, P.O. Box 399, Milwaukee, WI 53201; (414) 229-6282, nacis@nacis.org; www.nacis.org.

North American Serials Interest Group, PMB 214, 2103 N. Decatur Rd., Decatur, GA 30033-5305; info@nasig.org; www.nasig.org.

Northeast Document Conservation Center, 100 Brickstone Square, Andover, MA 01810-1494; (978) 470-1010; nedcc@nedcc.org; www.nedcc.org.

OCLC Online Computer Library Center, 6565 Frantz Road, Dublin, OH 43017-3395; (614) 764-6000, (800) 848-5878; oclc@oclc.org; www.oclc.org.

Ontario Library Association, 100 Lombard St., Suite 303, Toronto, Ontario M5C IM3, Canada; (416) 363-3388, (866) 873-9867; info@accessola.com; www.accessola.com.

Oral History Association, Dickinson College, P.O. Box 1773, Carlisle, PA 17013-2896; (717) 245-1036; oha@dickinson.edu; omega.dickinson.edu/organizations/oha/.

Patent and Trademark Depository Library Association, www.ptdla.org.

PEN American Center, 568 Broadway, Suite 303, New York, NY 10012-3225; (212) 334-1660; pen@pen.org; www.pen.org.

Poetry Society of America, 15 Gramercy Park, New York, NY 10003; (212) 254-9628; www.poetrysociety.org.

Poets House, 72 Spring St., 2nd Floor, New York, NY 10012; (212) 431-7920; info@poetshouse.org; www.poetshouse.org.

Popular Culture Association/American Culture Association, c/o Michael Schoenecke, Professor of English, Box 43091, Texas Tech University, Lubbock, TX 79409-3091; (806) 742-1617; mkschoene@aol.com; www.h-net.org/~pcaaca/pca/pcahistory.htm.

Program for Cooperative Cataloging, Regional and Cooperative Cataloging Division, Library of Congress, Washington, DC 20540-4382; (202) 707-2822; cast@loc.gov; www.loc.gov/catdir/pcc/.

Progressive Librarians Guild, P.O. Box 2203, Times Square Station, New York, NY 10108; (973) 623-7642; eharger@agoron.com; www.libr.org/PLG/.

ProLiteracy Worldwide, 1320 Jamesville Ave., Syracuse, NY 13210; (315) 422-9121, (888) 528-2224; info@proliteracy.org; www.proliteracy.org.

Radical Reference, info@radicalreference.info; www.radicalreference.info.

Reading Is Fundamental, 1825 Connecticut Ave., N.W., Suite 400, Washington, DC 20009; (202) 673-0020, (877) 743-7323; contactus@rif.org; www.rif.org.

Reforma: National Association to Promote Library Services to Latinos and the Spanish Speaking, c/o Sandra Rios Balderrama, P.O. Box 25963, Scottsdale, AZ 85255-0116; (480) 471-7452; reformaoffice@riosbalderrama.com; www.reforma.org.

RLG, 2029 Stierlin Court, Suite 100, Mountain View, CA 94043-4684; (650)

691-2333, (800) 537-7546; ric@notes.rlg.org; www.rlg.org.

Seminar on the Acquisition of Latin American Library Materials, Benson Latin American Collection, Sid Richardson Hall 1.109, University of Texas, Austin, TX 78713-8916; (512) 495-4471; sandyl@mail.utexas.edu; www. library.cornell.edu/colldev/salalmhome.html.

Slainte: Information and Libraries Scotland, 1st Floor Building C, Brandon Gate, Leechlee Road, Hamilton ML3 6AU, United Kingdom; +44 (1698) 458888; slic@lslainte.org.uk; www.slainte.org.uk/SLIC/.

Society for Scholarly Publishing, 10200 W. 44th Ave., Suite 304, Wheat Ridge, CO 80033-2840; (303) 422-3914; info@sspnet.org; www.sspnet.org.

Society of American Archivists, 527 S. Wells St., 5th Floor, Chicago, IL 60607; (312) 922-0140; info@archivists.org; www.archivists.org.

Software and Information Industry Association, 1090 Vermont Ave., N.W., 6th Floor, Washington, DC 20005-4095; (202) 289-7097; www.siia.net.

SOLINET, 1438 W. Peachtree St., N.W., Suite 200, Atlanta, GA 30309-2955; (404) 892-7879, (900) 999-8558; knevins@solinet.net; www.solinet.net.

Special Libraries Association, 331 S. Patrick St., Alexandria, VA 22314-3501; (703) 647-4900; sla@sla.org; www.sla.org.

Substance Abuse Librarians and Information Specialists, P.O. Box 9513, Berkeley, CA 94709-0513; (510) 642-5208; salis@salis.org; salis.org.

Theatre Library Association, c/o New York Public Library for the Performing Arts, 40 Lincoln Center Plaza, New York, NY 10023; martilomonaco@ optonline.net; tla.library.unt.edu.

Urban Libraries Council, 1603 Orrington Avenue, Suite 1080, Evanston, IL 60201; (847) 866-9999; info@urbanlibraries.org; www.urbanlibraries.org.

Writing a query letter

by Rachel Singer Gordon

WHILE COMPOSING an effective query letter and/or book proposal is the single best means of getting your work accepted for publication, there are a number of simple yet commonly ignored steps you can take to improve your odds. Editors both want to find new authors to work with and need to find new material to publish, and they are thrilled when they find writers who are distinguished by their attention to detail and professionalism. Remember that editors' success rests on constantly providing new and useful material to readers; publications and presses need writers as much as writers need them.

Unfortunately, newer and aspiring authors often fail to recognize the importance of seemingly minor details throughout the publication process (from spell check to proper manuscript formatting to familiarity with the journal), feeling that their work's strength should be inherently obvious. Successful writers realize, however, that failure to attend to detail can prevent editors from even getting to their content, and that professionalism and thoroughness can provide the "in" you need to get your work taken seriously.

Tips and Tricks for Publishing Success

1. Let it rest. Resist the urge to turn in a manuscript the instant it is complete; put it away for a week so that you can read it over with a fresh eye before submitting.
2. Follow guidelines. Publishers provide these for a reason; ignore them at your peril.
3. Meet deadlines. Publishers are on a calendar and need time to put an issue together or to edit, print, and publish titles expected in a certain season.
4. Know your audience. Editors always have the target market of their journal or press in mind, and the most important factor in accepting or rejecting your manuscript is whether it meets the needs of that market.
5. Know your publishing outlet. Familiarity with the articles or titles it publishes allows you to conform to its requirements and style and prevents you from submitting manuscripts or queries that are clearly outside of its scope.
6. Deliver what you promise.
7. Learn to prize clarity and conciseness; avoid excessive jargon.
8. Ensure that your work makes a unique contribution to the literature.
9. Ensure that your research findings are statistically significant and clearly presented.
10. Write what you enjoy. If you try to write on subjects for which you feel little interest—let alone passion!—your apathy will inevitably show.

While the tips in the sidebar above may seem like simple common sense, they reflect editors' most common pet peeves about their interactions with authors—and potential authors. Assimilating these suggestions and making a habit of interacting professionally with editors can dramatically increase your odds of being published, regardless of the inherent quality of your writing.

Increasing the odds for acceptance

Matching the content and style of your queries to particular publications' needs is of major importance. A common mistake beginning writers make is to blindly send a manuscript or query out to all the "big name" publications without taking the time to consider how their work fits into these journals and how they can tailor an inquiry to each. Pick one journal at a time, study its contents and needs, and customize your contact accordingly.

This is another instance where making a habit of reading regularly in the literature will pay off. Watch for editorials from journal editors discussing topics they would like to see submitted to their publication and for announcements of thematic issues. You will want to pick up on such editorials and announcements while they are still fresh, before the editor is overrun with ideas on his/her suggested themes or their timeliness has diminished.

Providence College Reference/Instruction Librarian Edgar Bailey shares an experience that helped him learn the importance of targeting publications' current needs and foci:

> Familiarize yourself with the types of articles published in the various journals. Submit to ones that focus on the area of your interest. Everyone would like to be published in *JAL* or *C&RL*, but there are many more specialized publications where you will have a better chance. Read the instructions to authors as well. I made the mistake of submitting an article to *RQ* just at the time when it was seeking to become more scholarly. Even though I wrote my article reporting a research project, I wrote it in the informal style which had previously

characterized *RQ*. Although the article was ultimately accepted, I had to completely rewrite it to conform to the new policies.

Also consider sending your initial queries to smaller or lesser-known publications. While you may crave the recognition a well-known journal provides, publishing in smaller venues will both enhance your writing résumé and provide clips you can then send to larger journals. Prestigious peer-reviewed journals have a very high rejection rate since everyone wants to write for these publications. Working for smaller journals also allows you to practice your writing skills and can allow you to publish more controversial and more informal material than is acceptable at most of the bigger-name outlets.

Look at writing for smaller outlets just as you would approach applying for an entry-level position. When you start out in the library field, you may begin by working for a smaller library or in a less-than-ideal position; then a year or two later use your experience to move on to a location more suited to you. The same applies to publication in the library field—your experience with smaller publications or creating shorter pieces builds your résumé so that you are later ready to tackle larger projects. Experienced writer GraceAnne A. DeCandido suggests that beginning librarian authors "start small—book reviews and Letters to the Editor are an excellent place to begin." Massachusetts Board of Library Com-

missioners Consultant Shelley Quezada concurs: "Also, I think it is a great idea for folks to 'start small'—that is, begin by writing small articles for local state newsletters or contribute to your city or town newsletter. If they do not have one, then suggest beginning one. Writing . . . requires practice."

Alternatively, you may find that you actually prefer being a big fish in a smaller pond. You can spend your entire writing career happily writing for smaller or more informal publishing outlets, just as some information professionals prefer spending their whole library careers working in smaller institutions.

These smaller outlets include journals and newsletters published by your state library or library association. Such publications are always looking for contributors, and it can be easier to break into their pages than into national journals. They also may be more interested in descriptions of programs or projects in your library than larger journals, as you have the local angle working in your favor.

Whether submitting to local or national outlets, always keep any communication with editors professional and to the point. A query letter or manuscript full of typographical, grammatical, or spelling errors will be the kiss of death. Pay particular attention when composing emails to an editor, as it is easier to lapse into informality on-screen, and not all email clients have spell-check. Keep your manuscripts professional and clean as well. While a nicely formatted manuscript will not guarantee your acceptance, it can prevent your work from being rejected without being read. It will also prevent reviewers and editors from being biased against your work from the outset; they will not appreciate having to read a sloppy manuscript, and errors can easily distract them from the content of your writing. Take the opportunity to make a good first impression.

SOURCE: Rachel Singer Gordon, *The Librarian's Guide to Writing for Publication* (Lanham, Md.: Scarecrow, 2004), pp. 41–44. Reprinted with permission.

Getting published in scholarly journals

by Robert V. Labaree

THERE IS A PLETHORA OF LITERATURE offering guidance on how to get published. In general, it encompasses either didactic works providing detailed "dos" and "don'ts" or it represents the anecdotal musings of authors and editors outlining their own tormented journey to first authorship. Early career librarians and soon-to-be-graduating library science students planning to enter academia may find this literature overwhelming and often conflicted. For those librarians carrying faculty status, the need to publish original research as part of the tenure and promotion process can be perceived as an especially daunting responsibility.

Whether you must publish as part of your institution's promotion process, or you simply want to disseminate your research to a broader audience, future authors may find the following strategies helpful.

Read the professional literature

Subscribe to electronic content alert services, such as the *Informed Librarian* (www.infosourcespub.com/ilofreesubscribe.cfm) and the table of contents alerting services of journals in your areas of interest. Monitor contents for gaps in the literature where the insights of an academic librarian could be of value. Pay particular attention to the call for papers section of the *Chronicle of Higher Education* and other publications for opportunities to present a conference paper that could eventually lead to a published article.

Become a good writer

The fastest track to getting published is to be a good writer. However, becoming an accomplished writer is rarely something you can achieve, but more representative of a continual process of reflexivity and practice. For example, thanks to the advice of an early career mentor, I volunteer to write abstracts for *America: History and Life and Historical Abstracts*. The material benefit is that you receive free issues of the journal you abstract. Intellectually, writing abstracts forces you to read and carefully analyze scholarly literature, thereby gaining a better understanding of the style and jargon of "academic speak."

Rod Serling tells:

What every creative person should know about writing for money

Rod Serling, six-time Emmy Award winner, made TV writing an art form with *Patterns, Requiem for a Heavyweight* and *Twilight Zone*. He has also written many short stories and motion picture scripts.

The act of synthesizing a dense, scholarly article into a 300-word abstract also requires developing and enhancing skills important to good writing, such as identifying a study's research problem, presenting a pertinent review of the literature, and understanding how to link main findings to the methodology used.

Write book reviews. I currently write reviews for *American Review of Books Annual, Choice,* and *Review of Higher Education.* I began writing book reviews by simply contacting the editor and volunteering my time and expertise. Send a letter to the editor of your favorite journal expressing a desire to write reviews. Describe your qualifications and areas of academic expertise. Writing book reviews will help you become a better writer, and, as an additional incentive, you often get to keep the books, which can then be donated to your local public library.

Revisit papers from your academic past. Consider papers you wrote as an undergraduate or graduate student. These works may not have been written with an intent to publish, but reread them and think about opportunities to publish in relation to specific journals. Use your skills as a librarian to conduct further research about the topic of your paper (or a subtopic embedded within) that can help bring the manuscript to publication quality as a result of additional research and writing.

Read new publications. Competition is fierce, and most new journals cease publication within their first few years, but publishers of new titles may be more open to consider a manuscript to help ensure the publication's survival. This does not mean editors of new journals will accept works of lesser quality, but the fact is their journals have yet to build a strong reputation. Therefore, it is unlikely that they will have a large backlog of manuscripts waiting to be reviewed. Always look for announcements of new journal titles at professional conferences and in the mail.

Review journal manuscripts and conference papers. Contact the editors of your favorite journals and ask to be considered as a manuscript reviewer. Often these are invited positions. However, target new titles and look for opportunities to meet editors at professional conferences. Ask if any openings are available for additional reviewers. Some journals maintain a large pool of reviewers because the scope of research disseminated within the journal is so broad. Target them. Also, look for announcements requesting volunteers to review conference papers. Reviewing papers submitted for presentation at conferences gives you an opportunity to read and evaluate what is currently being studied before it is published, and it will help enhance your writing skills because reviewing papers forces you to critically evaluate the writing of others. Critiquing journal manuscripts gives you an inside track to publishing in that journal because you see firsthand what is accepted and rejected.

Consider professional education journals. In most disciplines there is at least one journal devoted to examining the development and improvement of pedagogical practice. For example, in my areas of academic expertise, there are the *Journal of Planning Education and Research* (urban and regional planning), *Perspectives on Political Science*, and the *Journal of Public Affairs Education* (which focuses on examining the scholarship of teaching in public administration). These journals offer a good opportunity to get published because a topic that has been broadly treated in the field of academic librarianship, such as information literacy, may be viewed as relatively groundbreaking in the professional education journal of another discipline.

Look at professional development activities

Any professional-development meeting, any poster session, any panel discussion, any volunteer opportunity you participate in can either provide you with a framework for developing a research article or give you ideas for developing one, as a result of working with someone or hearing them speak. For example, a paper I published in *Advances in Qualitative Organizational Research* (JAI Press, 1999), examining the discursive strategies university administrators use when confronting a public relations crisis, was first formulated as a result of attending a meeting at the American Educational Research Association conference in 1997.

Active participation is key, but think strategically about targeting professional activities that maximize your chances to realize publishing opportunities because, let's face it, you are a very busy person. One way to think strategically about linking professional development activities with publishing opportunities is to target activities that relate to current issues in librarianship and higher education. This will expose you to the ideas and opinions of others who are prolific writers, and it may help lay the conceptual groundwork for formulating your own ideas about a research project. Always look for opportunities to publish in areas of study outside of librarianship when you are participating in professional activities.

Attend "How to Get Published" panel discussions. Make it a priority at conferences to attend these types of sessions. If one is not scheduled, suggest to the chair of the organization's conference planning committee that a "how to get published" discussion forum would be of value to you and others, then offer to help organize it. Editors participating on these panels often provide helpful suggestions for getting published, and not just in general but as it may relate to the specific journal they are associated with.

Know your audience, know the journal's audience

It is important to write in different styles for different audiences. Therefore, identify early in your research which journal you are planning to submit the manuscript to after it has been completed. Read articles in that journal covering the past few years and pay particular attention to what has been published during the tenure of the current editorial board. This will help familiarize you with what type of articles have been published while they have served as editors. If you are unsure whether your research topic is appropriate for the publication's primary readership, contact the editor and ask. If the editor indicates that the topic is out of scope, ask him or her to suggest another journal that may be more appropriate. If your topic is deemed appropriate for the journal's audience, you have already succeeded in demonstrating to the editor your interest in publishing with them, and they may be on the lookout for your manuscript as a result.

Talk to publishers at professional conferences. Walk the exhibit hall at professional conferences and make note of the publishers in your primary areas of interest. Speak with publisher representatives about possible new journal titles that may need additional contributions from an author or manuscript reviewer. Ask them to identify editors within their company whom you can speak with about your research ideas.

Collaborate

This is closely related to the strategy of viewing every professional development activity as an opportunity to publish. With an idea in mind, seek out people with like interests and gauge if you can collaborate with them on a writing project or a professional activity that could then lead to publication. Take advantage of your outreach activities on campus when pursuing opportunities to collaborate. However, in these cases, be prepared to do the initial legwork, because your faculty liaisons may consider you a valued colleague, but not necessarily someone they would consider coauthoring an article with. Writing a rough draft of the paper or a detailed outline of the proposed research study can demonstrate that you are sincere in collaborating with them.

Have others review your manuscript

This is very important. Journal editors always encourage potential authors to have their manuscripts reviewed by others before submitting them for possible publication. Identify colleagues who possess good writing skills as a result of being a teacher, a writer, or an editor. Ask them to review your paper in exchange for a free lunch, for example. They may be brutal in their assessment, but the end result will be a much better paper more likely to be of publication quality. Always follow the journal's publication guidelines precisely and always point out in your cover letter that several people reviewed your manuscript.

Rejection

Most peer-reviewed journals include comments from manuscript reviewers regardless of whether your paper has been accepted or rejected. If the editor does not send them to you, request that he or she does. If your paper has been

rejected for publication, consider the reviewer's comments and suggestions carefully. It is part of becoming a better writer. Remember that a "not acceptable as is, needs major revision" statement is *not* a flat-out rejection of your work—do what the reviewers tell you and resubmit it. If you follow their suggestions, the chances of eventually publishing the paper will be increased. However, provide a detailed explanation in the cover letter accompanying your resubmitted manuscript describing precisely how you have addressed the concerns of each reviewer. And remember, if you are able to join a journal's pool of manuscript reviewers, you can avoid these pitfalls ahead of time because you will have seen others.

And finally . . .

You are a librarian! You have been trained in the arts and sciences of employing effective research strategies, understanding the processes involved with critically evaluating scholarly research, and thinking interdisciplinarily about issues and topics that intersect the field of academic librarianship. Use those skills to manage a research project and ask your colleagues to provide the feedback needed to ensure that your paper is of publication quality. Good luck!

SOURCE: Robert V. Labaree, "Tips for Getting Published in Scholarly Journals," *College & Research Libraries News* 65 (March 2004): 137–139.

Reviewing reference books

by the ALA Reference and User Services Association

DEFINITION. A reference book is a handbook or compendium that contains facts, statistics, definitions, formulae, or other basic information giving direction to researchers. It provides users with current information that will help them develop arguments, explanations, and/or expand their search for more specific or specialized resources. Reference materials may be single volume or multivolume sets. Types of reference books include dictionaries, encyclopedias, and handbooks.

The reviewer should have a good grasp of the subject matter covered in the work and be aware of, or investigate, other reference works in the field.

The review should contain a general description of the work, its purpose, scope, and publication history. If the work is a revision or new edition of an existing source, the reviewer should pay special attention to the portions that have been revised. Note any dated or obsolete material. Note if the book is a supplement to, rather than a replacement for, earlier editions. If the revision corrects mistakes or answers appropriate negative criticism of an earlier edition, this should be noted.

The authority of the author, editor, and contributors and their credentials or the lack thereof should be noted, if important to the evaluative process. Indicate if individual entries are signed. Do the contents of the work match the purpose and the scope?

Explain the organization of the work: alphabetical, chronological, topical, etc. Note ease of use, cross-references, table of contents, and indices. References within the text should be accurate. The currency of bibliographic citations should be noted. If appropriate, note type and number of illustrations, entries, and any special features such as tables, text boxes, etc.

Consider the audience for which the reference is written. Is the sophistication of language and concepts appropriate for that audience?

It is critical to compare the work to others in the field. Note any new contributions or indicate if it substantially duplicates similar items. If the work is unique to the field, be sure of this fact.

Check the format and physical characteristics of the book (binding, layout, etc.). If something is not acceptable (i.e., difficult to read due to lack of white space, binding that will not hold up under heavy use), indicate the problem.

Provide examples that support both positive and negative findings.

Provide a final evaluation, noting whether the work fulfills its stated purpose. Also make a recommendation for the type of collection that will use it.

Finalize the review

Adhere to deadlines; warn the editor as soon as you can if you will not be able to supply a review by the indicated deadline.

Polish the final review before submitting it to the editor: Use the active voice; avoid the passive voice. Avoid using language that may come across as cute, condescending, or obscure. Watch basic grammar (keep an eye on prepositions) and spelling. Get rid of nearly every *it, this, that, there, who, which.* Remove redundancies and unnecessary descriptors. Break up long sentences. When possible, avoid negatives and state it positively.

Beware of too much description and not enough evaluation. Don't present a laundry list or table of contents when describing an item.

Be sure to back up judgments and evaluations; offer support for evaluations.

The final recommendation for purchase should follow the test; don't give an item a negative review and then recommend it for purchase.

The reviewer should not be showcased; don't write about you and your reactions. Write about the material. Avoid subjectivity and be as objective as possible. If you can't be objective, ask the editor to assign the materials to someone else.

Be very sure of your ground and avoid making false claims or criticisms for an item. For instance: "This is the *only* book available on the subject."

SOURCE: Elements for Basic Reviews, May 2004 draft, ALA/RUSA CODES Materials Review Committee, www.ala.org/ala/rusa/.

MATERIALS
CHAPTER FOUR

"I despair of ever getting it through anybody's head I am not interested in bookshops, I am interested in what's in the books. I don't browse in bookshops, I browse in libraries, where you can take a book home and read it, and if you like it you can go to a bookshop and buy it."

—Helene Hanff, *The Duchess of Bloomsbury Street* (1973)

BOOKS

Earliest printed books in selected languages

by George M. Eberhart

PRINTING WAS FIRST DEVELOPED in ancient China using a block of wood on which characters were carved in reverse relief. The woodblock was then inked to produce multiple impressions on sheets of paper or parchment. The technique was eventually applied to books—collections of pages connected as a scroll or bound together along one edge within a cover. Movable type was also invented in China, but it only proved successful in Europe in the 15th century because of the limited character set of Indo-European languages.

No source that I know of identifies the earliest known printed books in various languages. This list contains a number of educated guesses as well as omissions, so if any readers know of earlier imprints or languages that I've missed, please contact me.

Diamond Sutra Or. 8210/P.2

Diamond Sutra scroll, courtesy of the British Library

Chinese. *Jin gang ban ruo bo luo mi jing* [Diamond Sutra scroll]. This is a copy of the Sanskrit *Vajracchedika-prajnaparamitasutra*, translated into Chinese by Kumarajiva, printed by Wang Jie in May 868, and discovered in 1907 by Sir M. Aurel Stein at the Dunhuang Caves. Although woodblock printing had already been in use in China for more than 150 years, this is the earliest printed book to bear an actual date. The document consists of seven strips of yellow-stained paper pasted together to form a scroll more than five meters long. Owned by the British Library, the scroll can be viewed online at www.bl.uk/onlinegallery/ttp/digitisation2.html. Movable type made of baked clay and glue was invented by the alchemist Bi Sheng in 1041, but never caught on because of the multiplicity of Chinese ideograms.

Japanese. *Busseltsu kokkuji jinshu ogyo* is the oldest surviving specimen of a Japanese woodblock book containing a publication date. It is owned by the Ishiyamadera Temple, and has a notation of the year 1052 in red ink.

Although they are not books, a unique set of eight *Hyakumantô darani* (Million Pagoda Charms), printed between A.D. 718 and 764 on the orders of Empress Shôtoku (718–770), constitute the earliest printed documents with authenticated dates to have survived to the present day anywhere in the world. They are owned by the British Museum.

Korean. *Baegun hwasang chorok buljo jikji simche yojeol* [Jikji] (Cheongju, Korea: Heungdeoksa Temple, July 1377). A collection of Zen Buddhist texts compiled by a Korean priest named Baegun, the second volume of this book is preserved at the Bibliothèque Nationale in Paris. This is the oldest extant example of movable metal type printing.

Metal type was used in Korea as early as 1234; in 1403 King Htai Tjong ordered the first set of 100,000 pieces of type to be cast in bronze. Early examples of Chinese woodblock printing have been found in Korea, most notably the *Mugujonggwang taedaranigyong* [Pure Light Dharani Sutra] scroll, perhaps the earliest extant printed document in the world. Discovered in 1966 in the Sokkatap Pagoda at Pulguksa, it presumably was put into Chinese characters by a monk named Mit'asan around the year 704.

Latin. *Biblia Latina* [42-line Gutenberg Bible] (Mainz, Germany: Johann Gutenberg, 1454). An estimated 180 copies, 140 on paper and 40 on vellum, of the first printed Bible were manufactured in Mainz. Today, 49 complete and incomplete Gutenberg Bibles are known to exist worldwide, of which only 12 are printed on vellum. The four complete vellum copies are located in the State and University Library of Lower Saxony in Göttingen, the British Library, the Bibliothèque Nationale, and the Library of Congress.

German. A pamphlet/calendar: *Eyn Manung der Christenheit widder die Durken* (Mainz, Germany: Johann Gutenberg, 1454). The first German Bible was *Biblia* (Strasbourg, France: Johann Mentelin, 1466?).

French. Raoul Lefèvre, *Recueil des histories de Troyes* (Köln, Germany, 1466).

Czech. Guido delle Colonne, *Kronika Trojánská* (Plzen, Czech Republic, 1468).

Italian. Francesco Petrarca, *Canzonieri* (Venice, Italy: Wendelin of Speier, 1470). The first Italian Bible was published by Wendelin of Speier in 1471.

Hebrew. Rashi, [Commentary on the Midrash] (Rome, Italy, 1470).

English. Raoul Lefèvre, *The Recuyell of the Historyes of Troye*, trans. William Caxton (Bruges, Belgium: William Caxton, 1474).

Spanish. *Les obres o trobes dauall scrites les quals tracten dela sacratissima verge Maria* (Valencia, Spain: Lamberto Palmart and Fernando de Córdoba, 1474).

Greek. Constantine Lascaris, *Erotemata: Epitome ton okto tou logou meron* (Milan, Italy: Dioysius Paravisinus, 1476).

Dutch. *Vetus Testamentum* (Delft, Netherlands: Jacob Jacobszoen van der Meer and Mauricius Yemantszoen, 1477) was the first Old Testament in Dutch. The first complete Dutch Bible was printed in Antwerp by Jacob van Liesvelt in 1526.

Caxton's *Recuyell*

Courtesy of Ron Koster / Psymon

English, first in the U.K. Mubashshir ibn Fatik, Abu al-Wafa', *Dictes and Notable Wyse Sayenges of the Phylosophers* (Westminster, Eng.: William Caxton, 1479).

Croatian. *Missale Glagoliticum* (Kosinj, Croatia, 1483).

Portuguese. *Pentateuco* (Faro, Portugal: Samuel Porteiro Gacon, 1487).

Serbian. *Ochtoechos, modes 1–4* (Cetinje, Montenegro, 1494).

Danish. *Den danske rimkrønike* (København, Denmark: Godtfred af Ghemen, 1495).

Swedish. Jean Gerson, *Aff dyäfwlsens frästilse* (Stockholm, Sweden: Johannes Smedh, 1495).

Slavonic. *Liturghierul lui Macarie* (Targoviste, Romania: Macarie, 1508).

Polish. Biernat, z Lublina, *Raj duszy* (Krakow, Poland: F. Ungler, 1510).

Armenian. *Urbat'agirk'* (Venice, Italy: Hakob Meghapart, 1512).

Ethiopian. [Ethiopian Psalms of David] (Rome, Italy: Johannes Potken, 1513).

Arabic. *Kitab salat al-sawa'i* (Fano, Italy, 1514).

Polyglot Bible, first. *Vetus testamentum multiplici lingua nunc primo impressum* [Complutensian Bible] (Alcalà de Henares, Spain: Arnaldo Guillén de Brocar, 1514–1517). Edited by a team of scholars headed by Diego López de Zúniga, including Alfonso de Zamora, Pablo Coronel, Alfonso de Alcala, and others under the patronage of Cardinal Jiménes de Cisneros, this Bible has parallel columns of Latin, Greek, and Hebrew or Aramaic for scholarly comparison.

Greek (modern). *Homerou Ilias* (Venice, Italy: Stefano de Sabio, 1526).

Estonian. Simon Wanradt and Johannes Koell, *Katekismus* (Wittenberg, Germany, 1535).

Nahuatl and **Spanish, first in the New World.** Juan de Zumárraga, *Breve y más compendiosa doctrina christiana en lengua mexicana y castellana* (México City: Juan Pablos, 1539).

Hungarian. *Úy Testamentu,* trans. Janós Sylvester (Sárvár, Hungary, 1541).

Finnish. Mikael Agricola, *Abckiria* (Stockholm, Sweden: Amund Laurentsson, 1543?).

Basque. Bernat Dechepare, *Linguae Vasconum primitiae* (Bordeaux, France: Bernat Dechepare, 1545).

Prussian. *Catechismus jn preüßnischer sprach vnd da gegen das deüdsche* (Königsberg [Kaliningrad, Russia]: Hans Weinreich, 1545).

Welsh. *Yny lhyvyr hwnn* (London: Edward Whitchurch, 1546).

Lithuanian. Martynas Mazvydus, *Catechismusa prasty Szadei* (Kaliningrad, Russia: Johann Weinreich, 1547).

Romanian. *Catehismul* (Brasov, Romania: Diaconul Coresi, 1559).

Russian. *Apostol* (Moscow: Ivan Fedorov, 1564).

Irish. John O'Kearney, *Aibidil Gaoidheilge, & Caiticiosma* (ambaile Athacliath, 1571).

Ukrainian. *Azbuka* (L'viv, Ukraine: Ivan Fedorov, 1574).

Tamil. *Thampiraan vaNakkam* (Goa, India: Henrique Henriques, 1578).

Icelandic. *Biblia Pad Er, Öll Heilög Ritning, vtlögd a Norrænu* (Hólar, Iceland: Jone Jons syne, 1584) was the first Icelandic Bible.

Latvian. *Katolu catechisms* (Vilnius, Lithuania, 1585).

Quichua. Provincial Council of Lima, *Confessionario para los curas de Indios* (Lima, Peru, 1585).

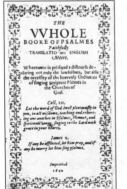

Bay Psalm Book,
courtesy of
the American
Antiquarian Society

Tagalog. Tomás Pinpin, *Librong Pagaaralan nang manga Tagalog nang uicang Castila* (Manila, 1610).

English, first in North America. *The Whole Booke of Psalmes Faithfully Translated into English Metre* [Bay Psalm book] (Cambridge, Mass.: Stephen Daye, 1640).

Vietnamese. Alexandre de Rhodes, *Catechismvs pro ijs* (Rome: Congregationis de propaganda fide, 1651?).

Wampanoag. John Eliot, *May, waj woh nashpe nutayi mun wahshâe wunauchemookae moeuweekomunk, ut oowesuonganit Jesus Christ* (Cambridge, Mass.: Samuel Green, 1658).

Montagnais. Jean-Baptiste de la Brosse, *Nehiro-iriniui aiamihe massinahigan* (Québec City, Canada: Broun and Girmor, 1767). This Indian catechism is said to be the first book printed in Canada.

Bengali. Nathaniel Brassey Halhed, *A Grammar of the Bengal Language* (Hugli, India, 1778).

Hindi. *A Grammar of the Hindoostanee Language* (Calcutta, India: Chronicle Press, 1796).

English, first in Australia. *New South Wales General Standing Orders* (Sydney, N.S.W.: George Howe, 1802).

Oriya. Mrtyuñjaya Bidyalankar, trans. [New Testament] (Shrirampur, India: Serampore Mission Press, 1807).

Tahitian. *Te aebi no Taheiti* (n.p., John Davis, 1810).

Malayalam. [New Testament] (Bombay, India: Courier Press, 1811).

Assamese. William Carey, et al., trans. [New Testament] (Shrirampur, India: Serampore Mission Press, 1813).

Telugu. *Grammar of Telugu* (Shrirampur, India: Serampore Mission Press, 1813).

Maori. Thomas Kendall, *A korao no New Zealand* (Sydney, N.S.W., 1815).

Hawaiian. [Gospels of Matthew, Mark, and John] (Rochester, N.Y.: Paiia ma ka mea pai palapala a lumiki, 1828–1829).

Cherokee. Elias Boudinot and Samuel Austin Worcester, *Cherokee Hymns* (New Echota, Ga.: J. F. Wheeler, 1829).

Afrikaans. C. P. Hoogenhout, *Eerste Afrikaanse printjies boeki vir soet kinders* (Paarl, South Africa: D. F. du Toit, 1879).

Out-of-print book terms and abbreviations

by Narda Tafuri, Anna Seaberg, and Gary Handman

4to, 8vo, 12mo, etc. Refers to the size of the book. This is based on the number of pages into which a single printed sheet has been folded to create the leaves that form the pages of a book. The fewer the folds, the larger the book. Most hardbound books are 8vo (octavo—6 by 9 inches, about the size of an average hardcover). To make an octavo book, a printed sheet would be folded eight times to form eight leaves. A leaf contains two printed pages, one on each side. A 4to is a quarto (9 by 12 inches). A 12mo is a duodecimo (five by eight inches, about the size of an average paperback).

Aeg. All edges gilt.

As new. *See* Condition.

Bdg. Binding.

Bds. Boards; the stiff front and back parts of hardcover books.

BOMC. Book-of-the-month club.

Brodart. Plastic cover used to protect a book's dust jacket.

Bumped. Dented; usually occurs on a book's edges and corners due to use.

Chipped. Small tears, or small pieces missing from the edges of pages or dust jacket.

Cocked. The spine is twisted so that the boards will not line up evenly with each other.

Condition. The following are standard bookseller terms generally used to describe the following conditions of a book. Abbreviations for these terms are: "near fine"—NF; "good"—G; "fine"—F; "very good"—VG; "poor"—P; "fair" and "as new" have no abbreviation. When two abbreviations or terms of condition are used together with a slash, the first term generally refers to the condition of the book and the second term to the condition of the dust jacket; for example, VG/VG means that the book is in very good condition and the dust jacket is also in very good condition. Term definitions below are quoted from the *AB Bookman's Weekly*.

As new: To be used only when a book is in the same immaculate condition as that in which it was published. There can be no defects, no missing pages, no library stamps, etc., and the dust jacket (if it was issued with one) must be perfect, without any tears.

Fine: Approaches the "as new" condition, but without being crisp. For the use of the term "fine" there must also be no defects, etc., and if the jacket has a small tear, or other defect, or looks worn, this should be noted.

Very good: Showing some small signs of wear—but no tears—on either binding or paper. Any defects must be noted.

Good: The average condition of a used book—worn, all pages or leaves present. Any defects must be noted.

Fair: Worn, with complete text pages (including those with maps or plates) but possibly lacking endpapers, half-title, etc. (which must be noted). Binding, jacket (if any), etc., may also be worn. All defects must be noted.

Poor: Sufficiently worn that its only merit is as a reading copy. Its text is complete and legible, but it may be soiled, scuffed, stained, or spotted and may have loose joints, hinges, pages, etc. Any missing maps or plates should still be noted.

Dust jacket (DJ). Also called dust wrapper; the paper cover, usually illustrated, placed around a book to protect its binding.

Dust wrapper (DW). *See* Dust jacket.

Ep. Endpapers; sheets of papers pasted onto the inside covers joining the text block to the cover. One side is pasted down onto the cover, the other is left free.

Exlib or ex-lib. A book that has been purchased from a library and will therefore have library stamp marks, pockets, due date slips, etc.

Fair. *See* Condition.

Ffep. Front free endpaper; the blank sheet that is not pasted down onto the cover.

Fine. *See* Condition.

First edition. The first printing of the first edition; the first time a book has appeared.

Foxed. Brownish spotting of paper usually due to acid content.

Good. *See* Condition.

Half leather. A book cover in which the spine and corners are bound in leather, while the rest of the cover is in cloth or paper.

Hinge. The joint (either outer or inner) of the binding of a book (the part that bends when the book is opened).

Ill. Illustrated or illustrations.

Insc. Inscribed.

Laid in. A piece of paper, leaf, letter, etc., inserted but not glued into a book.

Ltd. Limited edition.

Ms or mss. Manuscript.

Nd. No date.

Near fine. *See* Condition.

Pb or pbk. Paperback.

Pc or price clipped. The price has been cut out,

usually a small triangle from the inside dust jacket containing the price information.

Poor. *See* Condition.

Pub. Publisher or published.

Rubbed. Indicates that the outer layer of the binding material has been rubbed off.

Shaken. Book is no longer firm and crisp; textblock feels loose in the hinges.

Signed. Inscribed with the author's signature.

Slipcase. A container (usually cardboard) specially made to hold a book.

Spine. The bound outer edge of a book.

Teg. Top edge gilt.

Tipped in. A sheet or sheets added after the book was produced through the use of minute amounts of glue along the edges of the sheet(s) to be inserted.

Tp. Title page.

Uncut. Describes older books whose page edges were not trimmed.

Very good. *See* Condition.

Vol. Volume.

SOURCE: Narda Tafuri, Anna Seaberg, and Gary Handman, *Guide to Out-of-Print Materials* (Chicago: ALA Association for Library Collections and Technical Services/Scarecrow Press, 2004), pp. 41–43.

Outstanding reference sources

EACH YEAR THE ALA's Reference and User Services Association's Reference Sources Committee examines hundreds of reference works to identify those that are essential for small and medium-sized public or academic libraries. The following are their picks for 2003 though 2005, incorporating reference sources published between 2002 and 2004.—*GME.*

The arts

Atlas of World Art, ed. John Onians (Oxford University, 2004).

A Chronology of American Musical Theater, by Richard C. Norton (Oxford University, 2002).

Encyclopedia of American Folk Art, ed. Gerard C. Wertkin (Routledge, 2003).

The Encyclopedia of Sculpture, ed. Antonia Boström (Fitzroy Dearborn, 2004).

Encyclopedia of 20th Century Architecture, ed. R. Stephen Sennott (Fitzroy Dearborn, 2003).

Horror Films of the 1970s, by John Kenneth Muir (McFarland, 2002).

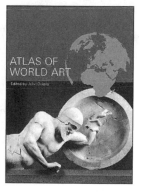

Business and economics

The Advertising Age Encyclopedia of Advertising, ed. John McDonough and Karen Egolf (Fitzroy Dearborn, 2003).

The Oxford Encyclopedia of Economic History, ed. Joel Mokyr (Oxford University, 2003).

History, culture, and civilization

Dictionary of American History, 3rd ed., ed. Stanley I. Kutler (Scribner, 2003).
Encyclopedia of African History, ed. Kevin Shillington (Fitzroy Dearborn, 2004).
Encyclopedia of American History, ed. Gary B. Nash (Facts on File, 2003).
Encyclopedia of Clothing and Fashion, ed. Valerie Steele (Scribner, 2005).
Encyclopedia of Food and Culture, ed. Solomon H. Katz (Scribner, 2003).
Encyclopedia of Modern Asia, ed. David Levinson and Karen Christensen (Scribner, 2002).
Encyclopedia of Recreation and Leisure in America, ed. Gary S. Cross (Scribner, 2004).
Encyclopedia of Russian History, ed. James R. Millar (Macmillan Reference, 2004).
Encyclopedia of the Great Plains, ed. David J. Wishart (University of Nebraska, 2004).
Encyclopedia of the Romantic Era, 1760–1850, ed. Christopher John Murray (Fitzroy Dearborn, 2003).
New Dictionary of the History of Ideas, ed. Maryanne Cline Horowitz (Scribner, 2005).

The Oxford Dictionary of the Renaissance, by Gordon Campbell (Oxford University, 2003).
The Oxford Encyclopedia of Food and Drink in America, ed. Andrew F. Smith (Oxford University, 2004).
Reader's Guide to British History, ed. David Loades (Fitzroy Dearborn, 2003).

Language and literature

The Beat Generation: A Gale Critical Companion, ed. Lynn M. Zott (Gale, 2003).
The Companion to Southern Literature: Themes, Genres, Places, People, Movements, and Motifs, ed. Joseph M. Flora and Lucinda H. MacKethan (Louisiana State University, 2002).
Encyclopedia of Holocaust Literature, ed. David Patterson, Alan L. Berger, and Sarita Cargas (Oryx, 2002).
Holocaust Literature: An Encyclopedia of Writers and Their Work, ed. S. Lillian Kremer (Routledge, 2003).
Literature of Travel and Exploration: An Encyclopedia, ed. Jennifer Speake (Fitzroy Dearborn, 2003).
The Oxford American Writer's Thesaurus, comp. Christine A. Lindberg (Oxford University, 2004).
The Oxford Companion to Chaucer, ed. Douglas Gray (Oxford University, 2003).

Law

Encyclopedia of Crime and Punishment, ed. David Levinson (Sage, 2002).
Legal Systems of the World: A Political, Social, and Cultural Encyclopedia, ed. Herbert M. Kritzer (ABC-CLIO, 2002).
Major Acts of Congress, ed. Brian K. Landsberg (Macmillan Reference, 2004).

Philosophy and religion

Encyclopedia of Buddhism, ed. Robert E. Buswell Jr. (Macmillan Reference, 2004).
Encyclopedia of Islam and the Muslim World, ed. Richard C. Martin (Macmillan Reference, 2004).
The Encyclopedia of Protestantism, ed. Hans J. Hillerbrand (Routledge, 2004).
The New Encyclopedia of the Occult, by John Michael Greer (Llewellyn, 2003).

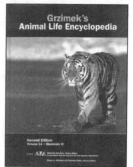

Science, health, and technology

Chemistry: Foundations and Applications, ed. J. J. Lagowski (Macmillan Reference, 2004).
Dogs: The Ultimate Dictionary of over 1,000 Dog Breeds, by Desmond Morris (Trafalgar Square, 2002).
Encyclopedia of Evolution, ed. Mark Pagel (Oxford University, 2002).
Grzimek's Animal Life Encyclopedia, 2nd ed., ed. Michael Hutchins (Gale, 2003–2004).
Magill's Encyclopedia of Social Science: Psychology, ed. Nancy A. Piotrowski (Salem Press, 2003).

Good Reference Books, Do's and Don'ts

Good reference works should include:
1. Clear, readable maps and photographs
2. Beautiful photographs and illustrations that enrich the text
3. Wide gutters, making photocopying easy
4. Sturdy bindings, strong construction
5. Readable, engaging text
6. Rich scholarship
7. Pleasing layout
8. Excellent indexing, with indented subheadings
9. Clearly stated selection criteria and purpose
10. Authoritative, well-documented information
11. Good cross-references
12. Broad audience appeal
13. Currency
14. Affiliation and background of contributors

Good reference works should exclude:
1. Fuzzy and poorly reproduced photographs
2. Indexing with run-on page numbers next to entries
3. Narrow gutters, making photocopying nearly impossible
4. Redundancy
5. Too many or too few volumes for the number of pages
6. Incomplete or nonstandard citations
7. Tiny typeface
8. Too much or too little white space
9. Weak construction or binding
10. Inconsistent length of entries
11. Unreferenced illustrations or photographs
12. Dated statistics

SOURCE: Reference Sources Committee, ALA Reference and User Services Association.

The Sage Encyclopedia of Social Science Research Methods, ed. Michael S. Lewis-
Beck, Alan E. Bryman, and Tim Futing Liao (Sage, 2004).
World Atlas of Coral Reefs, by Mark D. Spalding, Corinna Ravilious, and Edmund
P. Green (University of California, 2001).

Social issues and diversity

Encyclopedia of Aging, ed. David J. Ekerdt (Macmillan Reference, 2002).
Encyclopedia of American Social Movements, ed. Immanuel Ness (M. E. Sharpe,
2004).
Encyclopedia of Children and Childhood in History and Society, ed. Paula S. Fass
(Macmillan Reference, 2004).
Encyclopedia of Community: From the Village to the Virtual World, ed. Karen
Christensen and David Levinson (Sage, 2003).
Encyclopedia of Education, 2nd ed., ed. James W. Guthrie (Macmillan Reference,
2003).
Encyclopedia of Homelessness, ed. David Levinson (Sage, 2004).
Encyclopedia of Leadership, ed. George R. Goethals, Georgia J. Sorenson, and
James MacGregor Burns (Sage, 2004).
Encyclopedia of Lesbian, Gay, Bisexual, and Transgender History in America, ed. Marc
Stein (Scribner, 2004).
Encyclopedia of Terrorism, by Harvey W. Kushner (Sage, 2003).
Handbook of Death and Dying, ed. Clifton D. Bryant (Sage, 2003).
The Museum of Broadcast Communications Encyclopedia of Radio, ed. Christopher
H. Sterling (Fitzroy Dearborn, 2004).
Social Workers' Desk Reference, ed. Albert R. Roberts and Gilbert J. Greene (Ox-
ford University, 2002).

SOURCE: Reference Sources Committee, ALA Reference and User Services Association.

Notable books, 2004–2005

THE FOLLOWING BOOKS were chosen for their significant contribution
to the expansion of knowledge or for the pleasure they can provide to adult
readers. Each year the Notable Books Council of the ALA Reference and User
Services Association makes the selections, based on the criteria of wide general appeal and literary merit. More information on the books can be found by
consulting *Booklist, Choice,* or other review media.—*GME.*

Fiction

Ali, Monica. *Brick Lane* (Scribner, 2003).
Antunes, António Lobo. *The Inquisitors' Manual* (Grove, 2003).
Barnes, Julian. *The Lemon Table* (Knopf/Random House, 2004).
Boyd, William. *Any Human Heart* (Knopf/Random House, 2003).
Carey, Edward. *Alva and Irva: The Twins Who Saved a City* (Harcourt, 2003).
Casares, Oscar. *Brownsville: Stories* (Back Bay, 2003).
Christensen, Lars Saabye. *The Half Brother* (Arcade, 2004).
De Bernières, Louis. *Birds without Wings* (Knopf, 2004).
Dybek, Stuart. *I Sailed with Magellan* (Farrar Straus Giroux, 2003).
Haddon, Mark. *The Curious Incident of the Dog in the Night-Time* (Doubleday, 2003).

Hosseini, Khaled. *The Kite Runner* (Riverhead, 2003).
Jones, Edward P. *The Known World* (Amistad, 2003).
Khadra, Yasmina. *The Swallows of Kabul* (Nan A. Talese/Doubleday, 2004).
Lethem, Jonathan. *The Fortress of Solitude* (Doubleday, 2003).
Mda, Zakes. *The Madonna of Excelsior* (Farrar Straus Giroux, 2004).
Mitchell, David. *Cloud Atlas* (Random House, 2004).
Morrison, Toni. *Love* (Knopf/Random House, 2003).
Munro, Alice. *Runaway: Stories* (Knopf/Random House, 2004).
Niemi, Mikael. *Popular Music from Vittula* (Seven Stories, 2003).
O'Connor, Joseph. *Star of the Sea* (Harcourt, 2002).
Packer, ZZ. *Drinking Coffee Elsewhere* (Riverhead, 2003).
Roth, Philip. *The Plot against America* (Houghton Mifflin, 2004).
Saramago, José. *The Cave* (Harcourt, 2002).
Wolff, Tobias. *Old School* (Knopf, 2003).

Poetry

Espada, Martín. *Alabanza: New and Selected Poems, 1982–2002* (Norton, 2003).
Giovanni, Nikki. *The Collected Poetry of Nikki Giovanni, 1968–1998* (William Morrow, 2003).
Kooser, Ted. *Delights and Shadows* (Copper Canyon, 2004).

Nonfiction

Boyd, Valerie. *Wrapped in Rainbows: The Life of Zora Neale Hurston* (Scribner, 2003).
Chernow, Ron. *Alexander Hamilton* (Penguin, 2004).
Ehrlich, Paul R., and Anne E. Ehrlich. *One with Nineveh: Politics, Consumption, and the Human Future* (Island, 2004).
Faderman, Lillian. *Naked in the Promised Land* (Houghton Mifflin, 2003).
Fischer, David Hackett. *Washington's Crossing* (Oxford University, 2004).
Hagedorn, Ann, *Beyond the River: The Untold Story of the Heroes of the Underground Railroad* (Simon and Schuster, 2002).
Hays, Sharon, *Flat Broke with Children: Women in the Age of Welfare Reform* (Oxford University, 2003).
Henig, Robin Marantz. *Pandora's Baby: How the First Test Tube Babies Sparked the Reproductive Revolution* (Houghton Mifflin, 2004).
Hersh, Seymour M. *Chain of Command: The Road from 9/11 to Abu Ghraib* (HarperCollins, 2004).
Hughes, Robert. *Goya* (Knopf, 2003).
Kidder, Tracy. *Mountains beyond Mountains* (Random House, 2003).
King, Ross. *Michelangelo and the Pope's Ceiling* (Walker, 2003).
Krakauer, Jon. *Under the Banner of Heaven: A Story of Violent Faith* (Doubleday, 2003).
Kurlansky, Mark. *1968: The Year That Rocked the World* (Ballantine, 2004).
Lansky, Aaron. *Outwitting History: The Amazing Adventures of a Man Who Rescued a Million Yiddish Books* (Algonquin, 2004).
LeBlanc, Adrian Nicole. *Random Family: Love, Drugs, and Coming of Age in the Bronx* (Scribner, 2003).
Moats, David. *Civil Wars: A Battle for Gay Marriage* (Harcourt, 2004).
National Commission on Terrorist Attacks upon the United States. *The 9/11 Commission Report: Final Report of the National Commission on Terrorist Attacks upon the United States* (Norton, 2004).

Philbrick, Nathaniel. *Sea of Glory: America's Voyage of Discovery: The U.S. Exploring Expedition, 1838–1842* (Viking, 2003).

Pringle, Peter. *Food Inc.: Mendel to Monsanto—The Promises and Perils of the Biotech Harvest* (Simon and Schuster, 2003).

Quammen, David. *Monster of God: The Man-Eating Predator in the Jungles of History and the Mind* (Norton, 2003).

Sokolove, Michael. *The Ticket Out: Darryl Strawberry and the Boys of Crenshaw* (Simon and Schuster, 2004).

Taubman, William. *Khrushchev: The Man and His Era* (Norton, 2003).

Vine, Phyllis. *One Man's Castle: Clarence Darrow in Defense of the American Dream* (Amistad, 2004).

Von Drehle, David. *Triangle: The Fire That Changed America* (Atlantic Monthly, 2003).

SOURCE: Notable Books Council, ALA Reference and User Services Association.

20th-century literature in a nutshell

WORKS OF LITERARY CRITICISM have identified an extraordinary array of schools and movements that define the content and styles of novelists, poets, and dramatists who have flourished in the past 100 years. Here is a short list, culled from several different sources, that offers examples of prominent works and serves as a quick refresher course for reference librarians. —*GME.*

Abbey Theater, 1904–1930s. Irish nationalist drama centered on the famous Dublin theater founded in 1903: John Millington Synge, *The Playboy of the Western World* (1907); Sean O'Casey, *The Plough and the Stars* (1926).

Acmeism, 1910–1917. Russian poets who reacted against the mystical, vague, and allusive qualities of symbolism: Anna Akhmatova, *Chetki* (1914); Osip Mandel'shtam, *Kamen'* (1913).

Angry Young Men, 1950–1960. English writers who were disenchanted with the social and economic conditions following World War II: Kingsley Amis, *Lucky Jim* (1954); John Osborne, *Look Back in Anger* (1957); Alan Sillitoe, *The Loneliness of the Long Distance Runner* (1959).

Atheneum of Youth, 1910–1930s. Young Mexican writers who sought a return to traditional spiritual values: Alfonso Reyes, *Visión de Anáhuac, 1519* (1917); José Vasconcelos, *El desastre* (1938).

Beat Generation, 1950s–1960s. Disillusioned and rebellious American writers who were opposed to affluence and authoritarian control: Jack Kerouac, *On the Road* (1957); Allen Ginsberg, *Howl and Other Poems* (1956); William S. Burroughs, *Naked Lunch* (1959).

Black Mountain Poets, 1950s–1960s. Teachers and students of Black Mountain College (1933–1953) in North Carolina whose poetry was aligned with the rhythms and spontaneity of consciousness: Charles Olson, *The Maximus Poems* (1960); Robert Creeley, *For Love: Poems, 1950–1960* (1962).

Bloomsbury Group, 1905–1940s. Intellectuals who met in the Bloomsbury section of London and were characterized by a ferocious rejection of traditional value systems: Lytton Strachey, *Eminent Victorians* (1919); Virginia Woolf, *Jacob's Room* (1922).

Chicago Literary Renaissance, 1910s–1920s. A cosmopolitan literary movement centered on the Chicago-based *Poetry: A Magazine of Verse* and the literary journalism of the era: Vachel Lindsay, "General William Booth Enters into Heaven" (1913); Carl Sandberg, *Chicago Poems* (1916); Ben Hecht, *Erik Dorn* (1921).

Comedy of Menace, 1950s. English drama in which the characters appear to be menaced by a mysterious and indefinable terror that they cannot articulate: Harold Pinter, *The Birthday Party* (1958).

Concrete Poetry, 1950s–1960s. International poetic style incorporating graphic and spatial elements: Augusto de Campos, *Poetamenos* (1953); Eugen Gomringer, *Konstellationen* (1953).

Confessional Poets, 1950s–1960s. Autobiographical American poets who addressed the painful subjects causing postmodern malaise: Robert Lowell, *Life Studies* (1959); Sylvia Plath, *Ariel* (1965); Anne Sexton, *Live or Die* (1966).

Constructivism, 1920s. A Russian literary form employing technological motifs: Eduard Bagritskii, *Duma pro Opanasa* (1926).

Creation Society, 1920s. Chinese writers who emerged from the 1919 Cultural Revolution and countered the rise of realism: Kuo Mo-jo, *Nü-shen* (1921); Yü Tafu, "Ch'en-lun" (1921).

Cubo-Futurism, 1912–1930. Russian writers who saw themselves in revolt against sentimentalism, symbolism, and grammatical rules: Velimir Khlebnikov, "Zaklyatiye Smekhom" (1910); Vladimir Mayakovsky, "Oblako v shtanakh" (1915).

Cyberpunk, 1980s–1990s. American science fiction that portrays near-future societies radically changed by information technology and biomedical engineering, and centering on hacking, artificial intelligence, and megacorporations: William Gibson, *Neuromancer* (1984); Bruce Sterling, *Mirrorshades: The Cyberpunk Anthology* (1986); Neal Stephenson, *Snow Crash* (1992).

Dada, 1916–1923. European and American writers representing the radical anarchic temperament of the era in its violent abhorrence of any attempt to impose structure upon society or human creativity: Tristan Tzara, *La première aventure céleste de Monsieur Antipyrine* (1916); Raoul Hausmann, "Optophonetics" (1922); Kurt Schwitters, *Ursonate* (1921–1932).

Decadents (Burai-ha), 1940s. Japanese writers who autobiographically explored drug addiction, mental instability, and depravity as a reaction to the social upheavals of World War II: Dazai Osamu, *Ningen shikkaku* (1948).

***Diwan* School of Poets,** 1912–1919. Egyptian poets whose writings reflect the despair and alienation of the educated class, caught between the Arab world and the West: Ibrahim 'abd al-Qadir al-Mazini, *Al-Mazini's Egypt* (1983).

Edwardian Literature, 1900–1911. English and Irish writers who formed a bridge between the decaying Victorian literary tradition and the modernism that followed, mixing idealistic concepts of loyalty to the Empire with an appeal to popular audiences: Arnold Bennett, *Anna of the Five Towns* (1902); Joseph Conrad, *Nostromo* (1904); George Bernard Shaw, *Major Barbara* (1905).

Epic Theater, 1920s–1950s. German playwrights who reduced the emotional involvement of the audience to stimulate a critical scrutiny of reality: Bertolt Brecht, *Die heilige Johanna des Schlacthöfe* (1932).

Existentialism, 1940s–1990s. European fiction that promoted the belief

that humans must create themselves, their world, and their art in an essentially meaningless reality. Human beings are viewed as subjects in an indifferent and ambiguous universe. After 1970, existentialism dealt with themes of authenticity, the consciousness of death, alienation, and mundaneness: Albert Camus, *L'étranger* (1942); Jean-Paul Sartre, *La nausea* (1938); Michael Ende, *Die unendliche Geschichte* (1979); Chuck Palahniuk, *Fight Club* (1996).

Expansive Poetry, 1980s–1990s. American poetry that attempts to go beyond the short, free-verse, imagist, private, existentialist lyric that has become the modernist norm by using the inherent power of measured speech, even rhyme, and the power of narrative: Mark Jarman and David Mason, eds., *Rebel Angels: 25 Poets of the New Formalism* (1996).

Expressionism, 1910s–1920s. German writers, dissatisfied with naturalism, who wrote in compressed language using unconventional grammar and logic, symbolic imagery, and bold exaggerations and distortions: Georg Kaiser, *Von Morgens bis Mitternachts* (1912); Ernst Toller, *Die Wandlung* (1919). In America, a parallel movement was committed to ideals of social reform and the exposure of destructive aspects of modern life: Eugene O'Neill, *The Hairy Ape* (1922); Elmer Rice, *The Adding Machine* (1923).

Fantaisistes Group, 1910s. French poets who reintroduced elements of blithe irony and whimsical grotesqueness: Francis Carco, *Les innocents* (1916); Jean-Marc Bernard, *Sub tegmine fagi: Amours, bergeries et jeux* (1913).

Fringe Theatre, 1960s–1990s. Originating with acting companies in Edinburgh, London, Adelaide, Edmonton, and New York that were critical of both commercial theater and Western society, the movement now encompasses much avant-garde, edgy, and obscure dramatic experimentation: Howard Brenton, *Bloody Poetry* (1984); Caryl Churchill, *The Skryker* (1994).

Futurism, 1910s–1920s. Italian movement that proposed a radical way of looking at the world and allowed artists to create new visions and methods: Filippo Tommaso Marinetti, *Zang tumb tuum* (1914).

Gay Theater, 1960s–1990s. Drama that dispels the stereotypical portrayals of homosexuals and replaces them with definitions provided by the gay community itself: Mart Crowley, *The Boys in the Band* (1968); Larry Kramer, *The Normal Heart* (1985); Holly Hughes, *Clit Notes* (1990).

Georgian Poets, 1910–1922. British traditional poets who wrote with a clear message and realistic description of beauty and nature: Rupert Brooke, *Poems* (1911); Wilfred Owen, *Collected Poems* (1920); Walter de la Mare, *Come Hither* (1923).

Group Theatre, 1931–1941. A New York collective of actors, directors, and dramatists, the forerunner of the Actors' Studio, that rejuvenated dramatic performances: Clifford Odets, *Waiting for Lefty* (1935).

Hard-Boiled School, 1920s–1940s. Laconic and gritty short stories and novels dealing with crime that often featured as protagonist a lone, stoic, hero/antihero who operated beyond the fringes of the law yet adhered to a strict moral code: Dashiell Hammett, *The Maltese Falcon* (1930); Raymond Chandler, *The Big Sleep* (1939); Mickey Spillane, *I, the Jury* (1947).

Harlem Renaissance, 1920s–1930s. African-American writers in New York who made themselves an important part of the literary scene after World War I, emphasizing civil rights and equality: Alain Locke, ed., *The New Negro: An Interpretation* (1925); Langston Hughes, *Not Without Laughter* (1930); Rudolph

Fisher, *The Walls of Jericho* (1928); Zora Neale Hurston, *Their Eyes Were Watching God* (1937).

Heimatkunst, 1890s–1930s. Regional German writers who endeavored to create an authentically nationalist literature: Heinrich Sohnrey, *Der Bruderhof* (1897); Hermann Löns, *Die Häuser von Ohlendorf* (1917); Gustav Frenssen, *Jörn Uhl* (1901).

Hermeticism, 1915–1940s. Italian poetry characterized by unconventional structure and syntax, emotional restraint, and cryptic language: Giuseppe Ungaretti, *Il porto sepolto* (1916); Salvatore Quasimodo, *Acque e terre* (1930).

Imagism, 1909–1917. Anglo-American poets who advocated precise language, clear imagery, and forceful metaphor: T. E. Hulme, "Autumn" (1909); Lionel Johnson, *Post Liminium* (1911); H[ilda] D[oolittle], "Heat" (1916); Amy Lowell, "Patterns" (1916).

Inklings, 1940s. English authors with strong Christian beliefs and a preference for pre-19th-century poetry and myth: C. S. Lewis, *Perelandra* (1943); J. R. R. Tolkien, *The Lord of the Rings* (1954); Charles Walter Stansby Williams, *All Hallows' Eve* (1945).

Jazz Age, 1920s. American modernist writers concerned with the excitement and corruptive influences of 1920s capitalism: Sinclair Lewis, *Babbitt* (1922); F. Scott Fitzgerald, *The Great Gatsby* (1925).

L=A=N=G=U=A=G=E Poetry, 1970s–1990s. American genre, named after a New York poetry magazine, that questioned the attitudes to speech and assumed naturalness of language: Rae Armantrout, *Necromance* (1991); Ron Silliman, *In the American Tree* (1986).

Local Color School, 1860s–1900s. Regionalist American short fiction focused on atmosphere, setting, and locality: Bret Harte, "The Luck of Roaring Camp" (1868); Mark Twain, "Jim Smiley and His Jumping Frog" (1865).

Lost Generation, 1920s. American expatriate writers in Paris, identified as "lost" by salon figure Gertrude Stein, known for their critical and disenchanted portrayal of postwar society: Djuna Barnes, *Nightwood* (1936); e. e. cummings, *The Enormous Room* (1922); Ernest Hemingway, *The Sun Also Rises* (1926); Henry Miller, *Tropic of Cancer* (1934).

Magic Realism, 1950s–1990s. Latin American writings characterized by fantastic events, circumstances, and miracles in otherwise ordinary surroundings: Jorge Luis Borges, "Tlön Uqbar, Orbis Tertius" (1941); Gabriel García Márquez, *Cien años de soledad* (1967).

May Fourth Movement, 1916–1921. Chinese literary revolution that arose during the newly formed Republic of China to depose classical language and reinstate the vernacular: Lu Hsün, "The True Story of Ah Q" (1921).

Modernism, 1900s–1930s. A diverse multinational movement, with epicenters in Paris and London, that developed a new emphasis on the rhythms and internal structures of language and on the disillusioning realities of 20th-century life. It took a variety of forms at different times in various countries.

Austria and Germany, 1910s–1930s. Modernist authors uneasily accepted cosmopolitanism in a time of economic and social upheaval: Franz Kafka, *Der Prozess* (1915); Thomas Mann, *Der Zauberberg* (1924).

Denmark, 1950s–1960s. Experimentation came after World War II: Klaus Rifbjerg, *Konfrontation: Digte* (1960).

England and Ireland, 1910s–1930s. Modernist characteristics included requiring the reader to construct meaning out of fragments, allowing form to create content, and using imagery to fashion impressionistic collages: T. S. Eliot, *The Waste Land* (1922); James Joyce, *Ulysses* (1922); Ezra Pound, *The Cantos* (1917–1970); Virginia Woolf, *To the Lighthouse* (1927).

France, 1900s–1930s. French modernism was accompanied by the rise of the socialist movement, the appearance of anarchists in trade unions, and radical changes in the visual arts: Marcel Proust, *A la recherché du temps perdu* (1913–1927).

Italy, 1900s–1950s. Modernists rebelled against traditional sentimentality in favor of simplified language and themes: Eugenio Montale, *Ossi di seppia* (1916); Luigi Pirandello, *Sei personaggi in cerca d'auture* (1921); Ignazio Silone, *Pane e vino* (1937); Italo Svevo, *La coscienza di Zeno* (1923).

Latin America and Spain, 1880–1910s. Latin American and Spanish modernists stressed individuality of expression and used metaphorical language, mannered sentiment, and nostalgia: Rubén Darío, *Cantos de vida y esperanza* (1905); Juan Ramón Jiménez, *Platero y yo* (1914).

Russia, 1900s–1930s. Stylistic innovation was equated with revolution and the desire for a new society: Sergei Esenin, *Pugachyov* (1922).

Sweden, 1940s. Swedish modernists were influenced by the German expressionists and French symbolists: Gunnar Ekelöf, *Sent på jorden* (1932).

United States, 1910s–1930s. American modernists experimented with psychological fiction and intellectual inquiry: William Faulkner, *The Sound and the Fury* (1929); Wallace Stevens, *Ideas of Order* (1935).

The Movement, 1950s. Young British poets who preferred recognizable verse forms and a commonsense view of the central message: Philip Larkin, "Church Going" (1955).

Naturalism, 1860s–1920s. Writers who perceived the novel as a way to explore human behavior scientifically and objectively, with few moral trappings, in order to stimulate social reforms: Émile Zola, *Germinal* (1885); Max Kretzer, *Die Betrogenen* (1881); Stephen Crane, *Maggie: A Girl of the Streets* (1893); Theodore Dreiser, *An American Tragedy* (1925).

Négritude, 1930s–1960s. Literary movement begun by African and West Indian émigrés in Paris that called for the inversion of the values of European racial stereotypes to produce a culturally strong sense of identity and celebrate blackness: Aimé Césaire, *Cahier d'un retour au pays natal* (1939); Léopold Senghor, *Hosties noires* (1948).

Neo-Futurism, 1980s–1990s. Chicago-based theater group committed to enhancing audience interaction and putting the element of chance into performances: Greg Allen, *Too Much Light Makes the Baby Go Blind* (1988).

Neorealism, 1930s–1950s. Italian movement affected by the turmoil of Fascism and World War II that focused on the struggles of ordinary urban and rural people: Alberto Moravia, *Gli indifferenti* (1929); Cesare Pavese, *La luna e i falò* (1950); Elio Vittorini, *Conversazione in Sicilia* (1941). A similar Portuguese strain of neorealism concerned with social reform has been prominent since the 1920s: José Ferreira de Castro, *Emigrantes* (1928); Alves Redol, *Gaibéus* (1939).

New Journalism, 1960s–1990s. Innovative American approach to nonfiction prose that combines traditional journalism with such fictional techniques as dialogue, shifting viewpoints, and character sketching: Tom Wolfe, *The Right Stuff* (1979); Hunter S. Thompson, *Fear and Loathing in Las Vegas* (1971).

New Novel, 1950s–1960s. French genre using innovative narration to push fiction to new extremes: Michel Butor, *L'emploi du temps* (1956); Alain Robbe-Grillet, *La jalousie* (1957).

Objectivism, 1930s. American poets who treated the poem as an object and emphasized sincerity, intelligence, and the poet's ability to look clearly at the world: Louis Zukofsky, "Poem Beginning 'The'" (1926); Charles Reznikoff, *Jerusalem the Golden* (1934).

Postmodernism, 1965–present. American and European movement that argues for an expansion of the meaning of text, the celebration of fragmentation, and the progressive removal of barriers to social participation in power and art: John Fowles, *The Magus* (1965); John Barth, *Giles Goat-Boy* (1966); Thomas Pynchon, *Gravity's Rainbow* (1973); Vladimir Sorokin, *Queue* (1985); Don DeLillo, *White Noise* (1985); Salman Rushdie, *The Satanic Verses* (1989); Julian Barnes, *A History of the World in 10½ Chapters* (1989); Angela Carter, *The Passion of New Eve* (1977).

Post-Shingeki Theater, 1960s–1990s. Japanese drama that employs alternative venues for production as a way to protest artificial barriers between the audience and actors: Kara Juro, *Futari no onna* (1979); Satoh Makoto, *Nezumi kozo jirokichi* (1970).

Proletarian Literature, 1930s. Depression-era writers who critiqued American exploitation of the working class: James T. Farrell, *Studs Lonigan* (1935); John Steinbeck, *The Grapes of Wrath* (1939).

Provincetown Players, 1915–1929. Massachusetts acting company that devoted itself to new and innovative American drama: Susan Glaspell, *Trifles* (1916); Eugene O'Neill, *The Emperor Jones* (1920).

Realism, 1830s–1930s. An international literary trend influenced by the Industrial Revolution, scientific advancement, and skeptical philosophy. As with modernism, realism turned up at various times in different places.

Austria and Germany, 1848–1880s. Regionalism and psychological studies are typical German-language realism traits: Adalbert Stifter, *Der Nachsommer* (1857).

England, 1850s–1890s. Social reform was a dominant British theme: Charles Dickens, *Our Mutual Friend* (1865); George Eliot, *Middlemarch* (1872).

France, 1850s–1870s. French realism was predicated on the concrete, objective representation of ordinary people and events: Gustave Flaubert, *Madame Bovary* (1857); Guy de Maupassant, "Boule de Suif" (1880).

Italy, 1860s–1910s. Italian regional realism reacted to the overblown rhetoric of traditional literature: Luigi Capuana, *Profuma* (1890); Giovanni Verga, *I Malavoglia* (1881).

Latin America, 1910s–1930s. Latin realism took on a regionalist, indigenous form: Alfonso Hernández Catá, *El bebedor de lágrimas* (1926); Mariano Azuela, *Los de abajo* (1916).

Norway, 1870s. Norwegian realists were influenced by social philosophy and anticonservatism: Henrik Ibsen, *Et dukkehjem* (1879).

Poland, 1870s–1880s. Themes included corruption, poverty, and emancipation: Henryk Sienkiewicz, *Quo Vadis?* (1896).

Russia, 1852–1900s. Russian realists tempered social truths with moral and political insight: Anton Chekhov, "Dama s sobachkoi" (1899); Fyodor Dostoevsky, *Brat'ya Karamazovy* (1880); Leo Tolstoy, *Voina i mir* (1869); Ivan Turgenev, *Ottsy i deti* (1862).

Spain, 1870s–1890s. Spanish realists examined individual and social characteristics in the context of the nation's past and future: Benito Pérez Galdós, *Fortunata y Jacinta* (1887).

United States, 1880s–1910s. American realistic fiction mirrored actual, everyday life: William Dean Howells, *The Rise of Silas Lapham* (1885); Henry James, *The Portrait of a Lady* (1881); Mark Twain, *The Adventures of Huckleberry Finn* (1884); Edith Wharton, *Ethan Frome* (1911).

San Francisco Renaissance, 1950s–1960s. American avant-garde poetry with Asian cross-cultural influences: Kenneth Rexroth, *The Orchid Boat* (1972); Robert Duncan, *The Opening of the Field* (1960).

Scottish Renaissance, 1920–1950. Writers who revitalized Scottish poetry with an intense lyricism: Hugh MacDiarmid, "A Drunk Man Looks at the Thistle" (1936).

Socialist Realism, 1930s–1950s. An international style that emerged after the Russian Revolution of 1917, in which plot is a manifestation of history as class struggle and individuals are tied to the state: Maxim Gorky, *Mat* (1907); André Stil, *Le premier choc* (1953).

Surrealism, 1920s–1930s. An international movement that embraced philosophy and politics in a revolt against logical, rational, and systemized thought: Louis Aragon, *Le Paysan de Paris* (1926); André Breton, *Nadja* (1928); Paul Éluard, *Capitale de la douleur* (1926); Mário Cesariny de Vasconcelos, *Pena capital* (1957).

Symbolism, 1870s–1920s. An international movement born in France that used symbols to suggest a deeper level of existence. Like modernism and realism, symbolist writers flourished at different times in various countries.

Belgium, 1880s–1890s. Belgian symbolists used landscapes to evoke the inner world: Maurice Maeterlinck, *Pelléas et Mélisande* (1892).

Bulgaria, 1905–1920s. Social ethics was a major theme: Teodor Trayanov, *Regina mortua* (1908).

Czechoslovakia, 1890s. A blend of romanticist tradition and French symbolism: Otokar Brezina, *Vetry od pólu* (1897).

Denmark, 1890s. Danish symbolists favored intuition over scientific models: Helge Rode, *Hvide blomster* (1892).

England and Ireland, 1890s–1900s. Mystical and spiritual symbolism prevailed in the British Isles: William Butler Yeats, *The Wind among the Reeds* (1899).

France, 1870s–1890s. French poets insisted that symbols should suggest emotions and ideas rather than describe or directly represent them, using free verse, prose poems, alliteration, and musicality: Charles Baudelaire, *Les fleurs du mal* (1857); Stéphane Mallarmé, *Hérodiade* (1876–1887); Arthur Rimbaud, *Une saison en enfer* (1873); Paul Verlaine, *Romances sans paroles* (1874).

Germany, 1880s–1900s. Known as New Romanticism in Germany, symbolism made extensive use of classical allusions: Stefan George, *Hymnen* (1890).

Portugal, 1890s–1920s. Practitioners used bold imagery and metaphorical language: Eugénio de Castro, *Oaristos* (1890).

Russia, 1890s–1917. Russian symbolists featured end-of-the-century apocalypticism and malaise: Andrey Bely, *Zoloto v lazuri* (1904); Alexander Blok, "Dvenadtsat" (1918).

Theater of Fact, 1960s. German objectivist documentary drama: Rolf Hochhuth, *Die Soldaten* (1967); Heinar Kipphardt, *In der Sache J. Robert Oppenheimer* (1964).

Theater of the Absurd, 1950s–1960s. European and American drama that portrayed the world as essentially mysterious and unintelligible, and avoided presenting a rational narrative or character development: Samuel Beckett, *Waiting for Godot* (1954); Eugène Ionesco, *Rhinocéros* (1959).

Ionesco
Rhinocéros

Tremendismo, 1940s. Spanish writers who emphasized the absurdities and injustices of contemporary life: Camilo José Cela, *La familia de Pascual Duarte* (1942).

Unanimisme, 1908–1920. French genre based on the psychological concept of group consciousness and collective emotion and the need for the poet to merge with it: Jules Romains, *Mort de quelqu'un* (1911); Charles Vildrac, *Le Paquebot Tenacity* (1919).

White Birch School, 1910–1923. Japanese writers who espoused an optimistic humanism that was influenced by Western literature and art: Mushakoji Saneatsu, *Yujo* (1919); Shiga Naoya, *An'ya Koro* (1937).

SOURCES: Helene Henderson and Jay P. Pederson, eds., *Twentieth-Century Literary Movements Dictionary* (Detroit: Omnigraphics, 2000); Wikipedia; and other sources.

DOCUMENTS

What is an archives?

by Frank B. Evans, Donald F. Harrison, and Edwin A. Thompson

AN ARCHIVES IS (1) the noncurrent records of an organization or institution preserved because of their continuing value; (2) the agency responsible for selecting, preserving, and making available records determined to have permanent or continuing value; and (3) the building in which an archival institution is located.

SOURCE: Frank B. Evans, Donald F. Harrison, and Edwin A. Thompson, "A Basic Glossary for Archivists," *American Archivist* 37 (July 1974): 415–433.

The archival profession

by Susan E. Davis

THE COMMUNITY OF AMERICAN ARCHIVISTS is a 20th-century phenomenon. Archivists have been educated and worked in Europe for centuries, but the transition to American institutions was slow and took a shape somewhat different from their European counterparts. In the United States the archival tradition has two sets of roots. The first is the historical manuscripts tradition, shaped by private collectors and antiquarians who concentrated on collecting historical materials. The curators of these collections used techniques borrowed from libraries and combined a historical perspective with library techniques of cataloging and item-level control. The Massachusetts Historical Society, established in 1791 by the historian and minister Jeremy Belknap, was the earliest institution of this type. The American Historical Association (AHA) established a Historical Manuscripts Commission in 1895.

The second set of antecedents derives from European public archives. From the French came the principle of *provenance*, which emphasizes the connection records have to the agencies that created them. Prussian archivists formulated the concept of *Registraturprinzip* or *original order*, which means that records accumulate in a pattern that provides evidence of the function and purpose of the creating offices. These archivists were not interested in collecting historical materials but only in the management of an institution's own records. The AHA established a Public Archives Commission in 1899, an action that indicates that the organization distinguished between public records and historical manuscripts. Between 1900 and 1912, the commission surveyed state archives around the country and reported on their programs. The concepts of *provenance* and *original order* soon became two of the fundamental principles of archival theory on which the core of the profession's expert knowledge is based. These concepts now apply to both publicly and privately generated materials.

Initially the historical manuscripts tradition dominated in the United States, which delayed the adoption of distinct archival practices. In Europe, archivists believed that records were created by an organization in the course of ongoing activity, and preserved and made accessible by that organization, but should not be collected by a separate institution. The archivist's role was thus tied to the creating agency, and archivists developed a distinct occupational identity. In contrast, American archivists initially linked their work to that of librarians and historians, which postponed the development of an independent occupation. The profession thus needed to find middle ground between

---

Levels of Arrangement and Description

In its recent Statement of Principles, the Canadian–U.S. Task Force on Archival Description defined four levels of arrangement and description. The list here elaborates on these four, beginning with the largest level and continuing down to the smallest:

Record group—All the records created by an individual, family, organization, government, office, business, or other entity.

Series—A group of records filed together because they all relate to the same activity or function.

File unit—An organized group of records; at its simplest, a file folder of records that relate to the same subject, activity, or transaction. Often the description at the file-unit level takes the form of a sequential list of folder titles.

Item—One unit, normally a document. Description at this level may take the form of a list of each item in a folder, for instance. While such detailed description of textual materials is rare, it is sometimes used for very important correspondence or, say, an autograph collection. Item-level description is more common for nontextual items, such as maps and photographs.

More traditionally, archivists have recognized a fifth level, higher than the record group or collection level—the Repository level.

SOURCE: David W. Carmicheal, *Organizing Archival Records,* 2nd ed. (Walnut Creek, Calif.: AltaMira Press, 2004), p. 6. Reprinted with permission.

the historical manuscripts and public archives traditions, and this ongoing debate continued well into the 20th century.

In the 1930s, a series of events took place that shifted the direction of the archival profession. The National Archives was established in 1934, and the Society of American Archivists (SAA) was founded in 1936. Once SAA existed, AHA disbanded its Public Archives Commission. AHA originally intended to sponsor an institute for the leading practitioners, but it was recognized that such an institute would be too limited to meet the broader needs that a full professional association could serve. From that point on, archivists had in the National Archives a visible institution focused on protecting the nation's documentary heritage and one around which professional development could evolve.

THE SOCIETY of
AMERICAN ARCHIVISTS

The National Archives played a leading role in the early years of the American archival profession and SAA because it constituted the single largest and strongest professional repository. This situation did not change until the late 1960s and 1970s when a growing number of colleges and universities began to set up archival programs that frequently encompassed both institutional records and the private papers of faculty and alumni. It is estimated that two-thirds of the college and university archives listed in the 1980 *Directory of College and University Archives in the United States and Canada* had been established after 1960.

The college and university archives acted out the conflict between public records and manuscripts in that they frequently sought to preserve both the official records of their schools and the broader informational documentation of institutions of higher learning. Their growing numbers increased the mem-

---

Storage Conditions for Archival Records

Nothing contributes more to the long-term preservation of archival records than the proper environment. Not every small archives can achieve ideal conditions, but the following guidelines should be the goal of every archives.

Stabilize the temperature and humidity: The best temperature for most archival records is 65°F (some archivists recommend 68°F), with fluctuations of no more than ±2°F over a 24-hour period. The best humidity for most archival records is 45%RH, with fluctuations of no more than ±2%RH over a 24-hour period. While these conditions are difficult to meet, particularly if the collections must be stored in areas where people work, the archives should attempt to match them as closely as possible.

Reduce ultraviolet light: Cover windows to reduce the amount of sunlight reaching the records. Cover fluorescent lights with UV filtering sleeves.

Protect the collection from fire: Monitor the building to identify and eliminate fire hazards before they cause a disaster. Install sprinklers in storage areas. (There is some debate about the advisability of using wet pipe sprinkler systems, but it is safe to assume that wet records may be recoverable; burned ones are not.)

Use metal, open shelving: Metal shelving is preferable to wood, since wood shelves can release chemicals that are harmful to archival materials. Open shelves allow air to circulate, while closed shelves can trap gases that cause records to decay.

House the records in acid-free boxes and folders: Acid-free folders and boxes will slow the deterioration of archival records. Special folders are designed for the storage of photographs and negatives. Buy from a reputable archival supplier.

SOURCE: David W. Carmicheal, *Organizing Archival Records,* 2nd ed. (Walnut Creek, Calif.: AltaMira Press, 2004), p. 25. Reprinted with permission.

bership in SAA, and their identification with a profession and not just their employing institution shifted the dynamic among archivists. In addition, college and university archives were frequently organizationally situated within the library, thus increasing the ties between archivists and librarians. As library practices changed, archivists felt increasing pressure to accommodate automation and more uniform practices. Since the late 1970s, this has manifested itself in description.

The Research Libraries Group (RLG) played a very important role in the work of college and university archives. Established in 1974 as a "not-for-profit corporation devoted to the mission of 'improving access to information that supports research and learning,'" this powerful consortium combined the resources of a group of distinguished research libraries in a variety of cooperative ventures. RLG hosts the Research Libraries Information Network (RLIN), which created one of the first bibliographic utilities providing centralized access to research library collections around the world. RLG and its member libraries were major actors in the development of the MARC AMC (Archives and Manuscripts Control) format and its implementation by college and university archives. The resources and influence of RLG represented the only significant coalition of archival workplaces, in contrast to the norm of archival practice occurring in small institutions, and RLG's contributions to archival descriptive practice have been considerable.

The contemporary archival community continues to represent a diverse constituency. Archivists work in a wide range of institutions: governments at all levels, colleges and universities, public libraries, historical societies, museums, religious groups, corporations, labor unions, and a diverse array of not-for-profit organizations. At approximately 40%, college and university archivists represent the largest membership group within SAA, and almost two-thirds of the SAA membership work in small repositories (one to three FTE). Solo practice (or "lone arrangers," as single practitioners have often been called) is not uncommon.

The fact that so few archivists work in large archival institutions places a far greater emphasis on the role of the professional associations than might be  expected for other professions. In contrast, fewer librarians work alone, and the vast majority work in places familiarly labeled as libraries. Librarians thus have more access to colleagues and professional identification within their institutions than do archivists. SAA, as the national association, is the most visible, but archivists also join regional associations around the country.

Archivists invest a great deal of energy in these professional associations, which facilitate colleague communication, career satisfaction, visibility, credibility, professional identity, continuing education, and advancement of the profession. And within the professional associations the opportunity for leadership is often greater than it is within a specific workplace, where the archivist frequently is isolated. Approximately 25%–30% of the individual members of the Society of American Archivists attend the annual meeting each year, indicating that members strongly value this professional connection.

SOURCE: Susan E. Davis, "Descriptive Standards and the Archival Profession," in Martin D. Joachim, ed., *Historical Aspects of Cataloging and Classification* (New York: Haworth, 2003), pp. 291–308. Reprinted with permission.

Federal regional depository libraries

THE FRAMEWORK OF THE PRESENT depository library program was established in 1857 when a resolution was passed directing that printed documents be circulated to the public through official sources. In 1859, the statutory authority and responsibility to distribute all books printed or purchased for the use of the federal government was given to the Secretary of the Interior, except those for the special use of the Congress or the executive departments.

In 1860, Congress established the Government Printing Office to serve its printing and binding needs as well as the needs of the executive branch. The Printing Act of 1895 relocated the Superintendent of Public Documents from the Department of Interior to the Government Printing Office. Today, this position continues to be an important function of the Government Printing Office in disseminating federal information to the public through both the depository library program and publications sales program.

Congress established the Depository Library Program based upon three principles:

1. with certain specified exceptions, all government publications shall be made available to depository libraries;
2. depository libraries shall be located in each state and congressional district in order to make government publications widely available; and
3. these government publications shall be available for the free use of the general public.

In January 2005, the Government Printing Office proposed the elimination of nearly all print distribution to depository libraries beginning October 1, 2005. Superintendent of Documents Judith C. Russell announced that the GPO planned to request funding in FY 2006 that would cover little more than the distribution of 50 essential titles. The GPO had backed off from the full plan by September 2005, but it continues to explore ways to maintain standards of authenticity, preservation, version control, and public access in a predominantly digital environment. The proposed changes also include a print-on-demand (POD) allowance in which selected depository libraries would receive $500 and 53 regional depository libraries would get $1,500 for materials not on the essential titles list. Costs for additional print titles as well as for administration of the POD program would come from depository libraries' own budgets.

Libraries in the following list are regional depository libraries that (as of mid-2005) received all publications of the Depository Library Program.

Alabama—Auburn University at Montgomery, Library, 7440 East Drive, Montgomery, AL 36117-3596; (334) 244-3650; aumnicat.aum.edu/govtdocs/.

University of Alabama, Amelia Gayle Gorgas Library, Capstone Drive, Tuscaloosa, AL 35487-0266; (205) 348-6047; www.lib.ua.edu/govinfo/.

Arizona—Arizona State Library, Archives and Public Records, Research Division, 1700 West Washington, Phoenix, AZ 85007; (602) 542-3701; www.lib.az.us/is/feddocs/index.cfm.

Arkansas—Arkansas State Library, One Capitol Mall, Little Rock, AR 72201-1081; (501) 682-2869; www.asl.lib.ar.us.

California—California State Library, Government Publications Section, 914 Capitol Mall, Sacramento, CA 95814-4802; (916) 654-0069; www.library.ca.gov.

Colorado—University of Colorado at Boulder, Norlin Library, 1720 Pleasant

Street, Boulder, CO 80309-0184; (303) 492-8834; ucblibraries.colorado.edu/
govpubs/index.htm.

Denver Public Library, 10 West 14th Avenue Parkway, Denver, CO 80204-
2731; (720) 865-1712; denverlibrary.org/research/government/.

Connecticut—Connecticut State Library, 231 Capitol Avenue, Hartford, CT
06106; (860) 757-6570; www.cslib.org/gis.htm.

Florida—University of Florida, George A. Smathers Libraries, L120 Marston
Science Library, Gainesville, FL 32611-7011; (352) 273-0367; web.uflib.
ufl.edu/docs/.

Georgia—University of Georgia, Ilah Dunlap Little Memorial Library, 320
South Jackson Street, Athens, GA 30602-1641; (706) 542-3251; www.libs.
uga.edu/govdocs/index.html.

Hawaii—University of Hawaii at Manoa, Hamilton Library, 2550 The Mall,
Honolulu, HI 96822-2274; (808) 956-8230; www.sinclair.hawaii.edu/
govdocs/index.htm.

Idaho—University of Idaho Library, Rayburn Street, Moscow, ID 83844-2353;
(208) 885-6344; www.lib.uidaho.edu/govdoc/.

Illinois—Illinois State Library, 300 South 2nd Street, Springfield, IL 62701-
1796; (217) 782-7596; www.cyberdriveillinois.com/departments/library/
what_we_do/depository_programs/home.html.

Indiana—Indiana State Library, 140 North Senate Avenue, Indianapolis, IN
46204-2296; (317) 232-3678; www.statelib.lib.in.us/www/isl/whatwehave/
feddocs.html.

Iowa—University of Iowa Libraries, Washington and Madison Streets, Iowa
City, IA 52242-1420; (319) 335-5926; www.lib.uiowa.edu/govpubs/.

Kansas—University of Kansas, Anschutz Library, 1301 Hoch Auditoria Drive,
Lawrence, KS 66045-7537; (785) 864-4930; www.lib.ku.edu/anschutzlib/
govdocs/.

Kentucky—University of Kentucky, William T. Young Library, 1000 University Drive, Lexington, KY 40506-0456; (859) 257-0500, ext. 2141; www.uky.
edu/Libraries/deprds.html.

Louisiana—Louisiana State University at Baton Rouge, Troy H. Middleton
Library, Baton Rouge, LA 70803-3312; (225) 578-5652; www.lib.lsu.edu/
govdocs/.

Louisiana Tech University, Prescott Memorial Library, Everett Street at
The Columns, Ruston, LA 71272-0046; (318) 257-2231; www.latech.edu/
tech/library/govresources.htm.

Maine—University of Maine at Orono, Raymond H. Fogler Library, Orono,
ME 04469-5729; (207) 581-1673; www.library.umaine.edu/govdoc/
default.htm.

Maryland—University of Maryland at College Park, McKeldin Library, College Park, MD 20742-7011; (301) 405-9165; www.lib.umd.edu/GOV/.

Massachusetts—Boston Public Library, 700 Boylston Street, Boston, MA
02116-0286; (617) 859-2226; www.bpl.org/research/govdocs/index.htm.

Michigan—Detroit Public Library, 5201 Woodward Avenue, Detroit, MI
48202-4007; (313) 833-1440; www.detroit.lib.mi.us/index.htm.

Michigan Dept. of History, Arts, and Libraries, Library of Michigan,
702 West Kalamazoo Street, Lansing, MI 48915; (517) 373-1300; www.
michigan.gov/hal/.

Minnesota—University of Minnesota, Government Publications Library, 309
19th Avenue South, Minneapolis, MN 55455-0414; (612) 624-5073;
govpubs.lib.umn.edu.

Mississippi—University of Mississippi, J. D. Williams Library, Library Loop, University, MS 38677-9793; (662) 915-5857; www.olemiss.edu/depts/general_library/files/ref/govtran.html.

Missouri—University of Missouri at Columbia, Elmer Ellis Library, Lowry Mall, Columbia, MO 65201-5149; (573) 882-6733; web.missouri.edu/~govdocs/index.htm.

Montana—University of Montana, Mansfield Library, 32 Campus Drive, Missoula, MT 59812-9936; (406) 243-6866; www.lib.umt.edu/research/guide/gov_government.htm.

Nebraska—University of Nebraska at Lincoln, Don L. Love Memorial Library, 13th and R Streets, Lincoln, NE 68588-4100; (402) 472-4473; www.unl.edu/libr/govdocs/docs1.htm.

Nevada—University of Nevada at Reno Library, 1664 North Virginia Street, Reno, NV 89557-0044; (775) 813-6496; www.library.unr.edu/depts/bgic/Default.htm.

New Jersey—Newark Public Library, 5 Washington Street, Newark, NJ 07101-0630; (973) 733-7779; www.npl.org/Pages/Collections/govdocs.html.

New Mexico—University of New Mexico, Government Information/General Library, 1 University of New Mexico, Albuquerque, NM 87131-0001; (505) 277-5441; elibrary.unm.edu/govinfo/.

New Mexico State Library, 1209 Camino Carlos Rey, Santa Fe, NM 87507-5166; (505) 476-9702; www.stlib.state.nm.us/services_more.php?id=184_0_13_0_M64.

New York—New York State Library, Cultural Education Center, Empire State Plaza, Albany, NY 12230-0001; (518) 474-5355; www.nysl.nysed.gov/feddep.htm.

North Carolina—University of North Carolina at Chapel Hill, Walter Davis Library, 208 Raleigh Street, Chapel Hill, NC 27514-8890; (919) 962-1151; www.lib.unc.edu/reference/govinfo/federal.html.

North Dakota—North Dakota State University Libraries, 1201 Albrecht Boulevard, Fargo, ND 58105-5599; (701) 231-8886; www.lib.ndsu.nodak.edu/govdocs.

University of North Dakota, Chester Fritz Library, 3051 University Avenue, Grand Forks, ND 58203-9000; (701) 777-4646; www.library.und.edu/coll/government.jsp.

Ohio—State Library of Ohio, Government Information Services, 274 East 1st Avenue, Columbus, OH 43201; (614) 644-7051; winslo.state.oh.us/govinfo/slogovt.html.

Oklahoma—Oklahoma Department of Libraries, U.S. Government Information Division, 200 N.E. 18th St., Oklahoma City, OK 73105-3298; (800) 522-8116; www.odl.state.ok.us/usinfo/index.htm.

Oklahoma State University, Edmon Low Library, Stillwater, OK 74078-1071; (405) 744-6546; www.library.okstate.edu/govdocs/.

Oregon—Portland State University, Branford Price Millar Library, 951 S.W. Hall, Portland, OR 97207; (503) 725-5874; www.lib.pdx.edu/resources/govdocs/.

Pennsylvania—State Library of Pennsylvania, 333 Market Street, Forum Building, Harrisburg, PA 17126-1745; (717) 783-5986; www.statelibrary.state.pa.us/libraries/site/default.asp.

South Carolina—Clemson University, Robert Muldrow Cooper Library, Palmetto Boulevard, Clemson, SC 29634-3001; (864) 656-5168; www.lib.clemson.edu/govdocs/feddocs.htm.

University of South Carolina at Columbia, Thomas Cooper Library, 1322

Greene Street, Columbia, SC 29208; (803) 777-4841; www.sc.edu/library/pubserv/govdocs3.html.

Tennessee—University of Memphis, McWherter Library, 126 Ned R. McWherter Library, Memphis, TN 38152-3250; (901) 678-2206; exlibris. memphis.edu/resource/unclesam/.

Texas—Texas State Library and Archives Commission, 1201 Brazos Street, Austin, TX 78701-1938; (512) 463-5455; www.tsl.state.tx.us/ref/fedinfo/.

Texas Tech University Library, 18th and Boston, Lubbock, TX 79409-0002; (806) 742-2282; library.ttu.edu/ul/govdocs/.

Utah—Utah State University, Merrill Library, University Hill, Logan, UT 84321-3000; (435) 797-2684; library.usu.edu/Govdocs/.

Virginia—University of Virginia, Alderman Library, 160 McCormick Road, Charlottesville, VA 22904-4154; (434) 924-3133; www.lib.virginia.edu/govdocs/.

Washington—Washington State Library, 6880 Capitol Boulevard South, Tumwater, WA 98501-5513; (360) 704-5221; www.secstate.wa.gov/library/gov_publications.aspx?m=undefined,arl.

West Virginia—West Virginia University, Downtown Campus Library, 1549 University Avenue, Morgantown, WV 26506-6069; (304) 293-4040; www.libraries.wvu.edu/government/index.htm.

Wisconsin—University of Wisconsin at Madison, Memorial Library, 728 State Street, Madison, WI 53706-1494; (608) 262-3242; www.library.wisc.edu/guides/govdocs/index.htm.

Milwaukee Public Library, 814 West Wisconsin Avenue, Milwaukee, WI 53233-2385; (414) 286-3073; www.mpl.org/file/govdocs_index.htm.

SOURCE: U.S. Government Printing Office, www.gpoaccess.gov/libraries.html.

SPECIAL COLLECTIONS

Great New York Public Library collections I have known

by Kathie Coblentz

AT THE CORE OF THE ORIGINAL HOLDINGS of the New York Public Library is a once-private collection, that of James Lenox (1800–1880), who in 1870 incorporated his magnificent personal collection of rare books and manuscripts as the Lenox Library and opened it to New York City's reading public. The Lenox Library proceeded to acquire several other large private collections by donation or purchase, and then, in 1895, it merged with two other bodies: the Astor Library, New York's first public library, established in 1848 by the will of John Jacob Astor, and the Tilden Trust, formed from the estate of Samuel J. Tilden (1814–1886), who desired to create a more accessible public library for the metropolis. The Tilden Trust, too, came with an impressive private book collection, Tilden's own. The resulting institution is to this day known in its full official form as The New York Public Library, Astor, Lenox, and Tilden Foundations.

The Lenox Library's holdings have long since (1915) been merged with the rest of the library's collections, but the spirit of James Lenox lives on in a number of special collections, some of them separately housed with their own reading rooms, in the central building at Fifth Avenue and 42nd Street and the library's other research libraries. Indeed, one entire research library, the Schomburg Center for Research in Black Culture, was named in honor of a collector: Arthur Alfonso Schomburg (1874–1938), the Puerto Rican–born scholar and bibliophile, whose collection of materials by and about people of African descent throughout the world was added in 1926 to what was then the 135th Street Branch of the New York Public Library.

As a special collections cataloger in the Fifth Avenue building (known officially as the Humanities and Social Sciences Library), I have had the opportunity over the years to appreciate the workings of the minds and hearts of book collectors, as I have been privileged to examine an unending flow of extraordinary documents in the context of the collections for which they were acquired. Following are a few remarks about some of my personal favorites among these libraries-within-the-library. For more, explore the website of NYPL's research libraries, at nypl.org/research/.

Most of these collections were acquired along with generous endowments that have enabled their curators to continue expanding them in the spirit of the original collectors up to the present day. If anyone reading this is inspired to begin a collection that will one day be worthy of a special room in a public or university library, please be astute enough in your investments to allow for a donation of sufficient funds for its maintenance and expansion as well!

The Spencer Collection

This treasure trove of fine illustrated books, illuminated manuscripts, and books in extraordinary bindings was created in 1913 by the bequest of William Augustus Spencer (1855–1912), who went down with the *Titanic*. Besides his own modest-sized collection (several hundred mostly recent, mostly sumptuously bound French illustrated books, like that shown on the right), Spencer left the library a large endowment fund whose income continues to be used, 90 years later, to purchase "the finest illustrated books that can be procured, of any country and in any language . . . bound in handsome bindings representing the work of the most noted book-binders of all countries." Mr. Spencer's latest successors have given the collection (now more than 10,000 volumes strong) a modernist tinge—recent acquisitions include a large group of Dadaist books, pamphlets, and broadsides—but my personal favorites are the jewels of the illustrator's and bookbinder's art from the

past. Among those that have passed through my hands are volumes opulently bound and stamped in gold with the ciphers or armorial bearings of royalty and popes, and works from six centuries illustrated with original woodcuts and engravings, their pages bearing the marks of metal plates and woodblocks worked by the hands of great artists from Dürer to Picasso.

The Berg Collection of English and American Literature

First editions, rare books, autograph letters, manuscripts, and literary archives are the specialty here. The core of the collection was assembled by two book-loving physicians, the brothers Dr. Albert A. Berg (1872–1950) and Dr. Henry W. Berg (1858–1938), and presented to the library by Albert Berg in 1940. The emphasis is on authors from the age of Dickens onward, and holdings are especially strong in 20th-century writers, thanks in part to two other large private literary collections that Berg obtained or helped obtain for the library, those of W. T. H. Howe and Owen D. Young. The collection now includes around 20,000 printed items and 50,000 manuscripts. To mention just a couple of highlights, the Berg Collection possesses Ralph Waldo Emerson's copy of Thoreau's *A Week on the Concord and Merrimack Rivers,* inscribed to him by Thoreau himself, and the original drafts of T. S. Eliot's *The Waste Land,* annotated by Ezra Pound, some of whose advice Eliot followed.

The Arents Collection on Tobacco

Yes, tobacco. This eccentric assemblage of works on the history, literature, and lore of tobacco, tobacco products, smoking, and smoking paraphernalia was presented to the library in 1943 by George Arents Jr. (1875–1960), and

has been greatly expanded since by Arents and its curators. It now comprises more than 12,000 items. A true collector, Arents attempted to obtain the finest or most interesting copy available of an item he sought. The collection includes the expected: early accounts of America, tobacco's homeland; rare and beautiful herbals; early government edicts regulating the tobacco trade; compendiums of poems in praise of the "divine weed." But a work didn't have to be directly related to tobacco to catch Arents's eye—any obscure reference would suffice, if the work was interesting enough in some other respect. One of the gems of the collection is a manuscript in Oscar Wilde's hand of Acts I–II of the original four-act version *of The Importance of Being Earnest.* Connoisseurs of Wilde's masterpiece will recall the incident of Jack Worthing's cigarette case in Act I.

The Pforzheimer Collection of Shelley and His Circle

The creation of the financier Carl H. Pforzheimer Sr. (1879–1957), this multidisciplinary collection was donated to the library in 1986 by the Carl and Lily Pforzheimer Foundation. It contains around 25,000 books (some exceedingly rare), manuscripts, letters, and other objects minutely documenting the

life and times of Shelley, Byron, Keats, and other poets and social activists of the English Romantic movement, not forgetting those pioneers of women's rights William Godwin and Mary Wollstonecraft and their daughter, Mary Shelley. Among the extraordinary documents to be found here is the suicide letter of Harriet Westbrooke Shelley, the poet's first wife. The collection also possesses some remarkable realia, including fragments of Shelley's skull.

The Schlosser Collection on the History of Papermaking

This 1988 gift to the library by Leonard B. Schlosser, paper executive and connoisseur, comprises some 2,000 books, documents, and original samples, and covers the history of one of the most vital human artifacts (without which widespread dissemination of the written word would scarcely have been possible) from its invention in China, some centuries before our era, to the present day. It includes samples of papers as old as the 14th century and as new as the exotic papers crafted from such materials as carrot slices, wasps' nests, and blue jeans by young converts to the ancient art.

The Gross Collection of Voltaire and His Contemporaries

Begun in the 1980s by Martin J. Gross, this small but select collection was acquired by purchase in 1997 with the help of Mr. Gross and funds contributed by library trustee Barbara Goldsmith, and has since grown to comprise around 700 items published during their lives by the French Enlightenment superstars Voltaire, Rousseau, and Diderot, as well as some manuscripts. Dr. Robert Darnton, scholar of French culture and also a library trustee, declared, "With one great leap, the Martin Gross Collection makes the New York Public Library a major center for scholarship on the French Enlightenment." Here scholars will find 14 different editions and printings of *Candide* from its original year of publication, 1759 (one is surely the storied first, but which?), and such evocative items as Voltaire's only work composed in Italian—a pamphlet on fossils—accompanied by his handwritten letter (also in Italian) presenting it to a celebrated Parisian *salonière*, Mme. Dupin de Chenonceaux.

SOURCE: Kathie Coblentz, *The New York Public Library Guide to Organizing a Home Library* (Philadelphia: Running Press, 2003), pp. 122–126.

Exhibition design and preparation
by Andrew Dutka, Sherman Hayes, and Jerry Parnell

AFTER WE HAD COMPLETED our umpteenth exhibit this past year, Andy, Jerry, and Sherm were commiserating on the fact that we all had become (out of choice or necessity) accomplished exhibit designers and curators as part of our university library function at the University of North Carolina at Wilmington.

Upon reflection, we noted that none of us had received formal training, theoretical preparation, or even practical workshop training on how to successfully produce an exhibit. Initially some of us were unhappy with having to spend time and energy on exhibits because it took away from other duties. However, in the fall of 1999, the Special Collections at Randall Library expanded, doubling its size and including a large public space with display cases and walls suitable for displays. With the capacity increased, we were in the business by choice and opportunity. We assumed that in libraries it was mainly the few, large, and prestigious that had the time, energy, and resources to do displays.

Au contraire, the following examples demonstrate how we are creating exhibits and doing it regularly. Even our informal conversations with colleagues at public libraries, community colleges, small colleges, and other midsize universities indicate that scholarly and other types of display are becoming more useful as an outreach tool.

Why are exhibits important to libraries?

1. Teaching tool. An exhibit is a wonderful opportunity for the library to organize materials around a theme and present that to its audiences as a self-learning experience. While a lecture may be part of the process, or guided tours and printed materials may supplement an exhibit, most exhibits are useful because individuals can interact with the material at their own pace, and this interaction meets the individual's needs in an unmonitored learning experience. With all the ways we learn, exhibits continue to be a powerful and popular format.

2. Scholarly productivity. In addition to traditional forms of scholarly output, such as books and journal articles, we have accepted for our faculty exhibit creation as a legitimate form of scholarly output. Based on our informal survey of library tenure documents and anecdotal examples, it seems that other institutions are recognizing this scholarly effort.

There is no question that the standards for quality and comprehensiveness of such exhibits are not uniform. However, our experience shows that if approached correctly, the exhibit offers an opportunity for a library faculty member or team to create a scholarly product. Exhibits call for our best thinking, research, writing, planning, organizing, and time. The exhibit may even have supplemental products, such as exhibition catalogs, teaching bibliographies, websites, traveling products, summary articles describing the exhibit, or a formal curatorial lecture on the exhibited material. Most exhibits are time-based and not replicated for the professions like a publication. This should not minimize the potential professional growth offered by this type of scholarly endeavor.

3. Use of unique collections. Some collections, particularly materials in Special Collections and Archives, will seldom be seen or used unless they are physically presented.

4. Physical drawing card. Collections that are visual, oral, or tactile bring people into the facility. In order to teach and stimulate those who come into the facility and create new reasons to come in, we have created a coordinated exhibit strategy. We find that our interaction with potential and actual customers has changed over time. If an individual can get information via full-text searching for journals, he or she will no longer automatically come into our physical facility. Exhibits are just one method of drawing new customers.

5. Technological outreach tool. We are in the process of creating a virtual tour of fine art held in the library. This is a blend of new programming and permanent exhibit design. Electronic web exhibits may be temporary, promotional, or become permanent electronic resources. While there are unique issues in developing web exhibits compared to physical in-house exhibits, there are more commonalities.

6. Creating a buzz. Although our core businesses generate the greatest volume of service and usage, many times it is the special exhibit that creates excitement. The exhibit may get coverage in a local newspaper, even though only a few hundred come to see it. The thousands of books added or hundreds of classes taught, while central to your mission, seldom generate the publicity, buzz, or recognition.

7. Partnerships. The space that is available for exhibition can be a powerful tool for working with many different types of units on campus. Few departments have the materials, space, and staff that are available in the library. Recent exhibits produced in our spaces, led by library faculty, include alliances with the history, earth sciences, English, film studies, and theater departments; student publications; wellness center; university union; university relations; and the Museum of World Cultures.

In addition to library-designed exhibits, there may be opportunities to use your space for traveling exhibits, which involves less actual design by the library, but still involves planning, placement, and promotion. The partnerships help the library reach out to its patron base and develop ongoing relationships. The off-campus relationships may tie to existing collections, needed community service, potential donors, or other cultural organizations. There may be potential problems meeting the needs of community members who are not used to working within an academic environment, including raising and using resources, decision making, content, and exhibit design. Donors may want their gift displayed in a certain way or during a time period that does not fit the needs of the university.

8. Donor recognition and development. Many unusual items, including manuscripts and collections, are given to an academic library. The donor hopes and expects his or her special gift to be recognized, appreciated, and used. One of the most effective ways to do this is to construct an exhibit honoring the content of the gift and the donors. The exhibit and supporting events may be part of a bigger development effort that helps identify and cultivate new donors.

Components of exhibit design

Quality expectation. The public expects, based on experiences with other exhibits and commercial visual products, high-quality exhibits with professional visual impact and standards. The public makes no distinction between any of your products; all should be visually dynamic.

Who designs? The advent of the computer does not necessarily mean that we are all good graphic designers. We recommend that any librarian involved in displays understands the graphics packages available and visual products on the market. Although you may work with partners, the librarian should coordinate the design effort.

Key design elements. The exhibit has to have a hook that is tied to a theme or specific educational goal. First, one must choose the intellectual reason for the exhibit. What do you want your viewer to learn? Should the viewer be changed after participating in your exhibit (entertained, informed, emotionally affected, changed opinion, inspired, proud of institution)? We think that there should be a coordinated visual hook in addition to an educational hook.

Planning and integration. An exhibit, from idea to completion, is a complicated and, hopefully, a thoughtfully planned experience. In tackling any other scholarly work, one would plan, draft, involve colleagues, establish goals and objectives, and do all of the deliberate managerial steps to help ensure a successful product. Exhibits should not be different.

While many people are ready to help hang the exhibit, time should be spent planning early in the concept, writing textual support, layout, and preparing traffic patterns and visual goals before you just start "hanging." The text or other methods of presenting the information (audio, video, interactive computer) must be done in concert with the educational goals of the project. An integrated, planned exhibit at its many levels produces the best results. However, in defense of those who prepare and plan exhibits, there are spur-of-the-moment opportunities and demands that make complete planning an ideal, not always a reality.

Exhibits team. We recommend a collegial approach (project team, committee, task force, work group) to the exhibit process, since it is difficult to find one individual who has all the needed strengths in visual design, project conceptualization, marketing, layout, and writing. Examples of roles played by a variety of our library staff included: idea generator, layout designer, artifact preparer, labeler, bibliographer, procurer, builder, scheduler, writer, event planner, caterer, security planner, interpreter, photographer, videographer, lighting designer, marketer, and conservation specialist. Everyone can contribute something to the team, but there needs to be an overall coordinator.

Types of exhibit venues. You may be surprised how many potential exhibit spaces exist in your library. Samples of our found space include:

- Fixed display case at entry (traditional glass shelved unit best for attention-grabbing exhibits that need protection);
- Portable eight-foot-high exhibit wall that can be configured in multiple ways using Velcro technology to hold components. This is a nontraditional format for libraries, but common in trade shows; the material cannot be unique or protected, but this is a very flexible and quick venue.
- Stationary, flat display cases near Special Collections—a traditional tool best in supplementing Special Collections exhibits for material needing security.
- Curriculum materials center using a large bulletin board, similar to ones used in public schools, which is great for student art and flat exhibits not needing security.

- A 60-foot exhibition wall, approximately 12 feet high, with adjustable spotlights. This traditional exhibition space is supplemented with Plexiglas cases for showing three-dimensional artifacts. This area is used for major art exhibits and museum displays and is painted and repaired after each use.
- Special Collections room has an integrated display space, including a large, flat wall (reusable), two large glass security display cases, and various furniture surfaces.
- Archives has two sites, one inside of the room itself with some wall surfaces and portable cases, as well as a second long display wall outside of the room.
- Other open areas can be used with easels, ceiling hung displays, cabinet surfaces, and standing artifacts.

We have invested in a variety of display tools to support our exhibits, such as Plexiglas cases, book holders, pillows, portable Velcro walls, portable museum walls, glass clip frames, reusable picture frames, die cut letter machine and the requisite foam core, fabrics, glues, tools, and other supplies.

Venues can be categorized also by ownership, timeframe, cost, and learning delivery systems. It is important to classify the ownership of the exhibit to help identify responsible parties and budgetary divisions. The length of time the exhibit is displayed as well as the time within the academic year are key elements of strategy. We have constructed a library-wide exhibit calendar to help plan and coordinate our many venues. The frequency of change in the exhibit space is a negotiable item, and one needs to balance exhibit turnover with educational goals and resources so that the spaces are not changed haphazardly. Costs can be self-funded, grant-funded, partnership-funded, funded by the seat of your pants, unfunded, underfunded, overfunded, and disguised as funded from something else.

Venues can be flat surface informational, display case multidimensional, interactive, guided, web-based, or some combination of the above. The existing space and budgets dictate the best approach for your exhibit. The key is to include analysis of space, ownership, cost, timeframe, and delivery systems as part of your earliest planning discussions.

While none of us are ready to subcontract as exhibit designers, we feel that, ready or not, through study, trial and error, and mutual support we have all raised our professional abilities in the area of exhibit design, preparation, and management. We may have been surprised by our new roles, but we feel that the increasing emphasis on library exhibits is a vital part of our service mission.

SOURCE: Andrew Dutka, Sherman Hayes, and Jerry Parnell, "The Surprise Part of a Librarian's Life: Exhibition Design and Preparation Course," *College & Research Libraries News* 63 (January 2002): 19–22.

Borrowing special materials for exhibition

by the ACRL Rare Books and Manuscripts Section

TO ACCOMPANY A REQUEST LETTER, the prospective borrower should prepare a concise document describing the borrowing institution's exhibition program and facilities. For traveling exhibitions, a separate report should be submitted for each institution. If the borrower prefers to draw up its own facilities report, it should be written in a straightforward, narrative style. A standard facilities report may be obtained from the American Association of Museums.

The report can be organized under eight basic headings:

The borrower. State full name of institution, address, fax, and telephone numbers. Briefly describe the nature of institution. Indicate size of the staff and name(s) of staff member(s) in charge of the exhibition.

The building. Indicate date and type of building construction, size of the exhibition space, and its location within the building.

Fire protection. Describe in detail the fire detection and fire extinguishing/suppression system. The lending institution should decide what kinds of fire alarm systems and fire extinguishing/suppression systems are acceptable. For example, most institutions will not lend rare materials if an exhibition area fire alarm signal does not go directly to a central station. Some will not lend if it is protected by a sprinkler system; gas or dry powder systems may be preferred.

Security. Describe how items on exhibition will be properly safeguarded against theft or damage. Describe the exhibition cases and locks and the method by which framed items are mounted on the wall. Describe the intrusion alarm system in the exhibition area. If security staff are employed, give the number of security staff employed and the number on duty at any time. Indicate the days and hours that the exhibition will be regularly open. Indicate whether food and drink are ever allowed in the exhibition area, whether the space is rented to outside organizations, and if any other use is made of the space other than for exhibition viewing.

Environment. Indicate the range of temperature and relative humidity in the exhibition areas and the areas for packing and storage. Indicate the maximum variation percentage within a 24-hour period for temperature and relative humidity in those areas and how the readings were measured. Describe the types of monitoring equipment used, giving evidence of specific and well-calibrated measurements. The borrowing institution may be required to provide dated temperature and humidity records before and/or throughout the loan period.

Describe the lighting in the exhibition area. Identify the types of lighting fixtures in the exhibition and work areas and provide the exact light levels in foot-candles, indicating how these readings were taken. Explain how items on exhibition will be protected from ultraviolet radiation from natural or artificial sources in the exhibition and work areas.

Handling the lent objects. Indicate that the institution will use proper, accepted, professional standards at all stages of the exhibition process, including meeting lender's requirements concerning such matters as matting, framing, or the fabrication of custom cradles.

For some materials a fine-arts mover may be required, providing specially trained personnel and equipment, such as temperature/humidity controlled trucks with adequate theft protection. It is the right of the lending institution to refuse to send material with a carrier if its transportation requirements are not met. For certain items, the lending institution may require that one of its own staff members install and remove items from the exhibit cases.

Insurance. Describe the borrowing institution's fine arts insurance coverage and give the name of the insurer and broker. Offer to provide a copy of the policy, if requested. In most cases, the borrower will be expected to insure the object at the value specified by the lender on an all-risk, wall-to-wall basis. In most cases, the borrower's insurance policy should specify that the insured sum represents the true replacement value and that in case of damage, depredation, or loss there will be no recourse rights in the law to packers and carriers. The insurer will also be required to issue a certificate of insurance naming the lender as an additional insured before the objects will be released to the borrower.

The lending institution assigns a confidential valuation to each item lent for insurance purposes only. The lender may require that the borrowing institution pay for an appraisal by a qualified outside appraiser. Because of potential problems, a borrowing institution should never accept an appraisal by the lending institution's staff and should insist on one by a qualified outside appraiser. The lender should receive a certificate of insurance from the borrower's insurance company, indicating that insurance coverage is in full force before the item leaves the lending institution. The certificate should include a statement of the policy's standard exclusions.

Indemnity for international loans may be secured through the Federal Council on the Arts and the Humanities. Indemnity applications are reviewed twice yearly, and applications should be made at least one year in advance. Insurance valuations from a qualified outside appraiser are required. Please note that the entire cost of the necessary insurance coverage may not be awarded to the applicant.

It is the responsibility of the borrowing institution to cover the items involved with an all-risk, wall-to-wall fine arts insurance policy, with the lending institution named beneficiary or "additional insured," from the time the items leave the lending institution until they are returned.

References. Give a list of other institutions, with names of contacts, that have lent items to the borrowing institution for recent exhibitions.

SOURCE: Guidelines for Borrowing and Lending Special Collections Materials for Exhibition (January 2005), www.ala.org/ala/acrl/acrlstandards/borrowguide.htm.

4

Facetiae

by Bill Katz

COLLECTIONS OF ANECDOTES became popular during the late 17th and 18th century. "From 1769 until the end of the century the genre became a literary rage, and more than a hundred titles containing 'Anecdote' reached the public, several of them extending to five volumes or more," wrote James M. Osborn.

POGGIO BRACCIOLINI

Another form of the anecdote collection was the "facetia." The English adjective "facetious" comes from this Latin word, which describes a collection of witty and often licentious anecdotes. The Florentine Renaissance humanist Poggio Bracciolini (right) gave the title *Liber Facetiarum (Book of Pleasantries)* to his collection of anecdotes compiled in the middle of the 15th century. In explaining "facetiae" in his 1964 anthology *Wit and Wisdom of the Italian Renaissance*, Charles Speroni says it is "in general, a brief narrative that varies in length from a few lines to one or even two pages. Its main purpose is to entertain . . . by relating a humorous occurrence that often finds its conclusion in a pungent, well-timed repartee." The taste for facetiae, or pleasantries, increased throughout the Renaissance, particularly as a useful source of wit and wisdom in conversation. The appreciation for the skills of civil conversation and the rise of courtiers were celebrated in Baldassarre Castigione's *Book of the Courier.*

The English took over facetiae in the 17th and 19th centuries, and a number of titles were published that drew on translations of the Latin classics, for example, Thomas Brown (1663–1704), *The Works of Mr. Thomas Brown, Serious and Comical, in Prose and Verse* (London: Various publishers, editions 1703–to date). Actually most of the pages were filled with material from Horace, Cicero, and Martial. Some of the more "erotic" passages were given in Latin.

The descriptor "facetia" seems to have been rarely used in the subsequent century, although from time to time it surfaced. For example, in 1836 one Richard Gooch edited the third edition of *Facetiae Cantabrigienses* (London: C. Mason), which offers "anecdotes, smart sayings, satirics, retorts, etc. by or relating to celebrated Cantabs." (Cantabs is a shortening of Cantabrigian, i.e., a graduate of Cambridge University.) There were similar titles in European countries, but by the 20th century, facetiae have almost disappeared.

SOURCE: Bill Katz, *Cuneiform to Computer: A History of Reference Sources* (Lanham, Md.: Scarecrow, 1998), pp. 76–77. Reprinted with permission.

More unfamiliar genres

THE PREVIOUS EDITION of the *Whole Library Handbook* (pp. 250–252) offered a selected glossary of unusual book genres found in special collections. Here are a few more intriguing categories.—*GME.*

Big little books—small, thick, heavily-illustrated books, usually containing texts abridged from popular fiction.

Blow books—books with hidden nicks or tabs in the fore-edge so that various illustrations appear on different occasions of riffling.

Burlesques—literary or dramatic works that make a subject appear ridiculous by treating it in an incongruous way, as by presenting a lofty subject with vulgarity or an inconsequential one with mock dignity.

Calaveras—satirical broadside poems, usually in the form of mock epitaphs, illustrated with skeleton caricatures and issued around the Day of the Dead.

Chapbooks—small, cheap pamphlets with paper bindings that were sold door to door in England in the 17th and 18th centuries by itinerant peddlers ("chapmen"). They were illustrated with woodcuts and contained tales such as "Jack the Giant Killer," ballads, nursery rhymes, historical incidents, biographies, tracts, dream analyses, palmistry, and astrology. Most were published anonymously and few were dated.

Chiroxylographics—medieval block books with illustrations made from woodcuts and the text lettered by hand.

Clog almanacs—a primitive kind of almanac or calendar, formerly used in Norway, Denmark, and England, made by cutting notches, runes, or figures on the four edges of a clog, or square piece of wood, brass, or bone about eight inches long that could be hung up in a room or attached to a walking stick.

Colonial editions—cheap versions of British books printed for the colonial market between 1880 and 1910.

Convicts' addresses—confessions, last words, and the like, whether delivered to the public or to an individual for publication.

Emblem books—books in which the text is fancifully embellished with decorations showing heraldic or allegorical emblems expressing some thought or moral idea. The text, frequently consisting of proverbs, mottoes, or verses arranged in symbolic shapes, is frequently enclosed in a border.

Essay periodicals—A periodical, prevalent in the 18th century, each issue of which consisted of a single essay. Examples are *The Spectator* and *The Rambler*.

Harlequinades—the first printed items for children that can be described as movable books. In these books, pictures change when the reader moves a series of flaps. The idea came from Robert Sayer, a bookseller in Fleet Street, London, who began experimenting with his idea in 1765. The name originated because the harlequin, known from the panto-mimes in the theaters of that time, was often the star of the book's adventures.

House books—books that open up or fold out to form houses, castles, shops, or public buildings. Keith Moseley's *Victorian House Book* (Konemann, 1999) is unusual in showing both an interior and exterior; its front cover incorporates a useful booklet telling the social history of such buildings.

Merchant manuals—manuals containing information on trade routes, market locations, business practices, or merchant ethics.

Newsbooks—British publications printed in a small quarto volume of up to 24 pages and containing foreign news. Newsbooks were first published in 1622 at irregular intervals. They were not numbered until 1641 and dealt almost exclusively with the Thirty Years' War, ceasing in 1642 at the outbreak of the Civil War.

Pilot guides—nautical guides that describe coast lines, harbors, dangers, and aids to navigation.

Postcard books—booklets whose pages consist of postcards, suitable for mailing, that can be detached from the spine along a perforated edge.

Pull-tab movables—children's books with movable pictures. The first publisher to mass-produce them was Dean and Son in London, which issued many children's rhyme and story books with hand-colored pictures that could be animated by pulling a paper tab at the bottom of each page. The German satirical cartoonist Lothar Meggendorfer (1847–1925) designed a series of children's novelty books in which the plates sprang to life at the pull of a single tab, one picture often featuring five or six different movements. A forerunner of pop-up books.

Robin Hood plays—a rare group of plays that draw parts of their texts from the Robin Hood ballad tradition, found in a small area covering parts of Gloucestershire, Oxfordshire, Somerset, and Wiltshire.

Souvenir books—mid-19th-century compilations of poetry and prose, often profusely illustrated, elaborately decorated, and ornately bound. They were frequently issued in time for the Christmas season.

Utopian newspapers—newspapers associated with the expression of visionary or ideal schemes for the perfection of social or political conditions.

Volvelles—devices, whether individual or in books, consisting of one or more movable circles surrounded by other graduated or figured circles and intended for the calculation of astronomical or other data.

SOURCES: ALA Association of College and Research Libraries' Rare Books and Manuscripts Section; American Antiquarian Society; Ampersand Books, www.ampersandbooks. co.uk; Movemania, www.heino.speedlinq.nl; Margaret Haller, *The Book Collector's Fact Book* (New York: Arco, 1976); Ray Prytherch, *Harrod's Librarians' Glossary*, 9th ed. (Aldershot, Eng.: Gower, 2000).

A brief history of zines

by Julie Bartel

ZINES (PRONOUNCED "ZEEN," like "bean," rather than "line") are basically small, self-published magazines that are usually (though not always) written by one person and distributed through an intricate network of individuals and collectives. The only thing that all zines have in common is that

their existence is the result of passion rather than a desire for profit. Though accurate, this definition rarely satisfies the zine novice, since it fails to convey a clear understanding of the scope, breadth, and material reality of zines and zine culture. Perhaps because we've all grown up with guidelines and definitions and regulations for what is appropriate in various media, it's a struggle to accept that there are very few rules in the world of zines. We want a Definition, a definitive description, and restrictions which help us to define the boundaries. An exact, illuminating definition of "zines" is hard—if not impossible—to pin down, though; as Stephen Duncombe, author of perhaps the only scholarly work on zine culture (*Notes from Underground*, Verso, 1997), points out in the epigraph, it's difficult to convey their true essence without a show-and-tell session. So rather than attempting to formulate an authoritative definition, it's probably more helpful—and more accurate—to simply list some of the characteristics of zines and hope that we can come to a better understanding of what they are.

Each time I introduce the concept of zines to a group or classroom I end up answering the same questions, trying to help them understand zines by verifying what they are and can be. Even though (or perhaps because) I used the broadest terms possible to describe zines, listeners invariably seek assurance that they've understood the "correct" definition. "Can I do a zine about animals?" Yes. "What if I just took things from my journal and made them into something else. Is that a zine?" Yes. "Is it all right if I just draw pictures or cut things out of magazines?" Yes. "Do there have to be words?" No. "Can it be any shape that I want?" Yes. (After a flurry of similar questions, I usually just hand over a pile of zines and let them create their own personal definitions, but of course that doesn't work in print.)

Zines are about diversity, creativity, innovation, and expression. As a group, zines deliberately lack cohesion of form or function, representing as they do individual visions and ideals rather than professional or corporate objectives. With zines, anything goes. Anything. They can be about toasters, food, a favorite television show, thrift stores, anarchism, candy, bunnies, sexual abuse,

architecture, war, gingerbread men, activism, retirement homes, comics, eating disorders, Barbie dolls—you name it. There are personal zines, music zines, and sports zines, zines about politics, and zines about pop culture. There are zines about libraries (*Browsing Room, Nancy's Magazine, Library Bonnet*) and even more zines created by people that work in them (*Thoughtworm, Dwan, Transom*). There's even a zine just for zine librarians called, appropriately, *Zine Librarian Zine.*

I should make it clear right up front (in fact I should have done so sooner) that zines are *not* e-zines—that is, electronic magazines accessed through the internet. E-zines and zines—the terms are often used interchangeably, and incorrectly—are not the same thing, though their content is often similar. While often designated (and dismissed) as ephemera, zines spring from the desire to create a tangible material object, and the physicality of zines is what differentiates them in essential ways from their electronic counterparts. Zines are about paper and glue, staples, thread, and ink, not about HTML tags, links, and pop-ups. Creating an artifact which can be passed from one person to the next, which can be sent through the mail (the regular mail), is part of the appeal. As Duncombe so eloquently puts it, "There is something about the materiality of a zine—you can feel it, stick it in your pocket, read it in the park, give it away at a show"—that is integral to zine culture.

Zines come in all sizes and shapes, and while many are cut-and-paste, as seems to be the stereotype, others are hand-lettered (*A Renegade's Handbook to Love and Sabotage*), produced on a computer (*Low Hug*), printed on a letter-press (*Ker-Bloom*), or typed out on a manual typewriter (*Kitsch||artificial respiration*). Zinesters use handmade paper (*Brainscan*), linoleum-block prints (*All This Is Mine*), photographs (*Say Cheese*), and color collage (*Xenogenesis*) to enhance their work, and while many zines are simply folded in half and stapled in the middle, some are bound with  twine (*Twenty-eight Pages Lovingly Bound with Twine*), some are held together with intricate metal wiring (*Fragile*), and some employ the time-tested rubber band (*Night Ride Rambling*). There is infinite variety to be found in the content, format, and construction of zines, and there are no rules or restrictions to speak of. If you can imagine it and create it, you can make it into a zine.

You may be asking yourself: "Why would anyone do this? Creating a zine seems like a huge waste of time and money." Well, you're right. As I mentioned earlier, a desire for profit is not usually the motivating factor for creating a zine—which is good, because there is no profit to be made by making one. On the other hand, producing a zine requires time, money, and effort, all of which you must be willing to give in spades. But zines aren't about money (unless you count the money it will cost you to make one); zines are about making your voice heard and, especially, about defining and creating space within the dominant corporate media culture. "Zines, with all their limitations and contradictions, offer up something very important to the people who create and enjoy them: a place to walk to," writes Duncombe. "In the shadows of the dominant culture, zines and underground culture mark out *a free space:* a space within which to imagine and experiment with new and idealistic ways of thinking, communicating, and being."

Author and librarian Chris Dodge describes zines as "case studies in 'do-it-yourself' culture, a forum for those who don't like what's on TV and can't stand what they read in the daily paper." While the quality of individual zines may vary, each creation is invariably unique, a material representation of creativity and of the need to communicate. For zinesters, the satisfaction and gratification of communicating their vision is well worth the effort, whether they choose to seek a wide readership or not. As longtime zinester Chip Rowe explains, "they're Tinkertoys for malcontents," and while often considered (if they're considered at all) as part of an underground movement too radical for mainstream society, zines are a brilliant expression of the creative spirit.

Where did they come from?

Zines—the word is taken from the term "fanzines" (which is itself a shortened version of "fan magazines")—have been around in one form or another for hundreds of years. Small chapbooks of Shakespeare's works; Thomas Paine's pamphlet, *Common Sense;* and the myriad leaflets published during the 18th and 19th centuries could all be considered precursors to the modern zine. "Self publishing ventures of independent spirit and vitality such as American broadsides from Revolutionary days, Russian Samizdat material, Dada, and other avant-garde art, social movements' magazines and manifestoes, and beat poetry chapbooks," says Fred Wright, all embody the same spirit and vision—if not physical form—of today's zines. Their strongest historical connection, however, is with the science fiction fanzines of the 1930s, in which fans communicated with each other through elaborate letter columns.

While America certainly has no corner on the revolutionary pamphlet market (the number of treatises, leaflets, and brochures distributed during the French Revolution alone would argue otherwise), independent printing has been a hallmark of the American "independent spirit"—even before that spirit had a country of its own. Carl Berger, author of *Broadsides and Bayonets: The Propaganda War of the American Revolution* (Presidio, 1977), notes that "from the beginning it was a war of words as well as gunpowder, with each major protagonist seeking to subvert and weaken the enemy camp with carefully prepared arguments" which were disseminated via broadsides.

Perhaps the most famous, Thomas Paine's *Common Sense*, illustrates just how powerful this type of literature can be. R. Seth Friedman, former publisher of *Factsheet Five*, has pointed out on more than one occasion that Benjamin Franklin himself was a zinester. "He published his own thoughts using his own printing presses. It wasn't the magazine business. He did it all on his own."

Like their American counterparts, politically motivated dissidents of the Soviet Union self-published their work. "Samizdat," a Russian acronym for "self-publishers," was a term "coined by post-Stalin dissidents for the old Russian revolutionary practice" of "circulating uncensored material privately, usually in manuscript form—nonconformist poetry and fiction, memoirs, historical documents, protest statements, trial records, etc." It is clear that political motivations, while not always central, have often determined the course of self-publishers, since the act of publishing itself might be seen at times as criminal, let alone the contents.

Though perhaps not the stuff of treason or sedition, schools of art such as the Dadaists were deliberately subversive, attempting to shock and unsettle middle-class sensibilities by publishing manifestos which demanded, among other things, "the right to piss in different colors." "Like the participants in samizdat, the artistic rebels of Dada, particularly in the movement's beginnings in Zürich during World War I, had to resort to underground publishing in order to make . . . bold statements," and many of the techniques they used are still practiced by zinesters today. Dada magazines such as *Cabaret Voltaire*, *291*, and *New York Dada* incorporated rants (a zine staple), *detournement*

(taking something out of its appropriate context and giving it a context of one's own choosing, a practice zinesters have embraced), and collages, a near-necessity for beginning zinesters.

All these characteristics—political comment, literary and artistic expression, methods and means of form and distribution—found voice later in the beat poetry chapbooks and the political magazines and manifestos of America in the 1950s and 1960s. While their formats differed greatly—the beat poets often published exquisitely crafted chapbooks which were a far cry from the newsprint missives or handwritten manifestos of left-wing political groups—the attempt to communicate with others through self-publishing was the same.

Communication, perhaps the single motivating factor which most zinesters agree on, is the spark that generated the science fiction and fantasy fanzines of the 1930s and stimulated the spread and transformation of zines in the 1980s. In 1926 Hugo Gernsback started the first magazine devoted to publishing stories of science-based fiction, *Amazing Stories.* This magazine featured a letters column where fans debated story ideas, scientific concepts, and the credibility of the hypothetical science proposed by the magazine's featured authors. After a few issues, Gernsback "made a minor decision that changed the face of science fiction forever—he printed the full addresses of the letter writers so they could contact each other directly."

As the letter column grew in popularity, it caught the attention (as a means of communication which they could adopt) of the various fan groups and associations which formed as a result of their initial contact through *Amazing Stories.* One of these early fan groups, the Science Correspondence Club, began publishing in 1930, and the first issue of *The Comet*, the group's amateur publication, also marked the first fanzine. "In those days, a science fiction reader who wanted to share his opinions and enthusiasm would shove a ten-sheet carbon paper sandwich into a typewriter and hack out a three or four page fanzine to send to other fans." Fanzines sprouted across the country (and around the world) as devoted fans wrote in to discuss scientific concepts and developments, currents events, plots, characters, and, eventually, their own lives. Beloved serial stories were embellished and supplemented as fans wrote new, usually unauthorized, adventures to tide them over between installments, or to keep characters alive after a series ended.

"Like zines, the earliest fanzines were produced for personal and not financial reasons. They were predominately produced by aficionados of a certain subject, most frequently fantasy and science fiction literature, as documents to celebrate their devotion and interest." The words "fanzine" and "fan-mag," both of which were used to denote these small, nonprofessional publications, also indicated their origins (as well as distancing them from "prozines" such as *Amazing Stories* and *Weird Tales*). While many fanzine writers were content to keep their amateur status, others aspired to write for the prozines, and many did, notably Ray Bradbury, Robert Bloch, and Robert Heinlein. This golden age of science fiction not only allowed for occasional transitions from fan to professional, but also tended to foster and legitimize the fan experience. By communicating with each other through amateur publications and building networks of like-minded people, fanzine writers were able to encourage, perpetuate, and contribute to a world which they felt passionately about. Fanzines were empowering and addictive and allowed indi-

viduals to ignore, if not destroy, the distinction between those who create and those who consume.

This unique form of self-expression had
obvious appeal when the disaffected and disillusioned youth of the punk movement adopted it in
the 1970s. "The late '60s saw a synergy between
outspoken political commentary, literary experimentation, and heartfelt critiques of rock and roll
music," Friedman wrote. And then in the early
1970s something happened: "what was once the

SALT LAKE CITY PUBLIC LIBRARY ZINE COLLECTION

rebellious voice of a generation turned into the boring ol' establishment. The
excitement of rock and roll turned into the oppressive doldrums of overblown
stadium rock extravaganzas." In response to this seeming betrayal of musical
trust, a new kind of music evolved—punk—and with it came a new lifestyle,
complete with politics, dress code, and zines. Having perhaps more in common with early avant-garde artists such as the Dadaists than with science-
fiction aficionados, punks had high ideals of revolution, of escaping the mundane, of life as performance. Their anticorporate, do-it-yourself (DIY) lifestyle
advocated circumventing the system and producing, distributing, and promoting on their own. As with music, and true to their DIY reputation, when
the mainstream media failed to write and publish what they were looking for,
punk kids did it themselves, producing zines which featured interviews, record
reviews, travelogues, personal stories, and more.

By the 1980s, zines had become a staple of the punk lifestyle. With the rise
of cheap and accessible photocopying—and the spread of the personal computer—the "zine revolution" of the early 1980s really took off, and the medium exploded past the punk scene into an underground network of publishers, editors, writers, and artists. What really sparked the movement, however,
as I mentioned above, was communication.

In 1982 science fiction fan Mike Gunderloy decided to
simplify his letter writing by typing up a two-page tip sheet
describing the many interesting fanzines he came across.
This way he wouldn't have to duplicate his work when
corresponding with friends, and he could save a little time
(or so he thought).

He called his new creation *Factsheet Five*, after a short
story by science fiction author John Brunner, and sent
out a dozen copies. Within a couple of years *Factsheet Five*,
perhaps the most influential zine of all time, grew into a
full-size, internationally distributed magazine which
listed thousands of zines and had thousands of readers.
"By sending free copies . . . to the editors of zines reviewed in its pages," Chris Dodge explains, "Gunderloy fostered 'cross-pol-
lination' not only among zinesters, but also among all sorts of mail artists,
cartoonists, poets, and activists hungry for alternatives to mass-produced
media." These new connections between people "on the fringes" of society
turned out to be quite powerful, and the underground publishing movement as we know it today was born.

SOURCE: Julie Bartel, *From A to Zine: Building a Winning Zine Collection in Your Library* (Chicago:
American Library Association, 2004), pp. 1–9.

Why libraries should collect graphic novels

by Steve Miller

THROUGHOUT THEIR LONG HISTORY, COMICS—and now, graphic novels—were considered kid's stuff, at best. At its worst moment, comic art was seen as a disruptive social influence that created hooligans and delinquents. This misconception may still hold in the minds of some librarians and educators; this is the stigma that many people still subscribe to, and it raises the question, Why have comics in a library?

How can comics be seen in a new, more positive light? Consider these observations:

Graphic novels inspire art and imagination. They inspire a reader's active participation to bring the characters to life. Many young people take an interest in art, and they often express their own stories through comic art.

Graphic novels improve visual literacy. Children and teens are a visual generation. They are growing up with television, computers, and video games. They spend most of their time processing images and sounds rather than reading words. Our electronic age requires its citizens to process information visually. Comics provide a platform that shows words and images in a mutually reinforcing framework, one that promotes visual literacy. This can help students process information "beyond the words," one key to stimulating visual literacy.

Graphic novels and comic art are attractive to children and teens for recreational reading. Today's youth show a preference for comic art material. In 1999, a Newspaper Association of America report noted that 43% of American teenagers read the newspaper comic sections, more than the number of teens who look at the front page. Simmons, a marketing research company, published a study in 2000 reporting that comic books are the favorite reading material of 41% of children ages 6 to 11.

Graphic novels increase library traffic. A comic or graphic novel collection can attract new readers of *all ages*. Some libraries report as much as an 80% increase in patronage to their young adult area.

Graphic novels increase circulation of noncomic books. Many graphic

novels have tie-ins to books and, more recently, movies. Some libraries have reported 25% increases in overall collection circulation after adding graphic novels to their collections. A few have even noted that their few shelves of graphic novels circulate as much as a dozen shelves of young adult fiction.

Graphic novels attract reluctant readers. Illustrations work with the text to provide contextual reinforcement as the story progresses. This maintains the interest of challenged readers in a nonthreatening manner as they build reading confidence.

Graphic novels promote literacy. Many educators feel that reading anything will build literacy skills. Full-length graphic novels contain, on average, 168 pages and 12,400 words, while some reach as high as 20,000 words. Juvenile fiction novels can top 30,000 words, but reluctant readers can make it up in volume with graphic novels—teens often read multiple graphic novels, devouring thousands of words without realizing it. This is a very useful literacy tool for reluctant readers who ordinarily would not read a "regular" book. In many cases, literacy is such a high priority for public and school libraries that they are willing to try almost anything to help challenged or reluctant readers develop a love of reading.

Graphic novels help develop language skills. In comic art, the images support the text. This is helpful for ESOL (English for Speakers of Other Languages) students. The reader receives visual assistance in understanding the text. The inverse is also true—English-speaking students studying other languages can benefit from foreign editions of graphic novels in French, German, Spanish, Russian, Japanese, and other languages.

Graphic novels are used by public and school libraries. Many libraries and schools around the world are taking an interest in comic art and graphic novels. These popular books are used in classrooms and for library programs and are a dynamic part of library collections.

Why are they so popular? First, they are easy to read and comprehend. The visual images tell part of the story, lessening the burden on the reader. Second, comics often tell fun, exciting stories that draw the reader into the action. They are also quick to read—a graphic novel can be enjoyed in much less time than can a novel or even a short story.

An often overlooked reason why comics are popular is that it is rare to find a child who is *required* to read one. When children choose graphic novels, they sit down to read them because it is *their* idea. There is no pressure of being graded. It is not to *learn* something. It is just for fun! (The fun part, for the adults, comes when a teacher actually assigns a student to read a graphic novel. Most teens are excited to learn their teacher is actually *cool!*)

SOURCE: Steve Miller, *Developing and Promoting Graphic Novel Collections* (New York: Neal-Schuman, 2005), pp. 29–31. Reprinted with permission.

Notable multimedia for children, 2005

THE NOTABLE CHILDREN'S Videos, Recordings, and Computer Software list is compiled annually by three committees of the ALA Association for Library Service to Children to highlight multimedia materials. These are their selections for 2005.—*GME.*

Videos

Diary of a Worm (Weston Woods). With the thankless job of helping the earth breathe, a young worm gives us a view of his daily life from the underground up. The youthful voice of Alexander Gould brings to life this animated version of the humorous book written by Doreen Cronin and illustrated by Harry Bliss. Ages 5–9.

The Dot (Weston Woods). Discouraged by a blank piece of paper, Vashti is transformed from a frustrated young girl to a confident artist through the gentle nudging of a caring teacher. An inspiring animated adaptation of Peter H. Reynolds' book, perfectly narrated by Thora Birch. Ages 5–10.

Duck for President (Weston Woods). While campaigning for life, liberty, and the pursuit of happiness, Duck discovers it is very hard to run a farm, the state, and the country. Randy Travis continues to narrate Duck's animated escapades, as written by Doreen Cronin and illustrated by Betsy Lewin. Vote for Duck! Ages 5–8.

The ErlKing (National Film Board of Canada). Schubert's adaptation of Goethe's haunting poem is brought to life by Ben Zelkowicz's sand-on-glass animation. A kaleidoscope of disturbingly beautiful images form and reform, telling the story of the ErlKing's enticement of a young boy. Sung in German. Ages 12–14.

Fireboat: The Heroic Adventures of the John J. Harvey (Spoken Arts). The reactivation of an old fireboat on 9/11 is related in this iconographic adaptation of Maira Kalman's rendition of a true story. Framed by interviews with the author and the boat's crew. Ages 5–8.

I Stink! (Weston Woods). The roar of the garbage truck and Joel Goodman's jazzy music spring to life in this raucous animated version of Kate and Jim McMullan's stinky tale narrated by Andy Richter. Ages 2–8.

Journey of the Loggerhead (Environmental Media). Spectacular photography and interviews with marine scientists document the environmental odyssey of one of nature's endangered creatures, the loggerhead turtle. Ages 8–14.

Let's Get Real (New Day Films). In a powerful yet balanced documentary, real middle school students who are dealing with issues such as name-calling, bullying, racial and religious differences, disabilities, and perceived sexual orientation speak with candor about what is happening in their lives. A Columbine Award–winning, "in your face" video. Ages 12–14.

Liberty's Kids Series (WHYY-TV/PBS). A kid's-eye view of the American Revolution presented in a "you are there" manner. Celebrity voices bring to life a diverse mix of historical figures and fictional characters. Colorful animation makes history fun and educational. Ages 5–10.

Life on the Edge: A Guide to Pacific Coastal Habitats (Earthwise Media). Snorkel without getting wet in this beautifully photographed and informational film about Pacific Coastal habitats. Ages 8–12.

Pollyanna (WGBH Boston Video). Masterpiece Theatre's presentation of the beloved novel by Eleanor H. Porter breathes new life into the story of how a young orphan transforms her spinster aunt and an English village. Ages 8–12.

The Pot That Juan Built (Weston Woods). This variant of a favorite children's rhyme creates a magical journey into the life and work of Juan Quezada, a famous Mexican potter. Based on the 2004 Belpré Honor and ALA Notable Childen's book written by Nancy Andrews-Goebel and illustrated by David Diaz, this iconographic video, narrated by Alfred Molina, is complemented by a documentary visit with the potter. Ages 6–12.

Science, Please (National Film Board of Canada). Twenty-six short segments humorously explain scientific phenomena by the clever merging of old film footage and fun animation. The teachers' guide helps to match each clip with appropriate age and grade levels. Ages 5–14.

Thank You, Sarah: The Woman Who Saved Thanksgiving (Spoken Arts). A humorous look at Sarah Hale, the strong, determined woman who championed official recognition of the Thanksgiving holiday. This iconographic film, based on the book by Laurie Halse Anderson with illustrations by Matt Faulkner, also features an introduction by the author. Ages 6–10.

This Is The House That Jack Built (Weston Woods). Lively music and narration by Mandy Patinkin enhance this classic rhyme in a colorful animated film based on the book illustrated by Simms Taback. Ages 3–7.

Through My Thick Glasses (Pravda and National Film Board of Canada coproduction). A Norwegian grandfather tells his granddaughter the story of his disturbing experiences during World War II with Aunt Ella and the dreaded war machine. Director Pjotr Sapegin uses clay puppets to present a tragic, metaphorical drama, based on a true story. Ages 13–14.

The Wheels on the Bus (Weston Woods). The classic children's song takes a new turn on the way to the library in this version of Paul O. Zelinsky's adaptation. The Bacon Brothers' lively music perfectly matches the clever animation. Ages 2–6.

Recordings

Al Capone Does My Shirts (Recorded Books). Performed by Jonathan Heller. Grades 4 and up.

Beethoven's Wig 2: More Sing-Along Symphonies (Rounder Kids). Performed by Richard Perlmutter. All ages.

Bucking the Sarge (Listening Library). Performed by Michael Boatman. Grades 6 and up.

Dragon Rider (Listening Library). Performed by Brendan Fraser. Grades 4 and up.

Duck for President (Weston Woods). Performed by Randy Travis and Jorge Pupo. Preschool and up.

Fireboat: The Heroic Adventures of the John J. Harvey (Live Oak Media). Performed by Judd Hirsch. All ages.

Flipped (Recorded Books). Performed by Andy Paris and Carine Montbertrand. Grades 5 and up.

Heartbeat (Harper Children's Audio). Performed by Mandy Siegfried. Grades 4–8.

A House of Tailors (Listening Library). Performed by Blair Brown. Grades 3–8.

I Lost My Bear (Weston Woods). Performed by Kristen Hahn. Preschool–grade 2.

I Stink! (Weston Woods). Performed by Andy Richter. Preschool–grade 2.

Ida B. . . . and Her Plans to Maximize Fun, Avoid Disaster, and (Possibly) Save the World (Listening Library). Performed by Lili Taylor. Grades 3–8.

The Last Holiday Concert (Listening Library). Performed by Fred Berman. Grades 3–7.

Mike Mulligan and His Steam Shovel: A New Work for Narrator and Symphony Orchestra (Simon & Simon). Magic Maestro Music. All ages.

More Perfect than the Moon (Harper Children's Audio). Performed by Glenn Close. Grades 2–6.

Muncha! Muncha! Muncha! (Live Oak Media). Performed by William Dufris. Preschool–grade 2.

No More Nasty (Recorded Books). Performed by Johnny Heller. Grades 3–6.

Pincus and the Pig: A Klezmer Tale (Tzadik). Performed by Maurice Sendak and the Shirim Klezmer Orchestra. All ages.

The Pot That Juan Built (Weston Woods). Performed by Alfred Molina. All ages.

Princess in Pink: The Princess Diaries, Volume V (Listening Library). Performed by Clea Lewis. Grades 6 and up.

Rhinoceros Tap (Workman Publishing). Performed by Adam Bryant. All ages.

The Ruby in the Smoke (Listening Library). Performed by Anton Lesser. Grades 6 and up.

Sing Along with Putumayo (Putumayo Kids/Putumayo World Music). Performed by a variety of talented singers. All ages.

The Teacher's Funeral (Listening Library). Performed by Dylan Baker. Grades 4 and up.

When Marian Sang (Live Oak Media). Performed by Gail Nelson and Marian Anderson. All ages.

Computer software

Digital Curriculum, www.digitalcurriculum.com (AIMS Multimedia). This comprehensive interactive online learning resource integrates full-length videos, video clips, still images, encyclopedia content, teacher guides, lesson plans, and online assessments and assignments. Users can supplement learning at home and school with over 90,000 educational multimedia components for every subject. Includes correlations to state and national standards. Ages 7 and up.

I Spy Spooky Mansion Deluxe (Scholastic). Win/Mac. Fans of visual puzzles and wordplay will love this interactive trip into a haunted house. Fifteen I Spy picture puzzles must be solved before the resident skeleton guides the player out of the mansion. Once out, the skeleton invites the player back in for a new round of games and clues. Completing each of three rounds leads to a new challenge. Not only is the program easy to load and fun to play, it also sharpens visual and problem solving skills. Ages 6 and up.

Learn to Play Chess with Fritz and Chesster 2: Chess in the Black Castle (Viva Media). Win. Fans of the first Fritz and Chesster adventure will not be disappointed with this new game, this one focusing on chess strategy. Bianca and Fritz enter the creepy Black Castle to rescue their mentor, Chesster the Rat, who is being held hostage. Only by increasing their chess skills do they stand a chance of outwitting the nefarious King Black. With Bianca's handy Organizer, players can check on point values, learn strategies, store clues found throughout the castle and glean other helpful information. Ages 8 and up.

Photo Puzzle Builder (APTE). Win/Mac. Creating word and picture puzzles is a snap with this engaging program. Anagrams, crosswords, word searches, photo-scrambles, and photo jigsaws are just some of the puzzles users can create. Public domain images are included, but personal digital photos and graphics can be used as well. Puzzles can be edited and the final results can be saved, printed, exported, and posted on a website. Ages 6 and up.

Starry Night: Complete Space and Astronomy Pack (Imaginova). Win/

Mac. Discover the wonders of the night sky with this realistic planetarium program. Young astronomers can see the sky from any point on Earth, controlling time, location, elevation, and more. They can pilot the Deep Space Explorer up to 700 million light years from Earth for stunning views of the ever-expanding universe. Heavenly bodies can be viewed from any angle or distance and be rotated as well. This extensive package also includes Sky-Theatre, a full-length documentary on DVD, and an accompanying text, Starry Night Companion. Ages 9 and up.

SOURCE: ALA Association for Library Service to Children.

Unfamiliar graphic materials

THE LIBRARY OF CONGRESS Prints and Photographs Division has created a thesaurus of more than 600 terms for various visual materials in its collections. Here are some unusual ones.—*GME.*

A trois crayons drawings. Chalk drawings in three colors, usually red, white, and black.

Bank note vignettes. Engraved decorations primarily designed for use on bank notes or other currency but also commonly used on stock certificates and other securities. Pictorial or ornamental images from the 1790s to the present.

Carriers' addresses. Verses in broadside or pamphlet format presented at the start of a new year by newspaper carriers (and sometimes by other tradespeople) to request a gratuity.

Clipper ship cards. Printed cards made to attract freight consignments or passengers to clipper ships preparing to depart; chiefly 1850s–1860s; commonly 4 x 6.5 inches (10 x 16 cm.).

Collotypes. Photomechanical prints introduced commercially in the 1860s; commonly used in book illustration; can be difficult to distinguish from actual photographs.

Dotted prints. Metal relief prints in which white dots or stars, produced by punching a metal plate, punctuate otherwise dark background areas.

Exploded drawings. Graphic delineations showing the individual disassembled components of a structure or object. The parts are shown in their proper relationships with respect to their assembled positions.

Formation photographs. Photographs taken from an elevated vantage point of a large group of people assembled to form a particular design, such as an eagle or the United States flag.

Glamour photographs. Photographs portraying women or men and emphasizing their physical attractiveness. Subjects may be scantily clad, but desirability is conveyed, not erotica. Similar to Fashion photographs, which emphasize the product being modeled, and Publicity photographs, which are made for publicity or promotion purposes.

Optical toys. Toys comprised of a series of still images printed on disks or strips that engage the visual senses by creating the illusion of motion when viewed through specialized viewing devices.

Rewards of merit. Small printed or handwritten documents awarded in schools in recognition of good behavior or scholastic achievement. Common in the 1800s.

Satires (visual works). Graphic commentaries critical of the failings, weaknesses, and morals of the people, governments, or organizations depicted.

Sciagraphic projections. Two-dimensional graphic representations with shadows projected according to specific conventions in regard to the source of light. The projectors of the shadows are usually fixed as the diagonal of a cube from the top left corner to the bottom rear corner and at an angle of 45 degrees in plan and elevation.

Speakeasy cards. Identification cards that admitted the bearer to a speakeasy during the American prohibition era (1920–1933). Often appear to be a club membership card or contain only cryptic markings.

Tobacco package labels. Slips of paper or other material affixed or meant to be attached to a tobacco plug or container for identification, description, or decoration.

Ukiyo-e prints. Woodblock prints produced in Japan between 1615 and 1868. The term *Ukiyo-e* means pictures of the floating or sorrowful world. Formats include single and multiple sheet prints as well as book illustrations.

Watch papers. Circular papers used to ensure a tight fit between inner and outer cases of a pocket watch. Often contain watchmaker's or watch owner's name.

SOURCE: Thesaurus for Graphic Materials II: Genre and Physical Characteristic Terms (TGM II) (Washington, D.C.: Library of Congress Prints and Photographs Division, 1995), www.loc.gov/rr/print/tgm2/.

The practice of music librarianship
by Paula Elliott

DEBORAH CAMPANA HAS OBSERVED that "the close association among music librarians seems to have evolved because of the mission we share—to collect, preserve, and make accessible materials and information on the subject to which we all are drawn." This "subject to which we are all drawn" binds us not only to one another in professional practice but to our users in a common recognition of music's inestimable appeal. Bound by music, it is uniquely possible for us to see ourselves in our users, giving us a particular empathy with their needs. In providing people with the materials of music, we offer them something that is both immediate and immeasurable. Every aspect of our work allows us to support human imagination and celebrate creativity, past and present. "What is it that releases all the energy and the power we have gathered and made available?" asks Michael Gorman, the eminent librarian and thinker. "The presence of the people on whose behalf we work."

Who are those individuals for whom we do our work, those library users who justify our varied careers? They are musicians, professional and amateur. They are music lovers, some possessing a high degree of sophistication, others who simply "know what they like." They are academics and scholars: musicologists, historians, theorists, ethnomusicologists, and a population of music statisticians and computer enthusiasts. They are the people who write program notes and the booklets that accompany recordings. They are public and private school music educators and administrators. They are our neighborhood music teachers and the kids who go to them for lessons. They are the writers, readers, and listeners whose musical involvement may mean never playing an instrument or singing a tune. They are college, university, and conservatory students. Our users are people who listen to the radio, have jobs on the radio, read reviews and buy recordings, go to concerts, and download MP3s (sometimes on library workstations). Whether in flesh or in spirit, they are our culture's singers and dancers. In short, our users are much like us.

One profession, many careers

Within the library environment, the custody and delivery of music occurs in many ways, and opportunities to work with music in libraries are varied. Cataloging, providing reference assistance, instruction, database design and creation, the management of operations or human resources, and the use and understanding of technology all take on added significance when applied to the delivery of music services because working with music often requires fluency in another language—that of musical notation.

In addition to subject knowledge, catalogers possess sophisticated techniques to make materials in many formats accessible to users. Music reference librarians and catalogers alike are distinctively qualified to interpret musical materials, whether scores, sound recordings, reference books, or electronic databases. Reference librarians are skilled in discerning patrons' needs through artful conversation. Couched in a summary of daily activities is an insightful reminder from reference librarian David Lasocki: "Whether we are figuring out what users need, building relationships, teaching one-on-one, or using our research skills, music reference work is a wonderful training ground for compassion."

To make informed decisions about purchases, those involved in collection development gather information from many sources and review patron requests. Their other activities might include controlling or monitoring a budget, communicating with the library's fiscal officer, developing relationships with commercial vendors and potential donors, and submitting orders for purchase—a task that has been expedited by the welcome aid of technology.

The relationships that music librarians form with their vendors can be particularly congenial, perhaps because they share a love of the subject. Approval plans established with vendors often simplify selection. In the unique case of music, librarians work with their vendors to create appropriate profiles that deliver scores and sound recordings in addition to books.

Those who deal with rare or archival material depend on antiquarian catalogs and their relationships with antiquarian vendors to ensure that they are offered materials fitting their music collection's profile in a timely manner. And since much rare material is also acquired through donation, the music archivist must develop and nurture relationships with potential donors. In this environment, public relations and increasing public awareness of the library's collections go hand in hand with collection development.

The music librarian's collection responsibility also involves replacing worn or missing library items and sifting through gift material—"stuff in a box"—to determine its usefulness for the collection. Like all librarians, as budgets dwindle, music librarians continue to seek new means for resource sharing, whether arranging consortial purchases, taking a new look at interlibrary borrowing agreements, or collaborating on the creation of new online and print resources.

Public libraries

Among public libraries, which receive their support from city, state, or federal government, one finds a wide range of facilities, from large research libraries in urban settings to modest town libraries. All share a mission of serving the people in the area and are principally supported by tax revenues, though some enjoy the benefit of gifts and endowments. Collections reflect the needs of the community. In large urban libraries, particularly those with a strong research collection, users may be professional musicians and writers as well as enthusiastic amateurs. In contrast, small-town libraries might principally support their users' desires for recorded music.

"My situation isn't very typical of most music librarians in public libraries," says Steve Landstreet of the Free Library of Philadelphia, who chairs the Public Libraries Committee of MLA. "We're a bit like New York Public Library in that our music department has 14 full-time employees and one half-time library assistant. Of those, eight are librarians. There are also three music catalogers." Steve indicates that at this library, much attention is devoted to its special collections. "I work exclusively with music, except when I occasionally sub in the art department," he continues, "but that's only because it's something I enjoy. We don't have a combined department like the Boston or [Washington] DC Public Library—yet!" He alludes to the changes that many libraries are experiencing as downsizing affects their traditional modes of subject-specialized service. Unlike many public libraries that have abandoned subject divisions in favor of a centralized reference service point, the Free Library of Philadelphia is one that, at this writing, has managed to retain traditional subject divisions.

In many cities, music services are combined with fine arts, dance, recreation, and other "leisure" activities into an inclusive department often staffed by librarians with background in some aspect of the arts. This service model allows for the kind of interdisciplinary immersion that many patrons find satisfying. It also responds to traditionally American biases about "culture" in our society as being synonymous with entertainment, as pastime, as something apart from "work" (traditionally represented by the public library's business department).

Teens enjoying records at the Columbus (Ga.) Public Library, 1950s.

Columbus Ledger-Enquirer

"One of the great things about working at a public library reference desk is that you never know what's coming next," Landstreet says. "It might be a rapper who wants to protect his valuable intellectual property and has heard about copyright forms or our music business books, or the guy you thought was going to be that guy turns out to be an aspiring opera and lied singer and is looking for scores or info on competitions."

Unlike the large research library where Steve works, public libraries in small communities and local branches of urban systems are seeing that circulating CD collections make up the bulk of the music materials. In these libraries, limited collections of books and keyboard music often provide a needed supplement to the even more limited musical opportunities in the public schools.

And these same libraries offer what might be the last, best hope for the cultivation of a new generation of concertgoers. Librarians who offer music services in the country's public libraries have an opportunity to influence their communities in remarkable ways, as Anna Seaberg found out. Anna selects sound recordings for the King County Library System, which serves the more than 40 rural and suburban areas surrounding Seattle. "The kind of selection I do is an interesting mix of reflecting and anticipating people's tastes," she says. "There at least two reasons why people come to the public library: to find the familiar—a known quantity—or to find the unfamiliar—something they've never before encountered. The patrons and I take turns stretching each other. Occasionally, when I've felt that I have really gone out on a limb in the 'spinach music' direction (you know, 'eat this, it's good for you'), I find those can be the titles that generate the most interest."

Cathy Dixon works as a librarian/research specialist in the Music Division of the Library of Congress, bringing to her job prior experience as a music librarian and later as chief of the Music Division at the District of Columbia Public Library. While many of her responsibilities at the Library of Congress— "handling reference inquiries, using online resources, providing bibliographic instruction, preparing bibliographies and pathfinders, dealing with issues relating to the use of library materials"—are the same she had in her former job at DCPL, she admits that she is awed by the size and strength of the collections and feels privileged to work at LC. But she credits her years at DC Public Library for "the opportunity to be involved with diverse colleagues and clientele" that she knows will "serve her well in any job."

Such opportunities abound in public libraries. "The chance to deal with all types of music and all manner of people can make public librarianship with a music specialty an exciting and rewarding career," says Richard LeSueur, music specialist at the Ann Arbor (Mich.) District Library. A longtime student of music's place in public libraries, he is careful to point out that except in very large public library systems, "the music librarian is not *just* a music librarian. In some libraries, the holdings and activity in the music collection do not warrant a full-time music staff person."

LeSueur also remarks upon aspects of public library work that provide opportunities for interesting programming: "A series of noontime chamber recitals offers a nice break for the public from harried lunches. A lecture series highlighting an important upcoming musical event can bring the music collection into the public eye. So can creating displays which highlight music in the community." For this music specialist librarian, the joys of reference work in a public library are great: "Finding that song from 1933 for a 70th wedding anniversary, identifying a piece of music that is being whistled over the phone, or proving that Aunt Harriet really did sing at the Metropolitan Opera House." The satisfaction in helping "the shy student looking for an audition piece for the school musical or helping a young couple find the perfect music for their wedding can make even the coldest winter day a little nicer."

SOURCE: Paula Elliott, "A View of the Field: Landscapes and Faces," in Paula Elliott and Linda Blair, eds., *Careers in Music Librarianship II: Traditions and Transitions* (Lanham, Md.: Scarecrow, 2004), pp. 1–27. Reprinted with permission.

How to organize a map collection

by Angel Clemons and Claudene Sproles

MAPS ARE OFTEN ONE OF THE LARGEST and most uncontrolled of a library's ephemeral collections. But fear not! Gaining control of a map collection is not as difficult as one might think.

Maps are primarily issued in three different ways. Most people are familiar with monographic or single-issue maps such as an AAA map of Cincinnati or a map showing the movement of troops in Afghanistan. The second way in which maps are issued are as sets. Map sets are comprised of a limited number of map sheets that cover a particular topic. An example of this is the National Geographic set of *Peoples of the World*. The third way in which maps are issued is as series. Map series contain several map sheets covering a wide geographic area and often include updates and revisions. One of the most common map series is the U.S. Geological Survey's topographic series. Topographic maps show the contours and elevation of an area. The U.S. Geological Survey's topographic map series also shows development and changes in the landscape.

The U.S. Geological Survey topographic series is useful for a variety of patrons including planners, developers, geologists, geographers, and even hikers and vacationers. The primary U.S. Geological Survey series comes in three scales:

- 1:24,000 (7.5 minute)
- 1:100,000 (30 × 60 minutes)
- 1:250,000 (1 degree × 2 degree)

The smaller the scale number, the more detailed the map. A 1:24,000 scale map shows greater detail than a 1:250,000 scale map. The U.S. Geological Survey publishes other popular series, in addition to the topographic series, including several geological products, including mineral investigations resources (series C), geological quadrangles (series GQ), and oil and gas investigations (series OM). Due to budgetary reasons, however, not all of these titles are still being issued.

Besides topographical and geological maps, the U.S. Geological Survey also produces the 1:1,000,000 *Map of the World*, the *National Atlas of the United States*, satellite image maps, and Digital Raster Graphics (DRGs).

Obviously there are thousands of different types of maps published every year. It is unlikely that a single library will collect even a fraction of these maps. However, many libraries do have a map collection in some form, whether it is a historical collection, a miscellany of local interest, or government-produced maps. Guidelines for identifying and organizing these maps within a library's collection are outlined below.

Step 1: Identifying maps in a library's collection. Maps can be found several places within a library:

- Travel files—Travel files often contain commercially produced road maps such as folded Rand McNally street maps and official yearly state highway maps.
- Magazine inserts—Magazines such as *National Geographic* often issue supplemental maps to accompany articles.
- Government Documents collection—The United States government is one of the world's largest producers of maps. Common titles received on deposit include U.S. Geological Survey topographical and geological

maps, U.S. Forest Service maps, and Bureau of the Census maps. These can be in either a tangible or intangible format.

- Atlases—Atlases are often overlooked when assessing a map collection even though they are often the best source in helping patrons locate thematic, world, or historical maps. Also, they are often already cataloged in the collection.

It is a good idea to compare what is found in a library's collection to the ALA Map and Geography Round Table's (MAGERT) list of what a core map collection should contain. According to MAGERT, a basic, solid collection should contain the following:

- U.S. Geological Survey topographic maps for the area of interest at varying scales
- Current travel or state highway maps
- Thematic maps and maps of current interest (e.g., Iraq or local development)
- Locally produced maps
- Gazetteers of the library's state and the United States (magert.whoi.edu/pubs/larsg.html)

Any good map collection needs finding aids to assist in the location of specific geographical information. Paper indexes are available for most series issued, including the U.S. Geological Survey series. The U.S. Geological Survey also has map lists available online. Other important finding aids are gazetteers or geographical dictionaries which provide brief, general information about a specific location. Examples include the *Columbia Lippincott Gazetteer of the World*, the *Merriam-Webster Geographical Dictionary*, and the United States Defense Management Agency's gazetteers. The online Geographic Names Information System indexes features found on U.S. Geological Survey topographic maps. Searching this database is more efficient than poring over map sheets trying to find a geographic location. And lastly, invaluable to any map collection is Andriot's *Guide to USGS Publications*, which lists all the titles issued under the various geological series.

Step 2: Organizing the collection. Once maps within a library's collection are identified, the next step will be to decide how to catalog the collection. According to Mary Lynette Larsgaard, in her book *Map Librarianship: An Introduction* (Libraries Unlimited, 1998), there are several reasons to catalog a map collection. First, cataloging improves access to the collection. Users will be able to determine not only what the library has, but also where it is located and how it is organized. Second, cataloging reduces wear and tear on the collection. Single sheets of paper can be damaged easily if patrons are constantly browsing through an uncataloged collection. Also, cataloging can attract users that may not be interested in browsing or who do not know about the collection, especially if they are encountering map records in an automated system. And lastly, cataloging is more economical than not cataloging. Cataloging is done once, but the reference staff may recreate the same search for an uncataloged map hundreds of times.

Deciding how to catalog a library's map collection requires answering a few questions about the library's needs and capabilities. Below is a checklist of essential questions a librarian should ask before beginning a map cataloging project.

1. *Which items will be cataloged first?* The librarian has a choice between cataloging the most-used items or the less frequently used items first. Cataloging the most-used items allows library staff and patrons to locate, retrieve, and even circulate those items quickly and efficiently. Cataloging the less frequently used items or the things no one knows the library has can market those items to users.

2. *Who will be responsible for retrospective cataloging of maps and the cataloging of new maps?* In most libraries, this task will fall to the cataloging librarian. If the library is fortunate enough to have a map librarian, he or she may wish to get involved. A combination of the cataloger's expertise in cataloging and the map librarian's knowledge of maps would be an ideal team to organize the collection.

3. *Where will the bibliographic records come from?* Bibliographic records can either be purchased from a vendor, downloaded from a bibliographic utility, or created as original cataloging records by the library.

Purchasing records from a commercial vendor such as Marcive, Autographics, or OCLC's GovDoc service is a quick and easy way to get the records into the library's automated system. These vendors' services range from providing retrospective and ongoing cataloging records, to adding the library's symbol to the corresponding OCLC record as a holding institution, to providing smart barcodes, labels, and shelf list cards. While the process sounds simple, keep in mind that some database clean-up and minor editing of records will most likely have to be done.

There are costs and time involved in downloading records from a bibliographic utility, such as the OCLC database, as well. Not only is the library paying for a subscription to the service, there is the cost of searching records, the cost of setting holdings on OCLC, and the cost in staff time. If original records are being created for each map, the staff time involved can be more costly than either purchasing or downloading records.

4. *What will be the extent of the bibliographic description in each record?* If original records are created, the decision will need to be made as to how much information to include in each record. Is full cataloging preferred or will brief records be acceptable?

5. *What classification system will be used?* A choice between a standard scheme and a nonstandard scheme must be made. A standard scheme is an already established system for classifying materials such as SuDoc, Dewey, or Library of Congress. A nonstandard scheme is one that is created by someone within the library. If possible, use a standard scheme. When discussing nonstandard schemes, Larsgaard points out that "such schemes are seldom well documented and are very likely to be abandoned and the work later done all over again." Typically if records are purchased from a vendor or downloaded from a bibliographic utility, the decision to use a standard or nonstandard scheme will not be an issue. However, if original records are being created, the choice will need to be made between a standard and a nonstandard scheme.

Some libraries use the Library of Congress classification system to arrange their maps, even if their larger collection is not classed using it. Below are some advantages of using Library of Congress to classify a map collection.

- It is a very detailed system with each state, city, town, etc. having individual call numbers.
- Subject cutters have been developed for thematic maps.
- The schedule is updated regularly by Library of Congress staff.
- Online records with LC call numbers are available.

6. *What cataloging system will be used?* When deciding how to make cataloging information accessible to users, there are a few options: (1) a manual system, such as a card catalog, (2) an in-house database, such as Microsoft Access, or (3) an automated system, such as Voyager.

If the library is using a card catalog, then one option would be to integrate map records into the larger card catalog. The other option would be to create an in-house database. The advantage of this type of system is that it is flexible and easy to update. An in-house database can also be used if you already have an automated system. However, the information found in the database would not be available in other areas of the library, and patrons need to be directed to and taught how to use yet another database. The last option, the automated system, is the ideal system for a library to use. Adding map records to an automated system increases their visibility and improves access to the collection, benefits that the library may not receive if using an in-house database.

The Ekstrom Library at the University of Louisville currently uses an in-house database to catalog its map collection. Until January 2002, its map collection was uncataloged. In January 2002, the new government documents reference librarian began a project to inventory the collection and put the holdings in a database. She chose to put the holdings into a Microsoft Access database because she was not prepared to undertake a large map cataloging project immediately. Also, she did not have the background necessary for cataloging the maps into the library's automated system. Instead she searched each map in the OCLC WorldCat database and transcribed the information into an Access database. The database contains the following information about each map: title, edition, series, author, publisher's name, place of publication, year, description, subject headings, scale, Superintendent of Documents number, notes, location, and Library of Congress call number.

The government documents reference librarian found records for approximately 90% of the 1,500 maps the library owns and assigned call numbers to approximately 200 of those maps. The map database is available in the Reference Department and can be searched by any of the above-mentioned fields. Future plans for this database include continuing to add information about new maps as they arrive and eventually using the information to catalog the map collection in the library's automated system.

Once the map collection is cataloged, the next decision to be made is how to store the collection. Some questions you might ask are:

1. What types of maps will be stored? Are they large maps, small maps, map series, or frequently used maps?
2. Where will the equipment be located? How much space is available for a storage unit?
3. What is the present size and anticipated growth of the collection? Is it a historical map collection to which few maps will be added, or is it a collection to which new maps will be added on a regular basis?
4. What is the cost and availability of map storage units? What is the library's

budget and are there suppliers close enough to deliver so that shipping charges will not be incurred?

The two most popular methods of housing a map collection are to use either flat files or vertical files. Flat files allow maps to lay flat in large shallow drawers. The depth of the drawers, typically two to three inches, allows for easy browsing and extraction. Drawers typically come with a fabric dust cover that lies on top of the stack of maps and provides protection for them. Lock kits and fireproof cases are also available. The tops of these map cases can be used as a study area or as a refile shelf. An open base with a shelf at the bottom that can be used for extra storage can also be purchased. If the top or the open base will not be used for a study area or refile shelf, multiple cases can be purchased and stacked for additional storage. Overall, flat files are "the best combination of protection for the maps, accessibility to them, and ease of expansion," according to Larsgaard.

However, there are some disadvantages to using a flat file. First, these cases can be very heavy and not very mobile, especially if they are stacked. And, depending on the brand and style, these cases can be quite expensive. So, if mobility or price is an issue, a vertical filing system may be more appropriate for the collection.

Vertical files store maps in half the space as flat files and are excellent selections for narrow spaces. The files come in a variety of styles including wall-mounted and mobile units. The disadvantages of these files are that they are not as dustproof as flat files, they are not stackable, and there is no top or base that can be used as a study or refile area.

Once a decision is made about the type of storage system to be used, the next step is to contact a map cabinet supplier. Prices typically range from $550 to $8,500 per unit, so it is best to shop around before making a purchase. Another option is to look for retailers in the library's area that sell used equipment in good condition. The library can save money that way.

Here are some other things that a librarian will want to consider when organizing a map collection:

1. Does the library plan to acquire electronic spatial data? What special equipment and cataloging practices are required for these materials?
2. Will maps circulate? If so, are there special procedures for checkout that the circulation staff needs to know about?
3. What type of reference service will be provided and will the reference staff need to be trained to work with maps?
4. Will maps be available for interlibrary loan and, if so, how will they be transported?

Step 3: Maintaining the collection. Once maps within the library's collection have been identified and organized, the last step is to maintain that collection. Maintaining the collection can mean either acquiring new maps for the collection or keeping the core collection intact. New maps can be either ones that are newly produced or old maps that are new to the library's collection. One of the easiest ways to acquire new maps is to write to state highway departments, chambers of commerce, and travel and tourism bureaus for free maps. The U.S. Geological Survey is also a good source for inexpensive maps. There are also commercial map vendors such as Rand McNally and

DeLorme that sell individual maps, atlases, gazetteers, and other products. In the computer age, a popular request made to libraries is access to geospatial or GIS data. Even if the library cannot afford costly GIS equipment, patrons can still be directed to free sources of online information such as the USGS website.

In maintaining a collection, the library should also consider the historical importance of maps. Older editions of maps show changes in landscape over time. Historical maps of an area are particularly important in smaller locales where historical information about the landscape is more difficult to locate due to the lack of commercially produced sources. Historical maps provide patrons with a view of older locations of roads, developmental changes, and topographic changes such as the effects of strip mining on land. Space, too, is always an important issue, and many libraries simply do not have the room to accommodate a historical collection. Therefore, consideration should be given to the availability of geographical sources from other nearby libraries, archives, government offices, and online sources.

In summary, there are a variety of issues surrounding maps, and libraries need to have a plan in place before tackling a project such as organizing a map collection. Charles A. Seavey points out that "the map does not fit on conventional library shelving, does not convey information in textual format, does not conveniently fit into any cataloging code (present or past), is rarely treated as a topic in library schools, and often appears to be a vexatious problem to the harried library administrator." In spite of those problems, cataloged maps are much more valuable than uncataloged maps. The variety of information typically found in a map collection oftentimes cannot be found in other areas of the library's larger collection; therefore, it is worth the time and effort it takes to identify, organize, and maintain that collection.

SOURCE: Angel Smith and Claudene Sproles, "Don't Get Lost! The Basics of Organizing a Library's Map Collection," *Kentucky Libraries* 68 (Spring 2004): 22–27. Reprinted with permission.

CHILDREN'S MATERIALS

Newbery Medal winners

THE NEWBERY MEDAL, named for 18th-century British bookseller John Newbery, is awarded annually by the ALA Association for Library Service to Children to the author of the most distinguished contribution to American literature for children. These are the award winners since 2000.

2005—Cynthia Kadohata, *Kira-Kira* (Atheneum, 2004).
2004—Kate DiCamillo, *The Tale of Despereaux: Being the Story of a Mouse, a Princess, Some Soup, and a Spool of Thread* (Candlewick, 2003).
2003—Avi, *Crispin: The Cross of Lead* (Hyperion, 2002).

2002—Linda Sue Park, *A Single Shard* (Clarion, 2001).
2001—Richard Peck, *A Year Down Yonder* (Dial, 2000).
2000—Christopher Paul Curtis, *Bud, Not Buddy* (Delacorte, 1999).

Caldecott Medal winners

THE CALDECOTT MEDAL, named in honor of 19th-century English illustrator Randolph Caldecott, is awarded annually by the ALA Association for Library Service to Children to the artist of the most distinguished American picture book for children. These are the award winners since 2000.

2005—Kevin Henkes, *Kitten's First Full Moon* (Greenwillow, 2004).
2004—Mordicai Gerstein, *The Man Who Walked between the Towers* (Roaring Brook, 2003).
2003—Eric Rohmann, *My Friend Rabbit* (Roaring Brook, 2002).
2002—David Wiesner, *The Three Pigs* (Clarion, 2001).
2001—Judith St. George, *So You Want to Be President?* (Philomel, 2000); illustrated by David Small.
2000—Simms Taback, *Joseph Had a Little Overcoat* (Viking, 1999).

Batchelder Award winners

THE MILDRED L. BATCHELDER AWARD is given each year to an American publisher for the most outstanding children's book originally published in a foreign language or in another country. The ALA Association for Library Service to Children gives the award to encourage American publishers to seek out superior children's books abroad and to promote communication between the peoples of the world. The award is named for Mildred L. Batchelder, a children's librarian whose work over three decades has had an international influence. These are the award winners since 2000.

2005—Joëlle Stolz, *The Shadows of Ghadames* (Delacorte, 2004); translated from the French by Catherine Temerson.
2004—Uri Orlev, *Run, Boy, Run* (Houghton, 2003); translated from the Hebrew by Hillel Halkin.
2003—Cornelia Funke, *The Thief Lord* (Scholastic, 2002); translated from the German by Oliver Latsch.
2002—Karin Gündisch, *How I Became an American* (Cricket, 2001); translated from the German by James Skofield.
2001—Daniella Carmi, *Samir and Yonatan* (Levine, 2000); translated from the Hebrew by Yael Lotan.
2000—Anton Quintana, *The Baboon King* (Walker, 1999); translated from the Dutch by John Niewwenhuizen.

School librarians and early literacy programs

by Donna Shannon

WHILE ACCESS TO BOOKS and opportunities for reading are essential preconditions for reading proficiency, school library media specialists (SLMSs) have an important role and numerous opportunities every day to help children learn to select books—to find those just-right books. But what is just right?

Some educators depend on leveled books to direct children to books that they are capable of reading. (And there are plenty of commercial programs available to make this possible.) While easily decodable texts can develop fluency, one cannot minimize a child's interests or preferences as motivational factors. After all, unless children see books as appealing, they may lose interest in or develop negative attitudes toward reading: "When children want to read, their attitude toward reading improves. A positive attitude toward reading usually results in more reading, and this, in turn, helps students develop fluency." John Dewey described the importance of a child's personal and social interests in determining engagement (an interaction between students and what they study), which is essential to learning. In her analysis of Dewey's educational philosophy, Nel Noddings explained that "when students are forced to plod through material with which they are not really engaged . . . they lose interest in the material and confidence in themselves. They settle for giving answers and getting approval from their teachers. They give up the all-important belief that education has something to do with the construction of personal making."

In that delicate balance between gaining practice in reading and honoring individual preferences, the SLMS can guide children in making wise selections. In her book *Reading with Meaning* (Stenhouse, 2002), Debbie Miller recommends giving children choices but also providing a selection of mini-lessons that focus on text features, size of print, and readability. Even further, she advises us to teach students to consider whether they have sufficient background knowledge, reading experience, and motivation to read a particular book. Our goal, over time, is that children learn to choose a variety of texts at different levels of difficulty.

SLMSs can educate parents to help their children in finding those just-right books. Regie Routman includes three appendixes in her book *Reading Essentials* (Heinemann, 2003) that explain the concept and offer advice for teachers, parents, and children. The one specifically directed to parents explains that just-right books means that a child:

- Shows interest in the book.
- Can read and figure out almost all the words.
- Understands what he or she is reading (can tell you what the story is about or what he or she is learning).
- Can read fairly smoothly. If your child is stumbling over many words, she or he will not be able to focus on reading for understanding.

Leveling books

While leveling books to guide students to appropriate choices has become a common practice in schools across the country, it should be approached with caution. There is no one way to level books; publishers employ many different systems. Lucy McCormick Calkins argues that we should trust ourselves and our knowledge of individual children rather than accept levels as absolutes:

> Determining a book's level is approximate, messy work and it is tricky because every reader in the world is different and will find particular texts easy and particular ones difficult for reasons that are hers and hers alone. . . . The reasons readers experience difficulty are far more numerous, complicated and human than any overarching system can accommodate.

Teachers may find leveling schemes useful when selecting books to teach specific strategies during guided reading. However, if we rely solely on leveling schemes when recommending books for independent reading, children will not learn to use their own strategies and judgment for choosing their reading material.

In one sobering report from a teacher in a multiage classroom, Pierce found that her students tended to describe themselves as readers based on the level of the books they could read. She worried that children's focus on stepping through a series of leveled books could result in "ignoring, and possibly devaluing, other ways of defining or describing them as readers." Could we be doing children a disservice if we organize the library collection or label library materials using such schemes?

Informational texts

Several studies have revealed that expository or informational text is relatively scarce in primary grade classrooms. According to Nell Duke, Susan Bennett-Armistead, and Ebony Roberts, there are three unsupported beliefs frequently offered as reasons but for which there is no support from research. These beliefs state that young children: (1) cannot handle informational text; (2) do not like informational text, or at least prefer other formats of text; and (3) should first learn to read and then (at about fourth grade) read to learn.

In the March 2004 issue of *Educational Leadership* devoted to reading research, Duke offers four strategies for increasing children's comprehension of informational text: (1) increase children's access; (2) increase its use in instructional activities; (3) teach children how to read it; and (4) use it for authentic purposes. Certainly SLMSs can work with teachers to implement all of these strategies. Instructing children in how to read and how to use informational text for authentic purposes are part of the information literacy skills that SLMSs are responsible for teaching. These strategies provide opportunities for collaboration with teachers of young children and for involving students in research projects using school library resources. Several recently published professional books inform the efforts of classroom teachers and SLMSs to incorporate the use of informational texts into the curriculum and to engage children in expository writing activities.

Classroom collections and library collections

The allocation of funds to classroom collections at the expense of funds for library media resources is problematic. Classroom teachers will always want to have a sufficient and ready supply of books in their classrooms. The best possible scenario for equal access to a school or district's total resources is to direct monies to the school library media budget so that all teachers and students have the opportunity to use everything the school owns. Teachers could check out a classroom collection to support students' independent reading and refresh it as children finish books, as their reading abilities and interests develop, and as units of study shift to new topics. It is doubtful that teachers will give up classroom collections (nor should they), but one has only to look at how quickly titles go out of print and at the publishing gap between quality nonfiction hardback and paperback titles to recognize that the school library has more depth and breadth than any classroom library. In many cases SLMSs can resolve the issue by changing restrictive policies that prevent large numbers of library books to be taken to classrooms for extended checkout periods and by working diligently to see that children (and teachers) have access to and are welcome in the library media center at all times before, during, and after the school day.

In addition to providing books for classroom collections, the SLMS can work with teachers to choose books, assemble materials, and design activities for literacy-related centers within their classrooms. New teachers in particular will welcome the opportunity to partner with the SLMS, who is familiar with resources available in the school and beyond. Often classroom teachers do not know the standard selection tools and finding aids that can lead them to myriad resources on a wide variety of topics. This can be especially important for ensuring that both library and classroom collections are stocked with fiction and information books that reflect diverse culture as well as appropriate bilingual books and large print books, depending on the requirements of the school community.

Summer reading

Children from low-income families have less access to books both at school and home than do their peers from more advantaged homes. This is exacerbated during the summer, when most school libraries are closed. Results of research reveal that summer reading loss contributes to an achievement gap between children from economically advantaged and economically disadvantaged homes.

Anne McGill-Franzen and Richard Allington suggest that SLMSs can enhance summer access to books for children from low-income homes when they:

- allow children to check out library books for the summer;
- open the school library one night a week during the summer;
- hold a book fair supported by local businesses or grants so that children can choose one or more books for summer reading; and
- create an honor library at the entrance to the school from which children can select books and return them.

Reading aloud

While it may seem unnecessary to mention reading aloud, since most SLMSs already include it in their programs, Carol Avery and Katie Wood Ray remind us that reading out loud to children is teaching; how one reads to children and the talk that surrounds these events have an important impact on how children grow as readers and writers. In addition to providing cognitive benefits, reading aloud to a class of children contributes to their development as a learning community. The common experience of sharing powerful texts and subsequent engagement, reflection, and discussion permeate children's interactions with one another and with adults who are part of their learning communities.

Many different individuals will read to children in the early years of elementary school—classroom teachers, SLMSs, school administrators, guidance counselors, volunteers, and older children; each will have a unique style for doing so. Hints for effective read-alouds are available in many publications and include the following advice:

- choose books that you like and make sure you have read them in advance;
- read from a variety of genres;
- use expression in your voice;
- take your time—give children a chance to digest and respond;
- invite children to make comments and connections; and
- avoid recall questions—ask open-ended questions.

SLMS read-alouds can ignite interest in a new author. Combined with short booktalks, they stimulate appreciation of new genres. Skills such as identifying parts of books and locating books in the library can be reinforced during read-aloud sessions. For example, during a read-aloud session, the SLMS might engage children in comprehension strategies, such as predicting what will happen next, inferring meaning, and making personal connections or connections between texts. When done well, "reading aloud becomes a critically important means of teaching background knowledge, vocabulary, comprehension strategies, and knowledge of written language so crucial to becoming skilled and willing readers during the primary years and beyond."

One-on-one reading

It is well documented that children who have been read to and who have developed reading-like behavior have an advantage in school-based literacy activities. Children who have not had such experiences as preschoolers can benefit from opportunities to read with adults or other children. This pairing with a volunteer, an older child, or even a classmate can help the emergent reader discover what it means to be a competent reader. The SLMS can coach helpers to interact with emergent readers successfully, suggest appropriate books, and offer space in the library media center to carry out these activities.

Conclusion

Most SLMSs in elementary schools were first attracted to their job because of a love for books and reading. With so much national attention (and funding) being devoted to reading, and with so much interest in integrating the use of children's books across the curriculum, SLMSs have ample opportunities for partnering with teachers and parents to provide rich literacy experiences for children. With their knowledge of their school communities, standards, and curriculum, and armed with the research on literacy learning, SLMSs are well-positioned to play an integral role in their schools' early literacy initiatives.

SOURCE: Donna Shannon, "The School Library Media Specialist," *Knowledge Quest* 33 (November/December 2004): 15–21.

YOUNG ADULT MATERIALS

Top 30 best books for young adults, 2003–2005

EACH YEAR THE ALA Young Adult Library Services Association compiles a list of 10 titles that have potential appeal to young adults and exhibit either high literary standards or technical accuracy. The following list encompasses 30 titles from 2003 to 2005.

Anderson, Laurie Halse. *Catalyst* (Viking, 2002).
Anderson, M. T. *Feed* (Candlewick, 2002).
Braff, Joshua. *The Unthinkable Thoughts of Jacob Green* (Algonquin, 2004).
Brooks, Martha. *True Confessions of a Heartless Girl* (Farrar, 2003).
Curtis, Christopher Paul. *Bucking the Sarge* (Wendy Lamb, 2004).
Donnelly, Jennifer. *A Northern Light* (Harcourt, 2003).
Farmer, Nancy. *The House of the Scorpion* (Atheneum, 2002).
Frank, E. R. *America: A Novel* (Atheneum, 2002).
Haddon, Mark. *The Curious Incident of the Dog in the Night-Time* (Doubleday, 2003).
Hoose, Phillip M. *The Race to Save the Lord God Bird* (Farrar, 2004).
Johnson, Angela. *The First Part Last* (Simon & Schuster, 2003).
Korman, Gordon. *Son of the Mob* (Hyperion, 2002).
Lawrence, Iain. *The Lightkeeper's Daughter* (Delacorte, 2002).
Levithan, David. *Boy Meets Boy* (Knopf, 2003).
Levithan, David. *The Realm of Possibility* (Knopf, 2004).
Marchetta, Melina. *Saving Francesca* (Knopf, 2003).
Maynard, Joyce. *The Usual Rules* (St. Martin's, 2003).
Moore, Christopher. *Lamb: The Gospel According to Biff, Christ's Childhood Pal* (Morrow, 2002).
Morpurgo, Michael. *Private Peaceful* (Scholastic, 2004).
Nelson, Peter. *Left for Dead: A Young Man's Search for Justice for the USS Indianapolis* (Delacorte, 2002).
Nye, Naomi Shihab. *19 Varieties of Gazelle: Poems of the Middle East* (Greenwillow, 2002).
Oppel, Kenneth. *Airborn* (EOS, 2004).
Partridge, Elizabeth. *This Land Was Made For You and Me: The Life and Songs of Woody Guthrie* (Viking, 2002).
Pattou, Edith. *East* (Harcourt, 2003).

Rapp, Adam. *33 Snowfish* (Candlewick, 2003).
Rapp, Adam. *Under the Wolf, Under the Dog* (Candlewick, 2004).
Sáenz, Benjamin Alire. *Sammy and Juliana in Hollywood* (Cinco Puntos, 2004).
Stroud, Jonathan. *The Amulet of Samarkand* (Hyperion, 2003).
Thompson, Craig. *Blankets: An Illustrated Novel* (Top Shelf, 2003).
Weeks, Sarah. *So B. It: A Novel* (Laura Geringer, 2004).

SOURCE: ALA Young Adult Library Services Association.

Essential reads for British teens, 2005

LIBRARY STAFF IN TOWER HAMLETS, EAST LONDON, have compiled lists of recommended books for young adults since 2002. The books are well selected to tempt teens to read and retain their interest thereafter. There's no Jane Austen or Charles Dickens here. Themes range from sex and survival to school and surrealism, by way of bullying and bulimia, prejudice and pornography, football and families. Here are some of their selections for 2005. American editions are cited when applicable.—*GME.*

4

Adlington, L. J. *The Diary of Pelly D* (Greenwillow, 2005). Pelly D's diary tells of a future world where everyone has to be stamped with their genetic inheritance. The once-popular Pelly is now trapped in the lower grouping where she is forced to move home and faces the dangers of forced labor, disappearance, or execution.

Breslin, Theresa. *Divided City* (Doubleday, 2005). Two boys picked for soccer trials for the intercities league come from each side of the Glasgow divide. Will their friendship through soccer overcome their family backgrounds? There are no easy answers. A realistic book about prejudice and preconceptions.

Brooks, Kevin. *Candy* (Chicken House, 2005). A dark but touchingly innocent love story. Joe meets Candy and becomes embroiled in her world of pimps and heroin addiction while just trying to get to know her and ultimately get her out of the horrible situation she has got herself in.

Burchill, Julie. *Sugar Rush* (HarperTempest, 2005). Kim's mum runs off to a desert island with a millionaire. She has to change schools and falls in love with her best friend (a girl). The once-sensible Kim experiments with drink, drugs, and sex with the outrageous Sugar, but is more emotionally involved than her fun-loving friend, which can only lead to problems.

Dalton, Annie. *The Rules of Magic* (Egmont, 2004). An exciting and creepy story about the battle between good and evil. A teenage boy and girl become caught in a medieval plot by the devil and a search for a book written by angels that might just save the world. If you like *Buffy the Vampire Slayer,* you'll love this!

Gibbons, Alan. *The Defender* (Orion, 2004). Ian didn't understand why he and his father moved around so much until he discovers his father's secret past—he was once a member of a Protestant criminal organization in Northern Ireland. Many moral questions are posed, as the son has to come to terms with and deal with his father's past.

Higson, Charlie. *Silverfin* (Miramax, 2005). After a supremely scary open-ing featuring some terrifying mutated eels and a gruesome death, this story covers James Bond's early days as a 13-year-old at Eton in the 1930s. Staying with relatives in Scotland, he discovers a local laird is conducting horrific sci-entific experiments that prove he is very mad indeed and a threat to society.

Johnson, Catherine. *Face Value* (Oxford, 2004). A story set in East London across two generations: Paula and Ness become unlikely friends when Paula becomes sucked into the dangers of the modeling scene; and Lauren, a mixed-race girl is discovered by a modeling agent, which changes her life. The two stories are interlinked and the reader gets a fantastic cross-generational pic-ture of a vibrant, artsy area of London.

Jubert, Herve. *Devil's Tango* (Hodder, 2005). Genetic trackers cannot trace a mysterious, shadowy figure that seems to be randomly killing inhabitants of Basle. Roberta and her colleagues from the College of Sorcery have to find a way to catch the killer before the city is flooded and the power-crazy mayor takes over. Exciting, well imagined, and well written.

Kochka. *The Boy Who Ate Stars* (Egmont, 2004). Lucy befriends the autistic boy upstairs and discovers what autism is. She comes to realize that he has immense empathy and understanding of everything around him and she un-derstands that to look through his eyes is a liberating experience.

Marks, Graham. *Zoo* (Bloomsbury, 2005). Cam has been kidnapped and manages to escape, but this is just the start of his struggle. In his search for home he finds out he is the product of genetic engineering, which leads him to question his metaphysical as well as physical place in the world.

Naidoo, Beverley. *Web of Lies* (Puffin, 2004). Femi's family is waiting to hear if they are going to be granted asylum in Britain, but Femi's in trouble. He's joined a gang and is lying to his parents; but when the violence starts to spiral out of control he has to start telling the truth, even though it may put him and his family in danger.

Pausewang, Gudrun. *Traitor* (Andersen Press, 2004). An incredibly realistic and moving account of how one girl refuses to accept Nazi ideology and has the courage of her own convictions through hiding an escaped Russian prisoner of war. A riveting insight into how the war affected the Sudetenland and its German and Czech population.

Peters, Andrew Fusek. *Crash* (Hodder, 2005). A novel of love, death, loss, and heartache told through poems. Life seems to be perfect for Carl, his best friend, Nat, and his girlfriend, Kate, until a drunk driver smashes into Carl's car and kills Nat. There is a real sense of pain and guilt in Carl and Kate's trying to come to terms with their loss. This book is beautifully heartbreaking.

Rosoff, Meg. *How I Live Now* (Wendy Lamb, 2004). Evocative and beauti-fully written, a tragic love story of two cousins. The girl has eating disorder issues and is sent from the U.S. to live with her rural cousins in England with whom she has an unspoken psychic connection: They know what she's think-ing and feeling.

Saksena, Kate. *Hite* (Bloomsbury, 2005). Lee hates school and his dys-functional home life and doesn't want to join the gang on his estate. The only place Lee feels he can escape everything is on the roof of his tower block. One day he discovers someone else there invading his sanctuary—someone fascinating whom Lee can talk to. Suddenly life is full of all kinds of possibilities.

Singleton, John. *Skinny B, Skaz, and Me* (Puffin, 2005). Lee grows up in a tough neighborhood, his sister has leukemia, his best friend is unreliable, and he has gang trouble. It's time for Lee to find some real values and live by them.

Zephaniah, Benjamin. *Gangsta Rap* (Bloomsbury, 2004). This book brings to life the hip-hop scene. Three disaffected boys excluded from school enroll in a music project, which leads to them becoming the next big thing in the music industry. The real story is about the boys growing up, and how they relate to each other, their families, and their girlfriends. Some clever insights into life and who we are and what we believe in.

SOURCE: Essentialz (London: Tower Hamlets Public Libraries, 2005). Reprinted with the permission of the London Borough of Tower Hamlets Public Libraries and Schools Libraries Services.

Gaming for librarians
by Heather Wilson

I DON'T MEAN BRIDGE, Monopoly, or Trivial Pursuit. The games that teens are playing are far geekier, more imaginative and interesting, and harder to find. Whether it be computer and video games or role-playing and collectible card games, teens are playing and libraries are missing out. Because most librarians are not part of the gaming culture, this article is an introduction, opening a window to that world so that libraries can offer its delights to teens.

For four days in June 2004, I spent my time at Origins, a large gaming convention run by the Game Manufacturer's Association of America (GAMA), playing games with teens and talking to them. Held every summer in Columbus, Ohio, this convention attracts teens from as far away as California and Connecticut. While spending the weekend participating in some of their favorite activities, teens feel part of something larger and more accepting than they might find at home. One day they play a game in which they get to be a vampire, and the next day they have an epic battle with military miniatures.

Games come in many different types, including computer and video games; role-playing games; miniatures; card games with collectible or noncollectible cards; and board games.

Computer and video games

Comprising the broadest division of gaming, computer and video games require a device with which to play the game—either a computer or a console. Currently the most popular consoles are the XBox, the Sony PlayStation 2 (PS2), the Nintendo GameCube, and the Nintendo Game Boy Advance (GBA). The popularity of a system can change often, depending on how many games have been released for that system and how good they are.

Video games come in these major genres: action, adventure, driving, puzzle, RPG (role-playing game), simulations, sports, and strategy. In an action video game, the player's goals involve using speed or power to reach the objectives. Fighting games such as Mortal Kombat or movie tie-ins such as Spiderman 2 fit

the action genre. The adventure genre includes games such as Zelda; one plays a character who gains abilities through finding items and completing quests. In driving video games, players race each other to a finish line, often facing obstacles along the racecourse or completing objectives that might involve demolition derbies with other players, as in Burnout 3: Takedown. Puzzle games offer the challenge of solving a puzzle that might involve careful placement of pieces, as in the classic Tetris; or collecting items, as in the unique Japanese game, Katamari Damacy.

Computer role-playing games are similar to adventure games because the goal is to complete a task or quest; however, characters gain abilities through experience, actually changing through those experiences. These RPGs often offer the opportunity to play online in the form of MMORPGs—massive multiplayer online role-playing games—with as many people as the player wants.

Simulation games such as The Sims offer players the opportunity to set up situations for their creations and see how they react to those situations—or players might direct their creations' actions. War games can fall in either the simulation or strategy category. Some sports games are similar to simulation games in that players can recreate their favorite sports teams. Games such as ESPN NFL 2K5 also let players create a "dream team" of their favorite football players.

Role-playing games

In a nonelectronic role-playing game, players use different personas, called characters, who are specifically designed to interact in a world defined by the game and the person who is moderating or running it—the game or dungeon master. Conflicts within the game are usually resolved by rolling dice, using playing card values, or considering the character's statistics alone. The world in which the game is played is usually defined by the book containing the rules, with additions by the game master.

Dungeon & Dragons (D&D), the first truly popular role-playing game, has gone through several major rule revisions. (The first role-playing game was Chainmail, a set of wargame rules by Gary Gygax, whose combat system spawned Dungeons & Dragons.) Its current version uses a D20 combat system in which a 20-sided die resolves conflicts and decides statistics. This open-source D20 system can be licensed inexpensively to create D&D tie-ins or other games.

Miniature games

Generally based on a battle for contested territory, miniature games come in three varieties. Metal miniatures are painted by the players, with values assigned by a rulebook; prepainted "clicks" contain statistics on a plastic wheel attached to the figure's bottom that turns as those statistics change; and cardboard disks have abbreviated statistics printed on the edge. Miniature games can be played in a historical, fantasy, or science fiction setting.

At Origins, I had the opportunity to play a new type of miniature game, the Constructible Strategy Game. Called Pirates of the Spanish Main, the game is published and designed by WizKids, who are responsible for some of the most popular clicks games. Players pop puzzle pieces of a ship from a plastic card. They put the ship together and then play out a battle for treasure over a series of small cardboard islands. The ships can then be taken apart and popped back into the cards for ease of storage and transportation.

Collectible and trading card games

The two most well-known examples of collectible or trading card games are Pokemon and Magic: The Gathering. The player creates a customized deck of cards to play against an opponent who has done the same. Standard rules for the game can be overruled by individual cards if there is a conflict. As in miniature games, much of the strategy of collectible and trading card games comes from how well your deck is constructed to use the game rules to your advantage and overpower your opponent.

An impressive number of card games are playable straight out of the box with no customization. In Lunch Money by Atlas Games, players try to beat each other in schoolyard battles, with emphasis on trash-talking—name-calling and insulting your opponent's abilities—to make the game more interesting. Fluxx by Looney Labs has shifting goals and rules that constantly change as the game is played. Looney Labs also produces cards that players use for writing new goals or rules to make each game unique to its players. These cards have the same backs and borders as the normal game cards, but the main section is left blank for the players to add their own text.

Board games

Board games come in an impressive array of styles and subjects. They range from Settlers of Catan by Mayfair Games, about resource trading and city building, to Monkeys on the Moon by Eight Foot Llama, in which a player's goal is to send happy civilized monkeys from the moon back to earth. Along with role-playing games, board games were among the first in the subculture of gaming that sprang from the  strategy wargames of the 1960s and 1970s. Although board games such as Monopoly and Cranium are enjoyed by teens, the games played at conventions such as Origins place heavier stress on strategy; one game can take hours to complete. Risk is an example of a traditional board game that still enjoys great popularity. Its recent new versions include Risk 2210 A.D., with contested territory in outer space as well as on Earth.

Games as tie-ins

One thing that works for teens is that many types of games are tied in to some of their favorite franchises. For example, Buffy the Vampire Slayer from the television show has her own video games, board game, collectible card game, and role-playing game. Angel, a character originating in the Buffy show who spun off into his own show, also gets his own role-playing game—but no other gaming tie-ins at this point. The creepy and perennially popular Chthulu hor-

ror stories by H. P. Lovecraft and others have spawned their own role-playing and card games. WizKids produces Marvel and DC Comics HeroClix to tie in with favorite comic book characters. Their Cat Woman miniature (referred to as a mini) looks just like the recent movie version of that character. They also produce Indy HeroClix based on independent comic book characters such as Hellboy and Witchblade.

Recently I sat in the back of my library school class and heard people lament the fact that teens are playing video games and not reading. They are missing the point. Gaming often requires reading, problem-solving, and critical thinking. Through gaming, teens are learning in a way that is unfamiliar to most librarians. We penalize teens by not supporting their interest in gaming. Our library teen collections must include books that cover the activities that teens care about. Such books will get them reading—if that's our highest goal. We also must consider how to offer the games themselves in the library—what decisions we can make in our collection policies and what activities we can plan to support and encourage gaming.

Of the 48 teens with whom I spoke at Origins, only four thought that having games at the library was a bad idea. The other 44 not only thought that games were a great idea but also observed that having games available would get them into the library more often. Teens are looking for a place to be comfortable with their friends, a place without the material pressures of the mall where they can be themselves while participating in their favorite activities. For many teens, gaming is a top choice.

Bringing games into the library

How do you get games into your library? Adding role-playing game books and video game guides to your teen collection is one easy way to start. Your library also can be a place for teens to play their card, board, miniature, and role-playing games. Offering a function room for tournaments or open play is a way to attract teens who have no other place to play except commercial establishments such as coffee shops or game stores.

Your library could also lend video games the way they circulate CDs and DVDs. You could make consoles available for playing within the library. Computer games already appear in some library children's departments but not as often in YA sections. Loading computers with some of the most popular games would certainly bring teen traffic.

The primary goal of a library's YA space is to provide information to teens, in whatever form it is packaged. By overlooking games, librarians ignore a huge segment of the teen population. We can fill teens' gaming needs with just a few simple steps. To make gaming an option in your library, begin by talking to the teens in your community to find out what games they are playing. Then see what you can do to bring those games into the library.

SOURCE: Heather Wilson, "Gaming for Librarians: An Introduction," *Voice of Youth Advocates* 27 (February 2005): 446–449. Reprinted with permission.

OPERATIONS
CHAPTER FIVE

"In early days, I tried not to give librarians any trouble, which was where I made my primary mistake. Librarians like to be given trouble; they exist for it, they are geared to it. For the location of a mislaid volume, an uncatalogued item, your good librarian has a ferret's nose. Give her a scent and she jumps the leash, her eye bright with battle."

—Catherine Drinker Bowen, *Adventures of a Biographer* (1959)

Mansell revisited

by Danelle Hall

IT COST MORE TO PUBLISH than it did to build the Metropolitan Toronto Public Library. It took almost as long to complete as it did to build the Brooklyn Bridge 100 years earlier. Described at its inception as the greatest bibliographic feat in history, its completion in 1981 went nearly unnoticed; Art Plotnik lamented in the September 1981 *American Libraries*, "Can it be the biggest library news in 15 years is falling between the cracks?" And recently, when I suggested to a young librarian that he check Mansell for an older elusive title, he responded, "What's Mansell?"

Without doubt our profession is changing; but have we moved so far toward the future that we are losing track of major resources from the past?

Is it important that everyone know about Mansell? Not really. Is it essential that library education put our future librarians in contact with the important sources from the past? Without a doubt. Even more important, our future librarians need to know that once upon a time our profession dreamed a grand dream and made it happen.

So just what, exactly, is Mansell?

The complete title of this bibliographic wonder describes its purpose and scope: *The National Union Catalog, Pre-1956 Imprints: A Cumulative Author List Representing Library of Congress Printed Cards and Titles Reported by Other American Libraries, Compiled and Edited with the Cooperation of the Library of Congress and the National Union Catalog Subcommittee of the Resources Committee of the Resources and Technical Services Division, American Library Association.*

No wonder common usage has shortened the name to the Mansell Catalog, or simply Mansell, after its publisher, Mansell Information/Publishing Ltd.

The chronology of Mansell's conception and execution began with the acceptance in the late 1880s of uniform catalog cards as a norm for libraries across the United States. Its gestation continued as our own professional history unfolded. Its birth was possible when a company in Great Britain developed an automated camera for filming the catalog of the British Museum.

- In 1901, the Library of Congress began its union catalog project by obtaining copies of the catalogs of major libraries, including New York Public Library, the Boston Library, Harvard University Library, and the John Crerar Library. These records were added to its own catalog and arrangements made to receive updates.
- By 1926, the file contained over 2 million cards.
- From 1926 to 1932, "Project B," funded

by a grant from John D. Rockefeller Jr., added over 6 million records to the growing union catalog in an attempt to locate at least one copy of every important reference book in American libraries and register its location.

- From 1932 to 1943, the Library of Congress added an additional 3 million records.
- LC placed depository sets of these union catalog cards in selected research libraries, but this was labor-intensive and expensive. Researchers still had to travel to a site that had the card sets.
- In 1946 the first book catalog of these records was published. Book catalogs—a format that has since been abandoned by American libraries—were within the budgets of many libraries and were widely distributed.
- In the mid-1960s, the American Library Association decided to cumulate the pre-1956 imprints into a single alphabet to assist and simplify research.
- Two requests for bids were sent out before ALA and LC received a proposal that they felt met the needs of the library community to create this cumulation. Great Britain's Mansell Information/Publishing Ltd., the company that had created the British Museum catalog, received the contract in 1967.

It took Mansell 14 years to publish the 754 volumes of the Mansell Catalog. When completed, the project cost over $34 million and contained 528,000 pages of text. The complete set consumes around 130 linear feet of shelving space. Approximately five volumes of 600 to 700 pages per volume were published each month for each of those 14 years.

5

A cargo of cards

In order to meet Mansell's very ambitious publishing schedule, 20 to 30 LC cataloger/editors—first under the leadership of Johannes Dewton until his retirement in 1975 and then under David Alan Smith—edited, proofed, and massaged 20,000 library cards each week. Every Friday afternoon the mailroom staff raced to the airport to catch Pan Am Flight 106 from Washington to London and send 20,000 proofed, corrected, and edited library cards winging across the Atlantic. This operation was performed 603 times throughout the project. Deputy Librarian of Congress William J. Welsh, writing in the September 1981 *American Libraries*, said, "Not only was this shipping cycle carried out over 600 times, but not a card was lost."

The editing of the project was quite complex since the bibliographic entries represented the work of so many libraries. These libraries had created their catalogs over a period of more than 100 years—a span that saw changes in librarians, changes in internal procedures, and changes in cataloging rules.

The February 23, 1967, *Library of Congress Information Bulletin* described the steps that the editors had to perform to clean up the bibliographic records 20,000 times a week for 603 weeks: "Editing will consist of the combination of multiple reports for the same title into a single uniform entry, the revision of incorrect or ambiguous entries, the preparation of necessary cross references and added entries, the retyping of cards not reproducible by photographic techniques, the addition of location symbols in a standardized format, the assignment of a unique identification number for each book, and several proofreading steps."

In a process characterized in Welsh's 1981 article as "From Mess to Miracle," the editors not only had to go through the alphabet once creating the original 685 volumes; they then had to repeat the process to create the 69-volume supplement that listed all of the additional titles found and identified over the course of the project.

Frances Kennedy, my own library director at Oklahoma City University at the beginning of the Mansell project, was one of 1,350 directors in the United States and abroad who believed in the value of the effort so much that they made great financial sacrifices to continue purchasing the volumes as they came out over the 14-year period. It took most of the book budget of our medium-sized private-university library every year from 1968 to 1981 in order to purchase our set.

Like any dyed-in-the-wool librarian, Kennedy kept a file of brochures, correspondence, invoices, and other ephemera relating to the Mansell project. These bits and pieces of daily work have now become a history that gives a glimpse of what it must have been like to see this incredible project come to fruition.

From her file, an advertising brochure from Mansell (3 Bloomsbury Place, London WC1A 2QA, England) proclaims, "What can one say about . . . the bibliographic wonder of the world? Words such as monumental and invaluable cannot be used lightly; but if any publication merits their use, *The National Union Catalog, Pre-1956 Imprints* undoubtedly does." A small footnote at the bottom of the brochure suggests that Mansell borrowed these wonderfully extravagant words of praise from a review by J. R. Lowe in the June 1969 *Australian Library Journal.*

Mansell correspondence from March 1968, on thin onionskin paper and individually typewritten, offers the first set of 60 volumes at $873, a cost of $13.30 per volume plus $75 shipping and handling. The next 60 volumes would cost $23 apiece.

Mansell's burden

Kennedy's file contains letters expressing with grave British reserve regret at being forced to increase the per-volume cost, which the company had to do from time to time. The firm's initial cost estimates had been much too low for them to break even, much less realize a profit. The full cost of the project was borne by Mansell. The company even paid the salaries of the LC card editors on the other side of the Atlantic. In a transcription of a tape from a London meeting that was later published in the January 1970 *Catalogue and Index,* Mansell Chair John Commander discussed the financial side of the massive—and in his words, nightmarish—project: "Neither the Library of Congress, nor any branch of the U.S. Federal Government, has been prepared to finance any part of this project, from the initial accumulation of the National Union Catalog to its present phase of publication. Although LC is carrying out the editorial work and have recruited the staff to do it, it is we who are paying their salaries, and the whole project is financed by us."

The Mansell Company was hard hit by the energy crisis of the mid-1970s. In one of their newsletters that Kennedy kept, the company speaks of having electricity only three days out of the week. Their work on the other days had to occur during hours when natural light was available and the temperature in the building was not too extreme. In 1974, the company proudly announced the publication of volumes 300–304, probably thinking that they had reached the halfway mark in the project.

Dust-gathering dinosaur

Oklahoma City University and, I am sure, many other libraries across the United States now have all 754 volumes of "the greatest single instrument of bibliographical control in existence" (to quote from a sales brochure). It is a dinosaur, both in its size and its obsolescence. Even as the project progressed, the profession recognized that this "greatest single instrument" would be the last great bibliographic effort in a paper format. *Library Literature* has not used the heading "National Union Catalog" since 1994. Our set gathers dust in the library's technical services area.

At the time of Mansell's completion in 1981, it was estimated that 80% of its entries were not duplicated by the online network catalogs. Time, of course, has moved on and online resources now are far more extensive than 23 years ago. An admittedly very limited spot check of some Mansell entries in WorldCat revealed that every title I searched for was available in electronic format. It would seem that the primary value of this grand publishing venture may now be the history it provides of an bygone era.

Progress has swept us on toward better research solutions, but the Mansell Catalog, created by dedicated people on two sides of an ocean and at great cost in effort, money, and time, bears testimony to our profession's stubborn reverence for the book.

SOURCE: Danelle Hall, "Mansell Revisited," *American Libraries* 35 (April 2004): 78–80.

ACQUISITION & SELECTION

Collecting poetry in a sea of data

by Daniel Veach

LIKE MOST LIBRARIES, yours is probably awash with data. As librarians, we slosh through oceans of the stuff daily, helping our patrons net their shrimps and crabs, perhaps the occasional lobster. Data answers a lot of questions, of course, but there are certain types of questions that it does not answer. Questions the future will ask of us, like, "What was it like to be alive in the early 21st century?"

To those who come after us, this may be the most intriguing question of all. Our science and technology will seem primitive to them; our masses of data will be of interest only to historians. Only our lives, our human experience, will still appeal and speak to them, will still have meaning and value. Where will they find this? In novels and literary fiction, perhaps, in biography to some extent, but above all in poetry.

Haunting "houses"

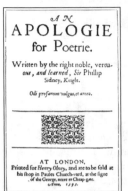

Shakespeare says that poetry "gives to airy nothing a local habitation and a name." These "airy nothings" are ideas, truths, or feelings that are difficult or impossible to grasp with ordinary language. To lure them down to earth, poets construct "local habitations" out of good, solid materials like metaphor: physical images that we can touch and taste and see. A well-made poem is a little haunted house, a tangible dwelling place for the spirit.

The spirit it provides a home for could be the spirit of *your* city, the unique quality of life in your place and time. There are poets who are trying to capture this elusive but all-important quality even now. And because good poetry is both local and universal, the building materials that poets find on the streets of your town can be used to construct an edifice of thought and feeling that will be admired in far-off times and places. That is, if anyone ever sees it. That's where you come in.

Stalking the local poet

And that's where the adventure begins. It's not hard to find the top names in national or international poetry. But the poet who's out there building habitations for the soul out of the bricks and mud of *your* city, that's a different story. (Unless, of course, you live in New York, where you have to be careful to avoid running over poets at intersections.)

Your own library staff may be a good place to start. Libraries are a frequent hiding place for poets, and you may turn over a log in cataloging and find one under there with the sow bugs and millipedes. No luck? (Watch out for those millipedes!) Maybe there's a poetry newspaper like Berkeley's *Poetry Flash* or a newsletter like *Poetry Atlanta* in my hometown. If not, try the "alternative" papers, or ask around at bookstores—Barnes & Noble and Borders stores often encourage poetry readings. Bookstores may have a shelf of local authors as well. Chances are, it will be cleverly concealed (perhaps under a log).

Don't be discouraged if you have trouble "logging on" to the poetry scene at first. Poets have a problem when it comes to publicity. They are (a) notoriously shy people who are (b) eager to become famous. Obviously, we are going to have to help them out here.

Out of the mainstream, into the surf

Local or state arts councils may be able to help you locate poets and writer's groups. You'll find them in the government pages of the phone book. Ask to speak with the literature grants person. One place you will probably *not* find anything is in your mainstream city newspaper or news media. They seem to take special pride in ignoring the local literary scene. Readers of Australia's

Sydney Morning Herald and the Singapore *Straits Times* have seen splashy feature articles on *Atlanta Review,* for instance, but readers of the *Atlanta Journal Constitution* are still completely in the dark about its existence. Like the prophets of old, no one is a poet in their own county.

Last but not least (and you've probably already done it first), you can surf the web for local poets. A Google search with "poetry" and the name of your town may yield some interesting results. Yahoo also has an extensive listing for individual poets. The Web is a godsend for unpublished poets, both good and otherwise. Most poetry is bite-sized and ideal for publication on the Web, where attention spans are byte-sized.

But how do you tell what's good out there? As a poetry editor myself, let me share with you the simple rule which has been the secret of my success: *If you like it, it's good.* There probably won't be any reviews or critical consensus about your local poets—indeed, there may be heated disagreement. Trust yourself, and trust your impressions from an actual live reading. That's where you'll find that poetry suddenly comes to life.

Close encounters of the verse kind

Your aim here is to find a local reading, or at least a writers group meeting, and go to it. This takes courage, not being something a normal person (assuming you fit the description) would ordinarily do. Mythical archetypes spring up: dope fiends, besotted with laudanum or absinthe, plotting revolution, or at least mixing metaphors in some dark, dingy dive. You might be disappointed to find yourself in Atlanta's top reading spot for the last 20 years: the library of the magnificent Callanwolde mansion. Brightly lit bookstores are also a common haunt. But if you really need *noir* you can still find a small cafe or a smoky bar with the real thing going on into the late hours.

What kind of people will you find there? Are they really monsters of nature, part god and part beast? Why did Plato ban them from his well-ordered Republic? After all the build-up, poets themselves may seem disappointingly gentle, humane, and good-humored, even "normal" on the surface. Their focus on "being" values and the quality of experience makes them outlaws of sorts in a society geared to "getting and spending." But, like the Pirates of Penzance, they are the most agreeable gang of outlaws you'll ever want to meet. And while there certainly are a few "starving" poets (I'm still on the thin side myself), you'll also find respected professionals in their ranks: doctors, professors, even (gasp) librarians.

The librarian as St. Peter

The moment of truth has arrived. You have tracked the poets to their secret lair, and are now in a position to sack their hoard of treasure and bring it back to your library in triumph. You will encounter very little resistance. Though they may breathe fire, these dragons are more than willing to share their wealth. Sit back, enjoy the show, and then ask the folks whose work you like if they might have a book you can buy.

Hopefully they'll have at least a *chapbook,* a small collection of 20 or 30 pages, often self-published. The word comes from the early English for "cheap book," and, compared to most library purchases, they certainly live up to their name. While you're there, don't forget to ask them to autograph it for you too. Who knows? The "cheap book" you buy today could someday be one of your library's crown jewels.

And please, be sure to tell them that your purchase is for the library's collection. Sure, it's only a few bucks, but what you are actually bestowing is much, much more. To a poet, being in a library is what being in a museum's permanent collection is to an artist. It's validation by Society (dashingly represented by you) of their life's work. Think of it: This gift is actually in your power to give. As librarians, we tend to take what we do for granted, but to a writer you are nothing less than St. Peter, the gatekeeper to literary eternal life.

"Original" cataloging

Of course, your catalogers may whine and moan when you get back home with your booty. What, no LC card number? No ISBN? Be firm. Point out that this is the supreme moment of their professional lives, the time for them *to boldly go where no LC cataloger has dared to go before*. Poetry makes everyone more "original," especially catalogers. In fact, Turner Cassity, one of America's most wryly original poets, recently retired from a career as an original cataloger at Emory University.

Care and feeding of your literary community

As a librarian, you can do more than just buy poetry—you can also encourage its development. The poets in your college or community are very simple to care for. Being poets, they have no expensive requirements. A few basic resources are all you need, and, from a librarian's point of view, they are almost ridiculously cheap.

For reference purposes, only two publications are really essential. *Poet's Market* (Writer's Digest Books) gives descriptions and contact information for nearly 2,000 poetry journals, plus contests, organizations, and poetry book and chapbook publishers. *Poets & Writers* is the trade journal of the serious literary community in America. A bimonthly, it has all the latest news and publishing opportunities, as well as interviews and feature articles. These two are all your poet really needs in the way of "professional" literature.

One might think that any magazine or directory for "writers" would also be good for poets. But in fact, poets get depressed when they read publications aimed at people who write for money. The basic ethos of publications aimed at freelance writers was expressed succinctly by Samuel Johnson: "Only a blockhead would write except for money." For better or worse, the writing of poetry is one of the few things in our society almost totally unconnected with money. In order not to make your poets feel like blockheads (at least while they are in your library), they need to have publications that understand what they are trying to do.

Poetry journals

Among poetry journals, there is one absolutely clear choice: Subscribe to *Poetry*. America's flagship poetry magazine, it comes out monthly and offers an engaging variety of top-level work. It is without question the "journal of record" for poetry in America. I believe I can say that most poetry editors, like myself, would gladly fall on our swords to defend it.

Of the 2,000-odd poetry publications available (some of them *very* odd), which ones should you get? Aside from a few big national names, my advice is to support your own literary community. If you're a Virginia library, people won't expect you to carry the *Samoan Samizdat*, but they will reasonably expect to find *Shenandoah* on your shelves. There's a convenient geographical index in *Poet's Market* you can use for this purpose. The *International Directory of Little Magazines & Small Presses*, another standard guide, also has a geographical index.

To add an exotic flavor to your collection, there are a small number of top-flight international publications you might consider: *Poetry Review* from London, *Poetry Ireland* (probably the only poetry magazine housed in a castle), and Australia's *Meanjin*. A freebie you can link to is Australia's high-quality poetry webzine, *Jacket* (jacketmagazine.com).

The incredible vanishing book

As predicted years ago, the massive wave of buyouts and mergers in the publishing industry has devastated major-press poetry publication. Poetry publishing has always been a *pro bono* activity. (Harper Brothers even gave Robert Frost a pension in his old age.) This sort of public-spirited concern is becoming a thing of the past. Only a handful of major American publishers remain committed to poetry, among them Farrar Straus and Giroux, Alfred A. Knopf, and W. W. Norton.

Fortunately, small presses and university presses have stepped forward to fill the void. Among university presses, Louisiana State University has a notable poetry publishing program, as do Iowa, Georgia, Illinois, Wesleyan, Chicago, Cleveland State, Pittsburgh, and a number of others. There are quite a number of small poetry presses which have grown both in size and distinction in recent years, among them Copper Canyon, BOA Editions, Graywolf, Milkweed, Hanging Loose, White Pine, and Alice James.

Poet's House produces a *Directory of American Poetry Books* with over 7,000 titles published since 1990. Their breakdown of poetry publishing indicates that 10% of poetry books are now produced by commercial publishers, 15% by university presses, and 75% by small, independent presses.

For an art form which has taken the vow of poverty, this is still quite a wealth of material to choose from. What to get? You'll want some big names, of course, Nobel and Pulitzer Prize and National Book Award winners. Beyond that, I would once again consult the geographical index of *Poet's Market* or the *International Directory*, and support the home team whenever possible. Just as poetry combines the universal and the particular, a poetry collector should both think global and buy local. It's the least librarians can do to keep the spirit of their time and place alive for the poets, and the readers, yet to come.

SOURCE: Daniel Veach, "A Local Habitation and a Name," in Abulfazal M. Fazle Kabir, ed., *Acquisition in Different and Special Subject Areas* (New York, N.Y.: Haworth, 2003), pp. 87–93. Reprinted with permission.

Faculty book-buying trips

by Malcolm H. Brantz

ACADEMIC LIBRARIANS CONSTANTLY STRIVE to buy the best books to support curriculums in an ever-changing world. Most book purchases are the result of approval plans, selections by librarians, and recommendations by faculty. A fourth buying channel, faculty book-buying trips, has evolved into a major source of new book purchases at a small liberal arts university in Colorado and is rapidly growing at a state community college. Faculty book-buying trips allow faculty to use library funds at super bookstores to purchase books that support their disciplines.

Two very different institutions

The university is a nondenominational, Christian liberal arts university offering 25 majors and three master's degree programs to 800 traditional and 1,000 adult students. Faculty book-buying trips began there four years ago when I was director of the library. Historically, the library had been poorly funded and students were guided to other metropolitan libraries for books and journals. The library continues to use faculty book-buying trips to keep its collection up to date.

The state comprehensive community college offers transfer courses, vocational education, workforce development, and community educational programs. Faculty book-buying trips have been used for the past year since I've become the Learning Resources Center (LRC) director. The LRC at the college incorporates a new 27,000 square-foot library housing 44,000 volumes, an online catalog, and 900 full-text electronic journals supplemented by 400 print journals.

Both libraries use Denver's Tattered Cover and Barnes and Noble bookstores, each of which stocks more than 150,000 unique titles. Faculty purchase orders from libraries have varied from $500 to $5,000 per trip, with more than 250 books bought at one time.

Prior to final purchase, the libraries check each title to see if it is already owned. The sales receipt, with duplicate titles crossed out, is sent to the faculty showing them what they purchased. These books are quickly cataloged and placed on the bookshelves. This method of buying books has proven to be extremely popular and productive for faculty and students at both libraries.

Using super bookstores

When the university library first began purchasing books at retail stores, library staff did the shopping. Librarians identified books for purchase and created a written list while at the superstores. We would then go back to the library to see if we owned any of the books and returned to the store to buy books not in the collection. On average, 10% of the selected books were already in the university library's limited collection of 39,000 books. Multiple trips proved to be labor intensive so we had a work-study student accompany librarians to the store and call a second work-study student to check titles at the library. This allowed for a single trip, reduced the amount of labor involved in writing lists, and proved acceptable in eliminating duplicate purchases. We began to enjoy the trips so much that we decided it was time to invite a faculty member to join us.

Taking faculty to super bookstores

The dean of humanities was invited to join us in the second year of the program. We generated a purchase order for $2,500 at the local Barnes and Noble store for the dean's purchase. He initially selected more than $2,500 worth of books, but the library already owned 10% of them. Several faculty members and two additional deans were invited on five more trips during the year. Our planning was minimal and invitations often depended on faculty being in the library at the right time.

During one trip, two members of the English Department invited a student to help with the book-buying and brought a list of literature books to purchase. This trip took more time and effort on their part, but both were pleased with the books.

However, we learned that bringing a prepared list of titles can be a mistake when the dean of the school of music brought a list of 200 music CDs to Barnes and Noble.

Although Denver's Barnes and Noble claims to stock 40,000 music CD titles, display categories used by the Barnes and Noble music department at that time were confusing and lacked consistency. The faculty member's experience of searching for specific CDs was slow and tiresome and resulted in less than 20% success. Instead of spending $2,000, we purchased less then $500 worth of CDs. The faculty member was frustrated and felt the retail CDs were overpriced.

After this experience, we changed our tactics. If faculty had a list, we asked that they give it to the library and we would use a traditional channel to buy the materials. Trips to the super bookstores were to be made without lists. The idea was to "let the store's bookshelves speak to their curriculum." This has had an immediate, lasting, and positive impact for speeding up the purchasing process and reducing work on the part of faculty. Faculty came back from the store saying they were pleasantly surprised by the variety of academic books on the shelves.

Keep it simple

We found that we needed to constantly remind faculty to keep their buying trips simple. Our goal was to make the trips a fun time for communicating with librarians and, most importantly, to offer faculty the opportunity to buy books. At the end of the second year, retail buying trips continued to be offered on an informal basis, with some faculty wanting to make trips but not being invited.

In the third year, our university's program became more formal by design and lost some of its personal touch. A memo was sent to six deans at the university, in which the library offered to purchase $5,000 worth of books for each school. Some deans formed buying committees, while others divided the funds by departments in the school. Due to faculty request, we expanded the retailers to include a local school of theology and a large university's bookstore. Becoming more formal actually reduced the number of buying trips in the year due to lack of follow-through by some schools.

In addition to the offer to each dean, we continued to make special trips with faculty to build specific subject areas. During one such trip, the chairman of the art department purchased $3,800 worth of books in 45 minutes! At the other extreme, a history professor felt buying new books was a waste of money. This faculty member selected three area used bookstores to visit. We generated a purchase order of $150 for each store. He completed his purchases and said he wanted to return only to the largest used bookstore. He eventually purchased another $800 worth of books from this store. We invited an art department faculty member to visit the same used bookstore because of its extensive collection in art and architecture books. After his visit, the faculty member expressed an interest in shopping at the used bookstore.

A community college's experiences

The community college's experience with faculty book-buying trips is limited. A book-buying trip was used to start a branch campus library at a center 10 miles from the main facility. The first trip produced 30 books valued at $1,000. To our surprise, the branch campus administration decided to pay for an additional $700 worth of books identified during this trip.

Faculty book-buying trips often produce external money to purchase library books at the community college. Last year, while spending $1,000 for branch campus books, the same administrators decided to supply $3,500 more from their 2000–2001 budget.

What was learned

Our experience is that books acquired from retail stores differ significantly from books supplied through approval plans. Not surprisingly, the approval books are more often academic. Yet, the number of scholarly monographs we have found on the superstore shelves surprised us. It does, however, take six months for the retail stock to change over to make second trips productive by the same faculty members.

It is possible to send faculty to bookstores by themselves and have them simply pull books and leave them at the institutional sales desk for later payment. Drawbacks to this method range from missing a great opportunity to meet with the faculty to confusion as to which superstore they should visit to the faculty's loss of focus about the purpose of the trip. From the library's perspective, retail purchase trips take time and effort and require library participation in order to maximize the benefits.

However, the library, faculty, and students all benefit from this method of buying new books. Any academic library is assured of obtaining books that are highly useful to their students. The library is also exhibiting its trust in the choices made by faculty and receives much praise for working closely with the faculty. Additionally, our libraries do not have the staff to specialize in many subject areas, and faculty can provide relief for this deficiency.

Faculty win in this process because they can build their part of the collection to augment the courses they are or will be teaching. They can also observe and examine new books which, if valuable, can be acquired on the spot, and they develop a better grasp for which books are in the library.

Students benefit from the book-buying trips in that books that are relevant to what the faculty discuss are in the collection and students are assured that faculty's recommended hooks have been purchased.

From a collection development perspective, we have received a higher rate of faculty input than before. From a purely marketing perspective, we get great publicity from this effort. While our budgets are not large, we are experiencing a steady increase in levels of support. Changes in the information flows of the late 1990s suggest that new players are joining the patron's information channels. In the foreseeable future, libraries will have even more competition for materials budgets with other library-like information providers and computer departments.

I believe it is crucial for the library to take a twofold approach to providing students and faculty with books. First, we must take advantage of the electronic advances in order to be efficient and functional. Secondly, we shouldn't turn our backs on spending quality time with our faculty and should use super bookstores to gain an advantage over our library-like competition.

SOURCE: Malcolm H. Brantz, "Library-Sponsored Faculty Book-Buying Trips," *College & Research Libraries News* 63 (April 2002): 264–266, 292.

CATALOGING

5

Cataloging 101 : Getting started
by Deborah A. Fritz

ANGLO-AMERICAN CATALOGUING RULE 1.0A was completely rewritten in the 2004 amendments to make it more obvious that the first step when cataloging a resource is to decide exactly what it is that we are cataloging.

The rule requires us to decide whether we are cataloging something that stands by itself or is actually a part of a larger entity (for example, a part of a multipart resource, or an individual work in a monographic series, or a single section of a website). If the latter is the case, then we must choose whether we are going to catalog the part (the single volume of a monographic series), or the larger entity of which it is a part (the monographic series).

If we decide that we are cataloging a single-part resource, then the rule tells us to base our description of it on the resource as a whole. On the other hand, if we decide that we are cataloging a multipart resource, then we have to decide whether it is a multipart monograph (a monographic series), or a serial, or an integrating resource.

Library of Congress Rule Interpretation 1.0 (amended in May 2003) calls this step deciding on the "type of issuance" and gives good definitions of the three types:

Monographs: "A bibliographic resource that is complete in one part or intended to be completed in a finite number of parts. The separate parts may or may not be numbered. Use rules in [AACR] Chapter 1 and the chapter(s) representing the carrier." Monographic resources include books (AACR Chapter 2), sound recordings (AACR Chapter 6), videos (AACR Chapter 7), etc.

Serials: "A continuing resource issued in a succession of discrete parts, usually bearing numbering, that has no predetermined conclusion. Use rules in [AACR] Chapter 1, Chapter 12, and the chapter(s) representing the carrier." Serial resources include periodicals, magazines, travel books, etc.

Integrating resources: "A bibliographic resource that is added to or changed by means of updates that do not remain discrete and are integrated into the whole. Integrating resources can be finite or continuing. Use rules in [AACR] Chapter 1, Chapter 12, and the chapter(s) representing the carrier." Integrating resources include websites (changing all the time), loose-leafs that are meant to be updated, etc.

In addition, you may sometimes find yourself with a resource accompanied by another resource, for example, a book accompanied by a video, or a video accompanied by a book. You will have to decide which format is predominant or most important, and then describe the primary format, and note the accompanying material.

Once you have decided what you are cataloging, you can move on to the following broad cataloging steps. These steps apply no matter what type of material you are cataloging.

Search for copycat records

Most of us would quite rightly rather copy someone else's record than make our own. To find records that you can copy, you first have to search for them, and searching can be an art in itself.

First, remember to take your search terms from the correct source. In other words, remember to think about where on the resource you are supposed to find the terms that you can use for searching, such as the appropriate "prescribed source of description" for the type of material.

Then think about which search terms are best for finding records. Sometimes a given term will work better for one type of material than another. For example, it is a good idea to try searching by a Library of Congress Control Number if you are looking for a record for a book, but it is unlikely that you will ever find an LCCN on a sound recording, a video, or an electronic resource. In addition, when you have to pay for each search that you do (as at OCLC), think about the possible results of our search, and try to use the best term for the specific resource.

Do not forget the individual quirks of your bibliographic utility. What might work for ITSMARC (from TLC) might not work for OCLC and vice versa. We are not going to cover how each different utility searches, because each utility is significantly different from every other in its searching techniques, as are local automated systems. However, some of the issues to consider are:

- whether UPPER CASE or lowercase is significant (or how to force a case-sensitive search)
- whether you search as you see, or use "derived" search keys
- whether you search with or without hyphens in LCCN/ISBN
- whether you enter or omit punctuation, e.g., apostrophes, commas
- whether you enter initial articles, or omit initial articles
- whether your system uses stop words (e.g., the names of states, in OCLC).

Match resources to records

Once you have found a record that you think you might be able to use, you have to decide whether it is an *exact* match for the resource in your hand.

Use the Quick Match Criteria table [available in chapters 4–8 of the author's book] that is appropriate for your type of resource to assist in your decisions about matching. The criteria in these tables come from:

- AACR, 2nd ed., 2002 revision, 21.2 and 21.3.
- OCLC bibliographic and format manual, "When to make a new record," at www.oclc.org/bibformats/en/input/.

Even if you are not using OCLC, you should still follow OCLC's guidelines for accepting or rejecting records for copying, since OCLC's document has become the de facto standard for this important step.

If you do not wish to follow all of these standards, then that is up to you, but you should document your decisions.

One of the first things to remember about matching is that you are looking for differences. You have searched using some search term and the system has presented you with a record that it says matches your search term. Now you have to prove to your satisfaction that it is *not a different record*. This is one time when it is better to be a pessimist than an optimist!

You should be aware that some knowledge of cataloging is required to match and copy records properly. For example, you must be able to decide whether minor differences between your resource and a record you have found are because:

- the resource described by that record truly is different
- the record is a CIP record
- the differences are because of mistakes made in cataloging the record
- the differences are because of different cataloging practices.

Another thing to remember about matching is that you are usually looking at a combination of elements. It is true that you might have to reject a record because of a difference in one field alone, e.g., a place of publication, or a date of publication, or an edition statement. Usually, however, there will be more than one difference between the record and your resource to make you call the record a no-match.

You should keep the Quick Match Criteria tables handy to make it easy to look up the list of fields you must check to ensure that a record truly matches a resource. Bear in mind that sometimes the absence of a field in a record can indicate a difference (e.g., if the record has no 250 edition statement, and your book says "Fifth edition"). If you are only looking at the record, you might not remember to look out for missing fields.

Edit records

Once you have decided that your resource truly matches the record that you have found, you will have to decide whether the record can be copied as is, or will need some minor (or major) editing.

Budgetary and staff constraints have forced some libraries to set as policy that they will accept LC copy without checking or editing. This will certainly save them time and money, but may not be good service to their patrons, because even LC can make mistakes:

> 46.2 percent of the sample LC records had at least one error or discrepancy from current practice somewhere in the MARC record. . . . In the aforementioned research, significant errors, defined as errors that would affect any kind of access points, were found in 19.6 percent of the records. The difficulty was that there was no way to predict which records would fall into this group without examining every record. . . . [In determining how much of the description will be accepted without change] a third factor may be the increased use of union catalogs and networks that service persons at some distance from the resource. Any library that is involved in these or that has even a remote possibility of being involved some day, must weigh its responsibilities to the distant as well as to the local clientele.—Arlene G. Taylor, *Cataloging with Copy* (Libraries Unlimited, 1988), p. 21.

Use the "Editing/cloning/creating records cheatsheets" in chapters 4–8 [of the author's book] to help remember the fields that you might need to edit. These cheatsheets outline what you should be checking in *all* records that you copy, time and budgets permitting. You do not have to follow everything suggested there, but you should at least make reasoned decisions about what you will and will not do.

Obviously, you will follow the most current standards for coding MARC records when you are creating original records or cloning records to make new records for different editions. However, you also need a policy about whether or not you will upgrade the MARC coding in older records that you copy for current acquisitions.

If your library has a small system that cannot see data that is in obsolete fields, then you must move that data to currently valid fields in order to be useful. You will have no choice but to update coding.

If your library has a more sophisticated system that can see data in both obsolete and current fields, then you do not have to update the coding in your records. However, you might want to update all new records that you add so that, eventually, your database will not contain any obsolete coding.

Some reasons for editing are:

1. Outdated copy—Pre-AACR2 (Desc: "i"), some differences include:

- edition numbers were abbreviated differently, e.g., 2d, instead of 2nd
- abbreviations were allowed in the title statement of responsibility area
- inclusive dates could be shortened, e.g., 1978–79 (now 1978–1979)
- geographical material designations were capitalized
- if a city was unknown, we could not give a state or country in 260$a
- an ampersand (&) was used for accompanying material information in the 300 instead of the plus sign (+)
- publisher is not repeated in 260 if it is the main entry
- publication date is in brackets ([ ]) if it is from the title page verso
- index is not indicated in a note, but coded in 008
- statement of responsibility is not always given if it is the same as the main entry

2. Outdated copy—Pre-AACR/ISBD (Desc: blank), e.g., publication dates may be different because of changes in rules:

- pre-ISBD said give printing date and copyright date if different
- ISBD/AACR said give publication date and copyright date if different, and, optionally, add date of later printing
- AACR says use publication date and, optionally, add copyright, if different; LC applies this option, and sometimes gives both copyright and printing date, if the publication date is missing

3. Limited Cataloging (LC 1951–1963)

- an LCCN with the suffix "/L" means that the cataloging in the record is very simplified, for example, titles are not traced.

4. Minimal Level Cataloging (LC 1980–) (Encoding level: 7)

- bibliographic description will be OK, but notes are minimal, with only bibliographic history (for example, originally published) and those needed for justifying access being provided; fixed field information is sparse; access is sparse (no subject headings or classification numbers are provided)

5. Shared Cataloging (LC 1966–1980) (015 indicates country). Some differences include:

- absence of statement of responsibility and/or publication data
- punctuation differences
- abbreviations differences
- differences in 260 data, e.g., copyright date is given in brackets as an inferred publication date instead of as a copyright date

6. Also, watch out for different uses of subject headings, or no subject headings at all, and for different choices of call numbers.

It is difficult for any human being to remember all of the changes that have been made to MARC over time, and even with careful checking it is still possible for the best of catalogers to miss changes or simple errors, e.g., filing indicators. Cataloging checker programs, such as MARC Report, can be extremely useful to help catch common errors.

Clone different edition records

Sometimes a record is nearly the same as a resource, but has a different publisher, or date, or one of the other differences that are "Not OK" according to the match criteria. In that case, you can copy the record but you must change it radically to make a brand new record from it.

You must be extra careful to remove all information that does not apply to the resource in hand so that your new record really does match your resource.

If you are using OCLC for your cataloging and you enter the "new" command, the OCLC software strips the record of certain data that might not apply to your resource; you must then enter new data and make a new record. Unfortunately, other systems do not do this for you, so if you are not using OCLC, you must remember which fields to change or delete.

For example, if you are creating a new record by copying and changing a similar record, you have to consider what to do with the 050 (LC classification number). Even if your library uses Dewey decimal call numbers, the LC class number could be useful information for another library, so you should not simply delete it. However, if you are going to keep the LC class number in your new record, then you will either have to change the second indicator to "4" (assigning library is not LC) or change the tag to an 090 (locally assigned LC-type call number). In either case, you must also change the date at the end of the LC class number to match the publication date of the resource.

Remember that when you are cloning a record for a different edition, all information in the new record must match your resource.

Create original records

If you can find no matching record to copy and edit, and no near match is available for you to use as a basis for cloning a different edition, then you must create an "original" record.

Every cataloging module will have some way to bring up an appropriate blank work form for entering information for different types of resources. Some systems allow you to customize these work forms to always include certain data, or always prompt for special fields. Learn how to set up your work forms to save steps, if that is an option in your software.

SOURCE: Deborah A. Fritz, *Cataloging with AACR2 and MARC21: For Books, Electronic Resources, Sound Recordings, Videorecordings, and Serials,* 2nd ed. (Chicago: American Library Association, 2004), pp. 2-3–2-8.

Machine-readable cataloging (MARC)

by Robert L. Maxwell

WHEN THE APPLICATION OF THE COMPUTER to library tasks began in the early 1960s, cataloging was one of the obvious candidates for automation. The computer could not simply digest a catalog record in card format, however, and generate a sensible result; furthermore, the possibilities of access to computerized records far surpassed access to the traditional card catalog, but only if the records were properly coded so that the machine could distinguish, for example, between a title and an author, or between a series and a subject heading. Thus various systems of encoding bibliographic data have grown up around the world.

In addition to improved access to the records, computerization of cataloging has also opened the possibility of shared cataloging. Large international databases (for example, RLIN and OCLC) have appeared, containing catalog records contributed by member libraries for most of the world's current publishing and a large percentage of earlier works. Such a project requires standardization of the computerized cataloging format used by the various libraries. Currently there is no single internationally accepted format, but efforts are under way for the reconciliation of formats so that the goal of easily exchangeable cataloging records around the world can be realized. The mechanism for worldwide transmission of data, the internet, is already in place and has become a catalyst for more serious efforts at standardization than have taken place in the past.

The Library of Congress was one of the first organizations to develop a machine-readable format for catalog records, and this format has evolved into what is currently called "MARC 21." MARC 21 is used almost universally throughout the United States and Canada and was adopted by the British Library in 2004. It is also widely used in other English-speaking countries. Use of a single standard greatly enhances the ease of information exchange in the Anglo-American cataloging world.

The MARC catalog record is divided into *fields*, which in turn are divided into *subfields*. These correspond to various aspects of the catalog record. The fields are all numbered with a three-digit numeric *tag*. Although not all numbers are used, there is a theoretical possibility of up to 999 fields (from 001 to 999). Following the field tag in the MARC record are two numeric digits called *indicators*. Each of these may either be blank or may contain a number, which normally instructs the machine to manipulate the data in some way (for example, for display or indexing purposes). Following the indicators are the subfields, which contain the actual cataloging data. Each subfield is preceded by a delimiter mark (often indicated by a double dagger) and a single letter or number, which tells what type of subfield is being used. This system can obviously become extremely complex, but it is organized in a logical fashion and incorporates a system of mnemonics that are very helpful.

(In the following discussion, the letter X in a field tag represents any number from 0 to 9. For example, 1XX can represent 100, 110, 130, etc.; X11 can represent 111, 711, 811, etc.)

The theoretically possible 999 MARC tags are divided into groups of 100.

0XX fields comprise mainly control fields and record various types of identification and classification numbers. A common field from this group is the 020 field, where the International Standard Book Number (ISBN) is recorded.

1XX fields record the main entry, including personal authors, corporate names, meeting names, and uniform titles. Because there may only be one main entry per catalog record, there will never be more than one 1XX field in a record.

2XX fields mainly contain title information. The most common of these are the 245 field, the title and statement of responsibility, and the 246 field, where variations on the title are recorded. Another 2XX field, not containing title information, is the 260 field, where imprint information is recorded.

3XX fields, which may be repeated, contain the physical description of the item.

4XX fields record series statements as found on the item; if the series has been established differently from that given on the item, the 4XX field is combined with an 8XX field.

5XX fields contain various types of notes.

6XX fields contain subject headings. AACR2 does not address subject access.

7XX fields contain added access points to the record, which may include headings for coauthors, illustrators, translators, etc.

8XX fields contain series added entries.

9XX fields are locally defined fields; each library may define these as it wishes in accord with its own policies. The number 9 in other positions, also, means locally defined: X9X fields (e.g., 590) are reserved for local use as well.

In addition to the division of the 999 numbers into ten blocks, certain mnemonic devices exist that cross these blocks. In the 1XX, 6XX, 7XX, and 8XX fields, the second and third digits of the tag have parallel meanings. The most commonly used are:

X00 signifies a personal name. For example, the 100 field contains a main entry heading that is a personal name.

X10 signifies a corporate name. For example, the 710 field contains an added entry heading that is a corporate name.

X11 signifies a meeting or conference name. A 111 field contains a main entry that is the name of a conference or meeting.

X30 signifies a uniform title not linked to an author.

SOURCE: Robert L. Maxwell, *Maxwell's Handbook for AACR2* (Chicago: American Library Association, 2004), pp. xix–xxi.

Cooperative cataloging programs
by Robert L. Maxwell

COOPERATIVE CATALOGING PROGRAMS have been in place in the United States for decades and have ranged from nationwide programs primarily designed to assist the Library of Congress in the production of cards for its card distribution program to local or statewide consortia that share cataloging responsibilities. The rise of mutually accepted record interchange standards, i.e., the MARC formats, has greatly facilitated these efforts.

The Program for Cooperative Cataloging

The most successful of these programs to date is the Program for Cooperative Cataloging. The PCC began in 1995 as a result of planning that had taken place since the early part of the decade. It currently has four components: NACO (Name Authority Cooperative Program); SACO (Subject Authority Cooperative Program); BIBCO (Bibliographic Record Cooperative Program); and CONSER (Cooperative Online Serials Program). There is not yet a component for the creation of genre/form authority records.

The most important goals of the PCC are to make more authoritative records (both bibliographic and authority records) available for sharing by all libraries and to develop mutually acceptable standards for record creation.

One of the reasons for the PCC's success is that it is self-governing. Most of the earlier national cooperative programs were controlled by LC, and participants were essentially imitating LC catalogers, as though the records they were creating were going to go into LC's own catalog. Although LC is still a very influential member of the governing boards of the PCC, it is no longer the final decision maker, and all full PCC participating libraries have an equal voice in most decisions.

In 2003, there were over 400 libraries participating in the PCC, including 419 participating in NACO, 46 in BIBCO, 127 in SACO, and 41 in CONSER (with many participating in more than one of the programs). Collectively, these libraries produced 167,163 new name authority records, 9,324 new series authority records, 3,509 new subject authority records, and 74,793 new bibliographic records.

Participating libraries are located in all parts of the world. The majority are in the United States, but there are also participants in Argentina, Australia, Brazil, Canada, England, Hong Kong, Ireland, Italy, Lithuania, Mexico,

PCC Programs Overview

New Zealand, Scotland, Singapore, South Africa, Swaziland, and Wales. The PCC is truly an international effort.

The PCC maintains a web page (www.loc.gov/catdir/pcc/) where further details about the program can be found.

NACO

The Name Authority Cooperative Program is typically the first PCC program a library joins. NACO participants are trained to create and revise name, uniform title, and series authority records and to contribute them to the Name Authority File (NAF).

New participants are trained in NACO procedures at a weeklong training session, typically at their own library, during which they learn guidelines for creating a consistent and predictable authority file. The training includes a review of AACR2 heading rules and MARC formatting for authority records. After training, the library begins submitting records to the NAF, which are for a time reviewed by the person who trained them. When the trainer is satisfied with the quality of the records, the library becomes independent. The library assigns a liaison to the program, who usually becomes the NACO trainer for catalogers at the library.

For more information on the NACO program, see its web page, available at www.loc.gov/catdir/pcc/naco/naco.html.

SACO

The Subject Authority Cooperative Program participants propose new subject headings to the Library of Congress Subject Headings (LCSH), as well as changes to existing headings.

They may also propose changes to the LC Classification schedules. Unlike the NAF, the Subject Authority File (SAF), where LCSH resides, is completely under LC control. Additions and changes proposed by SACO participants are discussed and approved (or not) at internal LC meetings, and therefore SACO participants cannot directly make changes in the SAF, as NACO participants can in the NAF.

There are good reasons for this. In the first place, LCSH, as its name implies, belongs to the Library of Congress, and LC understandably wishes to retain control over its contents. Even without that consideration, the thesaurus-like structure of the database is quite a bit more complex than the NAF and really needs a central body to ensure that changes do not damage that structure. Additionally, subject authority work is considerably more subjective than name authority work. In most cases there are less questions about choice and form of name for a person or corporate entity than with subject terms; with subject terms there are often many synonyms to choose from, and the relationships of the terms to other terms— the hierarchy of the thesaurus—is often subjective as well. It makes sense, then, that LC should retain control over the SAF.

Although it is possible to be a SACO participant without participating in NACO, very few libraries do this. Normally a library becomes a NACO participant, and then when its catalogers are comfortable with NACO, it begins participating in SACO. It is also possible for individuals at libraries not affiliated with the PCC to contribute to SACO, although as a practical matter institutional support is usually necessary for an individual cataloger to receive training in SACO procedures.

Training is on an as-needed basis. LC periodically gives training at the library in Washington, D.C., and usually conducts workshops in conjunction with the American Library Association's Annual Conference and Midwinter Meeting. The library will also send trainers out to individual libraries and consortia for regional training. The expense of this training is borne by the inviting library or institution(s).

For more information on the SACO program, see its web page at www.loc.gov/catdir/pcc/saco/saco.html.

BIBCO and CONSER

The Bibliographic Record Cooperative Program and the Cooperative Online Serials Record are the two PCC programs concerned with creating bibliographic records.

BIBCO participants produce authoritative bibliographic records in a variety of formats at either the core or full level. These records are marked as PCC records in RLIN and OCLC, which guarantees that (1) they were created according to AACR2 standards; (2) they contain all the MARC fields required by either the core or full standard, including a call number from a recognized scheme (most commonly either an LC or Dewey decimal classification number); and, most importantly, (3) all needed access points, both descriptive and subject, have been fully established in the authority files.

Because of the authority component of BIBCO, participants must at a minimum be independent NACO members. Most also contribute to the SACO program. Typically a library will be a NACO member for some time before applying for BIBCO membership.

New BIBCO libraries receive a two- or three-day training session from a regional trainer. Training focuses on standards, including introduction of the core standard. This standard was developed by the PCC in the hopes of offering catalogers a "less-than-full" standard that would still meet the needs of library users. Theoretically, use of this standard might allow PCC catalogers and others to produce more records than they would have otherwise. One of the major components of the training is the development of decision-making skills in catalogers, allowing them to apply their judgment in deciding issues such as which standard to apply.

For more information about BIBCO, see www.loc.gov/catdir/pcc/bibco/bibco.html.

CONSER is the oldest PCC program. In fact, it antedates the program itself, having begun in the 1970s; it joined PCC in 1997. CONSER participants create and maintain authoritative serial records that are then used by other libraries for their serial holdings. Such a program is more than a way to create more records available to be shared. Because of the dynamic nature of serials, individual serial records are constantly changing, and it is necessary to have an authoritative record that libraries can look to for the latest information. To produce as uniform records as possible, participants follow the guidelines in the *CONSER Editing Guide* and the *CONSER Cataloging Manual,* both available on *Cataloger's Desktop.*

CONSER records appear in RLIN, but the principal database of CONSER records resides in OCLC, and OCLC membership is currently required for CONSER participation.

For more information about the CONSER program, see its web page at www.loc.gov/acq/conser/.

SOURCE: Robert L. Maxwell, *Maxwell's Guide to Authority Work* (Chicago: American Library Association, 2002), pp. 258–261.

Great moments in the history of technical services

by W. Lewis and Manuel M. Urrizola

8560 B.C. Cultivation of emmer, barley, and other wild grasses begins on the steppes of Central Asia, leading to the development of specialized occupations, such as cereal catalogers.

4362 B.C. First evidence (from Anatolia, modern-day Turkey) of a four-wheeled book cart. Within two generations this design was adopted throughout Europe and Asia, replacing the more maneuverable, but much less stable two-wheeled book cart.

3193 B.C., spring. First serial title attested: *Publications of the Royal Sumerian Academy.*

3193 B.C., late summer. First serial title change attested: to *Royal Sumerian Academy Publications.*

537 B.C. The National Library of Babylon, finally switching to papyrus, ceases maintaining its clay tablet shelflist, but is unable to discard it for nostalgic reasons. Two years later, under siege by the Persians, the city finds a new use for the old tablets and manages to inflict severe losses on the besieging army by pelting them from the ramparts with large quantities of shelflist tablets.

43 B.C. First attested use of an ISBN (for the special collector's edition of Julius Caesar's *Gallic Wars* with an introduction by Mark Antony): IXIVVIIXVIIIVIIIVIVII.

A.D. 81. Second gospel of the Christian New Testament becomes the first document written in MARK format.

427. The Library at Alexandria decides to outsource its annual weeding project; Vandal hordes are the lowest bidder.

762, June 21. Death of St. Minutia, patron saint of catalogers. The birth date of St. Minutia is unknown. The only reliable chronicle has an unlucky lacuna: *Sa. Minutia in [.......an]no domini nata est,* where only the last two missing letters can be supplied with any certainty. Vitae of the saint written later naively abbreviate the ". . . no domini" as "n.d.," and this is the form traditionally cited for her birth. Minutia is said to have been born in the former Roman province of Nova Pannonia (part of the present day Czech Republic), in the village of Sineloco (modern day Odnikud). Her time and place of birth, therefore, are usually given as "s.l., n.p., n.d."

Happily, a generous amount of hagiographical material on St. Minutia has survived, perhaps the most popular of which is a collection of her homilies and sayings, including the motto most closely associated with her: *Non pilus tam tenuis ut secari non posit* (There is no hair too fine to be split). She appears to have had some interest in ecclesiastical architecture; one early vita has references to a church which was built using plans drawn up by Minutia herself. The actual building has not survived, but there is a fragment from a contemporary description: "On either side of the main entry, St. Minutia caused innumerable added entries to be placed, such that people marveled at the great multitude of doors, and rebuked the Saint for the labor wasted in putting them there. 'No labor has been wasted,' she answered them patiently, 'for by these means no one will be barred from my church through a lack of access.'" Another account explains that her plans were an improvement on earlier designs which had called for a single entry at the east end, near the tabernacle; the inconvenience of relying on this so-called corporate entry was immediately recognized and rectified by the saint.

She was, not surprisingly, an influential member of her convent. There are a number of references to her reorganization of its agricultural property: She is said to have divided the land into holdings devoted to permanent crops (fixed fields) and holdings given over to crop rotation (variable fields). The variable fields were further divided into smaller parcels (subfields) assigned individually to peasants attached to the convent. Minutia is also renowned for her role as a mediator between the warring factions so prevalent in those chaotic times. She was continually optimistic in even the most threatening circumstances and was careful never to anticipate a conflict, although she quickly resolved them when they arose.

1066. William the Conqueror defeats his cousin Harold at the Battle of Hastings and imposes the *Anglo-Norman Cataloging Rules*, 2nd ed. (ANCR2) on his new subjects. Ten years later he commissions the first systematic catalog of selected realia (the *Domesday Boke*).

1757. Lakota Indians begin recording information on the insides of their portable dwellings; this is the first known use of the teepee verso.

1778. A small group of Irish-American colonists from County Cork form the Dublin Corps to assist in the struggle for independence. By limiting themselves to only the most essential supplies, members of the Corps could be prepared and mounted more quickly than other militias.

1782, August 5. Birthdate of the Werke brothers, Gesammelte ("Gus"), Sämtliche ("Sam"), and Ausgewählte ("Wally"). In addition to being prolific authors, the brothers were devoted to their military music and appeared in countless Bands, always in uniform.

1870s. Widespread use of highly acidic paper for book production begins, thus introducing the first disintegrating resource.

1883–1884. Cattlemen at the Bar and Drum Ranch, outside Lone Stack, South Dakota, develop the "barcode" brand as a way to keep track of individual animals in the herd.

1916. Jean Arp, Marcel Duchamp, and others mount an assault on the traditional definition of art. Catalogers attempting to describe their work respond with the invention of metadada.

SOURCE: W. Lewis and Manuel M. Urrizola, *Great Moments in the History of Technical Services*, sun3.lib.uci.edu/~murrizol/ts_history/tshist.htm. Reprinted with permission.

Much about metadata

by Arlene G. Taylor

METADATA IS OFTEN DESCRIBED as "data about data." This definition assumes that an information package (a web page, an MP3 audio file, a book, etc.) is data. Therefore, a description of the attributes and contents of that information package (or MP3, etc.) would be data about data. This definition represents the very broadest level of the concept. In this context it has even been suggested that movie reviews are a form of metadata. In a cursory survey of terminology usage, numerous definitions can be found, ranging from the afore-mentioned "data about data" to more complex, lengthier definitions. What they all have in common is the notion that metadata is *structured information that describes the attributes of information packages for the purposes of identification, discovery, and sometimes management.* The term has come into use because of concern that some kind of standardized representation is needed for internet resources if we are ever to be able to discover the most useful and reliable information available for our information needs (a process called *resource discovery*).

FOLDOC: Free On-Line Dictionary of Computing (wombat.doc.ic.ac.uk/foldoc/) defines metadata as "definitional data that provides information about or documentation of other data managed within an application or environment. . . . Metadata may include descriptive information about the context, quality and condition, or characteristics of the data." This definition implies that metadata includes not only descriptive information such as that found in traditional retrieval tools, but also information necessary for the management, use, and preservation of the information package (e.g., data about where the package is located, how it is displayed, its ownership and relationships, its quality and condition, etc.).

Even among information professionals, metadata concepts can appear complex and confusing. This is due in part to the multifaceted nature of the topic. It is also due to the overly broad, pervasive "data about data" definition. With that as a primary description, it is no wonder that many refer to any number of interrelated concepts as "metadata." It is also important to remember that the term "metadata" may mean different things to different communities. When a librarian familiar with Dublin Core (a general purpose, user-friendly schema) speaks of metadata, she or he has a different notion of the concept than someone working with Federal Geographic Data Committee geospatial metadata (a highly detailed, more complex approach).

Metadata systems can be classified into three levels of complexity. The first level is the *simple* format, in which the metadata is really no more than some unstructured data found in the resource itself. This is reflected by the search engine approach to organizing the Web that uses automated indexing techniques. The second level is the *structured* format. This includes formal metadata element sets that have been created for the general user. This level of metadata may have a basic template for metadata creation and does not require professional-level description. The Dublin Core reflects this level of complexity. The third level of complexity is the *rich* format. Libraries, archives, and museums tend to use systems in this category. Information professionals use these formats to create comprehensive, detailed descriptions. They are more complex in nature and may combine metadata elements with encoding and content standards. Examples of rich formats are found in bibliographic

5

records that are created using MARC and AACR2 and in archival records created using the Encoded Archival Description.

People can mean many different things when they refer to metadata. Discussions of the topic may be about any of the following or any combination of the following conceptual components: the information package and its attributes, content standards (rules for describing the package), metadata schemas, metadata elements, metadata records, and encoding formats. While we may discuss these as distinct conceptual components, in practice it is not so clearly divided. The concepts are so intertwined that efforts to separate them often result in confusion. An example to illustrate this can be found in the MARC format. While many consider MARC to be only an encoding format, others refer to it as a metadata schema. MARC exhibits properties of both, and on close examination it even acts as a content standard by dictating the contents and formats of certain data elements, especially the fixed fields. So it is not surprising that there is some confusion about metadata.

The basics of metadata

Metadata may be divided into three broad types: *administrative metadata, structural metadata,* and *descriptive metadata.* These three categories are somewhat fluid, however. They are not necessarily the only ways to describe metadata types. Some authors may include four categories of metadata, while others might include seven. Because there is no formal metadata taxonomy, what one author might refer to as "use metadata," another author might call "structural metadata" or "administrative metadata." The three categories chosen here seem to reflect the most common usage today. All of the additional types of metadata are included as subtypes, mostly under administrative metadata. In this text, administrative metadata includes metadata for object management, rights management, maintenance and preservation, and meta-metadata.

Metadata can describe information packages at various levels of granularity. It can be created for individual information packages, for pieces of those information packages, or for entire collections of information packages. In other words, a single photograph found on a website might be described with metadata. Alternatively, the web page on which the picture is found could be the object of description, or an entire website containing several web pages and pictures might be described in the metadata record.

Different communities might describe information on any or all of these levels of granularity, depending on the information package, the community's approach to organizing information, and the needs of their users. Traditionally organized into units larger than a single item, archival materials are described at a less granular level than are library materials or museum objects. Digital

libraries may combine or alternate between collection-level and item-level descriptions, based on the nature of a particular collection, the size of the collection, and the users of the collection. In other words, a digital library might describe individual objects (a digitized map), individual collections (a digitized collection of 1,200 maps), or both.

The information package represented by the metadata may also be at various levels of intellectual expression. The metadata might describe a work, an expression of that work, a manifestation of the expression, or an individual item representing the manifestation.

These categories are from the *Functional Requirements for Bibliographic Records,* published in 1998 by the International Federation of Library Associations and Institutions (www.ifla.org/VII/s13/frbr/frbr.htm).

Metadata can be a header to a digital document, it can be wrapped in a digital object's packaging (e.g., descriptive metadata inside a METS object), or it can be a record that is separate from the resource that it describes. Metadata records that are separate can be collected into a single database, or they can be collected in a file such as an XML file, or they can be distributed among a variety of locations. Metadata records are often in the form of encoded, separate records that describe and substitute for information packages. These records are held in retrieval tools to allow users to browse or search for the records instead of trying to navigate through each individual item in the collection. Because metadata generally includes encoding, the term is rarely applied to records found in paper tools.

Metadata schemas

In order for it to be used to its full potential, metadata cannot be unstructured descriptions of resources; it must be standardized and controlled. Without formal rules, metadata description is no better than keyword access. The basic units of metadata are the *schema* and the *element*. Metadata elements are the individual categories or fields that hold the individual pieces of description of an information package. Typical metadata elements include title, creator, creation date, subject identification, and the like. Metadata schemas are sets of elements designed to meet the needs of particular communities. While some schemas are general in nature, most are created for specific types of information. Schemas have been designed to handle government information, geospatial information, visual resources, and many other types of information packages. As a result, schemas can vary greatly. They vary in the number of data elements, in the use of mandatory and repeatable elements, in encoding, and in the use of controlled vocabularies, among other things. While most schemas focus on descriptive elements to support resource discovery, some contain elements to support administrative and structural purposes. With the various needs of different communities, it is not possible to create a perfect, one-size-fits-all metadata schema.

According to Sherry Vellucci ("Metadata and Authority Control," *Library Resources and Technical Services,* January 2000, pp. 33–43), there are three characteristics found in all metadata schemas. They are: (1) structure, (2) syntax, and (3) semantics. *Structure* refers to the data model or architecture used to hold the metadata and the way metadata statements are expressed. Two examples of such models are RDF and METS. *Syntax* refers to the encoding of the metadata. This may be the MARC format for bibliographic records or an XML or SGML DTD for other types of metadata. *Semantics* refers to meaning, specifically the meaning of the various data elements. Semantics help metadata creators understand, for example, what "coverage" or "modification date" means in a given schema.

The semantics of a metadata schema do not dictate the content placed into the elements. This is the province of content standards (or content rules) and controlled vocabularies. Content standards determine such things as how the date will be formatted within the metadata elements. For example, it might

specify that all dates will be entered using the yyyy-mm-dd format. Controlled vocabularies refer to lists of words in which certain terms are chosen as preferred and their synonyms act as pointers to the preferred terms, thereby limiting the range of values that can be entered into a field. Controlled vocabularies are often used in object-type and in subject-related data elements. If such rules and systems did not exist, information retrieval effectiveness could be compromised.

Metadata characteristics

In order for metadata to be as useful as possible in meeting the diverse needs of information users, there are some special characteristics of the electronic environment that require attention. They are interoperability, flexibility, and extensibility.

Interoperability refers to the ability of various systems to interact with each other no matter the hardware or software being used. Interoperability helps minimize the loss of information due to technological differences. Interoperability can be further divided into semantic, syntactic, and structural interoperability. *Semantic interoperability* refers to ways in which diverse metadata schemas express meaning in their elements. In other words, does the element "author" in one schema mean the same thing as "creator" in another schema? *Structural interoperability* refers to how metadata records are expressed. Is the metadata statement understandable by other systems? *Syntactic interoperability* refers to the ability to exchange and use metadata from other systems. Syntactic interoperability requires a common language or encoding format.

Flexibility refers to the ability of "metadata creators to include as much or as little detail as desired in the metadata record, with or without adherence to any specific cataloging rules or authoritative lists," as Vellucci defined it.

Extensibility refers to the ability to use additional metadata elements and qualifiers as needed to meet the specific needs of various communities. Qualifiers help to sharpen the focus of an element or might prescribe a specific vocabulary to be used in that element. An example of extensibility can be found in the education community. In order to meet their specific needs, a standard element set was extended by adding new elements such as grade-level and audience. There is a note of caution about extensibility, however. As extensibility increases, interoperability tends to decrease. This is because as the schema moves further away from its original design (with additional elements or qualifiers), it is less understandable to other systems. This is a trade-off that needs to be considered carefully before being implemented.

Metadata and cataloging

Some definitions of *metadata* refer exclusively to electronic materials, but the term is not necessarily restricted to digital objects and web resources. Many

authors like to point out that the library profession has been creating metadata for millennia. Even the earliest Sumerian lists contained metadata in some form. Some authors equate creating metadata for electronic resources with the cataloging of books.

Some consider cataloging to be a subset of activities under the broader concept of metadata creation.

Parallels between the two processes certainly exist. The basic objectives of metadata creation and cataloging (providing a description of and access to items) are alike. The processes used to create the descriptions are also similar. Both focus on attributes that allow users to identify information packages and to select the packages that most closely meet their needs. Electronic and analog materials share many characteristics. Both generally have titles, creators, creation dates, subject matter, and publication sources of some sort. There are enough similarities between the two activities to see that a relationship exists between creation of metadata and cataloging.

While there are parallels, differences are also claimed. Some feel the dissimilarities are too great to equate metadata with cataloging. Stefan Gradmann, in "Cataloging vs. Metadata: Old Wine in New Bottles," *International Cataloguing and Bibliographic Control* 28 (October–December 1999): 88–90, states that the differences lie in who creates the metadata (nonprofessionals), why it is created (resource discovery, not just description), the process (more efficiently produced), and materials to be covered (electronic resources). It is puzzling that these are presented as distinctions. For at least three decades, much cataloging has been done by people called "paraprofessionals." The ideal of having authors create their own metadata is not coming to pass, and it is also being discovered that lack of consistency in metadata creation is a problem in resource discovery, the second difference listed. But cataloging has always been about resource discovery. That is why there has been such an emphasis on access points for names and subjects with a concentration on authority control for these. Classification has provided yet another way for users to discover resources by finding them beside other materials on the same subject. With respect to the third difference, "process," the processes of cataloging have become more efficient with the advent of computers. Finally, the conventions of cataloging have been expanded to apply to electronic resources, as seen in the 2002 revision of the *Anglo-American Cataloguing Rules*. In many ways it appears that metadata creation is a reinvention and/or extension of cataloging.

Most of the objections raised to the comparison tend to focus on certain characteristics of electronic resources. Electronic resources have particular differences that must be considered. These differences are important to acknowledge, even though they do not negate the relationship between cataloging and metadata creation. The first of these is more a perceived difference than a real one. It is the degree to which there is difficulty in determining what is an information package. There has always been some difficulty in deciding what is a "catalogable unit," but the world in which cataloging is done has had centuries to develop standards and practices. For the most part, one physical item has been equated with one bibliographic record. However, there  have remained the problems of when to provide just one record for multiple items (e.g., serials, multivolume sets) or when to provide multiple records for one item (e.g., anthologies of short stories, articles in journals). Now we have the same problem for digital resources. What is a describable unit on the Web or in a digital library? Do we create metadata for a single web page or for the entire site that contains it? Do we describe a digital image or a collection of digital images? This returns us to the granularity issues mentioned earlier.

In addition, with a digital object, what exactly is being described? Should the metadata describe the digital image only? Should it describe both the digitized photo and the original analog photograph? Should that be one record or two?

An obvious difference is that remote-access electronic resources have no physical carriers, unlike books, maps, or compact discs. A key feature of bibliographic cataloging is the physical description (e.g., 280 p. ; ill.; 26cm. *or* 1 videocassette (15 min.) : sd., col. ; ¾ in.). Except, perhaps, for the indications of illustrative matter, this is unnecessary for a website.

Another distinction between electronic and analog resources relates to the concept of edition. For some electronic resources, like commercial software, it is obvious when a new edition or version has been released. But for others, like websites, it is not so obvious. Websites can be ephemeral and/or unstable. Some websites simply disappear without a trace. Others can (and do) change often. While some sites may have relatively stable content, others are updated frequently. Unlike most tangible information packages (where updated information necessitates a new physical carrier), an updated website can be difficult to detect. This is complicated by the fact that the old site is generally gone for good. If a web page is slightly altered, does that make it a new edition? Probably not, but at what point does a new edition emerge? At what point is new metadata required? When changes occur, it is not always obvious whether the metadata for that website should also change.

Location information also differs. When metadata records and information packages are both encoded and accessible online, the encoded nature of the metadata records allows users to locate and access an information package almost simultaneously. Therefore, special attention must be paid to location/access metadata for electronic resources. URLs are far more likely to change than are call numbers in an average library.

The last major difference between analog and electronic resources is that found in their structure. Compared to the structure of an analog resource, the structure of a digital object can be very complex. For example, a digitized book requires more and different types of metadata than does a book upon the shelf. For the most part, the physical book requires mostly descriptive data, such as title, author, publisher, subject, with some administrative information in addition. The digital object, however, requires extensive structural metadata in order for the object to be displayed and to function properly. This is in addition to descriptive metadata about the digitized resource, descriptive metadata about its original analog equivalent (if such exists), and administrative metadata as well.

Objectives of an information system

One of the primary purposes of creating metadata is to help users find information packages that they might need. It is helpful then, when creating metadata, to look at the objectives that users may have when approaching an information retrieval system, so that their goals and needs may be met. The following list of tasks comes from IFLA's *Functional Requirements for Bibliographic Records.* These objectives include:

> **Find**—Users approach retrieval systems to search for information packages that meet certain criteria. They may wish to find all articles published by *Cataloging & Classification Quarterly* in 1999, all books written by

Ranganathan, or all video recordings of Puccini operas held by the Carnegie Library of Pittsburgh.

Identify—The metadata records found in retrieval tools help users to identify entities. This may involve distinguishing between similar information packages or identifying an item that corresponds to a citation in a bibliography.

Select—Systems help users to select information packages that are appropriate for their needs. This may involve such characteristics as language, edition, or system requirements.

Obtain—Users approach systems in order to acquire or gain access to information packages.

In addition to these four objectives, Elaine Svenonius (*The Intellectual Foundation of Information Organization,* MIT Press, 2000) adds a fifth objective—**navigate.** This objective takes into account the information-seeking behavior of some users who cannot articulate their information needs, but use the structure of the information system to help them find the information they are seeking. In order to meet the needs of users, as well as the needs of information professionals, metadata should be created with these objectives in mind.

Types of metadata

As mentioned above, there are three broad categories of metadata: administrative, structural, and descriptive. Until recently, most metadata discussions focused on descriptive metadata only. It is only within recent years that administrative and structural metadata needs have been recognized, or at least acknowledged, as "metadata issues."

Administrative metadata. Who decides what an object is called? Where is it held? Who decides when it needs to be updated or transformed? How are these processes accomplished? How did the object come into this collection? Was it digitized in-house, by an outside vendor, or was it born digital? These are questions that can be answered by administrative metadata.

Administrative metadata is created for the purposes of management, decision making, and record keeping. It provides information about the storage requirements and migration processes of digital objects. Administrative metadata assists with monitoring, reproducing, digitizing, and backing up digital information packages. It includes information such as:

- acquisition information (e.g., how and when the information package was created, modified, and/or acquired; administrative information about the analog source from which a digital object was derived)
- ownership, rights, permission, reproduction information (e.g., what rights the organization has to use the material; what reproductions exist and their current status)
- legal access requirements (e.g., who may use the material and for what purposes)
- location information (e.g., URL; call number)
- use information (e.g., use and user tracking; content reuse; exhibition records)
- use management (e.g., what materials are used, when, in what form, by whom)

- preservation information: integrity information (e.g., checksums), documentation of physical condition, documentation of actions taken to preserve (e.g., refreshing data; migrating data; conservation or repair of physical artifacts)

Some administrative metadata elements can be generated automatically (as can structural metadata elements). Unlike structural and descriptive metadata, administrative metadata elements can be repository-specific. They might focus on local requirements, such as who makes decisions about these information packages.

Administrative metadata may be described as having several subtypes. These include preservation metadata, rights and access metadata, and meta-metadata. Each of these is discussed in turn.

Preservation metadata. Technology changes rapidly. Data files from just a few years ago—our WordStar documents and VisiCalc spreadsheets—are now old and no longer functional. They have been lost because there were no plans to keep the data usable and no real understanding of how fast things change. With this in mind, we must consider how much more we are willing to lose. Will the Word documents and Access databases we create today be usable in 200 years? What about 20 years? Or 10 years, even? If we are going to save this information from oblivion, we must consider a number of questions. Should we preserve the look and feel of the software, or are we concerned with content only? Do we need a standards library? One hundred years from now, will users still know what a .jpg or a .tiff is? Without documentation, will they be decipherable? When we preserve an information package, how do we determine which version of that package needs to be preserved? In other words, how do we determine the best edition?

These questions are preservation metadata concerns. In recent years, OCLC and the Research Libraries Group, the National Library of Australia, and the CEDARS project in the UK have all initiated preservation metadata initiatives. Preservation metadata is the information needed to ensure the long-term storage and usability of digital content. It includes information about the processes used in preserving the digital content, including reformatting, migration, emulation, conservation or repair, file integrity, representation, provenance, and decision-making data. Typical preservation metadata elements might include structural type, file description, size, properties, software and hardware environments, source information, object history, transformation history, context information, digital signatures, and checksums.

Rights and access metadata. Who can access an information package and for what purposes? Who can make copies? Who owns the material? Are there different categories of information objects in the collection? Are there different categories of users who can access different combinations of those objects?

Rights and access metadata is information about who has access to information packages, who may use them, and for what purposes. It deals with issues of creators' intellectual property rights and the legal agreements allowing users to access this information. In rights and access metadata, information about parties, contents, and transactions can be found. These are issues currently being examined. The <indecs> project is the most widely known model for rights metadata (www.indecs.org/pdf/framework.pdf). It focuses on e-commerce applications. Typical rights metadata elements might include

---

What Is the Dublin Core?

The Dublin Core is a metadata standard used to describe web-based and other electronic resources. Named after Dublin, Ohio, where the first joint OCLC and National Center for Supercomputing Applications workshop on the standard took place in March 1995, the schema was created in order to have a basic set of elements that can be used by anyone— including publishers, database managers, librarians, software developers—who produces digital documents. The Dublin Core Metadata Initiative (DCMI) oversees the various implementations of the standard's element set, which consists of 15 broad descriptors:

1. Title	9. Format
2. Creator	10. Identifier
3. Subject	11. Source
4. Description	12. Language
5. Publisher	13. Relation
6. Contributor	14. Coverage
7. Date	15. Rights
8. Type	

This element set provides the basic categories of information about a resource that allows for its successful search and retrieval. Other metadata elements can be added to provide a richer description of resources. The DC-Library Application Profile, developed in 2002 and revised in 2004, adds 29 other descriptors useful in libraries or library-related applications and projects. See dublincore.org/resources/faq/ for more information.

5

access categories, identifiers, copyright statements, terms and conditions, periods of availability, usage information, and payment options.

Meta-metadata. If metadata is data about data, then meta-metadata is data about the data about data. Not only can metadata track administrative data about the information package, it can also track information about the metadata. Ensuring authenticity of the metadata and tracking internal processes are some of the uses of meta-metadata. While some meta-metadata resides within some descriptive records (e.g., the record creation information and modification dates in a MARC record), other meta-metadata must be tracked in other ways. In 1999, Renato Iannella and Debbie Campbell proposed to the Dublin Core Metadata Initiative (DCMI) *The A-Core: Metadata about Content Metadata* (metadata.net/admin/draft-iannella-admin-01.txt). "A-Core" stood for Administrative Core and seemed to be a core set of administrative metadata. DCMI preferred a tool for users of metadata to manage metadata, and so the proposal was revised in 2002 by Jytte Hansen and Leif Andresen as *AC-Administrative Components* (dublincore.org/groups/admin/proposal-20021007.shtml). AC focuses on elements that describe attributes of the metadata record, track changes and updates, and provide information for the interchange of records. It is currently out for comments at this writing.

Structural metadata. If an information organization received a digital object, one that it had no part in creating, could the object be opened? Would it be known what the object was? Would it be known what it does? Would the requirements for presenting the object be understood? If the digital object were a complex, multifile entity, would it be known how the pieces fit together? Without structural metadata, probably not.

Structural metadata is that which refers to the makeup or structure of the file, dataset, or other information package that is being described. It is the technical information that is needed to ensure that a digital information package functions properly. It refers to how related files are bound together and how the object can be displayed and disseminated on a variety of systems. It deals with what an object is, what it does, and how it works. Sometimes, structural metadata is referred to as technical metadata, display metadata, or use metadata. It includes the following kinds of information:

- hardware and software documentation
- technical information (e.g., file size, bit-length, format, presentation rules, sequencing information, running time, structural maps, file compression information)
- version control (e.g., what versions exist and the status of the information resource being described; alternate digital formats, such as HTML or PDF for text, and GIF or JPG for images)
- data to identify a version of an image and to define what is needed to view it
- digitization information (e.g., compression ratios, scaling ratios)
- data related to creation of the digital image (e.g., date of scan, resolution)
- authentication and security data (e.g., encryption keys, password methods)
- associated search protocols (e.g., Z39.50, common indexing protocol, CGI form interface)

Some structural metadata elements can be found in the headers of some file types, but others must be collected manually, or new processes must be developed to capture this metadata at low cost. At this time, the technological and financial resources needed to collect complete structural metadata and to take full advantage of that metadata are not yet here. In some metadata schemas, structural metadata is not well represented in the data elements. In others, it may be unnecessary or inappropriate. For example, with a single textual document in a word processing format, extensive structural data is not necessary. Once the information package becomes more complex, however, more structural metadata becomes necessary.

Implementations of structural metadata. The use of structural metadata is not new, but the terminology used to describe it is. An early, successful implementation of structural information is the page-turner model. A page-turner  is used for materials with contents that must be ordered in a definite sequence. It provides structure for the contents to be displayed and for the user to navigate through the information package as one normally pages through a book. The page-turner may allow the user to navigate through the resource on more than one level, that is, at a chapter level and at a page level. The page-turner uses structural metadata to bind together individual images of pages to form a complete object (again, this may be on the level of the e-book, a volume of a set, or a chapter). It also may use the structural metadata to associate a text file with each of those individual pages, so that the intellectual content of the page image is searchable. Structural metadata can also associate these images with thumbnail images of the pages, images of greater or lesser resolution, HTML- or XML-formatted pages associated with the web interface (though this may be done on the fly), or some other file.

Descriptive metadata. Descriptive metadata is that which describes the identifying characteristics of an information package along with analyzing its intellectual contents. It includes the following kinds of information:

- data that identifies an information package (e.g., title; author; date of creation or publication; information regarding the analog source from which a digital object is derived)
- intellectual organization data (e.g., authority control; collocation with related works, names, subjects, etc.; identification of relationships among entities)
- intellectual access data (e.g., subject headings; classification; categorization)

SOURCE: Arlene G. Taylor, *The Organization of Information* (Westport, Conn.: Libraries Unlimited, 2004), pp. 139–152. Reprinted with permission.

Romanization tables

ALTHOUGH YOU MIGHT NOT READ Russian or Greek, there may come a time when you have to transcribe some words into the Latin alphabet. Here are the Library of Congress–approved tables.—*GME.*

Russian

Upper Case	Romanization	Lowercase	Romanization
А	A	а	a
Б	B	б	b
В	V	в	v
Г	G	г	g
Д	D	д	d
Е	E	е	e
Ё	Ё	ё	ё
Ж	Zh	ж	zh
З	Z	з	z
И	I	и	i
І	Î	і	î
Й	Ĭ	й	ĭ
К	K	к	k
Л	L	л	l
М	M	м	m
Н	N	н	n
О	O	о	o
П	P	п	p
Р	R	р	r
С	S	с	s
Т	T	т	t
У	U	у	u
Ф	F	ф	f
Х	Kh	х	kh
Ц	TS	ц	ts
Ч	Ch	ч	ch
Ш	Sh	ш	sh

Щ	Shch	щ	shch
Ъ [1]	″ (hard sign)	ъ	″
Ы	Y	ы	y
Ь [2]	′ (soft sign)	ь	′
Э	Ë	э	é
Ю	IU	ю	iu
Я	IA	я	ia

1. Letter is disregarded in romanization when found at the end of a word.
2. Do not confuse with similar part of the letter Ы, ы (romanized Y, y).

Greek

Upper Case	Romanization	Lowercase	Romanization
A	A	α	a
B	B (V, v in modern Greek) [1]	β	b
Γ	G (n before medial γ, κ, ξ,)	γ	g
Δ	D	δ	d
E	E	ε	e
Z	Z	ζ	z
H	Ē	η	ē
Θ	Th	θ	th
I	I	ι	i
K	K	κ	k
Λ	L	λ	l
M	M	μ	m
Mπ	B	μπ	b (initial only)
N	N	ν	n
Nτ	D	ντ	d (initial only)
Ξ	X	ξ	x
O	O	ο	o
Π	P	π	p
P	R	ρ	r
ʻP	Rh[2]	ʻρ	rh[2]
Σ	S	σ	s
T	T	τ	t
Υ	Y	υ	y
Φ	Ph	φ	ph
X	Ch	χ	ch
Ψ	Ps	ψ	ps
Ω	Ō	ω	ō

1. The era of the modern Greek language begins with texts written after 1453. Texts written before 1454 are considered classical Greek.

2. Diacritical marks such as accents, the diaeresis, and the iota subscript (̗) are omitted in romanization. As the result of a presidential decree in Greece in 1982, monosyllabic words are now written without accents; polysyllabic words are written with the acute accent only.

SOURCE: ALA-LC Romanization Tables: Transliteration Schemes for Non-Roman Scripts (Washington, D.C.: Library of Congress Cataloging Distribution Service, 1997), www.loc.gov/catdir/cpso/roman.html.

CLASSIFICATION

Dewey decimal classification: The hundred divisions

MOST LIBRARY USERS KNOW the general structure of Melvil Dewey's decimal classification. First published in 1876, the Dewey decimal classification divides knowledge into ten main classes, with further subdivisions. Here is an outline of its 100 major subdivisions.

000 Computer science, knowledge, and systems

010   Bibliographies
020   Library and information sciences
030   Encyclopedias and books of facts
040   [not assigned]
050   Magazines, journals, serials
060   Associations, organizations, museums
070   News media, journalism, publishing
080   Quotations
090   Manuscripts and rare books

IN THIS GREAT AGE
YOU NEED THE
ENCYCLOPAEDIA BRITANNICA

100 Philosophy

110   Metaphysics
120   Epistemology
130   Parapsychology and occultism
140   Philosophical schools of thought
150   Psychology
160   Logic
170   Ethics
180   Ancient, medieval, Eastern philosophy
190   Modern Western philosophy

LUCRETIUS

200 Religion

210   Philosophy and theory of religion
220   The Bible
230   Christianity, Christian theology
240   Christian practice and observance
250   Christian pastoral practice and religious orders
260   Christian organization, social work, and worship
270   History of Christianity
280   Christian denominations
290   Other religions

Portrait Authentique
de Sainte-Bernadette

300 Social sciences, sociology, anthropology

310 Statistics
320 Political science
330 Economics
340 Law
350 Public administration and military science
360 Social problems and social services
370 Education
380 Commerce, communications, transportation
390 Customs, etiquette, folklore

400 Language

410 Linguistics
420 English and Old English languages
430 German and related languages
440 French and related languages
450 Italian, Romanian, and related languages
460 Spanish and Portuguese languages
470 Latin and Italic languages
480 Classical and modern Greek languages
490 Other languages

500 Science

510 Mathematics
520 Astronomy
530 Physics
540 Chemistry
550 Earth sciences and geology
560 Fossils and prehistoric life
570 Life sciences, biology
580 Plants (botany)
590 Animals (zoology)

600 Technology

610 Medicine and health
620 Engineering
630 Agriculture
640 Home and family management
650 Management and public relations
660 Chemical engineering
670 Manufacturing
680 Manufacture for specific uses
690 Building and construction

700 Arts

710 Landscaping and area planning
720 Architecture

730 Sculpture, ceramics, metalwork
740 Drawing and decorative arts
750 Painting
760 Graphic arts
770 Photography and computer art
780 Music
790 Sports, games, entertainment

800 Literature, rhetoric, and criticism

810 American literature in English
820 English and Old English literatures
830 German and related literatures
840 French and related literatures
850 Italian, Romanian, and related literatures
860 Spanish and Portuguese literatures
870 Latin and Italic literatures
880 Classical and modern Greek literatures
890 Other literatures

900 History

910 Geography and travel
920 Biography and genealogy
930 History of the ancient world (to ca. 499)
940 History of Europe
950 History of Asia
960 History of Africa
970 History of North America
980 History of South America
990 History of other areas

5

SOURCE: Summaries: DDC Dewey Decimal Classification (Dublin, Ohio: OCLC, 2005). Reprinted
with permission of OCLC Online Computer Library Center, Inc.

The story of
Library of Congress classification
by Jane Aiken

THE FIRST BOOKS PURCHASED for the Library of Congress arrived in
1801, and in its 12-page catalog (1802), the entries are arranged by size and
format: folios, quartos, octavos, duodecimos, and maps and charts. In 1808,
librarian Patrick Magruder issued another book catalog, also arranged by size
but with special types of material, such as statutes and other federal documents, listed separately. The first subject arrangement appeared in the 1812
book catalog. The 18 subject classes came from the Library Company of
Philadelphia, which had adapted a scheme developed from the English philosopher and statesman Francis Bacon's division of knowledge into memory,
reason, and imagination. To these the Library of Congress added two format

divisions: gazettes, and maps and charts. Within each subject class, however, arrangement was still by size.

When the British set fire to the Capitol Building in 1814, destroying the library, Congress replaced the books by purchasing the private library of Thomas Jefferson. Jefferson had his own classification of 44 "chapters," also based on Baconian principles. He devoted 15 chapters to history (ancient, modern, and natural); 14 to philosophy, including jurisprudence, ethics, government, mathematics, physics, and geography; and another 14 to fine arts (architecture, art, gardening, music, poetry, oratory, and criticism). The last chapter was for general or multidisciplinary works. But members of the Congressional Joint Committee on the library disliked classification schemes, and they wanted to dispense with Jefferson's arrangement altogether. Librarian Watterston did not agree, but he also modified Jefferson's arrangement. While not especially pleased with Watterston's changes, Jefferson graciously commented that the new arrangement might be easier for readers to use.

Librarians John Silva Meehan and Ainsworth Rand Spofford further modified Jefferson's scheme. Of the two, Spofford made the most extensive changes, but the paucity of space in the library's Capitol Building quarters defeated attempts to keep the books in strict order. As Spofford revised it to accommodate the rapidly growing collection, the classification still included 44 classes, but it had little resemblance to the original.

In 1897, librarian John Russell Young hired James Christian Meinich Hanson, an expert on cataloging and classification, to head the new Catalog Department that Young was establishing. Hanson decided that the old classification system was inadequate, and he persuaded Young to hire an expert classifier, Charles Martel, to build a modern classification scheme. They considered adopting the Dewey decimal classification, Charles Ammi Cutter's Expansive Classification, and others, but ultimately decided to devise their own system.

Developed over several years, the outline of the new scheme came partly from Cutter. Martel used Cutter's Book Arts class to develop Class Z: Bibliography and Library Science, which he had completed by the time Herbert Putnam became librarian in April 1899. Putnam wanted to reconsider the classification issue because he hoped to employ an existing system that would transfer readily to other libraries, and he thought the Dewey system would be adaptable for that purpose. Melvil Dewey, however, refused to allow the library to make any changes in decimal classification, which destroyed any hope of adopting it. Thus Putnam agreed that Martel should proceed. By 1903, the outline of the classification was complete, consisting of 21 classes and including three mnemonic classes: Music (M), Geography (G), and Technology (T).

The library's needs dictated classification priorities. Class Z had to be developed first because those books had to be organized first: the bibliographical material provided essential assistance in working on other classes. Similarly, Americana required early attention because of its importance in the library's collections, and Martel therefore began work on classes E and F (American History) next. Thereafter he moved to D, World History, in which he used double letters for subclasses for the first time. In D, each country has a different second letter; for example, DA for Great Britain.

Herbert Putnam

Under Martel's supervision, library subject specialistsdeveloped the detailed schedules. Class M, Music, appeared in 1904 and Class Q, Science, in 1905, but no more schedules were published until 1910, when Philosophy (B–BJ), Fine Arts (N), Geography (G), Political Science (J), the Social Sciences (H), Medicine (R), Technology (T), and  Naval Science (V) all appeared. General Works (A), Agriculture (S), and Education (L) followed in 1911; Americana (E–F) in 1913; Auxiliary Sciences of History (C), and General Literature and British and American Literature (PN, PR, PS) in 1915; and Universal and Old World History (D) in 1916. After the schedules were printed, at intervals the library has issued lists of additions and changes and, eventually, new editions.

After a long period when no schedules were issued, Religion (BL–BX) appeared in 1927; Classical Languages and Literature (P–PA) in 1928; the Modern European Languages and Literatures (PB–PH) in 1933, and the languages and literatures of Africa, Asia, Oceania, and America (PJ–PM) in 1935. In 1936 and 1937, Romance Languages and Literatures (PQ) completed the basic classification. Works of fiction were originally classed in PZ, but in response to requests from research libraries that wished to classify it with the appropriate literature classes, in 1968 the library began providing those class numbers and by 1980 had decided to apply literature class numbers to all fiction in English. A project begun in the early 1940s to construct Class K, Law, encountered many 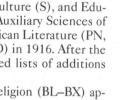 delays, but with the assistance of grants from the Council on Library Resources Inc., KF, American Law, finally appeared in 1969, with the other subclasses following. From time to time classifiers have thoroughly revised portions of the classification to reflect advances in knowledge, and they have further developed or established some subclasses, such as JZ (International Relations) and KZ (Law of Nations), both com- pleted in 1997. Class K was declared "essentially complete" in 2002 after nearly 30 years of development in consultation with the American Association of Law Libraries and libraries around the world. The entire  Library of Congress classification system was converted, over a 10-year period, to an online tool, which became available in 2003.

The Library of Congress classification was developed with the library's future needs in mind. Initially it did not seem especially suited to the needs of other libraries. Nevertheless, librarians were very interested in the classification, and by 1906 several federal libraries and one state library were planning to adopt it. In 1920, the five largest U.S. academic libraries (Chicago, Columbia, Cornell, Harvard, and Yale) were using the classification for all or part of their collections, and other institutions slowly followed. By the 1970s, nine-tenths of the largest U.S. libraries and over half of all U.S. academic libraries employed the Library of Congress classification system for all or part of their collections. Now available on compact disk and on the World Wide Web, the classification scheme is readily accessible by computer in libraries large and small. On the internet, when users search the online catalog, they may browse parts of the classification simply by typing in the class numbers that cover the relevant subject.

SOURCE: John Y. Cole and Jane Aiken, eds., *Encyclopedia of the Library of Congress: For Congress, the Nation & the World* (Lanham, Md.: Bernan Press, 2004), pp. 211–213. Reprinted with permission.

LC classification outline

THE LC CLASSIFICATION was developed and used at the Library of Congress beginning in 1899. It has become the system of choice for many large research libraries. This list gives the scope for most one- or two-letter designators, which may serve as an aid in learning the classification schedules in more detail.

A (General works)

AC	Collections, series, collected works
AE	Encyclopedias (general)
AG	Dictionaries and other general reference books
AI	Indexes (general)
AM	Museums (general), collectors and collecting
AN	Newspapers
AP	Periodicals (general)
AS	Academies and learned societies (general)
AY	Yearbooks, almanacs, directories
AZ	History of scholarship and learning

B (Philosophy, psychology, religion)

B	Philosophy (general)
BC	Logic
BD	Speculative philosophy
BF	Psychology, parapsychology, occult sciences
BH	Aesthetics
BJ	Ethics, social usages, etiquette
BL	Religions, mythology, rationalism
BM	Judaism
BP	Islam, Bahaism, theosophy
BQ	Buddhism
BR	Christianity
BS	The Bible
BT	Doctrinal theology
BV	Practical theology
BX	Christian denominations

C (Auxiliary sciences of history)

C	Auxiliary sciences of history (general)
CB	History of civilization
CC	Archaeology (general)
CD	Diplomatics, archives, seals
CE	Calendars, technical chronology
CJ	Numismatics, coins, medals
CN	Inscriptions, epigraphy
CR	Heraldry, chivalry
CS	Genealogy
CT	Biography (general)

D (History, general, and history of Europe)

D   History (general)
DA   Great Britain, Ireland
DAW Central Europe
DB   Austria, Liechtenstein, Hungary, Czech Republic, Slovakia
DC   France, Andorra, Monaco
DD   Germany
DE   The Mediterranean region, the Greco-Roman world
DF   Greece
DG   Italy, Malta
DH   Belgium, Luxembourg
DJ   Netherlands
DJK Eastern Europe (general)
DK   Russia, former Soviet republics, Poland
DL   Northern Europe, Scandinavia
DP   Spain, Portugal
DQ   Switzerland
DR   Balkan Peninsula
DS   Asia
DT   Africa
DU   Australia, Oceania
DX   Gypsies

E–F (History, America)

E   Indians, United States (general)
F   U.S. local history, Canada, Mexico, Central and South America

G (Geography, anthropology, recreation)

G   Geography (general), atlases, maps
GA   Mathematical geography, cartography
GB   Physical geography
GC   Oceanography
GE   Environmental sciences
GF   Human ecology, anthropogeography
GN   Anthropology
GR   Folklore
GT   Manners and customs (general)
GV   Recreation, sports, games, leisure, physical education

H (Social sciences)

H   Social sciences (general)
HA   Statistics
HB   Economic theory, demography
HC   Economic history and conditions (by region or country)
HD   Industries, land use, labor
HE   Transportation and communications
HF   Commerce

HG Finance
HJ Public finance
HM Sociology (general)
HN Social history, social problems, social reform
HQ Sex, the family, marriage, women, feminism
HS Societies (secret, benevolent)
HT Cities, communities, classes, races
HV Social pathology, social and public welfare, criminology
HX Socialism, communism, utopias, anarchism

J (Political science)

J   General legislative and executive papers
JA Political science (general)
JC Political theory
JF Political institutions and
    public administration (general)
JJ —North America
JK —United States
JL —Canada, Central and South America
JN —Europe
JQ —Asia, Africa, Australia, Oceania
JS Local and municipal government
JV Colonization, emigration, immigration, migration
JX International law (no longer used)
JZ International relations

K (Law)

K   Law (general), jurisprudence, comparative law
KB   Religious law and jurisprudence
KBM   Jewish law
KBP   Islamic law
KBR   History of canon law
KBU   Roman Catholic law, the Holy See
KD–KDK   United Kingdom and Ireland
KDZ   America, North America
KE   Canada
KF   United States
KG   Mexico, Central America, Caribbean
KH   South America
KJ–KKZ   Europe
KL   Ancient Orient
KLA–KLW Eurasia
KM–KPZ   Asia
KQ–KTZ   Africa
KU–KWW   Pacific area
KWX   Antarctica
KZ   Law of nations
KZA   Law of the sea
KZD   Law of outer space

L (Education)

L   Education (general)
LA History of education
LB Theory, teaching, teacher training, higher education
LC Forms, social aspects, religious education,
      other types, special classes, adult education
LD United States
LE America, except United States
LF Europe
LG Asia, Africa, Oceania
LH College and school magazines and newspapers
LJ Student fraternities and societies
LT Multisubject textbooks

M (Music)

M   Music
ML Literature on music
MT Musical instruction and study

N (Fine arts)

N   Visual arts (general)
NA Architecture
NB Sculpture
NC Drawing, design, illustration
ND Painting
NE Print media
NK Decorative arts
NX Arts in general

P (Language and literature)

P   Philology and linguistics (general)
PA Greek and Latin languages and literature
PB General European languages, Celtic
PC Romance languages
PD Germanic and Scandinavian languages
PE English language
PF West Germanic languages
PG Slavic, Baltic, Albanian languages
PH Uralic and Basque languages
PJ Egyptian, Libyan, Berber, Cushitic,
      Semitic languages and literature
PK Indo-Iranian languages and literature
PL East Asian, African, Oceanic languages
PM Inuit, American Indian, artificial languages
PN Literary history and collections, drama, journalism
PQ Romance literatures
PR English literature
PS American literature

PT   Germanic and Scandinavian literature
PZ   Juvenile belles lettres, miscellaneous literature

Q (Science)

Q   Science (general), information theory
QA   Mathematics
QB   Astronomy
QC   Physics
QD   Chemistry
QE   Geology, paleontology
QH   Natural history, biology
QK   Botany
QL   Zoology
QM   Human anatomy
QP   Physiology, animal biochemistry, experimental pharmacology
QR   Microbiology, immunology

R (Medicine)

R   Medicine (general)
RA   Regulation, public health
RB   Pathology
RC   Internal medicine, medical practice
RD   Surgery
RE   Ophthalmology
RF   Otorhinolaryngology
RG   Gynecology and obstetrics
RJ   Pediatrics
RK   Dentistry
RL   Dermatology
RM   Therapeutics, pharmacology
RS   Pharmacy and materia medica
RT   Nursing
RV   Eclectic medicine
RX   Homeopathy
RZ   Alternative systems of medicine

S (Agriculture)

S   Agriculture (general)
SB   Plant culture, pest control, diseases
SD   Forestry
SF   Animal culture, pets, veterinary medicine
SH   Aquaculture, fisheries, angling
SK   Hunting, wildlife management

T (Technology)

T   Technology (general), engineering (industrial), patents
TA   Engineering (general), civil engineering
TC   Hydraulic and ocean engineering

TD	Environmental technology, sanitary engineering
TE	Highway engineering, roads and pavements
TF	Railroad engineering and operation
TG	Bridge engineering
TH	Building construction
TJ	Mechanical engineering and machinery
TK	Electrical engineering, electronics, nuclear power
TL	Motor vehicles, aircraft, astronautics, UFOs
TN	Mining engineering, metallurgy
TP	Chemical technology
TR	Photography
TS	Manufactures
TT	Handcrafts, arts and crafts
TX	Home economics, hospitality industry

U (Military science)

U	Military science (general)
UA	Armies
UB	Military administration
UC	Maintenance and transportation
UD	Infantry
UE	Cavalry and armor
UF	Artillery
UG	Military engineering, air forces, air warfare
UH	Other military services

V (Naval science)

V	Naval science (general)
VA	Navies
VB	Naval administration
VC	Naval maintenance
VD	Naval seamen
VE	Marines
VF	Naval ordnance
VG	Minor services of navies
VK	Navigation, merchant marine
VM	Naval engineering, shipbuilding, diving

Z (Bibliography, library science)

Z	Books in general
Z 4–8	History of books and bookmaking
Z 40–115.5	Writing, manuscripts
Z 116–659	Printing, binding, the book trade, copyright, censorship
Z 662–1000.5	Libraries, library science, information science
Z 1001–8999	Bibliography
ZA	Information resources, electronic resources, government information

SOURCE: Library of Congress Classification Outline, www.loc.gov/catdir/cpso/lcco/lcco.html.

Cutter numbers

by Vanda Broughton

AFTER CREATING A CLASS NUMBER for a book, the cataloger must add information about the author and the date of publication. This is called the Cutter number, named after its inventor, Boston librarian Charles Ammi Cutter (1837–1903).—*GME.*

The author information takes the form of an encoded number representing the author's name. This system of encoding names was invented by the ubiquitous Mr. Cutter, and the resulting numbers are known as Cutter numbers, or sometimes simply as Cutters. Cutter numbers are not restricted to the Library of Congress classification, and U.S. libraries in particular use them for author numbers in conjunction with Dewey decimal classification and other schemes.

Cutters are constructed using the conversion table below that allows you to express the letters in a word as numbers. There is obviously a fundamental difficulty here as there are 26 letters and only 10 numerals, so one number is used to represent several letters. This makes use of the Cutters a bit less than exact, and in practice they often need manipulation to maintain the correct alphabetical sequence.

Table for Constructing Cutter Numbers

1. After initial *vowels*

For the second letter	b	d	l–m	n	p	r	s–t	u–y
Use number	2	3	4	5	6	7	8	9

2. After initial letter *a*

For the second letter	a	ch	e	h–i	m–p	t	u	w–z
Use number	2	3	4	5	6	7	8	9

3. After initial letters *Qu*

For the second letter	a	e	i	o	r	t	y
Use number	3	4	5	6	7	8	9

For initial letters *Qa–Qt,* use 2–29

4. After other initial *consonants*

For the second letter	a	e	i	o	r	u	y
Use number	3	4	5	6	7	8	9

5. For further expansion

For the letter	a–d	e–h	i–l	m–o	p–s	t–v	w–z
Use number	3	4	5	6	7	8	9

The Cutter number consists of the initial letter of the author's name, plus numbers representing the next two or three letters. These numbers differ according to whether the first letter of the name is a vowel, S, Q, or any other consonant. If further differentiation is needed, extra numbers can be added using section 5 of the table.

The Cutter number for Broughton will be B76, derived as follows: B plus 7 (representing R after a consonant other than S or Q) plus 6 (representing further expansion of O). Similarly, the Cutter for Stendhal is S74, for Beethoven B44, for Ivan the Terrible I93, and for Quasimodo Q37.

Cutter numbers are usually taken to two numerals, although where not many books are to be arranged one number might be enough, and very large collections might need more than two numbers. The purpose at the Library of Congress is to give each book a unique number, but other libraries are not necessarily aiming for that and so won't bother with very long Cutter numbers.

The above names are straightforward, but if you look carefully at the table you will immediately notice that some very necessary letters are not represented. For instance, there is no provision for "h" or "l" following a consonant, despite the frequency of these letter combinations in English. Slavonic (and other non-Western European) languages have many letter pairs that are not provided for at all. In cases like this you have to invent a number that will get the Cutter to file in the right place alphabetically. This seems to me greatly to undermine the value of the Cutters, since different classifiers in different libraries will make up different numbers; over a period of time, the adjustments necessary to maintain the correct order can move a long way away from the original table. It also worries beginners not to have a "right answer" or to see Cutters on a catalog record that "don't make sense," but you should be reassured that the problem is not with you. A more immediate difficulty for the beginner is that making up answers as an exercise has no context and you can only guess at an appropriate number. In a real library situation, you would be fitting your Cutter into an existing sequence, and see more clearly how this adjustment of numbers works.

Although Cutter numbers are primarily used to provide an "author" arrangement, difficulties arise when there is no personal author. Nowadays Cutters are linked to main entry, so if the main entry were to be something other than an author (the title, a corporate body or a named conference, for instance) you should make the Cutter for that instead. Editors can never be the main entry point, so you will never need to make a Cutter for an editor's name. If the state of your cataloging knowledge makes deciding on main entry a bit of a challenge, it is safest to make the Cutter for title when there is no personal author.

You add the Cutter to the classmark after an intervening full stop (period).

Sacred and the feminine : toward a theology of housework / Kathryn Allen Rabuzzi.
– New York : Seabury Press, 1982
    LCC Classmark: BL458
    Cutter for Rabuzzi: R33
    Call-mark: BL458.R28

Who's who in barbed wire. – [Texline, Tex. : Rabbit Ear Pub. Co.], 1970
    LCC Classmark: TS271
    Cutter for Who's who W5
    Call-mark: TS271.W5

In addition to the author Cutters, LCC also uses Cuttering as the basis of alphabetical subject arrangement. If you look at the alphabetical list of subjects in poetry you can see the Cutters added to the basic classmark.

PR1195.M2	Madrigals
PR1195.M22	Magic
PR1195.M24	Manners and customs
PR1195.M33	Medicine
PR1195.M53	Mice
PR1195.M6	Monsters
PR1195.M63	Mothers
PR1195.M65	Mountains

In theory you can add any other "Poetry by subject" to the list by making an appropriate Cutter. But LCC has not always applied the Cutter chart consistently in creating these lists of subjects. You can probably also see where the Cutters are not derived from the Cutter chart, and where difficulties could arise. How, for instance, would you deal with books of poetry about macaroni or moles? Nevertheless this use of the Cutter number is widespread throughout the scheme, so you must make the best of it.

Cutters are also used for A/Z geographical arrangement, another very common situation. In a situation where you have a subject or geographical Cutter, this precedes the author Cutter, and the two are separated by a space.

Step-by-step book about stick insects / David Alderton. – Neptune City, N.J. : T. F. H. Publications, 1992

LCC Classmark:	SF459
Cutter for subject (Stick insects):	S75
Cutter for author (Alderton):	A43
Call-mark:	SF459.S75 A43

Antwerp in the age of Reformation : underground Protestantism in a commercial metropolis, 1550–1577 / Guido Marnef. – Baltimore ; London : Johns Hopkins University Press, 1996

LCC Classmark:	BR828
Cutter for place (Antwerp):	A58
Cutter for author (Marnef):	M37
Call-mark:	BR828.A58 M37

Normally no more than two Cutters are used in a call-mark. If it happens that there are two subject/geographical Cutters (perhaps because an A/Z subject arrangement is further subdivided by A/Z geographical arrangement), the author Cutter is left out. This is because the point is to create a unique number (rather than provide information about the author), and two Cutters are likely to achieve this. LC completes the call-mark by adding the date.

Picture your dog in needlework / B. Borssuck, Ann Jackson. – New York : Arco, 1980

Classmark:	TT778.C3
Author Cutter:	B67
Date of publication:	1980
Call-mark:	TT778.C3 B67 1980

Again, this is aimed at producing a unique book number, and it's not very likely that libraries other than the Library of Congress will want to follow the practice, although in a large library it is a useful device for breaking up long runs of books at the same number.

SOURCE: Vanda Broughton, *Essential Classification* (New York: Neal-Schuman, 2004), pp. 154–160. Reprinted with permission.

The 55 Percent Rule

by Danny P. Wallace and Connie Van Fleet

A BRIEF ARTICLE IN A NORMAN, OKLAHOMA, newspaper in 2003 revealed a disturbing set of statistics. In an unobtrusive test conducted by investigators from the Treasury Department, employees of the Internal Revenue Service provided correct answers to 57% of questions asked. The direct implication is that nearly half a million taxpayers may have received incorrect answers between July and December 2002. Furthermore, that 57% can be subdivided into 45% of questions answered correctly and completely and 12% answered basically correctly but incompletely. Perhaps most disturbingly, for 12% of questions posed by the surrogate taxpayers, IRS employees instructed the questioner to find his or her own answer, a direct violation of IRS policy.

That figure of 57% is remarkably close to the infamous 55 Percent Rule that has aroused so much light and heat in studies of the success rates of reference librarians. The term appears to have been formulated in 1986 by Peter Hernon and Charles R. McClure, who summarized unobtrusive evaluation of reference services as revealing that "staff generally answer 50%–60% of the questions correctly." Earlier studies revealed similar success rates. A series of studies conducted at the University of Illinois Library Research Center in the 1980s emphasized that success rates can vary widely, even when the same methodology is applied consistently in repeated tests. A 2002 study by Neal Kaske and Julie Arnold suggests that the 55 Percent Rule may apply to chat and email reference. Recent work by John V. Richardson Jr. and Matthew Saxton has suggested that such studies are inherently flawed in that they used unacceptably small samples and unsophisticated models for assessing success.

Analogs from other arenas

The newspaper article regarding success rates for IRS employees provides a very close analog to studies of reference success and invites a search for studies of success in other arenas. The results of such a search in areas other than reference are interesting, and in some cases alarming. Here are just a few:

- Web usability expert Jakob Nielsen found that users of web pages successfully complete fewer than 50% of desired tasks.
- A study of estimates made by Wall Street analysts between 1974 and 1991 indicated that they accurately predicted investment earnings about 45% of the time and that their accuracy was declining over time.
- Although oral health problems are among the most common chronic conditions experienced by older adults, family physicians and geriatricians were able to correctly diagnose oral health problems in older adults only about 55% of the time.
- Sixty-four percent of Secret Service agents, 58% of psychiatrists, 57% of

judges, 56% of robbery investigators, and 56% of federal polygraphers are capable of determining whether an individual they are interviewing is lying.

How bad is 55 percent?

There are some environments in which a success rate of 55% would be viewed as exceptional or even unattainable. Examples from the world of sports are numerous:

- Ty Cobb's career batting average of .366 has never been equaled.
- Dan Marino holds the record for passing yards completed, with a success rate of 59.4%.
- Kareem Abdul-Jabbar hit 53% of attempted field goals.
- Thirty-seven percent of horses that won both the Kentucky Derby and the Preakness went on to win the Triple Crown.

The need for a benchmark

Studies of the accuracy of answers to reference questions have produced averages as low as 40% and as high as 90%. A key problem in evaluating studies of reference accuracy is that there is no obvious target against which to compare results. A common thread in discussions of the 55 Percent Rule is a sense that it just can't be correct, that reference librarians surely must be performing at a higher level than that. Many reactions to studies of reference performance have reached into the realms of outrage and accusation.

A confounding factor in interpreting studies of reference accuracy is the lack of a uniformly accepted standard for defining success. Rejection of studies that reveal low success rates in answering reference questions focus on the negative implications of seemingly low numbers. We can't believe that reality is reflected in such low percentages, but we don't have a meaningful benchmark for defining success. There is an implication that success in answering

---

The Song of the Reference Librarian
by Sam Walter Foss

See the Reference Librarian and the joys that appertain to her;
Who shall estimate the contents and the area of the brain to her?
See the people seeking wisdom from the four winds ever blown to her,
For they know there is no knowledge known to mortals but is known to her;
See this flower of perfect knowledge, blooming like a lush geranium,
All converging rays of wisdom focused just beneath her cranium:
She is stuffed with erudition as you'd stuff a leather cushion,
And wisdom is her specialty—it's marketing her mission.
How they throng to her, all empty, groveling in their insufficiencies;
How they come from her, o'er flooded by the sea of her omniscience!
And they know she knows things,—while she drips her learned theses
The percentage of illiteracy perceptibly decreases.
Ah, they know she knows she knows things, and her look is education;
And to look at her is culture, and to know her is salvation.

SOURCE: Sam Walter Foss, "The Song of the Library Staff," in *Songs of the Average Man* (Boston: Lothrop, Lee & Shepard, 1907).

reference questions is an all-or-nothing proposition in which nothing less than 100% success will do. Absolute success, however, can't be a realistic goal, so we are left with a serious problem regarding definition. Perfection is unrealistic, but we don't know what threshold value to use to define success. Although Richardson and Saxton's recent work is encouraging, there is still a real need to explore the nature of the reference process and establish the metrics that will engender a true understanding of success.

SOURCE: Danny P. Wallace and Connie Van Fleet, "Strange Bedfellows: Evidence of Accuracy in Professional Performance," *Reference & User Services Quarterly* 43 (Winter 2003): 109–110.

Things that make libraries look stupid

compiled by Chris Rippel

THROUGH THE PUBLIB ELECTRONIC DISCUSSION LIST, I asked librarians across the country to help make a list of "things that (1) may not get done or may fall through the cracks, but (2) could make the librarian, the library staff, and the library look incompetent and stupid." I thank everyone who contributed to the list below. Capital letters after the questions are the initials of contributors. Full names of contributors are at the bottom of the list. Questions without initials are anonymous.

Can everyone at the circulation or reference desks quickly produce:
* an up-to-date copy of the library's policies? CR, MY
* an up-to-date copy of the library's budget? CS
* applications for the Talking Book program and help fill out the form? LN

Does everyone behind your circulation and reference desks know:
* where today's programs and meetings in the library are being held? This apparently is the most common problem. One contributor asked front staff where a state library association meeting of 100 people was in their library and they didn't know about it. "State library association *here?*" CN, NP, AP, SH, MY
* where to register for library programs? AJ
* who is on the board of trustees? CN, LC, CS, JP
* who is president of the board of trustees? CN
* when and where the library board meets? JP
* how does one become a member of the library's board? AS
* who is in the Friends group and who is president of that group? CN
* who library sponsors and partners are? MY
* the library's mission statement? CS
* the hours branches are open? BK
* how to handle complaints about a book or video? KM, JJ
* the answer to the question, "Can I place a request for a book not yet released?" JJ
* policies on check-out times, renewals, and fines? LC
* about the library programs, especially the Summer Library Program? Patron to adult services librarian: "I guess you don't have anything for my kid to do." Adult services librarian: "Not really." All around were flyers and posters telling about their summer reading program with story times, performers, craft times, and other special events. JT, CN

5

- about library services and programs for "special needs?" LN
- how to sign up for the statewide or regional library card? KR1
- the URL of the library's website? MY
- how to use the library's website to answer questions about specific library programs and services?
- how many employees work in the library? JP1
- where the library gets its money (especially if you have a nonresident fee)? LC
- if you have a nonresident fee, how that fee is determined? LC
- who city and county officials are and their phone numbers? JP2
- what to tell parents asking where their children will be taken if a tornado warning sounds? I believe all parents, when signing up their children for library cards and story hour, should receive a document explaining library procedures during tornado watches and when tornado warnings are sounded. The document should instruct parents to tell their children what to do if, for example, you close the library during tornado watches, and, in the case of a tornado warnings, assure parents their children will be taken to a safe place and encourage parents to take shelter themselves rather than run to the library in the middle of a tornado. It makes us look caring and thoughtful. CR
- when the library was built? LC
- what kind of plants and trees are in the library's yard? LC
- where to find the list of elected officials after an election? BC
- how to handle requests for information by law enforcement officials? MY

If asked, can the library director:
- explain how library money is spent and give at least rough estimates of the amounts in each category? MH, JP
- state his or her email address? CR
- explain, "How can you spend money on [your service here] when you can't afford to keep the doors open?" JP
- explain what will be done if a tornado or flood damages the library? CR
- explain what to do with wet or moldy books? CR

Do all staff know:
- the library's hours? JT
- the proper way to answer the telephone? JT
- directions to the library? BK
- what to do in an emergency? KM, SD, TL
- what to do if fire occurs? SD, PH
- where the fire extinguishers are? LR
- how to use fire extinguishers? During the panic of fire few, few people will stop to remember what they saw in a video last year. Proper reaction to a fire requires repeated hands-on practice. CR
- where flashlights are in case of a power failure? JP2
- what to do in a tornado warning and tornado watch is sounded? SD
- how to respond to a natural disaster (e.g., tornado, earthquake)? JP2
- how to get the doors open if people get stuck in the elevator? CR
- what to do if a reporter shows up? PH
- how to close the library? PH

Other questions. Are the words on all your signs spelled correctly? Is the library's web page current? KR2

Does each page of the library's website have the name of library and address, including country? CR

Are signs and handouts correct in days and hours open? KR2

Are promised summer reading prizes delivered to library branches? AJ

Are summer reading incentives age-appropriate as related to choking? PH

Are frontline staff empowered and encouraged to waive fines, fees, etc., in the interest of customer satisfaction? (There is a difference between telling someone they have the power to do so, and actively encouraging them to use that power as needed.) MY

Contributors to the above list were:

AJ   Andrea Johnson, Cook Memorial Public Library, Illinois
AP   Amy Paget, Tippecanoe County Public Library, Indiana
AS   Andrew Smith, Williamsburg Regional Library, Virginia
BK   Bettye Fowler Kerns, Central Arkansas Library System, Arkansas
BC   Bonnie Case, Highland Park Library, Texas
CN   Catherine Newland, Morrill Public Library, Kansas
CR   Chris Rippel, Central Kansas Library System, Kansas
CS   Carol Simmons, Daly City Library, California
JJ   Julie James, Forsyth County Public Library, North Carolina
JP1 JoAnn Potenziani, New Lenox Public Library, Illinois
JP2 Jill Patterson, La Habra Branch Library/Orange County Public Library, California
JT   Julie Tomlianovich, South Central Kansas Library System, Kansas
KM   Kelly R. McBride, Russell Co. Public Library, Virginia
KR1 Kathy Rippel, Central Kansas Library System, Kansas
KR2 Kay Russell, North Central Kansas Library System, Kansas
LC   Linda Cannon, Joplin Public Library, Missouri
LN   Liz Nix, Southeast Kansas Library System, Kansas
LR   Leah Randolph, Abington Community Library, Pennsylvania
MH   M. Brooke Helman, Hinsdale Public Library, Massachusetts
MY   Mary Ann Yonki, Osterhout Free Library, Pennsylvania
NP   Nancy Polhamus, Gloucester County Library System, New Jersey
PH   Pamela J. Hickson-Stevenson, Portage County District Library, Ohio
SD   Sonya Dintaman, Carnegie Public Library of Steuben County, Indiana
SH   Susan Henricks, Carnegie-Stout Public Library, Iowa
TL   Tracy Luscombe, McKinney Memorial Public Library, Texas

SOURCE: Chris Rippel, in PubLib Archive, "Final List of Things Making Libraries Look Stupid," sunsite.berkeley.edu/PubLib/archive/0406/0036.html.

5

The Genealogy Search Process

by Laurie S. Francis

THE SEARCH FOR GENEALOGY INFORMATION is not a linear, closed process like that of a student research paper, but a more circular pattern. Patrons and professional researchers often find that the more information they locate, the less certain they may be about previous "facts." They must verify the information they already have, make corrections and additions to their data, and continually evaluate the authenticity of all sources. Patrons frequently find they must return to an earlier stage in the search process in order to reevaluate the method or the source. This process lends itself to a new search pattern that I have labeled the Genealogy Search Process (GSP).

Although the GSP can be compared to the research process of a regular library patron because it loosely follows Carol C. Kuhlthau's Information Search

---

Genealogy Search Process Model

Stages
Desire to search for ancestors
Search for a specific family or individual
Research process (Topic Exploration)
Concentrate on specific records or geographical areas (Focus Formulation)
Gain skills
Gather data (Resource Collection)
Change direction of research, new records, or locations
Closure (Presentation)

Feelings
Interested but uncertain
Optimistic
Confused, frustrated
Increased interest, curiosity, fascination, determination, or abandonment occurs
Confident
Encouraged, a sense of progress, or anger*
Determination, perseverance, or irritation, frustration, anger, impatience
Satisfaction, pride, accomplishment, or sad but realize there isn't anything more to do

Actions
Decision is made to begin searching
Ask questions, go to a library, enroll in a class
Search records often in a shotgun approach, contact others for assistance (librarians, pro-
    fessional researchers, others)
Search specific types of records, or particular localities
Learn research methods and skills
Note taking, letter writing, traveling, active research
Review and verify known information, widen research area, select another family
Print/frame family tree, publish book, article, or online version, help others with their
    research

*It isn't uncommon for some patrons to become angry and behave irrationally during and after their searches. Impatience and frustration with lengthy searches, copy costs, borrowing charges, postage and travel expenses, the cost of professional researchers, dead ends, inaccurate information, laws, and more can induce temper tantrums in the most docile patrons.

Process (ISP) model (*Seeking Meaning: A Process Approach to Library and Information Services*, Ablex, 1993), there are some exceptions. Inexperienced genealogy patrons begin their search with feelings of uncertainty; they want to know about their family tree but initially aren't sure where to start (Kuhlthau's Task Initiation stage). Frequently a well-meaning friend or relative, or even a newspaper article will lead them to believe that Aunt Mary, or a family history library, or even the internet will have all their answers. Patrons begin to feel optimistic. They are sure that locating the information they need should be easy and that a wealth of details will be available to them immediately (Topic Selection stage).

Most patrons choose a particular ancestor or family to learn more about when they begin their search for information. Once they begin exploring the various sources (Topic Exploration), they can quickly become confused and frustrated, again very similar to Kuhlthau's ISP. The assistance of a knowledgeable librarian can make a big difference to patrons at this stage. The librarian can assist patrons in narrowing sources, providing descriptions of what can be found in the sources, helping patrons to determine exactly what information they should be looking for, and recommending the best sources for that information (Focus Formulation stage).

It is at this point that most patrons either become hooked on genealogy or lose interest in the project. For those who continue, the search for information becomes a treasure hunt, with patrons taking on the role of investigators or detectives. Patrons begin to feel interest and ownership in the search. The librarian can assist them in locating sources, gathering information (Resource Collection stage), and providing instruction in how to use specific library equipment (computers, readers, indexes). By now, patrons are beginning to understand some of the methods involved in searching the records to find their ancestors. They have gained some new skills, and feelings of confidence and determination are common.

At this stage in the GSP, genealogy patrons and experienced researchers often diverge from Kuhlthau's model. It is common for researchers to spend months and even years researching a particular family line without finding the specific information they are seeking. Genealogy patrons do not necessarily experience the feelings of satisfaction and relief experienced by Kuhlthau's subjects as they complete their research and prepare a final presentation.

Unfortunately, an information search does not guarantee results. The needed material may only be available at another location that doesn't lend items through interlibrary loan, or the repository may not allow the general public to search its materials and a professional researcher or member of a historical society must be contacted to search the records. Frequently, for a variety of reasons, the records that might provide the information patrons are seeking may not be available due to natural disasters, man-made disasters, lack of appropriate preservation methods, prohibited access, translation difficulties, privacy laws, and more. Over the past century, records previously unavailable have been located and made available to the public, so it may also be a matter of just waiting until the records are made public.

Once patrons reach the point that they can no longer obtain accurate, pertinent information, they must return to an earlier point in the research process, review their information, and determine a new direction for the GSP. When patrons decide they have reached the end of their search, they move into the final phase, similar to the Presentation stage of Kuhlthau's model. Feelings of relief, pride in accomplishment, and genuine satisfaction in having learned more than just names and dates about their family are typical for genealogy patrons. Many choose to display the results of their searches as printed or framed family trees, others publish books detailing their research, or post it on the Web for others to appreciate.

Some patrons experience overwhelming feelings of possessiveness and selfishness about their final products, refusing to share their information, feeling that they have done the hard work, and so should others interested in the same data. Those who publish their research in books, magazine articles, and online formats have a right to expect protection of their intellectual property rights and appropriate citations for their efforts and information. But one's great-great-grandparents belong to all of their descendants, not just the researcher who located their information. However, those who would take another's research and try to pass it off as their own are practicing unethical and illegal behavior.

SOURCE: Laurie S. Francis, "The Genealogy Search Process," *PNLA Quarterly* 68 (Spring 2004): 12, 22. Reprinted with permission.

Religion at the reference desk

by Mike Wessells

LOOKING INTO THOSE EARNEST 10-year-old eyes, I sensed the immense importance of the question. I knew the answer from my other vocation as pastor of an evangelical Christian church; in that capacity, I can hardly wait for someone to ask the question. But here, behind that bulwark of neutrality, the library reference desk, how was I to deal with this youngster's sincere query: "Is God real?"

In years past and in distant lands today, blood has been regularly spilled over differences in faith. If history has taught us anything, it is that spiritual certitude and governmental power make an explosive mix. Over the years, our country has moved toward the opposite extreme, ruthlessly relegating spirituality in the public sphere to a matter of personal preference on a par with one's favorite baseball team. Current efforts to reinject religion into the public sphere have only confirmed the wisdom of caution.

In what public arena, then, may an individual seriously explore deep spiritual issues without touching off alarm bells? Not in the schoolroom, not in the courtroom, not in the legislative chamber. How about that bastion of neutral information nourishment, the public library? Yes, but only with a carefully selected collection and a sensitive staff.

Collection building in the area of religion has been historically unbalanced. The limitations of refereed religious publications and selective library review sources have narrowed the practical choices open to librarians. Many spiritual traditions were simply underrepresented in reviews or published by sectarian publishing houses, rendering those traditions unavailable for the most part on library shelves.

From agnostics to zealots

Today's more open climate of electronic instant publishing is subtly changing our role from information gatekeepers to gate evaluators. "What information can I trust and how do I know?" is the type of question we must teach our patrons how to answer, where in past ages we did it for them via our collection-development expertise. Ironically, this opens up vast opportunities for collection balance driven by patron demand rather than by the choices of mainstream publishers or review journals. In an area of knowledge such as spirituality, where truth is more elusive than professional consensus can encompass, we can ask those who know better than ourselves.

For instance, librarians can:

- Ask each of the faith communities in your service area to name the five works that would best reflect their faith to someone who did not share it. Surely they might know better than a reviewer or librarian not of their faith. Use their lists as a basis for collection development. Better yet, use the opportunity to solicit donations—what more motivated group could you find?
- Interact regularly with clerical groups in your area, explaining the library, building support, and gaining ideas for collection development and use.
- Cultivate religious youth groups for input on materials, especially in audiovisual, and include representatives on teen advisory councils.
- Rather than discourage on-the-job displays of the religious sensibilities of staff, tap into their affiliations to learn the language, modes of thought, and information needs of their religious fellows. It is just as important to have a staff member who speaks "evangelical" when serving that community as one who speaks Spanish to serve your Hispanic community. The key is mutual listening and respect.
- Develop your own spirituality. (No, I am not switching hats and trying to convert you.) A deeper look at your own spiritual depths will help you to recognize and respect those of your patrons, especially those whose spiritual conclusions differ from yours.

These last two points get to the heart of staff sensitivity. Recognizing the immense impact of spirituality on our patrons leads to understanding the intensity of their values and how the library can support those values, especially when those values might conflict with library policy. In intellectual freedom circles, we often say, "There should be something in the library to offend everyone"; we had best include ourselves among those who need to be offended from time to time. In fact, the willingness to operate outside our comfort levels must go along with spiritual openness among staff, or we run the risk of reenacting minireligious wars in our back rooms.

The liturgy of librarianship

Balancing a spirituality that mandates "witnessing" with the neutrality ethics of librarianship can be tricky, but the best sharing of anyone's faith is the simple living of it in front of others. Your life is the best testimony as to the value of your faith, and no faith is worth its salt when imposed by mandate or bullying. Each of us has reached our point in faith by a journey, and others must make their own. One of librarianship's strongest faith statements is that information has value, librarians must impart that value to patrons, and they must then build their own belief systems out of that imparted information.

So I looked my young patron in the eye and said, "That's the biggest and best question I've ever been asked. I'll show you how lots of other people have answered that question and you can see what is best for you." And together we headed toward the stacks and the terminals—on an adventure that lasts forever.

You probably have a better way to handle this question. Send it to me—I want to learn from you. After all, if reference were easy, anyone could do it. Instead, it's up to us. Librarians—the few, the proud, the chosen.

SOURCE: Mike Wessells, "Faith at the Front Desk: Spirituality and Patron Service," *American Libraries* 34 (May 2003): 42–43.

On-the-fly reference

by Jessamyn West

AS LIBRARIANS, WE CAN SEE THEM COMING a mile away. People
with questions. They see something in our eyes and know we have the answer, or know where to find it. We're mistaken for clerks in stores, hosts at
parties, and librarians in other libraries. No wonder librarianship is often described as more of a calling than a job.

Our dispositions indicate a willingness to help and not ridicule, and perhaps to even find the elusive answer. As a result, we often do information
work in our off-hours, either as volunteers or as ready reference for friends
and relatives.

This sort of on-the-fly reference is at once familiar and foreign. Many of us
reach instinctively for the keyboard that isn't there, or wish that we were back
with our books. Often we are working with or for nonlibrarians who have a
different idea of the job to be done. Makeshift information desks are often
added as an afterthought at large events, to keep the organizers free for more
managerial tasks.

I have frequently found myself doing on-the-fly reference. In August 2001
I staffed the Playa Info desk at Burning Man, a seven-day outdoor music and
art festival in Nevada's Black Rock Desert.

When I worked at Playa Info at Burning Man, I felt well prepared. My
ability to subtly queue people with a quick glance meaning, "I see you, and
you will be the third person I can speak with" amazed my colleagues. The top
questions were, as expected:

"What time is it?" "Where are the bathrooms?" "What are the upcoming
events?" However, the next tier of questions and concerns were all new to me:

"We're out of water and need to get some more, quickly."

"I can't find my friends, can you help me?"

"Is the nearest phone really 12 miles away?" It was.

In the public library, we rarely need to answer questions that
could immediately affect someone's health or welfare. At Burning
Man, many of the problems we solved were in this vein:

"I'm locked out of my car. What do I do?"

"My dog is missing. Who can help?"

"I'm out of my medication. Where can I find some?"

Add to that the fact that many of the questioners were sun-
burned, hungry, thirsty, tired, half-dressed or undressed, or under the influence of *something*, and our work was cut out for us. Conducting a reference
interview with someone dressed in a fuzzy bunny outfit is a unique challenge.

Similarly, at the library you mostly deal in facts, not rumors and rumor control. At events, you become a voice of authority and may have to answer questions like "What is that glass that turns purple in the sun that you see in the
sidewalks in Seattle?" and "Who's in jail?"

The editor of the local paper took to stopping by the Burning Man info
desk a few times a day just to find out what we'd heard. We talked to more
people at the event in a single day than almost anyone else there. Making sure
you have proper answers before you open your mouth becomes crucial. Once
rumors could be verified or debunked, then we'd add that information to what
was on hand, so that succeeding staffers had the straight scoop.

Filling more than information needs

When Chuck Munson worked at an information table during the 2001 International Monetary Fund protests in Washington, D.C., he found some interesting overlaps with library work. "Maintaining activist confidentiality is similar to patron confidentiality," he observed, "although at the library you don't have to worry about surprise police raids. Cops are always looking for information about who the activists are. When the police shut down the convergence center, several quick-thinking information-desk volunteers smuggled out the sign-up sheets and housing lists."

At Burning Man, making clear decisions about what information was or was not public was a major topic of conversation. Sure, there was a satellite phone available for extreme emergencies, but we had to determine what constituted a true emergency. And the Fornication Station, although wanting to keep its

---

On-the-Fly Tool Kit

So, you're going into an unknown situation and are expected to answer questions like you've been there all your life. How do you prepare? What do you need? Here's a tool kit for being an impromptu information superstar.

Things to bring:
Comfy shoes, snacks, and water. You may be standing in one place for a long time.
Timepiece. "What time is it?" is still the most frequently asked question.
Pens, paper, tape, and rocks. Pens and paper for drawing maps and makeshift signs; rocks and tape to keep things on the table.
Phone. Be aware that you may have the only local phone, and if people see it they may want to use it.
Local information. Bus schedules, maps, phone lists, and restaurant info.

Once you're there:
Take a walk. Learn the area, note some landmarks, gauge distances, and pay special attention to locations of phones, bathrooms, and ATMs.
Identify yourself. Make sure people know you are there to answer their questions—nametags that just say "Info" can be all it takes.
Talk to people. How do you contact other people, such as event organizers, that you may need to talk to for answers?
Survey info. What do you have available, and what might you need? Other people are often your best reference sources.

As you work:
Note and refer. See if there are ways to make handouts with oft-requested information. Posting a large FAQ list can cut down on repetitive questions, as can good signage.
Live and learn. In a multiple-day event, keep notes of what to bring on Day Two and speak to organizers about what would make the info area more productive.
Stay vs. roam. Some events work better with a central information location. In other situations it's best if you go to them; don't be afraid to get out from behind the desk.
Straighten and organize. Lots of stuff gets dropped at an info desk. Keep it clean and make essential information stand out.

Afterward:
Debrief. Talk to other workers about the events. See where there is room for improvement.
Self-assess. See if you learn anything about yourself and how you work in unfamiliar surroundings that could be useful in your professional life.
Offer feedback. Let organizers know what works and what doesn't for next time.

5

exact location a secret, had posted several events in the public calendar (safer-sex demos, nightly love-swing play) that garnered many tough-to-answer questions. The more we could offer a united approach to requests, the more the event looked well organized and the staffers looked well prepared. Sometimes the only interactions people have with event workers or administrators are via the help staff. Making sure that their interactions are smooth and fruitful is key. As in the library, the answer "I don't know" was out of the question.

This highlighted a major difference between the info-desk culture and the reference-desk culture: At the reference desk you are often providing pointers to existing materials. At the info desk you are often assembling information in order to create new reference materials. Working at information desks has shown me how experienced and talented many of us are at providing information compared to the average event volunteer, even though the work we do rarely feels like work to us.

It also hit home that there's *something* about librarians. If we don't find the patrons, they seem to find us. If situations are disorganized, we straighten them out, often explaining as we go. As Gerry, an Ohio librarian told me, "Sometimes librarianship is just gracefully telling people 'I don't know—but I'll find out, for your sake and mine.'"

SOURCE: Jessamyn West, "On-the-Fly Reference," *American Libraries* 33 (May 2002): 54–57.

CIRCULATION

Hard times and library use correlated

by Mary Jo Lynch

ON NOVEMBER 27, 2001, the *New York Times* carried a story headlined "Economists Make It Official: U.S. Is in Recession." The first paragraph noted that "The group of economists that tracks business cycles made official today what has been apparent to laid-off workers and struggling businesses for months: the longest economic expansion on record gave way earlier this year to the first recession in a decade."

The downturn, which began in March 2001, was also apparent to public librarians, who noticed that circulation was increasing, while their budgets were being cut. Those librarians began calling ALA, asking for evidence of what Stephen E. James once called "the Librarians' Axiom" that "public libraries prosper whenever the country is experiencing economic stringency."

According to an article by James in the Fall/Winter 1986 *Public Library Quarterly*, the relationship between library use and economic conditions had been discussed for over 100 years. He notes that one of the first references to the link is a statement by William Poole in the *1880 Annual Report* of the Chicago Public Library and mentions a later reference to the same idea in Bernard Berelson's classic 1949 volume on *The Library's Public.* James asserts that there is "ample evidence" from the time of the Great Depression to substantiate the link between business cycles and public library use. But his own research, a study of economic conditions and library use in 20 large cities from 1960 to 1979, did not establish "the Librarians' Axiom" as true. According to James, "overall the investigation suggests that when one uses the most rigorous statistical standards no relationship can be shown between local economic conditions and the use of public libraries."

The article by James was the only literature ALA could suggest to those who asked questions on this matter. As those questions increased and National Library Week 2002 approached, ALA's Office for Research and Statistics and the Public Information Office decided that the time was right for another study. Given budget constraints and the need to finish the work in early April 2002, we could not do anything as elaborate as James had done. Instead, we worked with staff at the Library Research Center (LRC) of the Graduate School of Library and Information Science at the University of Illinois/Urbana-Champaign to design a small study that would take a contemporary look at an old belief.

Because the LRC manages the Public Library Data Service under contract to ALA's Public Library Association, the staff at LRC is in touch with the people responsible for statistics at many public libraries. LRC staff contacted those people at the 25 public libraries in the U.S. serving populations of one million or more and asked them to provide monthly data on circulation and visits for the last five years. Twenty-three of the 25 agreed to cooperate and sent data. The visits data were not robust enough for statistical analysis. However, circulation data from 18 libraries were exactly what was needed.

Using that data and the standard methodology of time series regression analysis, LRC found that circulation has increased significantly in all the months since March 2001, when the National Bureau of Economic Research pegged the beginning of the latest recession. Additional analysis made this conclusion even more impressive. Statisticians have determined that variation of data values in any time series can be the result of four types of change:

1. normal growth or decline over a long period of time;
2. seasonal variation;
3. cyclical movement in the economy; or
4. residual or random factors.

Mathematical formulas have been established to remove the effects of the first two types of change. LRC applied those formulas to the data and found cyclical variation alone responsible (plus possible random variation). Circulation was 8% above trend in March 2001, the date when the recession officially began. It stayed well above trends, an average of 9.1% above, the rest of the year.

Does this prove that "the Librarians' Axiom" is true? It certainly seems true for those 18 libraries in this period of economic stringency. It would take much more research to establish that those results apply to other libraries and to other points in time. But the more interesting question is "Why?" A couple of obvious possibilities come to mind: People who are unemployed check out books to help themselves qualify for new jobs, and people with less money to spend get books at the library rather than buy them. To really answer the "Why?" question we need to know a lot more about how and why people use public libraries.

SOURCE: Mary Jo Lynch, "Economic Hard Times and Public Library Use Revisited," *American Libraries* 33 (August 2002): 62–63.

DISTANCE LEARNING

Managing distance learning library services

by the ALA Association of College and Research Libraries

DISTANCE LEARNING LIBRARY SERVICES refers to those library services in support of college, university, or other post-secondary courses and programs offered away from a main campus, or in the absence of a traditional campus, and regardless of where credit is given. These courses may be taught in traditional or nontraditional formats or media, may or may not require physical facilities, and may or may not involve live interaction of teachers and students. The phrase is inclusive of courses in all post-secondary programs designated as extension, extended, off-campus, extended campus, distance, distributed, open, flexible, franchising, virtual, synchronous, or asynchronous.

Philosophy

Access to adequate library services and resources is essential for the attainment of superior academic skills in post-secondary education, regardless of where students, faculty, and programs are located. Members of the distance learning community are entitled to library services and resources equivalent to those provided for students and faculty in traditional campus settings.

Management

The chief administrative officers and governance organizations of the originating institution bear the fiscal and administrative responsibilities, through the active leadership of the library administration, to fund, staff, and supervise library services and resources in support of distance learning programs. As the principal and direct agent of implementation, the librarian-administrator should, minimally:

1. assess and articulate, on an ongoing basis, both the electronic and traditional library resource needs of the distance learning community, the services provided them, including instruction, and the facilities utilized;
2. prepare a written profile of the distance learning community's information and skills needs;
3. develop a written statement of immediate and long-range goals and objectives for distance learning, which addresses the needs and outlines the methods by which progress can be measured;
4. promote the incorporation of the distance learning mission statement, goals, and objectives into those of the library and of the originating institution as a whole;
5. involve distance learning community representatives, including administrators, faculty, and students, in the formation of the objectives and the regular evaluation of their achievement;

6. assess the existing library support for distance learning, its availability, appropriateness, and effectiveness, using qualitative, quantitative, and outcomes measurement devices, as well as the written profile of needs. Examples of these measures include, but are not limited to:

    (a) conducting general library knowledge surveys of beginning students, reoffered at a midpoint in the students' careers and again near graduation, to assess whether the library's program of instruction is producing more information-literate students;

    (b) using evaluation checklists for librarian and tutorial instruction to gather feedback from students, other librarians, and teaching faculty;

    (c) tracking student library use through student journal entries or information literacy diaries;

    (d) asking focus groups of students, faculty, staff, and alumni to comment on their experiences using distance learning library services over a period of time;

    (e) employing assessment and evaluation by librarians from other institutions and/or other appropriate consultants, including those in communities where the institution has concentrations of distance learners;

    (f) conducting reviews of specific library and information service areas and/or operations that support distance learning library services;

    (g) considering distance learning library services in the assessment strategies related to institutional accreditation;

    (h) comparing the library as a provider of distance learning library services with its peers through self-study efforts of the originating institution;

7. prepare and/or revise collection development and acquisitions policies to reflect the profile of needs;

8. participate with administrators, library subject specialists, and teaching faculty in the curriculum development process and in course planning for distance learning to ensure that appropriate library resources and services are available;

9. promote library support services to the distance learning community;

10. survey regularly distance learning library users to monitor and assess both the appropriateness of their use of services and resources and the degree to which needs are being met and skills acquired;

11. initiate dialogue leading to cooperative agreements and possible resource sharing and/or compensation for unaffiliated libraries;

12. develop methodologies for the provision of library materials and services from the library and/or from branch campus libraries or learning centers to the distance learning community;

13. develop partnerships with computing services departments to provide the necessary automation support for the distance learning community; and

14. pursue, implement, and maintain all the preceding in the provision of a facilitating environment in support of teaching and learning, and in the acquisition of lifelong learning skills.

SOURCE: ALA Association of College and Research Libraries, Distance Learning Section Guidelines Committee, "Guidelines for Distance Learning Library Services," *College & Research Libraries News* 65 (November 2004): 604–611, www.ala.org/ala/acrl/acrlstandards/guidelinesdistancelearning.htm.

SYSTEMS

Overcoming the systems librarian imposter syndrome

by Rachel Singer Gordon

DUE TO THE NEWER NATURE OF THIS SUBFIELD of librarianship and the lack of formal technical training experienced by a number of systems librarians, many feel needlessly inadequate in their positions. An understanding of the importance of a library background and skills in the success of any systems librarian can help these individuals overcome their "imposter syndrome" and settle more comfortably into their positions.

"Mother," Meg pursued, "Charles says I'm not one thing or the other, not flesh nor fowl nor good red herring."—Madeleine L'Engle, *A Wrinkle in Time* (1962).

Like Meg in Madeleine L'Engle's classic YA novel, many systems librarians—especially those who originally entered librarianship intending to concentrate on another specialty—worry about failing to fit into the tidy categories that have traditionally marked our perception of the profession's subfields.

While categorization is a natural librarian impulse, systems librarians (and their employers) need to realize the futility of trying to package systems job descriptions into neat little boxes. Systems librarianship by its very nature fosters both overlap and ambiguity; systems librarians need both an understanding of the needs of each department and the ability to work with librarians in other specializations.

During any given week, a systems person in a public library may be helping technical services to write and implement policies in the automation system, adding links to the website for the children's department, and disassembling the PC at the reference desk to replace a broken CD-ROM drive. In an academic library, she might be negotiating electronic license agreements, adding new resources to the intranet, and teaching students effective database and internet searching. In smaller libraries, systems librarians can fill dual (or triple, or quadruple) roles in departments like reference and systems or cataloging and systems, rather than having the luxury of concentrating solely on the technological portion of their job. In any library, their actions impact and intersect all departments, since technology is so intertwined with both the institution's day-to-day activities and its larger mission.

The skills and philosophy underpinning the field, however, draw upon the foundations of librarianship itself; a library background is essential to the effectiveness of any systems librarian. Systems librarians who realize their inherent strengths and learn to use their existing library skills in dealing with changing technology both feel more secure in their positions and are better able to serve their institutions.

Faking it through

Unfortunately, it often takes library systems personnel years to settle comfortably into the ambiguity inherent in their jobs. Many originally entered librarianship with the intention of specializing in some other subfield of the profession, or completed their degree before an emphasis on technology was common. They lack formal training in technology management, troubleshooting, network administration, and many other duties as assigned. This lack, combined with the need to deal with constant change, leads many otherwise successful systems librarians to feel as if they are faking their way through their jobs. When those with an official IT background proclaim that there is but one true standard of expertise and education that defines systems librarianship, this only exacerbates the feeling that they fail to measure up. They go through their duties convinced that they will eventually be exposed, unable to resolve a critical issue or unable to answer a crucial question.

Joan Harvey talks about a syndrome called "the imposter phenomenon," in which otherwise successful individuals believe that others overestimate their talents, that their success is not due to their own ability, and that they will eventually be exposed as frauds in their position (Joan C. Harvey and Cynthia Katz, *If I'm So Successful, Why Do I Feel Like a Fake?* St. Martin's, 1985). While this syndrome occurs in people across all professions, those in positions that constantly require doing new tasks or taking on new roles are particularly susceptible to these feelings. Their cure lies in realizing that their success stems from their own abilities and actions rather than in some random or external force. The cure for systems librarians lies in realizing that, as long as they know (or can find out!) enough to keep the systems in their own institutions humming along, they are successes—and integral to the smooth functioning of their library.

New roles, familiar skills

Whether or not they do so consciously, systems librarians in all sizes and types of libraries draw on their existing skills and background in order to serve effectively in their positions. It is precisely because they have these skills to draw upon that they are able to be successful in a systems role, with or without formal technical training. Essential traditional library skills for systems personnel include many of those we are either taught in library school or learn on the job. The following observations show several ways in which systems librarians use these skills—and offer suggestions on how they can extend their knowledge and abilities to serve even more effectively in their positions.

Research. One academic librarian notes: "It has never ceased to amaze me how much better I am at finding solutions to problems in knowledge bases (like Microsoft's) than my technical staff, most of whom, frankly, can barely spell." A background in librarianship is an invaluable tool in navigating both online knowledge bases and offline manuals, researching problems, and locating answers. It serves us well as we build a personal collection of resources that will be useful in our own technological environment. A librarianship background gives us insight into whom to trust, where to start, what to look for, and how to evaluate potential solutions to our support dilemmas—and helps us to avoid implementing untrustworthy techniques that can create more damage than the original problem.

While each systems librarian's support toolbox and strategies will be unique to her situation, there are resources that will be useful in many environments, some of which can be found on the Accidental Systems Librarian website (www.lisjobs.com/tasl/). Many systems librarians also pick up tips from colleagues or from online discussion lists and make a habit of bookmarking sites and ordering reference materials they come across in their reading.

The skills that systems librarians have picked up through reference course work or while working on a public service desk are also valuable additions to their support toolbox. A typical technical support interview with a staff member or library patron eerily parallels a typical reference interview. In each, the trick is to work from the original inquiry to the actual problem by asking questions designed to narrow down the issue. Only then can we resolve the issue or answer the question. In each instance, we also need to know the point at which we need to call on an expert—in this case, vendor technical support or support personnel in our larger institution or system.

Networking. Karen Ventura, head of systems and technology at Novi Public Library, advises that systems librarians "collaborate with other library technology folks. . . . Together, we do much more than we could do on our own. And if there's something that I am not familiar with, chances are someone else at another library is. This way, the library technology world is much more manageable!"

Librarians are master networkers from way back; the sheer proliferation of professional email discussion lists, workshops, conferences, and interest groups attests to our reliance on each other's knowledge and experiences. The image of a solitary researcher toiling away in a back room is passé; our strength lies in our collaboration.

Systems librarians are no exception to this need to network. From mailing lists such as SYSLIB-L, Web4Lib, oss4lib-discuss, and LIBNT-L, to conferences that include Computers In Libraries and ASIS&T, specialized forums on technological issues serve every interest and level of expertise. The inclusion of tech topics in more general conferences and among the workshops offered by local library systems offers a further opportunity for systems librarians to enhance their technological skills while they keep a foot in the traditional library world. Successful systems librarians take these opportunities to learn from one another, share their own experiences, and, above all, to realize that they are not alone. Teaching and learning from others, beginning to feel part of a larger community, is a large step toward overcoming the sense of being an imposter.

Organization of knowledge. Any systems librarian who has needed to lay his hands quickly on a CD key, a grant number, a technical support phone number, or a video card model number knows the value of organization. As the computing environment expands, both physically and in complexity, well-organized records allow systems librarians to keep track of everything from installed systems and software to vendor information and institutional IP addresses.

Organization also helps us track and make use of the statistics of which library administrations are so fond. Electronic statistics include website usage statistics, information on electronic database usage, and reports generated through an institution's ILS (Integrated Library System). Knowledge—and the ability to find information—is power! The well-organized and informed systems librarian can justify his position and carry out his duties in relative calm.

Lifelong learning. In their quest to keep informed, empowered systems librarians are inveterate lifelong learners. Learning can be achieved in many ways—informed systems librarians make a habit of keeping up with developments in fields relevant to their library's environment and potential. Savvy systems librarians take advantage of a mix of on- and offline opportunities, which can include relevant reading, online tutorials, weblogs and announcement lists, formal coursework, and on-the-job education. Every professional activity is an opportunity for learning. The more knowledge a systems librarian acquires, and the stronger her background in both technology and librarianship, the more comfortable she will be in her position. Systems librarians who remain open to learning from every situation, and who make a conscious effort to improve their skills, are empowered by their own efforts.

Instruction techniques. University of Washington systems librarian Emalee Craft explains: "As a librarian, a lot of my skills involve how to communicate effectively with users in a way that will help fill their information needs. I think these same skills have been invaluable in relating technological terms and ideas to other staff members and users of the library."

Whether or not systems librarians are formally involved in technology instruction in their institutions, every tech support call and every computer-related interaction provides an opportunity to teach. Any technological knowledge they can communicate to their colleagues helps empower other library staff, making everyone's job easier. Any technological knowledge they can communicate to their patrons enables library customers to make effective use of institutional resources, making their colleagues' jobs easier and improving the image and effectiveness of the library. One of systems librarians' most important roles, therefore, is that of communicator—both imparting knowledge and translating technical terms and ideas.

A bridge between two worlds. Using traditional skills to fill new roles, systems librarians bridge the two worlds of technology and librarianship. They also benefit from the best of both worlds, using both sets of skills to confront changing technology as librarians, and in terms of the larger goals of their institution. Once they are able to relax into their positions, they are able to feel the excitement and possibility that comes from bridging these fields. As University of San Francisco Director of Library Systems Karen Johnson explains: "You will never get bored. If you like change, living on the edge (at least the edge of the library), then this is the job for you."

At the end of *A Wrinkle in Time*, Meg finds to her relief and delight that she is so much more than she imagined. It is precisely her unique combination of personal strengths and skills that make her able to face her fears and save the day—and her brother Charles. Successful systems librarians draw on their own unique combination of strengths and skills in situations ranging from the dramatic (the internet connection is down and classes are scheduled all day for database training) to the everyday (a printer failure, a press release needing to be posted on the website, a patron with a technical question). Neither flesh, nor fowl, nor good red herring—simply a necessary bridge between technology and librarianship.

SOURCE: Rachel Singer Gordon, "Overcoming the Systems Librarian Imposter Syndrome," *LIBRES* 13, no. 2 (Summer 2003), libres.curtin.edu.au/libres13n2/ess&op_singer_gordon.htm. Quotes are taken from answers to a survey on systems librarianship, which was posted online from late 2001 to early 2002. Reprinted with permission.

PRESERVATION & DISASTERS

Storage guidelines for disaster prevention

by Johanna Wellheiser and Jude Scott

GOOD STORAGE PRACTICES are a cornerstone of collection preservation. As well, proper storage methods can reduce hazards that could lead to fire and water damage. The following section covers storage as it relates to disaster prevention, rather than storage as a comprehensive topic.

Well-planned and well-designed storage is critical. Books stored off the floors or away from overhead pipes are at less risk from water damage. Collections stored near windows can face a triple threat from light deterioration and water damage as well as loss from theft. Relocating or reorganizing a storage area can be a relatively low-cost preventive measure.

Storage location checklist

- Avoid basement storage. When flooding occurs, water seeks the lowest level. Basements often have uninsulated outside walls, which leads to problems with dampness and eventually mold.
- Avoid attic storage. Attics are also often uninsulated, prone to leaks and subject to infestations.
- Avoid storage near or below service pipes.
- Separate storage areas from washrooms, darkrooms, labs, kitchens, and workshop areas.
- Storage areas should never be next to the physical plant operations due to the risk of fire.
- If basement storage is unavoidable, use it for collections that the organization considers less valuable.
- Store more valuable collections on main and upper floors.

Collection storage checklist

- Never store collections directly on the floor, even temporarily.
- Store collections at least 15 cm (6 inches) above the floor.
- Store collections on the top shelf of hooded shelving units only.
- Place more valuable, vulnerable, or irreplaceable collections on lower shelves but not the bottom shelves. For example, photographic media, which are susceptible to heat, could be housed on lower shelves. Disaster experts have noted that materials on top shelves are often burned beyond recovery, while those on bottom shelves are in good condition. Easily replaceable volumes could be placed on top shelves.
- If shelving cannot be relocated away from water hazards, cover it with plastic sheeting. This should only be done as a temporary measure, and the collections monitored for conditions of elevated humidity.

- Install shelving at least 5 cm (2 inches) away from inside walls and 30 cm (12 inches) away from outside walls to avoid damage from condensation, burst pipes within walls, etc.
- Consider orienting files within boxes perpendicular to their shelves.
- Avoid using carpet in storage areas. Carpets retain water, hamper drainage and hinder efforts to stabilize the relative humidity of the storage area after flooding.

Hazardous supply materials and storage checklist

The following storage guidelines aid in preventing fire. They apply not only to employees within the organization, but also to outside contractors. If the work involves flammable materials and sources of heat, the fire risk will be greatly increased.

- Store flammable and combustible supply materials in a safe, cool place out of sunlight, inside fireproof containers and cabinets.
- Store hazardous supply materials such as gas cylinders, solvents, and paints in accordance with safety regulations and standards.
- Provide training for staff in the correct handling, use, storage, and disposal of hazardous supply materials according to applicable legislation.
- Store hazardous supply materials in properly marked containers.
- Do not store large containers of hazardous supply materials on high shelves from which they may fall and break. "Shelf-lips" may be installed to help prevent materials from accidentally falling off.
- Keep all chemical and solvent containers closed, even during use, to minimize the escape of flammable and toxic vapors and dusts.
- Store and dispose of cellulose nitrate-based film according to applicable standards and fire regulations. The Canadian Conservation Institute recommends either storing it at low temperature—10°C (50°F)—and 30–40% RH, or having it copied by an experienced firm and disposing of the original. Kodak recommends a vault temperature of 2°C (35°F) and RH of between 20–30% for long-term storage, and a vault temperature of no greater than 21°C (70°F) and RH below 50% for extended-term storage. This film can be retained, however, if proper conditions for its handling, use, and storage are complied with. Failing the means to do this, some sources recommend immediate copying and storage of the original outside the facility.
- Enclose storage areas with fire separations (any wall, ceiling, or floor that effectively retards the passage of heat and smoke).
- Keep all fire-rated doors closed.

Shelving and cabinets

Steel shelving and cabinets coated with a baked enamel finish are generally recommended for library and archival storage. However, it has been suggested that organizations consider the use of sturdy wooden shelving due to its stability until consumed by fire—"metal shelves buckle and eject their contents at temperatures of 400°C–500°C [752°F–932°F], which can be reached in minutes."

The type of wood used for storage is a consideration, as some woods off-gas more then others. Oak, for example is not generally recommended. If wooden shelving is used, a coating should be applied as a barrier to the off-gassing of acid and other compounds from wood fibers, as well as any adhesives/binders present. Options include acrylic latex paint, acrylic urethane latex paint, and some acrylic urethane clear varnishes. Use of a semigloss or gloss finish will result in less wear and tear on books or containers. Some sources suggest lining shelves with polyester film as an added barrier. Any coating applied should be allowed to off-gas and cure completely before being used for collections storage.

Vital records storage

Some larger organizations store vital records offsite in separate fire-resistive buildings. Equipment and furnishings for such buildings should also be fire-resistant. These facilities have environmental controls (temperature, relative humidity, lighting, and ventilation), and appropriate security, fire detection, and suppression systems.

Failing the means to provide a separate building for vital records, other offsite locations could include: a commercial storage facility, a branch company office, or a cooperative arrangement (jointly owned and operated between other similar organizations).

While governments operate remote facilities, and some large corporations utilize branch plants for remote storage, most smaller organizations find that privately owned commercial record centers provide the most cost-efficient method of protecting and providing records services.

SOURCE: Johanna Wellheiser and Jude Scott, *An Ounce of Prevention*, 2nd ed. (Latham, Md.: Scarecrow, 2002), pp. 56–58. Reprinted with permission of the Canadian Archives Foundation.

Water damaged collections
and records recovery
by Johanna Wellheiser and Jude Scott

MOST DISASTERS TO LIBRARIES AND ARCHIVES involve water. The cause of the disaster may not be water per se, but water damage will surely be a consequence or secondary effect of fire or earthquake. Major concerns involving water are growth of mold on damp, wetted, or soaked collections and records; blocking of coated paper; distortion; and water-sensitive media and components. All wet materials should be considered fragile and must be handled with care.

> If there is one clear rule for response to water damage it is this: **The faster the correct action, the better the result.** The key word is "correct." Once wet, paper and film emulsion will swell, bindings distort, leather and vellum react. The quicker they can be brought under control, the less disastrous your emergency will be. (Sally A. Buchanan, *Disaster Planning, Preparedness and Recovery for Libraries and Archives*, UNESCO, 1988, p. 71)

As the majority of the damage to materials takes place in the first hours after a disaster, immediate action must be taken to control the environment and to stabilize the wet collections. Decisions must then be made about appropriate recovery techniques to be used. Where few items are involved, immediate decisions can usually be made. Larger amounts of wet material will require more extensive assessment and a larger recovery effort.

Some materials will pose particular problems. Wet coated paper, films, and magnetic tapes, for example, are susceptible to total loss and must not be allowed to dry out unattended. And collections of differing media require different techniques for recovery.

An understanding of the effects of water on various collections and records materials is essential to planning a successful recovery operation. This is because paper and other materials absorb water at varying rates and to differing degrees, depending on their nature, condition, and age. The affected collections will probably contain a mixture of wet, wetted, and damp materials.

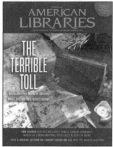

Paper absorbs water quickly, causing swelling and other problems. The percentage of water absorption can also be very high. Uneven wetness of paper is a particular problem: Such materials are unlikely to dry without distortion. Except for lengthy immersion situations, boxed materials will likely survive with less damage than shelved book materials, as the boxes will protect the contents. The level of protection will depend on the material of the box (type of board or plastic) and its design. Tightly shelved materials can, however, ward off considerable water.

Where large numbers of books are involved, the quantity of water to be extracted in the drying process can be estimated based on an average per-book dry weight and an appropriate water absorption percentage. In general, pre-1840 books and documents will absorb water to an average of 80% of their original dry weight, although some may absorb as much as 200%. More modern books, except those with brittle paper, will absorb an average of up to 60% of their original dry weight.

Peter Waters (palimpsest.stanford.edu/bytopic/disasters/primer/waters.html) stresses that recovery action should be determined by the water content of the material, and not by the relative humidity of the environment. The water content of the materials may stay dangerously high, even when the area's RH has been successfully lowered. He suggests using a moisture meter, or if one is not available, a mirror placed within, but not touching, the textblock. Condensation will form on the mirror's surface if moisture is present. Less than 7% water content is considered dry.

Waters also stresses that any drying-service contracts drawn up must specify that the acceptable water content of all the book's composite materials be less than 7%. An average reading of water content is not acceptable, as some composite materials may be far less than the desired 7% and other materials, such as book cover boards, may exceed this percentage.

Other materials, such as magnetic tapes, are not affected by water in the same way as books and other paper materials. Paper can absorb water quickly and fully, while tapes are hydrophobic and thus, water absorption is both low and slow. Tapes are more sensitive to damage by extremes of heat and cold. Newer tapes are more resistant to damage by moisture than older tapes. Moisture and water cause tapes to fail when absorbed by the tape binder, causing it to become soft and gummy. However, a wet tape is not immediately in danger, unless the water contains organic or corrosive components, such as sea water and sewage, that may degrade the tape. The recovery of wet paper should take precedence over wet tape.

Photographic materials vary in their resistance to water damage. Starch prints (early color photographic processes) will not survive immersion, and thus, prevention of water damage is essential. For other materials, such as wet collodion glass-plate negatives, immediate appropriate action is critical to successful recovery.

Cleaning wet materials

Wet paper-based materials can be cleaned; however, it is usually best to do so once the materials are dried. No cleaning should be done of wet, rare, or valuable materials, fragile materials, or materials with water-sensitive or friable media or components. All moldy materials must be dried before being cleaned. Cleaning of wet, fire-damaged materials is not recommended.

Wet, film-based materials, some photographic materials, and computer media should be rinsed in clean water as part of the recovery process. Dirt, mud, and other debris and contaminants should not be allowed to dry on these materials.

The cleaning of moldy or sewage-covered materials requires the use of protective equipment and clothing as well as special precautions.

Wet-stabilization

Wet-stabilization is an interim measure, an option to be used only for a limited period of time until treatment can be undertaken. Materials (such as coated paper, some film, and magnetic materials) once wet, should be stabilized by wet packing until they can be freeze-stabilized or dried as appropriate, either in-house or at an external recovery company. This is to prevent materials from sticking together (blocking) permanently in a solid block as they dry and to prevent debris from drying onto their surfaces. If the water was contaminated, however, materials such as films and magnetic tapes should first be rinsed before wet packing. Wet-packed materials should be kept cool to avoid or reduce the opportunity for mold growth. Materials cannot be kept wet indefinitely—six to eight hours is the general rule of thumb for coated papers, and 48 hours for film-based materials. However, this will depend on the nature and condition of the materials. Already damaged materials are extremely vulnerable to further damage. Immediate freezing is preferable for wet coated paper, followed by vacuum freeze-drying.

Note: Wet-stabilization packing methods are different for paper- and film-based materials.

Wet-stabilization has many advantages:
- It prevents coated paper from blocking.
- It prevents film-based materials from sticking to one another or their enclosures.
- It prevents debris from drying onto film-based materials.
- It provides a period of time, albeit limited, in which to organize systematic drying operations, carry out further damage assessments, etc.

Wet-stabilization also has disadvantages:
- It is labor intensive.
- The bags containing paper-based materials must be removed prior to drying.

- Further damage to materials may result, such as increasing solubility of paper coatings.
- Loss of identification markings or labels may result.

Freeze-stabilization

Freezing is the preferred method for the stabilization of large quantities of water-damaged, paper-based, library and archival materials prior to drying (often by vacuum freeze-drying or vacuum thermal-drying methods). Freeze-stabilization can also be used for smaller quantities that will later be air-dried. Many materials, including vellum, can be safely frozen. However, some materials, such as paintings and some photographs, can be further damaged by freezing. Further research needs to be done on some materials, such as magnetic tape, where the professional literature is not clear on the risks associated with freezing. Further research is required overall to more fully understand the physical and chemical reactions in materials.

However, paper-based library and archival materials, once frozen, can be stored indefinitely in that state without damage, while decisions are made as to how to dry them. It may be best to freeze everything that you might want to recover, rather than discarding at the outset.

Refrigeration of wet materials (at approximately 4°C or 39°F) should only be used as a temporary measure when other treatment options are not available. The rate of mold growth will be reduced, but heavy, persistent pigmentation will result.

Prolonged freezing will dry paper through a natural sublimation process, like the dehydration that materials undergo in the freezer compartment of a frost-free refrigerator. Drying time will depend on the efficiency of the freezer unit, volume and wetness of the material, the freezer temperature, and air circulation.

Freeze-stabilization has many advantages:
- Freezing arrests the condition of materials, preventing further distortions and blocking of coated paper. Saturated volumes swollen by immersion will increase slightly more in thickness during freezing; however, this has not been found to contribute further significant damage.
- Further damage caused by the diffusion of water-soluble components is prevented by freezing. Inks, dyes, etc., would otherwise continue to spread by the action of wicking, if left wet or if dried by conventional means from the wet state. Inks and dyes can run if air dried from the frozen state.
- Freezing reduces mold growth (right) by induc-
  ing the dormant state in the spores (conidia). It also kills germinating conidia and hyphae, but not dormant or activated conidia. Materials infested by mold should be either cleaned and returned to controlled environmental conditions or, if absolutely necessary, further treated.
- Freezing provides time in which to organize systematic drying operations, carry out further damage assessments, determine replacement requirements, estimate recovery costs, and plan for rehabilitation of the building.

Freeze-stabilization also has limitations and disadvantages:
- Moisture in materials remains high.

- Further damage to materials may result as a result of ice crystal formation, increased thickness, and porosity.
- Some materials cannot be safely frozen, e.g., some types of photographs.
- Costs can be significant, depending on the volume of collections to be frozen and the length of treatment.
- As compared to manual drying and cleaning alone, moldy materials once frozen and dried may be susceptible to reoccurrence of fungi as the spores may have entered a dormant state and thus be potentially viable.
- Materials still need to be dried (unless frozen long term for the purpose of drying).

Wet books and documents should be packed and frozen as rapidly as possible. This will minimize the size of the ice crystals formed within the materials and limit swelling and deformation. It is best to straighten out distortions before freezing, if that can be done safely.

The best freezing option is blast-freezing (with rapidly circulating air) at a commercial facility, which freezes materials swiftly. The British Library blast-freezes at –25°C (–13°F). Once frozen, it is generally recommended that cold storage temperatures be maintained at –20°C (–4°F) or less. If this temperature cannot be achieved, then maintain at whatever frozen state is possible. Commercial freezers can also be used—they generally operate at –10°C to –30°C (14°F to –22°F). Household freezers can also be used for smaller quantities of materials, although temperatures do not usually go below –10°C (14°F).

The type of transportation to the freezer facility will depend upon the particulars of the situation. If the freezer facility is close at hand and prepared for arrival of the material, transport by regular truck may be the best option. Refrigerated or freezer trucks are generally less available and considerably more expensive than regular trucks. Refrigerated trucks will only chill materials or keep already frozen materials from thawing. Freezer trucks do provide freezing temperatures, but do not offer blast freezing. In cold winter conditions, materials may be frozen outside in a secured area.

Mary-Lou Florian notes, in *Heritage Eaters: Insects and Fungi in Heritage Collections* (James and James, 1997), that if frozen wet materials are slowly thawed in a refrigerator, the vegetative growth of germinated fungi and a high percentage of hydrated conidia will be killed.

Note: The procedure used for freeze-stabilization of water-damaged materials is different from the freezing treatment used specifically for the treatment of insect-infested dry materials.

Drying

Many factors will determine which of the various methods of drying is best in a given situation. The type, number, nature, condition, value, importance, and frequency of use of the water-damaged items, as well as time constraints, should all be taken into account. The use of a number of different drying methods for different collections may need to be considered.

General guidelines for drying:
- Mass chamber or mass *in situ* drying methods are generally not suitable for rare or special collections. Vacuum freeze-dried books and paper documents can show good results (excluding leather, parchment, and vellum).
- Air drying is most suitable for smaller numbers of damp or slightly wetted books and documents. Blocking of bound coated paper may be a problem.

- It is the preferred method for works of art on paper, paintings, most photographic materials, and smaller numbers of other nonpaper media. It has the highest staff labor costs.
- Dehumidification-drying is most successful when used on damp or slightly wetted, rather than soaked, materials including books, documents, some microforms, computer media, and some sound and video recordings. It is generally faster than freezer-drying, vacuum thermal-drying, or vacuum freeze-drying, except where major structural drying is being done *in situ* at the same time.
- Freezer-drying is most suitable for smaller quantities of water-damaged book and paper-based material.
- Vacuum-drying at ambient temperatures can be used to dry computer media, some microforms, some sound and video recordings, and electronic hardware.
- Vacuum freeze-drying is considered the best overall option for water-damaged, paper-based library and archival materials, subsequent to freeze-stabilization. Coated paper is best recovered by this treatment. It is more expensive than vacuum thermal-drying.
- Vacuum thermal-drying is less expensive than vacuum freeze-drying and air-drying for larger numbers of paper-based materials. However, blocking of coated paper, distortion of books, etc., often results. Materials that have already suffered major damage may be the best candidates for this option. Some materials must not be treated by this method, such as parchment and vellum, photographic materials, microforms, etc.
- There is only a 50% success rate in drying clay or coated paper, no matter what drying method is used.
- Costs for all types of mass chamber or *in situ* drying provided by an external service company are roughly the same: generally from $50–$70 Can (U.S. $40–$56) per cubic foot or $6–$11 Can (U.S. $4.80–$8.80) per book, depending on the handling required. A large number of materials would cost less per unit.
- It is best to know the risks associated with each drying method and select accordingly for the materials that require treatment. Availability may also vary depending on timing and geographic location.
- Where weather suits, consider the low-tech option of natural freeze-drying outside.

Air-drying

Air-drying in a controlled, well-ventilated environment is the preferred method when the wet materials are manageable in number, in unbound form, are edge wet only or merely damp, or if other drying techniques cannot be used. The process consists of separating the individual wet sheets or fanning out book materials and laying them on paper-covered tables where they dry by evaporation. Absorbent papers can be used to encourage wicking of moisture from items. If only damp, pamphlets and thin volumes may be hung on support lines to dry. Drying outside in the open air may be an option depending on the time of year and weather. Irrespective of the technique used, ongoing monitoring of the items and the environment must be done.

Air-drying is the preferred method for most photographic materials, magnetic tapes, compact discs, and phonographic records.

The advantages of air-drying are:
- It is a low-tech option.
- The cost is relatively low if the number of items is not large.
- Sorting and manipulation of the materials can be carried out as necessary.
- It allows for control of individual material characteristics.
- Other associated treatments can be carried out by conservators.
- The state of the materials being dried can be easily assessed.
- It is next to impossible to overdry materials.
- Large quantities of freeze-stabilized items can be air-dried in batches.
- The drying costs are less than replacement costs.

The principal drawbacks of air-drying are:
- It is impractical for enormous numbers of items.
- For large numbers of items that require ongoing attention, it is very labor intensive.
- The cost can be high (labor and supplies). Staff training is required.
- Considerable space is needed if large numbers of materials need to be dried. And the dedicated space may be required for a long period of time.
- Controlled environmental conditions must be maintained.
- Some wet materials cannot be successfully air-dried, i.e., books with coated paper (pages may block), and water-soluble inks, pigments, etc., which may bleed or offset.

Dehumidification-drying

Dehumidification-drying has been used for many years to dry buildings and ships' holds. It has recently been used in the library and archives community to dry rooms and their contents *in situ*, and even entire facilities. A room onsite can also be set up as a drying chamber for collections. There are two types of dehumidification-drying: desiccant and refrigerant.

Desiccant dehumidification is drying whereby moisture is trapped and absorbed by a desiccant. A room (or building) is sealed to create a "chamber," and the HVAC system is locally deactivated. Dry air is then continuously circulated through the room and ducted through portable, desiccant dehumidification equipment, situated in or outside the building. The equipment extracts the moisture to the outside, and dry air is returned into the wet areas for moisture pickup and subsequent moisture removal.

Depending on the equipment, this type of dehumidification can be effective in small or large spaces, as well as in cold temperatures. The air can be dried down to 10% RH, so careful monitoring is required. The temperature should remain below 21°C (70°F) to prevent damage to materials. If handled and controlled properly, desiccant dehumidification can be just as effective as vacuum freeze-drying and is reported to be excellent for drying photographs, film, negatives, X-rays, microfilm/fiche, and Mylar.

Refrigerant dehumidification is drying whereby moisture is condensed on coils, then collected and flushed into a drainage system. This method uses portable equipment and is effective for small-sized applications and local control. The air can be dried down to 20% RH, and careful monitoring is required of temperature and the removal of water from the drainage system. Refrigerant dehumidification lowers the RH more quickly and to a lesser degree than does desiccant dehumidification.

In either case, the process continues until the room and its contents are dry and the desired level of ambient humidity is achieved. Library and industrial buildings, books, documents, carpeting, and equipment have been successfully dried in this way. Books and documents are best treated before any swelling or blocking has occurred. Water-damaged tapes may also be dehumidification-dried. The drying time averages seven to 10 days, where structural drying is not a significant issue. Monitoring of the items and the environment must be done on an ongoing basis.

The advantages of dehumidification-drying are:
- Labor costs and documentation needs are minimized.
- There is no need to pack and transport materials if done *in situ*.
- It is relatively fast.
- It reduces risks to health from bacteria, viruses, and mold.
- The drying costs are less than replacement costs.
- Materials can be treated from the frozen or wet state.

The disadvantages of dehumidification-drying are:
- It is not suitable for soaked materials.
- It is not suitable for some materials, i.e., photographic materials, parchment, and vellum.
- Inks, dyes, etc., can run.
- Paper can cockle and wrinkle.
- Coated papers can stick or become distorted.
- Adhesives in bound volumes can release.
- Materials can be overdried.

Dehumidification-drying can cause the above-noted problems, because the items stay wet until the moisture is removed. Thus, damp or slightly wet materials will generally show better results than soaked materials.

Freezer-drying

As mentioned in the discussion on freeze-stabilization, water-damaged materials will dry over time in a freezer. An alternative for drying up to 200–300 books is to use a commercial freezer that has been specifically modified for the purpose of drying library and archival materials. The Hussman freezer modified for this purpose is also capable of insect extermination. No experience of using this equipment for drying documents is reported in the literature; however, there is no technical reason why this could not be undertaken.

Prepared books are placed onto racks in the freezer. They are first stabilized by blast-freezing and then dried by temperatures just under freezing. The water moves as a gas from the frozen books in the book compartment (temperature approx. –7°C to –2°C or 20°F to 28°F) to the evaporator component of the freezer, at temperatures well below –40°C, preferably between –45°C to –50°C (–49°F to –58°F). On average, wetted books take two to four weeks to dry. Individual books can be removed when they are dry, and distorted books may be reshaped during freezer drying.

This method would be used onsite with your own equipment or offsite with that of a sister organization. If small numbers of materials are involved, these may also be dried over time in the freezer compartment of a frost-free refrigerator or a regular freezer.

The advantages of freezer-drying are:
- The unit allows for good control of the process because of accessibility.
- Wetted books can be straightened during the freeze-drying.
- Major relocation of materials is not required.
- Drying costs are less than replacement costs.

The disadvantages of freezer-drying are:
- Limited treatment capacity.
- Capital cost of equipment.
- No reported experience of use with documents.

High-frequency radiation-drying

Microwave and other forms of high-frequency radiation-drying are not generally recommended. This is because of problems associated with the metal inclusions and attachments found in documents and books in the form of staples, clips, stamping, security strips, etc., which can cause burning of materials.

Manual freeze-drying

Following the 1989 fire at the USSR (now Russian) Academy of Sciences Library, a process termed "manual freeze-drying" was developed by the USSR Ecological Safety Research Centre for drying some 200,000 books.

Larissa Shapinka, et al., in *Book and Paper Group Annual* 10 (1991): 221–223, described the process as follows. Subsequent to freezing, groups of 10–15 books of similar size were parceled together and tightly wrapped with absorbent cloth. Each parcel had an outside pocket on each of its six sides, each of which was filled with sawdust. No special requirements were established for the cloth or sawdust. The still-frozen parcels were then moved in lots of about 300 to shelves in a drying room in which air was vigorously circulated and continuously exhausted to the outside by ventilating fans. There was a 3,000–4,500 book capacity per cycle. Drying occurred at 25°C–35°C (77°F–95°F) and 25–35% RH. Books were normally dry after one week. If not, they were returned to the drying room for a second week.

The advantages of manual freeze-drying identified by Shapinka are:
- Books dry evenly from inside to outside.
- Books tightly tied together cannot move or change direction as they dry.
- Books can be straightened out after drying because they are not absolutely bone dry.
- There is no mold growth.

Aside from the onsite equipment needs, the apparent disadvantage of manual freeze-drying is that it is very labor intensive. The costs of this drying method are unknown.

Vacuum-drying

Vacuum-drying is a drying method where materials are dried in a vacuum chamber generally at ambient or near-ambient temperatures. Freezing or high temperatures are not used. The progress of drying is determined by weighing. The process may need to be halted and the chamber opened. This method is reported to be very successful for the drying of magnetic tapes and electronic hardware.

The advantages of vacuum-drying are:
- Materials are not likely to be overdried.
- Drying costs can be less than air drying for larger quantities of material.
- Drying costs can be less then vacuum freeze-drying.
- Drying costs are less than replacement costs.

The disadvantages of vacuum-drying are:
- Availability and size of chambers is limited.
- Books may distort during drying.
- Coated papers generally block.
- Inks and pigments can run.
- There is a danger of mold development during drying.
- Some materials cannot be successfully vacuum-dried, i.e., photographic materials, parchment, and vellum.

Vacuum freeze-drying

Vacuum freeze-drying is considered the least damaging and most successful method for drying large quantities of water-damaged library or archival materials. Frozen materials are dried in a vacuum chamber, and do not thaw out as they dry, thus greatly reducing certain types of damage. This is the important difference between vacuum freeze-drying and vacuum thermal-drying.

In the vacuum freeze-drying process, prefrozen materials are placed in a chamber at a commercial facility from which the air is removed to create a vacuum. Then carefully controlled heat is applied. Because of the lowered air pressure (vacuum), the water sublimates directly from the solid to the gaseous state (i.e., from ice to vapor), thus eliminating further damage by the liquid phase of water. As water in the ice phase (ice in the frozen books) passes into the vapor phase (sublimation), heat is lost. If this heat is not replaced, the temperature of the material is continually lowered, thus slowing the drying process due to evaporative freezing. Extreme care must be taken to ensure that the materials are neither under- nor overdried. Excess water removal will result in embrittlement of the materials being dried. The progress of drying is determined by weighing. The process may need to be halted and the chamber opened.

Peter Waters recommends that the internal temperature of a chamber (vacuum freeze- or vacuum thermal-drying) be no greater than 100°F (38°C). This is considered a safe temperature. For sensitive materials, he suggests lower temperatures be used to dry the material slowly and under carefully monitored conditions. The costs can be high. He further advises that the materials must remain completely frozen throughout the drying cycle (below 0°C [32°F] and preferably lower to reduce the size of the ice crystals), and the vapor pressure must be below 4.5 torr.

Blast-freezing and vacuum freeze-drying experiments have been carried out by the British Library on a variety of library materials including books, documents, vellum, computer and audio tapes, and microforms. Detailed descriptions of temperatures and pressures as well as results are provided in a number of published articles. A. E. Parker, in "The Freeze-Drying Process," *Library Conservation News* 23 (April 1989): 4–8, concludes that vacuum freeze-drying can be used successfully on a wide variety of library materials. Some problems have been experienced with some coated papers (early clay-loaded art papers), parchment, and vellum materials. Parker says a vacuum freeze-drying temperature of 30°C (86°F) produces good results, but is too hot. He indicates that future drying will be done at a maximum of 20°C (68°F), which will take longer but leave the materials less brittle.

The British Library has test-frozen and vacuum freeze-dried a number of materials in recent years. See A. E. Parker, "Freeze-Drying Vellum Archival Materials," *Journal of the Society of Archivists* 14, no. 2 (1993): 183–185. A great many materials were considered successfully dried (i.e., various papers, computer tapes, various bindings, diazo microfiche, etc.). Materials considered to be unsuccessfully dried or resistant to the procedure were reels of microfilm (silver-halide positives), art/glazed/machine-finished paper, liquid toner–type photocopy paper, and illuminated vellum.

The advantages of freeze-stabilization followed by vacuum freeze-drying are:
- It is suitable for large numbers of materials.
- Frozen materials may be selectively chosen for vacuum freeze-drying.
- Expansion and distortion of the materials being dried is minimal.
- Wicking of the materials' water-sensitive or water-soluble components is minimal.
- Rate of mold growth is reduced and germinating conidia and hyphae are killed. The effect on dormant or activated conidia is not clear.
- Results are good for coated papers and drafting linens. There is minimal blocking.
- Dirt and silt are pulled to the materials' surfaces more effectively than with vacuum thermal-drying, allowing for more effective post-treatment cleaning.
- Mobile units are available.
- Drying costs are less than replacement costs.

The disadvantages of vacuum freeze-drying are:
- The cost is more than that of vacuum thermal-drying due to the use of sophisticated equipment.
- Materials can be overdried, as for any vacuum method.
- Some materials cannot be successfully vacuum freeze-dried, such as some photographic materials.
- Limited availability. As many vacuum freeze-drying facilities in Canada are associated with food-processing plants, timing can be an issue. To prevent contamination, frozen collections must be kept separate from food being stored or processed.

Vacuum thermal-drying

Vacuum thermal-drying offers a less expensive alternative to vacuum freeze-drying for the treatment of large numbers of wet materials. Vacuum thermal-drying uses a vacuum to pull the water out, after which warm, dry air is pumped into the chamber to complete the drying. If frozen materials are vacuum-dried, some water will sublimate from ice to vapor. Most of the water, however, will first pass through the liquid state before vaporizing. As a consequence of the heat and reintroduction of water, materials will show distortion.

Damp or slightly wet materials will generally show better results than soaked materials. Adhesives may release resulting in the need for rebinding. Inks and dyes may run and coated papers may stick together. In addition to the process limitations, there is a problem with the limited capacity and availability of facilities currently available in Canada.

As previously mentioned, the disadvantage of any vacuum method is that some of the material can be overdried. Peter Waters recommends that the internal temperature of a chamber be no greater than 100°F (38°C). As the progress of drying is determined by weighing, the process may need to be halted and the chamber opened.

The advantages of vacuum thermal-drying are:
- It can be used for large numbers of materials.
- Frozen materials may be selectively chosen for treatment.
- If an onsite mobile unit is used, there is no need to pack materials for distance travel.
- Drying costs are less than replacement costs.

The disadvantages of vacuum thermal-drying are:
- Wet or wetted materials do not show as good results as damp materials.
- Materials may be distorted.
- Inks and dyes may run.
- Coated papers may block.
- Binding adhesives may release.
- Materials can be overdried.
- Some materials cannot be successfully treated, such as many photographic materials, leather, parchment, vellum, computer media, and microforms.

SOURCE: Johanna Wellheiser and Jude Scott, *An Ounce of Prevention*, 2nd ed. (Latham, Md.: Scarecrow, 2002), pp. 127–135. Reprinted with permission of the Canadian Archives Foundation.

5

Preservation and Copernicus
by Owen Gingerich

BOOKWORMS HAVE RIDDLED a number of copies of the first edition of *De revolutionibus* (1543) by Nicolaus Copernicus. I thought I had never laid eyes on a bookworm, living or dead. Many of my students suppose it's a mythical beast and are incredulous when shown pages perforated by their trails. I didn't remember even seeing a picture of a bookworm, so was taken by surprise to discover that one is shown in Robert Hooke's well-illustrated *Micrographia* of 1665. From the small, round bores in early books, I had always assumed that the hungry insect was a cylindrical worm, but Hooke's enlargement pretty clearly shows a silverfish. Hooke himself described the insect as "the silver-colour'd Book-worm" and reported that "this Animal probably feeds upon the Paper and covers of Books, and perforates them in several small round holes." In fact, the *Encyclopaedia Britannica* indicates that a variety of insects qualify as bookworms, with the silverfish *(Lepisma saccharin)* as the leading candidate.

I was pretty puzzled about how a silverfish could create round bore holes, but eventually found the answers from Nicholas Pickwoad, an English expert who was helping Harvard University on its numerous book conservation problems. The silverfish feasts on mold damage, so it proliferates in humid environments. Its damage is generally to the surface of a page or to a leather binding. In contrast, the round bore holes often seen in early books were caused by the hungry grubs of the death-watch beetle (family Anobidae), which can eat right through the pages of books on a library shelf or penetrate furniture. The beetle lays its eggs near a source of food, for instance, in a crack or crevice of a well-stocked bookshelf, and the larva bores its way through its food supply, sometimes taking as long as 10 years before it finally metamorphoses into a beetle.

Presumably, the really well-drilled copies of *De revolutionibus* have long since been scrapped.

Rodents can make even quicker work of an ill-fated volume. A few years ago the Carnegie Institution of Washington put its library in warehouse storage while its premises were being remodeled. The books were placed on sledges and carefully covered with tarpaulins to secure them against water damage; not until several weeks later did it finally occur to someone to include rat poison in the precautions, but it was already too late. Today the Carnegie Institution has a library with scores of missing spines nibbled away by the rodents.

Fire ranks low in the list of book destroyers. I have tried without success to document whether any copies of Copernicus' book were lost in the Great Fire of London in 1666. Possibly so, but there is no evidence. A copy was lost when the Great Tower burned in Copenhagen in 1728, presumably another when the Strasbourg Library was destroyed in the Franco-German War in 1870, and a first edition went up in flames when the retreating Nazis deliberately burned the National Library in Warsaw in the autumn of 1944. Demolition bombing in World War II brought about substantial losses of *De revolutionibus*, in Douai, Frankfurt, Munich, and Dresden.

SOURCE: Owen Gingerich, *The Book Nobody Read: Chasing the Revolutions of Nicolaus Copernicus* (New York: Walker, 2004), pp. 130–131. Reprinted with permission.

Crisis management
by Jan Thenell

IF THERE IS EVER A TIME when an organization must mobilize itself to speak as one body, it is during a crisis. When the *Exxon Valdez* oil tanker ran aground in Alaska's Prince William Sound in March 1989, company executives—lacking good information and with no clear communications direction—made inconsistent, even contradictory comments to the media. Their mistakes, along with other company blunders, engendered suspicion among the press and the public.

When one inside group contradicts another, however innocently, credibility suffers. The leader-spokesperson thus becomes *the* voice and symbol of the library during a crisis. Her office—or her designated public information or public relations office—becomes "information central." All information and information requests flow through this office.

As the public representative of the library during a crisis, the spokesperson must be a good communicator who understands the human need to hear concern first, reasons and rationale second. She must be an effective leader, an effective decision maker, and an effective speaker. She will have already established trust with the media and the public. She should possess good interview skills and be able to communicate well under pressure. She should be knowledgeable enough to speak easily about the crisis and about libraries in general. She should be a quick study, learning quickly from successes and mistakes.

Depending upon the scope of the emergency, others may also speak for the library, especially the public relations officer. The public, however, most often wants to hear from the "person in charge," and it is the director who can speak with the most knowledge, credibility, and impact. If the chosen spokesperson is someone other than the director, the initial statement to the press and the public should be made by a person who is perceived as *the* authority: the director, the library board chair, or the president of the library's board of governors.

Speaking with one voice

The anthrax scare that followed the 2001 terrorist attacks on the World Trade Center illustrates further the folly of failing to speak authoritatively with one voice. For days and weeks after the first anthrax letters were found, no clear, knowledgeable spokesperson emerged to provide credible information and allay public fears. As various agencies worked to get a handle on the scope of the problem, the public received a host of contradictory statements.

At the height of the outbreak, Secretary of Health and Human Services Tommy Thompson told television viewers that the government was prepared to deal with any kind of bioterrorism attack. Days later, it became clear that he had misspoken; government scientists had much more to learn about anthrax.

Contrast the public's perception of the anthrax scare with the press coverage of New York Mayor Rudolph Giuliani's actions after the terrorist attack.

> For weeks afterward, Giuliani was more than just a mayor. Day after day, his calm explanation of complicated, awful news helped to reassure a traumatized city that it would pull through and that someone was in charge. He attended funerals, comforted survivors, urged residents to dine out and tourists to come in, all the while exuding compassion and resolve, even as the new threat of anthrax emerged. (*Portland Oregonian*, December 31, 2001)

Checklist

Select your team. List team members' titles and duties as well as their names.
Designate a backup person for each team member.
Select your library's leader-spokesperson.
Establish a crisis chain of command. Team members will be working together closely, and knowing who's in charge will eliminate many problems when a crisis occurs.
Create a rapid response mechanism (telephone tree, cell phone list, email) for getting in touch with team members and their alternates. Practice it.
Let everyone in the organization know who's on the team and what the lines of authority are.

SOURCE: Jan Thenell, *The Library's Crisis Communications Planner: A PR Guide for Handling Every Emergency* (Chicago: American Library Association, 2004), pp. 18–19.

PLANNING

Using standards in
public library planning

by Thomas J. Hennen Jr.

A STANDARD IS A SPECIFIC AND MEASURABLE BENCHMARK for achievement. The two major types of library standards are *numeric*, which measure by counting, and *prescriptive*, which prescribe an action. An example of a numeric standard is the common state library standard for a given number of books or staffing per capita. Prescriptive standards include statements that a library should have a collection development policy, follow open meeting laws, or employ a properly certified director.

Most states have library standards, but these standards are usually advisory only. There is usually no penalty for failing to meet the standards set by a state, although there are exceptions. Effective library planners will carefully consider library standards in their state, especially if there are any mandatory standards. Voluntary standards can and usually should be fundamental to the plan developed.

Setting specific numerical targets for key input and output measures makes most of the key objectives in your plan easily measurable. You can set specific numerical targets for your library by examining the current measures on these factors of all similarly sized libraries in the country.

A brief history of standards

Until 1966, the American Library Association took an active role in setting standards. Since then, they have concentrated on variations on planning and have encouraged libraries to set their own standards. Individual state library agencies assisted by state library associations have taken on the job of setting standards. I believe that ALA should develop new standards for the 21st century based on the models set by England and a number of U.S. states, including Iowa and Wisconsin; however, it is highly unlikely that ALA will heed that advice.

Starting in the 1930s, the Carnegie Corporation spurred the push for standards and wider units of service. Carnegie was disappointed by the failure of individual libraries built with Carnegie grants to garner sufficient support to thrive. The Carnegie Corporation hoped that standards would help. The University of Chicago and Carleton B. Joeckel, among others, began to push ALA in the direction of national standards.

In 1956—the year that Congress enacted federal aid for public libraries—ALA published a compendium of standards for public libraries designed to be used by local boards and governmental officials. The document stated this dictum unequivocally: "Libraries working together, sharing their services and materials, can meet the full needs of their users.

State Public Library Standards

Ala.	www.apls.state.al.us/webpages/pubs/standardsdraft.doc
Alaska	none
Ariz.	none
Ark.	none
Calif.	none
Colo.	www.cde.state.co.us/cdelib/download/pdf/slplstan.pdf
Conn.	ct.webjunction.org/do/DisplayContent?id=6978
Dela.	none
Fla.	dlis.dos.state.fl.us/_move to archivedwebpages/standards/section1.html
Ga.	www.georgialibraries.org/lib/publiclib/standards-final.pdf
Hawaii	none
Idaho	*Standards for Idaho Public Library Services,* 1991
Ill.	www.cyberdriveillinois.com/departments/library/what_we_have/readyref/pdf/serving/ILA_Serving.pdf
Ind.	www.statelib.lib.in.us/www/isl/ldo/pubstan.html
Iowa	www.silo.lib.ia.us/for-ia-libraries/accr-and-standards/In-Service-to-Iowa-4th-Final.pdf
Kans.	skyways.lib.ks.us/KSL/development/standard2000.html
Ky.	www.kdla.ky.gov/libsupport/standards/manual.pdf
La.	www.llaonline.org/sig/public/standards2003.pdf
Maine	www.mainelibraries.org/standards/index.html
Md.	none
Mass.	mblc.state.ma.us/grants/state_aid/policies/
Mich.	*Library Laws Handbook: State Laws Relating to Michigan Libraries,* 2001–2002
Minn.	education.state.mn.us/mde/static/003580.pdf
Miss.	none
Mo.	www.sos.mo.gov/library/libstan.pdf
Mont.	msl.state.mt.us/admin/libstandards.html
Nebr.	www.nlc.state.ne.us/Statistics/Guidelines2004.pdf
Nev.	dmla.clan.lib.nv.us/docs/nsla/lpd/state/
N.H.	www.state.nh.us/nhsl/libstandards/stand2000.html
N.J.	www.njstatelib.org/LDB/Library_Law/lwaid002.php
N.Mex.	www.nmcpr.state.nm.us/nmac/parts/title04/04.005.0002.htm
N.Y.	www.nysl.nysed.gov/libdev/helpful.htm
N.C.	statelibrary.dcr.state.nc.us/ncplda/guidelines.htm
N.Dak.	in process
Ohio	winslo.state.oh.us/services/LPD/standards.html
Okla.	www.odl.state.ok.us/servlibs/l-files/stateaid.htm
Oreg.	olaweb.org/pld/standards.html
Pa.	Title 22 *Pennsylvania Consolidated Statutes,* Sect. 131
R.I.	www.lori.ri.gov/plstandards/default.php
S.C.	www.state.sc.us/scsl/pubs/PLstandards/
S.Dak.	www.usd.edu/sdla/PublicLibs/CA.htm
Tenn.	www.state.tn.us/tsla/lps/minimum standards.pdf
Tex.	www.txla.org/groups/plstand/plstand.html
Utah	library.utah.gov/documents/Standards%202002.doc
Vt.	dol.state.vt.us/gopher_root5/libraries/standards/minstand86.pdf
Va.	www.lva.lib.va.us/whatwedo/ldnd/govadmin/pfle/index.htm
Wash.	none
W.Va.	*West Virginia Library Commission Working Standards Manual,* 1992
Wis.	www.dpi.state.wi.us/dlcl/pld/standard.html
Wyo.	none

5

This cooperative approach on the part of libraries is the most important single recommendation of this document." The revision of the public library standards reiterated this premise and was entitled more precisely, *Minimum Standards for Public Library Systems, 1966.*

By 1980, ALA had abandoned standards in favor of locally defined planning processes. There are library standards for at least 40 states. At last count, 35 of the states' library standards were available on the Web.

Some states do not have library standards, and for most of the states that do, they are voluntary or advisory rather than mandatory. In a few states, however, receipt of state aid is contingent upon meeting the minimum standards outlined by the state. A few other states have authorized standards at the county or regional level as well.

Standards and excellence

Perhaps one of the fundamental reasons for the abandonment of national standards by ALA was the fear that minimum standards would come to be seen as maximums and hold back quality libraries. The output-measures focus epitomized by the 1980 edition of the ALA Planning Process document worried many who feared that catering to the circulation and numbers game diluted and potentially destroyed the public library's responsibility for building quality collections and achieving solid educational objectives. In response to this fear, many states have established varying levels of standards. Minimum standards are established to mean just that—minimums. Beyond these minimums are standards that set the bar at moderate, advanced, and excellent.

Library planners must address this issue head-on and decide what they want their library to be—basic, moderate, enhanced, or excellent. That decision will drive the objectives established for collection development, staffing levels, hours, and all other elements of library services. If the state has no established definitions for these categories, planners should strongly consider using the national comparison measures and percentiles.

Numerical standards

Mandatory minimum standards get some attention, but only a few states have implemented such standards for any but the narrowest of measures, such as certification of library staff and hours of service. At times, state aid or eligibility for grants are tied to meeting these minimum standards, so it is important for library planners to review them carefully where they exist.

Many states have target standards. These involve moving target standards pegged to some proportion of the median measures for a given library population. For example, a state may choose to peg the recommended standard for books per capita to the median for all libraries in the state. This standard will move over time as libraries change collections and the median shifts. Many libraries cannot meet these types of standards because half of all libraries will, by definition, always fall below the median. Such standards are advisory. Libraries seeking improvements often lament the lack of target standards, particularly the numerical standards for collection size, expenditures per capita, and the like; however, those libraries well above the targets fear such targets will hold them back and they push for community-based planning instead of hard standards.

Numerical versus prescriptive library standards

When we think of standards, what most often comes to mind is numerical standards such as the number of books per capita. Equally important are prescriptive standards that enquire about the existence of a challenged-materials policy, bylaws for the board, and internet-acceptable use policies. These standards represent items or processes that are necessary in all public libraries of every size, and effective planners will use such standards to determine if their library has all the necessary items in a plan.

Personnel certification

Quite a number of states have requirements for library staff that usually include the types of initial and continuing education required for directors or other paid staff. Sometimes, as in the case of New York, these requirements are written into state statute. More often they are published in state library documents that are easily obtainable from the state library agency. Find out whether there are such requirements in your state and if your library meets them.

Library certification

A few states, including Iowa and Nebraska, certify libraries. Certification may mean merely the prestige of meeting the grade, or it may include eligibility for state funds or federal grants controlled by the state library agency. In any case, it is important to be aware of these requirements and to know whether or not the library meets the certification criteria.

5

Standards in various states

A total of 40 states have public library standards and all but a handful of these standards are available on the Web. Carefully consider your library in relation to your state's standards, if any. Illinois, Kansas, Oklahoma, Texas, Virginia, and Wisconsin include very specific quantitative or numerical formulas for staffing ratios, collection size, budget levels, recommended technology, and other elements in their standards that might prove helpful if your state lacks standards. State standards are often voluntary documents developed by the state library agency or the state library association, and some are included in state law or administrative rules with the force of law.

Review the current state statutes whenever a planning process is undertaken. States constantly revise laws that affect libraries, and it is easy to drift away from both the letter and spirit of the law unless there are periodic reviews.

Consult the regional library system or state library agency staff on the issues. Often there is a simple checklist that has been developed for use by individual libraries to assure statutory compliance.

Libraries must also follow all legal requirements for public entities in addition to those aimed specifically at libraries. For example, there are open-meeting laws, fair labor standards requirements, and proper bidding procedures for large spending projects. The size and composition of the board and its meeting frequency are usually laid out in statutes, and the legal relationship between the library board and its parent municipality (city, town, city, county, parish, etc.) is most often outlined with some degree of specificity. State laws also deal with the sometimes contentious issues of whether the library board or city council is in charge of hiring and firing, the line items in the budget, or building a library or branch.

States vary in the latitude they allow. When reviewing plans and policies, ask the library's usual legal counsel to review statutes aimed at libraries and public organizations.

SOURCE: Thomas J. Hennen Jr., *Hennen's Public Library Planner* (New York: Neal-Schuman, 2004), pp. 120–125. Reprinted with permission.

Management models for library administration
by A. B. Credaro

CARGO CULT MODEL. Library administration is conducted from a remote location. No one ever sees who is in charge; no one ever knows when funding will arrive, or its magnitude. Everyone is very grateful for the fact that something arrives, but they are not sure what to do with it, or if it has a specific purpose.

Monolith model. One person is in charge of everyone and everything. Inflexible in approach, the administrator hardly ever leaves the office, but when this does occur, others are expected to move out of the way.

Gandhian model. Inspired by the actions of Mahatma Gandhi, the library administrator listens to everyone's "personal issues" and proposals for improvement or change, and serves as office peacemaker. Quietly spoken and philosophical in approach, this person makes management decisions that, to all appearances, have been considered in the light of all available data.

Faux-participative management. The hallmark of this model is the overwhelming number of committees and meetings that are generally conducted outside core working hours (i.e., on your personal time). Agendas may be formal, informal, obscure, or hidden. The library administrator does not take the chair at meetings, but it is shared in rotation through the committee members. Final management decisions are made by the administrator regardless of any discussions, proposals, or options that are considered.

Dispersed management. An organizational diagram shows multiple individuals sharing heirarchical positions. This means that no single person is accountable for disasters, whereas all can share the accolades for anything that actually does work well. The system serves as a retrenchment buffer but prevents any meaningful change, as no real decisions are ever made.

Novocaine model. Administrator needles the library staff until work is conducted in a numbed state. Communication is by barely comprehensible mumbling, and everyone is expected to "be brave."

School library model. The library staff (often consisting of one person) does everything, is accountable to everyone, receives nil recognition for any innovations, and does not appear on any organizational charts.

SOURCE: A. B. Credaro, www.warriorlibrarian.com. Reprinted with permission.

THE UNDERSERVED
CHAPTER SIX

"Any way you look at it, the more we expand libraries,
the less we'll expand prisons. Thanks to my mom and
the Chicago Public Library, I'm a writer now."

—Author Sandra Cisneros, *Denver Post*, April 8, 2005

ETHNIC GROUPS

Library services to Latino youth

by Oralia Garza de Cortés

GIVEN THE OFTEN DISMAL STATE OF AFFAIRS that Latino children and their families find in gaining access to first-rate library services and programs, one wonders if library professionals truly understand the seriousness of the shortcomings. What sort of measures can be put in place to hold administrators accountable for ensuring that they apply democratic principles equally? Unless public libraries begin to change their models and operate differently, Latino children will be condemned to the same inferior services they have received for most of the 20th century. Moreover, a lack of fundamental language development skills in young children, necessary for substantive language acquisition, may well contribute to the development of Latino children as one of the many "post-illiterates," defined by Barry Sanders in his thought-provoking social analysis *A Is for Ox: Violence, Electronic Media, and the Silencing of the Written Word* (Pantheon, 1994), as children dispossessed of "oral and written language."

What do we need to do differently?

We can begin by quantifying and qualifying the information and literacy needs of Latino children. Professionals serving Latino children need the facts that library schools should be substantiating and compiling for us. Where is the research on library use among Latino children? What percentage of Latino children participate in summer reading programs? How many Latino parents know that reading to their child is the single most important activity they can do with and for their child? Where is the proof we can take to city policy makers and funders on why they need to be investing in library programs for children now rather than pouring wasteful monies into juvenile detention programs that provide too little too late? Why is it so difficult for us to prove that becoming good readers may well be a direct result of access to free books and participation in story-hour programs that a child has experienced in our public libraries? As long as library professionals operate in the dark, libraries will continue to do business as usual with no new resources and no creative ways or political will to change current practices.

Latino children need programs, programs, programs! Infant and baby programs, Born to Read Programs, toddler programs, preschool programs, elementary age story-time programs, summer reading programs, and year-round reading programs are all essential to prepare a child for the many challenges of the 21st century. In addition, learning programs such as Hands-On-Science, poetry programs, art programs, multicultural programs, and even holiday programs in both English and Spanish all help to further develop a child's interest and curiosity. Programs are learning opportunities for children that enhance their literacy experiences and help them to develop their social, emotional, and intellectual competencies.

10 Steps for Effective Outreach to the Latino Community
by Ben Ocón

1. *Know your community*
   - Study the demographic statistics of your service area
   - Obtain a copy of the local school district's statistical profile of student enrollment
   - Get acquainted with community leaders (e.g., church, schools, elected officials)
   - Patronize the local Latino-owned businesses (and businesses patronized by Latinos)
2. *Develop your Spanish-language and Latino-oriented collection*
   - Get on the mailing lists of Spanish-language publishers and distributors
   - Become familiar with review sources of Spanish-language materials
   - Involve staff who have Spanish-language proficiency or expertise in multicultural materials
   - Seek input from Latino patrons
3. *Develop your library's services*
   - Identify library services that can be promoted to the Latino community
   - Children's services (e.g., story times, raising readers)
   - Book discussion programs
   - Internet instruction
   - Offer these services in Spanish (if possible)
   - Provide basic library signage in Spanish or in bilingual format
4. *Translate your library's basic library forms and brochures into Spanish*
   - Registration forms
   - Welcome brochures and loan-borrowing privileges
   - Hours of service
5. *Involve fellow staff members in outreach efforts*
   - Create opportunities for staff members to be informed of outreach efforts
   - Seek support from administrators, trustees, and the Friends
   - Support-staff training on service and sensitivity to diverse populations
6. *Market your library's collection/services*
   - In local newspapers (especially the Spanish-language press, radio, and television)
   - Post flyers in Latino businesses and church bulletin boards
   - Distribute information to faculty and students at local schools and PTA functions
   - Display the library's brochures at hospitals, clinics, and day-care centers
7. *Participate in local community events/activities*
   - Events in neighborhood (street festivals, parades, charity runs, activities in parks)
   - School activities held for the community
8. *Make presentations to Latino service organizations and ESL classes*
   - Form community alliances that will facilitate the library's outreach efforts
   - Identify ESL programs in your community; provide each class with an overview of library services
9. *Establish strategic alliances with community organizations*
   - Seek membership in key community organizations (e.g., Latino chamber of commerce)
   - Support special community projects
10. *Utilize technology in outreach efforts*
   - Incorporate technology training in special presentations to the Latino community
   - Facilitate access to Latino-oriented electronic resources and Spanish-language databases/sites
   - Utilize the new technology to improve access by Latinos to the library's resources

SOURCE: Ben Ocón, "Effective Outreach Strategies in the Latino Community," in Salvador Güereña, ed., *Library Services to Latinos: An Anthology* (Jefferson, N.C.: McFarland, 2000), pp. 183–193. Reprinted with permission.

Latino children need outreach services. If Latino children are not coming to the public library, we must find ways to reach them where they are. If there is one lesson that both Pura Belpré and Gabriela Mistral demonstrated, it is that we must take the story and services to the child, no matter if the child is in the rural farms of California, Ohio, or Florida, or the urban jungles of New York, Houston, or Los Angeles.

Latino children need libraries to serve as homework centers. Homework centers are places to get help after school with core subjects such as math and reading. But these homework centers must also be learning centers where students are taught the skills of research that will enable them to become information-literate and skilled investigators and to hone their inquiry skills. The public library must provide that creative space that will allow them to develop their curiosity and discover their talents and interests.

Latino parents need parenting programs in English and Spanish. Parenting programs are needed that provide information and enable parents to synthesize the vast amount of information that will help them to rear their children to be successful students and citizens. Thus, information on child development, early brain development, oral language development and language acquisition, the literacy development of young children, and the vast array of parenting information is essential for success as educated and informed parents.

Latino families need quality learning experiences through well-designed family literacy programs—en inglés y en español. These programs should use children's literature as the center of the curriculum and should serve to model story reading in the home. In addition, programs must provide meaning and context, incorporating cultural programs that go beyond music and dance to include the history of Latinos in that particular community, along with civil rights and immigration history of Latinos as a whole.

Latino children need competent, qualified, bilingual children's librarians and managers. These professionals must be able to communicate with their constituents and provide the best quality services possible; in short, they should meet all the standards and qualifications set out in the ALSC document *Competencies for Librarians Serving Children in Public Libraries.*

These professionally trained bilingual librarians must plan and collaborate with social service agencies, schools, churches, and other neighborhood groups. Moreover, they must be able to manage, conduct, and supervise programs such as Born to Read Programs and community-wide library literacy celebrations such as *Día de los Niños: Día de los Libros,* celebrated on April 30. To do this, they must have the organizational and managerial skills to launch community-wide bilingual reading initiatives that target Latino families. In addition, Latino children need bilingual community outreach workers who can act as library assistants, working closely with bilingual librarians.

Latino children need to view public libraries as friendly, useful places. They need to know how a library is organized, what the rules are, how to find information in a timely fashion, and how to use their research skills. They also need to learn to use online services effectively. By taking full advantage of the public library, Latino children can become better information seekers, readers, students, and citizens.

Latino children need advocates in the public library. Latino families need library professionals who are less proprietary and more sympathetic to local needs. These librarians need to remind themselves of their role as public servants. Library professionals must be willing to create new models and community partnerships that incorporate the needs of the community with best practices. This will entail rethinking, redesigning, and transforming local branch libraries from empty reading rooms into learning laboratories, much like models such as The Family Place.

Latino children and their families need comprehensive programs. Child development funders must be convinced that library services and programs are as critical to the future of Latino children as are Head Start programs, WIC programs, and other early child-care intervention programs. Programs such as those funded by the Lila Wallace–Readers' Digest Fund may well be the last, best hope for branches in underserved Latino communities.

As public services librarians we must be willing to challenge systems and institutions, our own public libraries included, that treat poor people as second-class citizens. If we have learned anything in this century it is that as an institution, we have not done a very good job of serving the needs of Spanish-speaking children and their families. Let us resolve that the little *Pepes* being born today are not left out of the public library literacy equation. In the 21st century, we must move beyond equal access and focus on quality and equal services for all children so that they achieve their fullest potential and blossom into bright, hopeful, healthy, intellectual, responsible, and productive citizens.

SOURCE: Oralia Garza de Cortés, "Give Them What They Need," in Barbara Immroth and Kathleen de la Peña McCook, eds., *Library Services to Youth of Hispanic Heritage* (Jefferson, N.C.: McFarland, 2000), pp. 89–97. Reprinted with permission of the author.

Communicating with Asian-language speakers

edited by Shelly G. Keller

6

WHILE THERE ARE MANY SHARED linguistic characteristics among Asian-language speakers, there are many differences. Depending on the country or nation of origin, an Asian-language speaker's pronunciation may be nasal or clipped, linguistic mannerisms may appear blunt, or gestures animated. Each cultural linguistics specialization reveals a combination of cultural influences, including the importance of the homeland. Other factors stem from influences of other groups such as the French in Southeast Asia, the Japanese in Korea and mainland China, the British in India, and the Spanish in the Philippines.

Of primary importance to providing good customer-centered library service is a staff that responds to the linguistic and cultural needs of the community. To that end, the staff should be trained in cultural and linguistic expectations and patron preferences. Staff members can learn common everyday phrases to make patrons feel welcome and open to learning about the library.

Recruitment, mentoring, and retention of a multilingual staff at all levels for public-service work are all factors essential to delivering effective library service to Asian-language speakers. This approach helps the library build a network of informed, concerned library staff members who exhibit behavior culturally appropriate to the outreach needs of the community. A multicultural staff can help colleagues understand cultural specifics, traditions, and taboos.

Often, library policies are in conflict with the expectations of many Asian cultures. These policies can include overdue books and subsequent fines or fees, and censorship of materials available to minors. To deliver effective service, the library must work with Asian-language-speaking patrons within their limits of understanding, respecting individual values while maintaining the library's professional standards. Flexibility in reaching a common understanding is the key to good communication.

Recommendations

1. The concept of the public library in America is new to many Asian-language-speaking immigrants. This is important when communicating with new patrons of Asian descent. To help them become familiar with the public library, translate all library brochures into the appropriate Asian languages to help them become acquainted with how library service works. Be sure to include information about loan period, fees, fines, any interlibrary loan charges, etc.

2. Promote the library's Asian-language collection by distributing brochures in Asian communities where people gather. Make sure the library staff is available to help Asian-language speakers become acquainted with the concept of the public library.

3. Give patrons the benefit of the doubt when dealing with problems. A patron can be wrong without being dishonest. There can never be too much understanding in providing service to people of other cultures.

4. While it is important to help people of other cultures understand the library's rules and policies, staff members should avoid reprimanding Asian-language-speaking patrons publicly.

5. Many behaviors are culturally based. Making eye contact and smiling are two examples of how culture affects behavior. Some Asians do not make eye contact because in their culture it is disrespectful. When Asian patrons smile and nod their heads, it is usually done to be polite, and does not necessarily mean they agree or understand what you are saying. Smiling does not come easily to some Asians. For example, in the deeply embedded Confucian values of Korean culture, a serious dignified look is more acceptable than a smile. On the other hand, a Vietnamese patron might smile for any number of reasons, i.e., lack of understanding, agreeing, or disagreeing but being polite. The staff should not conclude that an unsmiling patron is unhappy or disapproving.

6. Staff members can learn a few simple words and phrases to facilitate service. These can include welcoming phrases, common library terms, terms of respect, and library classification numbers.

7. There is one simple, surefire way to get the names of Asian-language speakers correctly: Ask them about their personal preferences. This is especially important with new immigrants, because some may still list their names in the style of their homelands (often with the family name listed first), while others may have already adopted American usages (family name listed last). Most Asian-Pacific Americans who have been in this country for a while will list their names in the American style—but it is important to always ask about preferences.

8. Physical contact is perceived differently from culture to culture. Physical contact is not necessarily a form of affection, endearment, or familiarity

in Asian cultures. Initiating physical contact with a patron is sometimes inappropriate. A nod or a smile goes further than a handshake or a pat on the back. Learn what is acceptable before making physical contact.

9. Taking photographs of someone from an Asian culture can be misconstrued because some cultures or individuals view photographs as too intrusive or as undesirable exposure. When taking photos to document programming and services, be sure to ask permission.

10. When a library staff person who speaks an Asian language is not available, library staff may ask a patron who speaks the same Asian language to help translate.

11. When the staff members cannot communicate in the spoken language, they can sometimes communicate through the written word.

12. Libraries can create a welcoming environment and enhance communication with non-English-speaking patrons by providing appropriately translated signage, pathfinders, fliers, forms, and instructional materials. It is also helpful to create a "community information center" by providing translations of voter registration and other information as well as information on community-based organizations.

13. Hiring bilingual staff members is the ultimate commitment a library can make to serving Asian-language speakers. Providing even a little language training to staff members willing to learn can also have a tremendous impact on how well a library serves its Asian-language-speaking patrons.

SOURCE: Shelly G. Keller, ed., *Harmony in Diversity: Recommendations for Effective Library Service to Asian Language Speakers* (Sacramento: California State Library, 1998), pp. 16–18. Reprinted with permission.

6

Indigenous peoples and information technology

by Loriene Roy and Antony Cherian

INDIAN COUNTRY IS HOME TO CHALLENGES and innovations in information technology. Challenges are seen in providing access to even basic technologies. According to a 1995 U.S. census survey, 53% of Native homes do not have a telephone. On the Pine Ridge Reservation, 39% of the homes lack electricity, and many do not have indoor plumbing.

In 1995, the U.S. Congress issued a report on telecommunications in Indian country. It stated, "Absent some kind of policy interventions, Native Americans are unlikely to catch up with and probably will fall further behind the majority society with respect to telecommunications," U.S. Office of Technology Assessment, *Telecommunications Technology and Native Americans: Opportunities and Challenges,* OTA-ITC-621 (Washington, D.C.: U.S. Government Printing Office, August 1995).

Yet indigenous communities in the United States are using information technology in a variety of efforts. Key among these is Native language revitalization. The health of its language may be the greatest indicator of the well-being of an indigenous culture. Once, between 300 and 600 indigenous languages were spoken in North America. Now, only 211 languages are spoken, and only 32 of these are spoken by people of all ages.

Much attention is being given to Native language revitalization, due in large part to the passage of the Native American Languages Act of 1990. The act declares, "It is the policy of the United States to preserve, protect, and promote the rights and freedom of Native Americans to use, practice, and develop Native American languages."

Information technology can support language recovery because it reaches many people in a variety of formats. The University of Alaska provided a for-credit distance learning class on Deg Xinag, the Ingalik Athabaskan language spoken in central Alaska. Native speakers conversed with one or two students by telephone for an hour each week. Radio station KTNN has served as the Voice of the Navajo Nation since 1986, providing programming in Navajo that includes the morning livestock report, local and regional news, weather, and the Navajo Word of the Day. The Intertribal Wordpath Society of Oklahoma produces *Wordpath*, a weekly half-hour television show on Indian languages of the state.

The University of Hawaii at Manoa has used electronic discussion lists, the Hawaii Interactive Television System, and collaborative writing software (Daedalus) for communication and content delivery. Students and faculty have also used multimedia to author websites to support Hawaiian language study. Other key organizations and events for language recovery include the Indigenous Language Institute (New Mexico), the annual American Indian Language Development Institute (Arizona), and the Sovereign Nations Preservation Project (Texas).

Tribal community libraries are becoming important partners in language recovery efforts. A Tewa language study group meets in the Santa Clara (New Mexico) Pueblo Community Library. Elders of the Pala Band of Mission Indians in California are available in the library to offer Cupeno language tutoring and to assist in developing Native language curriculum. The tribal community library serving the Wiyot (California) tribe developed a living language website. Other libraries develop and house language collections, including unique oral history materials.

Will technology support tribal sovereignty or contribute to the erosion of Native culture? Craig Howe, an Oglala Sioux, defines tribal sovereignty as consisting of four aspects:

- spatial (geographical or connection to the land)
- social (personal identity)
- spiritual (morality and ethics)
- experiential (ceremony and observance)

Technology alone will not enable a person to lead an indigenous life, but it can be a powerful tool if paired with cultural respect, tribal community ownership, and thoughtful community-centered discussion.

SOURCE: Loriene Roy and Antony Cherian, "Indigenous Peoples and Information Technology," in Robin Osborne, ed., *From Outreach to Equity: Innovative Models of Library Policy and Practice* (Chicago: American Library Association, 2004), pp. 58–60.

Library groups serving the underserved

by Tiffeni Fontno

DIVERSITY IS IN MOTION in the library profession. We are collecting, archiving, organizing, advocating, and reflecting the changes in our world. To encourage and facilitate communication and awareness of our efforts to diversify the profession, it is important to identify and have access to those organizations promoting change.

African American Studies Librarians Section, ALA Association of College and Research Libraries; www.ala.org/ala/acrl/aboutacrl/acrlsections/africanam/afashomepage.htm.

African American Subject Funnel Project, Library of Congress; Dorothy Washington, (765) 494-3093; dwashin2@purdue.edu; www.loc.gov/catdir/pcc/saco/aframerfun.html.

Asian, African, and Middle Eastern Section, ALA Association of College and Research Libraries; www.ala.org/ala/acrl/aboutacrl/acrlsections/aames/aameshomepage.htm.

Committee on Cataloging Asian and African Materials, ALA Association for Library Collections and Technical Services; www.ala.org/ala/alctscontent/catalogingsection/catcommittees/catalogingasiana/catalogingasian.htm.

Ethnic and Multicultural Information Exchange Round Table, American Library Association; www.ala.org/ala/emiert/aboutemiert/aboutemiert.htm.

Instruction for Diverse Populations Committee, ALA Association of College and Research Libraries, Instruction Section; www.ala.org/ala/acrlbucket/is/iscommittees/webpages/idp/index.htm.

Libraries Serving Disadvantaged Persons Section, International Federation of Library Associations and Institutions; www.ifla.org/VII/s9/index.htm.

Libraries Serving Special Populations Section, ALA Association of Specialized and Cooperative Library Agencies; www.ala.org/lsspsTemplate.cfm?Section=LSSPS.

Library Service to People Who Are Deaf or Hard of Hearing Forum, ALA Association of Specialized and Cooperative Library Agencies; www.ala.org/ala/ascla/asclaourassoc/asclasections/lssps/lspdhhf/lspdhhf.htm.

Library Service to the Impaired Elderly Forum, ALA Association of Specialized and Cooperative Library Agencies; www.ala.org/ala/ascla/asclaourassoc/asclasections/lssps/lsief/lsief.htm.

Library Services to Multicultural Populations Section, International Federation of Library Associations and Institutions; www.ifla.org/VII/s32/index.htm.

Library Services to Special Population Children and Their Caregivers, ALA Association for Library Service to Children; www.ala.org/ALSCTemplate.cfm?Section=alsccommrosters&Template=/MembersOnly.cfm&ContentID=22672.

Library Services to the Spanish-Speaking Committee, ALA Reference and User Services Association, Management and Operation User Services Section; www.ala.org/ala/rusa/rusaourassoc/rusasections/mouss/moussection/mousscomm/spanishspeaking/libraryservices.htm.

Middle East Librarians Association, An-Chi Dianu, Library of Congress, RCCD/MENA; president@mela.us; www.mela.us.

6

National Library Service for the Blind and Physically Handicapped, Library of Congress; www.loc.gov/nls/.

Outreach to Young Adults with Special Needs Committee, ALA Young Adult Library Services Association; www.ala.org/ala/yalsa/aboutyalsab/outreachyoung.htm.

Services to Multicultural Populations Committee, ALA Public Library Association; www.ala.org/ala/pla/committeework/servicesmulticultural.htm.

Women's Studies Section, ALA Association of College and Research Libraries; libr.org/WSS/index.html.

SOURCE: Tiffeni Fontno, "Library Diversity Who's Who," *Versed,* March–April 2004, www.ala.org/ala/diversity/versed/versed2004/march2004abc/librarydiversity.htm.

Milestones in African-American library service

by Maurice B. Wheeler and Debbie Johnson-Houston, with Heather Boyd

1816: A school and library are established for African Americans in Wilmington, Delaware.

1828: The Reading Room Society, the first social library for African Americans, opens in Philadelphia.

1831: The Female Literary Society, the first African-American women's social library, is founded in Philadelphia.

1833: The Philadelphia Library Company of Colored Persons is organized as a literary society.

1886: The main library and the first four branches of the Enoch Pratt Free Library open in Baltimore, providing service to users of all races.

1894: North Carolina A&T State University's Bluford Library is founded in Greensboro.

1896: The U.S. Supreme Court decision *Plessy v. Ferguson* establishes the "separate but equal" law that legalizes segregated libraries.

1901: A Carnegie library is built at Tuskegee Institute in Alabama.

1902: A black patron is featured in a stereo view of the Boston Public Library.

1903: The Cossitt Library of Memphis, Tennessee, provides books and a librarian for a collection to be housed in the LeMoyne Institute for African-American students.

1904: Carnegie library buildings begin construction at Alabama A&M, Atlanta University, Benedict College, Talladega College, and Wilberforce University.

1904: In Henderson, Kentucky, a one-room annex opens August 1 at the rear of the Eighth Street Colored School to serve as a library—the first structure built specifically to offer public library service to African Americans.

1905: A branch of the Rosenberg Library in Galveston, Texas, opens in an addition to Central High School in January to serve as a public library for African Americans.

1905: The Brevard Street Library for Negroes opens in Charlotte as an independent institution. It is the first public library for blacks in North Carolina.

1905: The Western Colored Branch Library of the Louisville (Ky.) Free Public Library, the first branch of a public library system to offer service exclusively to African Americans, opens September 1 in three rooms of a private residence.

1905: Carnegie libraries are established at Cheyney State Teacher's College, Johnson C. Smith University, Livingston College, and Fisk University.

1906: A Carnegie library is erected at Wiley College in Marshall, Texas.

1907: Carnegie libraries begin construction at Howard University and Knoxville College.

1908: Louisville's Western Colored Branch Library relocates to a new building paid for by Carnegie.

Louisville, Kentucky
Western Branch Library

1910: James H. Gregory of Marblehead, Massachusetts, funds a traveling library service for southern blacks, known as the Marblehead libraries, that is administered by Atlanta University.

1914: The Eastern Colored Branch of the Louisville Free Library opens, making Louisville the first city to have two branch libraries that offer service to African Americans.

1914: Howard University's Moorland-Spingarn Research Center has its origins in a gift of 3,000 items from the Rev. Jesse E. Moorland.

1921: The first meeting of ALA's Work with Negroes Round Table is held.

1923: Bibliotherapy pioneer Sadie Peterson Delaney establishes a library in the Veterans Hospital in Tuskegee, Alabama.

1926: The Schomburg Center for Research in Black Culture begins when the personal collection of black scholar Arturo Alfonso Schomburg is added to New York Public Library's Division of Negro Literature.

1926: Eastern Baptist Theological Seminary Library is founded in Philadelphia.

1926: Louisville Free Public Library Director George T. Settle reads a paper on the "Status of Work with Negroes" at the Fourth Biennial Conference of the Southeastern Library Association.

1927: The first Negro Library Conference is held at the Hampton Institute Library School in Virginia, March 15–18.

1928: The West Virginia Supreme Court rules that Charleston libraries cannot exclude black patrons since, as taxpayers, they are equally entitled to library service.

1929: Julius Rosenwald, a merchant and philanthropist, helps fund libraries in 13 southern states to be used in both urban and rural areas, regardless of race.

1932: The first Faith Cabin Library opens in Saluda County, South Carolina.

1932: Vivian G. Harsh, Chicago Public Library's first black librarian, establishes a research collection of African-American history and literature that is now housed at CPL's Carter G. Woodson Regional Library.

1932: Howard University School of Divinity Library is founded.

1935: Kennedy-King College Library opens in Chicago as Woodrow Wilson Junior College Library.

1941: Yale University announces the acquisition of the James Weldon Johnson Collection of African-American writers and artists.

1954: *Brown v. Board of Education* Supreme Court decision declares "separate but equal" facilities based solely on race unconstitutional.

1956: ALA holds its first integrated annual conference in Miami Beach after years of avoiding the South as a meeting place due to racial segregation.

1960: The first library sit-in is held in Petersburg, Virginia, resulting in the arrest of 11 students for trespassing.

6

Danville (Va.) Public Library

1960: The Danville (Va.) Public Library reopens in September on a trial basis with no tables and chairs in its reading room in order to allow for gradual integration. A local court had ordered the library closed after five blacks were denied entry.

1961: ALA amends the Library Bill of Rights to support "the rights of an individual to the use of a library should not be denied or abridged because of his race, religion, national origins, or political views."

1962: In response to a number of library sit-ins, the Carnegie Library in Albany, Georgia, closes in August, but opens to blacks for the first time in March 1963 after 1,600 whites sign a petition asking the library to integrate its services.

1963: While trying to apply for library cards September 15 at the all-white public library in Anniston, Alabama, two young ministers are attacked by an angry mob.

1964: Twenty-five Freedom Libraries are established throughout Mississippi by a group of librarian volunteers in the civil rights movement.

1966: In *Brown v. Louisiana,* the U.S. Supreme Court rules that five African-American demonstrators arrested during a 1964 sit-in at the Audubon Regional Library in Clinton, Louisiana, should not be charged with disturbing the peace. It is the only library segregation case to be argued in the U.S. Supreme Court.

1969: The Cooperative College Library Center, the first consortium of black academic libraries, opens in Atlanta.

1970: The Black Caucus of the American Library Association is formed at the ALA Midwinter Meeting in Chicago "to mobilize the power necessary to ensure that the fullest and most relevant library service is made available to black people."

1972: The Martin Luther King Memorial Library opens in Washington, replacing the old District of Columbia Central Public Library.

1976: Clara Stanton Jones is inaugurated as ALA's first African-American president and the association adopts a "Resolution on Racism and Sexism Awareness."

1977: The Intellectual Freedom Committee recommends to ALA's Executive Board that the resolution be rescinded, but President Clara Stanton Jones demands that the fight against racism and sexism in librarianship be upheld. The resolution stands.

1994: The Auburn Avenue Research Library on African-American Culture and History opens as a special branch of the Atlanta-Fulton County Public Library System.

1999: The Vivian G. Harsh Research Collection of Afro-American History and Literature, the largest collection of its kind in the Midwest, opens as an expanded wing of Chicago Public Library's Woodson Regional Library.

2002: The African-American Research Library and Cultural Center opens as a branch of the Broward County Libraries in Fort Lauderdale, Florida.

2003: The Blair-Caldwell African American Research Library opens as part of the Denver Public Library system.

SOURCE: Maurice Wheeler and Debbie Johnson-Houston, "A Brief History of Library Service to African Americans," *American Libraries* 35 (February 2004): 42–45.

PEOPLE WITH DISABILITIES

Library services for people with disabilities

by the ALA Association of Specialized and Cooperative Library Agencies

THE AMERICAN LIBRARY ASSOCIATION RECOGNIZES that people with disabilities are a large and neglected minority in the community and are severely underrepresented in the library profession. Disabilities cause many personal challenges. In addition, many people with disabilities face economic inequity, illiteracy, cultural isolation, and discrimination in education, employment, and a broad range of societal activities.

Libraries play a catalytic role in the lives of people with disabilities by facilitating their full participation in society. Libraries should use strategies based upon the principles of universal design to ensure that library policy, resources, and services meet the needs of all people.

ALA, through its divisions, offices, and units, and through collaborations with outside associations and agencies, is dedicated to eradicating inequities and improving attitudes toward, and services and opportunities for, people with disabilities.

For the purposes of this policy, "must" means "mandated by law and/or within ALA's control" and "should" means "it is strongly recommended that libraries make every effort to . . . "

The scope of disability law

Providing equitable access for persons with disabilities to library facilities and services is required by Section 504 of the Rehabilitation Act of 1973, applicable state and local statutes, and the Americans with Disabilities Act of 1990 (ADA). The ADA is the civil rights law affecting more Americans than any other. It was created to eliminate discrimination in many areas, including access to private and public services, employment, transportation, and communication. Most libraries are covered by the ADA's Title I (Employment), Title II (Government Programs and Services) and Title III (Public Accommodations). Most libraries are also obligated under Section 504, and some have responsibilities under Section 508 and other laws as well.

Library services

Libraries must not discriminate against individuals with disabilities and shall ensure that individuals with disabilities have equal access to library resources. To ensure such access, libraries may provide individuals with disabilities with services such as extended loan periods, waived late fines, extended reserve periods, library cards for proxies, books by mail, reference services by fax or email, home delivery service, remote access to the OPAC, remote electronic access to library resources, volunteer readers in the library, volunteer technology assistants in the library, American Sign Language (ASL) interpreter or real-time captioning at library programs, and radio reading services.

Libraries should include persons with disabilities as participants in the planning, implementing, and evaluating of library services, programs, and facilities.

Facilities

The ADA requires that both architectural barriers in existing facilities and communication barriers that are structural in nature be removed as long as such removal is "readily achievable" (i.e., easily accomplished and able to be carried out without much difficulty or expense).

The ADA regulations specify the following examples of reasonable structural modifications: accessible parking, clear paths of travel to and throughout the facility, entrances with adequate, clear openings or automatic doors, handrails, ramps and elevators, accessible tables and public service desks, and accessible public conveniences such as restrooms, drinking fountains, public telephones, and TTYs. Other reasonable modifications may include visible alarms in rest rooms and general usage areas and signs that have Braille and easily visible character size, font, contrast, and finish.

One way to accommodate barriers to communication, as listed in the ADA regulations, is to make print materials available in alternative formats such as large type, audio recording, Braille, and electronic formats. Other reasonable modifications to communications may include providing an interpreter or real-time captioning services for public programs and reference services through TTY or other alternative methods. The ADA requires that modifications to communications must be provided as long as they are "reasonable," do not "fundamentally alter" the nature of the goods or services offered by the library, or result in an "undue burden" on the library.

Collections

Library materials must be accessible to all patrons including people with disabilities. Materials must be available to individuals with disabilities in a variety of formats and with accommodations, as long as the modified formats and accommodations are "reasonable," do not "fundamentally alter" the library's services, and do not place an "undue burden" on the library. Examples of accommodations include assistive technology, auxiliary devices, and physical assistance.

Within the framework of the library's mission and collection policies, public, school, and academic library collections should include materials with accurate and up-to-date information on the spectrum of disabilities, disability issues, and services for people with disabilities, their families, and other concerned persons. Depending on the community being served, libraries may include related medical, health, and mental health information and information on legal rights, accommodations, and employment opportunities.

Assistive technology

Well-planned technological solutions and access points, based on the concepts of universal design, are essential for effective use of information and other library services by all people. Libraries should work with people with disabilities, agencies, organizations, and vendors to integrate assistive technology into their facilities and services to meet the needs of people with a broad range of disabilities, including learning, mobility, sensory, and developmental disabilities. Library staff should be aware of how available technologies address disabilities and know how to assist all users with library technology.

Employment

ALA must work with employers in the public and private sectors to recruit people with disabilities into the library profession, first into library schools, and then into employment at all levels within the profession.

Libraries must provide reasonable accommodations for qualified individuals with disabilities unless the library can show that the accommodations would impose an "undue hardship" on its operations. Libraries must also ensure that their policies and procedures are consistent with the ADA and other laws.

Library education, training, professional development

All graduate programs in library and information studies should require students to learn about accessibility issues, assistive technology, the needs of people with disabilities both as users and employees, and laws applicable to the rights of people with disabilities as they impact library services.

Libraries should provide training opportunities for all library employees and volunteers in order to sensitize them to issues affecting people with disabilities and to teach effective techniques for providing services for users with disabilities and for working with colleagues with disabilities.

ALA conferences

ALA conferences held at facilities that are "public accommodations" (e.g., hotels and convention centers) must be accessible to participants with disabilities.

The association and its staff, members, exhibitors, and hospitality industry agents must consider the needs of conference participants with disabilities in the selection, planning, and layout of all conference facilities, especially meeting rooms and exhibit areas. ALA Conference Services Office and division offices offering conferences must make every effort to provide accessible accommodations as requested by individuals with special needs, or alternative accessible arrangements must be made.

ALA publications and communications

All ALA publications, including books, journals, and correspondence, must be available in alternative formats including electronic text. The ALA website must conform to the currently accepted guidelines for accessibility, such as those issued by the World Wide Web Consortium.

SOURCE: ALA Association of Specialized and Cooperative Library Agencies, *Library Services for People with Disabilities Policy* (Chicago: American Library Association, 2001), www.ala.org/ala/ascla/asclaissues/libraryservices.htm.

GENDER ISSUES

Serving gay and lesbian teens
by Darla Linville

AS YOUNG ADULT LIBRARIANS, we hope that outcast, questioning, confused teens will find their way to the library, will find it a safe place, and will find the librarian impartial and helpful. We don't reach out to lesbian, gay, bisexual, transgendered, and queer and questioning (LGBTQ) teens as much as we could, at times because they are an almost invisible group, and at times because we don't want to single them out from the crowd or make assumptions about them that they might not yet be making about themselves. In our own communities, we might not know any gay teens, we might find that the books are checked out but never know who takes them, or we might find gay books hidden among the poetry books where someone has been surreptitiously reading them. We know statistically that queer youth must be there, but we might not know how best to serve them.

Note on terminology: Many people about my age (33) and younger use the word "queer" to describe themselves as "other than the white-picket-fence variety." We mean this word as an affirming and positive label, not in a derogatory sense. Queer is still considered a slur by some people, though. Here I use it interchangeably with gay and LGBTQ to describe a range of sexualities on the spectrum of human sexuality outside what is considered heterosexual or straight.

Offering vital materials and information

Real stories about real teens. Materials that will satisfy the requirements of gay teen readers include biographies of gay people, collections of coming-out stories, and photo-essay books, such as *The Shared Heart,* by Adam Mastoon (Morrow/

Avon, 1997), that profile young people with pictures and their stories. *In Your Face,* by Mary Gray (Haworth, 2003), is also a wonderful collection of real stories about real teens from all over the country talking about their home situations, how it is to grow up gay where they are, how they came to understand that they were gay, and what they are doing to reveal or hide their sexuality. *Love Makes a Family,* by Gigi Kaeser (University of Massachusetts, 1999), is a portrait of adults living together and feeling proud about being gay and raising kids. Kevin Jennings's books talk about coming out during school years and coming out of it alive, and Eric Marcus answers the basic questions that everyone has about queer people. These books also examine, via the stories of these individuals, what it means to be gay and how it changes or doesn't change a person's life. *They* reassure their readers that queer people are normal people.

Historical gay figures. Young people also benefit by knowing which famous people from history were gay. Many biographies written for teens skip over the fact that a famous historical person was gay or was married with lovers of the same sex. This practice is a disservice to young people, who need to know that queer people have always existed and that they also have always acted upon their desires. The Knitting Circle (myweb.lsbu.ac.uk/~stafflag/people.html) contains an alphabetical list of historical figures who, at least by some historical account, lived a queer life. This and other useful websites can be found by accessing the Library Q (library.cudenver.edu/libq/), a website with a reference shelf that contains wonderful resources for librarians. Although this resource has not been updated in a few years and some of the links are dead, the ones that remain contain a wealth of queer informa-

Oscar Wilde

tion. Teens need to hear what kinds of lives gay people had in other times, and how the expectations that we have about sexuality have changed. As librarians, we need to know which biographies tell about the real life of the person, letting the young queer person know that his existence has a history, too.

Community information. Libraries can help teens connect with local information, groups, and activism information, too. Again, one way is through the books in your collections. In a 2003 book, *GLBTQ: The Survival Guide for Queer and Questioning Teens,* author Kelly Huegel (Free Spirit, 2003) covers all the topics necessary to get anyone started on understanding identity. It has the most significant section on transgender teens in any book available, with a thorough resources section listing national organizations where teens can connect with others. This and other similar books, such as *Free Your Mind: The Book for Gay, Lesbian and Bisexual Youth and Their Allies,* by Ellen Bass and Kate Kaufman (HarperPerennial, 1996), are full of information as well as reliable connections for teens striking out on the internet. Libraries can also post flyers for local queer youth group meetings and LGBTQ centers (if your community has one), and make gay newspapers and magazines available.

Sexuality information. Elsewhere in the nonfiction collection are the teen sex and dating books. Find out which ones discuss gay teens equally with straight teens. One that I like is *Changing Bodies, Changing Lives,* by Ruth Bell (Random House, 1980). Know which ones talk frankly about gay sex, a very common question. Before they want to do it, many teens want to know what "it" is. They want to fantasize about it and see if they can imagine themselves doing it. There are not many good movie, television, fiction, or magazine representations, and they need some details. Ideally, libraries will be able to offer teens some images of gay sex that do not come from pornography distributors.

Making information accessible

Where are gay and lesbian materials? The teens that I surveyed loved the library. The focus groups and survey participants were self-selected and therefore very positive about using the library. Even within this library-happy group, however, I got some disturbing answers. Some teens

felt that the gay books were hidden in the library, as compared to a bookstore, for example, because there are no signs labeling a section as "Gay and Lesbian." They don't see displays, even though some branches have displays, especially for Pride Month. They note that the gay books say they are checked in but are often missing from the shelves, and don't get replaced when they disappear. The survey asked what teens were unable to find in the library. Answers included lesbian novels, current gay fiction, list of community groups for my community, disabled rights and empowerment, trans issues of all types, how to tell if someone is gay, famous gay people and gay people in history, and local gay news and events. These answers might mean that the library doesn't have these items or perhaps just that teens were unable to locate them. It certainly means that libraries need to do a better job of making queer resources visible.

Is it safe to ask? We can make the library a safe, authoritative, confidential, and accessible place for teens to do the information-gathering part of their search for sexuality and identity. In my research, many teens expressed some level of discomfort, fear, or reluctance to ask questions in the library. I hope that we can improve these statistics. When I asked my focus groups what would make them feel more comfortable, they suggested that "if you got different people to work, of different sexualities, . . . and they should wear a sign on their nametags . . . like a rainbow or a triangle, something that gives them away. Maybe they wear corduroy pants. Then you could find out the gay people who work there." Librarians have the power in the library to make the information available or to hide it, to make teens feel welcome or to make them feel unwanted. Even if librarians feel nervous talking or thinking about queerness, we must remember that searching young people are much more nervous than we are. We are the ones who can make them comfortable in our space.

What about labeling materials? In each of my focus groups, I asked teens about labeling books—especially fiction books—that contain queer content. The answers were not simple. Some teens relished having all the gay books in one section, both fiction and nonfiction, so they are easy to find, as in the bookstore. Some liked the idea of putting stickers (rainbows or triangles) on the spines of books that contain gay characters, so they are as easy to spot as science fiction. Others felt that each of these solutions would stick the label on their foreheads, pointing out to other teens that they are gay. A compromise that many teens liked was stickering one copy of the book and having other copies available without the sticker. Then they could easily browse the shelves to find the gay books, but wouldn't have to take out the copy with the glaring, "outing" sticker.

Will being seen with gay books be embarrassing? Also very important is the way that teens are treated when they want to take those books out of the library. If, as happened to one young man in my focus group, they go to the library to check out a book and the clerk retrieves the book from the shelf, laughs at the title with a colleague, and then doesn't look at the young person when checking it out, they will not feel welcome or safe at the library. One girl mentioned that she felt judged just by being a youth in the library. Many were comfortable when looking for books by themselves, but a few felt scared to approach the librarian with a question about sexuality. One person responded, "[My community] is closed-minded so I get afraid to ask questions."

What materials are available? Finally, it is important to make sure that everyone working on the information or reference desk knows how to find these resources. We who read gay teen fiction must make booklists of titles and authors. Find out which ones the library owns. Post the list where people can find it. Make a bookmark. Update it regularly, especially if the catalog doesn't include subject headings for fiction. Remember the short story collections. We have important work to do for all our readers, perhaps, and especially for the queer youth population, by highlighting the new books available in the genre, giving them lists of classics, and making sure that we can answer their questions and point them to reliable online sources, too.

About one quarter of the survey respondents said that they don't read gay fiction. For the rest, gay teen fiction is a staple in their reading diet. Most could list the books that they had read and loved. Teens want to see a new, broad selection of gay fiction in their local public library, not just the central library. Most libraries can fill patron requests from other branches, but teens want *their own branch* to have at least some of those books.

What do gay teens want to know when they walk into a library? They want to know that we know that gay people live in every neighborhood, not just in that gay neighborhood over there. And they want to know that we welcome queer people to the library.

SOURCE: Darla Linville, "Beyond Picket Fences: What Gay/Queer/LGBTQ Teens Want from the Library," *Voice of Youth Advocates* 27 (August 2004): 183–186. Reprinted with permission.

OLDER ADULTS

Serving seniors
by Celia Hales Mabry

6

THE NUMBER OF SENIORS hitting our reference desks is likely to grow in the coming years, as aging baby boomers—75 million of them, born between 1946 and 1964—move into the senior demographic of 55 and over. While we as professionals have the capability to serve people of any age with courtesy and aplomb, a few distinctive traits can make serving older adults a challenge.

Seniors fall into a wide age span, making them the most diverse group of individuals in our culture; they are also most prone to be stereotyped and targets of ageism by younger people. Moreover, the elders themselves—especially health-conscious boomers—may resist any attempts to pigeonhole them as aging. Our culture doesn't respect seniors to the extent that many others do, and this calls for our understanding of what seniors face in their daily interactions.

What is the reference staff to do? What do we need to keep in mind when interviewing seniors at the reference desk? The following list, prepared in consultation with practicing reference librarians and health professionals specializing in aging, can help smooth the way for the increased numbers of seniors soon to crowd our doorsteps.

Trust your instincts. Our senior patrons are, by definition, almost always older than we are, and except for comparing them to our parents or grandparents, we may not have enough life experience to form an accurate first impression. You often can choose the right words by letting your inner sense inform your response to a question. With seniors, the right tone in a reference interview goes a long way.

Listen attentively. This is a cardinal rule in life as well as reference work, but how many of us always follow it? "You have to hear them before you can help them," explains Dr. Robert L. Kane of the University of Minnesota School of Public Health, describing his bedside manner with older adults. "It is not even enough that you do hear them. They have to believe that you are listening." At the reference desk, we must listen to a senior's question without too quickly following up with one of our own. Kane's cogent advice reminds us of the overwhelming value of establishing rapport. While we aim to do this with patrons of any age, listening is especially important when dealing with such a wide range of individuals who have more life experience than we do.

Be patient. Seniors often move more slowly than we do—not necessarily from any disability, but as a normal accompaniment to the slower reaction times that come with aging. There is, of course, great variability among seniors as to the degree they are affected; those who exercise regularly can perform many tasks as well as young people. In our own too-fast-paced world, however, we must remember to adjust our responses to match the pace of those who *do* move more slowly.

Make no assumptions. Seniors who come to the reference desk are like all others who approach us; they temporarily need our help, and the mind behind their question may be very keen indeed. "Try not to judge someone approaching you by how frail or wizened they appear," cautions Karen S. Feldt of the University of Minnesota School of Nursing. "I'm always wonderfully surprised by the life experiences and perceptive questions of this population." Verbal abilities, in fact, remain stable until one is quite advanced in years, and life experience frequently has been shown to more than make up for any memory decline in older adults.

Don't embarrass. Between one-fourth to one-half of seniors, depending on age and gender, experience some hearing loss. When you face a patron with a hearing problem, don't shout, but instead speak more distinctly. Make these and other accommodations as unobtrusively as possible, and the senior will (perhaps silently) thank you.

Show respect. Terri Summey, associate professor at Emporia (Kans.) State University's William Allen White Library, described an encounter with a senior that followed a television documentary on syphilis. The patron was hesitant to speak aloud the name of the venereal disease, couching her information request in such general terms that Summey had to use all her skill to pinpoint the real question. Respecting the reticence of some seniors to articulate in language what they find socially unacceptable is a necessary part of showing respect for age and cultural differences.

Go the extra mile. A percentage of seniors need special help because of disabilities. Perquimans County (N.C.) Librarian Jeri Oilman offers "shopping for Betty": She borrows audiobooks for a vision-impaired patron named Betty from other libraries "since our collection isn't nearly large enough to satisfy her."

Appreciate the older adult's wisdom. Creativity in seniors is likely to be at a lifetime high; for example, the peak for history and literature scholars is as late as a person's 60s. Moreover, senior patrons are often returning scholars—a welcome boon to librarians.

Amanda Izenstark, reference and instruction lecturer at the University of Rhode Island Library, reports, "I've found older adults have the patience to actually *do* the research, not just look for a few full-text articles that they can print out."

Enjoy your work! When we have a moment to relax at the reference desk, our older-adult patrons may delight us. Sophie Brookover, youth services librarian at the Mount Laurel (N.J.) Library, gives one example: "On the afternoon of New Year's Eve, I was working with an older patron who wanted to buy the December 2002 issue of *Gourmet*, but couldn't find a single copy at any of the local bookstores. . . . While I waited on hold with the magazine's subscription offices to find out if any copies of the issue were still available for individual purchase, the patron complimented me on my (faux) pearl necklace, sparking a lively discussion about where to find the best costume jewelry at the best prices. We agreed that thrift shops and church rummage sales are tops. The patron left with the information she needed to place an order, and I was delighted that my $2 necklace had passed muster."

All too often we are unnecessarily serious about our work, our lives, our *everything*. Senior patrons can remind us that in life, as in reference work, appreciating the interaction is sometimes very nearly all that is truly important.

From the oldest baby boomer (age 60) to the current most senior adult (85+), seniors defy generalization. I recommend the utmost sensitivity to their individuality, and perhaps also the golden rule: Do unto others as you would have them do unto you. Certainly this rule is among the hardest to apply consistently, but, oh, the warm feelings we reference librarians will invite and the satisfied senior patrons we will have when we do!

SOURCE: Celia Hales Mabry, "Serving Seniors: Dos and Don'ts at the Desk," *American Libraries* 34 (December 2003): 64–65.

INCARCERATED PERSONS

6

Prison library trends

by Mike Geary

LIBRARY STAFF IS RARELY MENTIONED in the history of libraries in prisons. In contemporary times, though, library staff is omnipresent and often mandated by law. Today's prison library staffs must meet qualifications. A standardized test, the state civil service test for professional librarians, is one way of ensuring that library staff is qualified. One's application must detail minimum qualifications to satisfy the job description. Verification follows administration of the test. Unqualified personnel receive no score. Basically, a master's degree in library science qualifies the applicant. Lesser education credits, along with at least two years' job experience, also qualifies the candidate. Pennsylvania, along with many other states, hires its prison librarians in this way.

Ideally, then, each facility will have a qualified librarian. Larger facilities would have support staff as well. In Pennsylvania's Coal Township facility in

Shamokin, two full-time clerical staff members assist the librarian. In the George W. Hill Correctional Facility in Delaware County the librarian is a paralegal, not a library school graduate. His assistants are trustees. These are usually older prisoners who are better educated and more experienced. They are also serving the last two years of their sentences. This particular facility is a little different than most because the Wackenhut Corporation, a contracted prison service, runs it. Wackenhut provides a paralegal rather than a librarian because of their legal requirement to provide prisoner services. Wackenhut has a number of facilities in 10 U.S. states, Great Britain, Australia, and the Republic of South Africa.

It is logical to wonder if safety and security concerns weigh heavily on librarians who work behind bars. Chris Conboy was the most forthcoming of those interviewed. He said it depends largely on how one carries oneself. Self-confident prison staff members usually do not have problems with the inmates. An alarm system is within reach, and the staff has the power to curtail privileges of hostile inmates. It seems the library is one privilege no one wants to risk losing.

Judith Clark conveyed a routine attitude about safety and security issues. In her 17 years spent at the Bucks County (Pa.) Prison she has not had a specific problem where she has been in danger. It takes into account her occasional suspension of privileges of prisoners who might have overdue books or break library rules in some other way.

Prison librarians also have to work closely with other prison staff. As might be expected, that includes staff involved in education and training. It also includes the prison chaplains, who counsel prisoners about personal and religious problems. Some of the chaplains use a kind of bibliotherapy and work with the library staff to provide specific materials to a needy prisoner. The Wackenhut Corporation facility in Delaware County has a prison chaplain staff of four: two Protestant, one Roman Catholic, and one Muslim. Counseling and legal services often work hand-in-hand. The educational standards are mandated for prisoner release.

Library services

It is important to keep in mind that prison librarians are part of the organization that locks up the prisoners. They are professionals who serve the institution as well as the inmates. Basic beliefs in intellectual freedom, censorship, and public service may all be compromised. Censorship is probably the most onerous. Usually the librarian prides herself or himself on the ability to find information or reading materials at the behest of the needy customer. However, sometimes rules prevent that free flow of information to the incarcerated. For instance, no convicted felon in the state of Pennsylvania has internet access. It is difficult to find any state that guarantees that right to an incarcerated individual.

An example of censorship in prison libraries occurred in South Carolina. Unwelcome media attention about accountability for expenditures caused the director of the department of corrections to remove certain books from the 32 institutional libraries. These "prison classics" were mostly published by Holloway House and contained violence and explicit sex. The director of library services protested but was overruled. He felt that anything that kept the prisoners busy was good for all concerned. Many professional librarians feel it is a step backward in a state system considered to be innovative.

Literacy was an issue in the early history of the prison library movement, and it continues to be important. Trying to acquire a General Education Diploma (GED) is ubiquitous throughout contemporary penology. For Wackenhut prisons, it is a minimum standard to be attained prior to the prisoner's release. Many other prisons present it as an opportunity rather than as a requirement. Even jails provide opportunities for interested short-term prisoners.

Mandated legal services are a focal point in prison library service. Since 1977, when the Supreme Court ruled in *Bounds v. Smith*, state prisons have had to provide legal access through counsel or materials. Forty-seven out of 50 states have ensured that prison libraries have legal materials in-house.

The State of Minnesota has found success in providing legal materials to prisons through different means. It has formed a service called Law Library Service to Prisoners (LLSP). That state-sponsored service provides legal reference services to the incarcerated by sending out "circuit-riding" librarians. Minnesota prisons do not have organic libraries. Instead, they depend on public and civilian facilities to provide services to them as an outreach service.

Asked to estimate their time spent doing legal reference, one librarian answered that one whole day per week plus maybe 15% of other days was devoted to legal reference service, while another said that it comprised most of his time spent working. Conboy also detailed the online legal materials available to prisoners. Inmate library staff help other prisoners with these materials. These online materials are not connected to the internet. Minnesotan librarians take a slightly different approach to their legal research services. It is not confined to the boundaries of prison walls. They are allowed an internet connection at the location of their headquarters or wherever they are doing their work. The prisoners receive only the results of the research and do not participate or get to touch the materials themselves.

David Wilhelmus discusses mandated legal services to prisoners in the state of Indiana in the March 1999 issue of the *Journal of Academic Librarianship*. He identifies a new emphasis in these libraries: developing collections to support academic curricula taking place in the prison environment. As director of a Martin University program extended to the inmates of the Indiana Women's Prison, his concern is that materials there support his educational efforts. Wilhelmus extends the discussion to statistical returns from other prison educational programs and stresses the need for them to integrate their efforts for support to educational and rehabilitative programs at various levels. He identifies this correctly as collection development.

Wilhelmus also resurrects a unique idea presented by Charles Perrine in 1955 that took recreational reading to a new height. The idea is that the prison library must inculcate culture in the incarcerated. The library must be savior, uplifter, and the means of rehabilitation. This may be the most original and viscerally appealing idea discussed in library service roles.

Recreational reading is the most obvious role, besides legal research, that a prison library offers inmates. Reading dispels the dismal daily drudgery of doors dogged down tight. In the daily life of prisoners, anything that allows a mental escape or reduces conflict and violence is a good thing.

At the Coal Township, Pa., facility, James Lindberg spends two afternoons a week at the restricted facility for more serious offenders. On those afternoons he takes the prison bookmobile service for their recreational reading. The main prison population has access to the library on a scheduled walk-in basis.

At some facilities prisoners participate in special projects. For several years, the Bucks County Prison librarian, Judith Clark, has headed a project that produces Braille educational materials for public education. She works in partnership with a local Lions Club. This service organization has traditionally worked in areas that involve the blind and visually handicapped. The local club there buys the necessary materials and conveys them to the prison. The librarian then oversees inmate production of scripted materials for public education use. With a project like this, staff training becomes an issue. The Braille project is one of the very few technical jobs available to inmates. Clark tries to always have three inmates involved with production on a full-time basis. There must be other projects involving prison libraries, although documented sources are not evident now. That old idea of prisoners making license plates is long since passed away, but nothing has really replaced it in the public eye.

SOURCE: Mike Geary, "Trends in Prison Library Service," *Bookmobile and Outreach Services* 6, no. 1 (2003): 79–91. Reprinted with permission.

How to implement the ALA Poor People's Policy

by the ALA Hunger, Homelessness, and Poverty Task Force

THE AMERICAN LIBRARY ASSOCIATION POOR PEOPLE'S POLICY (www.ala.org/ala/ourassociation/governingdocs/policymanual/servicespoor.htm) was approved by ALA Council in June 1990. These are some suggestions from an ALA task force on how to set the policy in motion.—*GME.*

Actions for citizens

Challenge public policy that adversely affects low-income people, such as welfare reform, cutting tax credits, reducing food stamps, eliminating benefits to immigrants, or reducing health benefits.

Join local advocacy groups that work to promote resources being made available to poor people.

Promote full, stable, and ongoing funding for existing legislative programs in support of low-income services and for proactive library programs that reach beyond traditional service sites to poor children, adults, and families.

Promote the implementation of an expanded federal low-income housing program, national health insurance, full-employment policy, living minimum wage and welfare payments, affordable day care, and programs likely to reduce, if not eliminate, poverty itself.

Actions for library professionals

Related to library services and policies:

Examine your library's mission statement. Who is supposed to be served? Are all people welcome? Are all people being served? What are the barriers to people using the library? What steps could be taken to eliminate these barriers?

Work to insure people know how library policies are determined and are able to voice their concerns.

Evaluate library policies to ensure that they do not discriminate based on the ability to pay for access and/or service.

Promote the removal of all barriers to library and information services, particularly fees and overdue charges.

Enable the future success of all children by contributing to efforts that insure children know how to read and are encouraged to read.

Work with local literacy providers to publicize availability of adult basic education classes, GED, and ESL to help adults improve their literacy skills.

Related to staff training:

Promote training to sensitize library staff to issues affecting poor people and to attitudinal and other barriers that hinder poor people's use of libraries.

Promote training opportunities for librarians, in order to teach effective techniques for generating public funding to upgrade library services to poor people.

Related to budgets and funding:

Promote the incorporation of low-income programs and services into regular library budgets in all types of libraries, rather than the tendency to support these projects solely with "soft money" like private or federal grants.

Promote equity in funding adequate library services for poor people in terms of materials, facilities, and equipment.

Promote supplemental support for library resources for and about low-income populations by urging local, state, and federal governments, as well as the private sector, to provide adequate funding.

Related to outreach services:

Ask local community organizations what issues they're working on and how the library can contribute to their work.

Promote the determination of output measures through the encouragement of community needs assessments, giving special emphasis to assessing the needs of low-income people and involving both antipoverty advocates and poor people themselves in such assessments.

Have a special area of reports, brochures, and newsletters of local organizations and agencies with addresses, contact names, and purpose of groups so that interested people can get involved.

Fund and support outreach services that address community needs such as literacy programs, read-aloud programs, etc.

Promote networking and cooperation between libraries and other agencies, organizations, and advocacy groups in order to develop programs and services that effectively reach poor people.

6

Build partnerships with organizations in your community that serve low-income families.

Tell those organizations what you have, how the library works, and update them on new materials and services.

Promote among library staff the collection of food and clothing donations, volunteering personal time to antipoverty activities and contributing money to direct-aid organizations.

Promote related efforts concerning minorities and women, since these groups are disproportionately represented among poor people.

Compile a database of local community organizations and make it part of your library's web pages and/or online catalog and make this information readily available to patrons who may need it.

Sponsor public events (such as forums, speakers, community discussions, presentations by local organizations) so people can understand issues affecting them—taxes, child care options, job gap, corporate welfare, crime, etc.

Related to public awareness:

Promote increased public awareness—through programs, displays, bibliographies, and publicity—of the importance of poverty-related library resources and services in all segments of society.

Promote direct representation of poor people and antipoverty advocates through appointment to local boards and creation of local advisory committees on service to low-income people, such appointments to include library-paid transportation and stipends.

Collect, display, and make readily accessible current and up-to-date information on issues that are being debated such as the wage gap, lack of jobs, lack of child care, welfare reform, etc.

Promote the publication, production, purchase, and ready accessibility of print and nonprint materials that honestly address the issues of poverty and homelessness, that deal with poor people in a respectful way, and that are of practical use to low-income patrons.

Related to professional association activities:

Read ALA's Poor People's Policy and think about how its recommendations may be implemented in the libraries where you work.

Distribute copies of the Poor People's Policy to colleagues and initiate discussions at the libraries where you work and get your colleagues thinking about and discussing ways it can be implemented.

Ask ALA's Washington Office to actively support legislative initiatives that would contribute to reducing, if not eliminating, poverty (for example, living wage, more low-income housing, etc.).

Get involved in the ALA offices working on the issues of library services to the poor.

Document effective library services aimed at serving poor people and share information about these programs through ALA publications, conference sessions, electronic discussion lists, etc., as well as to groups outside ALA.

Encourage library science programs to offer courses on services to poor people.

Volunteer to develop and lead creative strategies within ALA and other professional associations that can bring visibility to the issue of library services for the poor.

SOURCE: ALA Social Responsibilities Round Table's Hunger, Homelessness, and Poverty Task Force, 2000.

PROMOTION
CHAPTER SEVEN

"I think the health of our civilization, the depth of our
awareness about the underpinnings of our culture and
our concern for the future can all be tested by how
well we support our libraries."

—Carl Sagan, *Cosmos* (1980)

PROMOTION

@ your library: The Campaign for America's Libraries

WHILE LIBRARIES ARE POPULAR, they are often taken for granted. While libraries are ubiquitous, they are not often visible. And, while libraries are unique, they are facing new challenges.

Out of these challenges was born @ your library®: The Campaign for America's Libraries, ALA's multiyear public awareness and advocacy campaign designed to showcase the value of public, school, academic, and special libraries and librarians in the 21st century. Based on research and crafted to target key audiences, the Campaign for America's Libraries is designed to remind the public that libraries are dynamic, modern community centers for learning, information, and entertainment. The campaign's goal is to increase awareness about the vibrancy, vitality, and real value of today's libraries, to galvanize public support and ultimately influence public policy and impact funding (www.ala.org/ala/pio/campaign/campaignamericas.htm).

While the campaign is national in scope, the riches that will bring the campaign to life and make it even more relevant to target audiences—the real-life stories and programs illustrating how libraries and librarians positively impact each and every individuals' personal lives— come from the grassroots. Libraries and library organizations across the country have already embraced the campaign, which launched in April 2001 with the help of First Lady Laura Bush. In fact, more than 20,000 libraries of all types in all 50 states have been reached.

The national campaign provides the foundation from which each of a series of targeted campaigns are being built. These campaigns provide the flexibility and the personal tailoring necessary to ensure the campaign is engaging all members of the library community and is proactively reaching their users. In 2002–2003, an Academic and Research Library Campaign began (www.ala.org/ala/pio/campaign/academicresearch/academicresearch.htm). A School Library Campaign (www.ala.org/ala/pio/campaign/schoollibrary/schoollibrary.htm) launched in 2003, followed by a public library initiative ("The Smartest Card" campaign) that kicked off during Library Card Sign-up Month in 2004 (www.pla.org/ala/pla/plaissues/smartestcardcampaign/smartestcardcampaign.htm).

External campaign goals. Increase awareness and support for libraries by increasing the visibility of libraries in a positive context and by communicating clearly and strongly why libraries are both unique and valuable.

Update the image of libraries and librarians for the 21st century, sustaining and strengthening their relevance.

Bring renewed energy to the promotion of libraries and librarians.

Increase library usage—at school, on college and university campuses, at work and in daily life.

Increase funding for libraries.

Bring librarians to the table at public policy discussions on key issues: intellectual freedom, equity of access, and narrowing the digital divide.

Positively impact recruitment efforts for the profession.

Internal campaign goals. Bring the entire library community together to speak with a unified voice.

Develop tools and materials to help libraries and librarians promote their value to their users and reach their specific audiences.

Extend the reach of the national campaign to the local, state, and regional levels, working with ALA chapters and sister library organizations as partners. Ensure the campaign is useful to libraries of all types—school, public, academic, and special—through close work with ALA divisions.

SOURCE: American Library Association, www.ala.org/@yourlibrary/.

45 ways to reach your faculty members

by Terri L. Holtze

UNIVERSITY OF LOUISVILLE Social Sciences Reference Librarian Terri L. Holtze offered these ideas, many contributed by colleagues, on establishing relationships with teachers to collaborate on promoting student instruction and information literacy.—*GME.*

Meeting your faculty

1. Invite them to lunch, coffee, a new faculty reception, or an appropriate library meeting.
2. Attend the events they might attend: grant writing or scholarly writing workshops, junior faculty lunches.
3. Meet the people around your faculty: departmental staff, administrators, graduate students.
4. Give new faculty a small amount of money to buy library materials they or their students will need.
5. Create a reading and writing center for students as a joint faculty effort.
6. Cosponsor a literacy service/learning event working with appropriate units, such as the Department of English or Education.
7. Meet with candidates for department positions to discuss what resources would be available to them.

Building relationships

8. Send a thank-you note for referring a student or colleague.
9. Provide a benefit, like free coffee or copies, to the department's liaison to the library.
10. Cultivate those professors who already use the library. They can be your best advocates.

11. Create exhibits in the library based on the lab or research work of faculty.

Communicating professionally

12. Create a "Faculty Guide to the Libraries" with all the essentials: phone numbers, course reserve procedures, etc.
13. Write a profile of a faculty member's contribution to library services for the library's newsletter.
14. Send an FAQ list or other useful handouts to share with classes.
15. Research and let them know about grant opportunities in their field.
16. Assess the needs of distance faculty.
17. Ask faculty to include the contact info of the library subject specialist on their syllabi.

Positioning the library

18. Apply for grants. Most universities announce grant winners in campus newsletters. This raises money and positive attention.
19. Make sure that library successes are promoted to the president and deans.
20. Establish the library as a central place on campus to go for research, writing assistance, computer labs, coffee, etc.
21. Get involved with learning communities.
22. Hold teaching and learning enhancement workshops.
23. Organize or participate in a program for faculty to mentor at-risk students.
24. Get on the list of campus experts or speakers bureau.

Knowing your stuff

25. Get an advanced degree in a subject-specific field.
26. Join the professional organizations of the faculty, not just library organizations.
27. When you get an opportunity to teach, prepare thoroughly. One source estimates that instruction preparation time should be two to three hours per hour of instruction.
28. Publish in the topic field journals, not just in library journals.

Tailoring to faculty interests

29. Advertise individualized research assistance for students and faculty.
30. Teach short courses for faculty on topics they want.
31. Do a study of faculty research habits.
32. Find out what new courses are in the works that may need collection support.
33. Keep a profile on each professor's research interests and accomplishments.
34. Create a faculty advisory board for library issues.
35. Work intensively with a particular faculty member to reinvent a course with an embedded research component.
36. Put together a seminar for faculty on detecting plagiarism.
37. Work with faculty designing distance-education courses.

Collaborating with faculty

38. Find out what kinds of activities mean the most for faculty promotions and focus your efforts there.
39. Coauthor an article.
40. Collaborate on a grant.
41. Create a class assignment together.
42. Partner with them to teach Web evaluation skills.
43. Teach a session for their class on research methods and resources specific to the class.
44. Coteach a class with IT.
45. Ask faculty to help provide content for the library's pathfinders.

SOURCE: Terri L. Holtze, "100 Ways to Reach Your Faculty," paper presented at an Office for Library Outreach Services preconference at the ALA Annual Conference in Atlanta, June 13–14, 2002, www.ala.org/ala/pio/campaign/academicresearch/reach_faculty.pdf.

30 ideas for outreach to students

EVERY CAMPUS OFFERS unique opportunities for communicating with students. In developing your library's promotional materials, consider the image you wish to convey. The colors and types of promotional materials you choose and how you distribute them are as much a part of the message as the words you use. Your goal should be to deliver the message in a way that is appealing to students and appropriate for your institution.

Aim to communicate a consistent image in all of your publicity and promotion efforts. Also keep in mind that some students may have had little library experience or perhaps a negative one. Presenting the library and its staff as inviting and helpful is key to overcoming these barriers. Also try for that element of surprise. Tell students what you can do for them that they might not expect. Bust the stereotypes with programs and activities that let them know the library is a changing, dynamic, and "with it" place staffed by people who understand and care about their needs. Advertisers know that for their message to be remembered, their audience must see/hear it a *minimum* of seven times. Aim to deliver your message as often and in as many forums as possible.

Ideas to get you started

1. Form a student advisory group or Friends of the Library group to advise and assist in developing programming and promotions directed at students. Take advantage of students who work in the library.
2. Seek to have a library message appear on student ID cards or provide stickers with the URL.
3. Put out a "Talk Back" suggestion box inviting students to ask questions or share what they like and don't like about the library. Post frequently asked questions and answers.
4. Publish an "It's an Information Jungle Out There!" survival guide for students. Distribute it during orientation and other events.
5. Distribute "tent cards" (similar to those often found on restaurant tables) featuring the library's website or other services on tables in dining halls and the student union.

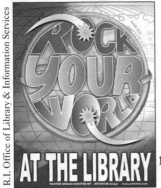

6. Have library messages appear on electronic message boards around campus. Explore getting electronic signage for the library.
7. Distribute door-hanger flyers in residence halls.
8. Use "A-frames" or easels inside and outside the library to display posters or a calendar of events. Sponsor contests both online and offline.
9. Plant "footprints" around campus—all leading to the library. Publicize their imminent appearance and offer a prize such as a free pizza coupon to the first 50 or so students who check in at the information desk.
10. Provide and publicize an idea exchange on the library's website for students to post their best tips for studying and using the library.
11. Host a "pizza night" or other special event during exam week.
12. Invite campus celebrities to appear on posters for the library.
13. Invite well-known graduates to do readings, give talks, or make appearances at the library. Ask for their testimonials to include in ads in the student newspaper and other library publicity materials.
14. Print a coupon for free coffee or copies at the library's café or bookstore.
15. Print messages on napkins, cups, or cup sleeves at the library café.
16. Run the library's message in campus planners/calendars.
17. Give away library brochures and promotional items such as bookmarks, highlighters, or pens in registration packets and at orientation.
18. Host tours or sponsor a reception for parents and alumni during orientation or homecoming.
19. Enter a float in the homecoming parade.
20. Ask faculty to include a library message, e.g., "Got questions? Get answers! @ your library," in course handouts.
21. Send brief and lively announcements of training classes, study tips, new materials, and other updates via email distribution lists.
22. Use screen savers and banners to highlight special messages on the library's website.
23. Have plastic book bags imprinted with the library message. Also give to campus bookstores to use.
24. Post flyers or posters on information kiosks and bulletin boards around campus, as well as in the library.
25. Ask bookstores to insert library flyers in shopping bags.
26. Distribute posters/flyers/other library promotional materials at the tutoring center and other student service centers, e.g., Office for Disabilities, ethnic student associations, job placement, etc.
27. Hang colorful banners outside the library, in dining halls, in the student center, and around campus.
28. Distribute library promotional materials during fraternity or sorority events. Include with rush materials or direct mail or email.
29. Give away earplugs in cases imprinted with the library's message at the information desk. Other ideas for giveaways: mouse pads, T-shirts.
30. Use chalk to graffiti the library message around campus. Get permission, if needed.

SOURCE: The Campaign for America's Libraries Toolkit for Academic and Research Libraries (Chicago: American Library Association, 2003), pp. 12–13.

Novelty marketing materials for youth

by Angela B. Pfeil

WHEN LIBRARIES PUT ON a special event or a special session of programming, often a novelty item is budgeted for and purchased to either give away or sell to the attendees. There are companies who work primarily with libraries in developing new and innovative items to distribute. The JanWay Corporation has been at the heart of custom library promotions since the company's inception in 1981. Its website (www.janway.com) offers easy navigability as well as unique ideas for library promotions. K-READ Custom Promotions offers a special "Reading Store" with library- and literacy-related items. Its website (www.k-read.net) is searchable by type of promotion as well as by keyword. Although capturing library users' attention is important, the marketing plan may call for attracting new users. Using novelty, or nontraditional, items may be most effective.

Pencils and pens. Pencils are relatively inexpensive, even when they are specially ordered and designed to your specifications. One drawback to using pencils as a novelty item is the small amount of display space on  the pencil for information. When using pencils, it is best to display the library or outreach program name and a web address. Pencils are easy to distribute and are necessary for most students in elementary school. If your library purchases pens to distribute and plans on giving them out at elementary schools, be sure that the color of the ink is the same as the mandatory ink color most schools require. Although the colorful and popular gel pens may seem to be more attractive to students, these will not be used for schoolwork and therefore may not be used on a daily basis. Distributing pencils and pens to children doubly benefits the library because they serve an educational need and the library marketing plan.

Stickers. Kids love stickers. Some children collect stickers, while others simply like to display them on notebooks, artwork, and in their homes. Distributing visually appealing library stickers will be a huge success with children. These stickers should be no larger than 3-by-3 inches, and they should include the library logo along with any other special library information, such as the kids' website or the name of the special outreach program. Some libraries create bookplate stickers for distribution. Kids can then apply these to the books in their personal libraries. Although this is a worthwhile idea, how often are kids going to look at the stickers on the inside covers of books they are not reading anymore? However you choose to format these stickers, it is important to remember your library's mission statement and purpose for printing the stickers. These stickers can be distributed as prizes for ongoing reading programs and can also be used to distribute during outreach. Although these are not serving any educational need of students, they will foster the brand recognition that the library is looking to attain.

Book covers. Many schools require or encourage their students to cover their textbooks. Parents scramble around to find the perfect paper, and teachers usually only have a limited supply of book covers. Creating book covers with library information, including useful library links, books, or e-resources related to the subject, and distributing these free to schools will meet the

needs of the students and take a burden off of the parents. When making book covers, be creative. You can create one layout that includes all the subjects, or you may choose to do different layouts for each of the subjects. All book covers may be printed on the same paper, or, if the covers are already separated by subject, each subject may be printed in a different color. Book covers remind students of the library daily.

Posters. Many libraries deem posters as too expensive to create and prefer to use the free posters librarians receive at local and national conferences or to purchase the standard Read posters from the American Library Association. These posters serve an important, dual purpose by showing celebrities reading and by promoting all sorts of books. Posters created by your library will serve the important purpose of promoting your library specifically. Be sure to include such information as the library logo, library website, address, and phone number. It's best to feature actual images of kids using the library or of staff performing a program. As with any large sign, these posters should be colorful, inviting, and intriguing. Teachers will gladly accept and display the library's promotional poster. Kids will see the poster each day, and when it comes time to prepare reports or projects, they will know they have a library they can go to.

Folders. Every student needs a folder at some point in the school year. Try producing a plain, colored folder with the library district logo in a visible but not overwhelming spot on the cover. Include suggested resource lists for various subjects on the inside, and this folder will meet the needs of both students and the library marketing plan. When creating content for the inside of the folder, remember to include the

library web address and specific directions on how to access the featured resources. If possible, create folders that have a perforated insert for business cards, and encourage students to keep their library cards in that spot.

Key chains. If you offer key-chain library cards, why not offer students a key chain for the cards? They will leave your library with a set of keys more rewarding and empowering than any set of car keys—you are giving them the keys to unlock the door to information.

Other novelty items. Anything that kids collect, no matter how small, can be created with the library logo on it. Consider yo-yos, pencil sharpeners, rulers, pencil cases, postcards, notebooks, book bags, temporary tattoos, magnets, and other items for your library promotions.

Marketing materials can be large or small, and they can meet a need or simply fulfill a desire. Whatever your library chooses to produce, be sure that it is not only a quality product but also one that meets the objectives of the marketing plan. Remember to include the library logo, name, and website on all materials.

SOURCE: Angela B. Pfeil, *Going Places with Youth Outreach* (Chicago: American Library Association, 2005), pp. 25–28.

Fundamentals of good press releases

by Jane Kessler and Carol Anne Germain

TIRED OF WRITING PRESS RELEASES that never make it to black and white? Do you feel your local news editor has something against the articles you submit? Do you really want the local public to read about what's going on in your library? Maybe the problem is your press releases. A "let's get published" strategy for all media outlets includes writing a good press release, making a connection with the news source, and following publication guidelines.

Getting connected

Get your press release published by establishing and maintaining a good rapport with reporters and editors. "The existence of a personal relationship between the journalist and the public relations practitioner is likely to provide a high level of placement," note Timothy N. Walters, Lynne Masel Walters, and Douglas P. Starr in the Winter 1994 *Public Relations Review*. Start a positive working relationship by introducing yourself and your library to the news contact. Since you want this to be a long-term relationship, go out of your way to meet face-to-face. This could be as simple as extending an invitation to share a coffee break or go out to lunch. In this exchange, you will want to provide information about your library and find out important facts about your contact's publication.

Develop an informational folder for the news agency's reference files. It should contain contact information (including fax, email, phone numbers, and an evening contact), library background data and statistics, and details about regularly sponsored events. This file will serve as a handy reference when an upcoming story arises, making the writer's job easier.

Don't make it a one-way connection. Ask for their media packet, which usually outlines criteria for press release submissions and a profile of the publication. Read the publication. This will give you a better feel for press releases that are accepted. Also, this practice will help you choose the section or feature in which you'd like your release published.

In addition, get to know reporters and editors personally. Send holiday greetings, good wishes, and thank-you notes. Find out about their interests. Since you're a librarian, you may be able to help them with their research. Remember the old saying, "One hand washes the other." Ask for feedback and solicit suggestions—and then follow them!

To maintain a quality working relationship, follow the news source's guidelines. These include deadlines (which may be different for weekends, holidays, etc.), submission preference (email, fax, postal service), and article criteria (length, audience, style, spacing). Address press releases to the proper contact editor. If John Smith is the community page editor, send the release directly to John Smith, in care of the publication. Your release has a better chance of not being discarded if it gets into the right hands quickly. Be dependable. If you regularly submit interesting news pieces, the press will contact you for stories! Most importantly, write a good press release.

7

Shaping your press release

The key to writing an effective press release, one that editors publish and readers read, is to use the inverted pyramid style. The inverted pyramid style puts the most important information in the leading paragraphs and less significant details in succeeding paragraphs. Since editors cut from the bottom, using this style ensures that vital details are not deleted. In addition, people tend to skim articles, so convey the essential information at the start to be certain your message is read. Using this format greatly simplifies the process of writing press releases.

In the first paragraphs of a press release, address the five W's: Who? What? When? Where? Why? Provide answers to How? and So What? if space allows. Place library phone numbers in the initial paragraphs to guarantee readers will have a contact for additional information. All information should be complete and accurate.

In the latter paragraphs, provide descriptions and background about the event or news item. For example, if your library has received a grant to present a children's program on reptiles, provide descriptions of reptiles, facts about the handlers, and don't forget to mention the snake-shaped cookies. Highlight hands-on components of the event to encourage attendance.

Additional paragraphs may contain a direct quote from key persons. Don't use quotes if they are banal and insipid. For example, quotes such as "It'll be a fun day for the children" don't normally work. Of course it will be a fun day! Instead, a statement from the reptile handler might work better. An example may be, "Surprisingly, girls are not squeamish when touching the snakes and lizards."

Content

Write simply; make it readable. Newspaper sentences average 22 words, and the average word length is one-and-a-half syllables. Don't drown readers with big words and complicated ideas. Avoid abbreviations, jargon, and acronyms. You want readers to understand the content of your release.

Don't be a passive writer. Use an active voice. When writing with an active

---

Helpful Tips

Submit the release early (preferably a week).
Label photo back with release title.
Editors and reporters are busy—don't pester them.
If a release is not published, follow up with a quick call or email and solicit ideas for improvement.
Make sure cited web pages are still available.
Know the material you're promoting and an appropriate contact for follow-up information.
Develop a media list (with pertinent information).
Find out about institution and campus press-release policies.
Be available for interviews (positive or negative news).
Make sure essential people read the release before it is sent out.
Don't send duplicate press releases.
Double-check facts.
Have colleagues proof once, twice, three times.
Don't expect all "news" to be published for free; buy advertisement space when necessary.

voice, the subject of the sentence performs the action; with passive voice, the subject receives the action. For example:

Active: The editor accepted the press release.
Passive: The press release was accepted by the editor.

Journalists write 71 active voice sentences to every one passive voice sentence. Readers with an 11th-grade education can read and understand their copy. However, numerous studies reported that readers must be juniors in college to read and understand most press releases. For a list of active verbs, see www.albany.edu/~cg219/averbs.html.

Should your headlines scream?

There is some disagreement in the literature about the use of interesting or catchy headlines in press releases. Some writers argue for a "just the facts" approach to press release writing. Moira Duncan states,

> Obviously, there should be a headline, but don't get in a flap about this and start gibbering about it having to be "catchy" and "punchy." It need be nothing of the sort: what it must do is give a clear indication as to what the story is about. Leave the puns and witticisms to the sub-editors. ("Totally Unique! How Not to Write a Press Release," *Managing Information*, September 1994, p. 39)

Contrary to this point of view is Tony Sutton's perspective on the need for arresting headlines, in *Quill*, May 1995: "Good headlines that are both informative and captivating are as rare as hen's teeth. Make yours the exception to the rule that seems to say that headlines should be dull and unreadable."

The headline should grab the reader's attention so that the release is read. To write an effective headline, make it short, use power words and active verbs, and summarize the press release. Make this the last step in writing the press release. For the above example, "Get Wrapped Up in Snakes!" would draw an audience.

Copy preparation

7

After writing a great release, don't have it passed over for publication because of incorrect formatting. Editors are more likely to print a properly prepared press release, so always use standard press release format. The key components of standard press release format are:

- 8½" × 11" plain white paper
- minimum one-inch margins
- letterhead information at top of paper
- labeled as a press release
- date submitted
- release date
- contact information
- headline centered and in bold type
- [city, state] followed by the body of the release double spaced
- ### or END at end of release
- avoid **bold**, *italics*, or CAPS
- limit the press release to one page

If it's impossible to limit the release to one page, type "MORE" at the bottom of the first page. On the second page, retype the title and the date. Number the pages 1 of 2, 2 of 2, etc.

Common mistakes

With practice you'll learn what your target publication wants in a press release and you'll be successful. The authors surveyed 25 different news publications, large and small, nationwide, to determine pet peeves and mistakes often made in press releases. Editors identified the most common error as length. They noted lengthy releases often wind up in the wastebasket and stated that if the editor tires of the text, certainly their readers will, too. Poorly written articles are also a regular problem; many releases contain poor sentence structure, misspellings, and grammatical errors. The editors also discouraged opinionated pieces, late entries, and handwritten articles. Overuse of superlatives in a release is annoying, since the editor already knows that your story is superexcellent. Other problems included little or no contact information, omitting important details—such as event costs, dates, locations, and times—and incorrect facts. This latter difficulty is not only time-consuming for writers and editors, since they have to double-check material, but embarrassing if mistakes are published because the publication receives the blame.

Where to publish?

What you wish to publicize influences where you publish. Should you submit the release to a publication with a small, medium, or large circulation? To get an audience for an event, you'll want a local venue, so use the area newspaper. Don't stray too far from your community unless your event is big: Other communities will publish "their" news first. For bigger stories, such as grants and building projects, submit the release to a state or national publication, such as *American Libraries* or *Public Libraries*. News in national and state publications can be re-reported and highlighted in local newspapers. *Gale Directory of Publications and Broadcast Media* provides lists of news publications by state, subject, and media type. Contact information and circulation figures are included.

Getting your press release published is not a matter of luck. By developing a relationship with news sources, writing a good press release, and avoiding common mistakes, you'll get your release released!

SOURCE: Jane Kessler and Carol Anne Germain, "Extra! Extra! Extra! Read All About It! Fundamentals of Good Press Releases," *Public Libraries* 42 (October 2003): 300–302.

State associations get the news out
by Jennifer Burek Pierce

THINK GLOBALLY, ACT LOCALLY has been a slogan for everything from political activism to, with minor modification, a microbrewery in my home town. In many respects, this pithy contemporary aphorism also describes the aims of newsletters written for state library association members. Conversations with two newsletter editors whose publications stand out among their peers reveal editorial interest in both the big picture and the thumbnail sketch, the national and the regional news. As a result, one need not hail from New Mexico or Illinois to find information or enjoyment in the pages of these state publications.

Getting personal in New Mexico

Robert Upton's responsibilities at the New Mexico State Library include editing *The Hitchhiker*, a weekly newsletter published both in print and on the Web. Upton said the publication's subscription list includes 860 addresses, while the subscription list for email notification is around 300. Available online at www.stlib.state.nm.us since 1996, *The Hitchhiker* is a popular feature of the state library's site. "It's by far the largest hit on our website," Upton said.

"Having a clear idea of who my audience is and addressing them as individuals rather than as an amorphous group is my main goal," Upton commented. "Because the library community in New Mexico is small, we know each other well. It's a very personal kind of reporting."

Upton estimates that librarians make up 80% of his readership, but the remainder includes some legislators. Citing hearing and committee reports, Upton notes that *The Hitchhiker* "does have an effect on the legislative level." The general readership, too, reported much satisfaction in a recent survey, offering appreciation for topics covered, particularly national ones like the USA Patriot Act. Upton said readers want to know still more about the workings of the state library and activities in other area libraries, including academic and tribal libraries.

He observed that one important feature of the publication is that "it's a historical document as well as a current document. It's the only record of library activity in New Mexico" and serves as "a unified picture of New Mexico library activity."

Reporting from Illinois

In Illinois, Robert Doyle is both editor of the *Illinois Library Association Reporter* and the association's executive director. Available both online (www.ila.org/pub/reporter.htm) and in print, the *Reporter* has a run of approximately 3,500 copies and is mailed to ILA's 3,000 members. Extras are sent for distribution to the state's two library schools in an effort to promote the state library association. In considering the advantages of print versus electronic access, Doyle observed, "I still like the paper copy. In my opinion, it's one tangible benefit they get as members of the association." At the same time, web publication promotes availability. "I want people to have access to it," he said. "That's the important thing."

Doyle includes information that he believes will have broad appeal. He explained, "What we're trying to do is present interesting and well-written articles that our members might not be able to get anywhere else." With respect to including sensitive or controversial content, Doyle said, "One reason I put that in is to encourage people to think, 'Are we prepared for a situation like this?'"

One factor that Doyle credits with the positive reception enjoyed by the *ILA Reporter* is member involvement. An active publications committee selects a

theme for the year's feature content, developing assignments for related stories and recruiting content. This year's theme, for example, is Doing More with Less, "reflecting current economic realities that libraries face," Doyle observed.

The committee's involvement contributes to useful perspectives, he said. "My suspicion is that for many groups, publishing a newsletter is a little burdensome. I want to see how we can keep it fresh."

This means certain types of information, like board minutes and candidate statements, aren't found in the *ILA Reporter.* "I don't want this newsletter to be a housekeeping vehicle," Doyle said. "I think there's more effective ways of doing that. I'd rather have articles that represent the totality of the Illinois library community."

Upton shares Doyle's perspective. "Librarians are isolated one from the other," he said, referring to New Mexico's sparse population. "They won't meet for lunch except on rare occasions." In editing *The Hitchhiker,* Upton strives to provide information and connection.

SOURCE: Jennifer Burek Pierce, "Grassroots Report: State Associations Get the News Out," *American Libraries* 35 (October 2004): 63.

FUND-RAISING

Make yourself indispensable

by Marylaine Block

MARKETING IS AN UNGODLY, COMPLICATED PROBLEM for librarians. Like some corporate octopus, we offer an immense range of products—information, books, reading itself, the internet—to an immense range of audiences, from children to parents, public officials to business people, toddlers to seniors. So when we talk about improving our marketing, we need to define which product we want to sell, and to which audience.

The marketing effort that concerns me most is convincing the local power structure that we are the "go-to" people for information. In *A Place at the Table: Participating in Community Building* (ALA Editions, 2000), Kathleen de la Peña McCook surveyed library literature and funding information for urban redevelopment; she found that libraries were virtually invisible to the movers and shakers who wanted to revitalize their communities.

Perhaps our key error is waiting for them to come to us. If we want the influential people in our service areas to regard us as full partners in community building, we need to know their information needs before *they* do, and get the resources into their hands that will facilitate their decision-making *before* they realize they need it.

Cozying up to the fourth estate

Building such relationships with reporters requires our understanding that their work is driven by the "news peg"—the fourth estate's operating principle that no matter how interesting an idea or issue may be in the abstract, it won't make the editorial cut unless it's connected to a breaking news story.

Reporters won't write about the issue of underage drinking and fake IDs until Jenna Bush is arrested. They probably won't develop a feature on the dangers of nuclear energy until the 20th anniversary of Three Mile Island, or reflect on World War II until an anticipated blockbuster movie such as *Pearl Harbor* is about to be released. Journalists are almost guaranteed to write about women's issues in March during Women's History Month and African-American achievements during Black History Month in February, but not during the other 10 months of the year. In other words, reporters will welcome story ideas and information that are pegged to news events, past and present.

Because journalists have to do their research on short deadlines, we can earn their gratitude by offering them story ideas and prepackaged research. Librarians need to teach them by example that we can find better information than they can with their quick internet searches.

How might we do that? One way is a regular library newsletter (by mail, email, web page, or all three) that includes a "This Month in History" feature that highlights interesting historical and cultural milestones of 25, 50, or 100 years ago—votes for women, the first Barbie doll, the first IBM PC—and recommends excellent books, articles, magazines, and online resources for each.

We can do the same thing for current issues, both local and national. Where flood control is an ongoing concern, we could recommend books on the history of efforts to control local waterways, and online documents such as Corps of Engineers reports and historical statistics. Library web pages could include scanned photos and news accounts of previous floods, and reading lists and on-site displays could offer that same information for library visitors.

Librarians can be equally proactive with leaders of local government. First, study their immediate and continuing issues, and their individual hobbyhorses and pet projects. How? Make a point of attending city council meetings or at least reading their minutes, which, in many towns, are posted on the internet. You can then research those issues, and supply city officials with pertinent articles, websites, and other documents that indicate how other cities have dealt with similar problems.

As the keepers of the city's history, we can give community leaders background information about how today's community problems developed in the first place, how their predecessors dealt with those issues, and why our current laws are written as they are.

As to your area's local business leaders, many may already know the kinds of business reference materials libraries stock. But they may not be fully aware of key business resources on the internet and that librarians are experts at finding them; they also may not know about the library's access to full-text article databases. One useful way we could call to business leaders' attention both the information available and our expertise in finding it is by emailing them a daily weblog linked to relevant news stories and new business or statistical resources. Perhaps the weblog could also pose a "question of the day" item featuring a business question, its answer, and the resources we used to answer it. How about going a step farther, and developing a variety of weblogs for patrons' different interests: business, leisure reading, crafts and hobbies, etc., each maintained by the acquisitions librarian for that area?

7

Another marketing resource librarians may not be mining is our public meeting rooms. Odds are that community leaders attend events in our library meeting rooms at least once every few months—everything from book-discussion groups to quilting-club meetings and folk-music presentations. Knowing in advance what interests each scheduled group, you could maintain a shifting display outside the meeting room of materials that would appeal to each group. You could also publish brochures recommending particularly good books, websites, magazines, and reference sources on those topics.

Meme's the word

In addition, library officials need to examine their organizations' human links to influential groups and individuals in their communities. To what nonlibrary groups do each of your staff members and trustees belong? In each of those groups, those staffers should make a point of routinely supplying timely and accurate information to aid in decision making.

Meme theory—the premise that ideas spread contagiously through society like a virus—can also be a useful tool for identifying the people and organizations librarians need to influence. Start by ascertaining all the voluntary organizations in your service area; then plot the overlapping memberships held by staff members. People who are active in several groups are connectors who can spread ideas and enthusiasm (i.e., memes) among those who share few common interests. These connectors are the people we want on our side as library supporters.

You also want to know who the community's innate salespeople are—those who are good at convincing others to undertake projects, spend money, and offer their time and effort. You need these people on your side as well. If librarians and board members already know some of these people, you have a relationship to build on, and knowledge of their interests. If you don't already know them, find a way to reach them. Arrange to join groups they're involved in, or to work with them on community projects, such as "Race for the Cure" or fundraising for a new Gilda's Club.

If you don't already do so, make a point of letting these community live wires know when a new book comes in that will pique their attention. You should also go out of your way to show them the library's new toys that will capture their imaginations—the newest databases, redesigned web pages, reference books, magazines, and the like.

Stretching for dollars

You may be reading this and saying, "In what possible universe will I have time to do all this stuff and still serve the people who are already coming to us?" And you're right; there's a limit to how far we can stretch. Librarians can't do all the things I'm recommending.

But if we don't do *some* of them, we will continue to be invisible. If we don't want to settle for being good at what we do but want to be known to be good at what we do, we have to put marketing time and money into reaching out to the people who make things happen in our community.

SOURCE: Marylaine Block, "The Secret of Library Marketing: Make Yourself Indispensable," *American Libraries* 32 (September 2001): 48–50.

Marketing your library

by Mark Y. Herring

MANY LIBRARIANS ARE FINDING the profession we entered 20 or more years ago *vastly* different from the one we find ourselves in today. Welcome to the world of change, and whether you know it or not, that world is yours if you are in a Friends group. It began when computers waltzed into the library in the early 1970s. Our tried and true professional prejudices about formats have now been dashed to bits, our easy rules about cataloging shaken (how do you catalog a website, and should you bother?), and our comfortable notions about annual budgets devoured by skyrocketing inflation and the multiplicity of media. We have one verity left to us and it is not an easy one: We can be certain that what we know about libraries today will change in a few years, if not in a few months. Like Heraclitus, from this day forward, librarians will know only flux.

So, for the rest of us, what are some principles of marketing libraries?

Product ownership and tough sells

Libraries are a tough sell. This may seem like reverse psychology but it is not. Stop and think about it. Every library can produce a warm fuzzy, but no one really owns it. Like air, no one really owns it, or rather, *every* patron who walks in the door does. While this might make one think product ownership is easy, it isn't. When everyone owns it, no one does. Think a minute about your demographics for a moment. A library's demographics might look like this:

- Age: 3–95
- Race: all
- Households: every one of them
- Household incomes: 0–millions
- Sex: evenly divided between men and women
- Geographic location: in town and around the world

The bad news is that it's hard to target *one* group. The good news is that it's hard to miss any target group you choose. So the first principle might be this: Look for the good in what you do. The trouble with marketing something everyone owns is that *everyone else* thinks the other person is supporting it. The trick is to think about what you do, encapsulate it in a few easy-to-remember points, and then begin the process of selling it to your clientele—*all of them.*

But if everyone owns it, isn't it already sold? Not really. It is not until those few or many actually put *their* money into *your* Friends group. Most patrons already know why they come to the library. What they do not know is why you need their money, and therein lies the rub. Much of library marketing is teaching others about the cost of your product and how underfunded it really is.

The library as value

In the end, as David E. Gumpert wrote in *How to Really Create a Successful Marketing Plan* (1996), "[M]arketing is the process of identifying prospects [patrons] and determining best how to turn them into customers [friends]." The task is formidable but it can be done if care is taken how one goes about it. One especially important aspect is value. In order to *market* a product, one has to convey to target groups why such a product is valuable.

For example, how often in the past year have you conducted a user-satisfaction survey *and* used it to change what's being done? User-satisfaction surveys are common in libraries. What may not be as common is *changing what you do because of what your learn even it'll means doing something non-librarian-like*. While it's considered a colossal blunder in the marketing world, how many libraries, after spending a tenth as much money, would have cancelled an entire offering if it crashed and burned like the new Coke? Yet, the Coke company turned that blunder into a boom. These surveys can also be very useful in helping us establish our own market segmentation.

Even though anecdotal evidence is limited to small audiences, it is nevertheless such ideas that help Friends groups understand what the library does and how it helps its clientele in ways not readily apparent. Moreover, it also provides solid examples of real value. It is up to Friends groups to ferret out such examples and present them to potential donors to complete the cycle of successful marketing, unless of course your group plans to recruit all new members every year.

Marketing library needs

Marketing library needs to create successful fund-raising is another way to exploit the gamut of publicity. The Friends of the Redwood Libraries in Eureka, California, did this in a remarkable manner. When a budget shortfall threatened this system with severe cutbacks, or worse, the Friends began looking at their options. The group sent a letter to their 600 members explaining that if everyone who got the letter gave $5, this particular shortfall would be avoided. The Friends allocated $2,000 for the campaign and ended up spending $1,900. The result? Nearly $45,000 was raised, averting the budget disaster.

What makes the Redwood experience noteworthy, in addition to its obvious success, is the number of successes and failures within the campaign. First, the Friends group recognized it had to have a budget for this campaign—following the old adage that you must spend money to make money—and stick to it. But it also had failures. While they were successful in raising funds overall, individual attempts (for example, donations from professional organizations) failed. This roller-coaster life cycle is nearly every company's experience with marketing, and further underscores why it's important to keep track of what you do. Some things will succeed while others will not. It's good to know what does and *does not* succeed for the next venture. One key to successful marketing is a willingness to revisit the same issue often, just to be sure that what worked one year is working the next. Marketing is not a one-shot, one-time encounter. It must be constantly revised, reimplemented, and updated.

Marketing your group's library services and needs must take a backseat to nothing. We all have clienteles we must satisfy. In order to do this we must get feedback on the programs we now provide. This means examining marketing survey data (though those of us may not want to call it that). Many libraries may find that they are dissatisfied with the results of the data, with their efforts to improve, or both. But that speaks less to effectiveness of the ideas, and more to our execution of them. Not only are resources ready at hand to help, but so also are many resources available through FOLUSA, ACRL, and many other library organizations. It may be necessary to provide library training after hiring a person effective in public relations *but without a library degree.* We can easily teach the one while we may not know how to begin with the other.

If all of this seems overwhelming, it need not be. Most changes in what we do will mean fine-tuning what we are already doing. For example, up-to-the-minute status reports on interlibrary loans. Many may do something like this already. All we need to add is a simple report that we generate for ourselves anyway and get them to our clients who need the information far more than we do. There is no doubt that much of this talk about marketing and clients will leave some cold. It will prove better in the long run, however, if we can get over this before we discover that our clients have gotten over us.

SWOT analyses

You may be wondering at this point how your group can begin marketing its library. The best place to begin is to find out if the library has ever done a SWOT analysis. If not, *now* is the time to do one. You may realize that marketing is important, even essential to your Friends groups. You may also realize that you have something to tell your community about—library programs and projects, Friends programs, local and regional events. The one lacking puzzle piece is where to begin. Discovering the Strengths, Weaknesses, Opportunities, and Threats (SWOT) of the library will provide the Friends group the fodder it needs to feed the marketing machine.

Most libraries do these analyses routinely, but if yours has not, you need not fear for there is no better time to begin than the present. A SWOT analysis is an investigation into the library's strengths, weaknesses, opportunities, and threats. What comes out of this analysis will provide excellent data for a baseline marketing audit. It is important that the library examine environmental forces by taking a snapshot of where the library is and placing it where it wants to be in the near future. Given that the library's current environment today is very different from what it was only five years ago, it's a good bet that it will not be in the same place five years from now.

Furthermore, the SWOT analysis helps the library assess what it has been doing, how those things it is doing well can be strengthened, and how those things that are not being done well can be done better. It is helpful to remember during this process that if the services are not serving your clientele—your patrons—or not serving them well enough, then either the services should be stopped or changed so that they are more successful. As you go through the SWOT process it should become obvious again why the library's head must be intimately involved in the Friends process.

Strengths. What does your library do well? What is it that your patrons *always* come to you for first? This may not be as obvious as it seems. If it is your computers alone, then do not delude yourself,

because they can gain *that* access elsewhere. Figuring out why your strengths work well will come when you spend time brainstorming your many strengths together. You will be surprised what you discover *together* as you go through this exercise. Writing everyone's thoughts on butcher paper or a grease board is also helpful. Whoever records this—and it probably should be the library's head—should not make any value judgments. These will come later.

Once completed, and everyone has said all he or she wants to say, try grouping these strengths into categories: services, programs, and the like. Once you have done this, have someone write everything down and circulate it among staff. It is best to do this over a few days as other ideas will naturally occur after a few days of reflection. Once everyone has agreed on what has been recorded, you are ready to tackle step two. Group your strengths into categories so they will be easier to assign later on.

Weaknesses. At first, these will be harder to come by so persistence will be needed. Like the Lake Wobegon effect where all children are above average, it will be hard to pinpoint real weaknesses for it is the *other* libraries, not yours, that aren't up to snuff. The first to emerge will be easy ones that may or may not be actually true weaknesses: low budgets and low salaries. Even if you assume these are legitimate weaknesses (and they undoubtedly will be), more will come. This is why it is important to get feedback from other sources: patrons of every description and category. Without these important sources, your weaknesses may only be straw men.

One very beneficial aspect of examining weaknesses is not only that they eventually come after a few false starts, but also that staff are quick to resolve them. If the library head were to say, "I want you to do such and so," the response might legitimately be, "How can I? I'm swamped as it is." But if these are singled out through the SWOT process, the likelihood that they will be undertaken and solved is very high.

Equally important in this process are certain ground rules, such as no person or department is singled out in an inflammatory way, only *services*. As soon as someone says, "Circulation really doesn't do it's job," the game is lost. Circulation personnel must now defend themselves and will inevitably launch a retaliatory volley against the person or the department (or both) that launched the preemptive strike. Establish these rules early in the process and all should go well. Susan Carol Curzon argues in *Managing Change* (Neal-Schuman, 1989) that a key to effective brainstorming is the separation of staff from their ideas.

Another benefit of the weaknesses process is the understanding that each library has a way to go, has unreached goals. All of us know this but we may not know it operatively—just metaphorically, which is to say, not at all. This is especially true of staffs that have been together for a number of years. You may find it necessary to ask pointed questions about certain areas in order to challenge assumptions or rock preconceived notions. Using a book such as Spencer Johnson's *Who Moved My Cheese?* (Penguin Putnam, 1998) may help staff come to grips with the change-thinking process needed to accomplish this and other important tasks. Once it can be admitted that you are not perfect, beneficial and necessary change is at least possible.

One final word. Do not go fishing where there is no water. It is possible that only a few items will result. Perhaps there are areas you see that need change. Suggest one or two and if they are shot down, do not press them. Revisit them later. Do not demand they be included if they are not generally accepted.

Opportunities. What are areas suggested by this process that you should seize upon? Most of the time, these will reveal themselves as both weaknesses and threats that you can reassign as opportunities. While not really earthshaking, we discovered that *communication* was one area in which we could do better; so we listed a number of opportunities we could turn to our advantage (and of course to an eventual strength).

Threats. Equally important to the overall success of your marketing scheme are the threats that can come out of this analysis. In my years of doing this I have found that some librarians are not as keen on these threats as they should

be. For example, *every* library must come to see the internet as a threat to its own existence. While professionally we *know* it cannot really compete with a full-service library, we also know many of our strongest supporters see it as doing our jobs as well or better. Obviously then, threats are both real and imagined ones that need to be cited.

Other kinds of threats will also become obvious. For example, Barnes and Noble is not really a threat to a library. But the *service* it provides, as well as the setting, are. If this were not true, libraries would not be adding cafés in their foyers, and designing their layouts in imitation. Other such threats will also emerge, and all need to be listed.

Through? SWOT yet done

Are you finished? Not yet. Although this is not obvious on a SWOT analysis for it is not part of the mnemonic, it should be understood as an important part of the process. With your categories in place and assignments made, participants in the process need to know everything possible about the strengths, weaknesses, opportunities, and threats. You may know what your collection contains, but do you know what it *should* contain? What is the latest technology? What parts of it will you use or ignore? Why? A SWOT analysis will help you identify what you need to do to move your library into the future. This process may take several weeks and will yield not only more strengths once it is complete but should also reveal more weaknesses, opportunities, and threats.

For example, when we went through this process, we learned how more and more libraries not much larger than our own were moving into 24/7 reference services. We wanted to learn more, and the group in charge of reference services did just that. They reported a number of aspects that while generally known, were not known well enough for us to make an assessment. After thorough research into this, we still did not think it something we should divert scarce funds to. The exercise was not futile. This will occur with a number of items. Even if you decide not to use them, you should still list them as part of the analysis. Once this part is completed, and all that you wish to have incorporated is included, you are ready to make a final analysis. Research is critical to this success of this enterprise.

There is no such thing as overkill when it comes to marketing who and what you are to the people you serve. If this were true, you would never hear another bread, beer, or broomstick commercial.

Now what?

Some final points are in order. If the library has not gone through a stakeholders process, this may be the time to do that as well. One must judge carefully about information overload, but if staff have not thought through who it is they serve it will be impossible—or at least exceedingly difficult—to think through the process of marketing to target groups. Many of those to whom library marketing is aimed are, of course, stakeholders. Especially important is looking at each process through the patron's eyes.

Whatever you do, you will need a budget. It is just not possible to have a marketing plan without one. Within a university, this may seem easier than at first glance. Call your PR office and ask what you can do to help with this process. Show them your SWOT analysis and ask them in what ways you can aid the delivery of information about the university (and therefore your library) to the constituencies. It may be that you can coordinate deliveries of the information and pool your budgets. The important point is to try. Get out in the marketplace and market what you have.

SOURCE: Mark Y. Herring, *Raising Funds with Friends Groups* (New York: Neal-Schuman, 2004), pp. 64–71. Reprinted with permission.

TECHNOLOGY
CHAPTER EIGHT

"The computer is here to stay; therefore, it must be kept in its proper place as a tool and a slave, or we will become sorcerer's apprentices, with data everywhere and not a thought to think."

—Jesse Shera (1983)

LOW TECHNOLOGY

Things we use in libraries and when they were invented

by George M. Eberhart

Air conditioner, 1906. American engineer Willis Haviland Carrier devised a system to control heat and humidity for the Sackett-Wilhelms Lithographing and Publishing Company in Brooklyn. The firm had been unable to print reliable colors at times because of fluctuations in ambient temperature and humidity that caused paper to expand or contract and ink to flow or dry up.

Audiocassette tape deck, 1965. Marketed by the Phillips corporation as an improvement over reel-to-reel recorders and players. It enclosed both reels of the recording tape in a small case that eliminated the need to thread the tape through individual reels.

Automated catalog, 1951. King County Public Library in Seattle issued possibly the first machine-produced book catalog, generated from punched cards and printed on an IBM Tabulator.

Automated catalog (union), 1962. The Monsanto Company's information center in St. Louis produced a book-form catalog for its seven libraries using a computer-based system.

Automated circulation system, 1962. The U.S. Army's Picatinny Arsenal in New Jersey was perhaps the first institution to convert its bibliographic records to a homegrown digital catalog, using IBM punch cards. The Illinois State Library in Springfield set up an early online system in 1966, which merged transactions into the main circulation file once a day via batch processing.

Ballpoint pen, 1938. Hungarian journalist László Bíró developed a pen with a rotating tip that picks up ink from a cartridge as it turns in its socket. It became the first commercially successful ballpoint. A Massachusetts inventor named John Loud had patented a ballpoint pen for marking rough surfaces in 1888.

Bar-code reader, 1974. The first successful retail bar-code reader was used on June 26 to scan a pack of Wrigley's Juicy Fruit chewing gum at the Marsh supermarket in Troy, Ohio. Bar-code technology had been patented by Norman Joseph Woodland and Bernard Silver in 1952.

Book catalog, 3000 B.C. The oldest known catalog is a 62-item list of titles that appears on a Sumerian tablet found at the ancient city of Nippur, located northeast of Ad Diwaniyah in modern Iraq.

Bookmobile, 1858. A "perambulating library" was begun in England in 1858 by the Warrington Mechanics' Institution. The first bookwagon service in the United States was started in 1905 by Mary Titcomb, the first librarian at Washington County (Md.) Free Library in Hagerstown (see p. 50).

Card catalog, 1860. Ezra Abbot, assistant librarian at Harvard College, is credited with devising the first alphabetical library card catalog system in the United States, complete with the grouping of minor topics under more general headings. Melvil Dewey's Library Bureau in Boston encouraged the standardization of card size to 3-by-5 inches in 1890, began manufacturing drawers with a single row of cards in 1891, and patented the first drawers with metal rods that entered from the front in 1894. The Library of Congress began printing catalog cards in 1898 and started distributing them to other libraries in 1901.

Card index tabs, 1896. American inventor James Newton Gunn started using tabbed cards to subdivide membership records for the Akron YMCA. The tabs were positioned so they would not obscure the view of another tabbed card in a drawer. In 1897, Gunn sold the rights to Melvil Dewey's Library Bureau, where he began work as a consultant.

Central heating, 100 B.C. Roman fish farmer Gaius Sergius Orata invented a way to keep his fish tanks warm by circulating hot air from a nearby furnace. Later, Roman engineers applied the principle to create the *hypocausum*, a heating system in which wood fires heated the air in the basement tanks of Roman baths, which then circulated through pipes or hollow bricks along the floor and into the walls.

Clock, 723. A mechanical astronomical clock using water as a power source was invented by the Chinese Buddhist monk I-Hsing. Richard of Wallingford's mechanical clock at St. Albans Abbey in England (ca. 1330) appears to be the first automatic striking clock with a modern escapement.

Compact disc, 1982. Sony and Phillips introduced the first CD players. The first commercial audio CD was *52nd Street* by Billy Joel. CD-ROMs were adapted by the computer industry for low-cost storage of large computer programs and databases in 1985; the first application was *Grolier's Electronic Encyclopedia*. In 1995, Microsoft's *Encarta* published the first hybrid online/CD-ROM encyclopedia; this version could be updated monthly by downloading content from the internet.

Dust jacket, 1833. *The Keepsake*, an annual illustrated anthology of poetry and prose, published in London in 1833 by Longman, Rees, Orme, Brown, Green, and Longman, possibly had the first commercially printed dust jacket, although a seven-volume set of Sir Walter Scott's *Poetical Works* published in 1824 by R. W. Pomeroy in Philadelphia may have had paper wrappers provided by the publisher.

DVD, 1996. The first DVD players were available in Japan, followed by the United States in 1997. *Batman* was the first of 50 DVD titles released by Warner Home Video in March 1997.

Electronic mail, 1970. Douglas Englebart at Stanford Research Institute's Augmentation Research Center developed the first large-scale implementation of email. In 1971, Ray Tomlinson, a computer scientist at the Bolt, Beranek, and Newman engineering firm in Cambridge, Massachusetts, wrote the first email program to send messages across a distributed network; in March 1972 he introduced the @ sign to separate the name of the addressee from the name of the computer location.

Electronic mail spam, 1978. The first instance of mass unsolicited email was perhaps the announcement of a product presentation sent on May 3 by a Digital Equipment Corporation salesman to several hundred scientists and researchers on the ARPAnet. The first instance of the use of the word "spam" occurred on March 31, 1993, when Usenet administrator Richard Depew inadvertently posted the same message 200 times to a discussion group; adopting a term previously used in online text games, outraged Usenet users branded the excessive message posting "spam."

Elevator, 1852. Elisha Otis invented the first freight elevator with a safety guard that prevents the elevator from falling if the cable is cut. He demonstrated it at New York's Crystal Palace in 1854, and installed the first safety-equipped passenger elevator in a Manhattan china and glass store at 488 Broadway in 1857.

Fax machine (photos), 1902. German physicist Arthur Korn developed a method of sending photographs over wires by electrical signals. In 1907, he  sent the first intercity fax when he transmitted a photo from Munich to Berlin.

Fax machine (writing), 1865. Italian physicist Giovanni Caselli introduced the pantelegraph, based on earlier ideas by Alexander Bain and Frederick Bakewell. Three of his machines transmitted handwritten messages in France until 1870.

Filing cabinet, 1892. Melvil Dewey's Library Bureau in Boston invented the first filing cabinet in which papers are stored vertically rather than flat. It was designed for the Charity Organization in Buffalo.

Fire extinguisher, 1816. The first compressed-air extinguisher was invented in London by Captain George Manby. It consisted of a three-gallon copper vessel containing a potassium carbonate solution.

Fluorescent lamp, 1926. German inventor Edmund Germer coated an ultraviolet arc lamp with fluorescing powder to transform UV light into visible light. The patent was picked up by General Electric and brought to commercial use in 1938.

Flush toilet, 1775. British watchmaker Alexander Cummings invented the S-trap toilet that uses standing water to seal the outlet of the bowl.

Full-text searching, 1960. The University of Pittsburgh demonstrated the first instance of computer searching of full-text information.

Glass windows, 60 B.C. The oldest glass windowpane at Pompeii was found in a building in the Forum built around this date. It was fixed in a bronze frame that turned on two pivots, allowing the window to open.

Inkjet printer, 1988. The first commercially available printer using inkjet technology was the Deskjet introduced by Hewlett-Packard, although the technology had been developed in the 1960s.

Integrated library system, 1972. Stanford University's BALLOTS was the earliest successful implementation of a multifeatured technical processing system. Later adopted as the online bibliographic component of the Research Libraries Group's RLIN, BALLOTS allowed for MARC record searching, acquisitions tracking, and cataloging.

Internet, 1969. UCLA engineering professor Leonard Kleinrock and student Charley Kline attempted to send a message at 10:30 p.m., October 29, from one Honeywell computer to a similar unit at the Stanford Research Institute in Palo Alto—the only two nodes on the fledgling ARPANET. The message was supposed to be the word "login," but the system crashed as they typed in the letter "g." The first internet message, then, was "lo." Kleinrock was able to complete Leonard Kleinrock the message one hour later.

Kurzweil reading machine, 1976. Raymond Kurzweil announced the first print-to-speech reading machine for the blind January 13 at a televised press conference. After seeing a demonstration on the *Today* show, singer Stevie Wonder purchased the first production model.

Liquid Paper, 1956. Dallas secretary Bette Nesmith Graham (the mother of Monkee Michael Nesmith) began marketing her typewriter correction fluid as "Mistake Out."

Loose-leaf ring binder, 1854. The first was patented by Henry T. Sisson of Providence, Rhode Island.

Magazine, 1663. A German monthly started in 1663 by Hamburg poet Johann Rist, *Erbauliche Monaths-Unterredungen,* is said to have been the first magazine. The first British magazine was the *Oxford Gazette,* established in 1665 and still published as the *London Gazette.* The first scientific journals were the *Journal des Sçavans* (1665) and the *Philosophical Transactions* of the Royal Society (1666). The first women's magazine was the *Ladies Mercury* (1693), and one of the first periodicals to use the word "magazine" in its title was the *Gentleman's Magazine,* founded in London in 1731, which became the most influential general-interest journal in the 18th century. In America, the first magazines were Andrew Bradford's *American Magazine* and Benjamin Franklin's *General Magazine,* both published within days of each other in 1741. The earliest magazine in Canada was the *Nova-Scotia Magazine* (1789).

Microfilm reader, 1925. The British optician John Benjamin Dancer had successfully produced and sold microphotographs by 1858. Rear Admiral Bradley A. Fiske of the U.S. Navy had invented a Fiskeoscope reader in 1919, but it was never developed. New York banker George McCarthy obtained a patent in 1925 for his Checkograph machine, which used motion picture film and a conveyor belt to photograph checks before they were returned to bank customers. In 1928, the Eastman Kodak company's Recordak division purchased the rights to the invention. In 1935, Recordak began publishing the *New York Times* on microfilm.

Mouse, 1963. American inventor Douglas Engelbart designed the first device to move a cursor on a computer monitor and issue simple commands. Made in a shop at Stanford Research Institute, the casing was carved out of wood. It had only one button.

Newspaper, 1609. The first weekly newspaper was possibly *Avisa Relation oder Zeintung, Was Sich Begeben und Zugetragen Hat,* published in Augsburg, Germany, by Lucas Schulte. In the early 1620s, Schulte moved his operation to Oettingen, where the paper eventually became the *München-Augsburger Abendzeitung.* The first English-language paper, *The Corante, or, Newes from Italy, Germany, Hungarie, Spaine and France* (1621), was a translation of an Amsterdam weekly.

Online bibliographic retrieval, 1964. The New York World's Fair offered the first public demonstration of online bibliographic retrieval at its Library/USA exhibit. The general public could view bibliographic information and interact remotely with reference librarians through a computer using standard telephone lines. Produced by Joe Becker and cosponsored by the American Library Association and members of the data processing and publishing industries, this was the first online system to allow multiple users to search one database simultaneously. In 1968, the State University of New York launched a Biomedical Communications Network that provided nine libraries with phone-line access to a medical database; it was the first system to provide regular service on a long-term basis to a wide network of users. It consisted of 500,000+ records and was the first to incorporate library holdings information with specific output records.

Online bibliographic utility, 1971. Chartered in 1967 and launched in 1970 with offline batch processing, OCLC (then the Ohio College Library Center) in Dublin, Ohio, in 1971 licensed terminals that allowed its member libraries to search its database online and order catalog cards.

www.oclc.org

Online public access catalog, 1970. IBM put the Experimental Library Management System (ELMS) into operation at its Los Gatos Laboratory library. Designed by Robert Alexander, the system included bibliographic descriptions, order information, and circulation status. Shortly afterward, in December 1970, Ohio State University launched one of the first campuswide systems with its innovative, IBM-developed Library Control System.

Paper, 105 A.D. The Chinese court official Cai Lun was the first to mention the modern method of making paper from cotton rags.

Paper clip, 1899. William Middlebrook of Waterbury, Connecticut, patented a machine for manufacturing paper clips of the type made by the Gem Paperclip Company in England since 1890. A less functional clip was invented the same year by a Norwegian, Johan Vaaler.

Pencil, 1565. Swiss naturalist Konrad von Gesner described a wooden pencil filled with graphite. The first pencil to have an eraser at the tip was invented by Hyman Lipman of Philadelphia in 1858.

Pencil sharpener, 1847. Frenchman Therry des Estwaux is said to have invented the first manual pencil sharpener. Henry C. Haskell patented a combination pen rack, cleaner, and mechanical pencil sharpener in 1860.

Personal computer, 1973. The Xerox Corporation developed the Alto computer at the Palo Alto Research Center, complete with monitor. It was the result of a joint effort by Ed McCreight, Chuck Thacker, Butler Lampson, Bob Sproull, and Dave Boggs, who were attempting to make a device that was small enough to fit in an office comfortably, but powerful enough to support a reliable operating system and graphics display. The first commercially successful personal computer was the Apple II, launched in 1976.

Phonodisc, 1890. Thomas Edison had invented the phonograph in 1877, which recorded sounds on a rotating metal cylinder. In 1890, the German inventor Emile Berliner founded a company (which later became Deutsche Grammophon) to produce the first flat records for his gramophone invention. In 1892, he incorporated the United States Gramophone Company in Washington, D.C., which marketed the first non-toy, five- and seven-inch disc records on the Berliner Gramophone label. One of the earliest musical disc recordings was George J. Gaskin singing *I Don't Want to Play in Your Back Yard* on October 29, 1895. Cylinder recordings continued to compete with the growing disc record market into the 1910s, but discs won out when Columbia (which had been making both discs and cylinders) switched exclusively to discs, and the Edison company started marketing its own disc records.

Phonodisc (78 rpm), 1903. The first 12-inch, 78-rpm records were made by the Victor Talking Machine Company featuring songs by the Italian opera tenor Francesco Tamagno. The earliest record sleeves are possibly those issued in 1905 by Victor for recordings by the Australian soprano Nellie Melba.

Phonodisc (33-1/3 rpm), 1926. The first 33-1/3-rpm recording was produced by Vitaphone Corporation to synchronize with the motion picture *Don Juan*. The first successful release of long-playing vinyl 33-1/3-rpm microgroove discs (developed by Peter Goldmark and William Bachman in 1945) was announced by American Columbia in June 1948.

Phonodisc (45 rpm), 1949. The first seven-inch, 45-rpm discs were introduced by RCA Victor in various shades of colored vinyl.

Phonodisc (stereo), 1957. The first commercial stereophonic discs were made by Emery Cook of Stamford, Connecticut, in 1957, although the first stereo recordings were actually produced by Pathé in France between 1910 and 1914.

Photocopier, 1938. American physicist and attorney Chester F. Carlson and his German assistant Otto Kornei made the first xerographic copy (the words "10.-22.-38 ASTORIA" in India ink on a microscope slide) on October 22, 1938, in Astoria, New York. In 1944, Carlson signed a royalty-sharing agreement with the Battelle Memorial Institute in Columbus, Ohio, which developed the process further. In 1947, Battelle granted the right to develop an "electrophotography" machine to a small photographic-paper company run by Joseph C. Wilson in Rochester, New York, called Haloid, which decided (after Battelle consulted with a Greek scholar at Ohio State University) that the new machine would be called "XeroX." In 1959, the Haloid company, which later changed its name to Xerox, introduced the first plain-paper xerographic office copier, called the 914 because it could make copies up to 9 × 14 inches in size.

Plumbing, 2700 B.C. Joinable earthenware pipes of standard size were in use by the Indus Valley civilization of India and Pakistan.

Post-it note, 1974. 3M researcher Art Fry applied a weak adhesive developed by his colleague Spencer Silver to create bookmarks for his hymnal in church choir. 3M began distributing them nationally in 1980.

Rubber stamp, 1862. Invented in the early 1860s and made of vulcanized india rubber, the first stamps are variously credited to James Orton Woodruff, John Leighton, L. F. Witherell, and Henry C. Leland.

Sprinkler system, 1874. Henry S. Parmalee of New Haven, Connecticut, invented the first practical automatic sprinkler head by improving on Philip W. Pratt's 1872 patent and creating a better sprinkler. In 1874, he installed his system into the piano factory that he owned.

Stapler, 1914. The Boston Wire Stitcher Company developed the first desk-model staplers, in which staples were inserted loose or in paper wrappers. The company switched to a new model in 1923 that allowed staples to be inserted in long rows. Earlier, heavier models were patented by Samuel Slocum in 1841, the Patent Novelty Manufacturing Company in 1866, and George W. McGill in 1867.

Subject index (computerized), 1958. *Biological Abstracts* published the first computer-produced subject index in April.

Subject retrieval engine, 1954. The U.S. Naval Ordnance Test Station at China Lake, California, developed a batch-oriented retrieval engine using Mortimer Taube's Uniterm system on an IBM 701 calculator for an Armed Services Technical Information Agency file of 15,000 documents. It could add new information, delete information on discarded documents, match search requests against a master file, and produce a printout of document numbers.

Telephone, 1876. Although Alexander Graham Bell has long gotten the credit, Italian inventor Antonio Meucci built a working telephone model in 1855 and filed a caveat (notice of intent) with the U.S. Patent Office in 1871.

Telephone (coin-operated), 1889. Inventor William Gray installed the first public coin-operated phone in the Hartford (Conn.) Bank. Customers deposited coins after calls were completed.

Telephone (touch-tone), 1962. Introduced at the Seattle World's Fair in 1962, touch-tone phones—which used tones in the voice frequency range rather than pulses generated by rotary dials—

Antonio Meucci

had been developed by Bell Telephone as early as 1941. In 1963, the first modern touch-tone phone, the Western Electric 1500 with only 10 buttons, became available commercially.

Telephone (mobile), 1973. Although mobile phones with direct dialing have existed since the 1950s, the first modern instance of mobile telephony is considered to be April 3, 1973, when Motorola employee Martin Cooper placed a call to rival AT&T's Bell Labs while walking the streets of New York City talking on a Motorola DynaTAC, the first mobile phone to receive FCC acceptance. The first text message (Short Message Service) took place December 3, 1992, when messaging engineer Neil Papworth of the British technology company Sema Group sent the (premature) greeting "Merry Christmas" from a personal computer to the mobile phone of Richard Jarvis, a director of the Vodafone company, on the Vodafone GSM network.

Telephone booth, 1883. First created by Thomas A. Watson, assistant to Alexander Graham Bell. His model used fine wood, screened windows, and a desk with pen and ink.

Television, 1941. Commercial broadcasting began in the United States when the FCC issued its first commercial license, and NBC and CBS begin transmitting programs and commercials in 1941 in New York City. Scottish engineer John Logie Baird had demonstrated that a semimechanical analogue television system was possible with the transmission of a static image of Felix the Cat in London in February 1924. On October 30, 1925,

How to make a Simple Televisor

Specially described and tested for Television" by our Technical Staff.

Baird transmitted the first moving image, a grainy image of a ventriloquist dummy's head, and later sent a live image of a local boy he had paid to take part in his experiments to a crowd of amazed onlookers. A fully electronic television system with a vacuum-tube display was first demonstrated by Philo Taylor Farnsworth on September 7, 1927, when he transmitted the image of a simple straight line at his own laboratory at 202 Green Street, San Francisco.

Theft detection system, 1964. Possibly the first electronic system was installed at the Grand Rapids (Mich.) Public Library.

Turnstile, 1928. American inventors John Perey and Conrad Trubenbach patented the first tripod-arm mechanical turnstile.

Typewriter, 1868. Milwaukee printer Christopher Latham Sholes patented the first non-cumbersome typewriter, complete with the "qwerty" key layout, which he then licensed to the Remington company of Ilion, New York. The "Sholes & Glidden Type Writer" went on sale in 1874, with the "Remington No. 2" (improved with a shift bar allowing for upper- and lower-case letters) going on sale in 1878. One of the first customers was Mark Twain, who claimed in 1904 he had been the first author to deliver a typewritten manuscript to a publisher (*The Adventures of Tom Sawyer*, 1876).

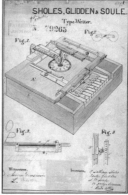

Videocassette, 1975. Sony introduced the first consumer videocassette recording and playback system, the Betamax. It was successful at first but later failed in the marketplace against JVC's 1976 VHS because its initial maximum recording time of one hour was a disadvantage that it could not overcome, even when it later offered five-hour recording times. Earlier, in 1958, Ampex had taken a color video tape recorder to Russia and demonstrated it before Vice President Richard Nixon and USSR Premier Nikita Khrushchev; a color recording was brought back and broadcast on American television.

Wi-Fi wireless adapter, 1999. Introduced by Apple in its new iBook computers, under the brand name AirPort.

Word processor, 1976. Designed by Harold Koplow and David Moros, the first computer-based word processor was introduced by Wang Laboratories of Tewksbury, Massachusetts. Each workstation looked like a typical terminal of its day, but contained a Z80 microprocessor and 65K of RAM (roughly comparable in power to a 1982 IBM PC).

World Wide Web, 1990. In November, British software developer Tim Berners-Lee created the first web page, nxoc01.cern.ch/hypertext/WWW/TheProject.html (no longer maintained, but a later version is archived at www.w3.org/History/19921103-hypertext/hypertext/WWW/News/9201.html). It appeared on the first web server, hosted by CERN (European Organization for Nuclear Research) in Switzerland, and was located at nxoc01.cern.ch, which later changed to info.cern.ch. It provided an explanation about what the Web was, how one could own a browser, and how to set up a web server. It became the world's first web directory, since Berners-Lee later maintained a list of other websites apart from his own. The program ran on the NeXT operating system; not many people used it. CERN released web client software in July 1992, and about 23 servers were operating by November. The explosion in popularity of the Web began after the National Center for Supercomputing

NeXT workstation used by Tim Berners-Lee as the first web server

8

Applications at the University of Illinois at Urbana-Champaign developed Mosaic, a graphical browser running originally on Unix but soon ported to the Apple Macintosh and Microsoft Windows platforms. Version 1.0 was released in September 1993. Marc Andreessen, who was the leader of the Mosaic team at NCSA, quit to form a company that would later be known as Netscape Communications Corporation.

SOURCES: Bryan Bunch and Alexander Hellemans, *The History of Science and Technology* (Boston: Houghton Mifflin, 2004); Gerri Flanzraich, "The Library Bureau and Office Technology," *Libraries and Culture* 28 (Fall 1993): 403–429; Kevin Desmond, *A Timetable of Inventions and Discoveries* (New York: M. Evans, 1986); Dennis Reynolds, *Library Automation* (New York: R. R. Bowker, 1985); Robert and Celia Dearling, *The Guinness Book of Recorded Sound* (Enfield, Eng.: Guinness, 1984); Laird Whitmire and Lisa Gieskes, Chronology of Information Science and Technology, www.libsci.sc.edu/bob/istchron/iscnet/ischron.htm; Wikipedia; History of Office Equipment, www.ideafinder.com/features/everwonder/office.htm; Roger Darlington, Fascinating Facts and Figures about All Aspects of the Information Society, www.rogerdarlington.co.uk/FFF.html; and other internet sources.

The monster under the bed

by Martin H. Raish

One of the diseases of this age is the multiplicity of books; they doth so overcharge the world that it is not able to digest the abundance of idle matter that is every day hatched and brought forth into the world.

—Barnabe Rich, ca. 1613, cited by Derek de Solla Price
in *Little Science, Big Science* (1963)

WE HAVE ALL HEARD THE MANTRA: Knowledge is doubling every [insert your favorite number] years/months/days/hours, and so on. Knowledge is a monster of hideous proportion. *Or is it?*

The "knowledge is doubling" specter in its various guises has haunted us for generations, as illustrated by the Barnabe Rich quotation, but it gained increased attention with the rise of the internet and the development of personal computers in the early 1980s. Today many people, including librarians, seem to be frightened by this beast, judging by the hundreds of times it is mentioned in books, articles, speeches, news reports, and websites. A tiny sample (a half-dozen years' worth) of such statements follows. I could have included many other examples (my most recent Google search for "knowledge is doubling" returned over 600 hits), but these will suffice. They are arranged chronologically:

- "Knowledge is doubling every six months."—Mountain Brook City (Ala.) Schools' Technology Plan, Spring 1994.
- "Our worldwide knowledge fund doubles every six to seven years." —Phoenix *Arizona Republic*, Feb. 26, 1995.
- "We are in a period when knowledge is doubling every 16.7 months." —National Association of County Agricultural Agents, Aug. 1995.
- "Knowledge is doubling every 350 days according to those who calculate such things."—SUNY Potsdam, New Student Convocation, Aug. 24, 1995.
- "Knowledge is doubling every 16–18 months."—*Forbes*, Dec. 4, 1995.

- "It is estimated that the amount of medical knowledge doubles every two years."—*JAMA* 275 (1996): 1637–1639.
- "Knowledge is doubling every 3–5 years."—*Daily Motivator,* Mar. 27, 1996.
- "At the current rate, the entire body of scientific knowledge will double every two years."—*American Druggist,* June 1996.
- "The total of all printed information doubles every five years."—*Professional Reading Guide for Educational Administrators,* Feb./Mar. 1997.
- "Human knowledge is doubling every 30 or so years."—4th Hong Kong (AsiaPacific) Medical Informatics Conference, Oct. 1997.
- "The reservoir of world knowledge is doubling every two years."—Kuala Lumpur *New Straits Times,* Dec. 2, 1997.
- "Human knowledge is doubling every 10 years."—London *Times,* Mar. 16, 1998.
- "The store of human knowledge is doubling every five years."—*Journal of Commerce,* Mar. 26, 1998.
- "Recorded knowledge is doubling every 15–20 years."—Los Alamos National Laboratory, *Research Library Newsletter,* Jan. 1999.
- "Scientific and technological knowledge doubles every three to five years."—Tokyo *Daily Yomiuri,* Jan. 25, 1999.
- "In 25 years, knowledge will double every three months."—*San Jose Mercury News,* Sept. 15, 1999.
- "All printed knowledge doubles every five years."—Kuala Lumpur *New Straits Times,* July 20, 2000.
- "The total of all printed knowledge doubles every four or five years." —Jack Trout, *Differentiate or Die* (Wiley, 2000).
- "The amount of available knowledge is doubling every 18 months." —Bayer Group Webzine, Sept. 12, 2001.
- "Advances in technology and technique now double the total information astronomers gather annually."—*Washington Post,* Oct. 30, 2001.

I have long had serious reservations about statements such as these. Let me explain why.

Data, information, knowledge

My first concern is simply the lack of precision about what exactly is growing. While most of the statements speak of "knowledge," I discovered the majority of them while searching for "information." They were taken from speeches and articles about "The Age of Information" or "the information explosion," yet they cite how rapidly knowledge is growing. Information and knowledge, however, are not the same thing. (Nor is either the same as data, another term people sometimes confuse with them.) We need to understand clearly the distinctions among these terms.

Pieces of *data* are things lying about. They can be natural phenomena—the temperature of the air, the size of a seed, the weight of a lion, the composition of the soil, and so forth; or they can be man-made—prices of goods, sports scores, dimensions of buildings, and so forth. There seems to be no end to data.

Information is more than data. (As Clifford Stoll in his book *Silicon Snake Oil* [Doubleday, 1995] has observed, "Data isn't information any more than fifty tons of cement is a skyscraper.") It has been defined in many ways, but two of my favorite definitions are "facts without context and therefore without priority" (Wendell Berry, *Orion Online,* Oct. 30, 2001), and "the meaning that someone assigns to data" (Peter J. Denning, *The Invisible Future* [McGraw-Hill, 2002]). The critical aspect is that for information to exist, a person must gather and ponder data and arrive at some decision that usually results in an action being taken or at least a choice being made. This action or choice may be immediate, or the information may be filed away for future use.

And just as information is built from data, so is *knowledge* built from information. Knowledge is information that has been internalized, that has become "mine" and is different from "yours." It is what results when I gather and ponder information, evaluate various conflicting ideas and experiences, then apply it to my circumstances to make it part of my life. It is also something that rarely results from anything other than sustained effort or direct experience. Thus, it generally has longer staying power. It is more permanent, less open to the winds of change.

Knowledge is also difficult to communicate. When you try to share with me what you know, it comes to me not as knowledge but as information or perhaps even as data, if there is distance between us either in time or in the number of intermediaries who have translated, reworded, or summarized the ideas along the way. I must recreate my own knowledge with the information I have received. Thus in the quotes above, the term "printed information" is acceptable, but "printed knowledge," "recorded knowledge," and even "available knowledge" are more difficult for me to accept.

One way to illustrate the differences in these concepts is to picture yourself driving in your car toward a railroad crossing on Main Street in your town. The tracks are data: they are just there. The times of departures and arrivals are also data.

Information is formed when you see the tracks, read the timetable, and recognize it as the correct one for your location. You then combine this with data such as the day of the week, the time of day, and the fact that you plan to be in town several times this week.

Knowledge is the realization not only that the train arrives at 12:05 on Tuesday afternoon but also that the day is Tuesday, the time is 12:04, and you are approaching the crossing. All the data and information you have gathered and considered now combine to become valuable to you. (Wisdom, of course, is to stop your car and wait for the train to pass.)

All this is probably moot, however. The people who made the doubling statements likely never thought about my concern. For them the terms are almost certainly interchangeable.

I have no doubt that the amount of data is growing at an astounding pace, as we discover more about our natural world and create mountains of artificial data in our man-made world. If these statements spoke of "data" instead of "knowledge" or "information," I would have a much smaller quarrel with them. The fact that they do not discriminate between the terms is a serious weakness they all share.

Measuring or guessing?

My second reservation with these statements is their significant disagreement as to exactly how rapidly information/knowledge is growing.

The differences cannot be explained because of the years in which the words were written, as if the pace of growth were accelerating. The two quotes about "scientific knowledge" illustrate this problem: It is doubling every two years in 1996 but every three to five years in 1999. It is also important to note that the extremes are separated by only two years: We have 30 years' doubling time in 1997 but only 12 months doubling time in 2001.

Similarly in 1995, different statements have this doubling occurring within years, months, and even days. Either we are not all using the same instrument to measure growth, or the tool we are using is inaccurate. It is also possible that we are not using any measuring instrument at all but only making educated guesses, based on limited observations of data that is sketchy at best.

Furthermore, in order to claim that something is growing, we must not only measure it now but must have also measured it sometime in the past using the same (imprecise) tool. Has this been done? Yes, but rarely, since there are few situations where accurate measurements are even possible. One is to count the number of publications in a particular field and calculate how rapidly it increases. For example, we can determine how long it took Chemical Abstracts to index its first millionth entry, its second millionth, and so forth. Because fewer years elapsed between each milestone, it is reasonable to conclude that the number of publications in the field of chemistry is growing. But the data simply does not support the contention that any sort of doubling is occurring very quickly.

If we define "doubling" as the total number of items cited since Chemical Abstracts began keeping track, the data shows that the most recent doubling took about 17 years, from 9,904,000 items in 1983 to 19,754,000 in 2000. If we define "doubling" as the number of citations listed each year, the data shows an even longer period: In 2000 there were 725,195 citations, but we must go back to 1975 to find a figure about half this size. Thus, the data reveals periods of 17 or 25 years, not two or three or five, as these experts claim. (A similar analysis of Biological Abstracts showed that the literature of biology increased by about 80% between 1984 and 1994—a faster pace than that of chemistry but still far from doubling in just a few years.)

Even if we acknowledge that the pace of scientific publication is accelerating, can we conclude that all knowledge is growing at a similar rate? Such an extrapolation, I believe, is unjustifiable.

Documentation

The third factor that erodes the value of these statements is that the authors provide no documentation for their claims. One statement does mention "those who calculate such things," and others (not cited here) occasionally make passing reference to the number of articles or books published in a year, or some similar bit of data that could be verified (or not). But every time I have tried to uncover the source of a growth number, I have run into a dead end.

For example, a scholar was quoted in *American Libraries* as saying that "the amount of electronic information is doubling every 60 minutes" (Aug. 2000, p. 34). I contacted him and asked for his documentation. I learned that what he was really talking about was the number of electronic records generated everyday, including short-lived banking and business transactions, and satellite downloads of weather and military surveillance data that are not really "information." He had gotten his figures from a colleague, who in turn had read them in a 2000

Collaborative Electronic Notebook Systems Association report, the methodology of which was described as being "at best, back of envelope."

What originally appeared to be a rare case of a well-documented study of the growth of information proved to be a mirage. (I should also note that the source where I first found the statement neglected to mention that it was a prediction, that the growth was not happening today, but was expected to occur "within 10 years.")

It is undoubtedly true that data is being discovered and generated at a fantastic pace and that the amount of information we deal with daily is prodigious, but none of the statements about the doubling of knowledge have enough real evidence to persuade me that it is increasing at anywhere near the rate many people are claiming.

This leads me to conclude that the "Knowledge Is Doubling" monster is, to a large extent, more a mirage than a reality. Some sort of creature is lurking under the bed, and it is probably large, but it is not so huge that we should be paralyzed by its mere shadow. Shining a flashlight on it reveals its lack of substance and shrinks it to a manageable size.

SOURCE: Martin H. Raish, "Shining Some Light on the Monster under the Bed: A Closer Look at the 'Doubling of Knowledge,'" in Martin H. Raish, ed., *Musings, Meanderings, and Monsters, Too* (Lanham, Md.: Scarecrow, 2003), pp. 145–156.

LIBRARY SYSTEMS

Trends in integrated library software

by Marshall Breeding

THE MAINSTREAM LIBRARY AUTOMATION SYSTEMS available in 2004 can all be considered fully developed, at least regarding the core ILS functionality. Although each product has its strengths and weaknesses relative to its competitors, all the products include the major modules and sophisticated functionality within each module.

As the table on page 431 illustrates, some systems on the market benefit from more than 20 years of product development and evolution. Although some systems have evolved significantly in their underlying components, the features available in the system have grown steadily. Even the newest of the current systems have been on the market for more than five years.

Having developed previous generations of automation software, some companies offer history and experience that exceed the development history of their latest product.

The expected feature set of library automation systems has been evolving even longer. The basic methods and procedures associated with library automation were established in the precursors of these systems that have since become extinct.

Few multiuser library automation systems have entered the market in the last five years. The Destiny product released by Follett Software Co., which debuted at the National Educational Computing Conference in July 2003, remains as one of the few new systems introduced in recent years. Since this system was developed by the dominant company in the school library automation market, it is a system to watch.

Year of Product Introduction	
Product	*Year introduced*
Aleph	1980/1995*
Horizon	1991
Library.Solution	1996
Innopac/Millennium	1985
Polaris	1997
Unicorn	1982
Virtua	1995
Voyager	1992/1995**

*Aleph began as a mainframe-based system in about 1980. Aleph 500, the fourth generation of this product, began development in 1995.

**MARCorp, formerly Carlyle Systems, began development of a library automation system called Voyager Library Series in 1992. Endeavor Information Systems acquired that product when Endeavor became a company in November 1994. The original Voyager code base was replaced by programming developed by Endeavor starting with the version released in 1995.

Consolidation of companies and systems

One of the major trends in the library automation industry involves consolidation—both on the library and the vendor sides. Results of this trend are less diversity in the systems operated by libraries over time and for implementations of library automation systems to be larger, each supporting a large number of libraries.

A consolidation of library automation companies has transpired over the course of the last five years. A smaller number of library automation companies are offering fewer library automation systems.

Note, however, that the degree of consolidation among the library automation companies has not been as aggressive as that seen in other information services industries. Yet, the mergers and acquisitions that have taken place in the last 10 years have been the largest single factor in determining the systems available today.

The library automation industry has seen many consolidations take place through corporate acquisitions. The process initially involves one company acquiring one its competitors.

In the initial period following the acquisition, the acquiring company offers reassurance to the customers of the acquired company that its products will be supported and developed for a reasonable time. Whether stated or unstated, the years following the merger involve a steady process of coaching the libraries to adopt the company's flagship system.

All the mergers that have taken place in the industry have eventually resulted in a consolidation of systems—even if accomplished gradually. Ideally, each library automation company strives to develop and support a single library automation system.

Legacy systems and those gained though acquisitions ultimately will need to give way to a single flagship system on which the company can focus its resources. Ongoing development and maintenance of multiple systems cannot be sustained indefinitely.

Extending the ILS

The traditional ILS focused on the library's print collections of monographs, serials, and physical media (videos, CDs, DVDs). The universe of the current library automation must be much broader if it is to serve the library successfully.

The core functionality of the library automation can be considered fairly well defined, and the major library automaton systems all achieve almost complete compliance with that functionality. Yet, that core functionality focuses mostly on managing and providing access to the library's physical collection.

Although the part of library automation defined by the traditional ILS is mature, a whole new set of automation expectations is emerging. The solutions in these areas are in an early stage.

These new expectations center on the modern library's need to manage collections with ever higher proportions of electronic content and to provide services to library users through the Web, while still continuing to manage physical collections and provide traditional in-library services.

To serve a library well, a library automation environment must manage both physical and electronic resources. Earlier conceptions that libraries would evolve into mostly virtual organizations have not come to pass.

Although some areas—especially scholarly journals—have seen print resources diminish as electronic content expands, books continue to be a mainstay. E-books have made a relatively small impact on libraries, and the collection and circulation of physical books will be a permanent part of library operations.

The range of materials managed, though, must expand to include the library's collection of electronic journals, abstracting and indexing (A&I) databases, and collections of digital objects (images, video, and sound).

One of the largest challenges lies in managing collections of periodicals and journals that are partially electronic and partially print. Library users want electronic journals they can click through and read from the convenience of their web browser—whether they are at home, in their office, or even in the library.

A basic issue addresses accessing article-level information. Library catalogs tend to work best at the title level for books and journals.

Beginning in the late 1980s, many libraries experimented with loading article citation databases in their online catalogs. The NOTIS Multiple Database Access System was but one example of such a system that allowed libraries to load large sets of citations from A&I databases into their local catalogs as bibliographic records that could be searched alongside the library's traditional database, using the same commands and interface. These locally mounted article databases were valuable at the time, since the alternatives in the form of mediated searching and printed indexes were inconvenient for library users.

Citation databases next became commonly distributed on CD-ROM, packaged with PC-based search-and-retrieval software. These CD-ROM–based products expanded into local area networks, allowing multiuser access within the library—a significant advance at the time.

The main disadvantages of this system included having to physically visit the library to use the resources. An additional limit occurred with the number of libraries that could use any given resource imposed by the physical number of PCs on which the software was made available or the number of simultaneous users allowed by the distribution license.

The next step in the evolution of citations involved web-based resources. This approach takes advantage of the ubiquitous infrastructure of the Web, allowing library users to access many different citation databases to which the library may subscribe from outside the library.

The model of web-accessible citation databases, while providing a level of convenience for its users, also presents some challenges. As a separate brand-name product, the library user may not even be aware that the product is made available by license fees paid for by the library, even if they link to it from the library's website.

Library users also have difficulty in knowing what kind of information is provided by each of the many different citation databases their library might make available to them. Although all the web-based citation databases follow the same general set of conventions for entering searches and viewing results, differences among them exist. Figuring out how to use each citation database can burden library users.

Using a citation database isn't an end in itself, but rather a tool for finding articles and other resources relating to the searcher's research topic. Linking from the citation to full text has become a standard expectation of the current information environment. Providing links that reliably take library users from a citation database to full text or from citations within one article to the full text of another article also is an expected capability.

Several technologies, such as OpenURL-based link resolvers and federated searching, have emerged to address many of the issues that surround the library's involvement with article-level information and electronic content.

Electronic resource management

Core ILS functionality includes detailed functionality related to print subscriptions. Serials modules with predictive check-in capabilities, the ability to load subscription invoices and produce claims for missing issues, renewals, routing list management, and the like are all standard fare.

The traditional ILS modules are ill-suited to managing the library's collection of electronic journals and databases. Many aspects of electronic resources, especially those related to the licensing agreements, do not fit well within functionality designed for managing print journals.

A typical license agreement will specify the number of simultaneous users allowed to access the system, the effective dates of the license, conditions under which the license can be terminated, whether remote access to the resources is allowed, whether the resource can be used to fill interlibrary loan requests, and many other details.

Also important to record are the telephone numbers and email addresses for customer assistance or technical support. Having a scanned digital image of the signed contract available and the full text of the contract searchable may even be beneficial.

Many libraries have informal systems for managing the licenses associated with their electronic content. But, in the same way that most libraries outgrew manual or homegrown systems for managing their book budgets and implemented acquisitions modules specifically designed for the task, many librar-

8

ies have far more licenses for electronic content than they can track without an automated system.

Automated tools for managing electronic resources are just beginning to emerge. The Digital Library Federation launched the DLF Electronic Resource Management Initiative, which involves many projects and activities. Efforts undertaken so far include conducting a survey of the current library practices and some of the local systems that have been developed and exploring a conceptual model of the processes involved. It also has conducted a workshop in partnership with NISO and documented the data elements that need to be tracked.

In 2004, only one ILS vendor offered an electronic resources module. Innovative Interfaces offered software called Electronic Resources Management that operates either as an extension of the Millennium serials and acquisitions modules or as a stand-alone application for libraries that use other automation systems.

Integration beyond the library interface

As libraries implement an expanding arsenal of web-based applications, they need to be concerned about how the applications work together. A library web environment includes at a minimum HTML pages that provide descriptive information about the library and its services and the web-based online catalog. But it also may offer an interlibrary loan system, electronic reserves, digital library collections, proxy services to allow remote access to restricted resources, link resolvers, and federated searching.

Libraries need to ask if a single information architecture underlies the components, or does each manage its part of the library's information resources independently? Do they share a common look and feel? Do they each require library users to log in separately, or does the library's environment have a single login that carries the proper credentials through all the applications and services?

In this view, the ILS and its web-based catalog are but a part of the overall library web environment. In the selection and implementation of the ILS, consider what features it offers that foster integration with other library-provided applications and services.

The current model of library automation centers on a web-based online catalog, however enhanced, that offers information about the library's offerings and delivers end-user services through a dedicated web interface. Though that model will no doubt continue indefinitely, libraries will increasingly have an interest in participating in higher-level portals.

A university library may, for example, want to create a portal environment for its students that includes courseware, the library catalog, email, and other web-based services in a single interface. They can all be integrated in ways that not only share a common look and feel but that also work together to share a single login and allow the student to navigate easily among the functions available.

As this model of organizational portals takes hold, library automation systems will need to be less concerned with owning and controlling the landscape of the user interface directly but will need the ability to offer data and user functions as services provided through higher-level applications and interfaces.

SOURCE: Marshall Breeding, "Integrated Library Software: A Guide to Multiuser, Multifunction Systems," *Library Technology Reports* 40 (January/February 2004): 8–13, 16–17.

DIGITIZATION

Questions to ask before beginning a digital project

by the Collaborative Digitization Program

WHAT IS YOUR PURPOSE? There are many reasons for digitizing collections. Some of the first questions you should ask are:

- For what purpose do you want to use the digitized materials, and what are the benefits of having this collection in digital form? Is there a demand for the content of these materials in digital form?
- What are the goals of your project? What do you hope to accomplish? Is the main goal increased access or decreased handling of fragile originals (preservation)? Or both?
- Will the digital images replace or supplement existing originals? Will the digitized materials complement existing collections in online or print form, or might they fill a lack of digitized materials in a certain unique subject or topical area?

See Dan Hazen, Jeffrey Horrell, and Jan Merrill-Oldham, *Selecting Research Collections for Digitization* (Washington, D.C.: Council on Library and Information Research, August 1998), www.clir.org/pubs/reports/hazen/pub74.html.

Who is your audience? Other important questions to ask at the outset of any digitization project are:

- Who is your intended audience? This will determine the parameters of the project at all stages of digitization.
- Often your audience can be divided into primary (in your service area), secondary (related to your service area), and tertiary (internet users at large) user groups.
- What are the needs of your users, and how can you best serve them? This question may apply to modes of access, what search features and web interfaces will be most helpful to your users, what types of browsing might be appropriate, how users intend to use the information, scanning practices appropriate to intended use of the materials, etc.

See CDP's Market Segments and Their Information Needs, www.cdpheritage.org/digital/reports/rsrcUsers.cfm.

What are the physical characteristics of the collection?

- What is the physical condition of the materials? How do the originals need to be handled during scanning to prevent further deterioration?
- What is the format of the collection (negatives, black and white, color, text and graphics, etc.)?
- What size are the materials? Do you have the capability to scan oversize materials?

8

- What is the quality of the originals? This will determine what resolution you will scan at (scan at the highest resolution appropriate to the quality of the object you are scanning is a general rule of thumb), as well as file size and storage considerations.
- In what format and in what way will the digitized images be stored (on CDs or tape)? If you intend to store images online, do you have appropriate server space?

Who owns it? Copyright is a big deal and it is essential to understand issues of ownership and intellectual property rights.

- Who owns the materials?
- Are they in the public domain? If not, can permissions be secured?

See CDP's Legal Resources, www.cdpheritage.org/digital/legal.cfm.

What is your timeframe? This is an important consideration, especially for grant-funded projects. As a rule, everything usually takes longer than you plan for. It is helpful to break the project schedule down into proposed durations, with milestones and expected completion dates.

How is the project being funded?

- Have you secured a funding source for this project?
- Have you considered local, state, national, philanthropic, and collaborative sources?
- What parts of the project will funding support (physical resources, hardware, software, networked access, personnel, dedicated space, vendor services, etc.)?
- What about plans for maintaining access into the future (ongoing costs)? Is there a long-term institutional commitment to this project?

See CDP's Funding Resources, www.cdpheritage.org/alpha/digital/projectManagement/funding/fundingResources.cfm.

Who will be responsible at different stages of the project? The allocation of staff is also an important consideration.

- What areas and levels of staff expertise are available to you?
- Who will be responsible for selection and evaluation of the materials?
- Who will be responsible for preparation of materials prior to scanning?
- Who will be responsible for image capture, quality control, and post-scanning manipulation of images (if any)?
- Who will be responsible for indexing and cataloging of image records?
- Who will determine the best way to make the images accessible to users?

All of these responsibilities could involve the collaboration of subject experts or bibliographers, curators, librarians, archivists, imaging technicians, indexers and catalogers, conservators, computer network and system folks, and webmasters. See CDP's Project Management Resources, www.cdpheritage.org/alpha/digital/projectManagement/pmResources.cfm.

How will you perform the actual digitization?

- Where will the digitizing take place—in a central location or off-site? If off-site, does the vendor have adequate, safe storage facilities?
- What is the level of image quality (resolution) you hope to obtain (according to user needs and the quality of originals you are digitizing)?

- Will you perform any manipulation of the images postscanning (faithful reproduction vs. image optimized for presentation)?
- What is your criteria for an "acceptable image" when performing quality control?
- How will you store copies of the digitized images? CD-ROM, magnetic tape?
- Are there specific image guidelines specified by your funding source that you must adhere to?
- Will you create an "archival image" as well as derivative files for viewing and downloading?
- What are the limitations of your hardware and software (file size, file format standards, proprietary file formats, interoperability, scanner limitations, etc.)?

See Western States Digital Imaging Best Practices, January 2003, www.cdpheritage.org/resource/scanning/documents/WSDIBP_v1.pdf.

What metadata scheme are you planning to use?

- What type of description already exists for the collection, and at what level (item level, collection level)?
- What metadata or finding aid scheme do you plan to use (Dublin Core, MARC, VRA, EAD, etc.)?
- If there are several versions of an original, which version will you catalog?

See Western States Dublin Core Metadata Best Practices, January 2003, www.cdpheritage.org/cdp/documents/CDPDCMBP.pdf.

How are you going to provide access to the collection?

- Will the images be linked to existing bibliographic systems, or will it be necessary to develop a new access method for the images?
- At what level will this access be provided: item or collection level or both?
- Will the images be accessible and deliverable via a central or distributed site?
- Will you provide a search mechanism? How will users be able to search the collection?
- Will your audience be local or global? Will access be restricted or password protected?
- How will you distribute your collection (over the Web, at dedicated CD-ROM stations, by interactive media device, etc.)?

See Thomas K. Fry et al., *A Comparison of Web-Based Library Catalogs and Museum Exhibits and Their Impacts on Actual Visits: A Focus Group Evaluation for the Colorado Digitization Program*, www.cdpheritage.org/resource/reports/cdp_report_lrs.pdf.

8

How are you planning to maintain the collection into the future?

- How do you plan to store archival images and where?
- What kind of a backup mechanism do you have in place in case of hardware/software failure?
- What plans have you considered for data migration and refreshment?
- What level of long-term institutional commitment have you secured for your project?
- Do you have funding resources secured for maintenance of the digitized collection into the future?

See CDP's Digital Preservation Resources, www.cdpheritage.org/alpha/digital/preservationResources.cfm.

SOURCE: Collaborative Digitization Program, www.cdpheritage.org/digital/projectManagement/. This site is updated frequently. Reprinted with permission.

THE INTERNET

Basic problems with information on the internet

by Diane K. Kovacs and Kara L. Robinson

SOME BASIC PROBLEMS WITH INFORMATION obtained from the internet, or just about anywhere else for that matter, are listed here in the order of their observed frequency on the Web.

Typos. The information provided on the internet comes from many sources. Typos are one of the most prevalent problems, because *anyone* can publish information on the internet and often no editors or publishing agencies review the information. The two most likely causes of typos are inaccurate typing because of the informality of the medium and ignorance of the language. English is the lingua franca of the internet, but many varieties or dialects of English exist. Some typos may in fact be spelling variants rather than errors. Terry Ballard and Tina Gunther, in Typographical Errors in Library Databases (faculty.quinnipiac.edu/libraries/tballard/typoscomplete.html), publish the results of their ongoing analysis of the typos that occur in library catalogs, websites, and other library-related sources.

Factual errors (accidental or deliberate). These usually happen because people simply are not checking, or sometimes are just recalling information from confused memories. During an internet searching workshop taught in 1993, the only answer we could find on the internet to the question, "What was the year of the first Thanksgiving?" was 1676. According to Infoplease (www.infoplease.com), the actual year of the first Thanksgiving is either 1621, 1789, or 1863, depending on whether you mean the first celebration, or the year that it was declared a holiday by George Washington or Abraham Lincoln. The answer we found in 1993—at a site that no longer exists—was supplied

by a 6th grader at a suburban Chicago school. This example is not meant to imply that 6th graders are always a source of inaccurate information. Some 6th graders might publish accurate information if they acquire the facts from an authoritative source (teacher) and/or document their source (encyclopedia, almanac, or website).

Opinion stated as fact. Throughout the internet, users can find opinion stated as fact. This problem is very prevalent. Do you question the veracity of something *just* because of who published it? Where the internet is concerned, yes, you must question the

veracity of information based on who said it. You have
to ask, "Did the person/doctor/6th grader have
training or do research that gives them the authority
to provide the information?"

A related issue is the fact that the actual live
person who publishes information on the internet
can create an online identity that looks good, but
has no connection to the reality of the person's real
life. This means that checking offline sources to
verify authority and credibility is essential.

Can that person provide documentation/proof that
what he or she says is accurate? What type of information is provided online to
make these determinations? We do the same kinds of evaluation when we
work with print resources. Look at the authors of articles and find their sources,
research, training, and background before you believe what they say or write.

Editors evaluate the veracity of content as well as the
authors producing that content at the acquisition stage
of publishing, and libraries rely on a publisher's reputation in making their purchasing decisions. During the
acquisitions process, librarians rationalize that if a particular publisher accepted and published a book or journal, then it must by association be of good quality.
Internet research evaluation is more difficult. It involves more primary research than we are used to doing. One factor is that much information on the
internet was originally part of a conversation. Discussion lists, newsgroups, MUDs, and chat transcripts may
be text based, but they are really more akin to speech than to publications.
The difference between speech and published information is primarily for-
mality of the language. A three-judge panel that heard the initial arguments in
ACLU v. Reno, 521 U.S. 844; 117 S. Ct. 2329 (1997) found that on the internet
"tens of thousands of users are engaging in conversations on a huge range of
subjects. It is no exaggeration to conclude that the content on the internet is
as diverse as human thought." Some transcripts of this worldwide conversation are literate and/or authoritative, and others are not.

Out-of-date information. Considering how easy it can be to update web
pages and other internet information sources, the amount of out-of-date information online is surprising. But people don't always have the time or ability to
update information, or to take it offline when it is obsolete. For example, student project websites might remain online long after the project is finished and
the student graduates. Another problem is that so much information on the
internet is actually archives of discussion lists and newsgroups. It is important
to check the dates of the individual postings in such archives, as well as on any
other web resource that might be included in your elibrary collection.

Bias. Bias is a bigger problem with all sources of information than many
people realize. Many internet sites—as well as every other publication medium—provide slanted information to influence how people think about something. An illustrative example is the "Dihydrogen Monoxide Research Division" (www.dhmo.org). The website uses hyperbole, negative statistics, and
words that are meant to scare and alarm people; e.g., dangers, alerts, truth,
cancer, "DHMO Kills." Not much documentation supports these claims. Yet

8

none of the information or facts are false. The bias used in presenting the information gives a skewed sense of the meaning of the information. Only when the user pauses to consider the identity of dihydrogen monoxide does it become clear that this site is intended to illustrate the problems of bias. This site also illustrates the need for selection of resources that take into account educational attainment, reading level, and information needs. The reader needs to have at least some basic chemistry education. Di- (two) hydrogen atoms—H_2, plus mono- (one) oxygen atom—O, makes H_2O. The DHMO site is all about water.

They're Not Just Using Websites
by Paul O. Jenkins

A fear often expressed by today's academic librarians is that students at their institutions are using websites at the expense of more reputable resources, such as books and journals. In order to study just how true this perception might be at the College of Mount St. Joseph, a private college in Cincinnati with an enrollment of 2,500, I requested faculty to forward to me bibliographies in student papers. Six faculty members, each from a different discipline, responded, leaving me to compile statistics from a total of 116 papers. The results from this sample are discussed below.

Percentage of citations by resource type

Discipline	Citations	Articles	Books	Websites
Sociology	260	20%	36%	44%
Physical therapy	234	82%	18%	0%
Religion	149	20%	54%	26%
Humanities	83	11%	42%	47%
Nursing	66	41%	56%	3%
Chemistry	62	48%	27%	24%
Total	**854**	**41%**	**35%**	**24%**

As the table indicates, the papers yielded 854 citations. A look at the totals reveals that the traditional research sources—articles and books—remain those most often used. Together they made up 76% of the citations, websites accounting for the remaining 24%. Exceptions to this pattern are the sociology and humanities papers, for which websites were used more than any other resource.

No consistent pattern emerged from an examination of course levels for the papers submitted. The only upper-level courses were those from humanities and religion. The physical therapy and nursing courses were midlevel, and those from sociology and chemistry were lower level. Resource requirements outlined by instructors varied from course to course and had a more profound effect.

The physical therapy instructor did not allow the use of any websites; the nursing instructor required that students obtain the permission to use them as sources for their papers. As the numbers indicate, the instructors in the other disciplines adopted a more lenient stance.

Certainly the addition of websites has influenced how students conduct research. If my institution is any true indicator, faculty acceptance of websites as legitimate resources is by no means universal, but seems to have become valid for many. Students have embraced websites and use them with books and articles. For the time being, however, the more traditional resources remain in the ascendancy.

SOURCE: Paul O. Jenkins, "They're Not Just Using Web Sites," *College & Research Libraries News* 63 (March 2002): 164.

<blockquote>
From Mr. Edwin Worsh
NO 268 hosipital road,
Box 1287 Port Shepstone
Chaka -South Africa.

Dear Friend,
We want to transfer to overseas
($36,000.000.00 USD)Thirty six
million United States Dollars) from
a Bank in South Africa. I am
looking for a reliable and honest
person who will be capable and fit
to provide either an existing bank
account or to set up a new Bank a/c
immediately to receive this money,
even an empty a/c can serve, as
long as you will remain honest to
me till the end for this important
business, trusting in you and
believing in God that you will
never let me down either now or in
future.
</blockquote>

Election campaign information is biased, almost by definition. For that matter, so is all advertising information. Probably every piece of information reflects bias of some kind, due to the subjectivity of writing. The degree, type of, and reason for bias must be considered in evaluating information.

Deliberate fraud is a rapidly growing problem, given the ubiquity of the Web. Medical fraud on the Web has increased. Business or consumer frauds are also common. The best defense is to know where to check to see if an offer or claim really is too good to be true. Medical claims made on websites might be checked out using the Federal Trade Commission's Operation Cure-All site (www.ftc.gov/bcp/conline/edcams/cureall/) on which the FTC reports ongoing health fraud investigations and warnings, or the Quackwatch website (www.quackwatch.com). Other valuable sources of information are Quatloos!—Cyber-Museum of Scams and Frauds (www.quatloos.com), ScamOrama (www.scamorama.com), and Scambusters (www.scambusters.org).

SOURCE: Diane K. Kovacs and Kara L. Robinson, *The Kovacs Guide to Electronic Library Collection Development* (New York: Neal-Schuman, 2004), pp. 22–24. Reprinted with permission.

Libraries and internet filtering, 2005

by Lori Bowen Ayre

LIBRARIES BEGAN USING INTERNET FILTERS in the late 1990s due to community pressure and the Children's Internet Protection Act (CIPA). CIPA is a federal law that requires all computers in a public library to be filtered if that library accepts any federal funds for computers that access the internet or the costs associated with a connection to the internet. It took effect on July 1, 2004. According to the National Conference of State Legislatures, 21 states have filtering laws that apply to schools or libraries. While most of these laws require publicly funded institutions to adopt internet use policies, some mandate filters. Legislators are convinced that filters effectively protect minors from harmful, web-borne internet content. To the extent that filters are expensive and may pose a threat to free speech or open access, legislators (and much of the public) have decided that the protections for children outweigh any such concerns.

The use of filters in public libraries has increased steadily. Norman Oder reported in the January 2002 and January 2005 issues of *Library Journal* that the percentage of public libraries filtering increased from 25% in 2000 to 65% in 2005, yet many librarians argue that filters have no place in a library.

The American Library Association fought CIPA in the courts and took the position that "the use of filtering software by libraries to block access to constitutionally protected speech violates the Library Bill of Rights." Some libraries refused to install filters and gave up federal funding instead. Filters were seen as antithetical to the mission of the library.

8

While some libraries were developing internet policies explaining their reasons for not using filters, other libraries were quietly installing them. The libraries installing the filters soon found that filters alleviated many thorny problems they'd been grappling with. It turned out that filters did prevent children from bumping into unexpected and unwanted websites and advertisements. Filters served as a deterrent for public porn browsers. Libraries found that with some effort, they could implement and enforce their internet-use policy. For the first time, libraries had a way to control how their public computers were being used. The filters didn't do the job perfectly, but the fact was, there were no more complaints from patrons after the filters were installed. The filters were *good enough*.

How filters work

Filters operate on a system of categories. Websites, or sometimes individual web pages, are categorized by filter companies. The library's filter administrator utilizes the categories to build filter profiles. For example, the adult filter profile might allow all categories of content to pass through except items categorized as "sexually explicit." The children's filter profile would undoubtedly block the "sexually explicit" content as well as other categories deemed inappropriate for children such as "hate," "firearms," and "violence."

The filter company decides how each site will be categorized. Filter companies fiercely protect their process for categorizing websites and equally fiercely protect the websites identified within each category. Part of the value of the filter is in the number of websites categorized, because sites that have yet not been categorized will not necessarily be blocked.

Ironically, librarians—professionals trained to catalog and evaluate content—subcontract their cataloging job to software companies when they install a filter. Unlike librarians, the subcontractors are not information professionals, and they typically use automated methods to classify the 3 billion web pages on the internet.

The features available in state-of-the-art filters are too numerous to recount here. For a thorough summary of filter features and to compare filters, feature-by-feature, visit libraryfiltering.org. However, certain features are particularly important for libraries, such as the ability to control what is blocked, how to override blocked pages, how granular the blocking is (site, page, domain, IP address), and what information is presented to end-users when they encounter a blocked page.

Most library filters leave the choice of what to block in the hands of the system administrator, who sets up filter profiles and selects the categories to block. Filters that don't allow for different filter profiles might be suitable for home use but are not appropriate in a library setting.

Most filters provide some mechanism for overriding blocked pages either on the fly using an administrator password, or by adding sites to an "always allow" list that supersedes the block on a page caused by its categorization.

This override capability provides the local administrator the ability to fix errors the filter company has made in its classification process, or to modify the filter company's classification system to more closely match the library's policies. Because most filters do not disclose the websites contained within each category, these adjustments to the filter categories must by made by the filter administrator as they are discovered.

Some filters provide more granularity in their blocking behavior than others. For example, a small number of filters allow the administrator to block certain file types (such as GIFs, JPEGs, BMPs, TIFFs) within a category. This enables the filter administrator to block the images without blocking the text on the page. Other filters are more gross in their blocking behavior and block the entire page or even the entire domain. Some filters convert the domain to an IP address and block any websites sharing that IP address. Blocking shared IP addresses always results in overblocking.

Some filters rely solely on lists of URLs within categories. Other filters use a system of dynamic filtering. Dynamic filters analyze websites as they are accessed by the end-user and categorize the page based on its analysis. As filters become more and more sophisticated, more companies are using a dynamic filtering process to at least supplement their URL lists, if not replace them entirely.

When end-users encounter a blocked page, they are usually presented with a message advising them so. The default block page is often customizable and can be used to provide useful information about why the page has been blocked and what to do if they'd like the page unblocked. Filters that block pages without advising the patron that they've been blocked should be avoided.

Best practices

Libraries using filters should take special precautions to do so in accordance with the library's mission. The following guidelines are provided to assist libraries implementing filters.

Protect patron privacy. Because of the way filters work, it is easy to accidentally invade patron privacy. Many of the filters have real-time monitoring features that should be turned off. Filters generate logs containing websites visited by patrons, and these logs should be erased according to a written retention policy. It is important to understand all the features associated with filters and turn off the unwanted features. Administrators should also ensure that only authorized filter administrators have access to the filter server.

Minimize blocking. By default, most filters will block far more content than is appropriate in a library setting. It is important to cycle through several iterations of tweaking and tuning your filter configuration before determining that your filter is set to block as little content as necessary to comply with your internet use policy.

Monitor blocking accuracy. Ensure that someone on your staff is monitoring blocked sites and that the filter is adjusted as needed when sites that should be allowed are being blocked. Do not rely upon patron complaints to tell you whether your filter is working, because experience shows that most patrons do not complain when a site is blocked.

Make unblocking easy and quick. Many filters provide features that enable adult patrons to turn off blocking for themselves, either for a single site or for all sites for the duration of their session. Use these auto-selection features as much as possible to accommodate all patrons.

If patrons cannot unblock the sites for themselves, there must be a way for staff to perform this function for them quickly and easily. Some filters enable the user to request a site be unblocked via the blocked page itself. Others require the patron to locate a staff person to unblock the site by entering a password or changing a setting on the server. Be sure your library has  established a policy for handling unblocking requests swiftly and that the process is easy for both patrons and staff.

Keep patrons informed. Regardless of what your filter policy is, which filter you use, or how you handle unblocking sites, it is important to keep your patrons informed of the underlying reasons for filtering the internet and all the procedures associated with implementing that policy. The internet use policy should be readily available for all users accessing the internet on library computers. Handouts about the filter and how to turn off filtering or request that a page be unblocked should also be readily available to patrons. If multiple filter profiles are available to choose from, make sure there are instructions for patrons to make the choices that suit them.

Conclusion

More public libraries are using filters than are not using filters ("Budget Report, 2005," *Library Journal,* January 15, 2005). How they are implemented varies from state to state and library to library. Some libraries filter all computers. Some libraries filter only the children's computers. Some state libraries, such as Kansas and Maine, offer statewide filtering. Others install individual filters in each branch. It can be done in any number of ways.

Filters today are powerful and feature-rich. Though they are still imperfect, they are a far cry from the simplistic filters that blocked an entire site because of an "offensive" word. Today's filters are much better at evaluating content, and their features provide the library with many options.

If your library is using a filter, it is your responsibility to do so with integrity and transparency. Work closely with patrons, staff, and library boards to agree on and implement a policy of filtering. Monitor the performance of your filter, make adjustments, and work closely with your community.

Take advantage of today's broad range of features to provide a flexible filtering environment for your patrons. The requirement to filter may have been mandated by legislators, but the implementation of your filter need not be so unyielding.

Key resources

ALA Office of Intellectual Freedom, "Filters and Filtering," www.ala.org/ala/oif/ifissues/filtersfiltering.htm. News, ALA policies and statements on filtering, Internet Toolkit, legal information, and more.

ALA Washington Office, "CIPA," www.ala.org/CIPA/. ALA's position on the Children's Internet Protection Act, information about implementing CIPA filtering, legislative history.

Libraryfiltering.org. Lori Bowen Ayre's filtering software comparisons. Summary of filters available for libraries including contact information, pricing, and product features.

Lori Bowen Ayre, "Filtering and Filter Software," *Library Technology Reports* 40, no. 2 (March/April 2004). Comprehensive reports covering the history and development of filters, selecting a filter for a library, library best practices, sample library internet use policies.

SOURCE: Special report for the *Whole Library Handbook 4* by Lori Bowen Ayre, who is the founder and principal technology consultant for The Galecia Group in Petaluma, California (galecia.com). ©2005 The Galecia Group/Lori Bowen Ayre. All original material created by Lori Bowen Ayre for inclusion in this book is licensed under a Creative Commons License (creativecommons.org/licenses/by-nc-nd/2.0/).

Glossary of blogging terms

WEBLOGS CAUGHT ON IN THE LIBRARY WORLD early, both as a way for librarians to express their opinions freely and as a resource for finding current library news and views. This glossary, primarily borrowed from Samizdata.net, has been augmented with a few other terms.—*GME.*

Advocacy blog. A blog focused on political advocacy. Although most blogs are overtly partisan, an advocacy blog's content will be pointedly structured to deliver an activist message. Advocacy blogs are a subset of *Pundit blogs*, but usually have a less strict emphasis on current news and are more polemical in nature.

Aggregator. Software used by *Bloggers* and others who want to check a large number of news sources or blogs on a daily basis. Aggregators regularly check selected *RSS* feeds for new content and display a list of results, usually listing the most recently updated links first, allowing bloggers to quickly catch up on the latest news and comment from around the web. There are a variety of aggregators available: some are web-based, some work in tandem with other pieces of software such as Microsoft Outlook, while others are separate pieces of software.

Anti-idiotarian. Someone opposed to a whole raft of political values that are derived from a fundamentally irrational world view. Anti-idiotarians can be found across a wide section of the political spectrum and are primarily characterized by vocal, rational judgmentalism, generally hawkish sentiments, and transcendent loathing of Noam Chomsky. *Usage:* "Like most anti-idiotarians, I cannot but marvel at the sight of the Palestinian leadership forming yet another circular firing squad at the first grudging sign of reasonable behavior by the Israeli government."—*Perry de Havilland.*

Audioblog. A blog in which the posts consist mainly of voice recordings.

Barking moonbat. Someone on the extreme edge of whatever their -ism happens to be. Coined by Perry de Havilland. *Usage:* "Definition of a 'barking moonbat': someone who sacrifices sanity for the sake of consistency."—*Adriana Cronin.*

Biblioblogosphere. The community of library-related blogs.

Biz blog. Business blog. This can mean a blog writing about business issues or (increasingly) actually run and maintained by a business as part of its day-to-day operations. Generally biz blogs are outward facing (that is, written to communicate with customers or business peers), but the term is occasionally used for an internal company blog used as a knowledge-management system. Also called b-blog. See *K-log*.

Blawg. A weblog written by lawyers and/or one concerned primarily with legal affairs. Probably coined by Denise M. Howell.

Bleg. To use one's blog to beg for assistance (usually for information, occasionally for money). One who does so is a "blegger."

Bliki. Combination of a blog and a *Wiki*; a blog that can be edited by readers or an approved group of users.

Blog. 1. *noun.* A contraction of "weblog," a form of online writing characterized in format by a single column of text in reverse chronological order (most recent content at the top) with the ability to link to individual articles. There is usually a *Sidebar* displaying links, and the content is frequently updated. Probably coined by Peter Merholz. *Usage:* "Glenn has written an interesting article about the folly of gun control on his blog." Earliest use was apparently in 1999.

2. *verb.* To write an article on a blog. *Usage:* "Steven Green has just blogged about the joys of vodka today."

The majority of blogs are still nonprofessional as of 2005 and are run by single writers. However, a differentiating factor between a blog and other online formats (such as forums and *Wikis*) is that the main articles (as opposed to comments) are written by the blog's owners or members and *not* by the general public. Although there are several competing definitions on what makes a blog a blog, it can be convincingly argued that a true blog must be readily accessible in the *Blogosphere*. Reverse chronological order is a defining feature of a blog, but that alone is not enough. If the individual articles cannot be linked via a *Permalink* (rather then just linking to the whole site), then the site in question is not a blog. This means some ostensible blogs are not really blogs at all—they are merely bloglike in appearance.

Blog digest. A blog that regularly reports on or summarizes a number of other blogs, typically on a daily basis. Blog digests are extremely useful but they are difficult to sustain, and unfortunately tend to have short operational lives. Also referred to as digest blog.

Blog people. Deprecatory term for *Bloggers* who, in the words of librarian Michael Gorman, "have a fanatical belief in the transforming power of digitization and a consequent horror of, and contempt for, heretics who do not share that belief" (*Library Journal,* February 5, 2005).

Blog-site. 1. A blog. 2. A hybrid blog/website, featuring website features such as a conventional online company brochure (for example) but also incorporating a blog in a sidebar as a supporting feature on the same page. The latter usage was coined by Adriana Cronin.

Blogathy. When you just don't give a damn about posting in your blog that day. Coined by Michele Catalano.

Blogger. 1. A person who owns or writes for a weblog. 2. Blogger.com, the most widespread blog publishing software package, created by Evan Williams at www.blogger.com.

Blogger ecosystem. A chart or lists showing the links between blogs. Also called blog ecosystem.

Bloggered. Having one's reputation or credibility torn down by members of the *Blogosphere*.

Bloggerel. Variant of "doggerel." Opinion put forward on a blog that has previously been repeated over and over and over again until it makes people sick. Coined by The Pontificator.

Blogistan. The totality of blogs; blogs as a community. However, the term is sometimes used to mean the totality of just *Warblogs* or *Pundit blogs*, rather than the entire *Blogosphere.*

Blogiversary. The birthday of the establishment of a blog.

Blognoscenti. Blog connoisseurs. Also known as Blogerati.

Blogopotamus. A very long blog article. *Usage:* "Paul Marks has done another Blogopotamus on Samizdata.net."

Blogorrhea. An unusually high volume of articles on a blog. *Usage:* "Well, 48 hours and 4,195 words later, we're reaching for our dictionary to check the definition of 'significantly.' After that, we're going to look up blogorrhea."— *William Quick.*

Blogosphere. The totality of blogs; blogs as a community; blogs as a social network. Coined by William Quick. *Usage:* "The blogosphere has been abuzz with the Trent Lott story for the last few days and many of the blogs are baying for blood!" Also called Bloggerverse or Blogiverse.

   The key to understanding *Blogs* is understanding the blogosphere. Blogs themselves are just a web format, whereas the blogosphere is a social phenomenon. What really differentiates blogs from webpages or forums or chatrooms is that blogs (at least properly implemented ones) are designed from the outset to be part of that shifting internet-wide social network. There have been many attempts to design "social software" but thus far the only effective example is the blogosphere, which was not designed by anyone but is an emergent phenomenon.

Blogroach. A reader who infests the comment section of a weblog, disagreeing with everything posted in the most obnoxious manner possible. Coined by Stacy Tabb.

Blogroll. 1. A list of links in the *Sidebar* of a blog, often linking to other blogs. Also called blog roll. 2. A blog link-management system, such as www.blogrolling.com.

Blogspot. The blog hosting servers operated by Blogger.com. In 2005, more blogs were hosted on blogspot than anywhere else.

Blogstipation. 1. To be unable to think of anything to blog about; writer's block for bloggers. 2. To be unable to post an article on your blog because Blogger.com is down yet again. Latter usage coined by Jim Treacher.

Blogule, *noun.* A concept or point within an article on a blog that is not quite grandiose enough to be a *Meme.* Coined by Brian Micklethwait.

Blogware. Commonly used in reference to tools used to write blogs, such as WordPress or Movable Type.

Blurker. 1. One who reads many blogs but leaves no comments behind; a silent observer of blogs. 2. One who reads many blogs but has no blog of their own; a blog-watcher or blog voyeur. *Usage:* "But, Mikey, I can't have a blog of my own! I'm a blurker!"

Comment spam. Spam is unsolicited online messages, generally of a commercial nature and usually delivered as email (virtual junk mail). Comment spam, however, is when someone posts off-topic commercial remarks with links in a blog's comment section. Some comment spam is overt, but just as often it takes the form of innocuous remarks such as "I agree with your article!" or "Hey, great site!" in a blog's comment section. The spammer's payload is in the personal details link, which takes you to a dubious (often pornographic) site. One reason comment spam is a major problem is that if readers visit the spammer's link, the site often tries to install browser hijackers, tracking cookies, or other adware/malware on the duped reader's computer. Most comment spam is entered by *Spambots* rather than actual people.

Commentariat. The community of people who leave comments on a blog. *Usage:* "We got some useful suggestion from the commentariat today on how to deal with the spammer problem."

Commenter. A person who leaves remarks in the comments section that many blogs offer.

Crisis blog. A company blog, or *Biz blog*, set up to handle a public-relations crisis for a company or institution. This can be either to handle internal communications or to allow a company to present its side of a story in a frank, credible, and timely manner when a situation is developing rapidly.

Crud. Unintentionally visible code—rather than a clickable link, special character, or formatted text—that results when a blog is published with incorrect html.

Dead-tree media. Paper newspapers and magazines; also known as *Old media*.

DNQ/DNP. Do not quote/Do not print. May be used in online correspondence, to clarify that these words/comments should not be posted on the other person's blog. Adapted by Gary Farber from common science-fiction fandom usage.

Dowdification, noun. *Dowdify,* verb. The willful omission of one or more words so the meaning of the statement is no longer understood but suits the needs of the writer in launching an ad hominem attack, whether or not the construction is truthful or grammatically complete. Named after *New York Times* columnist Maureen Dowd, from her manufacture of a quote attributed to President George W. Bush in her May 14, 2003, column, as first reported by Robert Cox on TheNationalDebate.com. Coined by James Taranto.

Edublog. An education-oriented blog.

Ego-googling. Looking up one's own name in Google to check on its prominence. Also called e-googling or self-googling.

Event blog. A blog set up for only a limited period to cover some event, for example, Hurricane Katrina. Event blogs are often commercial in nature.

Fact-check. To use internet search engines to ascertain the veracity of dubious claims made in the press. Coined by Ken Layne.

Fisk. To deconstruct an article on a point-by-point basis in a highly critical manner. Derived from the name of British journalist Robert Fisk, a frequent target of such critical articles in the *Blogosphere*. *Usage:* "Orrin Judd did a severe fisking of an idiotic article in the *New York Times* today."

Flame. To make a hostile, intemperate remark, usually of a personal nature. *Usage:* "Andrew has seriously flamed Brian over his views on abortion again."

Flame war. A hostile exchange of views via the internet characterized by highly intemperate language. The term is by no means exclusive to blogs and is found in wide use throughout the internet.

Google bomb. To intentionally insert words or phrases into as many blogs as possible to increase the ranking on the Google search engine. Held by some to be a form of *Meme war*. Coined by Adam Mathes.

Group blog. A blog with more than one regular contributing writer.

Hitnosis. Being unable to stop yourself constantly refreshing your browser to see if your hit counter or comments section has increased since the last time you did it (i.e., about one minute ago). This often occurs when a specific number is coming up (such as a blog's hit counter crossing 10,000 or 100,000 or 250,000 visitors) or after an unusually large surge of posted comments. Coined by Perry de Havilland.

Idiotarian. A term of abuse for an advocate of what are deemed to be irrationalist and subjectivist values that have very little reference to the workings of the real world. Idiotarians are often socialist (quintessentially Noam Chomsky), but can also be paleolibertarian or paleoconservative. The defining phrase of idiotarianism is "it is all the fault of the United States": This is usually applied to geopolitics but is sometimes encountered with regard to cultural issues, economic issues, environmental issues, the weather, or socks lost in the laundry. The term is obviously highly partisan but is in widespread use by many blogs. However, it is not a term used exclusively by neoconservatives; many left-of-center or libertarian blogs have used it to describe the more surrealist wings of their particular branch of political thought. See also *Anti-idiotarian.*

Instapundited. To have your blog mentioned on Instapundit.com. Also termed an "instalanche." *Usage:* "Holy shit, look at the hit counter! We must have been Instapundited!" See also *Slashdotted.*

Interblog _____ war. A series of exchanges between two or more blogs contesting some factual, political, or philosophical issue. Coined by Natalie Solent. *Usage:* "Aintnobaddude.com, Heretical Ideas, and Samizdata.net have started another Interblog Gun War."

Journal blog. A personal diarylike blog. Personal journal blogs are by far the most common type of blog. Most have extremely small daily readerships (albeit sometimes very dependable). Also called diary blog. Journal blogs form one of the three primary distinct (and largely separate) cultural groups within the blogging world, the other two being *Tech blogs* and *Pundit blogs.* See also *Kittyblogger.*

Kittyblogger. Technically, someone who uses a blog to write about her cats, but mostly used to describe mundane *Journal blog* content.

K-log. Short for "knowledge log." Usually internal blogs (i.e., on an intranet and not visible to the general public) that are used as highly effective knowledge management systems and/or internal company communication systems (such as project blogs).

Klogger. Someone who writes for a corporate *K-log.*

Linguablog. A specialist blog dealing with regular postings about linguistics, language learning, translation and localization, endangered languages, or other language-related subjects. Coined by Enigmatic Mermaid.

Link orgy. When a *Blogger* finds that he has been linked by multiple sites, or has been added to several *Blogrolls,* in a short time. Coined by James Martin.

Link rot. Over time, any large list of links will contain an increasing number of dead links.

Link whore. A *Blogger* who will go to any lengths to get other bloggers to link to them (the term is usually intended to be humorous). Also called link slut. Both terms are in fact gender nonspecific.

Linklog. A blog carrying only a simple list of interesting links, without extensive commentary or illustration. Sometimes a linklog will run alongside fuller journal entries or other commentary.

MSM. Acronym for mainstream media.

Mediasphere. The conventional media collectively.

Meme. A discrete idea that replicates itself. There is an assumption that memes replicate themselves and are propagated by people through social and technological networks, much like both real and computer viruses.

Coined by Richard Dawkins. *Usage:* "The sarcastic meme of 'Our friends, the Saudis' continues to spread across the internet." Although not, strictly speaking, blog-specific, the term is widely used in the *Blogosphere*.

Meme hack. Intentionally altering a concept or phrase, or using it in a different context, so as to subvert the meaning. *Usage:* For example, the use of "socialist" imagery to advocate capitalism.

Meme war. Using *Comment spam, Google bombs,* hostile *Trackbacks,* and other technical means to propagate *Memes.*

Metablogging. To write blog articles about blogging.

Minarchist. Derived from anarchist. An advocate of minimal government, often described as the night-watchman state, in which the state exists legitimately only to enable appropriate law and order and to deal with collective territorial defense. Such a state can exist to reinforce the liberty of individuals but not to "do things" and is therefore a largely apolitical polity guarding the boundaries of civil society. Although this is not a blog-specific term, it is often used on *Pundit blogs,* many of which are libertarian.

Misting or **MiSTing.** Similar to *Fisk* in that it is a refutation of another's views, but misting is less aggressive and usually humorous. Mistings usually take the form of an imaginary exchange of views. The term is derived from the Comedy Central show MST3K, *Mystery Science Theater 3000,* about characters who were captured by a mad scientist and forced to watch terrible sci-fi movies. They responded by commenting (rather hilariously) on the movies.

Moblog. A blog maintained via mobile hardware, typically a mobile phone (cell phone) with a built-in digital camera. Moblogs are usually photo journals rather than text-intensive (though this varies). Although a moblog is generally run from a phone, it can also be run from a laptop, palmtop, or web-enabled PDA. The defining element of a moblog is that it is used to blog away from the desk.

MP3 blog. A blog that hosts downloadable music in the MP3 audio format.

News blog. See *Pundit blog.*

Old media. Newspapers, magazines, and major network television. Also called *Dead-tree media.*

Permalink. 1. A link to a specific article in the archives of a blog, which will remain valid after the article is no longer listed on the blog's front page (i.e., after it is archived). 2. A link in a *Blogroll.*

Pilger. Named after London-based antiwar journalist John Pilger. To destroy facts in a John Pilger fashion, to pillage the truth using poor or no fact checking, wild accusations, and conspiracy theories. Coined by Auberon Waugh.

Ping. 1. *noun.* An automated packet of information (64 bytes) sent from one network to another to establish the status of a target system. 2. *verb.* To send a small automated packet of data to actuate some expected function, such as a *Trackback.* PING is an acronym for Packet INternet Grouper.

Plog. 1. A project blog set up to chronicle a particular (business) project. 2. Online bookseller Amazon.com has experimented with offering its customers personalized weblogs called plogs. Although Amazon has trademarked the name, it is already in use with other meanings.

Plogging. 1. Short for presidential blogging (as in the president or CEO of a company), which bypasses the entire PR apparatus, as well as the traditionally blah forms of published speech by CEOs. Think of it as "do-it-yourself PR" for the people best positioned to make hay with it. Coined by

Doc Searls. *Usage:* "Schwartz and Cuban are playing the plogging game." 2. Project blogging.

Podcasting. A form of *Audioblog* created by Adam Curry, a former MTV Host, and Dave Winer, the founder of Userland Software. Its name comes from the targeting of audio posts to Apple's iPod audio player, although podcasts can be listened to on competing players and on computers.

Progblog. A progressive blog that expresses various left-wing political views.

Pundit blog. A blog focused on news punditry. The bulk of a pundit blog's content is dissection of, or pointers to, stories currently running in the *Old media.* Pundit blogs form one of the three primary distinct (and largely separate) cultural groups within the blogging world, the other two being *Journal blogs* and *Tech blogs.* The archetypal pundit blog is Instapundit.com.

RDF. RDF is a web content syndication format that stands for Resource Description Framework.

Reciprocal link. If you *Blogroll* link to our blog, we will blogroll to your blog.

RSS. RSS is a web content syndication format that stands for (variously) RDF Site Summary, Really Simple Syndication, or Rich Site Summary.

Sidebar. One or more columns along one or both sides of most blogs' main pages, usually used for *Blogroll* links or contact information.

Slashdotted. To have your blog mentioned on Slashdot.org. See also *Instapundited. Usage:* "Our hosting server has just used up the whole month's bandwidth in the last 12 hours! We must have been slashdotted!"

Spambot. Online code that automatically generates large numbers of unwanted messages and directs them at members of the public. Within the context of blogging, it is code that enters unsolicited *Comment spam.* A spambot can enter dozens or even hundreds of unwanted spams in a matter of minutes into the comments of an unprotected blog.

Splog. A blog created solely to increase the page rank of affiliated websites or to get ad hits from visitors. Also known as Spam blog.

Stripblog. A cartoon- or comic-related weblog.

Tech blog. A blog focused on a technical subject. A high proportion of tech blogs are also *Group blogs.* Tech blogs form one of the three primary distinct (and largely separate) cultural groups within the blogging world, the other two being *Journal blogs* and *Pundit blogs.*

Thread. A series of remarks posted by people in a public-comment section of a blog that follows a conversational and topic-related sequence. Although used on blogs to describe related comments under a single blog article, this term is more specifically associated with online forums, many of which use a threaded format that indents related digressions from the main conversation in a branching manner, making it clear to which previous comment a person is replying. Although some blog-forum hybrids also use this threaded format within their public comments section, the term is more commonly associated with forums rather than blogs.

Trackback. 1. A system by which a *Ping* is sent to another trackback-aware website (usually another blog) to notify the site that a link to it has been created (usually within a posted article). The objective is to notify subjects of an article that they have been mentioned in another article elsewhere. 2. To follow a trackback ping from the target weblog to the source weblog.

Troll. 1. *verb.* To post a provocative article purely in order to generate an angry response (usually followed by sending a mass email shot to the target audience) and commensurate increase in hit rate. 2. *noun.* A person who trolls.

8

Usage: "Justin Raymondo has just trolled the Warbloggers again." Troll is widely used as an epithet in newsgroups and elists as well as blogs.

Turing test. A test that determines if the party on the other end of a remote communication is a human or a computer program. This is germane to blogging because many comment sections on blogs use nonmachine-readable systems to prevent *Spambots* from entering *Comment spam.*

Warblog. 1. One of a large number of blogs that sprang up shortly after September 11, 2001. Most, at least initially, were created to provide *Anti-idiotarian* commentary in the aftermath of Al Qaeda's attack upon the United States. Warblogs are essentially a subset of *Pundit blogs.* Someone who runs a warblog is a warblogger. 2. Any blog largely or primarily dedicated to coverage of terrorism, the war or terrorism, and conflict in the Middle East, regardless of when it was started. 3. Any blog that takes an editorial position generally in favor of military intervention by the United States in one or more Middle Eastern or Central Asian nations linked to terrorism. Probably coined by Matt Welch. It would be fair to say that the term is now only of historical significance. Although many of the former self-described warblogs are still publishing, the term is now largely unused.

Weblog. See *Blog.*

Whoring for hits. Posting things on a blog purely to generate an increase in visitors. The term is often intended humorously, but not always.

Wiki. A type of collaborative online software that allows readers to add content on a subject, which then can be edited by others. For example, Wikipedia. The major difference between a blog and a wiki is that the primary objective of a blog is for the owners to express themselves to their target audience. A wiki is about collaboration (in a general sense) rather than expressing views.

XML. A markup language used for (among other things) syndication formats used on blogs. Acronym for eXtensible Markup Language.

SOURCES: Blogging Glossary, Samizdata.net, www.samizdata.net/blog/glossary.html; Neil McIntosh and Jane Perrone, "Weblog Glossary," *The Guardian,* December 18, 2003, www.guardian.co.uk/online/weblogs/story/0,14024,1109020,00.html; and Duncan Riley, "Understanding Blog Speak," Blog Herald, www.blogherald.com/2005/04/07/understanding-blog-speak/.

OTHER TECHNOLOGY

RFID and libraries

by Lori Bowen Ayre

RADIO FREQUENCY IDENTIFICATION (RFID) tags, like bar codes, are used to identify individual books, CDs, DVDs, and other circulating items. Unlike bar codes, RFID tags can be read without someone knowing it and they can contain more information than a bar code, which is limited to a single sequence of numbers. RFID tags communicate via radio signals, whereas bar codes operate optically. Bar codes require a reader to be held up to the bar-code tag—line-of-sight—whereas an RFID tag does not require line-of-sight. If the reader is close enough to the item, the RFID tag can be read inside the patron's book bag as they leave the library.

Benefits

Libraries are choosing RFID systems to replace (or sometimes supplement) their bar-code systems because of the streamlined workflows that become possible. Inventory-related tasks can be done in a fraction of the time with RFID as with bar-code readers. For example, a whole shelf of books can be read by the reader with one sweep of the portable reader, which then reports which books are missing or misshelved.

RFID-based circulation systems can process many more books in a shorter period of time with less strain on staff. Self-check systems have become very popular with both patrons and staff, and RFID self-check systems allow patrons to check in or check out several books at a time. RFID-enabled self-check systems reduce the number of staff needed at the circulation desk. Because the readers do not require line-of-sight, multiple items can be read simultaneously by passing a stack of books near the reader. Some say that the RFID self-check systems are easier to use than their optically based counterparts, making it easer for patrons to serve themselves.

For archivists handling sensitive materials, the ability to inventory items without handling them is another benefit of RFID. And while it has net yet been proven, some libraries believe RFID systems will reduce repetitive stress injuries associated with checking out books using bar-code-based systems.

Costs

While there are many benefits of RFID, the costs are high. Each circulated item must have its own tag. The tags cost anywhere from 50 cents to $1.50 each. Plain tags used in books range from 50 to 70 cents. Customized tags containing the library logo are more expensive. The costs go up when tags are placed on other media such as CDs, DVDs, and tapes ($1 to $1.50).

Each tag must be programmed. This can take months to accomplish and often involves everyone on staff plus volunteers. It is sometimes possible to order pretagged books from vendors.

New security gates, circulation readers, self-check stations, sorting equipment, and inventory wands must be purchased for the RFID system, and the interfaces between the library's integrated library system (ILS) and the RFID system must be configured.

Estimates for implementing an RFID system range from $70,000 to over $1 million. One library reports spending $650,000 to convert its 500,000-item collection to RFID.

Technology still new

While RFID technology is not new, the use of RFID tags in libraries is very new. In 2000, the first California library to implement RFID went live with their system. Today, approximately 300 libraries are using RFID nationwide. One problem for early adopters is that library RFID tags are not interchangeable. Therefore, once a library installs their tags, they are generally "married" to the vendor that supplied the RFID system.

Another issue for early adopters is that standards for the communication between item-level tags (ISO 18000) and the format of the data on the tag (data model standards) are still very much in flux. Therefore, first generation tags will likely need to be replaced to conform to the new standards.

Privacy and RFID

There are privacy costs as well. Because of the nature of RFID, tags can be vulnerable to unauthorized scanners reading the information stored on the tags. For this reason, most RFID tags used in libraries contain a minimal amount of information—essentially the same information stored on the bar code. But even if the tag contains nothing more than a unique identifier (like a bar code), there are privacy concerns.

In the paper "Privacy and Security in Library RFID: Issues, Practices, and Architectures" (www.cs.berkeley.edu/~dmolnar/library.pdf), David Molnar and David Wagner state that the potential threats to patron privacy are unauthorized tag reading and writing, hotlisting, eavesdropping, and tracking.

Unauthorized tag reading can occur when the data between the reader and the tag is unencrypted. This makes it easier for an unauthorized reader to read the data.

Unauthorized tag writing occurs when an unauthorized reader inserts data onto the tag during the normal read-write process. For example, the unauthorized reader could illegally reset the security bit, allowing the user to walk out of the library with an unchecked-out book.

Hotlisting is the process of illegally capturing data from the tag and matching it with a specifically targeted item. Eventually the interloper could build up a database of tag codes and the title of the item associated with each tag.

Tracking is the process of using the tag located in a book to keep track of the movements of an individual. In order for tracking to be effective, the individual being tracked must carry the tagged book and there must be unauthorized readers wherever the person travels.

In "Considering RFID: Benefits, Limitations, and Best Practices," *College & Research Libraries News,* January 2005, Laura Smart points out that "all of these privacy and security threats are labor intensive. The controversy stems from the potential of RFID technologies to erode privacy and civil liberties." She continues, "RFID is increasingly being used in commercial applications, and in its ubiquity lies its danger. As the technology evolves, stronger readers could emerge and start popping up everywhere like cell phone signal transmitters."

How library RFID systems work

An RFID system consists of tags, readers, programming stations, and the various interfaces involved in communicating or linking with other systems.

Tags. RFID tags are small radio receivers (antennae) with a microchip. The microchip is programmed with distinctive information about the item that can be directly imported from an integrated library system at the tag programming station. It is possible to include many types of information on the tag (such as book title, patron circulation information, date/time stamps), but a tag would typically only contain bar-code information.

Readers. There are many different types of tag readers or scanners. Typically, the reader is responsible for generating the electrical impulse that causes the tag to be read because the tags used in libraries are usually passive—

meaning they don't have their own source of power. The reader interrogates the tag, which then replies with the information stored on the tag.

Readers can be located at the circulation desk, self-check stations, book drops, sorting machines, exit sensors, and in hand-held wands. Some readers store the information captured from the tags while others capture the information and immediately pass it through to the database, or integrated library system.

Readers built into the exit sensors check the tag to ensure that the item was checked out. If it was not checked out, the alarm sounds. This process can be handled in one of two ways. Some vendors use a "theft bit" to indicate whether the item was discharged. Others require that the ILS be queried as the patron leaves the library.

Readers placed at the circulation desk and at self-check stations allow staff and patrons to pass stacks of books over the reader, which detects all the tags inside the books. It is not necessary for each item to be scanned individually.

Inventory wands act as readers and as portable databases that store shelf lists. Library staff can use the wands to scan all the items on a shelf and detect which items are out of order or missing.

Programming stations. In order to convert to an RFID system, all library material must be tagged and programmed. Programming, or conversion stations, are used to affix the tags to the items and program them (usually via the existing bar code).

Interfaces. Many RFID systems have a server that collects the information from each of the library's readers. The RFID server then communicates with the circulation system. SIP2 provides the standard for most communications between the ILS and other systems. All library RFID vendors are SIP2-compliant; however, compliance does not ensure smooth communications because some vendors have modified the protocol to suit their needs.

The National Information Standards Organization (NISO) is developing a new protocol to encourage better interoperability between RFID and ILS systems. The new standard, Z39.83-2002 or NCIP (National Circulation Interchange Protocol), has not yet, as of late 2005, been implemented by library RFID vendors.

Best practices guidelines

Best practices guidelines and RFID-specific privacy guidelines are being developed by early adopters of RFID technology. Below is a summary of best practices guidelines for library RFID use:

- The library should be open about its use of RFID technology, including providing publicly available documents stating the rationale for using RFID, objective of its use, any associated policies and procedures, and whom to contact with questions.
- Signs should be posted at all facilities using RFID. The signs should inform the public that RFID technology is in use and how this technology differs from other information-collection methods. It should also include a statement about how the patron's privacy is being safeguarded.
- Only authorized personnel should have access to the RFID system.
- No personal information should be stored on the RFID tag.
- Information describing the tagged item should be encrypted on the tag even if the data is limited to a bar-code number.
- All communications between tag and reader should be encrypted.
- Only passive RFID tags should be used.
- All RFID readers in the library should be clearly marked.

As Smart (2005) notes, RFID technology has the potential to improve physical access to library materials, but there are significant privacy implications. She encourages librarians to continue to "[monitor] the technology and maintain their professional obligation to protect patron privacy if they are going to choose RFID."

For more on RFID in libraries, visit the ALA's RFID page at www.ala.org/ala/oif/ifissues/rfid.htm, and RFID in Libraries at www.libraryrfid.net/wordpress/.

SOURCE: Special report for the *Whole Library Handbook 4* by Lori Bowen Ayre, who is the founder and principal technology consultant for The Galecia Group in Petaluma, California (galecia.com). ©2005 The Galecia Group/Lori Bowen Ayre. All original material created by Lori Bowen Ayre for inclusion in this book is licensed under a Creative Commons License (creativecommons.org/licenses/by-nc-nd/2.0/).

Types of CDs and DVDs
by Fred R. Byers

CDs are single-sided—one recorded layer or recordable layer on one side of the disc. *DVDs* come in several flavors: DVD-ROM, DVD-Video (commercially available prerecorded DVDs) can be single- or double-sided with one or two data layers on one or both sides of the disc (four data layers maximum). DVD-R, DVD+R, DVD-RW, DVD+RW are only available as single-sided, single layer (SS/SL). DVD-RAM is available in double-sided, single-layer (DS/SL).

Disc	Type	Storage capacity	Typical uses
CD-ROM, Audio-CD, Video-CD	Read only	650MB	**Commercially available:** Computer programs, music
CD-R	Record once	650MB	User recording music,
CD-R	Record once	700MB	computer data, files, applications
CD-RW	Rewritable	650MB	User recording computer
CD-RW	Rewritable	700MB	data, files, applications
DVD-ROM, DVD-Video, DVD-Audio			**Commercially available:**
Single-sided, one layer (SS/SL)	Read only	4.7GB	Movies, interactive
Single-sided, two layers (SS/DL)	Read only	8.54GB	games, programs,
Both sides have one layer (DS/SL)	Read only	9.4GB	applications
DVD-R (general)	Record once	4.7GB	**General use:** One-time video recording and data archiving
DVD-R (authoring)	Record once	3.95GB or 4.7GB	**Professional use:** Video recording and editing
DVD+R	Record once	4.7GB	**General use:** One-time video recording and data archiving
DVD-RW	Rewritable	4.7GB	**General use:** Video recording and PC backup
DVD+RW	Rewritable	4.7GB	**General use:** Video recording and editing, data storage, PC backup
DVD-RAM			**Computer data:**
Single-sided	Rewritable	2.6GB or 4.7GB	Storage repository for updateable computer data,
Double-sided	Rewritable	5.2GB or 9.4GB	backups

SOURCE: Fred R. Byers, *Care and Handling of CDs and DVDs* (Washington, D.C.: Council on Library and Information Resources and National Institute on Standards and Technology, October 2003), pp. 27–28, www.clir.org/pubs/reports/pub121/pub121.pdf. Reprinted with permission.

ISSUES

CHAPTER NINE

"I didn't realize librarians were such a dangerous group. They are subversive. You think they're just sitting there at the desk, all quiet and everything. They're like plotting the revolution, man. I wouldn't mess with them."

—Michael Moore, in BuzzFlash, March 13, 2002

CORE VALUES

Librarianship: A personal view

by Karen Schneider

WE ARE NOT IMPARTIAL. We are on the side of open access to information, literacy, lifelong learning, the pursuit of happiness, the joy of a novel on a summer afternoon. We believe in information as a common good. We are opposed to many things—censorship, the assault on privacy, less access to government information—and we are in favor of many things, such as better funding for libraries.

Librarianship is one of the most radical of professions. Society says, "This is how we teach you." Libraries say, "You can learn what you want when you want, and you can read for the sheer joy of it."

Society says, "Tune in at 8:00 for *Friends.*" Libraries say, "Find your own path, on your own schedule."

Society says, "Some things are only for the wealthy." Libraries say, "Here it is, no matter who you are."

Librarianship is really a subversive profession. One reason many of us became librarians was in rebellion with the one-truth model choked down our throats in public schools.

Society says education will happen at this and that point in your life, doled out in didactic spoonfuls. Libraries say learning can be lifelong and at your own pace.

Society says to use these textbooks and those measurements. Librarianship says there are no textbooks and measurements, only the information you want and need.

Society says education is to be endured through endless hours in dolorous classrooms. Librarianship says reading is a joy. Do it in the library, in your home, on a streetcar, on a blanket at the beach. Read novels and histories and joke books and newspapers and *People* and *American Scholar.* Read blogs all day. Write blogs all day. Read the last page of every John Cheever story. Play podcasts backward. Read two books a day or one a year. Go for it! Information is not a nasty-tasting medicine but a lily of the field.

Essayist Gretel Ehrlich made reference to her nascent ideas as "crystals in the air, beginning to congeal." The world is filled with such crystals. Ranganathan saw them, too: His fifth and last law was that the library "is a living organism."

Even the commitment to provide impartial service to everyone who walks in is not at all impartial. That's a radical notion, standing in opposition to the dominant cultural imperatives of our day.

SOURCE: Karen Schneider, adapted from a message on the ALA Council discussion list, July 13, 2004, and a posting on Free Range Librarian, May 29, 2005.

INFORMATION COMMONS

The emerging information commons

by Nancy Kranich

FOR DEMOCRACY TO FLOURISH, citizens need free and open access to information. In today's digital age, this means access to information online. In the early days of the internet, new technologies promised exactly that—abundant open access to an infinite array of resources that foster political participation and enrich people's lives. Indeed, the arrival of the information age in the last half of the 20th century inspired dreams of a utopia where people could connect with myriad ideas and with each other instantly, no longer constrained by location, format, cost, time of day, onsite rules, or other barriers.

But the same technology that enables unfettered access can also restrict information choices and the free flow of ideas. Instead of a utopia, large portions of the internet were soon dominated by media corporations that developed "technology protection measures," licensing terms, and other "digital rights management" techniques to restrict access to information and control its use. As a result, much online content is now wrapped, packaged, and restricted—treated as private rather than common property.

This "walled garden" or "enclosure" online creates an inequitable and often inaccessible information marketplace. Today, many Americans have little access or ability to use the new technologies. Others find their access restricted because they cannot afford the high prices or comply with the rules created by media corporations.

Public interest advocates—librarians, civil liberties groups, scholars, and others favoring open access to information and ideas—have struggled against enclosure. Despite impressive efforts, they have faced an uphill battle to influence outcomes in Congress and the courts. Now, however, the public interest community is coming together around the emerging concept of the *information commons*, which offers a new model for stimulating innovation, fostering creativity, and building a movement that envisions information as a shared resource.

Applying the commons to information

Just as common property scholars are presenting a framework for understanding and governing the commons, scholars in other fields have recognized the importance of shared information spaces for promoting democracy and the free flow of ideas. Civil society researchers such as Harry C. Boyte, Peter Levine, and Lewis Friedland emphasize that shared public spaces are needed to rekindle civic participation. Others who document the impact of technology on society, like Lawrence Grossman, Anthony Wilhelm, and Douglas Schuler, accentuate how access to cyberspace presents both promises and challenges for

9

wider participation in a 21st-century democracy. Legal scholars have grasped the idea of the commons as a new approach to understanding the nature of information, and to countering restrictions imposed by copyright rules and digital rights management techniques. Joining these scholars are librarians and other public-interest advocates who see the commons as a useful tool to reclaim public space and promote the public interest in the digital age.

A leader in the field has been David Bollier, who considers the commons a critical contribution to a community of shared moral values and social purpose. The value of the information commons thus goes far beyond maximizing economic utility. Bollier and his colleague Tim Watts explain in *Saving the Information Commons* (New America Foundation, 2002): "A commons analysis gives us a way to speak coherently about another matrix of concerns that are not given sufficient attention: democratic participation, openness, social equity, and diversity."

Moving from theory to practice, library science professors Karen Fisher and Joan Durrance have examined how information communities unite people around a common interest through increased access to a diffused set of information resources. The internet is often the hub of these communities, facilitating connections and collaborations among participants, the exchange of ideas, distribution of papers, and links with others who have similar interests and needs. They describe five characteristics that distinguish these internet-based information communities:

- information-sharing with multiplier effects;
- collaboration;
- interaction based on needs of participants;
- low barriers to entry; and
- connectedness with the larger community.

According to Fisher and Durrance, online communities that share the production and distribution of information are likely to experience increased access to and use of information, increased access to people and organizations, and increased dialogue, communication, and collaboration among information providers and constituents.

Civil-society scholars Lewis Friedland, Harry Boyte, and Peter Levine have tested the idea of the commons by establishing information communities in St. Paul, Minnesota, and Prince George's County, Maryland, in order to promote civic engagement, particularly among young people. Levine believes that such commons are appealing because they are not controlled by bureaucrats, experts, or profit-seeking companies, and they encourage more diverse uses and participation. Yet he also recognizes the vulnerability of such endeavors if they fail to adopt appropriate governance structures, rules, and management techniques so that they are equipped to survive in the face of rival alternatives, and avoid the anarchy that Garrett Hardin describes in "The Tragedy of the Commons," *Science* 162 (1968): 1243–1248.

Friedland, Boyte, and Levine acknowledge the historic role of institutions such as newspapers, schools, libraries, and community festivals in providing opportunities for democratic participation and a collective deliberative voice. To promote and sustain newly emerging information commons, they urge continued sponsorship and collaboration with such institutions, along with careful attention to governance structures.

In November 2001, the American Library Association sponsored a conference on the Information Commons, with commissioned papers on information equity, copyright and fair use, and public access (www.info-commons.org/arch/1/issue1.html).

In 2002 and 2003, the journals *Boston Review, Knowledge Quest,* and *Common Property Resource Digest* devoted full issues to the concept of the information commons. The Friends of the Commons, started with help from David Bollier and funding from the Tides Foundation, published its first annual report, *The State of the Commons,* in October 2003 (www.friendsofthecommons.org/stateofcommons0304.pdf). At the World Summit on the Information Society in December 2003 (www.itu.int/wsis/), the advocacy group World-Information.org issued a newspaper for delegates focusing on the topic, and posted other articles on its website (world-information.org).

All of these activities are calling attention to the commons as a new, dynamic approach to serving the public interest in the digital age. At the same time, initiatives sponsored by scientists, librarians, nonprofit groups, and many others have demonstrated that the information commons can actually flourish.

SOURCE: Nancy Kranich, *The Information Commons: A Public Policy Report* (New York: Free Expression Policy Project, Brennan Center for Justice, NYU School of Law, 2004), pp. 2–3, 12–15. Reprinted with permission.

Librarians and copyright: A match made in heaven

by Carrie Russell

WHY SHOULD LIBRARIANS KNOW AND CARE about copyright law? There are lots of reasons. We are concerned about infringement and want to make sure we are following the law to the best of our ability. Library users, teachers, faculty, and students often deem librarians the "copyright experts," so we must remain engaged in the topic. The law actually addresses a lot of what librarians do—circulation, interlibrary loan, public performances, and preservation—and of course, our library users exercise fair use in our libraries. Definitely, libraries are places where people learn by exploring, sharing, and building on the copyrighted works of others to advance the progress of science and the useful arts.

There is a more fundamental reason why librarians should know and care about copyright—librarians have a unique social responsibility to protect the interests of the public, which depends on information to lead full, engaged, informed, and rewarding lives. As a profession, we value equitable access to information, the privacy rights of users, the free flow of information, and preservation of the cultural record—grand ideas that are affected by copyright law and other information policies. As lofty as it sounds, libraries are "cornerstones of democracy," institutions that symbolize the freedom to know for all people.

Copyright law sets restrictions on how the public can lawfully use information, creative works, and knowledge, but only to ultimately serve the public

Jessica Abel

interest. Copyright law is about the dissemination of information—it allows creators the right to market their works so they are encouraged to *reveal* those works to the public. Of course, information is not cost-free, and librarians do not expect it to be. Librarians do, however, expect that information be "free-flowing." Copyright law facilitates broad free-flow by ensuring that information is made available, albeit through a market-based model. In this country, we pay people to create when they are willing to share (for a fee) their creations.

There are other models for ensuring that the public has access to information, creative works, and knowledge. Some creators willingly share their works without compensation. Some cultures pass knowledge on to future generations through story telling and direct communication with one another. Each model has advantages and limitations. The U.S. copyright model is successful when the rights of users of information are in balance with the rights of authors, creators, or other copyright holders. Our job as librarians is to monitor that balance. Copyright does not work when user rights are unduly restricted.

The current copyright environment

Congress has modified the copyright law throughout its history. On the one hand, it has strengthened the rights of copyright holders by adding additional exclusive rights, extending the copyright term, adding additional penalties and other remedies for copyright infringement, eliminating requirements for copyright protection, and creating new restrictions on access to information (such as the anticircumvention provision of the DMCA). On the other hand, it has carved out exceptions for users (including fair use and library-related exemptions). Have these modifications affected the balance of copyright law?

The answer to this question, of course, depends on whom you ask. Library associations and other public interest groups argue that the copyright balance has been tipped against the user, for a number of reasons:

- User access to copyrighted works is restricted by criminalizing circumvention of access controls.
- Fair use, the lawful yet unauthorized use of a work for legitimate purposes, is eroded by criminalizing the creation (and therefore use) of tools to circumvent copy protection technologies.
- User choice of how to use lawfully acquired materials is restricted by technology employed to control where, when, and how materials may be used.
- The public domain is eroded by the continual extension of the copyright term, which prevents copyrighted works from entering the public domain for longer and longer periods of time.
- Restrictive licensing and international agreements tend to export enforcement and protection but not fair use and other user exemptions.
- The creation of new works is limited by copyright holders who charge exorbitant fees for the use of copyrighted works.
- Free expression is suppressed when copyright holders use the law to restrict criticism and commentary.

- The public interest becomes a secondary consideration when Congress drafts copyright law in the interests of large corporations who control the majority of copyright-protected works.
- There are continual and ongoing efforts to further restrict user rights through new legislation, federal regulation, and the development and implementation of technological controls and devices.

These are extremely complex and controversial policy issues that most of us would rather ignore, but librarians have a responsibility to pay attention, remain informed, and ask the tough questions.

Making time to be copyright savvy

Admittedly, it is difficult to be a librarian with a full set of work responsibilities *and* be cognizant of the copyright law and other information policies that affect library users *and* take action to effect change for the betterment of your library community. However, as librarians, you must take the lead and be socially responsible to your users. Frequently, we get so caught up in our work assignments that we begin to identify with the work itself and forget about our larger role in society. Your job responsibilities may involve reference duties, managing user services, cataloging, and helping others use digital media applications, but you are a *librarian* first and foremost. In other words, you *are more than what you do.* We hope that information in this chapter will help you be a successful advocate for balanced (and therefore) effective copyright law and help you teach others about copyright.

Being a library advocate

Librarians understand the importance of the library in our communities, and we must carry the message of library users to members of the legislature, both on the national and local levels. Surprisingly, members of Congress know very little about libraries. It is difficult to capture the attention of legislators who have many issues to attend to, some of which are quite critical. Nonetheless, the information needs of our users are critical to the health of a well-informed citizenry. While information policy may not be the sexiest arena of policy and law, libraries serve millions of users who are potential voters. The sheer size of our constituency is key to our power to influence policy.

Making an impact with a complex issue. If you are willing to advocate for balanced copyright law but feel you do not have the expertise to discuss it with a member of Congress, you are not alone. Copyright is a complex law, and very few people feel comfortable talking about database legislation, fair use, or circumvention technologies. The library associations have expert copyright lobbyists to advocate on our behalf in the halls of Congress, *but don't let them fight the battle alone!* Although it may seem insignificant, librarians should write to their congressional representatives about their copyright concerns and the importance of fair use, especially when library lobbyists call for letters addressing pending copyright legislation. The American Library Association's Washington Office provides general guidelines, tips, talking points, and congressional contact and address information to help you craft the perfect letter. In addition, you can personalize your letter by sharing your "library stories," expounding on the importance of fair use or other copyright exemptions to your community of library users.

9

More directly, you can influence copyright and information policy at the institutional level. This is where librarians live and breathe copyright on a day-to-day basis, and where we are often already leaders in the copyright arena. This is the leadership role we must embrace and nurture.

Becoming a copyright leader in three easy steps. Becoming a copyright leader is not as hard as it sounds. *Staying informed about copyright developments and making the commitment to educate yourself* is the first step. There are several ways to do this:

- Keep abreast of new legislation by participating in legislative briefings given by associations such as the ALA Washington Office.
- Regularly visit and read library association websites that focus on copyright concerns.
- Attend legislative meetings for any state association or group to which you belong.
- Read a good newspaper, with a particular focus on the business section, where many emerging copyright concerns are reported.
- Sponsor your own informal in-house library meetings to discuss copyright concerns.
- Attend local and conference programs on copyright, ask tough questions, and contribute to the discussion.

The second step is to *participate in copyright policy development at your institution:*

- Volunteer to serve on the library committee charged with the responsibility of drafting the library copyright policy.
- Play the role of user advocate on the committee and ensure that fair use be a central feature of the finished policy.
- Write a "plain language" version of the finished copyright policy for library users, instructors, students, faculty, and staff, so it will be meaningful to them.
- Identify and develop an ongoing relationship with your institutional copyright officer or legal counsel and ask that they review your copyright policy.
- Make connections with other librarians responsible for or interested in copyright and share ideas on ways to improve or expand on copyright policies and other related matters.

The third step is to *teach others about copyright.* We cannot expect library users and our other clientele to understand copyright law—they probably don't even think about it! We must help them follow the law as well as help them understand their rights under the law:

- Develop and implement a copyright education program for library personnel.
- Create copyright fact sheets and guides focused on the needs of your user community or specialized group.
- Develop a "copyright basics" presentation and take it on the road locally; then test it out at the next state or regional library conference.
- Write articles about copyright for your regional newsletter or favorite library journal.

SOURCE: Carrie Russell, *Complete Copyright: An Everyday Guide for Librarians* (Washington, D.C.: ALA Office for Information Technology Policy, 2004), pp. 133–137.

LEGISLATION

Library lobbyists

by Bernardine E. Abbott-Hoduski

EVERY CHANGE IN POLICY starts with an individual. That individual identifies a problem, realizes that the solution is a policy change, and then lobbies to get the policy changed. The individual may act on his or her own or may persuade an association or institution to take up the cause. Following are some of the individuals who have impressed me with the courage and tenacity they have shown in pursuing their causes. They persuaded others to support their causes, sometimes at the loss of their own jobs.

Maryellen Trautman, a member of the Depository Library Council from 1973 through 1975, persuaded the Depository Library Council and the Government Printing Office to hold federal depository libraries accountable for serving the public. She worked to improve the standards used by GPO to grade and inspect those libraries. She urged GPO to hire knowledgeable librarians to inspect the libraries in person, not by mail, and to require that libraries post signs indicating that they are depositories and open to the public. Some libraries at the time denied access to anyone but their own faculty and students or when they did provide access made it difficult for the public to find the documents and use them. Some did not open their boxes of documents for months or even years and others did not catalog, bind, or shelve the documents. Trautman changed policy by first convincing Superintendent of Documents Robert E. Kling Jr. to resurrect the defunct depository library advisory committee in 1973 and then by being appointed to it and convincing Kling to appoint other working documents librarians like myself to the council. She met Kling at a Special Libraries Association conference and asked whether she could spend her vacation learning about the depository library operation. When he agreed, she sweetened their meeting at GPO by bringing his book, *The Government Printing Office*, for an autograph and a sample of her homemade wine. He was so charmed that he gave her a personal tour and called her later to ask her for suggestions about whom to appoint to the committee, insisting that she would be the first one appointed.

Zoia Horn (left) started the Right to Know Project at the Data Center in Oakland, California, and persuaded the American Library Association to establish the Coalition on Government Information. She served on the ALA committee that organized the coalition, using the list of organizations that she had prepared as part of her Right to Know Project.

Roberta Scull of Louisiana State University, **Karlo Mustonen** of Utah State University, and **Richard Leacy** of Georgia Tech, while members of the Depository Library Council, lobbied for the inclusion of scientific, technical, and agricultural government documents and contractor reports in the federal depository library program. They also argued that these documents should be cataloged using AACR2 and included in the *Monthly Catalog of United States Government Publications.* In response to their efforts, the Department of Energy (DOE) was an active participant in the electronic pilot projects for depository libraries. DOE and GPO have launched several cooperative electronic services that provide libraries and the public with free online access to thousands of scientific and technical reports as well as information about ongoing projects and scientific journal articles.

Richard Leacy, documents librarian at the Georgia Institute of Technology, spearheaded the effort to keep the economic census in the depository library program in the early 1970s. A census official had decided not to publish the census through the government and instead allow a private publisher to have sole rights to publication. Leacy launched a very effective campaign to alert other depository librarians about the potential loss to the public and persuaded them to lobby members of the congressional appropriations committees to keep the Commerce Department from privatizing public information.

Elizabeth Morrissette, while director of the library at the University of Montana School of Technology, persuaded the International Federation of Library Associations and Institutions to establish a working group on peace. She did this during the cold war and at IFLA meetings behind the Iron Curtain in Czechoslovakia and East Germany. She enlisted the aid of E. J. Josey, longtime American Library Association councilor, and me in persuading IFLA powers to allow the working group, but she was the driving force that made it happen. Morrissette also coordinated and energized a peace task force within the Social Responsibilities Round Table of ALA.

Joan Marshall and **Sandy Berman** (right) waged lifelong struggles to eliminate biases, prejudices, and cultural insensitivity in subject headings used by libraries. Marshall spent several months at the Library of Congress analyzing subject headings assigned to books about women and wrote *On Equal Terms: A Thesaurus for Nonsexist Indexing and Cataloging.* She lived at my house during that time and gave me a daily education on how to
change an institution for the better. Berman issued a cataloging bulletin that provided alternative terms to those used by the Library of Congress. When Marshall, Berman, and I represented Round Tables on the ALA committee that rewrote the cataloging rules in the late 1970s, we learned that asking for and getting changes in something as sacred as cataloging rules and subject headings takes patience and diplomacy. It also requires lobbying every member of the committee since rational arguments alone will not sway those who consider cataloging an art and not a science.

E. J. Josey (right) forced the American Library Association to fight segregation in libraries by expelling chapters whose states allowed racially segregated libraries. He served as ALA president and spent 29 years on the ALA Council persuading ALA to adopt policies that encouraged the recruitment of minority librarians, the provision of library services to minorities, and the diversification of library collections to reflect the communities that use them.

Stephen Hayes, documents librarian at Notre Dame, courageously confronted Donald Fossedal, superintendent of documents, about depository libraries being unable to serve the public because of the lack of government documents due to the microfiche disaster of the late 1980s. The GPO contractor was years behind in producing the fiche, and the fiche produced was of such poor quality that it was unreadable. Libraries that had chosen microfiche rather than paper did not receive any publications. Hayes (right) confronted GPO officials at ALA and DLC meetings. At the DLC meeting in Charleston, South Carolina, he explained that faculty were complaining about not having access to publications that were available for sale but not sent to depository libraries. He demanded that GPO live up to its slogan of "demand-driven, service-oriented."  Fossedal responded that the libraries should buy the publication while waiting for the depository copy. Hayes did not agree, urging librarians to stop asking GPO to solve the problem and lobby Congress instead. The Joint Committee on Printing was listening and after an initial investigation determined that the problem was that GPO had only one contractor and that contractor was not providing quality fiche on a timely basis. GPO then terminated its contract with the sole contractor and broke the work out into nine separate contracts. The terminated contractor won one of the nine bids and protested several others that it failed to win. The ongoing dispute further disrupted distribution of the fiche to libraries. JCP then asked the General Accounting Office (GAO) in July 1988 to investigate the problem and report back to JCP. As a result of the GAO report, additional steps were taken by GPO to institute quality control procedures to assure that only qualified contractors were awarded contracts. Hayes's campaign was a public one, but unknown to the library community, the GPO staffer responsible for the day-to-day operation of the microfiche program resigned in protest over the refusal of other GPO officials to disqualify the contractor for poor performance.

Carl LaBarre, superintendent of documents, chose to fight to keep 27 out of the 30 GPO bookstores open rather than close them down as directed by Dan Sawyer, public printer, in 1981. LaBarre, with the help of the bookstore managers, marshaled statistics showing that the stores paid their own way and were needed by the public. When this data failed to convince the public printer, he gave the information to the Joint Committee on Printing and resigned rather than implement a decision he believed to be detrimental to the public's right to know. JCP was convinced by the statistics and an outcry from the public and librarians and voted to keep the bookstores open.

John Gordon Burke, editor of the *Missouri Library Association Newsletter* and *American Libraries,* insisted on editorial independence so the journals could objectively report about library and policy issues. He believed so strongly in that principle that in 1974 he resigned as editor of *American Libraries* after he was forced to fire a reporter for investigating the financial reimbursement of commissioners on the National Commission on Libraries.

LeRoy Schwarzkopf, regional depository librarian at the University of Maryland and longtime editor of *Documents to the People,* helped bring down a superintendent of documents by taping his speeches at public meetings and courageously taking those tapes to the deputy public printer. As a depository librarian whose library was inspected by that superintendent, he could have suffered for complaining to the superintendent's boss.

Arne Richards, documents librarian at Kansas State University, lobbied Congress in the 1960s and 1970s to provide congressional committee prints to depository libraries. Committee prints are special reports and studies issued by committees. When I was hired by the Joint Committee on Printing in 1974, that became my first project, and now the majority of the prints are in libraries.

9

SOURCE: Bernardine E. Abbott-Hoduski, *Lobbying for Libraries and the Public's Access to Government Information* (Lanham, Md.: Scarecrow, 2003), pp. 48–52.

INTELLECTUAL FREEDOM

The Library Bill of Rights

THE AMERICAN LIBRARY ASSOCIATION affirms that all libraries are forums for information and ideas, and that the following basic policies should guide their services.

1. Books and other library resources should be provided for the interest, information, and enlightenment of all people of the community the library serves. Materials should not be excluded because of the origin, background, or views of those contributing to their creation.
2. Libraries should provide materials and information presenting all points of view on current and historical issues. Materials should not be proscribed or removed because of partisan or doctrinal disapproval.
3. Libraries should challenge censorship in the fulfillment of their responsibility to provide information and enlightenment.
4. Libraries should cooperate with all persons and groups concerned with resisting abridgment of free expression and free access to ideas.
5. A person's right to use a library should not be denied or abridged because of origin, age, background, or views.
6. Libraries which make exhibit spaces and meeting rooms available to the public they serve should make such facilities available on an equitable basis, regardless of the beliefs or affiliations of individuals or groups requesting their use.

Since 1948, when the *Library Bill of Rights* was first adopted, ALA Council has affirmed 18 interpretations that elaborate its provisions:

Access for children and young adults to nonprint materials. Adopted 1989; amended 2004.
Access to electronic information, services, and networks. Adopted 1996; amended 2005.
Access to library resources and services regardless of sex, gender identity, or sexual orientation. Adopted 1993; amended 2000, 2004.
Access to resources and services in the school library media program. Adopted 1986; amended 1990, 2000, 2005.
Challenged materials. Adopted 1971; amended 1981, 1990.
Diversity in collection development. Adopted 1982; amended 1990.
Economic barriers to information access. Adopted 1993.
Evaluating library collections. Adopted 1973; amended 1981.
Exhibit spaces and bulletin boards. Adopted 1991; amended 2004.
Expurgation of library materials. Adopted 1973; amended 1981, 1990.
Free access to libraries for minors. Adopted 1972; amended 1981, 1991, 2004.
Intellectual freedom principles for academic libraries. Adopted 2000.
Labels and rating systems. Adopted 1951; amended 1971, 1981, 1990, 2005.
Library-initiated programs as a resource. Adopted 1982; amended 1990, 2000.
Meeting rooms. Adopted 1991.

Privacy. Adopted 2002. (See pp. 481–482.)
Restricted access to library materials. Adopted 1973; amended 1981, 1991, 2000, 2004.
The universal right to free expression. Adopted 1991.

SOURCE: ALA Office for Intellectual Freedom, www.ala.org/ala/oif/.

The freedom to read

THE FREEDOM TO READ is essential to our democracy. It is continuously under attack. Private groups and public authorities in various parts of the country are working to remove or limit access to reading materials, to censor content in schools, to label "controversial" views, to distribute lists of "objectionable" books or authors, and to purge libraries. These actions apparently rise from a view that our national tradition of free expression is no longer valid; that censorship and suppression are needed to counter threats to safety or national security, as well as to avoid the subversion of politics and the corruption of morals. We, as individuals devoted to reading and as librarians and publishers responsible for disseminating ideas, wish to assert the public interest in the preservation of the freedom to read.

Most attempts at suppression rest on a denial of the fundamental premise of democracy: That the ordinary individual, by exercising critical judgment, will select the good and reject the bad. We trust Americans to recognize propaganda and misinformation, and to make their own decisions about what they read and believe. We do not believe they are prepared to sacrifice their heritage of a free press in order to be "protected" against what others think may be bad for them. We believe they still favor free enterprise in ideas and expression.

These efforts at suppression are related to a larger pattern of pressures being brought against education, the press, art and images, films, broadcast media, and the internet. The problem is not only one of actual censorship. The shadow of fear cast by these pressures leads, we suspect, to an even larger voluntary curtailment of expression by those who seek to avoid controversy or unwelcome scrutiny by government officials.

Such pressure toward conformity is perhaps natural to a time of accelerated change. And yet suppression is never more dangerous than in such a time of social tension. Freedom has given the United States the elasticity to endure strain. Freedom keeps open the path of novel and creative solutions, and enables change to come by choice. Every silencing of a heresy, every enforcement of an orthodoxy, diminishes the toughness and resilience of our society and leaves it less able to deal with controversy and difference.

Now, as always in our history, reading is among our greatest freedoms. The freedom to read and write is almost the only means for making generally available ideas or manners of expression that can initially command only a small audience. The written word is the natural medium for the new idea and the untried voice from which come the original contributions to social growth. It is essential to the extended discussion that serious thought requires, and to the accumulation of knowledge and ideas into organized collections.

We believe that free communication is essential to the preservation of a free society and a creative culture. We believe that these pressures toward conformity present the danger of limiting the range and variety of inquiry and expression on which our democracy and our culture depend. We believe that every American community must jealously guard the freedom to publish and to circulate, in order to preserve its own freedom to read. We believe that publishers and librarians have a profound responsibility to give validity to that freedom to read by making it possible for the readers to choose freely from a variety of offerings.

The freedom to read is guaranteed by the Constitution. Those with faith in free people will stand firm on these constitutional guarantees of essential rights and will exercise the responsibilities that accompany these rights.

We therefore affirm these propositions:

1. It is in the public interest for publishers and librarians to make available the widest diversity of views and expressions, including those which are unorthodox, unpopular, or considered dangerous by the majority.

2. Publishers, librarians, and booksellers do not need to endorse every idea or presentation they make available. It would conflict with the public interest for them to establish their own political, moral, or aesthetic views as a standard for determining what books should be published or circulated.

3. It is contrary to the public interest for publishers or librarians to bar access to writings on the basis of the personal history or political affiliations of the author.

4. There is no place in our society for efforts to coerce the taste of others, to confine adults to the reading matter deemed suitable for adolescents, or to inhibit the efforts of writers to achieve artistic expression.

5. It is not in the public interest to force a reader to accept the prejudgment of a label characterizing any expression or its author as subversive or dangerous.

6. It is the responsibility of publishers and librarians, as guardians of the people's freedom to read, to contest encroachments upon that freedom by individuals or groups seeking to impose their own standards or tastes upon the community at large; and by the government whenever it seeks to reduce or deny public access to public information.

7. It is the responsibility of publishers and librarians to give full meaning to the freedom to read by providing books that enrich the quality and diversity of thought and expression. By the exercise of this affirmative responsibility, they can demonstrate that the answer to a "bad" book is a good one, the answer to a "bad" idea is a good one.

We state these propositions neither lightly nor as easy generalizations. We here stake out a lofty claim for the value of the written word. We do so because we believe that it is possessed of enormous variety and usefulness, worthy of cherishing and keeping free. We realize that the application of these propositions may mean the dissemination of ideas and manners of expression that are repugnant to many persons. We do not state these propositions in the comfortable belief that what people read is unimportant. We believe rather that what people read is deeply important; that ideas can be dangerous; but that the suppression of ideas is fatal to a democratic society. Freedom itself is a dangerous way of life, but it is ours.

SOURCE: ALA Office for Intellectual Freedom. Adopted 1953; revised 1972, 1991, 2000, and 2004 by the ALA Council and the AAP Freedom to Read Committee; full statement available online at www.ala.org/oif/.

More Silly and Illogical Reasons to Ban a Book
by Beverly Goldberg

The *Whole Library Handbook 3* (2000) and the *Whole Library Handbook 2* (1995) contained lists of silly reasons to ban a book. Since then some other candidates have turned up:

1. It accurately describes the history of life on earth. Juliet Clutton-Brock's *Horse* was challenged at the Smith Elementary School in Helena, Montana, in 2004 because a concerned parent said there were "too many questions with evolutionary theory to present it as a fact." She specifically objected to the passage: "It took about 55 million years for the present family of horses, asses, and zebras to evolve from their earliest horse-like ancestor."

2. It's too flatulent. Glenn Murray's *Walter the Farting Dog* was challenged at the West Salem (Wis.) Elementary School in 2004 after a former school board member pointed out that the words "fart" and "farting" occur in the text 24 times altogether. In a letter to the local paper, the board president explained that the school district's mission to "help guide and nurture our youth into adulthood with some semblance of dignity and manners" is not served by "the graphical depiction of flatulence being blown into someone's face."

3. It miffs Muggles. The Harry Potter series of books was challenged at the Bend–La Pine (Oreg.) school district in 2000 because some parents thought its magical theme tended to foment "hatred and rebellion" among young people. Called a "masterpiece of satanic deception" by an Arizona pastor who organized a New Mexico book-burning in December 2002, J. K. Rowling's popular novels made it into the top 10 of ALA's "most-challenged" list from 2000 to 2004.

4. It inspires excremental art. The grandmother of a 2nd-grader in the John F. Kennedy Elementary School in Riverside, California, objected in 2003 to Dav Pilkey's *The Adventures of Super Diaper Baby* after she discovered her grandson sketching a picture of excrement because he was depicting the book's villain, Deputy Doo-Doo. "He was drawing a piece of poop," she said in the June 3 *Los Angeles Times.* She added, "There's just no moral value to that poop character."

5. It has swearing soldiers. In 2003, the George County, Mississippi, school board removed two novels about the Vietnam War from high-school library shelves because of profanity, Walter Dean Myers's *Fallen Angels* and Tim O'Brien's *The Things They Carried.*

6. It might bite. Bette Green's *The Drowning of Stephan Jones* was pulled from the middle schools of the Horry County (S.C.) School District in 2002 after a complainant likened the novel's sympathetic portrayal of gays to "a rattlesnake [that] needed to be killed right then and right there."

7. It unleashes lust. The *Guinness World Records, 2001* was challenged in 2002 in the Waukesha, Wisconsin, schools because boys clued each other to photos of models in a bikini, diamond-studded underwear, and a short tube dress. "It could start with one picture or one magazine," a complainant said, citing serial killer Ted Bundy's claim that pornography drove him to murder.

8. It's riddled with prejudice. That was the complaint lodged in 2001 against Mildred D. Taylor's *Mississippi Bridge*—a young-adult novel about Depression-era segregation—in the Henrico County, Virginia, schools.

9. Reading might erupt. "These books point to an addictive nature," explained the sexual-addiction counselor who tried to get the Springdale (Ark.) Public Library to withdraw the works of Western-genre authors Jon Sharpe, Jake Logan, and Tabor Evans in 2001.

10. It ruins reputations. The mother of a Bozeman, Montana, middle-schooler challenged *On the Bright Side, I'm Now the Girlfriend of a Sex God,* by Louise Rennison, in 2005 because an unstable person seeing a girl reading it might get the wrong idea and stalk her.

11. Divine right of way. A teacher's prayer group cautioned the Russell County, Kentucky, school board in 2002 that more than 50 books about ghosts, cults, and witchcraft "may need to be removed" from the high school library because God "can not come into a place that is corrupted."

9

In defense of America's freedoms

by Tom Teepen

REPORTING ON HIS OWN 1735 TRIAL for seditious libel for his disrespect of the Crown, colonial printer and *New-York Weekly Journal* Editor John Peter Zenger wrote that when the jury brought in a verdict of not guilty "there

were three huzzahs in the hall." Americans who prize their press and speech freedoms have been cheering ever since. Zenger's release, after 10 months in jail for publishing articles critical of New York Colonial Governor William Cosby, was a milestone on the way to the Bill of Rights, with its First Amendment admonition that "Congress shall make no law . . . abridging the freedom of speech, or of the press."

These 14 words were a second American revolution in their own right, indeed a revolution in human affairs, though one still sadly incomplete in most of the world. For all that the principle is embraced in the United Nation's Universal Declaration of Human Rights, the rights to free speech and a free press remain far from universal. Few nations even approach the breadth of protected expression that is secured by the U.S. Constitution's First Amendment.

Even here, our own freedoms to publish, distribute, and openly debate information and opinion remain under stress. Free speech is perhaps the purest example of the liberty whose price is "eternal vigilance," abolitionist Wendell Phillips said.

That vigilance is maintained in large part by a number of organizations committed to the free speech that too many Americans—often in positions of political power—would honor in principle while undermining it in practice. Among those defenders, count the American Civil Liberties Union, the American Booksellers Foundation for Free Expression, the Association of American Publishers, and the Freedom to Read Foundation (FTRF). Established in 1969 by the American Library Association, the FTRF was formed in recognition of the fact that a robust defense of the First Amendment is fundamental to the very essence of libraries as the crucial nexus that offers unimpeded access to society's wisdom, wit, folly, and frolic in all their confounding and sometimes cussed variety.

An offshoot of ALA's Office for Intellectual Freedom (OIF), the FTRF has been in court more or less constantly throughout its 35-year history and currently has more than a dozen active cases. The FTRF concentrates on issues that impact librarians and library practices but additionally joins with other First Amendment defenders in broader free-speech cases. The foundation recognizes that any chipping away at the First Amendment weakens it.

The real protectors

In its first year, the FTRF helped to defend a librarian who had been fired from the Missouri State Library for writing a letter to a local newspaper protesting the suppression of an underground newspaper. It helped a Maryland man challenge his conviction for selling an allegedly obscene issue of the *Washington Free Press;* a state appellate court overturned the conviction. And the foundation helped defray the financial hit that the city librarian of Martinsville, Virginia, had taken after coming under fire for challenging the constitutionality of a religious course taught in the city schools.

ALA's OIF set up shop in 1967 to chart censorship trends and alert librarians to them, as well as to provide resource materials to local libraries that found items in their collections being challenged. The office could back up local librarians with national reviews of besieged books and suggest effective talking points. With ready access to such reinforcement, local librarians were both more willing and better able to defend the content of their shelves. Judith Krug, director of OIF from its beginning, says, "When people began to realize they had support here, they began to develop backbones." Before then, Krug says, local librarians who tried to resist pressure to reject or remove books were "the lone voice in the wilderness."

Understandably, many shied away from that role. But as helpful as all that support was, and remains, Krug and others quickly realized that libraries also needed access to ready, committed, and expert legal support. As much as they needed advocacy in the political and social arenas, they need a champion in the legal lists, too.

The FTRF was created as the First Amendment legal arm of ALA, not formally attached to the association, but connected: Four ALA officers hold interlocking memberships on the 15-member FTRF board. Ten members are elected by an annual mail ballot of FTRF members, many of whom also belong to ALA. Krug, also a board member, wears a second hat as the foundation's executive director, and for years served as its only staff member. There is now one other full-time staffer, and some ALA staff do double duty working for the foundation.

OIF Director Judith Krug and attorney Bruce Ennis during a 1997 news conference celebrating the Supreme Court's ruling on the Communications Decency Act.

An early and key decision by the FTRF board based the foundation revenues primarily on membership funding, rather than on contributions from large private or corporate donors, helping to insulate the FTRF from the pressures major givers sometimes try to apply and keeping it free of the strings some might want to attach. The membership, drawn mainly from ALA's ranks, hovers around 1,800. The basic dues are $35 annually.

At first, ALA counsel represented the foundation, but as the FTRF caseload increased in both number and complexity, it became clear that the FTRF needed its own attorney. It has been represented by the Washington, D.C., office of Jenner and Block, a firm that specializes in First Amendment law.

Key court battles

Sometimes the FTRF files legal challenges directly, especially when the core mission of libraries is at risk. For instance, it joined with ALA in 1996 to contest the Communications Decency Act, a law that, like many before and since,

9

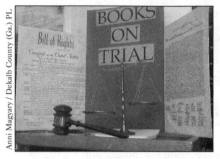

used a declared concern for children as a means to attempt much broader suppression of materials some might consider risqué. In 2001, the foundation once again joined ALA in a lawsuit challenging the Children's Internet Protection Act—a law requiring libraries receiving federal funds to defray telecommunication expenses to install filters on their internet computers. Although the Supreme Court ultimately upheld CIPA as a legitimate condition of funding, the justices made it clear that adults could not be blocked from accessing constitutionally protected material on the internet by emphasizing that libraries must disable filters at the request of adult users.

The foundation has, of course, soldiered through many wars over denounced books—from Kurt Vonnegut's *Slaughterhouse-Five* (Delacorte, 1969) through Eldridge Cleaver's *Soul on Ice* (McGraw-Hill, 1967) and the anonymously penned *Go Ask Alice* (Prentice-Hall, 1971) to Michael Willhoite's *Daddy's Roommate* (Alyson Wonderland, 1990) and Lesléa Newman's *Heather Has Two Mommies* (Alyson Wonderland, 2000) and such classics as *Lysistrata* by Aristophanes and Geoffrey Chaucer's *The Miller's Tale*.

It is through amicus briefs that the foundation most often appears in court. These friend-of-the-court filings broaden and add weight to ongoing First Amendment claims against a variety of legislation and local policies that would restrict access to published material.

With the singular "press" of Zenger's *New-York Weekly Journal* having long since proliferated into the plural "media," First Amendment issues have multiplied and become increasingly complex. Recent years have found the FTRF particularly busy opposing harmful-to-minors and child-protection legislation that sponsors use as a backdoor method to restrict material, including even scientific reports, that is intended for adults. Consistent victories in federal courts have not stopped Congress from passing virtually the same legislation over and over again, with the wording tweaked a little this way or that. And state legislatures frequently mimic even those federal statutes that already have been declared unconstitutional, requiring still more litigation.

National challenges

While much of the foundation's legal work involves it in cases bearing broad, national implications, the FTRF also jumps into community challenges. In 1999, the foundation helped the library in Wichita Falls, Texas, prepare a successful legal challenge to a city ordinance requiring it to move titles from its children's area to the adult section if 300 people signed a petition requesting it. Library circulations of videotapes and CDs have brought new challenges, adding struggles over images to the traditional tug-of-war over words. Internet issues are now so numerous that they are becoming a body of case law in their own right. And globalization is producing new and increasingly worrisome threats. An FTRF amicus brief supported Yahoo! against a French court's findings that the internet provider was liable for hosting customer pages on its United States site advertising Nazi and racist memorabilia that are illegal in France.

The USA Patriot Act, hastily drawn and enacted in reaction to 9/11 terrorism, has created a bewildering new array of First Amendment jeopardies. In coordination with other civil liberties organizations, the FTRF is in the thick of the legal fights over the act's extraordinary reach. The Patriot Act's infamous Section 215, for instance, expands the FBI's authority to demand library records and requires library workers to keep such intrusions secret.

The FTRF has argued that both the gag order and the act's failure to require any showing of relevance to a terrorist threat violated the constitutional right to freely transmit and receive information. The FTRF also supported an ACLU challenge to the Patriot Act's Section 505 provisions allowing the FBI to issue national security letters without judicial oversight, arguing that it threatens the rights of libraries, bookstores, and their patrons as well as internet communications in general.

Andrew Hamilton, John Peter Zenger's attorney, praised the jury that vindicated the printer in 1735, declaring that the verdict had "baffled the attempt of tyranny" and had "given us a right to liberty of both exposing and opposing arbitrary power . . . by speaking and writing truth." The FTRF's filings add to the growing body of First Amendment precedents upholding that tradition. They are often cited in court rulings and are so respected that, at one point, a New York judge held off making a decision until he could consult the foundation's views.

"We bring to this area," Krug said, "a reputation that we do a societal good."

SOURCE: Tom Teepen, "In Defense of America's Freedoms," *American Libraries* 35 (December 2004): 54–56.

Why people challenge library materials

by James LaRue

IN THE PAST 14 YEARS AS A LIBRARY DIRECTOR, I have received over 200 "requests for reconsideration"—typically, requests to remove library books, audiotapes, and movies from our collections. In 2004, I pulled out all my responses (I answer all such challenges personally) and read them through again to see if I could discover the underlying pattern. I made a surprising discovery that leads me to think that I now understand why we have gotten so many challenges.

Who are the people who challenge libraries? Overwhelmingly, they are:

• parents of children between the ages of 4 and 6, and
• parents of children between the ages of 14 and 16.

I have two children myself, and I do understand. In the first blush of parenthood, I found myself absorbed and charmed by my daughter. I quickly learned all those habits of protectiveness—moving the drinking glasses away from the edge of the dinner table, holding her hand when we crossed the street, snatching her up when I saw a loose dog.

At about the age of 4, children begin interacting with the world in a way less purely physical, and more concerned with language and social behavior. It's about this time that parents start cleaning up their own language, and start being annoyed by their childless friends, who swear as much as they always had.

The idyll of infancy has come to a close. Parents begin to see that the dangers of the world are both larger, and less well defined, than the potential harm of broken glass, speeding cars, and big dogs. Sometimes, parents reach this realization . . . at the library.

Consider the story of the Buddha: Prince Gautama's father sought to protect his son from any knowledge of the world's suffering. The young Gautama was not to see illness, or old age, or death. Eventually, of course, he encountered them anyhow. In his shock and horror, Gautama did just what his father feared: The child abandoned his family, fleeing pell-mell to his own, independent future.

Until their children reach the age of 4 or so, parents feel that the world is controllable; a generally safe environment can be created and maintained. But library collections, even in the children's room, provide ample evidence of the world's woes. No matter that you have told your child that it's not nice to call anyone names: One day he picks up a book of insults and finds it hilarious. Or you're working hard to have your child be neat and tidy—then she falls in love with a book about a happy slob.

So many of the challenges libraries receive have an emotional content that seems, at first, puzzling and disproportionate. Why? Because parents have just realized that the world is not controllable; that there are a wide range of influences in the world exactly contrary to the messages parents want to send their children. Thus parents' first reaction is a kind of stunned anger: Why are you, a public institution paid for by tax dollars, deliberately sabotaging their conscientious parenting?

It is often their own dedication that leads some parents to crusades, and blinds them to their own arrogance. They volunteer to review every book in the children's area, because librarians clearly don't understand the effect of literature on young minds. Out with all the disturbing influences! In with innocuous literature like—the Berenstain Bears!

Eventually, most parents come to a resigned adjustment. By then, their children are off in public schools, and the library isn't quite the threat it used to be. Now it's TV, and peer pressure, and how to dress your child so he won't be publicly belittled, and the lessons of soccer sportsmanship. Parents may even learn a new respect for librarians and their now-welcome skills at research and reader's advice. The library becomes again what it was at the beginning: a social asset.

The wonder years

The next crisis point comes with puberty. Suddenly, your children don't even look like children any more. They're taller than you are. They have breasts and body hair. You begin to notice all the teenagers with driver's licenses.

You remember all too clearly the night you borrowed your father's car, and crossed a distant state line for purposes that, even then, you knew were questionable.

Then there's the age-old irony of battling generational sensibilities. Just as you're settling into a period of maximum conservatism (you are, after all, saving for college and retirement), your children enter their period of maximum radicalism. They start questioning everything.

They stop going to church, or they go to churches whose beliefs baffle you.

They take drugs. Your children could go to jail, or be shot, or overdose.

They have sex. Your son has grown furtive, your daughter brazen. The holding pattern of adolescence is breaking up, and there are a host of new worries: pregnancy, disease, licentiousness. Just when you long to enfold your children back into swaddling clothes, to pull them closer to your memory, your heart, you realize they are drawn instead to other, wilder arms.

Despite all the hype about internet pornography, two of the three challenges I've gotten based on real circumstance involved 15-year-old boys caught in the act of exploration by their fathers. One exasperated dad banged his fist on my desk and said, "I caught my son looking at girlie pictures on your library's computers!"

"Tell him to stop," I said. "We don't appreciate that kind of behavior here, and that's not why we bought those computers."

It stopped him cold. And I could see his deep despair—"The library can't control him either." He left, defeated.

And we can't control his son, other than in the grossest sense of monitoring detectable violations of courtesy and law. We can oversee, remonstrate, attempt to redirect, and exile. That's all. Institutions do assist in the process of promoting general social stability; but institutions, like parents, always have people probing the perimeters.

Eventually, of course, parents make another adjustment. They negotiate new limits, and define new consequences. They try to find a new way to communicate with these suddenly strange beings, these changelings. Parents find themselves, again, reflecting that there are no shortcuts to experience. Control is an illusion. There is only love, and longing, and, perhaps, the faint whisper of early influence.

The good news

Yet there is much good news about this observation concerning the typical source of intellectual freedom challenges.

Consider: First, the parents use the library. They value literacy.

Second, they brought their kids to see us. And their children use the library, too.

Third, these parents actually pay attention to, and care about, their children's library use.

Fourth, the parents typically have a very clear sense of their values, and are working hard to communicate those values to their offspring.

Fifth, they have taken the time, inconvenient and uncomfortable as that might be, to talk directly to decision makers in public institutions about one of the core services of that institution: the quality and kind of the collection.

All of these things are rarer than they should be. The library should encourage, not punish, such behavior. To put it another way, the library should value such people. They are among the best building blocks we have for community support—providing, of course, that we take them seriously, that we do provide materials of use to them, and that we maintain service standards that reflect our mission and purpose in public life.

We must not, we cannot view them with contempt.

However the challenge arrives, there are six fairly simple rules to follow when dealing with an initial complaint.

9

Rule number one: Apologize. In general, people don't complain just for the fun of it. Taking the time to notify an institution of a problem often involves personal discomfort on the part of the person doing the complaining. In these litigious times, many of us are reluctant to express any sympathy, lest it be turned into an admission of blame. Nonetheless, I believe a simple apology is both appropriate and polite. Say, "I'm sorry!" and mean it. You're sorry that they had so unpleasant an experience that it upset them. Before you is a human being who may be facing a difficult thing. Let us be kind.

Rule number two: Don't be defensive; listen. The most common mistake made by library staff is wild defensiveness. There is nothing inherently aggressive about differences of opinion. If a patron were to say, "I hate this carpet color," you probably wouldn't take it personally. You might agree, disagree, or have no opinion one way or the other, and just make a polite reply.

Your job is not to silence the speaker, but to pay attention.

Ask, "What is your concern?"

Rule number three: Restate the problem until the patron agrees that you understand. Again, people raising challenges may be emotionally riled up, and subsequently have difficulty communicating. A simple model for communication is one person who says, "I'm sending a message. Do you copy?" and another person saying, "I copy." The second half of listening, and the key next step for library staff, is repeating or restating the message.

The mission of library staff at this point is to move the concern into clarity, into specificity. It is not to prejudge that concern, defend library principles or practices, or to change the complainant's mind. It is simply to understand the nature of the complaint.

When the case is stated clearly, library staff should repeat it: "Your concern, then, is . . . ?" Then wait to get that restatement validated by a nod, or a "Yes, exactly."

Very often, after hearing that library staff grasp the nature of the concern, the complainants are satisfied. They've had their say; someone got it. That clears the deck for the next step.

Rule number four: Offer service. Once you understand the problem, offer alternatives. Say, "Can I help you find something else for your child?" Or the question might be, "Were you looking for something in particular?"

This might put the patron right back into the rant. "Well, I wasn't looking for this!" Appropriate responses might be, "No, I understand! But what were you looking for?" This opens a dialogue that might move to, "What sort of books does your child most enjoy?"

The underlying assumption of this exchange is that the patron came to the library seeking service, and instead found something upsetting. After expressing the concern, the patron is presumably still interested in what brought him or her there to begin with. The goal of library staff is to have patrons walk out with something that satisfies their library need—a positive service transaction.

Rule number five: Offer additional information. Despite your best efforts, however, and even if in fact you succeed in providing a book the patron is pleased with, the patron may want to pursue the original concern further. How will you know?

The patron will tell you. The subject will be reopened, perhaps with questions such as, "Who orders these books?" It might be more direct: "I'd like to do something about this book."

In the case of questions, you should respond as you would to any other reference question: Give accurate information. In the event that the patron clearly is seeking some further action, then pass them quickly to the next step, which will vary with local library policy.

Rule number six: Follow up. Briefly, follow your procedures, in as timely a manner as possible. If the process takes a subjectively long time—five or six weeks—then a letter should go out the first week to describe the process and tell how long it might be before the patron hears back from the library.

Most of the time, alas, the library will not do precisely what the complainant is seeking. But responsiveness doesn't mean appeasement or agreement; it means that something happens. In the case of reconsideration, the library is obligated to give a thorough, thoughtful look at the item or service being challenged, and to communicate that process, the decision, and the reasoning behind it as promptly as possible.

Finally, follow-up is a balance of personal and institutional: personal courtesy and institutional consistency to mission and process.

The transition from childhood to maturity is profound, challenging not only the persons undergoing that transition but also their guardians.

Ultimately, however, Gautama's path took him not from safety, but from ignorance. And it took him not to danger, but to compassion. Interestingly, both of his parents eventually joined him on the other side of that journey. Surely, even in the modern age, that is still possible, and still worthwhile.

SOURCE: James LaRue, "Buddha at the Gate, Running: Why People Challenge Library Materials," *American Libraries* 35 (December 2004): 42–44.

First Amendment websites

TO KEEP UP WITH FIRST AMENDMENT ISSUES, check out these websites.—*GME.*

American Association of University Professors, www.aaup.org/Com-a/.
American Booksellers Foundation for Free Expression, www.abffe.org.
American Civil Liberties Union, www.aclu.org/FreeSpeech/FreeSpeechMain. cfm.
American Communication Association, www.americancomm.org.
American Library Association, Banned Books Week, www.ala.org/ala/oif/ bannedbooksweek/bannedbooksweek.htm.
American Library Association, Office for Intellectual Freedom, www.ala.org/ ala/oif/firstamendment/firstamendment.htm.
Americans for Radio Diversity, www.radiodiversity.com.
Americans United for Separation of Church and State, www.au.org.
Article 19, Global Campaign for Free Expression, www.article19.org.
BeSpacific, www.bespacific.com.
California Library Association, Library Privacy, www.libraryprivacy.org/ index.php.
Canadian Civil Liberties Association, www.ccla.org.
Canadian Journalists for Free Expression, www.cjfe.org.

9

Censorship and Intellectual Freedom Page, ezinfo.ucs.indiana.edu/~quinnjf/censor.html.

Center for First Amendment Rights, www.cfarfreedom.org/index.shtml.

Chilling Effects Clearinghouse, www.chillingeffects.org.

Computer Professionals for Social Responsibility, www.cpsr.org.

Copley First Amendment Center, www.illinoisfirstamendmentcenter.com.

Cyber-Rights and Cyber-Liberties, www.cyber-rights.org.

Electronic Frontier Foundation, Computer and Academic Freedom, www.eff.org/Censorship/Academic_edu/CAF/.

Electronic Frontier Foundation, Online Censorship and Free Expression, www.eff.org/Censorship/.

Electronic Privacy Information Center, epic.org.

Federation of American Scientists, Project on Government Secrecy, www.fas.org/sgp/.

Feminists for Free Expression, www.ffeusa.org.

FindLaw, caselaw.lp.findlaw.com/data/constitution/amendment01/.

First Amendment Center, www.firstamendmentcenter.org.

First Amendment Foundation, www.floridafaf.org.

First Amendment Handbook, www.rcfp.org/handbook/.

First Amendment Law, www.law.umkc.edu/faculty/projects/ftrials/firstamendment/firstamendmenthome.htm.

First Amendment Law Review, falr.unc.edu/indexmain.html.

First Amendment Project, www.thefirstamendment.org.

First Amendment Schools, www.firstamendmentschools.org.

Free Expression Network, www.freeexpression.org.

Free Expression Policy Project, www.fepproject.org.

Free Speech Network, www.freespeech.org.

Freedom Forum, www.freedomforum.org.

Freedom to Read Foundation, www.ftrf.org.

George Washington University, Freedominfo, www.freedominfo.org.

Georgia First Amendment Foundation, www.gfaf.org.

Human Rights Watch, Free Expression and the Internet, hrw.org/doc/?t=internet.

Index for Free Expression, www.indexonline.org.

Information Commons, www.info-commons.org/blog/.

International Federation of Library Associations and Institutions, Free Access to Information and Freedom of Expression, www.ifla.org/faife/.

Legal Information Institute, www.law.cornell.edu/topics/first_amendment.html.

Library Law Blog, blog.librarylaw.com/librarylaw/.

National Coalition against Censorship, www.ncac.org.

Norwegian Forum for Freedom of Expression, Beacon for Freedom of Expression, www.beaconforfreedom.org.

PEN American Center, www.pen.org.

People for the American Way, www.pfaw.org.

Student Press Law Center, www.splc.org.

Tech Law Journal, www.techlawjournal.com.

Thomas Jefferson Center for the Protection of Free Expression, www.tjcenter.org.

World Wide First Amendment Radio, www.wwfar.com.

Youth Free Expression Network, www.yfen.org.

PRIVACY

Privacy: An interpretation of the Library Bill of Rights

by the ALA Office for Intellectual Freedom

PRIVACY IS ESSENTIAL to the exercise of free speech, free thought, and free association. The courts have established a First Amendment right to receive information in a publicly funded library. Further, the courts have upheld the right to privacy based on the Bill of Rights of the U.S. Constitution. Many states provide guarantees of privacy in their constitutions and statute law. Numerous decisions in case law have defined and extended rights to privacy.

In a library (physical or virtual), the right to privacy is the right to open inquiry without having the subject of one's interest examined or scrutinized by others. Confidentiality exists when a library is in possession of personally identifiable information about users and keeps that information private on their behalf.

Protecting user privacy and confidentiality has long been an integral part of the mission of libraries. The ALA has affirmed a right to privacy since 1939. Existing ALA policies affirm that confidentiality is crucial to freedom of inquiry. Rights to privacy and confidentiality also are implicit in the *Library Bill of Rights'* guarantee of free access to library resources for all users.

Rights of library users

The *Library Bill of Rights* (see pp. 468–469) affirms the ethical imperative to provide unrestricted access to information and to guard against impediments to open inquiry. Article IV states: "Libraries should cooperate with all persons and groups concerned with resisting abridgment of free expression and free access to ideas." When users recognize or fear that their privacy or confidentiality is compromised, true freedom of inquiry no longer exists.

In all areas of librarianship, best practice leaves the user in control of as many choices as possible. These include decisions about the selection of, access to, and use of information. Lack of privacy and confidentiality has a chilling effect on users' choices. All users have a right to be free from any unreasonable intrusion into or surveillance of their lawful library use.

Users have the right to be informed what policies and procedures govern the amount and retention of personally identifiable information, why that information is necessary for the library, and what the user can do to maintain his or her privacy. Library users expect and in many places have a legal right to have their information protected and kept private and confidential by anyone with direct or indirect access to that information. In addition, Article V of the *Library Bill of Rights* states: "A person's right to use a library should not be denied or abridged because of origin, age, background, or views." This article precludes the use of profiling as a basis for any breach of privacy rights. Users have the right to use a library without any abridgment of privacy that may result from equating the subject of their inquiry with behavior.

9

Responsibilities in libraries

The library profession has a long-standing commitment to an ethic of facilitating, not monitoring, access to information. This commitment is implemented locally through development, adoption, and adherence to privacy policies that are consistent with applicable federal, state, and local law. Everyone (paid or unpaid) who provides governance, administration, or service in libraries has a responsibility to maintain an environment respectful and protective of the privacy of all users. Users have the responsibility to respect each others' privacy.

For administrative purposes, librarians may establish appropriate time, place, and manner restrictions on the use of library resources. In keeping with this principle, the collection of personally identifiable information should only be a matter of routine or policy when necessary for the fulfillment of the mission of the library. Regardless of the technology used, everyone who collects or accesses personally identifiable information in any format has a legal and ethical obligation to protect confidentiality.

Conclusion

The American Library Association affirms that rights of privacy are necessary for intellectual freedom and are fundamental to the ethics and practice of librarianship.

SOURCE: ALA Office for Intellectual Freedom. Adopted June 19, 2002, by the ALA Council.

USA Patriot Act guidelines

by the ALA Washington Office

MANY LIBRARIES HAVE ALREADY SEEN an increase in law enforcement inquiries following the September 11th terrorists' attacks. In libraries and other institutions, law enforcement authorities have sought access to patron records, including electronic mail and other electronic communications. With passage of the USA Patriot Act on October 26, 2001, many new questions have been raised about how to comply with the new law and how the Patriot Act provisions relate to current laws governing criminal and foreign intelligence investigations as well as to state and local privacy laws.

As always, the best course is to prepare before the "knock at the door." ALA provides the following guidelines for librarians to share with their staffs and local legal counsels. This is *not legal advice* but suggested guidance and direction so that local libraries—whether academic, public, or school libraries—can prepare themselves to do what is legal and appropriate.

Before

Consult your local legal counsel. These issues are complex, and absolutes that apply to every situation are rare. You will need legal experts familiar with your unique situations and local and state laws to help make sure that your policies and procedures are appropriate and legal. You will want to make sure that your local counsel is aware that legal inquiries under the USA Patriot Act may be an issue for your institution.

Review your policies. The USA Patriot Act does not require institutions to make changes in policies or computer systems. However, with a possible increase in requests from law enforcement and the pervasiveness of technology in the daily transactions of libraries, you will want to review and address your policies on retention of and access to all types of information. Make decisions regarding data, logs, and records of all types—digital and paper—to be discarded or saved. Establish a system for referring requests for operational records as well as other types of information within your institution. Plan for service continuity in the event that workstations, servers, or backups are removed or made inoperable.

Train your staff. Every member of your staff should understand your policies for three important reasons:

1. Anyone on your staff could be approached by law enforcement. Every staff member should know what to do if he or she is presented with a request. A system for referring requests from law enforcement should be clearly communicated to all staff so that everyone from the circulation assistant to the library director knows what to do. Often a library or institution will designate one staff person to receive all such requests.
2. Technology has made data ubiquitous and access to it effortless. Many people within your organization may have unexpected roles to play in implementing your policies. Your policy is only as good as the trained people who carry it out.
3. Knowledgeable staff will assure that your library is complying with all appropriate laws and protect against any institutional or personal liability.

During

Follow your policies. Sound policies can provide order and justification during what can be a chaotic time. They can help prevent surprises and help ensure that the best possible thinking and judgment go into your responses. Policies and plans will not help you if they are not understood and followed by all of the institution's employees.

Consult your local legal counsel. Most inquiries made by law enforcement are lawful and in good order; however, it is imperative to call on your own legal counsel when presented with a request. Legal counsel will help you respond appropriately and legally while protecting you and your staff from possible liability due to an unlawful request. Legal counsel can help you sort through your responsibilities under the myriad federal, state, and local laws that both protect privacy and require access.

Document your costs. The Patriot Act provides for some reimbursement of costs if an entity is asked by law enforcement to perform certain types of assistance in data collection. It is unclear what the guidelines will be for reimbursement. Document all costs incurred.

After

Consult your local legal counsel. Once law enforcement leaves your premises, your responsibilities may not be over. There are different rules for sharing information with others about who is being investigated or what types of information you have provided law enforcement. With whom you are allowed to speak and what you are allowed to talk about varies depending upon whether the inquiry is made under criminal or foreign intelligence investigation laws. You will want to consult with your local counsel to be sure that you and your staff meet any legal requirements to conceal the inquiries of law enforcement or conversely to fulfill any affirmative legal requirements to disclose what records may have been released.

Follow up

Consult with counsel; implement your policies; pursue any appropriate reimbursements. Determine whether you will have to maintain any subsequent information or records. The Washington Office will be tracking the impact of this legislation, so when allowed by law and the advice of counsel, inform the Washington Office of your experiences.

SOURCE: ALA Washington Office, January 19, 2002.

ADULT LITERACY

Why assess your literacy program?

by Suzanne Knell and Janet Scogins

IDEALLY, THE INFORMATION a literacy provider gathers, analyzes, and interprets during the course of an assessment will be valuable to all stakeholders. However, it is more likely that some data will be useful to all stakeholders, while other specific data may be requested and used by just a few or only one of the stakeholders. For example, the answer to the question "How much progress are the learners making in the literacy program?" is one that is of interest to all stakeholders. However, answers to the question "In what areas are the learners making progress?" may result in different stakeholders having varying degrees of interest in the specific response.

Government funders may be interested in how many learners obtained employment, received a GED, or advanced from one level to another. Other funders may be interested in achievements in life skills such as reading newspapers, developing general work-related skills, teaching their children, or using library resources. Learners, on the other hand, may be more interested in their progress toward achieving goals in life skill areas such as talking to a doctor, comparison shopping, reading specific materials or documents, or learning technology skills.

Following are a number of reasons why assessment is important to the different stakeholders, and how these reasons affect literacy programming.

Libraries provide sources of support for literacy programs through the library budget or the Friends of the Library. In addition, libraries provide space, book collections, reference desk resources, and staff time to support library-based literacy programs. Library directors and boards must determine if literacy programs are worth the investment. Assessment answers the questions:

Does the literacy program help forward the library's mission? Does the literacy program provide underserved populations with access to information and materials? Does the literacy program enhance the library's position in the community? Is the library literacy program a good use of tax dollars, library space, and staff time?

Literacy providers want to ensure that the literacy program is achieving its goals and that learners are making progress in specific areas. Providers use assessments to establish program accountability; to create program changes in curricula, instruction, and training; and to determine what the adult is learning. Assessment results can be motivating for the program staff and learners as they see how the results create lasting improvements within the program or for the learner. Often providers must conduct assessments in order to report results to boards of directors and funders.

Learners want to know if they are making progress and in what areas. Most learners are interested in scores from standardized tests, but also want to be informed regularly about their incremental progress. Often, site-developed assessment tools provide the information that demonstrates progress to the learner more tangibly and in smaller chunks. Learners also want to see and experience how learning is tied into their life. Discussions between the learner and teacher about progress is crucial in determining success and identifying needed program adjustments.

Funders. Most adult literacy programs receive support from a combination of public and private agencies, foundations, library boards, corporations, and other entities. In recent years, funders have focused more on program accountability and documenting effectiveness in adult literacy. Funders are constantly reevaluating the rationale for funding certain programs and not others. They compare the purpose and effectiveness of a large pool of literacy programs and reward successful programs. Government funders must adhere to federal and state regulations, while private funders are answerable to their boards of directors and may have specific guidelines to follow. In general, private funders are more "provider driven" while government funders are more "regulation driven." Therefore, funders may require different kinds of assessment data based on the policies and regulations under which they dispense funds.

Policymakers are dedicated to creating national and state policies that work. In order to move literacy-related policy ahead in the United States, literacy providers need to provide convincing data regarding the effectiveness of their programs. Development of strong policies in adult literacy is currently progressing slowly, however, because stakeholders are still struggling with the question: "What constitutes success in adult literacy programming?"

New projects of varying design have emerged to examine issues, solutions, and best practices in adult literacy programming assessment and evaluation. Regardless, the literacy community must be able to tell its story about what the adult learner is learning, how the learning affects the adult's life role and experiences, and how the literacy program, in turn, affects the economy, community, and society as a whole.

SOURCE: Suzanne Knell and Janet Scogins, *Adult Literacy Assessment Tool Kit* (Chicago: ALA Office for Literacy and Outreach Services, 2000), pp. 2–4.

Is your library literacy-ready?

by Dale Lipschultz

THE TERM "LITERACY-SET" was used in the late 1970s by Don Holdaway to describe a stage of children's early literacy development. Holdaway observed that children who have early experiences and interactions with books, print, and supportive adults come to school ready to learn how to read. In other words, they are literacy-set.

We assume that most schools are also literacy-ready. That is, they are prepared to teach children how to read. They have the tools and the teachers.

I think that we can also assume that libraries are literacy-ready. Libraries certainly have the books. Libraries also have librarians.

- Librarians are uniquely qualified to guide adults and children of all ages and stages toward and through the reading process.
- Librarians know the depth and breadth of the library's collection.
- Librarians not only know what's in the library, but they know the paths that lead to finding just the right book or poem or resource.

But it takes more than a library, a staff of librarians, and a collection of books to move from being literacy-ready to offering programs and services for adult learners.

What does "literacy-ready" look like?

1. The library has a literacy program with dedicated staff.
2. The library has facilities to meet the needs of a literacy program.
3. The library has a literacy department.
4. Library staff receive training about adult literacy, adult learners, and library literacy.
5. The library has a book collection for adult learners, tutors, and teachers.
6. The library also has a collection of video and audio instructional and educational materials.
7. The library has resources and educational materials in native languages to support reading and literacy development of ESOL adults and their children.
8. The library has an outreach program that informs adult nonreaders, new readers, and other underserved populations about the range of library services available at the main and branch libraries.
9. The literacy program has visibility in the community.
10. The library collaborates and networks with other literacy providers and social service agencies in the community.
11. The library is user-friendly. The library staff is cordial, willing to help, and takes the initiative to provide help and support.
12. The library director supports the literacy program.
13. The literacy program is integrated into the library.
14. The library staff understands and is responsive to the needs of adult learners.
15. The library supports the literacy program with funding and fund-raising activities.
16. The library has a bookmobile to reach adult learners in rural and remote areas.

17. The library literacy program offers direct small-group instruction for adult learners.
18. The literacy program staff is qualified and consistent.
19. The library offers a mentorship program for adult learners.
20. The library receives media support that showcases its literacy services and programs.
21. The library has signage that is appropriate for adult learners and others.
22. The library has developed multiple ways for adult learners to locate the literacy program.
23. The library has the resources and technology to meet the needs of adult learners.
24. The library and the community understand that libraries are not just for readers.
25. The literacy program has an assessment plan that measures learner progress and library usage.
26. The library has adult learners as spokespeople, mentors, tutors, and staff.
27. Literacy students interact regularly with library staff and patrons.
28. The library has greeters at the door.
29. The library finds an alternative to the word "literacy."

SOURCE: Dale Lipschultz, "Making Your Library Literacy-Ready," www.ala.org/ala/olos/outreachresource/makingyourlibrary.htm.

INFORMATION LITERACY

Information-literacy collaboration
by Jo Ann Carr and Ilene F. Rockman

IN 1989, ALA's Presidential Commission on Information Literacy concluded, "Out of the superabundance of available information, people need to be able to obtain specific information to meet a wide range of personal and business needs. These needs are largely driven either by the desire for personal growth and advancement or by the rapidly changing social, political, and economic environments of American society." One of the social changes driving the need for information literacy—the ability to locate, evaluate, and use information effectively—is the changing educational face of our society.

According to the Center for an Urban Future's 2001 report, "Building a Highway to Higher Ed," in three years 75% of today's high school seniors would become students at trade schools, community and liberal arts colleges, and comprehensive and research universities. Fifty percent of these students, the report adds, would fail to earn a degree. In today's information-rich world, a contributing factor to that high rate of failure is the inability of students in higher education to find and use information effectively. The need to increase retention and completion rates for students in higher education is a compelling reason for academic librarians to collaborate with their K–12 colleagues in developing information-literacy activities across K–20 education.

9

A July 1, 2003, *USA Today* article said that in 1997 almost 100% of certified teachers in our public schools were graduates of our colleges and universities, up from 84% in 1961. Since college is where nearly all teachers learn how to teach, school library media specialists must collaborate with academic librarians if we are to have teachers who know the value of information literacy and who can collaborate with K–12 library media specialists.

The survival of our school libraries is also at stake: The percentage of the population with a bachelor's degree or higher increased from 20.3% in 1990 to 25.6% in 2000, according to the 2001 *Digest of Education Statistics.* Citizens with college educations have been shown to be more likely to vote. If these voters learned the value of information literacy in college, that should translate into more support for school libraries when they consider school bond issues or participate in school-based management councils or their PTAs.

In 2003, the Association of American Universities and the Pew Charitable Trusts published *Understanding University Success: A Report from Standards for Success* to answer the question, "What must students know and be able to do in order to succeed in entry-level university courses?" More than 400 faculty and staff from 20 research institutions responded to that query over a two-year period. Not surprisingly, the contributors addressed both content knowledge and habits of mind. The report noted that "these habits of mind are considered by many faculty members to be more important than content knowledge." They include problem-solving, analytical and critical thinking, com-

---

Information Literacy Standards: AASL vs. ACRL

AASL/AECT, *Information Power* Standards

The student who is information literate:
  —accesses information efficiently and effectively
  —evaluates information critically and competently
  —uses information accurately and creatively
The student who is an independent learner is information literate and:
  —pursues information related to personal interests
  —appreciates literature and other creative expressions of information
  —strives for excellence in information seeking and knowledge generation
The student who contributes positively to the learning community and to society is information literate and:
  —recognizes the importance of information to a democratic society
  —practices ethical behavior in regard to information and information technology
  —participates effectively in groups to pursue and generate information

ACRL, *Information Literacy Competency Standards for Higher Education*

The information-literate student determines the nature and extent of the information needed
The information-literate student accesses needed information effectively and efficiently
The information-literate student evaluates information and its sources critically and incorporates information into his or her knowledge base and value system
The information-literate student, individually or as a member of a group, uses information effectively to accomplish a specific purpose
The information-literate student understands many of the economic, legal, and social issues surrounding the use of information and accesses and uses information ethically and legally

munication skills, and the ability "to discern the relative importance and credibility of various sources of information."

Despite the importance of information literacy to all levels of education, ALA's professional associations for school and academic libraries have, until recently, worked independently in developing and articulating information-literacy competencies and standards for higher education. ALA's American Association of School Librarians' 1998 *Information Power* provides nine standards in the three areas of information literacy, independent learning, and social responsibility (www.ala.org/ala/aasl/aaslproftools/informationpower/ informationliteracy.htm). ALA's Association of College and Research Libraries' *Information Literacy Competency Standards for Higher Education,* published in 2000, delineates five standards that focus on determining information need; accessing information; evaluating information; using information effectively; and understanding economic, legal, and social issues surrounding information (www.ala.org/ala/acrl/acrlstandards/informationliteracycompetency.htm). The standards at the two levels, as shown on p. 488, differ not only in content but in emphasis; in the March/April 2002 *Knowledge Quest,* Ellysa Cahoy described the K–12 standards as more theoretical and called the higher-education standards practical and detailed.

Sharing common goals

Despite differences in their standards, school and academic librarians share similar information-literacy goals. These include:

- helping students to formulate an information need;
- how to carefully select and evaluate information;
- how to communicate information to others; and
- how to use information responsibly by acknowledging the work of others, giving credit appropriately, citing information correctly, and using information ethically and responsibly.

In addition, school and academic librarians recognize the value of collaboration with their faculties, and with each other, to help all students achieve their highest potentials. School librarians work with classroom teachers in planning lessons and units of study to integrate information-literacy principles into the curriculum, and then to actively deliver and assess that instruction. Academic librarians also collaborate with their discipline-based faculties to integrate information literacy into courses and the curriculum, to develop active learning assignments, and to teach and assess student learning outcomes.

Together, school library media specialists and academic librarians develop outreach programs for students in secondary-school and community-college libraries to help young people understand what will be expected of them as university students.

Successful collaborations

Across the nation, programs to assist students to succeed in college and collaborations between academic librarians and those in the K–12 community are beginning to appear.

Among initiatives within the 23 California State University campuses is one at Fresno that sponsors a two-week summer library camp for middle-school students as part of the federally funded Migrant Scholars Program. The students strengthen their research skills and learn to communicate their ideas by developing a PowerPoint presentation and a web page. The Northridge campus, in consultation with the Los Angeles Unified School District, has developed a series of workshops for 17 feeder high schools and eight nearby community colleges. Aimed at teachers and librarians, the workshops have resulted in a handbook of lesson plans, shared information-literacy competencies, websites, and a bibliography for further study.

Other collaborative efforts can be found throughout the country:

- At Ohio State University, the library teaches a revised version of the university's information-literacy course for 9th- and 10th-grade special-education students. This is part of a larger project of transition skills funded by the U.S. Department of Education and the U.S. Office of Special Education.
- The University of Delaware and the K–12 education community in the state of Delaware created UDLib/Search, which provides state-funded access to networked electronic resources for all Delaware public high schools and middle schools. The service, maintained by the University of Delaware Library, is a step forward in helping students develop knowledge of database content and learn how to critically evaluate source materials, and how to effectively and efficiently search various electronic databases prior to entering the state's public higher-education institutions.
- At Washington State University, the library is represented on the local school district's Library Advisory Committee to establish a plan for systematic information-literacy instruction across the K–12 curriculum.
- The University of Nevada at Reno, in collaboration with area schools, supports the Learning and Resource Center to assist the ability of K–20

Words Students Don't Understand

More than 40% of some 300 undergraduates taking an initial questionnaire for a library skills lab did not understand the following library terms.

Word	% who did not understand it
Boolean logic	91.9
Bibliography	85.1
Controlled vocabulary	81.9
Truncation	72.3
Precision	68.2
Information need	65.1
Descriptors	64.2
Abstract	63.8
Article	53.0
Citation	48.3
Bibliographic information	45.3
Authority	42.3
Collection	40.3

SOURCE: Norman B. Hutcherson, "Library Jargon: Student Recognition of Terms and Concepts Commonly Used by Librarians in the Classroom," *College & Research Libraries* 65 (July 2004): 349–354.

educators "to enhance their instruction so as to facilitate greater learning for their students."

- At the University of British Columbia, teacher-librarians from area schools serve as mentors for students in teacher-education programs. Through this mentoring experience, the future teachers learn to work with teacher-librarians and enhance their abilities in information literacy and resource-based learning.

Only by collaborating to ensure a curriculum rich in information literacy for all students at all levels can we have a society that is prepared to recognize the value and need for information in a democratic society.

SOURCE: Jo Ann Carr and Ilene F. Rockman, "Information-Literacy Collaboration: A Shared Responsibility," *American Libraries* 34 (September 2003): 52–54.

PATRON BEHAVIOR

The medieval patron
by Wayne Wiegand

IN 1345, THE FEW students of library management who lived on the European continent were just beginning to hear about a new book by Richard de Bury (1287–1345) titled *Philobiblon* (1345), one of the first textbooks for the education of librarians. At the time, the library as an institution was mostly a collection of books. Although those charged with responsibility for managing this institution had to worry mostly about book collections, they had no program of education in place to prepare them for that responsibility. *Philobiblon* provided a bit of guidance, some of which still applies at the beginning of the 21st century to anyone who is taking an MLS into employment in our much-more-varied information marketplace.

For example, de Bury advises all managers of information-resource collections to watch out for the "stiff-necked youth sluggishly seating himself for study, and while the frost is sharp in winter time, his nose, all watery with the biting cold, begins to drip. Nor does he deign to wipe it with his cloth until he has wet the books spread out before him with the vile dew."

And that same person, warns de Bury, is capable of other transgressions involving body fluids. "With endless chattering he ceases not to rail against his companions and, while adducing a multitude of reasons void of all sensible meaning, wets the books spread out in his lap with the sputtering of his spittle."

But not all sins by library users against the physical properties of information resources are moisture-based. "Soon doubling his elbows," de Bury further describes this patron, "he reclines upon the book and by his short study invites a long sleep and, by spreading out the wrinkles, bends the margins of the leaves, doing no small harm to the volume."

Practicing librarians can probably cite thousands of instances in which contemporary patrons have visited as many similarly egregious behaviors on the collections of information resources for which they have management responsibilities. Now, as then, librarians have had to develop policies and articulate rules to deal with such patron deportment. But for the last 100 years, they at least have been able to complain that "we certainly didn't learn anything about this stuff in library school!" Seems to me that's another useful thing you can do with a MLS.

SOURCE: Wayne Wiegand, "This Month, 656 Years Ago," *American Libraries* 32 (April 2001): 104.

Creating a safe environment
by Anne M. Turner

THERE ARE SEVERAL THINGS library staff can do to create an environment that is less likely to provide opportunities for sexual harassment of patrons. One is to implement features that help make your building secure: Insist on good sight lines for staff in any new building, ensure that the restroom entrances are not hidden behind stacks or down dark hallways, and make the restrooms lockable so that staff can control the number of users.

Another is to ensure that all staff are trained to be alert to potential problems (*"Why* is that guy lying on the floor to read?") and to adopt a straightforward attitude toward enforcing the library's rules. If a page sees someone lying on the floor, for example, s/he should be prepared to say, immediately, "I'm sorry, sir, but lying on the floor to read causes a hazard for other patrons. Will you please move to a chair?" It shouldn't be necessary to call in a supervisor before acting, although resistance by the patron or fear on the part of the page obviously would justify this step.

Working with the police

Establishing a working relationship with local law enforcement officials is particularly well advised in dealing with sexual harassment incidents. It is astonishing how much the police know about what is going on (and who is doing it), and how helpful they can be if the library staff reaches out for assistance.

Reaching out is a means for jumping the real gap that often exists between library staff values (information for everyone, confidentiality above all) and those of the police (our job is to enforce the law; no one knows as much as we do about how horrible people really are). Police officers invited to consult with library staff—to lend their expertise to finding ways to handle problems—develop a new understanding of how the library works, why it does what it does, and why its staff seem to be so tolerant of all those "weirdos" who use it. Once achieved at the command level, this is an understanding that will eventually be passed down the ranks within the police force, and will be an enormous help to the staff in the long run.

Among other things, the police can help lay the groundwork for getting permanent restraining or trespass orders against habitual offenders, sexual or otherwise. Another option, again requiring police understanding of the library situation, is to make staying out of the library a condition of probation. The latter usually takes less legal paperwork.

Most important, a police department that knows the staff at the library also knows that the staff will not call unless there is a real emergency or a problem of high priority.

Ensuring the safety of children

Providing a safe environment for children involves special problems. A library cannot (and surely doesn't want to) make a blanket rule that forbids adults unaccompanied by children from visiting the Children's Room. Staff also cannot approach people and ask them to leave, based upon their dress or other aspects of their physical appearance. Presence in the Children's Room can be limited to those who are using the children's collection, but this is not a rule all libraries care to make.

What the staff *can* do is keep their eyes open for suspicious behavior, such as a patron gazing steadily at a child who is clearly not a relation, and find a way to interfere. For example, the staff person can approach the starer and say, "Is there something in this collection I can help you find?" Linda Luke of the Alachua County Library in Gainesville, Florida, calls this the "Killing Them with Kindness" approach.

"We don't have a rule forbidding people to use the children's room," she says, "But if we spot someone who is acting like he is after kids, we try to drive him crazy with helpfulness: Can I help you with that computer? Are you sure there isn't something I can find for you? And so forth. It usually works."

Constant vigilance seems to be one key to providing a safe environment for children. Another is ensuring that the staff has its priorities straight. On the one hand, staff should not be so nervous and suspicious that they move on any adult male who dares to show his face in the Children's Room. Ninety-nine percent of all adult and teenaged men are not child molesters or voyeurs. On the other hand, when in doubt, the staff should act on behalf of children, and worry about the rights of adults later.

Boys are the targets of pedophiles as well as girls. But from an early age girls are trained and warned far more frequently about danger from "strangers." Boys unfortunately tend to lack the radar girls develop for sensing inappropriate sexual approaches—and often, as a consequence, have less panache in handling them.

There was, for example, the wonderful child in Eugene, Oregon, who was sent off alone to the bathroom by her parent ("*Why* do parents *do* that?" asks the library director) and ran into a man who exposed himself to her. "The bathroom is over there," she told him matter-of-factly.

A picture is worth . . .

Polaroid cameras, loaded with film and ready for immediate use, are a handy tool to have in any library's emergency kit. You never know, after all, when an earthquake or hurricane will hit and you have to document the twisted shelving and books on the floor for the Federal Emergency Management Agency when there isn't a drug store open for miles. Polaroid cameras can also be used to back up staff documentation of criminal behavior, particularly sexual harassment.

9

When an exhibitionist is reported or observed, a member of the staff can immediately spot the perpetrator, and take his picture. The result can be used for identification purposes, to help the police, or simply as an aid for staff on the lookout for someone who is known to prey on children. Using photography can help a library strengthen its reputation as a place where sexual harassment of staff and patrons is *not* tolerated, but it is also a tool that should be used with caution. It is legal to take photographs without the consent of the subject when there are reasonable grounds to believe that the subject is engaged, or was engaged, in criminal behavior. "Reasonable grounds" would be a patron or staff person reporting the incident. Taking the picture may frighten the perpetrator into a hasty exit from the library, but at least the staff then has something to give the police.

It is also very important for the library staff not to fall into the practice of taking pictures of anyone who looks suspicious, or behaves in an unusual way. Women who wore trousers were once viewed as very suspicious indeed. Access to the information public libraries provide is a basic right of all the people, protected by the First Amendment to the Constitution of the United States. Photography is only appropriate when criminal behavior is being investigated.

Handling harassment situations

The cornerstone of any staff response to a report of an incident of sexual harassment in the library must be meeting the needs of the victim. Although it is important to call the police as soon as possible, staff should be trained to give their highest priority to the victim, and let law enforcement worry about catching the perpetrator. The standard procedure is:

1. Drop everything to pay attention to the victim.
2. Treat the victim with compassion and sympathy.
3. Extract as much information as possible about the incident from the victim.
4. Armed with a description, try to identify the perpetrator. Take a Polaroid picture of him if you can.
5. Call the police and get the victim to file a formal complaint.

When a child reports that s/he has been sexually harassed by someone, or "bothered" by an adult, most manuals advise following the same procedures as those for an adult, modified by the age of the victim, and the presence or absence of the child's parent.

Note: Many states *require* that all cases of sexual harassment and sexual abuse involving children be reported by the public official who observes them. Library management should verify whether library workers are included in the definition of "public official" under their own state's law, and the library's procedures should include instructions for staff telling how to do it (e.g., report the incident to the police).

SOURCE: Anne M. Turner, *It Comes with the Territory: Handling Problem Situations in Libraries* (Jefferson, N.C.: McFarland, 2004), pp. 48-52. Reprinted with permission.

Customer complaints

by Rebecca Jackson

CONSIDERING THE NUMBERS OF PATRONS who walk through the doors of our libraries on a daily basis, we can assume that the numbers of complaints at our libraries are consistent with those of businesses. Libraries, however, have their own complexities. For instance, John C. Stalker, in *People Come First* (ACRL, 1999), has pointed out that "many library users are reluctant to reveal problems with reference service: In some cases, they do not know that they have problems, and in other cases, they are unaware that their problems can be solved." Often patrons have no idea what services are available to them, nor do they understand what tools they can use to solve their information problems. In a survey done at the Iowa State University Library, users requested several services that were already available to them, such as online forms for interlibrary loan requests and specific online catalog search options.

How many of us have worked with patrons who had no idea that indexes were available to help them access periodical articles on a particular subject? Stephen K. Stoan refers to academic libraries when he wrote in *College & Research Libraries* in 1984 that "Faculty complaints . . . derive in no small measure from the [faculty] perception that, not understanding research, librarians end up organizing the library, its services, and its resources in terms of their own logic, not that of researchers." Faculty members are probably not the only patrons who feel that the library's organizational scheme does not serve their needs.

When patrons do complain, their problems can be categorized into several consistent types. Darlene Weingand, in *Customer Service Excellence* (ALA, 1997), lists the typical patron complaints:

1. Customer is unable to locate materials or information.
2. Telephone is not answered promptly when customer calls.
3. Length of time until a reserve material is available seems too long.
4. Library staff is not friendly or helpful.
5. Library staff appears to be busy or unapproachable.
6. Parking is not available nearby.
7. Line at checkout is too long.
8. Librarian is not available to assist in locating material or information.
9. Customers are notified at inappropriate times that requested items have arrived.
10. Library staff interpret policies literally and display a lack of flexibility.
11. Library hours are not convenient.
12. Customers must wait at the service desk while staff answers the phone.

9

In addition, the introduction of computers and electronic resources have added their own set of inconveniences: The printer is out of paper or ink; the computer is frozen; the patron cannot get into a particular database, usually from home; or the patron simply cannot find the information she needs. The survey done at Iowa State also indicated problems with the library's facilities, such as the lighting in some of the stacks areas and the temperature of the building. All of these things can lead to the patron becoming disgruntled, not wanting to use the library, and spreading bad publicity about the library.

Weingand includes a wonderful table in her book that demonstrates how a library employee's perceptions may differ from a library patron's perceptions. Here are just a few of her examples:

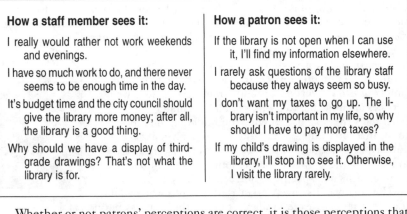

How a staff member sees it:	How a patron sees it:
I really would rather not work weekends and evenings.	If the library is not open when I can use it, I'll find my information elsewhere.
I have so much work to do, and there never seems to be enough time in the day.	I rarely ask questions of the library staff because they always seem so busy.
It's budget time and the city council should give the library more money; after all, the library is a good thing.	I don't want my taxes to go up. The library isn't important in my life, so why should I have to pay more taxes?
Why should we have a display of third-grade drawings? That's not what the library is for.	If my child's drawing is displayed in the library, I'll stop in to see it. Otherwise, I visit the library rarely.

Whether or not patrons' perceptions are correct, it is those perceptions that determine whether or not a person will become or remain a loyal library user:

> Long-term nurturing of the library-customer relationship has an outcome far beyond the obvious increase in customer satisfaction: the development of both internal and external stakeholders. . . . Stakeholders do more than simply use the library: they *care* about its success, they promote its activities, and they are active *lobbyists* in its behalf. (Weingand, 1997)

Those are the kinds of patrons we need if the library is to remain a vital part of the community.

Complaint management

So how can we turn every customer contact into an opportunity to solidify the relationship with our patrons? One suggestion from a management researcher is

> by making the environment knowable and predictable; by creating a customer-friendly environment in which people feel smart, competent and important, and comfortable; and by offering them choices. . . . [Though] providing customers with too many choices may overwhelm them and result in compromised feelings of competency and control. (*Sloan Management Review*, Fall 1999)

Specific ways to ensure this type of environment come from the business world:

1. Offer opportunities to complain. Consider again the statistics concerning how many people actually complain when they are dissatisfied. Part of the reason for lack of complaints is that people may not know where to go to complain. Make sure they have plenty of opportunities. Place suggestion boxes in different areas in the building, with large signs indicating their purpose. Conduct user surveys on a regular basis. Keep complaint forms at all the service desks. Make sure your websites have prominent suggestion links on each page.

Encourage patrons, in one-on-one interactions, to let you know of problems they encounter. Let your patrons know that their opinions are important.

2. Prepare library staff. Our service desks *are* our frontlines. Often staff at these locations provide the only human contact the patron has with the library. Frequently, these desks are staffed by students or nonlibrarian permanent employees. These people need to know from day one what it means to be customer driven. They need to be thoroughly oriented to the building and the services, so they know where and when to make referrals. Continuous customer service training must be provided to all employees, including students. They need to understand how what they do contributes to the perceptions our patrons have of our libraries, and how important those perceptions are. They need to know how far they can go to resolve a patron's complaint. They should be allowed the satisfaction that comes from making a patron happy. And they need to be rewarded for good service.

Knowledge about resources is equally important. The business librarian at the Iowa State University Library was confronted by a new faculty member who questioned why the library did not subscribe to a database he had used at another institution. The librarian prepared a presentation for that faculty member, demonstrating that another database the library did subscribe to not only provided a good alternative to the faculty's preferred database, but also offered options the first did not. The delighted faculty member went back to his department and told his colleagues about the wonderful resources in the library and the knowledgeable staff; the librarian felt good about making the library look good. Training, knowledge, and a customer-driven culture are critical to a library's success.

3. Plan for complaint management. "Management's responsibility begins with the preparation of written policies and procedures for speedy and fair complaint resolution" (U.S. Department of Commerce brochure, 1992). Libraries collect data on all kinds of transactions; keeping track of complaints should be part of that data collection. Suggestions in suggestion boxes or from library websites provide written documentation that can then be logged and categorized. Trends can be tracked and underlying problems can be resolved. Surveys provide means by which a collection of patrons, as well as nonpatrons, can voice their opinions about particular services and products. At service desks, there should be policies for documenting the types of complaints patrons bring to the staff; this could be done fairly simply with forms, either at the desk or online.

Policies for resolving complaints also need to be documented. Under what circumstances should a fine be waived? When can a faculty member take a periodical out of the library, and for how long? With the proper training, frontline staff should be able to resolve all but the most complex problems.

4. Respond to complaints. Sometimes a thank-you is enough. Sometimes just having a listening ear helps dissipate the frustration. By tracking complaints, libraries can often make policy decisions that will result in higher patron satisfaction, without having a major impact on the library. For instance, if you have a steady stream of patrons complaining that coming into the library to renew books is terribly inconvenient, then make it possible for them to renew books over the phone or by email. Some complaints are not so easy to

9

resolve. Constant complaints that students cannot find books on the shelves that should be there could be the result of different underlying problems. One could be that students do not know how to read call numbers correctly; in that case, education is definitely in order. Another reason could be that the books are not shelved correctly. The library will have to explore all of these possible causes, and often the solution may be complicated. However, a solution is required if we want to maintain our users' satisfaction.

If your library has suggestion boxes, it is a good idea to publicly exhibit, either in a prominent place in the library or online, representative suggestions and responses to them. Of course, not all suggestions or complaints will be of interest to all library users. But if a number of people tell you the building is too warm, it will make them feel better to know you have heard them, and that you are taking steps to make the building more comfortable. If one patron suggests renewals by phone, then probably many more would like that option; if it is already available, a public posting of the suggestion and the means for renewing by phone will help your patrons and your library's image.

5. Follow up on complaints. If a patron bothers to complain rather than just leave the library, it is in your best interest to acknowledge the contribution that person has made to your operations. If possible, send a letter or an email to that person, thanking him or her for the interest in your library, and explaining how you are working to resolve the problem. If patrons come to a service desk with a problem, check with them later on to make sure your response was satisfactory; that can be as simple as approaching those patrons at a workstation and asking if they are finding what they need or if that particular database worked for them. If a problem will take some time to resolve, stay in contact with the customers, letting them know where you are in the process, and when you hope to have results for them. Even if you cannot give all patrons exactly what they want, it makes them happier to know that you care and are interested in seeing that they are satisfied with what you *can* do.

SOURCE: Rebecca Jackson, "The Customer Is Always Right: What the Business World Can Teach Us about Problem Patrons," in Kwasi Sarkodie-Mensah, ed., *Helping the Difficult Library Patron* (New York: Haworth, 2002), pp. 205–216. Reprinted with permission.

ETHICS

ALA Code of Ethics

AS MEMBERS OF THE AMERICAN LIBRARY ASSOCIATION, we recognize the importance of codifying and making known to the profession and to the general public the ethical principles that guide the work of librarians, other professionals providing information services, library trustees, and library staffs.

Ethical dilemmas occur when values are in conflict. The American Library Association Code of Ethics states the values to which we are committed, and embodies the ethical responsibilities of the profession in this changing information environment.

We significantly influence or control the selection, organization, preservation, and dissemination of information. In a political system grounded in an informed citizenry, we are members of a profession explicitly committed to intellectual freedom and the freedom of access to information. We have a special obligation to ensure the free flow of information and ideas to present and future generations.

The principles of this code are expressed in broad statements to guide ethical decision making. These statements provide a framework; they cannot and do not dictate conduct to cover particular situations.

1. We provide the highest level of service to all library users through appropriate and usefully organized resources; equitable service policies; equitable access; and accurate, unbiased, and courteous responses to all requests.
2. We uphold the principles of intellectual freedom and resist all efforts to censor library resources.
3. We protect each library user's right to privacy and confidentiality with respect to information sought or received and resources consulted, borrowed, acquired, or transmitted.
4. We recognize and respect intellectual property rights.
5. We treat coworkers and other colleagues with respect, fairness, and good faith, and advocate conditions of employment that safeguard the rights and welfare of all employees of our institutions.
6. We do not advance private interests at the expense of library users, colleagues, or our employing institutions.
7. We distinguish between our personal convictions and professional duties and do not allow our personal beliefs to interfere with fair representation of the aims of our institutions or the provision of access to their information resources.
8. We strive for excellence in the profession by maintaining and enhancing our own knowledge and skills, by encouraging the professional development of coworkers, and by fostering the aspirations of potential members of the profession.

SOURCE: Adopted by ALA Council, June 28, 1995.

Lessons school librarians teach others

by Doug Johnson

THE SCHOOL LIBRARY MEDIA SPECIALIST (SLMS) has stepped up to the professional plate as a primary policymaker, staff trainer, and expert on information and technology ethics in our schools.

9

We place equal or greater importance on the teaching of safe and ethical use of complex technology than on teaching the simple technological "how-tos." Protecting one's privacy, guarding one's property, and stressing the safe use of technologies, especially the internet, are among the most important ways we "safeguard the rights and welfare of all employees of our institutions," as the ALA Code of Ethics suggests. We have accepted that as part of our mission, and take charge of the ethical education of our students and, to some degree, their parents and our fellow educators.

One of our longstanding roles—teacher—has grown in importance; another—watchdog—has grown in complexity. It has always been part of our job to help ensure copyright compliance by both staff and students in our districts—not just through training, but by monitoring as well. This is not a task most of us would choose for ourselves, but one that is thrust upon us because of the resources we control. Being asked to make unauthorized copies of print and audiovisual materials, to load software on more workstations than permitted by a license, or to set up a showing of a videotape that falls outside of public performance parameters are not uncommon requests. In these cases, we have learned to quietly, politely, and firmly just say "no" and explain how such an action violates not only the law, but our personal and professional ethical values as well.

But the ethical leadership of school library media specialists extends beyond being the copyright cops of our schools. We face five other major ethical challenges on a daily basis.

1. Encouraging intellectual freedom in a filtered environment. To a large degree, the Children's Internet Protection Act has taken the decision of whether to use internet filters out of the hands of local decision makers. Districts that receive federal funding, including e-rate telecommunications discounts, must install and use internet blocking software to be in compliance. Nonetheless, a strong commitment to intellectual freedom on the part of the SLMS is possible even in a filtered environment.

Internet blocking software offers a wide spectrum of restrictiveness. Depending on the product, its settings, and the ability to override the filter to permit access to individual sites, filters can either block a high percentage of internet resources (i.e., specific websites, email, chat rooms) or a relatively small number of sites. In our role as proponents of intellectual freedom, we strongly advocate for the least restrictive settings and most generous use of override lists by our school's internet filter. We make sure that the SLMS has available at least one machine that can access the complete unfiltered Web so that patrons can review questionably blocked sites and, when the contents of those URLs are found to be useful, restore immediate access for staff and students. In turn, when anyone asks that a specific internet site be blocked, we treat the request like any material challenge.

The SLMS also has the ethical responsibility of helping ensure patrons use the internet in acceptable ways by:

- Helping write and enforce the district's acceptable use policy.
- Developing and teaching the values needed to be self-regulating internet users.
- Supervising, and possibly limiting, computers with internet access and making sure all adults who monitor networked computers are knowledgeable about the internet.
- Educating and informing parents and the public about school internet uses and issues.
- Creating learning environments that promote the use of the internet for accomplishing resource-based activities to meet curricular objectives.

2. Preventing plagiarism, an offense that digital resources make easier than ever to commit. It's hard to remember, but intellectual-property theft existed prior to electronic cutting and pasting, peer-to-peer music-sharing services, and free term-paper sites. It's just that the speed, availability, and ease with which digital property can be copied have all led to greater instances of piracy, plagiarism, and even disdain for copyright laws.

The SLMS teaches students to respect the property of others as well as protect their own property from being abused. Students need to know that copyright law protects their own original work and that they have a right to give or withhold permission for others to use it.

But the major challenge for the SLMS is in helping teachers stem the tide of plagiarism washing through our schools—a trend that has been exacerbated by new technologies. For example, when Rutgers University Business School Professor Don McCabe conducted a 2000–01 survey of 4,500 students at 25 high schools, he found that more than half the respondents admitted to either passing off as their own work a paper they had downloaded from the internet or to pasting passages found online into their own work without citing the source (www.academicintegrity.org/cai_research.asp).

While we need to acknowledge that this is a serious problem, educators often spend too much effort trying to catch plagiarism in student work. The best SLMS plans with teachers to find ways of preventing plagiarism before it happens, such as:

- Teaching what plagiarism is, when and why to paraphrase, when using another's words is appropriate, and how to cite sources in all formats.
- Instituting a school or districtwide cheating policy that includes the definition of and consequences for plagiarism.
- Brainstorming with faculty on creating assignments worth doing: work that is relevant to students' lives, that demands creativity and originality, and that is assessed in thoughtful ways.

3. Protecting privacy and confidentiality in an increasingly networked information environment. School librarians help students become knowledgeable about technology issues related to privacy so that they can both protect their own privacy and honor the privacy of others. Students need to understand that businesses and organizations use information to market products, and that information is often gathered electronically, both overtly and covertly. They need to remember that a stranger is a stranger, whether met on the playground or on the internet, and that personal information shared with a stranger may put themselves and their families at risk. Students need to be aware that schools have the right to search the electronic files they create and store on school-owned hardware. Students need to be taught to respect the privacy of others: that just because information is displayed on a computer screen doesn't make it public, and that it is inappropriate to view information just because it was inadvertently left accessible.

We help the school set good guidelines. Helen Adams's booklet *The Internet Invasion: Is Privacy at Risk?* (Follett, Professional Development Articles, 2002) lists specific school topics related to privacy, and the SLMS should understand the privacy issues surrounding each and be able to help make good school policy related to them.

9

4. Imparting information evaluation skills of materials on the free internet. The internet and online services have given us access to an unimaginable spectrum of opinions, now readily available to students and staff in even the smallest of school library media centers. Everyone from scholars and 7th-graders to pundits and crazies can—and do—publish "information" online, often indistinguishable in appearance from reliable information. The information presented by businesses, nonprofits, think tanks, and others may be accurate but heavily biased.

The availability of misinformation or biased opinions is often confusing at best; at worst it can lead students, and even researchers, to make choices or reach embarrassingly misguided conclusions. Increasingly, students are using the internet to meet personal needs as well as to research school assignments that ask them to solve genuine problems. Making good consumer choices, health decisions, and career choices are a part of many districts' curricula. Gaining historical background and perspectives on social, scientific, and political issues through research is a common task expected by many teachers.

We teach our library users to be able to evaluate information for themselves. Were I the Grand Panjandrum of Libraries, I would instantly add Johnson's 9th Statement to ALA's Code of Ethics: *We teach our library users to be critical users of information.*

Established guidelines for the accuracy and reliability of information, understandable by even our youngest students, include the concepts of authority, age of the information, verifiability, and bias.

5. Closing the ongoing digital divide. The SLMS advocates for liberal access to electronic resources for all students in a school. But home and public library access to information technologies alone will not close the digital divide. We serve on building technology teams and advocate for access to technology for all students. Too often, technologies are acquired by individual departments, grade levels, or teachers within schools, only to be sequestered by them. As the equity counterweight, the SLMS voices the need for library access to information technologies that are available before, during, and after school hours. Our profession's "whole-school" view puts us in a unique position of knowing which children are getting technology skills and access in our buildings.

The professional mission of the school library media specialist remains constant even as it constantly evolves, as contradictory as that may sound. Information technologies offer new tools, opportunities, and challenges that those of us who did not grow up with technology may find confusing or frightening. But as a professional, the SLMS remains committed to making sure the students in our charge are effective, ethical, and safe users of information and ideas that can help them solve real problems and answer genuine questions.

We will remain the "teachers of teachers."

We will remain committed to the ideals of intellectual freedom in all formats.

And most of all, we will remain committed advocates for all children.

SOURCE: Doug Johnson, "Lessons School Librarians Teach Others," *American Libraries* 35 (December 2004): 46–48.

GLOBAL CONCERNS

Libraries in the Islamic world
by John Walbridge

SEVERAL FACTORS CONTRIBUTED to the prevalence of libraries in the medieval Islamic world. First, manuscript books were relatively cheap. Papermaking technology arrived in the Islamic world in the 8th century, providing Muslims with a material cheaper than the papyrus used previously in the Middle East and far cheaper than the parchment and vellum made from animal hides used in medieval Europe. Moreover, the Arabic script with its cursive forms and many ligatures could be written much faster than the medieval versions of the Roman alphabet.

Second, the medieval Islamic world was a literate culture. Men and even women of the upper and middle classes were almost always literate. Both religious and secular literatures were popular, and scholarly and literary attainments were respected. Islamic rulers, constantly hungry for legitimacy, collected books for the same reason they built monuments and patronized scholars and poets—to acquire reputations as cultivated rulers. Libraries of elegant manuscripts and learned treatises were thus appropriate possessions for kings and those who imitated them, and it was not uncommon for Islamic rulers, military officers, and high officials to have well-earned reputations for literary taste and scholarship.

Third, books were central to Islamic religious life. Despite a stress on oral learning in medieval Islam, books were necessary to record the masses of traditions of the Prophet, legal rulings, information concerning transmitters of religious lore, and linguistic lore that were the raw material of the Islamic sciences. Even the oral transmission of knowledge usually involved the production of a dictated book, so that studying a book involved producing a copy of it.

Fourth, medieval Islamic bureaucrats were accustomed to using books: encyclopedias of useful information, literary manuals useful for producing elegant official documents, literature for amusement, and such things as manuals of occult sciences.

Finally, the Islamic law of *waqf,* charitable endowments, allowed Muslim bibliophiles to donate their books to the libraries of mosques and *madrasas* with reasonable hope that their collections would be maintained intact.

The earliest Islamic libraries were the collections of Qur'ans that accumulated in mosques. Qur'an reading was an important Islamic devotional practice, and both copying Qur'ans and donating them to mosques were acts of piety. Larger mosques often acquired more diverse libraries, mostly through gifts. When a mosque was built or renovated, the donor often gave a collection

9

of books as the basis of the library. Bibliophiles and scholars, particularly those who taught in a particular mosque, often willed their books to the mosque library. Books copied in class were often given to the mosque library. To this day, many of the most important collections of Islamic manuscripts are in mosque libraries—for example, al-Azhar in Cairo and Suleymaniyyeh in Istanbul.

There are records of royal libraries as early as Umayyad times, the earliest associated with the scholarly Umayyad prince Khalid bin Yazid. The zenith of Islamic royal libraries was in the Abbasid period. The Abbasid caliph al-Ma'mun (reigned 813–833) founded the Bayt al-Hikma, the house of wisdom, which was the center for translation from Greek, Syriac, and Pahlavi and which was the basis of a caliphal library that survived for more than a century. The Umayyad royal library at Cordoba, founded by al-Hakam II (reigned 961–976), was supposed to have had 400,000 manuscripts. The greatest of the royal libraries was that of the Fatimids in Cairo, founded in 1004 by the caliph al-Hakim (reigned 996–1021). It survived, despite some vicissitudes, until it was ordered closed by Saladin in the late 12th century and its collections were dispersed and partly destroyed. The royal libraries sometimes had aggressive programs of commissioning both the copying and the composition of books. Both the Abbasid Bayt al-Hikma and the Mogul royal library in Delhi commissioned extensive translations, in the latter case often of Sanskrit Hindu literature of all sorts. Most of the great illustrated and illuminated Islamic books are the product of royal commissions.

There were also public libraries known as *dar al-'ilm*, houses of knowledge. These were more or less public libraries, often established for sectarian purposes. These institutions played a role in the establishment of *madrasas*, Islamic seminaries. With the rise of *madrasas* in the 11th century, their libraries became increasingly important.

Premodern Islamic libraries

Medieval accounts mention libraries containing hundreds of thousands or even millions of books, notably the royal libraries of Baghdad, Cairo, and Cordoba. Individual scholars are mentioned whose libraries consisted of some thousands of books. The higher numbers are scarcely credible. Istanbul, for example, has more than 100 manuscript libraries or collections dating from Ottoman times, some four centuries old, yet in 1959 a careful survey indicated that there were only about 135,000 Islamic manuscripts in the city, the largest collection containing about 10,000. It certainly is credible, however, that the larger medieval Islamic libraries contained tens of thousands of manuscripts and that wealthy individual scholars and bibliophiles possessed libraries of several thousand volumes—collections dwarfing anything in Europe at the time.

At their finest, Islamic libraries were large, well-organized institutions with specially built facilities for book storage and reading, professional staff, regular budgets and endowments, catalogs, and even lodging and stipends for visiting scholars. Public access varied, depending on the nature of the libraries, but established scholars could generally gain access to most collections. Books were usually stored on shelves or in cabinets, stacked on their sides with a short title written on the upper and lower edge of the book to aid in finding it. (Traditional Islamic bookbindings do not usually contain the title or author.) Catalogs were either bound handlists, the *waqf* documents donating the books, or lists posted on the doors of the cabinet. Collections were organized by subject. Avicenna describes visiting the royal library in Bukhara, for example, where rooms were devoted to different subjects. Paper, pens, and ink were sometimes furnished for the use of patrons.

Smaller collections had less elaborate facilities. Most mosques and madrasas had libraries. Private libraries and individual books were often donated to such institutions as *waqf*, endowment, and the terms of the gift would be carefully recorded on the flyleaf. Donated collections were often kept as separate units. There were also family libraries. In a society where professions were often hereditary, some families produced scholars and clerics generation after generation for centuries. Not uncommonly, a library would accumulate in the family home over many generations. Examples include the al-Husayni, al-Khalidi, and al-Budayri libraries in Jerusalem, each of which dates from the 18th century.

Destruction and dispersal of libraries

Islamic chronicles mention the destruction of many libraries, either deliberately or, more commonly, accidentally. Apart from a few places and times, warfare was endemic in the Islamic world and took its toll. Few surviving libraries in the Islamic world predate the older Istanbul libraries. While the story that the Muslim invaders burned the library of Alexandria has long been known to be false—it had been destroyed in Roman times—the sack of cities did often result in the destruction of libraries. Most of the major libraries of Abbasid Iraq were destroyed during the Mongol invasion. The Islamic library in Tripoli was destroyed when the city was sacked by the Franks during the First Crusade, beginning in 1095. The American invasion of Iraq in 2003 apparently resulted in the destruction of much of the collection of the National Library in Baghdad.

Sometimes the destruction was ideologically motivated. Mahmud of Ghazna (right) burned the heretical works in the library of the wazir Isma'il bin 'Abbad and confiscated the rest. The books on philosophy and the natural sciences in the library of al-Hakam II in Cordoba were burned by the orthodox during his son's reign. The mass destruction of Arabic books was part of the Catholic kings' program to suppress Islam in Spain, including the burning of Arabic books in Granada at the order of Cardinal Cisneros. There also was a curious tradition of scholars destroying their own books at their death, either to suppress embarrassing or incomplete works or to avoid unauthorized transmission of hadith and other texts that ought to be transmitted orally.

Finally, lack of supervision led to the decay of many libraries, with books stolen by readers or dishonest librarians or lost to damp and insects, the latter a particular menace in South and Southeast Asia, where insecticide is still sometimes sprinkled between the pages of books.

The destruction of libraries in wartime was not always, or even usually, deliberate. Books were valuable, and thus were better stolen than destroyed.

9

There is a report that when Constantinople fell to the Ottomans, the sultan ordered the surviving Greek manuscripts in the city collected for the palace library, and there can be no doubt that the size and quality of the manuscript collections in Istanbul are in good part the result of the imperial reach of the Ottoman armies. Likewise, many of the Islamic manuscript collections in Europe were, to some extent, the product of colonial wars. The great Islamic manuscript collections in Russia are the product of the Russian expansion into Central Asia in the 18th and 19th centuries. The treasures of the Mogul royal library were dispersed after the 1857–1858 mutiny, and many of the finest items ended up in London.

Libraries in the modern Islamic world

With some exceptions, the library situation in modern Islamic countries falls short of the glories of the medieval period. Some premodern libraries have survived and prospered. In Ottoman Turkey a stable bureaucratic tradition and internal stability meant that most of the old *waqf* libraries survived as functioning institutions until they were taken over by the modern Turkish state. Several of the larger Ottoman libraries in Istanbul are still functioning, and the collections of most of the smaller libraries have been gathered in a central library in the Suleymaniyyeh mosque. Al-Azhar University in Cairo has a library that has functioned for centuries in one form or another.

Most of the libraries of the Islamic world are of more recent date. These may be divided into two classes: libraries of traditional type founded in the 19th and 20th centuries, and Western-style libraries founded by colonial administrations or modern independent Islamic states.

Even after the occupation of most of the Islamic world by European colonial powers and the establishment of modern nation-states in the Islamic lands, libraries continued to be established that, despite occasional appurtenances of modern libraries and the prevalence of printed books, were indistinguishable in style and purposes from those established centuries earlier. The libraries of the Muslim rulers and nobility of princely states in British India were

royal libraries of the old sort—for example, the Raza Library in Rampur, based on a collection started by the Rohilla Nawabs of Rampur in the 18th century, and the Salar Jung Museum Library (left) in Hyderabad, Deccan. New mosques and madrasas had libraries indistinguishable from those of previous centuries, apart from the presence of printed books. A notable example is the Mar'ashi library in Qom, founded by a bibliophilic grand ayatollah in the mid-20th century, which emerged as a major library after the Iranian Revolution of 1979.

The colonial period marked a major change, with the introduction of European-style libraries intended to promote the diffusion of modern knowledge and to support the new systems of education and, to a lesser extent, to support modern industry. At the top of the pyramid are national libraries, supported by depository laws and national bibliographies. In some cases, such as Egypt and Iran, these libraries emerged from earlier royal libraries and are themselves important repositories of Islamic manuscripts. In other cases, such as Pakistan, they are new foundations rivaled or overshadowed by older university and traditional libraries. The introduction of modern educational systems led to the creation of school and university libraries. University libraries are well established across the Islamic world, though in general only a few of the older universities have really major libraries: Istanbul University, American University of Beirut, and Punjab University in Lahore, for example. Many newer universities have very limited library facilities. The high cost of foreign monographs and periodicals poses particular difficulties for academic libraries in the poorer Islamic countries, and the lack of such materials is one of the most difficult problems faced by academics in the Islamic world. The increasing importance of computers and electronic resources is an additional burden that few academic libraries in the Islamic world can afford.

Elementary and secondary school libraries are generally weak or nonexistent. Public library systems are also usually inadequate and rarely have much priority in competition for scarce public resources. Public libraries exist in major cities, but much less commonly in provincial cities or small towns. Translations of foreign works are relatively scarce. Cultural factors sometimes hinder progress. Where public libraries exist, there may be restrictions on circulation, subscription fees, or educational requirements that hinder free access, as is the case for the best public libraries in Pakistan. The Islamic world has not

yet had its Andrew Carnegie, endowing mass self-education through free public libraries. As a result, foreign institutions such as the British Council still play a significant role in providing library facilities, despite their existing only in the largest cities. The new Biblioteca Alexandria (right) being built in Egypt in emulation of the ancient library deserves mention, though it is far from clear that it will be able to achieve its goal to become a world-class research library.

There have also been challenges applying modern library techniques. The mixture of Arabic and Roman script books has posed problems for cataloging and computerization. The Dewey decimal system has been widely adopted, despite the inadequacies of its treatment of Islamic and Middle Eastern topics.

SOURCE: John Walbridge, "Libraries," in Richard C. Martin, ed., *Encyclopedia of Islam and the Muslim World* (New York: Macmillan Reference, 2004), vol. 1, pp. 414–416. Reprinted with permission.

Jobs in international librarianship

by Robin Kear

DO YOU ENJOY TRAVELING? Do you dream of cultures and places you haven't seen? Can you be alone? Do you own well-thumbed Lonely Planet books? Do you wish you were there when someone describes a faraway place? Are you comfortable in unknown places and situations? If you answer yes and want to find out if international work is for you:

- Talk to colleagues who have worked abroad and ask what they thought of the experience.
- Do some armchair traveling or try the real thing.
- Read the regular *College & Research Libraries News* feature "Jobs of a Lifetime."
- Read library journals from other countries.
- Look up their national associations.

9

- Shadow an international librarianship discussion list.
- Ask yourself if living and working abroad will make you happy.

Skills that will help you get the job

Because of expense, you may have to present yourself and your credentials by email and telephone. Here are some skills, knowledge, and aptitudes that will help get that international job.

- Knowledge of a foreign language or two;
- International travel experience;
- Genuine interest in working abroad;
- Knowledge of international issues;
- Work experience appropriate for the position you are applying for;
- Ability to apply practical and basic library and organizational skills for jobs in developing countries;
- Ability to work without the aid of technology in developing countries; and
- Membership in one or more international organizations, such as the International Federation of Library Associations and Institutions (IFLA), the International Society for Knowledge Organization (ISKO), and the ALA International Relations Round Table (IRRT).

For short-term experience (less than one year), consider internships, library exchanges, travel grants, and academic cruise ships. For positions lasting longer than a year, consider the military, nongovernmental organizations, the United Nations, universities with international campuses, and foreign universities.

Ways to get there

The United Nations offers a shortcut for its professional level positions known as the National Competitive Recruitment Examinations Programme. To be eligible, you must be under 32 years old and your country and profession must be underrepresented in the UN. For the last three years, the United States and librarianship have been underrepresented and thus eligible for the NCREP. If you pass the written test and interview, you are placed on a list of qualified applicants for professional librarian positions and almost guaranteed to receive the jobs as they open. Some jobs in the United States offer international opportunities. Look for libraries that have exchange programs with sister libraries abroad. Some academic appointments allow you to take a semester off for research or professional development.

Things to keep in mind

Living in a foreign country may present challenges for you and your family including homesickness and even hostility. You may be exposed to poverty, suffering, and danger. That being said, places are seldom as bad as the outsider imagines. If you are open, courteous, and respectful of custom, you are likely to have a good experience. Choosing to live and work in Kenya was the best thing I ever did, and I highly recommend the experience.

SOURCE: Robin Kear, "International Librarianship: Getting There from Here," *International Leads* 18, no. 4 (December 2004): 5–6.

Cultural concerns
in building a website

by Linda Main

DESIGNERS AND USERS OF WEBSITES may have very different cultural backgrounds. Culture can be defined as something that an individual learns while growing up with peers in a community or society. Culture is grounded in the group experience. It is an individual's sense of identity within the group; it is his or her relationship to other humans, to things, to animals, to gods, and to the cosmos. A culture often contains several subcultures, and cultures overlap.

The website designer must always remember that although he or she is thinking in terms of the global reach of the website, the user is coming to the website from a local perspective. Also, the variety of high-level, easy-to-use authoring tools for building websites makes it easy to create visuals, such as buttons, windows, and scroll boxes. However, the general look and functionality of the website is thus more or less preset and does not take into account the subjective and objective cultural issues specific to target cultures.

Subjective culture: Models

Subjective culture is psychological and deals with attitudes. Inevitably, researchers and writers have developed different models of and ways of looking at cultures. Geert Hofstede, in *Cultures and Organizations* (McGraw-Hill, 1991), saw culture as the collective mental programming of the people in an environment. People with different mental programming perceive the same object in different ways. Hofstede studied IBM employees in 50 countries and identified the following five cultural dimensions that impact work, home and family life, and education and that appear in a nation's or culture's symbols, heroes, rituals, and values:

- Power distance (the measure of inequality in a society and the degree to which people accept that inequality);
- Individualism and collectivism;
- Femininity and masculinity (masculine cultures have social roles clearly defined by gender, whereas these roles overlap in feminine societies);
- Uncertainty avoidance (the extent to which members of a culture feel threatened by the unknown); and
- Long-term time orientation (how well a culture adapts its traditions to modem perspectives).

Hofstede's model of culture has been criticized for ignoring diversity within national cultures and for viewing the individual as simply the passive recipient of culture. In a 2001 paper, however, Aaron Marcus and Emile W. Gould considered how Hofstede's dimensions of culture might affect user interface designs. They use many examples from the Web to illustrate his cultural dimensions. For example, cultures that are high in uncertainty avoidance prefer links that follow a strict sequence. The following briefly illustrates how Hofstede's conclusions can be applied to web pages designed for a Chinese audience.

9

Impact of power distance

Power distance is the extent to which less-powerful members expect and accept unequal power distribution within a culture. Hofstede found that countries like the United States and Britain had a small power distance index and thus favored an egalitarian ethos. Countries with a Chinese majority, or that had undergone Chinese cultural influences, however, had medium to upper-medium power distance indexes. Chinese people therefore "[a]ccept and appreciate inequality but feel that the use of power should be moderated by a sense of obligation." Thus, web pages designed for Chinese users should include references to characteristics associated with large power distance indexes, including the following:

- References to authority, power, expertise, and wealth;
- A strong focus on expertise, authority, official stamps, and logos;
- Prominent organizational charts that emphasize the organization's hierarchy;
- Clear statement of any special titles that have been conferred on members of the organization so that they can be properly addressed; and
- Significant or frequent emphasis on the social and moral order (e.g., nationalism and government leaders) and its symbols.

Impact of collectivism

Hofstede found American society to have the highest level of individualism among the 50 countries that he studied. Individualistic cultures value freedom and material rewards at work and are very direct in business communications. Hofstede considered the Chinese to be collectivist in nature. Collectivist cultures value harmony, and their business communications are much less direct than those of more individualistic cultures. Since the Chinese culture is a collectivist one, web pages designed for Chinese users should do the following:

- Place little emphasis on personal achievement;
- Define success in terms of sociopolitical, rather than individual, goals;
- Promote group solidarity rather than individual self-interest;
- Include links to other organizations to illustrate a strong group network;
- Be written in an indirect, impersonal style; and
- Emphasize tradition and history.

Impact of masculinity versus femininity

Masculine cultures have clearly distinct social gender roles, while these roles overlap in feminine cultures. Hofstede's study did not explicitly mention China's masculinity index. According to ITIM Culture and Management Consultants, however, China has a medium masculinity index slightly lower than that of the United States. As a result, a website localized for Chinese users does not require any of the design features advisable for either very masculine or very feminine societies.

Impact of low uncertainty avoidance

Uncertainty avoidance reflects the extent to which members of a culture feel threatened by the unknown. China, Chinese-speaking countries, and countries whose population includes a sizeable Chinese minority have a low uncertainty avoidance. Aaron Marcus and Emile W. Gould recommend that websites designed for users from low-uncertainty-avoidance cultures, such as the Chinese cultures, should include the following:

- Many choices and a large amount of information; and
- Minimal control over the user's navigation around the site with an emphasis on encouraging wandering by the user.

Impact of long-term time orientation

Hofstede found China to have the highest long-term orientation index of all the countries he surveyed. A high long-term orientation index indicates that a culture adapts tradition to modern perspectives and displays patience in pursuing goals. Websites aimed at users from cultures with high long-term orientation indexes should therefore emphasize the following:

- Perseverance and patience in pursuing goals;
- Future orientation;
- Content with a practical application; and
- Relationships as a source of information.

The model developed by Edward T. Hall, which has become widely accepted among sociolinguists, can help web designers in understanding what target cultures can and will accept. Hall compares the cultures of the world on a scale ranging from high-context to low-context (see Table 1). In cultures that are closer to the high-context end of the scale, important information is transmitted in nonverbal or indirect ways. Meaning is implied. Nothing is expressed directly; body language, tone, the status of individuals, and pauses and silences are important. Group-oriented cultures, such as the Chinese, Japanese, Korean, Latin American, Mediterranean, Middle Eastern, and Vietnamese cultures, tend to fall into this category. France also places close to the high-context end of the scale. In cultures that are closer to the low-context end of the scale, virtually all information is communicated with a direct statement. People say what they mean. In low-context cultures, the individual takes precedence over the group. Countries that place closer to this end of the scale include the United States, Canada, the United Kingdom, Australia, Germany, and most of Western Eu-

Table 1. Characteristics of High-Context and Low-Context Cultures	
High-context culture	*Low-context culture*
Implicit messages	Explicit messages
Internalized messages	Plainly coded messages
Nonverbal coding	Verbalized details
Reserved reactions	Reactions on the surface
Distinct in-groups and out-groups	Flexible in-groups and out-groups
Strong people bonds	Fragile people bonds
High commitment	Low commitment
Open and flexible time	Highly organized time

9

rope, including Scandinavia. Following Hall's theories, web pages designed for a Chinese audience should focus on the following:

- Communications that rely on highly developed personal relationships rather than detailed facts and agreements;
- Providing a variety of views and topics; and
- An orientation toward people rather than tasks.

Yvonne Cleary examines the role of subjective cultural issues on the usability of the Louvre Museum official website (www.archimuse.com/mw2000/papers/cleary/cleary.html).

Subjective culture: Some things to consider

The website designer should avoid jargon, slang, idioms, religion, race, sex, politics, stereotypes, humanized animals, humor, and references to parts of the body. It is important to state what something is rather than what it is

called (for example, use the term *stock exchange* not *Dow*). Use visual images, but remember that not everybody reads from left to right, so the sequencing should be appropriate for the target culture. In particular, remember that humor is very culture-specific. What is funny in one culture may not be readily understood in another culture or, worse, may be offensive.

At a minimum, the following should be considered when putting together a web page.

Authority. How is status determined? Is age important? Is money?

Colors. The colors of screens and icons can have different cultural implications. In China, white is associated with death and red with marriage and festivity. S. W. Chu, however, observes that red and white are often used together in Chinese society. He argues that Chinese users only find the use of the color white on a website unappealing or inappropriate if it is used in images of people holding white flowers or wearing white clothes. The Japanese also connect white with death, but red spells danger in Japan. In Western Europe, black is associated with death, white with purity and virtue, and red with danger. Western Europeans associate yellow with caution or cowardice, but in Arab countries, yellow signifies happiness. While the color green is acceptable to a Chinese audience, an image of a green hat is not because the expression *wearing a green hat* is used in China to refer to a man who is a cuckold. In Arab countries, green is a holy color. Phrases such as *in the red* or *in the black* may not be understood in cultures that do not use colors as adjectives.

M. E. Holzschlag suggests that blue is the most globally accessible color, safe in almost any culture, and it is therefore the best choice for a site designed for a worldwide audience. A study of international students by Elke Duncker, Yin Leng Theng, and Norlisa Mohd-Nasir reported that European and U.S. students more or less preferred a bright background, black text, and few moderately colorful objects. English students liked pastel color schemes with a lot of gray and low contrast. Scandinavian students tended to prefer dark colors, also with low contrast. Students with a Jamaican background preferred strong and bright colors with high contrasts. African students preferred black as the ground color. No particular pattern seemed to emerge in the use of colors by Asian students. A second survey later in the semester showed that students' color preferences were also affected by the degree of cultural mixing between the country of origin and the local (sub)cultures.

Gestures. How do people stand when they talk to each other? Which hand gestures are acceptable or unacceptable? The "OK" hand gesture is often used as an icon in the United States. In many countries it carries the same meaning as the middle-finger gesture in the United States.

Individuality. Some cultures embrace individuality; others find it offensive.

Learning styles. Should the style be chatty and friendly; or formal, instructional, and scholarly? If the style is informal, will the website be viewed as insulting to users accustomed to receiving a certain amount of respect? There are many studies on different learning styles in different cultures. R. Kaplan noted different organizational styles in English prose written by native speakers of French, Arabic, English, and the Asian languages. J. M. Ulijn found that Dutch readers preferred a direct linear organization, whereas French readers preferred a more digressive organization. In a 1991 study, R. G. Hein found that German readers liked background information giving historical and contextual perspectives. They wanted to see how something fits into the overall scheme of things, and above all they wanted precise information. B. L. Thatcher came to similar conclusions in a 1999 study of South American accountants. The participants in this study wanted contextual and historical information and detailed narratives, which was interesting, as South Americans are regarded as a high-context culture on Hall's scale. Three studies have found Japanese writing to be inductively organized, with the topic statements appearing late in the text. Another study contradicted this and found that if the topic is factual, Japanese readers prefer writing to be deductively organized.

Prejudices. Is there racial equality in the culture? What is considered beautiful or ugly? What are the attitudes toward aging, leisure time, and outsiders?

Roles of men, women, and children. Are the sexes considered equal? How is sexuality treated? Are families large and extended or small and nuclear? Should graphics take into account a disparity between gender roles?

Sense of time. Is time considered linear and critical, or elastic and unimportant relative to other things? The phrase "as soon as possible" means "immediately" in the United States; it often means "when convenient" in other cultures.

Sounds. If using sounds, it is important to remember that telephones, alarms, and sirens sound different in different countries. Also some cultures, such as the Japanese, dislike the use of sounds to correct a user's error.

Symbols. Do shapes, numbers, animals, or food carry meaning? For example, chopsticks in a rice bowl signify the Cantonese symbol of death. The significance of a shamrock as a good luck charm is lost on

9

most non-Western cultures. Thirteen is considered unlucky in the West; four is considered unlucky in Asia, but eight is very lucky. A piggy bank illustrates savings in most parts of the Western world. There are, however, countries where pigs are considered unclean. In the United States, a mailbox with a flag is often used to indicate that there is new mail. Mailboxes look different elsewhere. A better symbol would be an envelope. Similarly, the American shopping cart icon for ecommerce does not translate well because in many other countries shoppers use baskets, not carts.

Taboos. Are there religious principles pertaining to certain foods, colors, or behaviors that cannot be violated? What are the culture's attitudes toward body parts? For example, the left hand is offensive in some cultures, so it is better to say "on the left hand" or "left side." Eyes and feet should be avoided as they have negative significance in many cultures.

SOURCE: Linda Main, *Building Websites for a Multinational Audience* (Lanham, Md.: Scarecrow, 2002), pp. 35–43. Reprinted with permission.

LIBRARIANA
CHAPTER TEN

"Libraries are brothels for the mind. Which means that librarians are the madams, greeting punters, understanding their strange tastes and needs, and pimping their books. That's rubbish, of course, but it does wonders for the image of librarians."

—Guy Browning, *The Guardian,* October 18, 2003

WORDS

The word "library" in 131 different languages

Afrikaans	biblioteek	Dakota (Sioux)	wowapiopahi
Akan (Twi)	nhomakorabea	Danish	bibliotek
Alabama	holisso aachikìika	Dutch	bibliotheek
(Muskogean)		Egyptian	
Albanian	bibliotekë	(ancient)	𓇌𓏏𓈖𓆷𓏤
Amharic	ቤተ፡መጻሕፍት		st n 3š' w
	biblioteca	Esperanto, Ido	biblioteko
Arabic	بيتكلا راد	Estonian	raamatukogu
	اوحتو بيتكلا خضوبة	Faroese	bókasavn
	khīzana,	Farsi	كتابخانه' قرائتخانه' كتابفروشی
	hizâna-t kutub,		ketābkhune,
	kutubhâna,		kitab-khana,
	maktaba		ketâb-khâneh
Armenian	գրադարան	Fijian	vale ni wilīvola
	krataran, qradun	Finnish	kirjasto
Azeri	kitabxana	French	bibliothèque
Baluchi	kytabjah	French Creole	bibliyotèk
Basque	liburutegi	Frisian	bibleteek
Belorussian	biblijateka	Fulani	móoftirde defte
Bengali	পুস্তকসমূহ	Gaelic	leeberary
	pustAghawr	Georgian	ბიბლიოთეკა
Bobangi	libôkô li minkāna		bibliotek'a
Bosnian	biblioteka,	German	Bibliothek
	čitaonica	Greek	βιβλιοτεκα
Breton	levraoueg	Guaraní	kuatia renda
Bulgarian	библиотéка	Gujarati	વાચનાલય
Burmese	စာကြည့်တိုက်	Hausa	lābàrārī
Catalan	biblioteca	Hawaiian	hali waihona puke
Cebuano	basahonan	Hebrew	סִפְרִיָּה
Cherokee	gowili		sifriya
	deganvdigoliyedi	Hiligaynon	balasahan, librerya
Chinese	图书馆	Hindi	१.पुस्तकालय,
(Cantonese)	to sùe gwóon		वाचनालय
Chinese	圖書館		pustakālaya,
(Mandarin)	tú shū guăn		laibrarī
Chinese	t'u shu kuan	Hmong Daw	tsev khaws-qiv ntawv
(Wade-Giles)		(Miao)	nyeem
Clallam	spukáw'txʷ	Hungarian	könyvtár
Cornish	lyverjy	Icelandic	bókasafn
Czech	knihovna	Ilocano	bibliotéka

Indonesian	perpustakaan	Sindhi	لائبرري
Irish	leaḃarlann	Sinhala	පුස්තකාලය, පොත්ඟුළ
	leabharlann	Slovak	knižnica, knihovňa
Italian	biblioteca	Slovene	knjižnica
Japanese	図書館	Somali	libreriya,
	toshokan		maktabad
Kannada	gramthaalaya	Sotho	laebrari,
Kazakh	кітапхана		bokgobapuku
Khmer	បណ្ណាល័យ	Spanish	biblioteca
Kikuyu	mabukumongañitio	Sudovian	laiskabutan
	gĩkundi	Sumo-Mayangna	wauhtaya ûni
Konkani	pustakañsāl	Swahili	nyumba cha kuwekea
Korean	도서관		vitabu,
	tosŏgwan		maktaba
Kosraean	laepracri	Swedish	bibliotek
Kyrgyz	китепкана	Tagalog	aklatan
Lao	hohng sai muit	Tahitian	paepae buka
Latin	bibliotheca	Tamil	புத்தகசாலை
Latvian	biblioteka		pusthagasâlai
Lithuanian	biblioteka	Tatar	китапхане
Malay	perpustakaan,	Telugu	గ్రంథాలయం
	taman pustaka		granthaalayam
Maltese	librerija	Thai	ห้องสมุด
Manx	lioar-hasht		(f)hawng!
Maori	whare pukapuka		sa-(l)moot!
Maranao	roang a ribro	Tibetan	དཔེ་ཁྲིད་ཁང
Marathi	'लाइब्ररि		kun-dga-ra-ba,
Marshallese	ļāibrāre		pe-chha-khang
Mennonite	Bieliotäkj	Turkish	kütüphane
Low German		Turkmen	kitaphana
Michif	ita lee leevz	Uighur	kütüpkhana
(Metis)	kaw-ashtayki	Ukrainian	бібліотека
Mongolian	номын сан	Ulwa	buktak ûka
Nepali	पुस्तकालय	Urdu	کتب خانہ
	pustakālaya		katabkhānā
Norwegian	bibliotek	Uzbek	кутубхона
Occitan	bibliotèca	Vietnamese	thư viện
Ojibwa	agindaasoowigamig	Wakashan	bu'gwilas
Pampangan	aklatan	Welsh	llyfrgell
Panjabi	ਪੁਸਤਕਾਲਾ, ਲਾਇਬ੍ਰੇਰੀ	Xhosa	ilayibri,
	laibrerī		indlu yeencwadi
Pashto	kitab-khāna	Yiddish	ביבליאטעק
Polish	biblioteka		biblyotek
Portuguese	biblioteca	Yoruba	ilé ìkàwé
Romanian	bibliotecă	Zulu	iqoqo lamabhuku
Russian	библиотéка		
Saami	girjerádju		
Samoan	fale faitautusi		
Sanskrit	pustakâgāra		
Sardinian	bibblioèca		
Serbo-Croatian	knjižnica		

American Sign Language:
The "L" handshape makes a small circular movement.
International Morse Code:
• — •• •• — • — — • — • • — • — •
— • — —

10

50 more library quotations from the Molesworth Institute

by Norman D. Stevens

AMONG MY NEVER-TO-BE-FINISHED PROJECTS is expanding a collection of more than 1,000 quotations about libraries and putting them into an online database. I once thought that such a database might reveal the truth about the role of libraries in society. I have come to realize that what I have assembled is little more than a plethora of platitudes that either laud the library as the bulwark of society or decry it as a repository of dead books. Ignorant or learned persons will continue to express their views on libraries as long as librarians continue to invite readers and speakers to offer such ruminations. For *The Whole Library Handbook 3*, I selected 50 library quotations gathered by the staff of the Molesworth Institute to represent diverse points of view. Here are 50 more of the delightful, obscure, and valuable entries in our archive.

1. "A library is a building where books are kept for people to borrow."
   —Martha Alexander, *How My Library Grew: By Dinah* (1983), p. [3].

2. "I realized that if the books [in the library] held as much magic as the word of the old ones, then indeed this was a room full of power."
   —Rudolfo A. Anaya, in *The Magic of Words* (1982), p. 12.

3. "Perfect tranquility of life . . . is nowhere to be found but in a retreat, a faithful friend, and a good library."
   —Aphra Behn (right), *The Lucky Mistake* (1689).

4. "Restitution, *n*. The founding or endowment of universities and public libraries by gift or bequest."
   —Ambrose Bierce, *The Devil's Dictionary* (1911).

5. "[A library] offers the easiest escape from the depressing monotony of everyday life."
   —E. A. Birge, in *Material for a Public Library Campaign* (1907).

6. "In libraries it is well not to hurry."
   —Catherine Drinker Bowen, *Adventures of a Biographer* (1959).

7. "The only subject of lamentation is—one feels that always, I think, in the presence of a library—that life is too short."
   —John Bright, speech at the opening of the Birmingham New Free Library, June 1, 1882, cited in *The Book-Lover's Enchiridion* (1888), p. 339.

8. "I prefer the free public library to most if not any other agency for the happiness and improvement of a community."
   —Andrew Carnegie (right), in *Material for a Public Library Campaign* (1907), p. 36.

9. "To describe a library . . . authors use a certain number of words and expressions which have become stereotypes [such as] rats, worms, dust, silence, ladders, sanctuaries, cemeteries, labyrinth . . . [or an adjectival form] universal, eternal, solemn, impressive, innumerable, monumental."
   —Anne-Marie Chaintreau and Renée Lemaitre, in *The Image of the Library* (1994), p. 42.

10. "And to be a library is to convey acquired information from generation to generation which, according to the laws of biology, only living things are supposed to be able to do. To be a library, then, is to be a miracle."

—Roger L. Conover, "Excursis Poesis," *Rotch Library of Architecture, Commemorative of the Opening Celebration* [Massachusetts Institute of Technology], December 5, 1991.

11. "Then [when capitalism is abolished] the library will be, as it should be, a noble temple dedicated to culture and symbolizing the virtues of the people."

—Eugene V. Debs (right), in *The Weekly People*, April 7, 1901.

12. "A library of wisdom, then, is more precious than all wealth, and all things that are desirable cannot be compared to it."

—Richard de Bury (1287–1345), *Philobiblon* (1960 ed.), p. 29.

13. "Old libraries have wings like attics in houses where families have lived for many generations."

—Michael Dorris and Louise Erdrich, *The Crown of Columbus* (1991), p. 185.

14. "Libraries are as forests, in which not only tall cedars and oaks are to be found but bushes too and dwarfish shrubs; and as in apothecaries' shops all sorts of drugs are permitted to be, so may all sorts of books be in a library."

—William Drummond of Hawthornden (1585–1649), *Works* (1711), p. 233.

15. "[Libraries] are the home and refuge of our heritage. All that is good in our history is gathered in books."

—Will Durant, in *Modern Maturity*, August/September 1972, p. 25.

16. "I can stand in a library and hear the myriad voices around me as though I was standing in the middle of a vast choir, a choir of knowledge and beauty."

—Gerald Durrell, *The Picnic and Other Inimitable Stories* (1980), p. 142.

17. "The whole idea of a library is based on a misunderstanding: that a reader goes to the library to find a book whose title he knows. . . . The essential function of a library is to discover books of whose existence the reader has no idea."

—Umberto Eco, in "De Bibliotheca," *Bostonia*, Spring 1993, pp. 39–42.

18. "Do you foresee what you will do with [your library]? . . . The real question is, What will it do with you? You will come here & get books that will open your eyes, & your ears, & your curiosity, & turn you inside out or outside in."

—Ralph Waldo Emerson (right), *Journals and Miscellaneous Notebooks*, vol. 16 (1866–1882), p. 296.

19. "[The library] would not be a lounging place for idlers, but a quiet retreat for persons of both sexes who desire to improve their minds."

—Edward Everett, in *Boston Daily Evening Transcript*, August 13, 1850, p. 1, col. 6.

20. "The library is, in these deepest depths of what is after all its soul, the very antitheses of its public conception; there is little quiet calm, and peace here."

—David E. Fisher, *Katie's Terror* (1982), p. 180.

10

21. "Libraries are the vessels in which the seed corn for the future is stored."

    —Dorothy Canfield Fisher (right), in *The Library of Tomorrow* (1939), p. 27.

22. "The progressive library is a fisher of men. . . . The good library does not wait for its readers to come to it; it goes to its readers."

    —Sam Walter Foss, in *Christian Science Monitor,* October 6, 1909.

23. "Both [bicycle and libraries] move people forward without wasting anything. The perfect day: riding a bike to the library."

    —Pete Golkin, on a postcard issued by ALA's Write for America's Libraries campaign (1993).

24. "For myself, public libraries possess a special horror, as of lonely wastes and dragon-haunted fens. The stillness and the heavy air, the feeling of restriction and surveillance, the mute presence of these other readers, 'all silent and all damned,' combine to set up a nervous irritation fatal to quiet study."

    —Kenneth Grahame, *Pagan Papers* (1894), p. 57.

25. "Future generations will bless the memory of the man who gives libraries and books."

    —Thomas Greenwood, *Public Libraries* (1894), p. 6.

26. "Libraries are reservoirs of strength, grace and wit, reminders of order, calm and continuity, lakes of mental energy, neither warm nor cold, light nor dark. The pleasure they give is steady, unorgastic, reliable, deep and long-lasting. In any library in the world, I am at home, unselfconscious, still and absorbed."

    —Germaine Greer, *Daddy, We Hardly Knew You* (1989), p. 70.

27. "Why be prepared only for the library just because you've decided to go to the library?"

    —Timothy Hallinan, *The Man with No Time* (1993), p. 15.

28. "We learned from you to understand, but not to change."

    —Randall Jarrell, "The Carnegie Library, Juvenile Division," *Little Friend, Little Friend* (1945), p. 24.

29. "Coffined thoughts around me, in mummy cases, embalmed in spice of words. Thoth, god of libraries, a birdgod, moonycrowned."

    —James Joyce (right), *Ulysses* (1922), p. 186.

30. "If a society cannot provide work for all, the idle—chronic or temporary—are much safer with a book in the library than elsewhere."

    —T. L. Kelso, in *Arena,* vol. 7 (1893), p. 711.

31. "Not having to go to a library is a very important improvement in providing library service."

    —Fred Kilgour, in *New Yorker,* April 4, 1994, p. 78.

32. "And a library, after all, was just a library."

    —Stephen King, *Four Past Midnight* (1990), p. 413.

33. "Public libraries are anonymous places, most people come to them in silence and alone."

   —Gavin Lambert, *In the Night All Cats Are Grey* (1976), p. 25.

34. "Libraries are keels to the ship of state that keeps us stable and upright amid the winds of passion that from time to time blow over any society."

   —Richard Marius, in *The UTK Librarian*, Spring 1994, p. 13.

35. "I would go so far as to say that education is but a key to open the doors of libraries."

   —André Maurois, *Public Libraries and Their Mission* (1961), p. 9.

36. "The new library . . . [is a] marvelous place for children, but it corrupts them with false information in that first part *lie*. It has got to be *truthbrary*."

   —James Michener, *Caribbean* (1989), p. 552.

37. "The Treasure House of Literature is no more to be thrown open to the ravages of the unreasoning Mob, than is the Fair Garden to be laid unprotected at the Mercy of a Swarm of Beasts."

   —Edmund Lester Pearson, *The Old Librarian's Almanack*, June 1774 [1909].

38. "A town with a library can be distinguished easily from one with a lack of any such collection of books."

   —Charles F. Richardson, *The Choice of Books* (1881), p. 194.

39. "How much do you think we spend altogether on our libraries, public or private, as compared to what we spend on our horses? . . . If public libraries were half so costly as public dinners . . . even foolish men and women might sometimes suspect there was good in reading."

   —John Ruskin (right), *Sesame and Lilies: Of King's Treasures* (1865), 32 (I.); *The Works of John Ruskin* (1905), vol. 18, pp. 84–85.

40. "For some, this wondrous place is a retreat where they are saved from the external world with all of its dangers and adversities, like a church in the middle ages."

   —Valeria D. Stelmakh, *The Image of the Library* (1994), p. 13.

41. "It is the indispensable and primary use of a research library to preserve the records of the past so that research can make our knowledge less imperfect than it is."

   —Lawrence W. Towner, *Past Imperfect* (1993), pp. 125–126.

42. "See here these huge columns, these vast heavy stones: 'Tis the tomb of the Books, 'tis the high place of Bones."

   —Jones Very, *Poems and Essays* (1886), p. 525.

43. "Will not the increased value of their real estate, in consequence of having . . . a library, exceed a hundred fold all that they [who might object to a library] have expended in its establishment, or may yet expend in its augmentation?"

   —John B. Wight, "A Lecture on Public Libraries" (1854); unpublished manuscript cited in *Foundations of the Public Library* (1949), p. 197.

10

44. "There are, of course, worse places to wait for someone than in a library."
    —Valerie Wolzien, *All Hallows Evil* (1992), p. 84.

45. "[The library provides] nourishment for the soul."
    —Inscription on the Berlin State Library derived from an inscription on the library at Alexandria; cited in *The Book Lover's Enchiridion* (1888), p. 1.

46. "[The library is] a safe asylum for hands and brains that might, through forced idleness and discouragement, be led to harm."
    —*Annual Report of the Brookline* (Mass.) *Public Library* (1878); cited in *Library Journal*, May 1878, p. 122.

47. "The big public library is for all, and to meet all requirements it must contain many books, not only more than any one human being of the most omnivorous taste would care to read in a lifetime, but more than any one except a librarian and a catalogue would care to know even by their titles."
    —Editorial, *New York Times*, October 18, 1911, p. 10.

48. "The library is inside."
    —Said to have been uttered at the dedication of the Sterling Library at Yale University in the 1930s.

49. "In a liberry it's hard to avoid reading."
    —Anonymous student, in *New York Times*, July 23, 1976, p. A21.

50. "The public house is the ante-room of the gaol, while the library is the doorway of the knowledge which is power. . . . The public house is the high road to perdition; the library the wicket of truth."
    —"The Rivals: The Public House and the Free Library," in *Middlesex Courier* (ca. 1891).

SOURCE: Norman D. Stevens, *Roses & Thorns* (Storrs, Conn.: Molesworth Institute, 1999).

Famous librarians' favorite books

WHAT DO PROMINENT LIBRARIANS have to say about their favorite books? In previous editions of *The Whole Library Handbook*, library leaders have identified the publications that have given them great enjoyment or have significantly affected their professional or personal lives and philosophies. This edition adds the fond favorites of 10 new individuals to the reading list. I defined the term "book" as loosely as possible, to allow them to select anything from incunabula to websites.—*GME.*

CAMILA A. ALIRE, Dean of Library Services, University of New Mexico, Albuquerque.
   1. Rudolfo A. Anaya, *Bless Me, Ultima* (1972). Considered a classic in Chicano

literature, this novel renewed in me a sense of ethnic and cultural pride that continues to this day.

2. John Grisham, *A Time to Kill* (1989). Everyone should read this novel. It is full of moral dilemmas for any reader to suffer through in terms of "what would I do in this situation?"

3. Amy Tan, *The Joy Luck Club* (1989). Anytime I can learn more about a culture, even superficially through a novel, I am appreciative. The story was timely for me because it was most helpful in my understanding and working with Chinese-American women.

4. Mary Doria Russell, *The Sparrow* (1996). Different than anything I had ever read, this story takes place in space. It is a story that constantly questions one's morals and ethics and that left an impression on me. I am amazed that more people I know have not read it.

5. Theodore Dreiser, *An American Tragedy* (1925). The first adult novel I read, this story taught me that the end does not justify the means—the inconvenience of one's predicament in life does not justify the taking of another life.

DEBORAH L. JACOBS, City Librarian, Seattle (Wash.) Public Library.

1. Charles Dickens, frankly any title, but will choose *Great Expectations* (1861). Every winter I reread one Dickens because his stories and characters draw me deeply inside. I choose *GE* however, because everyone "gets" the reference to Miss Havisham!

2. John Irving, *A Prayer for Owen Meany* (1989). Like Dickens, Irving draws me into his world, and no world is richer than that of Owen Meany. Another book I read again and again.

3. David James Duncan, *The Brothers K* (1992). Among the most powerful family sagas; taking place at a time I remember, in a location I love. And again, baseball!

4. Doris Kearns Goodwin, *Wait Till Next Year* (1997). Baseball, New York, what's not to love. Also—a book about community and a book about a time that will never exist again!

5. Sydney Taylor, *All-of-a-Kind Family* (1951). As a child, I read the series again and again . . . finally a story about me, a rambunctious Jewish girl!

6. Jonathan Raban, *Hunting Mister Heartbreak: A Discovery of America* (1991). I read this right after meeting Raban and found it spot-on and funny to boot!

7. John Le Carré, *Tinker, Tailor, Soldier, Spy* (1974). God, why didn't George Smiley pick me! I am terribly in love with him and with almost everything Le Carré writes.

8. Hergé, the *Tintin* books (1930–1974). I will always love Tintin, Snowy, and the gang because so many hundreds of happy hours were spent reading and rereading them to my son, even after he learned to read (first book he read: *Tintin* in a carwash) by himself.

LARRY HARDESTY, Library Director, University of Nebraska at Kearney.

1. Patricia B. Knapp, *The Monteith College Library Experiment* (1966). I read this book after my first year as a librarian. I remember reading it into the wee hours of the night because I could not put it down. I kept thinking, "Here is someone who understands why students do not use the library more." It should be a must read for all academic librarians.

10

2. Harvie Branscomb, *Teaching with Books: A Study of College Libraries* (1940). This is another timeless library classic that is a must read for all academic librarians. I first read it more than 30 years ago. I remember discussing it with Lewis Kaplan, who had been the library director at the University of Wisconsin at Madison Library and was then teaching at its library school. He recalled when it first was published and reading it with disbelief as to how little students used the library. I believe that many of the conclusions reached by Branscomb are still valid today.

3. Landon Y. Jones, *Great Expectations: America and the Baby Boom Generation* (1980). I first read this book 25 years ago. The author was the first to impress on me the impact the Baby Boom generation would have as it continues to age.

4. Eric Hoffer, *The Ordeal of Change* (1963). This book harkens back to my undergraduate days. In simple words and profound logic, this longshoreman turned philosopher impressed on me the resistance we often have to even the simplest of changes.

5. Jim Hightower, *Thieves in High Places: They've Stolen our Country—and It's Time to Take it Back* (2003). Hightower has become one of my favorite authors in recent years. This Texas good-old-boy recognizes that we live in dangerous and troubling times with the erosion of basic freedoms and the increased concentration in the country of power and resources in the hands of fewer and fewer.

6. Frederick Lewis Allen, *Only Yesterday: An Informal History of the Nineteen-Twenties* (1931). I first discovered this book as an undergraduate history major and realized just how much fun history could be and how much was left out of the standard textbooks. While cultural and social history is accepted today, I think Allen was well ahead of his time in writing about how ordinary folks experienced events of the time.

LEONARD KNIFFEL, Editor and Publisher of *American Libraries* and author of *A Polish Son in the Motherland: An American's Journey Home* (Texas A&M University, 2005).

1. The Bible. N.T. (A.D. 50–150). As a Catholic child, I was never encouraged to actually read the Bible, certainly not the Old Testament with all its risqué content. Still, hearing the New Testament read and interpreted in church every Sunday for about 20 years had a profound effect.

2. Laura Ingalls Wilder, the Little House series (1932–1943). In the 3rd grade, these books and a wise teacher who read them to our class taught me that reading could be a joy. I remember my sadness when Wilder died in 1957.

3. Nathaniel Hawthorne, *The Scarlet Letter* (1850). I learned in high school that not all the "classics" were boring.

4. D. H. Lawrence, *Lady Chatterley's Lover* (1928). Though there is no agreement that this is Lawrence's best work, it made an English major out of me.

5. Anaïs Nin, *The Diary of Anaïs Nin* (7 vols., 1966–1980). These were the right books at the right time for me. Never had I read anything so passionate and personal.

6. Philip Larkin, *The Whitsun Weddings* (1964). Although the Beat poets really got me started on poetry, Larkin made me understand how beautiful contemporary language could be, as exemplified in a deceptively simple poem called "Home Is So Sad." And he was a librarian!

7. Czeslaw Milosz, *The Issa Valley* (1981). This Polish author's work and the

poetry of Wislawa Szymborska really inspired my search for my own ethnic background.

8. Jeffrey Eugenides, *Middlesex* (2002). This book answers the question, "So what have you read lately?" It's about immigration, my hometown of Detroit, and sexual identity. What more can you ask for in a book?

NANCY PEARL, former Director of Youth Services and Washington Center for the Book, Seattle (Wash.) Public Library, from an interview in *American Libraries*, May 2005.

1. Guy Gavriel Kay, *The Last Light of the Sun* (2004) and *Sailing to Sarantium* (1998). I have gotten back into reading fantasy and science fiction, so I am totally engrossed in reading Kay.

2. Dan Simmons, *The Crook Factory* (1999).

3. Sue Miller, *Lost in the Forest* (2005).

4. Meg Wolitzer, *The Position* (2005).

5. I loved Stacy Schiff, *A Great Improvisation: Franklin, France, and the Birth of America* (2005), about Benjamin Franklin's time in Paris.

6. David Thomson, *The Whole Equation: A History of Hollywood* (2005).

7. Children's fantasies like Eva Ibbotson, *Island of the Aunts* (2000).

8. Lauren Willig, *The Secret History of the Pink Carnation* (2005).

9. Adam Hochschild, *Bury the Chains: Prophets and Rebels in the Fight to Free an Empire's Slaves* (2005). As you can see, I am not only an addicted reader, I am also promiscuous—I'll read anything as long as it has interesting characters and good writing.

KAREN G. SCHNEIDER, Librarian's Index to the Internet.

1. Daniel Defoe, *Robinson Crusoe* (1719), a book I have been enjoying for over four decades. Dear Crusoe, slogging it out by himself, carefully reinventing the universe, and so pleased to find a friend!

2. Vladimir Nabokov, *Speak, Memory: An Autobiography Revisited* (1967), the loveliest, most erudite memoir-of-ideas, which traveled with me for 25 years so that I could again sit in a classroom discussing it, an experience which made my eyes sting with tears afterward. This is one of those books I truly love, love, love, really love, with that heart-thumping ardor of a true biblioholic.

3. Jane Austen, *Persuasion* (1818), is my favorite of all the Austen novels, with its nautical flavor and its mature, forward glance. It's less snarky than the others—though Austen is queen of the elegant, understated snark, a skill lost on most modern writers—and has a gentle quality, yet it is filled with the lively parlor politics and sexual issues of all of her writing.

4. Charlotte Brontë, *Jane Eyre* (1847), is anything but gentle, with its stormy, formal language, its slap-your-face symbolism, and its high drama. Sometimes when I cannot sleep but cannot quite stay awake I open *Jane Eyre* to any page, dreamlike book that it is, and segue to rest.

5. Emily Brontë, *Wuthering Heights* (1847), is all sound and fury signifying everything, but for true aficionados, I recommend Anne Brontë, *The Tenant of Wildfell Hall* (1848). Anne was not as great a writer as her sisters, but a lesser Brontë is nothing to sneeze at. Stick me on an island somewhere and forget about me forever, but leave me Austen and the Brontës.

6. *The Snow Queen, and Other Tales* (1961), a tattered book of Russian fairy

10

tales absent from my life for two decades before I realized my sister had it. It's an edition with extraordinary illustrations, Russian-style, by Adrienne Ségur for Golden Press, and the best stories, including "Winter's Promised Bride," "The Snow Queen," "The Nutcracker."

7. Then there are the books I haven't read through in 25 years, but love to quote and rummage among: James Boswell, *The Life of Samuel Johnson* (1791); Boswell's travel diaries; Shakespeare. I thought I would never reread any plays by Shakespeare, much as I wanted to, until last fall when while writing an essay I got a craving to quote from *The Tempest* (1611), and found myself reading the play end-to-end as easily as if it were a newspaper, something I could not do when I first studied these plays. Why was Shakespeare so hard to read in college? Was it because we were overreading the texts and I was trying too hard, or is it because Shakespeare is easier to read when you're older?

8. Would it be so terrible to list A. A. Milne's *Winnie-the-Pooh* (1921), or E. B. White's *Charlotte's Web* (1952), dear old tattered friends of my childhood, still on my shelves? What if I included Robert Heinlein and Isaac Asimov, who fueled my tween-age reveries, strapping me into galaxy-bound rockets that lifted me away from my fat, pimply misery?

R. N. SHARMA, Director of Libraries, West Virginia State University.

1. Anita Schiller (photography) and Susan Noyes Anderson (poems), *His Children* (2003). This book changed the way I view the world.

2. John Kenneth Galbraith, *Ambassador's Journal: A Personal Account of the Kennedy Years* (1969), inspired me to work harder in life.

3. Jawaharlal Nehru, *The Discovery of India* (1947), introduced me to the panorama of India's past and provided accounts of how a great nation can become weak and helpless.

4. Vladimir Zaitsev, Yelena Barkhatova, Liudmila Buchina, and others, *The National Library of Russia, 1795–1995* (1995), introduced me to the magnificent treasure of books in one of the largest libraries in the world.

5. Mohandas K. Gandhi, *An Autobiography: The Story of My Experiments with Truth* (1957), gave me mental peace to know that the truth always prevails.

6. Salman H. Abu-Sitta, *The Atlas of Palestine, 1948: A Most Comprehensive Record of the Mandate and al Nakba* (2004), enhanced my knowledge of the history and landscape of Palestine through the beautiful maps and historical accounts included in the atlas.

7. Russell A. Mittermeier and Cristina Goettsch Mittermeier, *Megadiversity* (1997), enriched my knowledge about the greatest biological wealth of the nations on the earth.

ANN SPARANESE, Head of Adult and Young Adult Services, Englewood (N.J.) Public Library.

1. Dee Brown, *Bury My Heart at Wounded Knee: An Indian History of the American West* (1970). Native American history they don't teach you in school, but it is, in my mind, essential stuff to understanding our national character. An unstoppable, unforgettable, almost unbearable read.

2. Anne Frank, *The Diary of a Young Girl* (1952) had a enormous impact on me when I read it as a preteen in the late fifties. Because Anne was such an inspired writer and enormously courageous human being, her self-absorption—my state at the time—was transformed into a sublime expression of the human spirit.

3. Zora Neale Hurston, *Their Eyes Were Watching God* (1937). After having two babies in succession, I was beat, and had pretty much given up serious reading in 1982. A woman's bookstore owner in my town handed me this novel, a stunner that brought me back to the reading life. How had I survived without it? I've read this one five times at least.

4. Lee Lockwood, *Castro's Cuba, Cuba's Fidel* (1967). A serendipitous acquisition from my college bookstore, this exciting book of photos and text by an American journalist sparked an interest that became lifelong, took me many times to the island, and has embroiled me in endless controversy.

5. Alice Walker, *Meridian* (1976). My favorite of Alice Walker's novels, it is a story of the civil rights movement and a young woman's personal growth in it. Like Malcolm X's *Autobiography,* which is also a favorite, I love how it describes growth and change in human beings, as they engage in the struggle for a better world.

JESSAMYN WEST, librarian.net.

1. Richard Powers, *The Gold Bug Variations* (1991). How can we use our research to show our love, or discover the love of others? A smart librarian drinks wine with geniuses and learns to uncover the language of music. I wanted to be that librarian.

2. Richard Brautigan, *The Abortion: An Historical Romance, 1966* (1971). The book that made me want to be a librarian, albeit in an impossible future where I could live in the library I worked in, and perhaps never leave.

3. Bryan A. Garner, ed., A *Dictionary of Modern American Usage* (1998). My mother used to embarrass me in front of my friends by telling people I read the dictionary for fun. Now I read this metadictionary for fun, and also to remind me that the descriptive can often overrule the prescriptive, in grammar and elsewhere.

4. Ftrain.com. A website that sets the bar high for moving others with the power of words, and tells funny stories about cats. My father used to tell me that he never wanted to see Emmylou Harris in concert for fear that he would run away [with her?] and never come back. I have similar feelings about Paul Ford.

5. *Co-op Currents,* the newsletter of the Washington Electric Cooperative in East Montpelier, Vt., reminds me that people everywhere want to make the world a better place and that our most basic choices don't come without some political baggage.

6. Margaret Wise Brown, *The Little Fur Family* (1946), embodied comfort and security in just a few short pages and taught me to love books before I could read.

7. *Dr. Seuss's ABC* (1963) helped me, at a very young age, dream of a world beyond Z.

BLANCHE WOOLLS, Professor Emeritus, San Jose State University School of Library and Information Science.

1. My early grade-school reader had a story about children visiting a farm and eating cooked carrots; I have eaten cooked carrots ever since.

2. William Pène Du Bois, *The Twenty-One Balloons* (1947), with a drawing illustrating a bed with automatic sheets being scrolled through washing cycles, was an appealing solution to perceived drudgery especially in my teenage years.

10

3. Reading my students' doctoral dissertations meant they were ready to graduate.

4. Mystery stories, from Nancy Drew to Rex Stout, Sue Grafton, and Josephine Tey, take you away from the world's problems for a breather on airplanes and just before turning out the light at night.

Academic and research librarians in detective fiction

MURDER IN THE UNIVERSITY LIBRARY holds a certain peculiar fascination for readers. Here are a few titles to get you started.—*GME.*

Catherine Aird, *Parting Breath.* London: Collins, 1977. Librarian Peter Pringle is one of the victims in a series of murders following a sit-in at the University of Calleshire in England.

David Beasley, *The Jenny: A New York Library Detective Novel.* Buffalo, N.Y.: Davus, 1994. Based on a true incident, the plot involves the theft of the misprinted 1918 airmail stamp known as the "inverted Jenny." New York Public Library security detective Rudyard Mack solves the case with the help of library union leader Arbuthnott Vine.

Gwen Bristow and Bruce Manning, *The Gutenberg Murders.* New York: Mystery League, 1931. Nine leaves from a Gutenberg bible have been stolen from the rare books collection of the private Sheldon Memorial Library in New Orleans. The chief suspect, assistant librarian Quentin Ulman, turns up dead. Head librarian Dr. Prentiss—"a scholar of pictures and legends, tall and slender, with a droop to his shoulders that suggested much bending over a desk, and long delicate hands that seemed made for caressing the crumbly pages of old books"—may not be the quiet bibliophile he seems.

Elisabeth Carey and Marion Magoon, *I Smell the Devil.* New York: Farrar and Rinehart, 1943. Cowabet College rare books librarian Miss Christopherson is stabbed in the back, and the mystery seems to revolve around a rare set of St. Cyprian's sermons. The library allegedly bears some resemblance to the Hatcher Graduate Library at the University of Michigan.

Terrie Curran, *All Booked Up.* New York: Dodd, Mead, 1987. After an English professor discovers that a 15th-century edition of Ranulf Higden's *Polychronicon* printed by Wynkyn de Worde is missing from the privately funded Smedley Library in New England, director Giles Moraise is murdered.

Umberto Eco, *The Name of the Rose.* New York: Harcourt, 1983. In 1327, Brother William of Baskerville investigates heresy and murder in the labyrinthine library of an Italian abbey.

Dorsey Fiske, *Academic Murder.* New York: St. Martin's, 1980. Ernest Garmoyle, the head of the Prye Library at Cambridge's Sheepshanks College, dies after drinking arsenic-laced port, and soon afterwards a recently discovered holograph copy of Shakespeare's poem "Cupid and Psyche" disappears.

Robert Foster, *Murder Goes to College.* Elgin, Ill.: Tenth Muse, 1998. Retired librarians Bernardine and Blanche Badger help out their English professor nephew, John Badger Smith, solve a series of thefts and murders at Carlton-Stokes College in Walton, Missouri.

Charles A. Goodrum, *Dewey Decimated.* New York: Crown, 1977. After accusations of a forged Gutenberg bible surface at Washington's Werner-Bok Library, retired librarian Edward George helps piece together a tale of theft, fraud, and murder. Other Werner-Bok whodunits are *Carnage of the Realm* (1979) and *A Slip of the Tong* (1992). *The Best Cellar* (1987) centers around the disappearance of the original collection of the Library of Congress in 1814. Goodrum was assistant director of the Congressional Research Service in the 1970s.

Will Harris, *The Bay Psalm Book Murder.* New York: Walker, 1983. Link Schofield, curator of special collections at Los Angeles University, is stabbed to death in his garage, but the murderer has left the scene with the murdered man still clutching the library's first edition of the *Bay Psalm Book* in his hand. The plot revolves around the book's provenance.

Marion B. Havighurst, *Murder in the Stacks.* Boston: Lothrop, Lee, and Shepard, 1934. Donald Crawford, the reclusive assistant librarian at Kingsley University, is found dead. Two other library staff are among the suspects, Bertha Chase and head librarian Mark Denman, and the center of the mystery is an essay by Charles Lamb.

Vernon Hinkle, *Music to Murder By.* New York: Belmont, 1978. The librarian sleuth was modeled on Harvard's Isham Memorial Library music librarian Larry Mowers.

M. R. Hodgkin, *Student Body.* New York: Scribner's, 1949. Most of the staff of the Carodac College library are suspects in the murder of three undergraduates.

Hugh Holman, *Up This Crooked Way.* New York: Mills, 1946. Young librarian Jackie Dean of Abecton College in South Carolina is one of the suspects in the murder of unpleasant landlord Walter Perkins.

Hazel Holt, *The Cruellest Month.* New York: St. Martin's, 1991. Irascible part-time librarian Gwen Richmond is killed by a falling *Encyclopedia Britannica* in the New Bodleian Library at Oxford, but British literary critic Sheila Malory suspects foul play.

W. Bolingbroke Johnson [pseud. of Morris Bishop], *The Widening Stain.* New York: Knopf, 1942. Library patrons are dying at the Cornell University-like Wildmerding Library, and chief cataloger Gilda Gorham decides to investigate.

Allen Kurzweil, *The Grand Complication.* New York: Hyperion, 2001. Bibliophile Henry James Jesson III hires New York Public Library reference librarian Alexander Short to identify the missing object in an 18th-century cabinet of curiosities. Involved in the intrigue is George Speaight, the curator of the erotica-oriented Center for Material Culture, whose nickname is the "Librarian of Sexual Congress."

Ross MacDonald, *The Chill.* New York: Knopf, 1963. Dolly Kincaid, a student and part-time library worker at Pacific Point College in California, disappears on her honeymoon, and her husband hires detective Lew Archer to find out what happened.

Peter Malloch, *Murder of a Student.* London: Long, 1968. A female librarian and a student are murdered by a demented history student at a provincial British university.

D. B. Olsen [pseud.of Dolores Hitchens], *Enrollment Cancelled.* Garden City, N.Y.: Doubleday, 1954. Two female undergrads at Clarendon College in southern California are murdered, both of them known to straitlaced thirty-something librarian Miss Pettit.

10

Bernard Peterson, *The Caravaggio Books.* New York: HarperCollins, 1992. Two faculty members of Kingsford (N.J.) University are murdered in the library, and police discover that the solution centers on three books about the 16th-century artist Caravaggio.

Stella Phillips, *The Hidden Wrath.* London: Hale, 1962. Four public librarians volunteer some free time cataloging books at Braseley Adult College in rural England. One of them, June Grant, is killed in a suspicious swimming-pool accident after she lets the others know she's hip to their secrets.

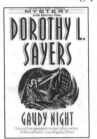

Dorothy L. Sayers, *Gaudy Night.* London: Gollancz, 1935. Unusual happenings at Shrewsbury College, Oxford University, include missing manuscript proofs from the library tended by Miss Burrows, who complains, "The trouble is, that everybody sneers at restrictions and demands freedom, till something annoying happens; then they demand angrily what has become of the discipline."

Veronica Stallwood, *Oxford Exit.* London: Macmillan, 1994. Former Bodleian cataloger Kate Ivory travels to several U.S. and British libraries in an attempt to solve both the murder of a library conservationist trainee and systematic book thefts from Oxford University. Oxford's Leicester College librarian, Kevin Newton, is singularly uncooperative.

Margaret Truman, *Murder at the Library of Congress.* New York: Random House, 1999. The murder of a Hispanic scholar in a carrel at the Library of Congress seems to involve the existence of an unknown second diary of Columbus's voyages written by Bartholomé de las Casas. Librarian Cale Broadhurst has to deal with the situation.

Jill Paton Walsh, *The Wyndham Case.* New York: St. Martin's, 1993. This tale of a two-story bookcase in the Wyndham Library at St. Agatha's College in Cambridge involves an attempted theft, a bizarre codicil to a 17th-century endowment, and a feud between the Wyndham special collections curator and the college librarian.

Percy D. Westbrook, *Infra Blood.* New York: Phoenix, 1950. Rare book librarian Miss Sauerman is killed in the same spot in the Banks College, Maine, stacks as a Shakespearean scholar. Library director Dr. Hoffman-Walter is a suspect, and the college's professor of criminal psychology tries to trap the culprit in the stacks after hours.

SOURCES: John E. Kramer, *Academe in Mystery and Detective Fiction* (Lanham, Md.: Scarecrow, 2000); Grant Burns, *Librarians in Fiction* (Jefferson, N.C.: McFarland, 1998); Bibliomysteries, www.bibliomysteries.com; Candy Schwartz, Simmons GSLIS Bibliomystery, web.simmons.edu/~schwartz/bibmyst-w.html.

Odd book titles

IN 1998 RUSSELL ASH AND BRIAN LAKE published a second edition of their book-length collection of odd titles. Here are some of their most unusual, plus a bunch from my own collection.—*GME.*

Ronald A. Beck and Fred Beck, *I Fought the Apemen of Mt. St. Helens* (n.p.: The authors, 1967).

Evelyn Cheesman, *Six-Legged Snakes in New Guinea* (London: George G. Harrap, 1949).

Hans Cory, *Wall-Paintings by Snake Charmers in Tanganyika* (London: Faber and Faber, 1953).

Theata Iona Crowe, *How to Cook a Bigfoot* (Hillsboro, Oreg.: Western Bigfoot Society, 2000).

HOW TO COOK
A BIGFOOT

BY THEATA IONA CROWE

Charles V. A. Eley, *How to Save a Big Ship from Sinking Even Though Torpedoed* (London: Simpkin, Marshall, Hamilton, Kent, 1915).

Tim F. Flannery, *Throwim Way Leg: Tree-Kangaroos, Possums and Penis Gourds* (New York: Grove, 1998).

Marion C. Fox, *The Supernatural History of Worms* (London: Friends' Book Centre, 1931).

R. Ruggles Gates and P. N. Bhaduri, *The Inheritance of Hairy Ear Rims* (Edinburgh: Mankind Quarterly, 1961).

E. Haldeman-Julius et al., *The Serious Lesson in President Harding's Case of Gonorrhea* (Girard, Kans.: Haldeman-Julius, 1930).

Marion Hall, *Let's Make Some Undies* (n.p.: W. Foulsham, 1954).

William Hyde, *I Smote Him on the Boko with My Whangee* [sheet music], n.d.

Alfred Bray Kempe, *How to Draw a Straight Line* (London: Macmillan, 1877).

Holger Kersten, *Jesus Lived in India: His Unknown Life before and after the Crucifixion* (Shaftesbury, Eng.: Element, 1986).

Alan T. Kitley, *The Big Problem of Small Organs* (Colchester: The author, 1966).

Björn Kurtén, *How to Deep-Freeze a Mammoth* (New York: Columbia University, 1986).

Tony Lesce, *Escape from Controlled Custody* (Port Townsend, Wash.: Loompanics, 1990).

Malaclypse the Younger, *Principia Discordia, or, How I Found Goddess and What I Did to Her When I Found Her* (Mason, Mich.: Loompanics, 1980).

John Charles Melliss, *The Sewage Question Solved* (London: E. Wilson, 1875).

James W. Moseley and Karl T. Pflock, *Shockingly Close to the Truth! Confessions of a Grave-Robbing Ufologist* (Amherst, N.Y.: Prometheus, 2002).

Burgo Partridge, *A History of Orgies* (London: A. Blond, 1958).

George R. Pisani, ed., *Herpervertlogical Review* (Lawrence, Kans.: Society for the Study of Amphibians and Reptiles, 1977).

Kevin Pope, *The Day Gravity Was Turned Off in Topeka* (New York: St. Martin's, 1985).

MOVIE STARS
IN
BATHTUBS

Compiled by
Jack Scagnetti

Gustaaf Johannes Renier, *The English: Are They Human?* (London: Williams and Norgate, 1931).

D. Scott Rogo and Raymond Bayless, *Phone Calls from the Dead* (Englewood Cliffs, N.J.: Prentice-Hall, 1979).

Jack Scagnetti, *Movie Stars in Bathtubs* (Middle Village, N.Y.: Jonathan David, 1975).

Phyllis Siefker, *Santa Claus: Last of the Wild Men* (Jefferson, N.C.: McFarland, 1997).

Margaret Stearn, *Embarrassing Medical Problems* (New York: Hatherleigh, 1998).

Mrs. Alec Tweedie, *Through Finland in Carts* (London: A. & C. Black, 1897).

Douglas B. Vogt, *Gravitational Mystery Spots of the United States: Explained Using the Tof Multidimensional Reality* (Bellevue, Wash.: Vector Associates, 1996).

H. E. White, *Music in the Typewriting Room* (London: Sir Isaac Pitman, 1947).

SOURCE: Russell Ash and Brian Lake, *Bizarre Books* (London: Pavilion, 1998).

10

Fun facts about the OCLC Top 1000

by OCLC Research

OCLC RESEARCH COMPILED A LIST in 2005 of the top 1,000 titles owned by member libraries—the intellectual works that have been judged to be worth owning by the "purchase vote" of libraries around the globe (www.oclc.org/research/top1000/default.htm). The OCLC staff has extracted the following factoids for your amusement.—*GME.*

How many works by Shakespeare made the list? 37.

How many works by Stephen King made the Top 1000 list? Zero, to our surprise. *Gunslinger* ranked 1080, though.

Which author has the most works on the OCLC Top 1000 list? William Shakespeare (with 37 works). He is followed by Charles Dickens (16 works) and John Grisham (13 works).

How many different authors are on the OCLC Top 1000 list? 576 authors made the list, not counting the anonymous ones.

How many of the OCLC Top 1000 works are anonymous? 59 works are anonymous or do not have a single author. (In library parlance, there are 59 "title main entry" works.)

What work on the Top 1000 list has the richest publication history, i.e., the most manifestations, as represented by OCLC libraries' holdings? The *Bible*, followed by the *Haggadah*. *Divine Comedy* was third, and the *Koran* fourth.

If all the Harry Potter books were bundled together, how would they have stacked up? We didn't bundle them together, but if we had, these books would have ranked fifth on the Top 1000 list (and first on the Top Fiction list, second on the Top Children's list). Considered together, 44,976 Harry Potter items are held by libraries and they are represented by 496 different bibliographic records.

Which author on the list is most held by OCLC libraries? William Shakespeare, followed by the United States government, Charles Dickens, Mark Twain, and Giuseppe Verdi.

How far down the OCLC Top 1000 list do you have to go to get to a live author? Jim Davis's *Garfield* is number 15 on the list. (Four of the five top works by living authors are cartoons!) And in case you're wondering, Harper Lee's *To Kill A Mockingbird* is the highest-ranking work by a living *female* author. It ranked 146.

What is the highest-ranking work written by a woman? *Wuthering Heights* by Emily Brontë ranks 28 on the list. *Jane Eyre* by Charlotte Brontë is ranked 30. Jane Austen's *Pride and Prejudice* ranks 32.

Who is the most written-about person in WorldCat? Jesus Christ.

What's the top mystery novel held by libraries? *The Adventures of Sherlock Holmes*. It ranks 192.

You've acknowledged that the Top 1000 list has a United States slant. How many U.S. presidents authored works on the list? John F. Kennedy (for *Profiles in Courage*), George Washington (for his *Farewell Address*), and Ulysses S. Grant (*Personal Memoirs*). James Madison, who along with Alexander Hamilton and John Jay coauthored *The Federalist Papers* under the pen name Publius, also made the list, though anonymously. (Madison and Hamilton also drafted Washington's *Farewell Address*.) Abraham Lincoln is not on the list.

How does the U.S. constitution rank? 237.

Kissin' don't last, cookin' do. *The Joy of Cooking* ranked 269 on the OCLC Top 1000 list. *Joy of Sex* did not make the Top 1000 list, or come anywhere close.

Fighting like cats and dogs. Garfield is number 15 on the list. Snoopy is 69.

How about animals generally? Garfield is the top-ranking animal overall. Moby Dick, at 34, was the second-highest ranking animal. Neither Lassie nor Bambi made the OCLC Top 1000 list. (*The Yearling*, though, ranked 281.)

What is the top-ranking bird? Does Mother Goose count? She was third on our list.

What about plants? *Leaves of Grass* ranked 49.

What's the top fruit? The top vegetable? The top mineral? It's *your* turn to look.

Who is the top monster? Dr. Frankenstein's monster. Ranking 43, he beat both Count Dracula (75) and Edward Hyde (*Dr. Jekyll and Mr. Hyde* ranked 141). The vampire Lestat ranked 927, but Shrek failed to make the list.

It was a dark and stormy night. The work *Paul Clifford*, by Edward George Bulwer-Lytton, did *not* make the list.

What cartoons made it to OCLC's Top 1000 list?
   Garfield, by Jim Davis (ranked 15).
   Peanuts, by Charles Schulz (ranked 69).
   Calvin and Hobbes, by Bill Watterson (ranked 77).
   Doonesbury, by Garry Trudeau (ranked 88).
   Far Side, by Gary Larson (ranked 115).
   Dilbert, by Scott Adams (ranked 399).
   Fox Trot, by Bill Amend (ranked 773).

What was the 1001st item? *Ecclesiastical History*, by Eusebius of Caesarea.

SOURCE: Fun Facts about the OCLC Top 1000, www.oclc.org/research/top1000/factoids.htm. Reprinted with permission of OCLC Online Computer Library Center, Inc.

MEDIA

Libraries and librarians in film, 1999–2005

by Martin Raish, Antoinette Graham, and George M. Eberhart

THESE FILMS WERE RELEASED after the publication of *The Whole Library Handbook 3*, which offered a comprehensive list through 1998.—*GME.*

Abandon (2002). Melanie Lynskey is Mousy Julie the librarian and Joan McBride is a library assistant at an academic institution (filmed at McGill University) where student Katie Burke (Katie Holmes) is stalked in the stacks. Robert Burns plays an archivist.

After Twilight (2005). Bookish Christine M. Auten as Jen Frazier becomes a freedom fighter against a theocratic regime that occupies the state of Texas,

10

and she carries a mysterious package to the underground resistance. In so doing, she makes the ultimate sacrifice, and the contents of the mysterious package are revealed to the audience. Saying any more, including which character is the librarian, would spoil your viewing of the film.

Age to Age (1999). Dot Braun plays a librarian in this independent science-fiction adventure set in North Carolina.

All the Queen's Men [Die Männer Ihrer Majestät] (2001, German/Austrian/US). Nicolette Krebitz as Romy is a sexy librarian and underground resistance fighter in Nazi Germany who operates a safe house in the library's attic. When four Allied soldiers parachute behind the lines and show up dressed in drag, they mistakenly contact the male assistant librarian (played by Heinrich Herki), who calls the Gestapo. Romy uses book titles to warn the good guys that they are in danger and show them an escape route.

Angel's Dance (1999). Caroline Alexander plays a worker at a library where Sheryl Lee as Angelica Chaste finds books on refrigerator repair and assassin avoidance.

Autumn in New York (2000). An older man (Richard Gere) follows a young woman (Winona Ryder) into what appears to be a museum, going upstairs past the library. The librarian (played by Delores Mitchell) asks if she can help him. He wants to know the name of the young woman. The librarian says, "I'll tell her you're here," to which the man says no and the scene ends.

Battlefield Earth (2000). Set in the year 3000, this film includes two scenes of libraries in ruins. First is the Denver Public Library, where the hero reads the Declaration of Independence. The other is the Library of Congress, where he learns the secrets of radioactivity.

A Beautiful Mind (2001). Russell Crowe as Nobel Prize winner John Nash spends a lot of time at the Princeton University library and marks up the windows with formulas.

Because of Winn-Dixie (2005). Eva Marie Saint plays Miss Franny, a lonely spinster librarian who loves books and tells interesting stories, such as about the time she fended off a bear with a Tolstoy novel. She also hands out

MOST HORRIFIC MOVIE LIBRARY SETTING. In Lucio Fulci's *The Beyond* (*E tu vivrai nel terrore—L'aldilà*) (1981), Martin Avery (Michele Mirabella) is attacked by four or five tarantulas that pull the flesh off his face in the New Orleans "Town Hall" library, right after he falls off this library ladder.

bittersweet candy called Litmus Lozenges, invented by her grandfather when he returned home from the Civil War to find his family had been wiped out. One of the ingredients in the candy is sorrow.

Before Night Falls (2000). Javier Bardem as the Cuban writer Reynaldo Arenas goes to Havana and gets a job in the José Martí National Library.

Billy Elliot (2000, British/French). A young lad (Jamie Bell) in a mining town in northern England prefers ballet to boxing but he must practice in secret, since his family and friends would not understand. In one scene he visits the bookmobile but is told by the librarian (Carol McGuigan) that he cannot take out a book because it is in the adult section. So he steals the book when she is distracted.

Blade (1998). This tale of vampires includes a portrayal of an archivist named Pearl, who is so fat that it is difficult to know if she is male or female. She is referred to by the feminine pronoun, but the actor who portrays her is named Eric Edwards. In any case, she is in charge of the vampire culture's archives, all computerized. She announces that no one can possibly translate the old texts, except that the villain manages to do so.

Blood Work (2002). Clint Eastwood as retired FBI agent Terry McCaleb does a computer database search in the library and, with no visible assistance, retrieves two newspaper articles—precisely the ones he needs!

Bookies (2003). Johnny Galecki as student Jude works as a Kingston State College library assistant in order to run an illegal sports betting operation with two pals. Bets are placed and payments exchanged by placing them in certain library books: "We made sure to use books that had never been checked out in the history of the school. Philosophy, the unabridged works of Plato, or anything in a foreign language."

Buongiorno, Notte (2003, Italian). This film tells the story of the 1978 kidnapping and murder of Italian Prime Minister Aldo Moro (Roberto Herlitzka) from the perspective of one of the terrorists—a young woman named Chiara (played by Maya Sansa) who works in an academic library but is also a member of the Red Brigade. One scene shows her dealing with a male colleague who keeps asking her out for drinks.

The Caveman's Valentine (2001). Samuel L. Jackson as Romulus uses a microfilm reader to research newspaper articles about a photographer. He also converses with a hallucination of his wife at a younger age. She dissolves into a stout woman (Deborah Lobban) in a dark suit jacket with a bun high on her head who wakes him up and tells him that if he doesn't leave, she'll call the police. A card catalog and bookshelves are in the background.

Chichi to Kuraseba [The Face of Jizo] (2004, Japanese). This film explores the relationship between a young librarian, Rie Miyazawa as Mitsue, and a shy, bespectacled man, Tadanobu Asano as Kinoshita, who is using the library to research the bombing of Hiroshima. The first scene shows her rushing home in a thunderstorm, frightened out of her wits because she had barely survived the atomic bomb attack on the city not many years before.

Collateral (2004). Tom Cruise as hit-man Vincent stalks a victim (Jada Pinkett Smith as Annie) in a corporate law library late at night.

Compensation (1999). The film presents a pair of African-American love stories, each about a deaf woman and a hearing man. The story set in Chicago in the 1990s revolves around children's librarian Nico Jones, played by John Jelks. He is in his 30s, loves his work, and offers a poignant and positive model of a librarian. Nirvana Cobb plays a library assistant who reads a poem to children that is simultaneously translated by an interpreter into American Sign Language.

The Crimson Rivers [Les Rivières Pourpres] (2000, French). The first victim in this tale of two gruesome murders is a 32-year-old academic librarian whose mutilated body has been found high in the mountains. One scene shows the police investigators visiting the (mythical) Guernon University library, a beautiful old building in the French Alps that is cinematically made to appear sinister and evil.

The Day after Tomorrow (2004). After an ecodisaster, some teenagers take refuge in the New York Public Library, where they burn books to keep warm. They have a short debate about which ones to burn and decide to torch the "whole section of tax laws." A librarian (Tom Rooney) saves the Gutenberg Bible because, even though he does not believe in God, it symbolizes "mankind's greatest achievement"—the printed word. Another librarian (Sheila McCarthy) helps identify the condition of a girl who develops blood sepsis when she cuts her leg.

Dinotopia (2002, TV miniseries). After the airplane in which they are riding crashes, two boys find themselves on an island where humans and dinosaurs live together in peace. (They all speak English, too.) One of the main characters is a librarian named Zippo (voiced by Lee Evans). He is also a Stenonychosaurus—a small theropod dinosaur (now classed as Troodon).

Don't Look under the Bed (1999). In one scene in a library the 14-year-old heroine is talking to her invisible guide Larry Houdini (played by Eric "Ty" Hodges II) and a librarian shushes her several times. Later, the guide magically inhabits a film some children are watching, and their loud laughter drives the librarian frantic.

Double Jeopardy (1999). Daniel Lapaine as a handsome internet expert helps Ashley Judd as Libby Parsons do some web searches in a library.

Drop Dead Gorgeous (1999). Claudia Wilkens as Iona Hildebrandt reminisces about winning the Mount Rose, Minnesota, beauty pageant in 1945. She was the town librarian at the time.

Dungeons and Dragons (2000). In the mythical kingdom of Izmer, Zoe McLellan is Marina Pretensa, minor Mage and library worker. She has a bun and glasses and complains about shelving books until she gets caught up in an adventure involving dragons, dwarves, a rod, and a scepter. After she ties up two thieves in the library with a magic bracelet, one (Justin Whalin as Ridley) comments, "It must be the only way she can get guys to come home with her." But she counters with, "I'll have to put a feeble mind spell on myself to want to take you home."

Elephant (2003). A Columbine-like massacre takes place in a Portland, Oregon, school library. Kristen Hicks as Michelle works as a shy student library aide.

The Emperor's Club (2002). Molly Regan is the stern librarian Miss Peters at the St. Benedictus School for Boys who argues with a student (Emile Hirsch as Sedgewick Bell) over a book he wants to take to his dorm to study. She stands by policy until Bell's teacher imposes, and the librarian unhappily turns over the book.

Everything's Jake (2000). Debbie Allen plays a librarian, Stephen Furst an assistant librarian, and Andrew DiSimone a library onlooker.

An Extremely Goofy Movie (2000). Goofy Goof (voiced by Bill Farmer) loses his job and decides to go college to earn a degree. There he meets college librarian Sylvia Marpole (voiced by Bebe Neuwirth) stamping and shelving books, since she's apparently the only one working there. At first she is typically prim and proper—she wears glasses, shushes him, and says something about having respect for the Dewey decimal system—but she quickly sheds the stereotype and offers to help. They strike up a conversation and learn that they both like the 1970s and disco. Since it's a Goofy cartoon, there's the requisite scene with the bookcases toppling domino-style.

The Final Cut (2004). Mira Sorvino (right) as rare-book librarian Delila has an on-and-off fling with Robin Williams as Alan W. Hakman, a morose man whose job is to edit the memories recorded on mental microchips of the recently deceased. Alan asks Delila, "Is Suicide under Self-Help?"

Finding Forrester (2000). Sophia Wu is a librarian at the New York Public Library, where Rob Brown as Jamal Wallace and Sean Connery as William Forrester conduct some research.

Firestarter 2: Rekindled (2002, TV miniseries). Marguerite Moreau as pyrokinetic student Charlene "Charlie" McGee works part-time in the campus library and explains to Vincent Sforza as researcher Danny Nucci that he must search through a huge collection of declassified government documents by himself. There is a shortage of librarians to catalog them because students just aren't taking an interest in library science like they used to. With Star LaPoint and K. C. Clyde as student library users.

Follow the Stars Home (2001, made for TV). Blair Brown as Hannah Parker is a librarian who retires from her job to help care for her handicapped granddaughter. One scene takes place in the library and involves a younger librarian, played by Debra Orenstein.

The Girl Next Door (2004). At the end of this spunky loss-of-virginity film, we see a sex video being shot in a high school library. No librarians, simply a library (briefly) as setting. Entertaining but fluffy. You'll love it if you're an adolescent boy.

Harry Potter and the Chamber of Secrets (2002). Once again the library is the source of important information that helps solve the mysterious goings-on at Hogwarts. It is also where students quietly study amid wonderful leather-bound books with no computer in sight.

Harry Potter and the Sorcerer's Stone (2001). A scene takes place in the Hogwarts library (filmed in the Bodleian Library at Oxford University) where the students look up information on magic. The impression is that information can help solve problems and that the library is where you find information. Another scene is a nighttime visit to the "locked section" of the library, where dangerous books are kept.

Last Life in the Universe [Ruang rak noi nid mahasan] (2003, Korean). A young Japanese obsessive-compulsive assistant librarian (Tadanobu Asano as Kenji) at the Japan Culture Center in Bangkok is intent on committing suicide. Fate interrupts at every turn (hanging, shooting, smothering, a leap off a bridge, hara-kiri). His apartment looks like a library, with towering but neat piles of books and metal shelving. Even his shoes and clothes are neatly categorized and labeled. The clean

10

plates drying by the spotless kitchen sink are lined up in a row. He gets involved with a Thai woman (Sinitta Boonyasak as Noi) who is his polar opposite. They communicate through broken English. The running theme is lizards, as in the Japanese children's book he carries around (*The Last Lizard*, who even misses his enemies).

The League of Extraordinary Gentlemen (2003). There are two gorgeous libraries in this film, one in the secret wing of the British Museum where the Gentlemen meet, and the other the private library of Stuart Townsend as Dorian Gray. (There's also a grubby library that catches fire in Richard Roxburgh as M's "summer retreat," a snow-covered fortress.)

The Librarian: Quest for the Spear (2004, made for TV). Noah Wyle as Flynn Carsen is in his early 30s, loves books more than girls, is single, and lives with his mother. He also has 22 college degrees (but not an MLS), apparently having worked his way through the alphabet beginning with ancient languages, anthropology, archaeology, and astronomy, and ending with technology and zoology. Along the way he learned "Dewey Decimal and Library of Congress," how to do research and even how to create an RSS feed. Thus he is well qualified to become the Librarian at the Metropolitan Public Library. This is the most special of special libraries, since it houses not only miles of rare books but also artifacts such as the Ark of the Covenant, Pandora's Box, and Excalibur. Someone breaks through the elaborate security and steals a section of the spear that pierced the side of Christ. If the thief is able to join this to the other two sections, he will have power over life and death, so Carsen is charged to find the spear and return it to the library. He joins forces with Sonya Walger as Nicole, who also works for the library but does not describe herself as a librarian, and Bob Newhart as his boss Judson. Kyle MacLachlan plays former librarian Edward Wilde. At one point, Carsen and Judson are in a museum where they face a room full of bad guys. Carsen is about to express his doubts about how much help the much older man will be when Judson grabs a bad guy, smashes him into a giant stone sculpture, and knocks him out. Carsen says, "You're a bad mother." Judson replies, "I was a librarian, too, you know."

The Librarians (2004). This film has nothing to do with librarians. Rather, it is about a team of vigilantes ("Three Men and One Woman on the Wrong Side of the Law, Doing the Right Thing") who are called the Librarians "because they collect overdue people, just like a librarian collects overdue books."

The Lord of the Rings: The Fellowship of the Ring (2001). Needing to learn more about the Ruling Ring, Ian McKellen as Gandalf goes to a library in the city of Minas Tirith where, after poring through many ancient books and scrolls, he finds a passage that reveals how it can be identified, and how it can be destroyed. No librarian is shown, but in the book the Steward, Lord Denethor, calls himself the "master of lore" of the city. Gandalf smokes his pipe and sips from a goblet while examining manuscripts at least 1,000 years old. You'd think there would be more stringent rules! Michael Elsworth plays a Gondorian archivist.

Lovers and Leavers [Kuutamolla] (2002, Finnish). The film details the transformation of 30-year-old bookstore clerk Iiris Vaara (played by Minna Haapkyla) from a lonely girl waiting for her Prince Charming into a wiser, self-assured woman. One scene intended to demonstrate this positive growth shows her as a smiling librarian behind the reference desk.

Magnolia (1999). Young genius Jeremy Blackman as Stanley Spector is reading a stack of books by phenomenologist Charles Fort, anomalist William Corliss, freemason Albert Mackey, and magician Ricky Jay (who is the film's narrator) in a school library as it's raining frogs outside.

The Manchurian Candidate (2004). Denzel Washington as Captain Marco researches a politically powerful and corrupt international corporation at the New York Public Library. Using the internet, microfilm, and a lot of coins in the copy machine, he compiles damning evidence against the company.

The Matrix (1999). Marcus Chong as Tank sits in front of a group of some 16 computer monitors looking up documents and manuals that help the main characters save the world.

Men of Honor (2000). An ambitious black man (played by Cuba Gooding Jr.) needs tutoring to help him pass the navy's dive school tests, and turns to the resources of the public library in Harlem where he meets the woman who will later become his wife. It's refreshing to see a black librarian, a positive (albeit very brief) portrayal, circa 1950. Actress Demene Hall as librarian Mrs. Biddle is beautiful, and her bun is actually stylish (okay, the glasses are a bit much, but remember the times). Her character doesn't fuss when the two young people stay after hours. Mrs. Biddle directs him (with a twinkle in her eye) to her unmarried assistant Jo (played by Aunjanue Ellis), who is putting herself through medical school by working in the library. She helps him pass his exams with high scores and along the way they fall in love. Several scenes take place in the library. (They were filmed in Portland at Multnomah County Library's Title Wave Bookstore, a Carnegie building that was retrofitted to look like the library it once was.)

Miranda (2002). Frank, a lonely and somewhat nerdy librarian (played by John Simm) meets the beautiful and mysterious Miranda (Christina Ricci) when she walks into the "library" (actually a counter and a bookcart that is otherwise irrelevant as a setting). He immediately falls in love with her and they begin a passionate affair. Then she suddenly disappears. He follows her to London where he discovers that she has three identities—as a dancer, a dominatrix, and a conwoman.

The Mothman Prophecies (2002). One scene was filmed in the library at Carnegie Mellon University in Pittsburgh. The library is in an older building with some areas that exude a Gothic look and feel, with no signs of technology.

The Mummy (1999). Rachel Weisz plays Evelyn Carnahan, a young Egyptologist and librarian in Cairo in the 1920s who becomes involved in a dangerous, action-packed (and ultimately romantic) adventure to kill the mummy that has returned to take his revenge on the world. In an early scene she manages to topple all the ranges of books in the library ("Oops!"). Later, sitting around the campfire in the midst of ancient ruins, and after consuming a few drinks, she says, "I may not be an explorer or an adventurer or a treasure seeker or a gun fighter, but I am proud of what I am." "And what is that?" Rick (Brendan Fraser) asks. "I . . . I'm . . . I am a librarian!" she proclaims. In the beginning scene she needs her glasses to shelve books, but later she manages to read hieroglyphics without them. Weisz reprised her role in the sequel, *The Mummy Returns* (2001), but not as a librarian.

The Music Man (2003, made for TV). Kristin Chenoweth plays River City (Iowa) Public Librarian Marian Paroo. The Internet Movie Database lists

10

as a goof (although bibliographically speaking, it's not): "Marian mentions ordering the *Indiana State Journal of Education* for 1901–1910, but when the book arrives, it's clearly labeled 1890–1910."

National Treasure (2004). Two would-be thieves do some research in the Library of Congress, trying to find a way to break into the National Archives so they can steal a priceless historical document. Diane Kruger plays Abigail Chase, the U.S. Archivist who has a foreign accent.

Never Been Kissed (1999). Two girls talk in the school library about getting dates to the prom.

The New Guy (2002). DJ Qualls as Dizzy Harrison is that geeky new freshman, requisite icon of coming-of-age films, who must learn how to make himself cool. When he is expelled from school and briefly jailed, he learns from a con (Luther, played by Eddie Griffin) what it takes to be respected. Dizzy demonstrates his new-found bad-boy skills at another high school, and darn if they don't work. What made him want to change schools in the first place? Total humiliation: "Yesterday an 80-year-old librarian broke my penis!"

The Ninth Gate (1999). Johnny Depp as Dean Corso, rarebook dealer, tries to track down a demonic text titled *The Nine Gates of the Kingdom of the Shadows*, published in Venice in 1666 by Aristide Torchia. His search takes him to several libraries and archives. Corso remarks, "It's an impressive collection. You have some very rare editions here. Are you sure you want to sell them all?" Joe Sheridan as the Old Man's son replies, "They're of no use to father. Not anymore. Not since he's been this way. His library was his whole world. Now it's just a feeble memory."

Notre Musique (2004, French). Jean-Luc Godard depicts the ruined Bosnian National Library in Sarajevo, where Spanish novelist Juan Goytisolo recites poetry and residents throw books onto a pile on the floor as the librarian watches. One character comments, "Humane people don't start revolutions, they start libraries . . . and cemeteries."

Ophelia Learns to Swim (2000). Dian Kobayashi is the Librarian, a superheroine who is a fount of knowledge.

Osmosis Jones (2001). In one scene, Chris Rock as white blood cell Osmosis Jones and David Hyde Pierce as cold pill Drix are doing research in a library—the host's Brain Memory Bank—whose librarian tells them that "we're really all about sports statistics here."

The Photograph (2003). This low-budget Texas feature tells the story of a woman who is unhappy with her life and becomes obsessed with a famous movie star. She finds an ancient book that might help her but to use it she must face grave danger. Screenwriter James McDonald wanted to show scenes in an old library with a basement and underground tunnels, but he could not find one. A newspaper article led him to the Commerce (Tex.) Public Library, where he found exactly what he had in mind.

Possession (2002). Aaron Eckhart as Roland Michell is researching Queen Victoria's poet laureate in a London library and finds a letter from the poet to his mistress in a book. He hides from librarian Hugh Simon and steals the letter. If you're a purist you'll cringe whenever Michell handles old books and letters (no gloves, too much creasing, not to mention the occasional letter pocketed in his quest for answers). As an American and lowly research assistant, Michell gets no respect, hence the dirty tactics. Notable quote re working as a researcher: "This is not a job for grown-ups." But he does get to zip around the stacks on a rolling chair.

Rare Books and Manuscripts (2005, British, short). In the reading room of the British Library, Jess falls in love from afar with the gorgeous Heinz. Too shy to talk to him, she starts sending him books spelling out her feelings for him. When she starts receiving books in turn—and not from Heinz—will she able to pluck up her courage to meet her admirer?

Read or Die (2001, Japanese). This anime film consists of three episodes of a wildly popular TV series about a superheroine (Yomiko Readman or "The Paper," voiced by Kimberley Yates in the English version) who paranormally manipulates paper into weapons, shields, or any other tools she happens to need—she deflects bullets and swords with a simple index card or dollar bill, shoots flypaper to blind her opponents, and constructs functioning machines. A substitute teacher attached to the Royal British Library's Division of Special Operations (the bookworm's equivalent of MI5), Yomiko's library card is one of her greatest weapons. Note especially the orgasmic delight Yomiko experiences as she rushes through the collection, touching spines and squealing. The librarian who helps her is a bit clumsy, wears glasses, and is dedicated to books, but she also helps save the world from evil.

Red Dragon (2002). A detective visits a library to track down the source of a quote by Hannibal Lecter. The librarian is a gum-cracking young blonde who finds the quote and other sources for him.

Revelation (2001, British). The three protagonists learn, from searching the Isaac Newton collection at Cambridge University, information that leads them to the Loculus, an artifact that contains the DNA of Jesus Christ. The librarian—a middle-aged man in glasses played by Derek Jacobi—eavesdrops after the library closes and is rewarded by being gagged with the gloves worn to preserve the books. Lacking a photocopier, James D'Arcy as Jake Marcel rips out a page and the librarian screams as best he can with his mouth full of glove. Filming emphasis is placed on the barred door that prevents anyone from stealing the books, but apparently not single pages. Best repartee: "How can an idiot be a librarian?" "How can a gunman be a priest?"

The Ring (2002). Naomi Watts as journalist Rachel Keller and Martin Henderson as her divorced husband Noah Clay go to a library to research a mysterious video. Guy Richardson plays a library clerk.

Scream 3 (2000). Two people try to use a movie studio archives to research the possible connection between Sidney's mother and the killer. The archives are in a dark basement. The archivist (Carrie Fisher as Bianca Burnette) is unwilling to help until she is offered a $2,000 ring. She is rude, uncaring, and just plain mean.

The Secret Life of Girls (1999). This raunchy high-school teen sex flick has one library scene. A girl is looking for a book in the stacks but can't find it. She approaches the librarian at the desk and explains that she can't find the book. The librarian, an older woman with white-blue hair and big glasses, says the book must be there because it isn't checked out. The student insists it isn't. The librarian insists it must be and she should check again. She gets upset, insisting it isn't on the shelf. The librarian eventually asks her if she would like to fill out a missing book slip, but this does not help the situation. The librarian gets alarmed and picks up the phone. A student interrupts the exchange, apologies to the librarian for the other stu-

10

dent, and then takes her to the reserve stacks. It turns out the book is there.

Shanghai Knights (2003). Jackie Chan as Chon Wang creatively fights bad guys in 1887 London in the private library of Lord Nelson Rathbone (played by Aidan Gillen) using rare books as shields and a bookshelf ladder as a weapon.

Shooting the Past (1999, British, TV miniseries). A British photographic archive of 10 million items, run by a small staff of librarians, is threatened when an American firm buys the building in order to turn it into a business school. Lindsay Duncan as head curator Marilyn Truman has one week to find a buyer for the collection or it will be destroyed. To persuade the new owner that it is worth saving, the archivists assemble a series of stories linked to various photographs in the collection—sort of an archival Scheherazade. It offers a fine portrayal of archivists as extremely resourceful,

able to find virtually anything in a noncomputerized collection, and very creative at putting together information. The theme of closure is also a powerful one, and the hard-fought battle is inspiring.

The Skulls (2000). College students join a secret club that does nasty things. Their videotape records are cleverly hidden in a secret room behind a bookcase in the campus library, accessed by moving a certain book After one boy is killed, his buddy tries to catch the culprit. He follows him into the library, but loses him in special collections. Later he is again spotted in special collections; perhaps he is a librarian!

Sky High (2005). An amusing romp about a high school for superheroes. Exteriors of the school were filmed at the Delmar T. Oviatt Library building, California State University, Northridge.

Somewhere in Between (2005). Adapted from Paul Gitschner's short play "The Diary Library," this the story of Franceska Lynne as Dawn, a befuddled young woman who wanders into a strange and cluttered library seemingly located on the edge of nowhere. She encounters Erica Engelhardt as Lib, a quirky and mysterious librarian charged with collecting and filing the diaries of all the library's previous visitors. As Dawn struggles to make sense of her eerie surroundings and to understand what fate has befallen her, she and the otherworldly Lib form a bond that reaches beyond reality and into the next dimension of time and place.

Soulkeeper (2001, made for TV). A young man helps two friends find information online. When their search is interrupted by a power outage, he says, "If you want anything else, you'll have to try the library." So they visit the library, a large building filled with dark wooden shelves and heavy light fixtures, where they use the card catalog to find the dusty tomes they need.

Star Wars, Episode II: Attack of the Clones (2002). Needing to find the location of a distant planet, Ewan McGregor as Obi-Wan Kenobi goes to the Jedi Library for information; but he doesn't find what he needs. A librarian/archivist (Alethea McGrath as Madame Jocasta Nu), with her gray hair in a bun, approaches him, asks a few questions, then declares that if the archive doesn't have it, the information doesn't exist. She does not help him search any further but instead turns her attention to helping a small boy. Obi-Wan soon gives up and leaves. In fact, the planet does exist, but someone has erased the information about it. Says one librarian and Star Wars fan, "Any librarian worth his weight in Imperial Credits wouldn't give up so easily." In this library the "books," which glow with an iridescent blue color, are lined up on shelves, with busts of famous Jedi at the ends of the ranges. (The one that Obi-Wan Kenobi stands by is young Count Dooku.)

The Station Agent (2003). A young man born with dwarfism (Peter Dinklage as Finbar McBride) ends up living in an abandoned train depot in rural New Jersey. He becomes entangled with an artist who is struggling with a personal tragedy and an overly friendly Cuban hot dog vendor. An attractive, young, blonde library staffer (Michelle Williams as Emily) helps him obtain a library card, but she won't issue one until he can confirm his address with a piece of mail, which is laughable when you know the mailbox next to his front door is more decorative than functional.

Stay until Tomorrow (2004). Barney Cheng as library worker Jim lets his childhood pal Nina (played by Eleanor Hutchins) stay at his place for a while. She tries to learn Italian at the library for her next job, but also manages to turn Jim's workplace into a site of comic, literary, and sexual escapades. Filmed in Providence, Rhode Island.

The Tao of Steve (2000). Donal Logue as Dex has standing-up sex with another man's wife (Ayelet Kaznelson as Beth) in the philosophy section of the library stacks.

The Time Machine (2002). Orlando Jones (right) is Vox #NY-114, a very cool virtual librarian of the future who is the compendium of (no less than) All Human Knowledge. He describes himself as a "third generation fusion card photonic with verbal and visual link capabilities connected to every database on the planet." He does a reference interview  and even holds story time for kids. We first encounter him in 2030, then later about 800,000 years into the future (although his source of power is never explained).

Tomcats (2001). In a fit of self-mobilization, Jerry O'Connell as Michael Delany declares in the library bathroom that he's going to bang the first woman he sees. But the second woman, as well as the first, is decidedly unattractive. Then Heather Stephens as librarian Jill (ho-hum stereotypical bun, dowdy, quiet, shy, glasses and cardigan) comes along, and he loves how she stammers "gosh, golly" when she invites him inside after their date. There he meets Marnie Crossen as Granny, who used to be a librarian. Faster than you can say DDC, he's handcuffed to the bed in a den of leather and pain. "This is a little unexpected." "Call me a misfit." She punishes him because "I know about boys like you . . . you don't take books seriously . . . you don't respect books . . . you break their bindings . . . you doodle in their margins." He is to get one whack for each day overdue. Then Granny joins in the fun.

The Wedding Cow [Die Hochzeitskuh] (1999, German). A young lady (Isabella Parkinson as Flora) on her way to her new job as a librarian in southern Germany has her money stolen and gets kicked off the train. A plumber gives her a ride. The cow in back of his truck is a wedding present from his aunt. He's traveling south to get married in just a few days. Many comedic troubles ensue.

Welcome to Mooseport (2004). The library in this film is actually an architect's prospective model of the Monroe Cole (played by Gene Hackman) Presidential Library. It is massive and modern, 40,000 square feet, shaped like a croissant as painted by Picasso. Dennis Akayama as Izuki Nami describes it as "European rationalism interwoven with American modernism, a metaphor of organic growth, a man-made mountain over which soars the eagle."

10

Wet Hot American Summer (2001). Two camp counselors ask a friend where they might find books on astrophysics and camp directing. They are directed to the library. The next scene shows them in the "Waterville, Maine" Public Library looking at books in the stacks marked "astrophysics" and "camp directing."

Where the Heart Is (2000). A teenage single mother in a small town in Oklahoma is helped by several somewhat eccentric local citizens, including the town librarian (James Frain as Forney Hull). Actually his sister is the librarian (Margaret Ann Hoard as Mary Elizabeth Hull); he just works in the library. But when she becomes ill, he assumes her duties. When he first meets the young lady he is rude, but he later becomes quite pleasant.

The Winslow Boy (1999). Based on a true case from 1910 England, this film depicts a father's efforts to defend his son, who has been accused of theft. His sister does much ad hoc research in the law library and finds cases that might be helpful.

SOURCES: Martin Raish, Librarians in the Movies: An Annotated Filmography, emp.byui.edu/raishm/films/introduction.html; Antoinette Graham, Movie Librarians, home.earthlink.net/~movielibrarians/index.htm.

Visual characteristics of librarians in films

by Ray Tevis and Brenda Tevis

THE IMAGE OF LIBRARIANS IN MOTION PICTURES has remained relatively stable; changes that occurred were infinitesimal and insignificant. On the whole, libraries and working librarians, as their image in films, changed very little during the 20th century. From a casual perspective, there were few meaningful visual modifications in libraries until the widespread use of computer applications revolutionized cataloging, public service, and reference functions. Libraries and librarians began converting to online catalogs, replacing cabinets with computer stations during the 1980s, but few films reflected this change.

Any filmgoer of any generation of the 20th century would immediately recognize a librarian in any motion picture released during any year. The visual characteristics associated with the stereotypical image—age, eyeglasses, hairstyle (bun or baldness), and clothes—that began to appear in 1917 with *A Wife on Trial* were displayed unabatedly in films released throughout the remainder of the century. The most apparent change was in clothing, which was affected most dramatically by the introduction and widespread use of color, primarily Technicolor and DeLuxe Color. Clothes prior to the use of color appeared onscreen as black, white, or a shade of gray; for reel librarians, already dressed in nondescript clothes, black and white enhanced the drab personality of their screen characters. Color provided a slight degree of relief to prosaic costumes, but many supporting actors portraying reel librarians were often dressed in darker hues, negating the effect of color. The majority of reel librarians who are or appear to be middle-aged or older dress conservatively, adhering to a real-life cliché that these individuals dress more conservatively than their younger counterparts.

The percentages of reel librarians displaying the visual characteristics of eyeglasses, receding hairline or baldness (in the case of males) or bun (in the case of females), and age, are shown in Tables 1 and 2. The clothing characteristic is not included in the tabulation. The data for these tables is compiled from 224 films released between 1917 and 1999.

Table 1. Visual Characteristics of Male Reel Librarians

Decades	*Glasses*	*Receding/ Bald*	*Ages*								
			Teens	*20s*	*30s*	*40s*	*50s*	*60s*	*70s*	*80s*	*Total*
Silent		1			1	1	1				3
1930s	4	2		1			2	2	1		6
1940s	4	3			1	2	2	1			6
1950s	2	2		1	3	2	1	2			9
1960s	7	3		4	5	7	2	3			21
1970s	2	1		1		1	1	1			4
1980s	11	4		5	4	2	3	5			19
1990s	6	7		5	6	2	8	1			22
Total	**36**	**23**		**17**	**20**	**17**	**20**	**15**	**1**		**90**
	40%	**26%**		**19%**	**22%**	**19%**	**22%**	**17%**	**1%**		

Table 2. Visual Characteristics of Female Reel Librarians

Decades	*Glasses*	*Bun*	*Ages*								
			Teens	*20s*	*30s*	*40s*	*50s*	*60s*	*70s*	*80s*	*Total*
Silent	1	3		5	2	3	1				11
1930s	7	7	2	6	3	3	3				17
1940s	6	11	1	11	5	9	3	1		1	31
1950s	4	7	1	6	8	6	3	2			26
1960s	6	10	1	9	5	2	5	1			23
1970s	11	6		8	8	1	4	1	1		23
1980s	19	9	1	6	17	8	7	3	1		43
1990s	26	13	1	14	14	10	10	11	1	1	62
Total	**80**	**66**	**7**	**65**	**62**	**42**	**36**	**19**	**3**	**2**	**236**
	34%	**28%**	**3%**	**28%**	**26%**	**18%**	**15%**	**8%**	**1%**	**1%**	

Of the 326 total librarians, 236 (72%) are women, and 90 (28%) are men. The three formative films of 1932 (*Forbidden, Young Bride,* and *No Man of Her Own*) had a combined total of 10 librarians; eight were women, a percentage that closely approximates the percentage for the entire century. The occupation is predominantly female, and this is reflected in motion pictures.

The percentages relating to visual characteristics for men and women reel librarians are remarkably similar. Some 34% of women and 40% of men wear or hold eyeglasses, while 28% of women sport a bun and 26% of men display a receding hairline or baldness. Three percent of women, but no men, are or appear to be younger than 20; 53% of women and 41% of men are between the ages of 20 and 40; 42% of women and 58% of men are between the ages of 40 and 70; and 2% of women and 1% of men are over the age of 70. Throughout the century, 59% of the men are 40 or older, while only 43% of the women are over 40.

The fact that 57% of women reel librarians are or appear to be younger than 40 has not impacted the elderly characteristic of the stereotypical image. This may be attributable to the size of the differential; 14% (32 reel librarians) may be significant statistically, but the data covers more than an 80-year time span and is based on only 236 screen characters. The numbers, quite frankly, are too insignificant to effect any change of the image. In the silent era and in every decade through the 1980s, the greatest number of women librarians are or appear to be younger than 40; in the 1990s, however, this trend changed. During this last decade of the 20th century, 54% of the women librarians are 40 or older. Whether the percentage of women librarians over 40 will continue to increase is unclear.

The stereotypical image of librarians is embedded deeply in the psyche of American popular culture, and librarians, on the whole, display some degree of concern about this image. Although many working librarians have expressed displeasure with the universally recognized stereotype over the decades, this aversion to the image has not effected one whit of change. Members of the occupation have acquiesced to the entertaining but ineffectual activity of talking among themselves about the stereotype; they have reached, in effect, a tenuous accommodation with the image. Librarians, however, need to embrace the stereotype, as have filmgoers and the general public. Acknowledging the validity of the century-old stereotypical image is essential to revolutionizing the image. Librarians laboring in concert, and with assiduity, have the intellectual capacity to modernize this image in the 21st century, provided they have the desire. The 20th-century salutation and, by extension, epitaph for librarians, "Old Lady Foureyes," will continue indefinitely until librarians accept the challenge to modernize the stereotypical image for the benefit of their cultural, social, and economic welfare. This occupational task must become the "manifest destiny" of librarians and their local, state, and national organizations and associations. Without such dedication on the part of librarians, the stereotypical image will persevere not only in films but in all media.

SOURCE: Ray Tevis and Brenda Tevis, *The Image of Librarians in Cinema, 1917–1999* (Jefferson, N.C.: McFarland, 2005), pp. 189–191. Reprinted with permission.

Myers-Briggs personality types of librarians in film

by Jeanine Williamson

THE AUTHOR EXAMINED 28 films with a total of 31 librarian characters and assigned personality types to each. The eight Myers-Briggs characteristics are Introverted (I), Extraverted (E), Sensing (S), Intuitive (N), Thinking (T), Feeling (F), Judgmental (J), and Perceiving (P). The listings below give the films, the characters' personality type, and selected evidence for the choice made.—*GME.*

The **Big Sleep** (1946). Carole Douglas as *librarian* at Hollywood Public Library (ISTJ). Tells Philip Marlowe (Humphrey Bogart) that he doesn't look like the type to read a book-collecting book.

Blade (1998). Eric Edwards as *Pearl* (ISFP). Fearful and quiet.

Bliss (1997). Lois Chiles as *Eva* (INFJ). Discusses details of rare book. Appears decisive.

The **Blue Kite** (1993). Quanxin Pu as *Lin Shaolong* (ISFJ). Concerned about upsetting family member. Xuejian Li as *Li Guodong* (ENFP). Playful.

Brazil (1985). Jonathan Pryce as *Sam Lowry* (INTJ). Obsessed with vision of escape with girl good with technology and systems. Ian Holm as *Mr. M. Kurtzman* (ISFJ). Concerned about a mistake.

Cal (1984). Helen Mirren as *Marcella* (ISFJ). Entertains, paints, is quiet.

The Convent (1995). Leonor Silveira as *Piedade* (INFP). Interested in literature, strong ideal of purity.

Desk Set (1957). Katharine Hepburn as *Bunny Watson* (ISTJ). Phenomenal memory, checks budget for errors, notices Richard Sumner's (Spencer Tracy's) mismatched socks.

Foul Play (1978). Goldie Hawn as *Gloria Mundy* (ISFJ). Kind to the couple in the car, quiet, pleasant.

Goodbye, Columbus (1969). Richard Benjamin as *Neil Klugman* (ENTP). Outgoing, humorous, observant, "not a planner, a liver," critical.

The Gun in Betty Lou's Handbag (1992). Penelope Ann Miller as *Betty Lou Perkins* (INFP). Interest in literature, has creative programming ideas, introverted.

Heart and Souls (1993). Charles Grodin as *Harrison Winslow* (INFP). Passion for music, dislikes aggression, appears to dislike closure.

Joe Versus the Volcano (1990). Tom Hanks as *Joe Banks* (ISFP). Moves in leisurely fashion, is attuned to bodily symptoms, decorates office, likes music, resourceful in times of crisis.

Major League (1989). Rene Russo as *Lynn Wells* (INFP). Passion for books, graceful and artsy attire, quiet.

The Mummy (1999). Rachel Weisz as *Evelyn "Evie" Carnahan* (INTJ). Deep knowledge of ancient documents, somewhat absent-minded (not aware of senses).

The Music Man (1962). Shirley Jones as *Marian Paroo* (ISFJ). Concerned with propriety, notices nature, becomes warm toward traveling salesman (Robert Preston), says he has caused the town to have "people to go out of your way for."

No Man of Her Own (1932). Carole Lombard as *Connie Randall* (ESTJ). Described as a "handful," assertive with Babe Stewart (Clark Gable), attempts to improve his organization and reminds him of appointments, said to "think of everything."

Party Girl (1995). Parker Posey as *Mary* (ESTP). Described as a major promoter, interested in parties and wardrobe, uses Dewey decimal classification for her own purposes. Sasha von Scherler as *Judy Lindendorf* (ISTJ). Quiet compared to Mary, good with details, responsible, often refers to past experiences such as her knowledge of Mary's mother.

Peeping Tom (1960). Anna Massey as *Helen Stephens* (ESFJ). Friendly, offers cake to a neighbor, curious, writing a children's book.

Scream 3 (2000). Carrie Fisher as *Bianca Burnette* (ESTP). Outgoing, knows tricks in the filing system, manipulative.

The Shawshank Redemption (1994). Tim Robbins as *Andy Dufresne* (ISFP). Likes geology and music, helps friends in prison (obtains beer, develops prison library, teaches prisoner to read), friendly but quiet.

A Simple Plan (1998). Bridget Fonda as *Sarah Mitchell* (ISFJ). Interested in home comforts, poor intuition, develops overcomplicated plans.

Sleeping with the Enemy (1991). Julia Roberts as *Sara Waters/Laura Burney* (ISFJ). Likes to decorate, charming, quiet, good at practical plans for escaping abusive husband.

Something Wicked This Way Comes (1983). Jason Robards as *Charles Halloway* (ISFJ). Caring, helpful, doesn't take risks.

Somewhere in Time (1980). Noreen Walker as a *librarian* (ISTJ). Dislikes nonroutine request to get magazines.

10

Soylent Green (1973). Edward G. Robinson as *Sol Roth* (ISFJ). Notices sensory details such as heat and poor food, remembers his past, loves nature.

The Spy Who Came in from the Cold (1965). Claire Bloom as *Nan Perry* (ISFJ). Likes to entertain, offers sandwich to coworker, loyal to Communism because it "organizes our emotions."

With Honors (1994). Patricia B. Butcher as *librarian* at Harvard's Widener Library (ISTJ). Tells homeless man (Joe Pesci) he can't stay, enforces rules.

SOURCE: Jeanine Williamson, "Jungian/Myers-Briggs Personality Types of Librarians in Films," in Wendi Arant and Candace R. Benefiel, eds., *The Image and Role of the Librarian* (New York: Haworth, 2002), pp. 47–59. Reprinted with permission.

COLLECTIONS

Stamps, cards, and covers: The New York Public Library and the American Library Association

by Larry T. Nix

THE FOLLOWING ARE EXTRACTS from Larry T. Nix's thematic display exhibit that tells the story of America's libraries using stamps, covers, and other paper artifacts. Its also documents the way libraries have used the U.S. postal system to conduct business.—*GME.*

The New York Public Library was created on May 23, 1895, when an agreement was signed that merged the Astor Library, the Lenox Library, and the Tilden Trust. *Library Journal* proclaimed that it was "the event of the year" in the library world.

At the time of the merger, the Astor Library was already one of the largest libraries in the nation. The postal card shown here, written in 1887, is from Charles Alexander Nelson, the chief catalog librarian at the Astor Library. From 1886 to 1888, Nelson produced a four-volume supplement to the Astor catalog, for which he received high acclaim. In 1887, he was also teaching at Melvil Dewey's School of Library Economy at Columbia College.

The message on the card reads: "Thank you for your letter of the 3d. I tried hard to find something to commend in N. Stockbridgis Catalog, and did not wish to be hyper-critical. He is one of the 'anybody-can-make-a-catalogue' class of men who are frequently found on library boards, and 'who know it all.' He has seen by this time, probably, the folly of ignoring authorities."

Completed in 1911, the NYPL building on Fifth Avenue was the largest and most expensive public library building built in the United States. This remained the case until 1960. It contained 10 million cubic feet of space. The building was designed by the New York firm of Carrere and Hastings. It was the largest marble building constructed in this country up until that time.

John Shaw Billings (right) was appointed director of the NYPL on January 15, 1896. Billings was a surgeon and had already achieved fame as "perhaps the most versatile American physician of his time." At NYPL he proved himself to be one of the outstanding librarians of his generation.

Only months before a declaration of war on Germany, the NYPL Acquisitions Division was communicating with the library in Nürnberg. This letter (to the right and below) was examined by censors in both countries.

The library had some difficulty (left) catching up with one of its more famous patrons, conductor Leonard Bernstein. Hopefully, it wasn't an overdue book that they were contacting him about.

The Maldives issued a souvenir sheet and postage stamp (right) of the New York Public Library at the Postage Stamp Mega-Event in New York City on October 18, 1992.

On November 9, 2000, the U.S. Postal Service held a first-day ceremony at the Jacob K. Javits Convention Center for a postage

stamp depicting one of the lion statues that flank NYPL's main entrance (see p. 550). Initially, the stamp design did not include the notation, "The New York Public Library." However, it was added when NYPL officials ex-

10

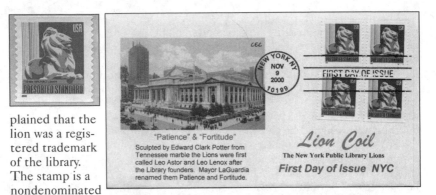

"Patience" & "Fortitude"
Sculpted by Edward Clark Potter from Tennessee marble the Lions were first called Leo Astor and Leo Lenox after the Library founders. Mayor LaGuardia renamed them Patience and Fortitude.

Lion Coil
The New York Public Library Lions
First Day of Issue NYC

plained that the lion was a registered trademark of the library. The stamp is a nondenominated (10 cents) self-adhesive coil stamp for use with presorted standard mail.

A perforated, lick-and-stick version of the coil stamp was released on February 4, 2003, in Washington, D.C., with no ceremony.

The American Library Association, founded in 1876, is the world's oldest and largest library association. The first "Librarians' Convention" (left) was held in Philadelphia, Pennsylvania, on October 4–6, 1876. Attendance at the convention included 90 men and 13 women. Today, its membership numbers more than 64,000. The invitation shown here is a replica.

When the association met in Pasadena, California, in 1911, attendance at the conference (below) was 582. ALA membership totaled 2,046.

LIBRARIANS' CONVENTION.

The Librarians of the City of Philadelphia request the pleasure of your company, on Friday Evening, Oct. 6, 1876, between the hours of 8 and 11, at the rooms of the Historical Society, No. 820 Spruce St.

PLEASE PRESENT THIS CARD AT THE DOOR.

ALA held a Midwinter Meeting in Philadelphia in 1999 (below).

The ALA played a major role in providing reading materials to our soldiers and sailors during World War I through the War Service Library (see p. 551, top left). This included operating camp and hospital libraries in the United States as well as distributing books in Europe. It also included conducting book drives though America's libraries and soliciting magazines for military hospitals. In Europe, the association was granted free franking privileges by General Pershing to facilitate the War Service Library's books-by-mail program (see p. 551, top right). The library program developed by ALA for World War I was the basis for our armed services libraries of today.

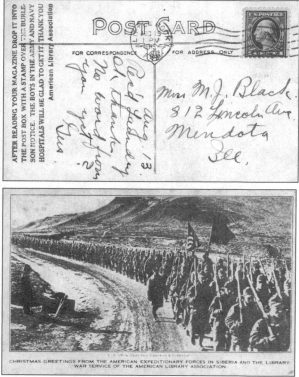

For a period during the war, American soldiers from the American Expeditionary Force were stationed in Siberia. The ALA Library War Service was also there. This ALA picture postcard (right) extending "Christmas Greetings" from the AEF forces in Siberia is one of only nine copies recorded as having survived.

SOURCE: Larry T. Nix, "America's Libraries," an exhibit at the National Topical Stamp Show, Milwaukee, Wisconsin, June 2005. The exhibit won three prizes, including a Gold Research Medal from the American Philatelic Society.

Library buttons

LIBRARIANS USE BUTTONS to convey a wide variety of messages. Here are a few that have turned up at ALA conferences over the years.

10

Jeffrey L. Baskin's 10 favorite library postcards

by Jeffrey L. Baskin

IN PREVIOUS EDITIONS of this handbook, librarians and postcard collectors Billy Wilkinson and Marjorie Warmkessel have shared their favorite cards depicting libraries. For this edition, I asked Jeff Baskin, director of the William F. Laman Public Library in North Little Rock, Arkansas, also an ardent appreciator of library postcards, to describe his 10 picks.—*GME.*

The Vallejo (Calif.) Free Public Library was established in its first location in Solano County in 1855. In 1902, a $20,000 Carnegie grant was secured for a new library building. Architects Werner and O'Brien designed the building in the Classical Revival

(Type B) style. The cornerstone was laid December 5, 1903, and the library was dedicated July 4, 1904. There was a small addition in 1905. The building was demolished in 1969. The postcard was published by the California Sales Co. in San Francisco and caught my attention immediately for two reasons: (1) for $20,000, I think Andrew Carnegie deserved to have his name spelled correctly; (2) the card's number, 569, eerily prefigures its demolition year.

Lyons (Kans.) Public Library. Andrew Carnegie donated $6,000 to build a library in Lyons, Kansas, and in 1909 the citizens agreed to support the library to the extent of $600 per year. The design was produced by E. F. Parker and Son, Architects, and the construction contract awarded to A. A. Shilkett. This postcard was proudly sent by Shilkett to his uncle after completion of the building. Luckily there is no "S" or "N" in Public Library on the façade. (The letters are inverted in the caption.)

The Parmly Billings (Mont.) Memorial Library was a gift from Frederick Billings Jr., a New York banker, in honor of his brother Parmly, who died at the age of 35. The town was named after their father, Frederick Sr., who was president of Northern Pacific Railroad. When

Frederick Jr. died, an additional $30,000 was donated to build east and west wings in his memory. This card shows the library before the wings were built. Notice the train, which was donated by the railroad to add reality to the children's story hour whenever they read Watty Piper's book.

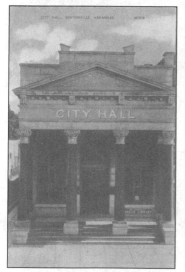

Bentonville (Ark.) Public Library. In 1977, the historic Massey Hotel building in Bentonville, Arkansas, was purchased by Wal-Mart heir Jim Walton and his parents, Mr. and Mrs. Sam Walton. The building was renovated back to its former glory with the idea of relocating the Bentonville Public Library where it is today. A new library is now under construction for opening in summer 2006. But here are its humble beginnings. I passed over this card several times before noticing the sign below the front window. The back of the card reads, "Bentonville . . . the chicken capital of the world." It still is, but it is now also the capital of the Wal-Mart Empire.

Sterling (Ill.) Public Library. Bentonville was not the only public library located in a city hall. But it was much better off apparently, than this one. Founded in 1874, the Sterling Public Library was relocated to the new city hall in 1889. Describing the library to Andrew Carnegie, R. S. Phillips wrote, "Very cramped quarters in City Hall over the room where the Fire Department horses are stabled; the stench from this in mornings is anything but inviting, not a fit place to sit and read." The new Carnegie Library opened in 1905. Books being sponges for odors, I wonder what the new library smelled like.

City Hall and Library, STERLING, ILL.

10

The Carnegie Library in Pittsburgh, Pennsylvania, was built in 1895 at a cost of $800,000. Between 1895 and 1910 someone decided to take the towers down and redesign the entry lobby. I like those towers; they remind me of Rapunzel and all the chivalric tales of my youth. Besides, what must the citizens have thought about those costly changes only 15 years after the original construction? I know that I would have been out of a job and up the proverbial tower without a rope or ladder for just suggesting the expenditure of those funds.

Peabody (Kans.) Public Library. The vice-president of the Atchison Topeka and Santa Fe Railroad, F. H. Peabody of Boston, Massachusetts, built and stocked a library in the town that was named for him. The first tax-supported public library in Kansas, the Peabody Public Library opened in 1874. In 1903, Carnegie agreed to replace the frame structure by providing $10,000 for a new building. The new library opened in 1914.

Interior, Cedar Rapids (Iowa) Public Library. I enjoy collecting the buildings, but seeing what they looked like on the inside is especially neat. These interior views are particularly hard to find so I treasure them. Built in 1901, this Carnegie library cost $75,000 and is

now part of the Cedar Rapids Museum of Art.

The Nora E. Larabee Memorial Library in Stafford, Kansas, was built in 1906 at a cost of $5,000 and expanded three times since. Information from the Stafford Chamber of Commerce states, "However unique its architectural features, the building became a public library only after a controversy which turned the town upside down. Public sentiment was so strong that the entire Stafford city council and mayor resigned before the deed was finally accepted." The problem was a clause in the deed denying membership on the library board to any descendant of the editor of the town newspaper in perpetuity. What does the library do in that town to get good press?

Paducah (Ky.) Public Library. This Carnegie Public Library was built in 1901 at a cost of $35,000. People sending postcards usually wrote hello-how-are-you-I-am-safe-and-sound, but rarely wrote anything about the library viewed on the card. But here for all to see and admire, I. B. says, "This is one of our finest build-

ings. It has so many nice books in it and is such a fine addition to the city." I love library supporters. Too bad the building was razed in 1969.

10

ANOMALIES

Haunted libraries

by George M. Eberhart

LIKE OTHER PUBLIC BUILDINGS that have seen long years of human activity, some libraries are allegedly haunted by the ghosts of former staff, patrons, or other residents. Most often the manifestations involve odd noises, cold spots, or objects moved; other times a visual apparition is reported. In many cases, phenomena can be attributed to the sights, the sounds, and the aura of a historic building. However, libraries offer such dynamic mental and sensual stimulation that if haunts are truly evidence for postmortem survival, I can't imagine anywhere else I'd rather spend my earthly afterlife than in a library, reading the news like old Dr. Harris in the Boston Athenaeum. (Beware, Ohio State!)

The following list represents a fairly comprehensive list of current and former library haunts.

United States

Alabama

Albertville Public Library. Some staffers say that early in the morning the elevator moves on its own and water runs in the bathroom spontaneously.

Bay Minette Public Library, Hampton D. Ewing Building. Lights turned themselves on and off and books tumbled from shelves, perhaps due to the paranormal presence of Annie Gilmer, who served as the first librarian, from 1922 to 1943. When operations moved across the street, the elevator behaved erratically.

Birmingham Public Library, Linn-Henley Research Library. The city's central library from 1927 to 1985, this facility now houses special collections and government documents. People have reported strange sensations, objects moved, and a spirit that occasionally sneaks a smoke.

Gadsden Public Library. The third floor is said to be haunted by the library's founder.

Tuscaloosa Public Library, former library on Greensboro Avenue. A creepy presence has been noted in a round room on the first floor, the main room at the window, the stairs leading to the top turret, and the lower basement level.

Tuscaloosa, University of Alabama, Amelia Gayle Gorgas Library. Built in 1941, the library is said to be haunted by Gorgas, who was university librarian from 1879 to 1906. Although the elevators can be locked so they don't stop on the fourth floor, where the special collections are housed, one elevator stops there anyway, with no passengers on it.

Arizona

Fort Huachuca, Colonel Smith Middle School. The ghost of a former student named Linda Landy can be seen through the library's tinted windows.

Arkansas

Benton, Saline County Library. The library's home from 1967 to 2003 was a converted theater building that frequently featured phenomena that made librarians suspect a ghost was afoot: phantom footsteps, paperback carousels rotating by themselves, books falling from the shelves, a self-operating photocopier, and a slamming book-return door. Once, late at night, Director Julie Hart heard the distinctive sound of a manual typewriter—but the library had long ago discarded theirs.

Helena, Phillips County Library and Museum. On this 1891 library's third-floor storage area and in the museum annex, the staff reports occasional footsteps, bumps, and bangs.

California

Alhambra, Ramona Convent Secondary School. Founded in 1889, this is one of the oldest operating schools in the state. Students have seen a nun in a white habit roaming in the library.

Chowchilla, Madera County Library, Chowchilla Branch. This new branch stands on the site of a bowling alley that burned down when its kitchen caught fire. The circulation area lies on the approximate position of the kitchen. Some say a cook who perished in the blaze can be seen in a flash of flame.

Clayton, Contra Costa County Library, Clayton Community Library. The library's heat-activated security system has gone off when no one is around, suggesting to a local ghosthunter that heat from a haunt is the cause. The clock and air conditioning also behave suspiciously, according to the *San Francisco Chronicle*, October 31, 1997.

El Centro, Central Union High School. Footsteps, talking, and doors slamming are heard in the library. In the library basement, where detentions were held in the 1980s, footsteps, crying, and laughing are heard.

Long Beach Public Library. The apparition of a young girl in Victorian attire was seen by a new employee in 1995 in the genealogy room. The north elevator behaved bizarrely in the late 1980s. One staff office featured strange rustling sounds and spontaneous equipment switch-ons. Appropriate books are said to serendipitously fall from the shelves.

Los Angeles, California State University, John F. Kennedy Memorial Library. In the late evening and early morning, locked doors open and faucets turn on in the third floor south area. Cold spots are reported in the restrooms.

Los Angeles Public Library, Cypress Park Branch. Ghost sightings have been reported since the library opened in 1924. The old fireplace, the men's room, and the occult section seem to be the centers for cold spots and whispers.

Riverside, University of California, Tomás Rivera Library. A female ghost haunts the older part of the library, mainly at night on the first and second floors. Maintenance men have reported sounds and cold spots.

Sacramento Public Library, Sacramento Room. This special collections area opened on the second floor of the central library in April 1995. The staff can hear sounds like Mylar rustling or someone shelving books. Two witnesses have seen and heard one of the glass doors close by itself. According to The Shadowlands website, "One employee working in the office a little before 7 a.m. heard the wooden shutters on the door leading into the copy machine area rattle. Thinking it was a custodian entering, he initially paid it no mind until he realized he had not heard the front door, which was locked, open." Needless to say, no custodian had been there.

10

San Bernardino, St. Thomas Aquinas High School. A student who hung himself is said to appear floating in the library.

Upland, Pioneer Junior High School. Books fall off the shelves spontaneously in the library.

Yorba Linda, Richard Nixon Library and Birthplace. Shortly after Nixon was entombed on the grounds in 1994, a night watchman reported seeing a luminous green mist over the president's grave. He also heard tapping sounds emanating from an exhibit room, according to the *LA Weekly*, September 30–October 6, 1994.

Colorado

Denver Public Library. Staff say there is a presence in the basement that shoves people.

Connecticut

Newtown, Cyrenius H. Booth Library. This 1932 public library was a posthumous gift to the town by benefactress Mary Elizabeth Hawley, who named it after her grandfather (a Newtown physician for 50 years) and provided a trust fund that kept it running without tax support until the early 1980s. She had a room on the top floor that she allegedly haunts, but it's been locked since a 1998 renovation.

Delaware

Dover Public Library. Not haunted, but the library's technical services department keeps the skull and a few loose teeth of notorious Maryland slave dealer and kidnapper Patty Cannon (d. 1822) in a hatbox. The staff is happy to show it to visitors on request.

District of Columbia

U.S. Capitol Building, Rotunda. The Library of Congress once inhabited the rooms to the west of the Rotunda. A male librarian allegedly haunts the area, looking for $6,000 he stashed in the pages of some obscure volumes. (The money was found in 1897 when the collection moved to the Jefferson Building.)

Florida

Miami, Southwest Miami Senior High School. Books in the media center are often rearranged and the lights flicker.

Tampa, Howard W. Blake High School. A cold spot can be felt around the tables in the back of the library.

West Palm Beach, Palm Beach Atlantic University Library. A janitor who disappeared mysteriously haunts the library near an old janitor's closet.

Illinois

Cairo, A. B. Safford Memorial Library. A ghost nicknamed Toby hangs out in the special collections room on the second floor of this 1884 building. Director Monica Smith said she has heard someone walking around upstairs when the library was closed and she was alone. Former librarian Louise Ogg and another staffer once saw a ghostly light rise up from behind a desk, pass slowly by her office, and disappear into the book stacks. There used to be a rocking chair in the library that made creaking noises by itself, as if someone were rocking it.

Decatur, Millikin University, Gorin Library. A room in the basement is supposed to be haunted by a maintenance worker who was accidentally killed there.

Godfrey, Lewis and Clark Community College, Reid Memorial Library. This institution started life in 1838 as Monticello College. Harriet Haskell, an ardent feminist who directed the college from 1868 to 1912, haunts the library that stands on the spot of a former chapel. One incident in the 1970s involved a young librarian who felt a hand touch her on the shoulder blade. She was so scared that she closed the library and left. Two prominent cold spots have been noticed in the reading room.

McHenry, McHenry East High School. The library metal detectors go off for no reason on the last day of the school year.

Normal, Illinois State University, Williams Hall. The ghost of ISU's first librarian, Angie Milner (d. 1928), has been seen by several faculty, staff, and students. Archives Specialist Jo Rayfield sensed a "kind, gentle" presence one day while looking at microfilm. Others have reported cold spots, a white figure, and books restacked in an odd fashion. The building is used for the Illinois Regional Archives Depository and stores infrequently used books owned by the Milner Library (named after Angie).

Peoria Public Library. Mrs. Andrew Gray, who owned the land where the library now stands, uttered a curse in 1847 that was said to have resulted in the untimely deaths of three library directors in the early 20th century. Employees have allegedly seen ghostly faces in the basement.

Peru Washington School. A disturbed school librarian supposedly killed three students and herself April 12, 1956, in the library. Since then, students have reported hearing screams and seeing an apparition.

Indiana

Evansville, Willard Library. A "lady in gray" has been seen in this 1884 Victorian Gothic building since 1937. The specter sports a scent of perfume that is often sensed near the elevator, near the rest rooms, or in the children's room. Occasionally staff will walk into cold spots. Former Director William Goodrich said the lady appeared once on a security monitor placed near the rest rooms. One theory is that the ghost is Louise Carpenter, the daughter of the library's founder. Louise once sued the library's trustees, claiming that her father was "of unsound mind and was unduly influenced in establishing [Willard] Library." She lost the suit and, as a result, her claim to any of the library's property. The *Evansville Courier and Press* set up three ghostcams in the research room, the children's room, and the basement; images can be examined at www.willardghost.com/index.php.

Fort Wayne, University of Saint Francis Library, Bass Mansion. A student suicide is said to be the source of cold spots and occasional apparitions.

Greencastle, DePauw University, Roy O. West Library. An old story has the ghost of James Whitcomb, Indiana's governor from 1843 to 1848, appearing to students who took home books that he had donated to the library.

Madison–Jefferson County Public Library. Women riding the elevator sometimes find themselves patted or caressed. A young man confined to a wheelchair is said to have lived in the Powell residence before the library moved to the site in 1930. The ghost has been nicknamed Charlie.

North Webster Elementary School. A young boy wearing khakis and a blue sweater is sometimes seen in the library trying to check out books.

10

Poseyville Carnegie Public Library. After the town expanded and rededicated this 1905 building in 2000, staff and volunteers began to feel that someone was watching them. Several staffers also reported sounds like someone was entering the building when the door was locked, though no one could be seen on the security camera. Library Assistant Sheryl Taylor was the first to see the ghost in the winter of 2001, a matronly woman surrounded by a hazy mist. The four computers in the old Carnegie section are always having problems, while those in the new section behave perfectly. For the full story, see www.indianaghosts.org/ghoststories/the_poseyville_carnegie_public_library_ghost.htm.

Iowa

Cedar Rapids Art Museum. Prior to 1985 this building housed the Cedar Rapids Public Library. An apparent case of "crisis apparition" occurred sometime in the late 1960s when a longtime patron was seen in the library shortly after she had died in a fire.

Cedar Rapids, Brucemore Mansion. Strange groans and laughter can be heard and objects move by themselves in the library of this 1886 home.

Council Bluffs, Union Pacific Railroad Museum. A 1903 Carnegie library until taken over and renovated by the museum in 1998, this building's basement was supposed to be haunted. Books would fly off the shelves, items disappeared, and people saw shadowy figures.

Kansas

Dodge City, Soule Intermediate Center. The library of this former high school used to be haunted by the ghost of a student who died in the school.

Hutchinson Public Library. The ghost of Ida Day Holzapfel, head librarian from 1915 to 1925 and 1947 to 1954, has been seen and heard since her death in California in 1954, according to the October 31, 1975, *Hutchinson News*. Library staffer Rose Hale said she saw a lady standing below the stairs one day. She did not know the woman's name, but when she described the woman to another library employee, Hale was told she had just described Ida Day. Other employees claim to have heard footsteps in the basement, and it became a shared joke that whenever anything was misplaced or missing, Ida Day took it. The stacks area in the southwest corner of the basement is notorious for cold spots, disembodied voices, and hazy apparitions.

Kentucky

Bowling Green, Western Kentucky University, Helm Library. A student who fell to his death while trying to open a window on the ninth floor is said to haunt the library.

Owensboro, Daviess County Public Library. The library hosts the apparition of a young boy with high red knee socks, a red vest, high shorts, and other clothing that seems to date from the 1920s or 1930s.

Maine

Eliot, William Fogg Library. A newspaper photo apparently shows a transparent skull floating above a staircase.

Maryland

Elkton, Old Library. This was the Cecil County Public Library from 1955 until the early 1990s. The Cecil County Historical Society occupies part of the space now. Former Mayor Henry Hooper Mitchell, who bought this building in 1925, haunts it and makes items move around or disappear.

Ellicott City, Howard County Law Library, Hayden House. Built in 1840 by the first county clerk, Edwin Parsons Hayden, this small building was part of the Howard County District Court complex in the 1970s. Former Judge J. Thomas Nissel said his secretary used to come to work early in the morning and smell eggs, toast, and bacon cooking, although there were no kitchen facilities. A rocking chair in the offices of the Department of Parole and Probation kept rocking on its own. The house was renovated before the library moved in, and the phenomena have apparently ceased.

Massachusetts

Boston Athenaeum Library. One of the oldest private libraries in the United States, the Athenaeum was founded in 1807 by the editors of the *Monthly Anthology and Boston Review*. Nathaniel Hawthorne used to read and write here in the 1840s when the Athenaeum resided in the James Perkins Mansion on Pearl Street (no longer standing). Hawthorne wrote a short story about seeing the ghost of Thaddeus Mason Harris (1768–1842) in the library, always reading the *Boston Post* as he used to do in life, on the day he died (April 3) and for several weeks thereafter ("The Ghost of Dr. Harris," written in 1856 but not published until 1900). Harris was pastor of the First Unitarian Church in Dorchester, but prior to that served as Harvard University librarian from 1791 to 1793.

Boston Public Library, East Boston Branch. The first branch library in the United States, the East Boston Branch opened in 1870. People have heard movements and talking in the basement where the restrooms are located.

Danvers, Peabody Institute Library. The ghost of an old man sits in a reading room of this 1892 building. Some say he has shushed people talking loudly.

Fairhaven, Millicent Library. The library's founder, Standard Oil magnate Henry Huttleston Rogers (1840–1909), had a daughter named Millicent who died of heart failure in 1890 at the age of 17. The 1893 library was named after her. Patrons sometimes see her walking the halls, outlined in bright blue light. At night, passersby have reported seeing a girl standing in the window of the turret in front. A woman dressed in black who runs her fingers along the shelved books has been reported from the upper floors, while a man dressed in a tweed jacket, purple bow tie, and small circular glasses has been seen mopping the basement floor.

Lowell, Dr. An Wang Middle School. The library is said to have a cold spot.

New Bedford Free Public Library. This Greek and Egyptian Revival building has been home to the library since 1910. An employee saw the apparition of an older woman with dark, gray-streaked hair and wearing a navy-blue coat in the lower-level children's room in 1999. A tall man with reddish-brown hair and a long tan coat has been observed on the second floor near the microfilm.

Norton, Wheaton College, Madeleine Clark Wallace Library. People have noted the unseen presence of a former librarian at night around the card catalog and stacks in this 1923 building.

Oxford Free Public Library. Books fall from the shelves and organ music is heard at night.

Michigan

Belding, Alvah N. Belding Memorial Library. In the children's room people have heard a girl laughing and felt a disturbing presence.

Dearborn Heights, Berwyn Senior Center. This former elementary school became a senior center in 1979. Seniors and neighborhood children say they've heard rattling, tapping, and moaning in the center's library. A school janitor is said to have hung himself in that location.

Detroit Public Library, Skillman Branch. The site of a former jailhouse where executions took place in the early 19th century, the library stacks sometimes reverberate with moans, rumblings, and other strange noises.

Muskegon, Hackley Public Library. Built in 1890 with funding from lumber baron Charles Hackley, whose ghost is accused of moving objects around and making noises.

Ypsilanti, Starkweather Home. This Italianate-style home was built in 1858 by local merchant Edwin Mills. It was later occupied by Maryanne Starkweather, who donated it upon her death to the Ladies Library Association in 1890. It was used as a library until 1964. Some claim to have seen Maryanne in the upper halls of the building or heard footsteps above them.

Minnesota

St. Cloud State University, James W. Miller Learning Resources Center. A 19th-century burial site was found in 1997 when the Miller Center's foundation was dug. The figure of a soldier has been seen wandering in the halls.

Mississippi

Tupelo, Lee-Itawamba Library System. This 1971 building was built on the site of the home of John Mills Allen (1846–1917), known as "Private John Allen," U.S. Congressman from 1885 to 1901. The doors and glass panels in the Mississippi Room are from his original dwelling. Allen's ghost is blamed for taking books off the shelf and putting them on the floor, as well as stealing items from the book drop.

Missouri

Mountain View, Southwest Baptist University, Mountain View Center Library. The Myrtle Glass Learning Center building was a warehouse of the Sharp Lumber Company, which went out of business in the 1970s. Books sometimes fall from the shelves, and people have heard a knocking on the floor.

St. Charles, Lindenwood University, Butler Library. Built in 1929, the library is one of the spots on campus said to be haunted by the ghost of college cofounder Mary Easton Sibley (1801–1878).

St. Joseph Public Library, Carnegie Library. Footsteps of the ghost of a former librarian, nicknamed Rose, can be heard at closing time on the second floor. Whispers, giggles, and shushes have also been reported, and books taunt the staff by reshelving themselves in the wrong spot.

St. Louis, University of Missouri, Thomas Jefferson Library. Basement Level One has a reputation for spooky goings-on. Former Director Dick Miller had a weird experience there on the first day of his job—phantom footsteps and a clear voice that spoke two words: "Hello, boy." The elevators go up and down frequently after hours, as noted by campus police.

Nebraska

Bellevue Public Library. The ghosts of an old man and a 10-year-old girl with large round glasses are said to appear occasionally.

Bellwood Elementary School. At night, the apparition of a severely burned woman has been seen standing in the library window.

Malcolm, Westfall Elementary School. The spirit of school founder Fern Westfall (d. 1996) knocks books off the library shelves.

New Jersey

Old Bernardsville Public Library. Phyllis the library ghost was so active at one time that the staff issued her a library card. Beginning in 1974, employees started seeing an apparition moving through the front rooms of the building, which was the Vealtown Tavern during the Revolutionary War. The ghost is said to be that of Phyllis Parker, the innkeeper's daughter, who suffered a nervous breakdown when her boyfriend, a British spy, was hung in 1777 and delivered to the tavern in a coffin. The fireplace in the former reading room was a focal point for phenomena. Local History Room volunteer Eileen Luz Johnston wrote a 46-page booklet about the spook titled *Phyllis—The Library Ghost?* in 1991. The new public library was built in the 1990s around the corner from the original building.

Raritan Public Library, General John Frelinghuysen House. Dating back to the early 18th century, this historic house was partially restored as a library in the early 1970s. Ghost hunter Jane Doherty sensed the presence of several specters here, according to the Bridgewater *Courier News*, October 14, 1999. One spook turns on lights and moves books after hours, and an elderly woman is seen both in a window and in the garden.

West Long Branch, Monmouth University, Murry and Leonie Guggenheim Memorial Library. Completed in 1905 as the summer home of mining and smelting entrepreneur Murry Guggenheim (1858–1939), the estate was converted into the college library in 1961. A lady in white walks down the staircase at midnight when the library closes.

New Mexico

Albuquerque/Bernalillo County Library System, San Pedro Branch. In the evenings, a disembodied voice has allegedly been heard to say, "Please come check out a book."

New York

Aurora, Wells College, Louis Jefferson Long Library. An eerie presence is felt on the third floor of this 1968 building.

Clinton, Kirkland Town Library. Phantom footsteps and whispers have been reported.

New York City, Joseph Papp Public Theatre. This building housed the Astor Library in the winter of 1859 when Library Director Joseph Green Cogswell (1786–1876) allegedly met the ghost of Austin L. Sands, a wealthy insurance executive, wandering in the alcoves on three separate nights. Lawyer and composer George Templeton Strong mentioned the event in his diary. The building became the Public Theatre in 1967 with the world premiere of the musical *Hair*.

Rochester, University of Rochester, Rush Rhees Library. A workman killed during the construction of the library in 1929 is said to haunt the old part of the stacks.

Tarrytown, Sunnyside. Several years after his death in 1859, three witnesses saw Washington Irving's ghost walk though the parlor and disappear into the library. Irving's spirit is said to pinch some female visitors, and the ghosts of his nieces tidy up the place at night after the interpreters leave.

10

North Carolina

Elizabethtown, Bladen County Public Library. A former janitor reported books and furniture moving around in the early morning hours.

Hickory, Patrick Beaver Memorial Library. Director Corki Jones said that her predecessor Elbert Ivey has visited the library long after his death. Staff heard his footsteps and doors slamming.

Marion, East McDowell Junior High School. Built on the site of an orphanage that burned down, the school's media center is haunted by the orphanage director, who died in the fire. Her figure can be seen on the upstairs balcony.

Mooresville, Brawley Middle School. The library is haunted by a middle-aged woman.

Raleigh, State Capitol, State Library Room. Capitol administrator Samuel P. Townsend Sr. visited the third-floor library in the late 1970s around 1 a.m. and felt cold spots at the doorway and north window. Capitol Curator Raymond Beck also had an uncomfortable feeling in the library late at night in 1981. Paranormal researchers from the Rhine Research Center in Durham detected cold spots and electromagnetic spikes during a 2003 investigation.

Saluda, Polk County Public Library, Saluda Branch. Librarians, volunteers, and patrons have heard muted sounds like people talking on the telephone and footsteps on the stairs in this 1919 building that became a library branch in 2000.

Taylorsville, Alexander County Library. Library staff saw a woman in a dark coat walk past the circulation desk one night and disappear when the library was closed. Employees have also heard someone rattling the locked door to the workroom and tidying the reference shelves after hours.

Washington, Beaufort-Hyde-Martin Regional Library, Old Beaufort County Courthouse. This building dates from about 1786 and was restored in 1971 to accommodate the library on the first floor. The sound of breaking glass is heard occasionally.

Wilmington, New Hanover County Public Library. The North Carolina Room harbors the ghost of a woman who frequented the library conducting Civil War research. Librarian Beverly Tetterton said some mornings she has found files spread out on a reading-room table when she had put everything away the night before. One book in particular, *The Papers of Zebulon Baird Vance*, has been left out frequently. Another employee once saw the glass door of a locked bookcase shake violently. The woman was seen and recognized on at least one occasion.

Winston-Salem, Salem College, Gramley Library. Screams are said to be heard on the third floor where two students were electrocuted in 1907.

North Dakota

Bismarck, Liberty Memorial Building. The offices of the North Dakota State Library occupy a basement area where the stacks of the North Dakota Historical Society were housed from 1924 to 1981. Society archivists reported strange presences, footsteps, and voices that they nicknamed the "Stack Monster" and attributed to Indian bones stored in the collections. Current library staff have reported no activity.

Harvey Public Library. Lights switching themselves on and chairs and book carts that rearrange themselves are said to be caused by the ghost of a woman who was murdered in a house where the library now stands.

Ohio

Ashtabula County District Library. The ghost of Ethel McDowell, who was appointed librarian when this Carnegie building opened in 1903, haunted the library prior to an October 1991 fire that took place during a million-dollar renovation. Odd footsteps were heard in the second-floor storage area, and apparitions and cold spots were reported in the basement hallway.

Circleville, Pickaway County Genealogy Library, Samuel Moore House. The ghosts of runaway slaves are said to haunt this 1848 building, a stop on the Underground Railroad. Slaves could have been kept in a secluded underground room connected with the basement beneath the sidewalk on Mound Street.

Dayton, VA Medical Center, Patient Library. Center Historian Melissa Smith said she has felt an uncomfortable presence in the library, while others have seen a ghostly woman standing at the upper windows.

Granville, Denison University, William H. Doane Library. A shadowy woman in an old dress sometimes wakes up napping male students on an upper floor.

Hinckley, Old Library. A young woman in an old-fashioned blue dress and a man with a hat have been seen in this 1845 structure. After the building opened as a library in 1975, librarians began to keep a file on the occurrences. Books left out the night before would sometimes be reshelved, while others (especially Anne Rice novels) would be flung to the floor during the night. Others have felt an odd presence in the upper rooms, occasionally paper clips sail through the air, and a furnace man once saw a ghostly figure on the basement stairs. The ghosts are believed to be those of Orlando Wilcox and his daughter Rebecca (1837–1869), who lived in a cabin on the site before the house was built. In 2003, the weight of the books and mold inside the walls forced the library to move to new quarters. A good summary of the haunt is Michelle Belanger's "The Haunting of Hinckley Library," *Fate* 56 (November 2003): 35–41.

Ironton, Briggs Lawrence County Public Library. The library staff has reported odd computer behavior and the sound of keys rattling, and Genealogy Librarian Marta Ramey said the hydraulic door to her office once closed abruptly three times in a row. The phenomena are blamed on Dr. Joseph W. Lowry, who was murdered in 1933 in a house on the current library site.

Kent Free Library, Carnegie Building. The first librarian to work in this 1903 Carnegie was Nellie Dingley, who died of pneumonia in France in 1918 while volunteering as a Red Cross nurse. She is said to haunt the place. The library moved to new quarters in 2005.

Paulding County Carnegie Library. One night in the 1980s, cleaners were in the building late at night when they looked up and saw a figure hovering in the north wing. The frightened workers refused to return to the library. In 2003, the director and board president were walking near the elevator when a large plant suddenly fell to the ground next to them.

Steubenville Public Library. This Carnegie library opened in 1902 with Ellen Summers Wilson as the first librarian. Her office was located in the central tower, and after she died in 1904 stories began to circulate about creaking sounds and footsteps in the unoccupied attic. Today the attic houses air conditioning equipment that mysteriously turned itself off—until the controls were moved downstairs.

Toledo–Lucas County Public Library, West Toledo Branch. Odd noises and bumps can be heard in the area near a fireplace on the west wall. The ghost of a man wearing clothing from the 1930s has also been seen there.

10

Oklahoma

Broken Bow Library. This 1998 building stands on the site of a former high school. Sometimes at closing, staff report a cold spot and argumentative voices in the southeastern corner of the library.

Inola Public Library. Books often move themselves forward and fall off the shelves in this small facility built in 1969.

Oregon

Pendleton Center for the Arts. Originally a 1916 Carnegie library, this building was the Umatilla County Public Library in 1947 when Assistant Librarian Ruth Cochran suffered a cerebral hemorrhage while she was closing the building October 11. She went to the basement to rest, but was found the next day and taken to the hospital, where she died. Spooky events in the library were blamed on Ruth until it moved to a new location in 1996. Once a custodian was alone in the building painting the children's room when the intercom system buzzed repeatedly.

Portland, Multnomah County Library, North Portland Branch. In the early 1990s, a man was seen several times on a security camera sitting in the second-floor meeting room when the room was closed and empty. On one occasion, a library assistant actually watched the figure vanish from the screen as a supervisor walked upstairs to investigate.

Union Carnegie Public Library. Strange noises emanate from a storage room in the basement.

Pennsylvania

Bellevue, Andrew Bayne Memorial Library. A woman dressed in Victorian clothing has been seen in this 1875 house. Many odd occurrences.

Bethlehem, Lehigh University, Linderman Library. A cantankerous ghost allegedly pesters students and staff. He is thought to be an elderly gentleman who frequented the library and was a general nuisance. Whether the phenomena will survive the library's current (2005–2007) restoration remains to be seen.

Cheltenham, former East Cheltenham Free Library, James Houldin House. When the library occupied a 200-year-old house on Central Avenue from 1957 to 1978, it shared quarters with a ghost. Head librarian Mrs. John Brockman said in the January 29, 1970, *Philadelphia Evening Bulletin* that she could smell coffee brewing in her office some afternoons around 4:30, and before closing time there was a "whole combination of cooking odors." Library Assistant Betty Stratton heard a "sniff or snort" on the second floor that she had a snorting dialogue with.

Dormont Public Library. Allegedly haunted by a former librarian named Alice, this 1962 library's books have a tendency to disappear and reappear. A man and woman laughing can sometimes be heard.

Easton Public Library. Spooky sounds and sensations are blamed on Elizabeth Bell "Mammy" Morgan (d. 1839, an innkeeper, amateur lawyer, and the widow of a doctor who perished in the Philadelphia yellow fever epidemic of 1793) and 513 others who were buried in a cemetery uncovered at this site when the library was built in 1903.

Gettysburg Borough Office Building. Home to the Adams County Public Library in the 1940s and 1950s, this Civil War–era building had a ghost named Gus who would move objects, turn on the water fountain, ride the elevator, and cook food in the building.

Hazleton, Bishop Hafey High School. Screams and loud noises are heard from the library at night, attributed to a student who committed suicide in the 1970s.

Immaculata College Library. KYW radio reported March 23, 2005, that library staff heard odd knocking noises after utensils and other artifacts from a nearby archaeological dig were put on display. The artifacts came from Duffy's Cut, a burial site of 57 Irish immigrants who died of cholera (perhaps aided by foul play) while working on the railroad in 1832.

Milton Public Library. Cold spots in the older section of this library built in 1974, computer high jinks, and phantom footsteps are blamed on the presence of a former librarian.

Philadelphia, American Philosophical Society, Library Hall. A cleaning lady claimed to have bumped into Ben Franklin's ghost, his arms full of books, in the 1870s or 1880s. The original structure was built in 1789 and demolished in 1888; the current building is a replica built in 1954.

Philadelphia, Civil War Library and Museum. Footsteps, an eerie presence, and phantom cigar smoke have been experienced here. In the Lincoln Room, the ghosts of soldiers playing cards have allegedly been seen.

Philadelphia, Historical Society of Pennsylvania. A spectral typist frequently heard in a room on the third floor is said to be the ghost of cataloger Albert J. Edmunds. Voices, footsteps, shadowy forms, and an address-label machine that operated without being plugged in have been well witnessed.

Selinsgrove, Susquehanna University, Blough-Weis Library. Student workers have felt a presence and seen an apparition while working late at night in the basement.

University Park, Pennsylvania State University, Pattee Library. According to The Shadowlands website, "Workers and students report that there have been strange screams echoing up from the basement levels, transparent girls thumbing through books, disembodied glowing red eyes, book carts being moved without anyone present, and all sorts of other phenomena."

University Park, Pennsylvania State University, Pollock Laptop Library. A grumbling voice has been heard in this facility, which was dedicated in 1999.

South Carolina

Columbia, University of South Carolina, South Caroliniana Library. Employees have seen the ghost of former USC President J. Rion McKissick (d. 1944) walking across the balcony. He is buried on the Horseshoe in front of the library, which was built in 1840.

McClellanville, Hampton Plantation. The sounds of a man sobbing and a chair that rocks by itself in the downstairs library are evidence of a ghost in this 1735 building.

Tennessee

Hendersonville, Robert E. Ellis Middle School. Formerly Hendersonville High School, this structure is haunted by a phantom known as the Colonel. A figure has been seen lurking in the windows of the second-floor library.

Johnson City, East Tennessee State University, Gilbreath Hall. The site of the library prior to 1998, the hall hosted a resident ghost that closed doors and windows left open by mistake and turned off unnecessary lights. One student claimed that she saw an apparition of founding President Sidney Gilbreath framed in an upper window one night.

Knoxville, University of Tennessee, James D. Hoskins Library. Footsteps of the "Evening Primrose," supposedly a former graduate student, are

10

sometimes heard after hours. The smell of cornbread is associated with her. A maintenance specialist said in 2004 that he's heard doors shutting and can sometimes smell cooking late at night.

Lebanon, Cumberland University, Doris and Harry Vise Library. Director John Boniol says that the library has a ghost cat. On March 5, 2001, he saw a "cat come floating across my office floor and disappear among the boxes stored under the table behind my desk. I did not see any legs or paws and no motion like a normal cat walking on a floor. The apparition was near the floor, about the right height for a cat, but it appeared to be gliding smoothly through the air instead of touching the floor. I couldn't tell if it came in through the door or came from under my desk." He's experienced eerie feelings in the Clement and Castle Heights rooms. A former librarian also reported the ghost of a little girl dressed in white with whom she used to play peek-a-boo around the circulation desk.

Memphis, University of Memphis, Brister Library. The university's main library from 1928 to 1994, the Brister ghost is said to be that of a raped student whose screams have puzzled campus security.

Rugby, Thomas Hughes Free Public Library. The ghost of Eduard Bertz, the librarian who organized this collection in 1881–1883, is said to have appeared to Brian Stagg in the late 1960s and provided hints on how to restore the library to its original shelf arrangement.

Texas

Alice High School. The library's ghost throws books off the shelf and is said to be a man who died when the library was built.

Boerne Public Library. Since 1994 the library has been housed in the Dienger Building, an 1884 structure originally built as a general store. Some can feel a presence inside, and at night people say the lights go on and off.

Brownsville, Dr. Garcia Middle School. TV sets are said to turn on at night, and books fall off the shelves.

Brownsville, University of Texas, Arnulfo L. Oliveira Memorial Library. Former Library Director Yolanda Gonzalez said she has seen the door to the Hunter Room open and close by itself and books in glass-fronted cabinets move slowly. She said in the October 29, 2004, *Houston Chronicle* that in her 47 years as a librarian she grew to accept that the spirits were there: "When I finally got a secretary, I told her don't be afraid of things that happen here." From 1948 to 1954 the UTB library was located in a wing of Gorgas Hall, which formerly served as the hospital for old Fort Brown and where a ghost nurse dressed in white was said to walk into locked offices and sit behind desks.

Corsicana, Navarro County Courthouse. Late-night users of the law library have heard someone walking on the stairs between the second and third floor. Speculation centers on a man shot by the sheriff after a political dispute.

Houston, Milby High School. A ghostly librarian has been reported.

Houston Public Library, Julia Ideson Building. The older section of the Central Library now houses special collections and archives, but it had the main collection from 1926 to 1976. Ghostly music could sometimes be heard drifting through the building. J. Frank Cramer, a night janitor who practiced playing a violin while wandering through the building after closing, was allegedly responsible. He lived in a small apartment in the basement until his death in 1936. Hattie Johnson, who came to work there in 1946, said the music could be heard on cloudy days and lasted a long time.

McKinney Public Library. A ghost is blamed for books getting misplaced or knocked onto the floor.

San Angelo, Fort Concho Museum. An active army outpost from 1867 to 1889, the fort's Officers' Quarters 7 Building now houses the museum library. Lights have been reported late at night, and in 1997 one librarian said the back door opened suddenly when she was sitting at the microfilm reader.

San Antonio, Hertzberg Circus Collection and Museum. Bequeathed to the San Antonio Public Library by Harry Hertzberg (1884–1940), this is the oldest public circus collection in the United States. Custodian Mario Lara has felt cold spots in the building, especially in the basement near the bookstore. Staff members have heard keys jangling in the rare books collection and footsteps in the third floor hallway. Ghostly voices, a strange light, and books rearranging themselves in closed stacks are also reported.

San Antonio, Institute of Texan Cultures Library. A ghost with crunching footsteps can be heard in the audiovisual room. Nicknamed Old John by the archival staff, he also rearranges books.

San Antonio, Marion Koogler McNay Art Museum. This 1929 Spanish colonial mansion was the former McNay residence. Researchers in the library in the Tobin Wing can sometimes hear a female voice singing an unrecognizable tune.

San Antonio, Our Lady of the Lake University, Sueltenfuss Library. A former janitor haunts the library basement.

San Antonio, Whittier Middle School. Strange noises and books and chairs moving around are attributed to the ghost of a 15-year-old girl who fell on the staircase leading from the library to the auditorium in the early 1950s.

Waco, Baylor University, Armstrong Browning Library. This special collection devoted to the works of Robert and Elizabeth Barrett Browning moved into its own building in 1951. Some say the spirit of Elizabeth Browning peers out of the top-floor library window at night.

Utah

Provo, Brigham Young University, Harold B. Lee Library. Moaning voices can be heard in the Music Library on level 4.

Salt Lake City Public Library, Chapman Branch. KSL-TV reported October 28, 2004, that Circulation Specialist Andrea Graham saw a ghostly form as she opened the 1918 Carnegie library one morning, and she also watched a puppet launch itself from a window ledge.

Vermont

Northfield, Norwich University, Chaplin Hall. From 1941 to 1993, this building housed both the library and a male ghost who knocked books off the shelves and played tricks with the lighting.

Virginia

Essex County, Blandfield. A male figure haunts the downstairs library of this privately owned 18th-century mansion.

Fauquier County, Edgehill. The ghost of Civil War Col. William Chapman has been seen in the library of this private 1790 house, and he is thought responsible for opening locked doors and making loud noises late at night.

Stratford, Stratford Hall Plantation. The apparition of Revolutionary War hero Henry "Light Horse Harry" Lee (1756–1818) has been seen at a desk in the library of the 1730s-era Great House.

10

Washington

Snohomish City Office Building, Old Carnegie Library. Catharine McMurchy, library director from 1923 to 1939, died in 1956 and her ghost could be seen or heard walking in the basement of this 1910 Carnegie before the library moved to modern quarters in 2003. In 1991, Children's Librarian Debbie Young was taking a break in the staff room when she saw an older woman walk down the stairs from a storage area and exit the room. For a while the library had a ghostcam to try to catch her appearances.

Spokane, Centennial Middle School. Students have seen an old woman with no legs floating around in the library.

Tacoma Public Library, Anna E. McCormick Community Rooms. This 1927 building served as the stacks area of the library until 1984, when a substantial addition was made to the north end. Maintenance workers reported disturbances in the old building for a three-week period in 1995, shortly after the terms of a bequest changed the name of the addition to the Anna Lemon Wheelock Library. Water faucets turned on, boxes fell to the floor, and one person saw the apparition of a gray-haired woman, possibly Anna McCormick, who had funded the original library.

Toppenish, Mary L. Goodrich Library. A man and woman have been seen looking out one of the top-floor windows.

West Virginia

Morgantown, West Virginia University Library. Ghostly sounds and an odd presence are sensed on the upper floor of the old section.

Wisconsin

Cornell Public Library. An overwhelmingly uncomfortable feeling permeates the basement where the restrooms are.

Madison, University of Wisconsin, Memorial Library. The ghost of the university's first librarian, Helen C. White, has reportedly been seen floating through the library stacks. One Christmas break when the library was closed, a student library assistant doing catch-up work in the reference stacks heard someone whisper "Sally Brown" when no one was around.

West Bend, University of Wisconsin Washington County Library. At night, lights switch themselves on, books fall, and doors slam.

Wyoming

Burns High School. The library walls are said to shake mysteriously.

Byron, Rocky Mountain High School. In 1952 or 1953 School Superintendent Harold Hopkinson heard footsteps walking down the hall and the library door open when no one was there. Custodians have reported blood-curdling screams and scary presences.

Green River, Sweetwater County Library. Lights have gone off and on mysteriously ever since the library opened in 1980. Former Director Patricia LeFaivre said that her staff has seen dots of light dancing on the walls in the art gallery room. Since 1993, the staff has kept a record of all odd goings-on in a Ghost Log. The library was built on top of a cemetery dating from the 1860s.

Thermopolis, Hot Springs County Library. Books strewn about, strange noises, and shadowy figures have been reported.

Canada

Calling Lake (Alberta) School. A dark, shadowy figure has often been seen in the library of this Indian school.

Montreal, Quebec, McGill University, McLennan Library. A man in an old-fashioned coat haunts the sixth floor of this 1969 structure. When people talk to him, he looks directly at them and disappears.

Timmins, Ontario, École St.-Alphonse. A small shadow leaps from shelf to shelf in the basement library.

Toronto, Art Gallery of Ontario, The Grange. Built in 1817 and occupied at one time by controversial essayist Goldwin Smith, this estate's library is home to a gaunt, shadowy haunt. Archivist Elayne Dobel Goyette said she recalled hearing about three different spirits when she worked there as a guide in the early 1990s.

Vancouver, University of British Columbia Library. An old lady in a white dress has been seen.

United Kingdom

England

Arundel Castle, Sussex. A "blue man" ghost, apparently dating from the late 17th century, has been seen browsing the bookshelves.

Blackheath Library, St. John's Park, London. The library in this former vicarage is inhabited by the ghost of Elsie Marshall (1869–1895), who grew up in the house. Lights come on when the building is empty, and an unseen presence brushes past people at the door.

Bristol Central Reference Library. The gray-robed monk who haunts Bristol Cathedral is said to visit the library next door to consult theological books.

British Library, Euston Road, London. If there are any spooks in the new facility that opened in 1999, no one is saying, but when it was under construction in 1996, workmen heard clanking sounds and one civil servant saw a "weeping man in 18th-century dress," according to the *Sunday Times*, May 19, 1996.

Combermere Abbey, Shropshire. A visitor to the abbey library, Sybell Corbet, took a time-lapse photo of Lord Combermere's favorite carved oak chair on May 12, 1891, at the same time that the man was getting buried four miles away. When developed, it showed a blurry image of a bearded man sitting in the chair (paranormal.about.com/library/graphics/lord_ghost_lg.jpg).

Farnham Library, Vernon House, Surrey. Charles I slept in this building one night in 1648 when he was taken to London for eventual trial and beheading. The room that he occupied, now an office area, has a "heavy psychic atmosphere."

Felbrigg Hall, Norfolk. The 18th-century scholar William Windham III haunts the library at this old estate. In 1972, David Muffon was working at a desk in the library when he noticed a gentleman sitting next to the fireplace reading. After about 15 seconds he faded away. For many years before the hall was acquired by the National Trust, the butler set out books on the table for the ghost to read.

Holland House, Cropthorne, Worcester. The ghost of Mrs. Holland is seen in the library of this Tudor retreat house.

Longleat House, Red Library, Wiltshire. Reputedly haunted by an elderly gentleman dressed in black. Librarian Dorothy Coates said the spirit was

10

friendly and could be the ghost of Sir John Thynne (1512–1580), who was responsible for the original building at Longleat.

Mannington Hall, near Cromer, Norfolk. Antiquarian Augustus Jessop (1823–1914) saw the ghost of a large man in an ecclesiastical robe as he was consulting books in the library late on the night of October 10, 1879. The figure was examining some of the volumes Jessop had piled on the table, disappeared at a slight noise, then reappeared briefly five minutes later.

Raby Castle, Durham. The library is haunted by Sir Henry Vane the Younger, who was beheaded for treason in 1662. His headless torso sometimes appears on a library desk.

Windsor Castle, Royal Library, Berkshire. Elizabeth I and Charles I are said to roam the stacks.

York Central Library. In 1954 the library was disturbed by a series of paranormal incidents involving a book titled *The Antiquities and Curiosities of the Church* (1897). Every fourth Sunday at 8:40 p.m., an unseen hand would remove the book from its shelf and drop it to the floor. An intense cold spot would presage the event, and on at least one occasion the caretaker reported seeing the outline of an elderly man searching for a book.

Scotland

Rammerscales House, Lockerbie, Dumfries. The library of this 18th-century stately home is haunted by its former owner, James Mounsey. A teacher and students that lived there during World War II were so frightened of the ghost that they preferred to sleep in the stables.

Ireland

Marsh's Library, Dublin. Founded in 1701 by Archbishop Narcissus Marsh (1638–1713), this was the first public library in Ireland. In the early 20th century, the inner gallery was said to be haunted by Marsh himself, wandering among the shelves and rummaging through volumes looking for a lost letter from his niece. But in the morning things were always found to be in order.

Russia

Kukoboi, Yaroslavl' Region. The birthplace of the Russian witch Baba-Yaga, this village's library once experienced a ghost, a young girl wearing an antiquated bonnet, who came in and disappeared after talking to the library staff, according to *Pravda*, August 18, 2004.

Philippines

University of the Philippines Diliman, Quezon City. The College of Science Library and the Main Library are two of the many haunted places on campus.

Australia

State Library of Victoria, Melbourne. This massive structure dates from 1856 and hosts many specters. The ghost of a female librarian named Grace keeps an eye on the children's books in the Arts Collection, and a mustachioed gentleman protects the music stacks and piano. A clairvoyant sensed a malevolent presence in room S200. Poltergeist phenomena have been reported in the Newspaper Room. Glowing balls of light appear on the stairs. Security guards witness many of these antics after the library is closed.

Mexico

Morelia Public Library, Michoacán. Library staff say that a "nun in blue" has haunted the 16th-century premises for many years. Director Rigoberto Cornejo said in Monterrey's *El Norte* newspaper, "When I leave the building, I feel the sensation of someone following me. In fact, I can even hear the footsteps." In 1996, library worker Socorro Ledezma requested a transfer because she felt paralyzed by an unseen presence standing behind her and blowing in her ear.

SOURCES: The Shadowlands, www.theshadowlands.net; George M. Eberhart, "Phantoms among the Folios: A Guide to Haunted Libraries," *American Libraries* 28 (October 1997): 68–71; Dennis William Hauck, *Haunted Places: The National Directory* (New York: Penguin, 2002); Dorothy Hodder, "Library Ghosts of North Carolina," *North Carolina Libraries,* Summer 2003, pp. 74–76; Julie Hart and Carolyn Ashcraft, "Libraries in the Twilight Zone," *Arkansas Libraries* 51, no. 5 (October 1994): 27–29; and many other sources.

Nina Grinyova, library school student and cryptozoologist

by Igor Bourtsev

DURING A 1980 RUSSIAN SCIENTIFIC EXPEDITION to Tajikistan in search of living examples of an alleged Central Asian wildman known locally as the "Gul," expedition volunteer Nina Grinyova, a Ukrainian library school student (now a journalist who lives in Krasnodon), had a close encounter with one of the creatures in the Varzob River gorge. The team was led by mountaineer Igor Tatsl and anthropologist Igor Bourtsev. In 1979, Tatsl had found hominid footprints in the area and nicknamed the individual "Gosha," so he returned the following year to try to get photographs of what he thought might be a relict population of Neanderthals. This is Bourtsev's report on the incident.—*GME.*

Igor Bourtsev with a plaster cast of a hominid track he found in Tajikistan, 1979.

[On August 20, 1980,] when I reached Tatsl and his group, he told me they had no hot news, though Gosha had been visiting the campsite area, judging by indistinct tracks and certain other signs, which other members of the group did not find convincing. After supper we sat around a fire and I told them of the work of the other groups and about my search on the Surshku Ridge. The discussion we had was long; we brewed tea twice. Around 11 p.m., I asked: "Where is Zaichik (Bunny)?" It was the nickname of a cheerful and robust 18-year-old girl, Nina Grinyova, a library student in Voroshilovgrad [now Luhans'k] in Ukraine.

Someone replied she had already turned in, and our talk continued. About midnight, we began preparing to turn in. Suddenly, I heard sounds as if a cat

10

Nina Grinyova (Zaichik) as an 18-year-old
library student, interviewing
a Tajik eyewitness in 1980.

was mewing, others said they heard a whistle. Svetlana Zaeka, a geologist from Kiev, who seemed to be agitated, whispered a few words to Tatsl, who called to Georgy Kirilyuk, and they dashed down the path to the river.

We shrugged our shoulders and went on preparing to go to bed. But after some time had passed and as our comrades had not returned, we began to worry. We then took flashlights and also made for the river. There we saw someone on the steep slope of the opposite bank leading another person by the arm. "That's Zaichik," someone exclaimed in surprise. Presently Georgy and Nina crossed the river by the ropes especially hung there because it was deep and very rapid at that point.

When I took a close look at Nina I could hardly recognize her. No trace of her former cheerful self, she looked withdrawn and remote. She spoke with difficulty and said from time to time, "Why did he go away?"

Though she was soaked in water to her waist and the night was very cold, she did not pay attention to that. She was made to change into dry clothes and then answer our questions. She found words only with difficulty.

I bitterly regretted that I had left my tape recorder in Dushanbe because Nina's first oral report was very impressive and its quality could not be reproduced later on. Here's what she said:

> At about 10 p.m., Tatsl helped me to cross the river. Only he and I were in on our plan. . . . When I was left alone on the other bank I was not afraid. At first the moon was shining. Through the trees I could see our camp fire burning. Then it went out. The sound of the river was coming up from beneath the slope. I sat singing songs and when I felt cold I danced. Then the moon went behind the cliff but continued to illuminate the high rock wall above me, still giving me enough light to see around.
>
> Soon after, I heard a noise coming from the area of the bushes upstream and began to look in that direction. Again there was a noise coming from the same area upstream and I turned there. Then, as if urged to do so, I made a sudden turn in the direction of the stone pounding sound I had heard earlier and saw him. It was Gosha. He was standing some 25 meters away, facing me and piercing my very soul with his gaze. It was not aggressive, rather well wishing, but piercing. The eyes were big and glowing. They were not bright but did glow. In fact, all of his body was sort of glowing. He was dark and at the same time, somewhat silvery. I could see his body was covered with hair but it was not shaggy. Maybe it was wet, anyhow the color had a silvery tinge. He was about two meters tall. [Nina said that Gosha was 10–15 cm taller than I am. My height is 187 cm.—I.B.]

His figure looked very hefty, square, and straight from shoulder to hip, with a short neck, the head put forward; also the arms were hanging down freely in a somewhat forward position.

When I saw him I was not scared and began slowly to advance toward him. Having gone about five steps, I held out and pressed, two or three times, a rubber toy in the shape of a bird, which made a squeaking sound. It was given to me by Tatsl in order to attract Gosha's attention with its sound. But it was this that spoiled our contact. Gosha made a sharp turn and quickly slid down the slope to the river and disappeared beyond the steep bank. I noted the softness and grace of his walk, though he moved very fast. It was not a human walk but as of an animal, as of a panther. Despite boulders and other obstacles, he moved quickly, softly, and even gracefully. He must have a perfect sense of balance because he negotiated the steep and uneven slope with no more difficulty than we would walk along a paved road. I was greatly disappointed by his retreat. But nothing could be done. I turned around and started to walk in the opposite direction, towards the crossing. At that point my memory faded and I don't remember what I did. No, I was not frightened. On the contrary, I regretted very much that he had gone. But I must have passed out. I don't know how I reached the water and what I did there. I came round only when Georgy was shaking me. Then I showed Georgy where I had seen Gosha.

Judging by the fact that Nina was wet to her waist, she had walked into the river and been in mortal danger. But somehow she had escaped the worst. This is what Kirilyuk told us: "When we were preparing to turn in, Tatsl came up to me and said, 'Take your flashlight and come along!' I grabbed a miners' lamp and rushed after him to the crossing place. On the way I thought: Maybe a mountain climber had gotten into trouble or something. When I got to the other bank I saw someone sitting there. Coming closer I saw it was a girl and she was sitting motionless. I shone the light into her face and realized it was Zaichik. She did not react to the light. I took her hand—her pulse was even but the hand was quite limp. I took her by the shoulders and began to shake her. She came to and her first words were: 'Why did he go away?' I said, 'How are you?' but instead of answering she said, 'Do you want to see the place where I saw him?' I said, 'If you're able to show me, go ahead.' She got up and led me straight to the place, telling me what had happened. Then we returned to the crossing place and I helped her cross the river using the ropes."

Lastly, to dot the i's, here's what Igor Tatsl had to say: "The idea of a contact with Gosha was not a new one. That is the goal of our whole expedition. Taking into account his telepathic ability, I've always demanded that the expedition members 'tune' themselves up accordingly. When we came to this place this summer, and it's my seventh visit here, we began, as usual, to make track zones in the vicinity of our camp and to install phototraps made by Igor Kolesnik. The track zones were also made on the other side of the river, which is practically inaccessible to humans. We loosened the soil as far as we could there and set up a pole with a red flag, hoping the bright color might interest and attract any hominoids. Indeed, we noticed their footprints but they were very indistinct. And no wonder, considering the hard soil in that place.

"It was then that Zaichik volunteered to 'date' Gosha on the other side of the river. The two of us discussed the plan in detail but to avoid complica-

10

tions, did not tell anyone else. The experiment has proved that the hominoid can affect a human's mind and react to a human's thoughts or maybe feelings. Otherwise how can one explain the fact that though Nina was not frightened by Gosha, she had experienced a blackout?"

Tatsl also said that a fortnight earlier another member of the group spotted a silvery-gray creature during daytime and standing among bushes on a mountain slope, quite a distance from her in the vicinity of the camp. The sighting was short and perhaps questionable. She only told Tatsl, so Nina did not know of that sighting.

When I listened to Nina I asked myself: "Perhaps it had been a hallucination?" After all, she had been preparing herself for a rendezvous and the tension and suspense of waiting in a lonely place at night may have played tricks with her senses. But the details she recalled and the circumstances of the encounter seemed to rule that out. When we inspected the place next morning we discovered indistinct hominoid tracks by the river, especially traces of heelmarks where he had slid down the very steep slope of the bank, just where Nina had seen him do this, a place where no human would have risked going.

Just a few words regarding Gosha's "vibes" affecting Nina's mind. Besides Tatsl's belief in such a possibility, there are accounts of witnesses who claim to have experienced a certain sensation even before they actually saw a hominoid. There are also reports of people who have become sick after an encounter with a hominoid. This raises the interesting question posed by Boris Porshnev in his monograph *On the Beginning of Human History*, published posthumously in 1974: "Has not the science of anthropogenesis overlooked the vast potential of man's highly organized ancestors to affect the central nervous system of animals and their higher nervous activity? . . . The speed and capacity of their [man's ancestors] nervous processes were greater than in other animals."

Thus contact has been made. We must thoroughly ponder its significance and implications before proceeding with our search.

SOURCE: Dmitri Bayanov, *In the Footsteps of the Russian Snowman* (Moscow: Crypto-Logos, 1996), pp. 91–98. Reprinted with permission.

A dozen solutions to all library problems

by Walt Crawford

IN HONOR OF APRIL 1, I'd like to share a special set of precepts to eliminate library problems and end the need for new library buildings, if you follow them to the letter.

    1. Every good library is the same. That's true for Barnes & Noble—and don't all librarians want to make their facility just like Barnes & Noble? Consider how much you'll save by treating your library just like all the other libraries.

2. Outsource: Profit = efficiency = effectiveness. You outsourced most cataloging years ago. You don't build your own integrated systems, publish your own books, or manufacture your own shelving. Why do local collection development, reference work, or anything except circulation? Outsourcing takes care of union problems and overpaid employees; it's as good for libraries as for any other bottom-line business.

3. Follow the Pareto Principle. Focus 80% of your library's budget and attention on the 20% of your customers who represent 80% of your business. Satisfy your best customers (the word to use!) and you can't go wrong. Those who get left behind probably don't pay much in taxes anyway, and won't help when you start your NPR-style pledge drives. Forget them.

4. Give 'em what they want. Period. Buy enough copies of the latest bestsellers to fill all demand. For academic libraries, get all the full-text journals you can possibly afford: Students love 'em. Why worry about materials that serve the next generation? You'll be retired by then anyway. What did the next generation ever do for you?

5. If it hasn't circulated in two years, dump it. Keep those shelves clear for the stuff your best customers want. If nobody's used it in two years, chances are it's worthless for today's top customers.

6. Never offend your community. Who are you to purchase materials that offend community members? Once you move to an inoffensive collection policy, you won't have to explain to trustees why they should care about intellectual freedom and minority needs.

7. Ignore your community. Do you have a growing Spanish collection to serve your growing Hispanic population? How about ESL and adult literacy programs to help struggling community members? Are you investigating and serving changing community needs? No? Then why bother? You're the professional here. That's why they pay you the big bucks.

8. Kids these days do everything on computers and they'll never change. Out go the bookshelves. In go the WiFi networks and ebook systems. Today's young mutants don't care about books, story hours, or anything that isn't on a

---

How Many Academic Librarians Does It Take to Change a Light Bulb?

by Blake Carver

One archivist to preserve and catalog the old, burnt-out light bulb;

One acquisitions librarian to order the new light bulb;

One cataloger to catalog and classify the new light bulb when received according to AACR2 standards, noting wattage, color, fluorescent or incandescent, etc.;

One reference librarian to ascertain that the light bulb ordered is what the patron *really* wants;

One media services librarian to make sure the bulb meets standard instructional objectives;

One government publications librarian to check that the bulb meets federal standards;

One circulation librarian to check out the bulb;

One dean of libraries to oversee the entire process; and

One student worker to actually change the light bulb.

SOURCE: Blake Carver, "How Many Academic Librarians Does It Take to Change a Light Bulb?" LISNews, posted February 5, 2002, www.lisnews.com.

10

cell phone/PDA or notebook computer. They never will. Aren't you just the same now as you were 20 years ago? You can see the wave of the future: Surf it or drown.

9. Technology solves all problems. If technology creates a problem, you just need more technology to solve the problem. You need to spend more time paying attention to new technological solutions—those are the only ones that matter.

10. Keep shifting to shiny new toys. How many neat new technologies and devices have you investigated this year? If you're not hooking up something new every week or two, you're falling behind. You're not some sort of Luddite, are you? It's new, it's neat, it's shiny: You must work it into your library plans.

11. You have your MLS. You can stop learning. Do you *really* want to spend time reading boring professional literature? If something matters, someone will alert you to it—and, after all, it's only the shiny new toys that matter. Institutes and conference programs are great excuses for drinking and dining, but the exhibits should teach you everything you really need to know.

12. Fight stereotypes at every turn. You could raise the status of librarians by providing professional, tailored services to those who need them most—but isn't it more fun to complain about media portrayals of hair in buns, sensible shoes, and shushing? As lawyers have demonstrated, the path to success is constant whining about stereotypes.

13. Embrace inevitability. The print serial is dead and the print book is dying. Nobody wants to go to a library. Book reading is a lost art in any case, and Google gives you all the research anyone really needs. That's the way it is. It's inevitable. Live with it.

There they are: A baker's dozen of ideas (some useful in small doses) that will end all your problems when taken to extremes. Enjoy!

SOURCE: Walt Crawford, "A Dozen Solutions to All Library Problems," *American Libraries* 35 (April 2004): 88.

The Librarian's Song
by Jack Campin

There's nought but books in ilka hand,
Now ev'ry hour that passes O,
For ilka lad is readin' mad,
Wi' bonny readin' lasses O.

CHORUS
Green grows the rashes O,
Green grows the rashes O,
A fig for a' your books sae braw,
If it werena for the lasses O.

Lang may our brethren read an' think,
An' act an' crack ay cautious O,
Till ilka line ay gar them shine,
An' ay respect the lasses O.

Lang may they thrive an' ay contrive,
To get baith books an' lasses O,
Our noble plan enlightens man,
An' maks him mair sagacious O.

We've books o' lair, Hume, Young an' Blair,
Wi' sermons snug to asses O,
Which surely suits land lugged brutes,
That caresna for the lasses O.

Some says I ha'e a fickle job,
Baith troublesome an' fashious O,
To keep the books, but sweet's the looks,
That I get frae the lasses O.

SOURCE: Jack Campin, "The Librarian's Song," in *Music of Dalkeith*, 2001, www.purr.demon.co.uk/ dalkeith/Dalkeith.htm. Reprinted with permission.

INDEX

GEORGE M. EBERHART is a senior editor of *American Libraries* magazine for the American Library Association. From 1980 to 1990 he was editor of *College & Research Libraries News*, the news magazine of ALA's Association of College and Research Libraries division. He has also written on the subjects of UFOs, cryptozoology, and postcard collecting. Eberhart holds a bachelor's degree in journalism from Ohio State University and an MLS from the University of Chicago.